BRITISH WRITERS

BRITISH WRITERS

JAY PARINI
Editor

SUPPLEMENT XVIII

CHARLES SCRIBNER'S SONS
A part of Gale, Cengage Learning

GALE
CENGAGE Learning

Detroit • New York • San Francisco • New Haven, Conn • Waterville, Maine • London

British Writers Supplement XVIII

Editor in Chief: Jay Parini

Project Editor: Lisa Kumar

Permissions: Leitha Etheridge-Sims

Composition Specialist: Gary Leach

Buyer: Cynde Lentz

Publisher: Jim Draper

Product Manager: Philip J. Virta

For product information and technology assistance, contact us at **Gale Customer Support, 1-800-877-4253.**
For permission to use material from this text or product, submit all requests online at **www.cengage.com/permissions**
Further permissions questions can be emailed to **permissionrequest@cengage.com**

LIBRARY OF CONGRESS CATALOGING-IN-PUBLICATION DATA

British Writers. Supplement XVIII / Jay Parini, editor.
  p. cm.
  Summary: "Biographical and critical essays on 18 British writers"-- Provided by publisher.
  Includes bibliographical references and index.
  ISBN-13: 978-1-4144-8026-8 (alk. paper)
  ISBN-10: 1-4144-8026-1
  1. English literature--History and criticism. 2. English literature--Bio-bibliography. 3. Commonwealth literature (English)--History and criticism. 4. Commonwealth literature (English)--Bio-bibliography. 5. Authors, English--Biography. 6. Authors, Commonwealth--Biography. I. Parini, Jay.

PR85.B688 Suppl. 18
820.9--dc23   2011020417

The paper used in this publication meets the requirements of ANSI/NISO Z39.48-1992 (Permanence of Paper).

Charles Scribner's Sons
an imprint of Gale, Cengage Learning
27500 Drake Rd.
Farmington Hills, MI 48331–3535

ISBN-13: 978-1-4144-8026-8
ISBN-10: 1-4144-8026-1

Printed in Mexico
1 2 3 4 5 6 7 15 14 13 12 11

Acknowledgments

Acknowledgment is gratefully made to those publishers and individuals who permitted the use of the following material in copyright. Every effort has been made to secure permission to reprint copyrighted material.

BURKE, GREGORY. From *Hoors.* Faber and Faber, 2009. / O'Donoghue, Noelle. From *Resource Learning Pack.* Traverse Theatre. Reproduced by permission. / *The Guardian,* July 6, 2002. Copyright © 2002 by Guardian News & Media Ltd. Reproduced by permission of Guardian News Service, LTD. / *The Sunday Times,* April 25, 2009. Copyright © 2009 Times Newspapers Ltd. Reproduced by permission.

DACRE, CHARLOTTE. "The Kiss," in *Hours of Solitude. A Collection of Original Poems, Vol. 1,* 2000. Reproduced by permission of British Women Romantic Poets Project, General Library, University of California, Davis. / "The Unfaithful Lover," in *Hours of Solitude. A Collection of Original Poems, Vol. 1,* 2000. Reproduced by permission of British Women Romantic Poets Project, General Library, University of California, Davis. / "To the Shade of Mary Robinson," in *Hours of Solitude. A Collection of Original Poems, Vol. 1,* 2000. Reproduced by permission of British Women Romantic Poets Project, General Library, University of California, Davis.

DEANE, SEAMUS. From "After Derry, 30 January 1972," in *Gradual Wars,* Irish University Press, 1972. Copyright © 1972 Seamus Deane. By kind permission of the author c/o The Gallery Press, Loughcrew, Oldcastle, County Meath, Ireland. / From "Eleven," in *Gradual Wars,* Irish University Press, 1972. Copyright © 1972 Seamus Deane. By kind permission of the author c/o The Gallery Press, Loughcrew, Oldcastle, County Meath, Ireland. / From "Great Times Once," in *Gradual Wars,* Irish University Press, 1972. Copyright © 1972 Seamus Deane. By kind permission of the author c/o The Gallery Press, Loughcrew, Oldcastle, County Meath, Ireland. / From "High in San Franscisco," in *Gradual Wars,* Irish University Press, 1972. Copyright © 1972 Seamus Deane. By kind permission of the author c/o The Gallery Press, Loughcrew, Oldcastle, County Meath, Ireland. / From "Landscape into Art," in *Gradual Wars,* Irish University Press, 1972. Copyright © 1972 Seamus Deane. By kind permission of the author c/o The Gallery Press, Loughcrew, Oldcastle, County Meath, Ireland. / From "Seven," in *Gradual Wars,* Irish University Press, 1972. Copyright © 1972 Seamus Deane. By kind permission of the author c/o The Gallery Press, Loughcrew, Oldcastle, County Meath, Ireland. / From "Smoke Signals in Oregon," in *Gradual Wars,* Irish University Press, 1972. Copyright © 1972 Seamus Deane. By kind permission of the author c/o The Gallery Press, Loughcrew, Oldcastle, County Meath, Ireland. / From "Title Poem," in *Gradual Wars,* Irish University Press, 1972. Copyright © 1972 Seamus Deane. By kind permission of the author c/o The Gallery Press, Loughcrew, Oldcastle, County Meath, Ireland. / From "Two," in *Gradual Wars,* Irish University Press, 1972. Copyright © 1972 Seamus Deane. By kind permission of the author c/o The Gallery Press, Loughcrew, Oldcastle, County Meath, Ireland. / From "A World Without a Name," in *History Lessons.* Gallery Press, 1983. By kind permission of the author and the Gallery Press, Loughcrew, Oldcastle, County Meath, Ireland. / From "Breaking Wood," in *History Lessons.* Gallery Press, 1983. By kind permission of the author and the Gallery Press, Loughcrew, Oldcastle, County Meath, Ireland. / From "Daystar," in *History Lessons.* Gallery Press, 1983. By kind

ACKNOWLEDGEMENTS

permission of the author and the Gallery Press, Loughcrew, Oldcastle, County Meath, Ireland. / From "Guerillas," in *History Lessons.* Gallery Press, 1983. By kind permission of the author and the Gallery Press, Loughcrew, Oldcastle, County Meath, Ireland. / From "History Lesson," in *History Lessons.* Gallery Press, 1983. By kind permission of the author and the Gallery Press, Loughcrew, Oldcastle, County Meath, Ireland. / From "Send War in our Time, O Lord," in *History Lessons.* Gallery Press, 1983. By kind permission of the author and the Gallery Press, Loughcrew, Oldcastle, County Meath, Ireland. / From "The Party Givers," in *History Lessons.* Gallery Press, 1983. By kind permission of the author and the Gallery Press, Loughcrew, Oldcastle, County Meath, Ireland. / From "Title Poem," in *History Lessons.* Gallery Press, 1983. By kind permission of the author and the Gallery Press, Loughcrew, Oldcastle, County Meath, Ireland. / From "A Fable," in *Rumours,* Dolmen, 1977. Copyright © 1977 Seamus Deane. By kind permission of the author c/o The Gallery Press, Loughcrew, Oldcastle, County Meath, Ireland. / From "Middle Kingdom," in *Rumours,* Dolmen, 1977. Copyright © 1977 Seamus Deane. By kind permission of the author c/o The Gallery Press, Loughcrew, Oldcastle, County Meath, Ireland. / From "Migration," in *Rumours,* Dolmen, 1977. Copyright © 1977 Seamus Deane. By kind permission of the author c/o The Gallery Press, Loughcrew, Oldcastle, County Meath, Ireland. / From "Scholar II," in *Rumours,* Dolmen, 1977. Copyright © 1977 Seamus Deane. By kind permission of the author c/o The Gallery Press, Loughcrew, Oldcastle, County Meath, Ireland. / From "A Schooling," in *Rumours,* Dolmen, 1977. Copyright © 1977 Seamus Deane. By kind permission of the author c/o The Gallery Press, Loughcrew, Oldcastle, County Meath, Ireland. / From "The Birthday Gift," in *Rumours,* Dolmen, 1977. Copyright © 1977 Seamus Deane. By kind permission of the author c/o The Gallery Press, Loughcrew, Oldcastle, County Meath, Ireland. / From "The Broken Border," in *Rumours,* Dolmen, 1977. Copyright © 1977 Seamus Deane. By kind permission of the author c/o The Gallery Press, Loughcrew, Oldcastle, County Meath, Ireland. / From

"Reading Paradise Lost," in *Selected Poems.* Gallery Press, 1988. By kind permission of the author and the Gallery Press, Loughcrew, Oldcastle, County Meath, Ireland. / From "Return," in *Selected Poems.* Gallery Press, 1988. By kind permission of the author and the Gallery Press, Loughcrew, Oldcastle, County Meath, Ireland. / *New Statesman,* v. 125, August 30, 1996. Copyright © 1996 New Statesman, Ltd. Reproduced by permission.

DUFFY, CAROL ANN. Duffy, Carol Ann. From *Mean Time.* Anvil Press Poetry, 1993. Copyright © 1993 Carol Ann Duffy. Reproduced by permission. / Duffy, Carol Ann. From *Selling Manhattan.* Anvil Press Poetry, 1987. Copyright © 1987 Carol Ann Duffy. Reproduced by permission. / Duffy, Carol Ann. From *Standing Female Nude.* Anvil Press Poetry, 1985. Copyright © 1985 Carol Ann Duffy. Reproduced by permission. / Duffy, Carol Ann. From "Originally," in *The Other Country.* Anvil Press Poetry, 1990. Copyright © 1999 Carol Ann Duffy. Reproduced by permission of the author c/o Rogers, Coleridge & White Ltd., 20 Powis Mews, London W11 1JN. / Duffy, Carol Ann. From "Poet for Our Times," in *The Other Country.* Anvil Press Poetry, 1990. Copyright © 1999 Carol Ann Duffy. Reproduced by permission of the author c/o Rogers, Coleridge & White Ltd., 20 Powis Mews, London W11 1JN. / Duffy, Carol Ann. From "Translating the English," in *The Other Country.* Anvil Press Poetry, 1990. Copyright © 1999 Carol Ann Duffy. Reproduced by permission of the author c/o Rogers, Coleridge & White Ltd., 20 Powis Mews, London W11 1JN.

GRENNAN, EAMON. Grennan, Eamon. From "Cave Painters," in *As If It Matters.* Gallery Books, 1991. Copyright © 1991, 1992 by Eamon Grennan. By kind permission of the author and The Gallery Press, Loughcrew, Oldcastle, County Meath, Ireland. In North America by Graywolf Press. / From "Kitchen Vision," in *As If It Matters.* Gallery Books, 1991. Copyright © 1991, 1992 by Eamon Grennan. By kind permission of the author and The Gallery Press, Loughcrew, Oldcastle, County Meath, Ireland. In North America by Graywolf Press. / From / Grennan, Eamon. Rome, The Pantheon," in *Out*

ACKNOWLEDGEMENTS

of Breath. Gallery Books, 2007. Copyright © 2007 by Eamon Grennan. By kind permission of the author and The Gallery Press, Loughcrew, Oldcastle, County Meath, Ireland. In the United States by Graywolf Press. / From *personal correspondence,* August 4, 2010. Reproduced by permission of the author. / From "Two For the Road," in *So It Goes.* Gallery Books, 1995. Copyright © 1995 by Eamon Grennan. By kind permission of the author and The Gallery Press, Loughcrew, Oldcastle, County Meath, Ireland. In North America by Graywolf Press. / From "At Work," in *Still Life with Waterfall.* Gallery Books, 2001. Copyright 2002 by Eamon Grennan. By kind permission of the author and The Gallery Press, Loughcrew, Oldcastle, County Meath, Ireland. In North America by Graywolf Press. / From "Detail," in *Still Life with Waterfall.* Gallery Books, 2001. Copyright 2002 by Eamon Grennan. By kind permission of the author and The Gallery Press, Loughcrew, Oldcastle, County Meath, Ireland. In North America by Graywolf Press. / From "So this is what it comes down to," in *The Quick of It.* Gallery Books, 2004. Copyright © 2005 by Eamon Grennan. By kind permission of the author and The Gallery Press, Loughcrew, Oldcastle, County Meath, Ireland. In North America by Graywolf Press. / From "Autobiographical Sketch: God Help Us," in *unpublished manuscript.* Reproduced by permission of the author. / From "A Gentle Art," in *Wildly for Days.* Gallery Books, 1983. Copyright © 1983 Eamon Grennan. By kind permission of the author and The Gallery Press, Loughcrew, Oldcastle, County Meath, Ireland. In North America by Graywolf Press. / From "Facts of Life, Ballymoney," in *Wildly for Days.* Gallery Books, 1983. Copyright © 1983 Eamon Grennan. By kind permission of the author and The Gallery Press, Loughcrew, Oldcastle, County Meath, Ireland. In North America by Graywolf Press. / From "In Mount Auburn Cemetry," in *Wildly for Days.* Gallery Books, 1983. Copyright © 1983 Eamon Grennan. By kind permission of the author and The Gallery Press, Loughcrew, Oldcastle, County Meath, Ireland. In North America by Graywolf Press. / From "Lying Low," in *Wildly for Days.* Gallery Books, 1983. Copyright © 1983 Eamon Grennan. By kind

permission of the author and The Gallery Press, Loughcrew, Oldcastle, County Meath, Ireland. In North America by Graywolf Press. / From "Something After All," in *Wildly for Days.* Gallery Books, 1983. Copyright © 1983 Eamon Grennan. By kind permission of the author and The Gallery Press, Loughcrew, Oldcastle, County Meath, Ireland. In North America by Graywolf Press. / From "Speech," in *Wildly for Days.* Gallery Books, 1983. Copyright © 1983 Eamon Grennan. By kind permission of the author and The Gallery Press, Loughcrew, Oldcastle, County Meath, Ireland. In North America by Graywolf Press. / Mahon, Derek. From "Preface," in *Wildly for Days.* Gallery Books, 1983. Copyright 1983 by Eamon Grennan. By Kind permission of the author and The Gallery Press, Loughcrew, Oldcastle, County Meath, Ireland. / *The New Republic,* June 11, 1990. Copyright © 1990 by The New Republic, Inc. Reproduced by permission of *The New Republic.*

HADFIELD, JEN. From *Almanacs.* Bloodaxe Books, 2005. Copyright © 2005 by Jen Hadfield. Reproduced by permission. / Hadfield, Jen. From *Nigh–No–Place.* Bloodaxe Books, 2008. Copyright © 2008 by Jen Hadfield. Reproduced by permission. / *Financial Times,* February 27, 2010. Copyright © 2010 Financial Times Information Ltd. Reproduced by permission. / *The Times,* January 14, 2009. Copyright © 2009 Times Newspapers Ltd. Reproduced by permission. / *Times Literary Supplement,* May 23, 2008. Copyright © 2008 by The Times Supplements Limited. Reproduced from *Times Literary Supplement* by permission.

INGALLS, RACHEL. David Cowart, "Fantasy and Reality in Mrs. Caliban" *Critique,* 1989. Reproduced by permission of Taylor & Francis Group, LLC, http://www.taylorandfrancis.com and the author. / Alan MacDonald, "Re–Writing Hemingway: Rachel Ingalls Binstead's Safari," *Critique,* spring, 1993. Taylor & Francis Group, LLC, http://www.taylorandfrancis.com. / *Kliatt,* v. 40, March, 2006. Reproduced by permission. / *Library Journal,* October 15, 2005. Reproduced by permission. / William Packard, "The Pearlkillers: Four Novells by Rachel Ingalls," *Los Angeles Times,* August 16, 1987. / Anne

ACKNOWLEDGEMENTS

Bernays, "Brother Anselm, in a Family Way," *New York Times,* August 31, 1986. / *Publishers Weekly,* 2005. Reproduced from *Publishers Weekly,* published by the PWxyz, LLC, by permission. / *The Times,* January 27, 2000. Copyright © 2000 Times Newspapers Ltd. Reproduced by permission. / *Village Voice,* December 20, 2005. Reproduced with the permission of *Village Voice.*

LEVY, ANDREA. Scarman, Sir Leslie George. From *The Scarman Report: The Brixton Disorders, 10–12 April 1981.* Penguin Books, 1983.

POLIAKOFF, STEPHEN. Poliakoff, Stephen. From *The Lost Prince.* Methuen, 2003. / *The Guardian,* November 28, 2009. Copyright © 2009 by Guardian News & Media Ltd. Reproduced by permission of Guardian News Service, LTD.

RAINE, KATHLEEN. Raine, Kathleen. From *The Collected Poems of Kathleen Raine.* Golgonooza Press, 2008. Copyright © 2008 The Literary Estate of Kathleen Raine. Reproduced by permission.

SAMPSON, FIONA. Sampson, Fiona. From *Common Prayer.* Carcanet, 2007. Copyright © Fiona Sampson, 2007. Reproduced by permission of Carcanet Press Limited. / Sampson, Fiona. From *Folding the Real.* Seren, 2001. Copyright © 2001 Fiona Sampson. Reproduced by permission. / Sampson, Fiona. From *Rough Music.* Carcanet, 2010. Copyright © Fiona Sampson 2010. Reproduced by permission of Carcanet Press Limited. / Sampson, Fiona. From *The Distance Between Us.* Seren, 2005. Copyright © 2005 Fiona Sampson. Reproduced by permission.

THUBRON, COLIN. *The Independent,* October 10, 1999; November 19, 2006. Copyright © 1999, 2006 by Independent Newspapers (UK) Ltd. Both reproduced by permission. / *Los Angeles Times Book Review,* October 6, 1985. Reproduced by permission. / The Observer, July 28, 2002 for "Back to the Heart of Darkness" by Robert McCrum. Copyright (c) 2002 by Guardian Publications Ltd. / *Third World Quarterly,* v. 12, 1990–1991 for "Behind the Wall" by John Gittings. Copyright © 1990 Taylor & Francis Group, LLC.

List of Subjects

Introduction

"A classic is a book that has never finished saying what it has to say," said the Italian novelist and critic, Italo Calvino. I would take this even further to suggest that almost any good book —classic or not—succeeds by refusing to complete its meaning. That is, the more closely you read the book, and the more often you return to it, the more you learn as it opens more fully, revealing complexities and nuances. But this process of opening demands careful reading, which in turns means scrutiny at a level rarely accomplished in a single reading. In some case, this careful reading is accomplished with help from a good critic, and this brings us to the articles in this particular volume, which is designed to help readers in the pleasurable work of reading good books—poetry, fiction, plays, nonfiction—attentively.

One of the goals of *British Writers* has always been to examine the lives as well as the work of authors with intensity and expertise, helping the reader to make connections between the life and work, which are rarely separate. We have tried, in the seventeen volumes thus far published, to show in what ways the writer's reading may have figured, too, in the development of her or his own literary productions. The articles in this series represent intellectual biographies, tracking the growth of an author's career over a crucial period, when he or she was most fully engaged in creating a body of work. The author's historical context is also an important part of each article.

In this volume we bring together a range of essays on writers who have developed a substantial reputation in the world of literature. As in previous collections, the subjects were chosen for their contribution to the traditions of British, Irish, or Anglophone writing (being texts written in English, indebted to the British tradition to some extent, often written by authors from former colonial states. Such a definition includes, for example, Canadian, Australian, New Zealand, and South African writers—or any writer whose primary language is English). We hope readers will find these essays useful, and that they will prove helpful to those unfamiliar with the work of a particular writer yet also interesting to those who know it well. What these articles contain are close readings of poems, plays, memoirs, or novels and some analysis of the cultural context of the career as it unfolds in time, in a particular place. A considerable element of each essay is therefore biographical and historical as well as critical.

British Writers started life as an offshoot of a series of monographs that appeared between 1959 and 1972, the *Minnesota Pamphlets on American Writers*. These pamphlets on American authors were extremely popular at the time. They were well written and informative, taking into account the work of ninety-seven American writers in a format and style that attracted a devoted following. The series proved invaluable to a generation of students and teachers, who could depend on these reliable and interesting critiques of major figures. The idea of reprinting these essays occurred to Charles Scribner, Jr., an innovative publisher during the middle decades of the twentieth century. The series appeared in four volumes entitled *American Writers: A Collection of Literary Biographies* (1974). *British Writers* followed, gathering a series of essays originally published by the British Council. These proved popular as well, and fourteen supplements have now followed. The goal of the supplements has been consistent with the original idea of the series: to provide clear, informative essays aimed at the general reader. These essays often rise to a high level of

INTRODUCTION

craft and critical vision, but they are meant to introduce a writer of some importance, taking into account previous scholarship and recent critical thinking.

The writers of these articles are, by and large, teachers and scholars. Many have published books and articles in their field, often on the work of the author under review. As anyone glancing through this volume will notice, our critics have been held to high standards of clarity as well as sound scholarship. Jargon and theoretical reflections have been discouraged, except when strictly relevant. Each of the articles concludes with a select bibliography of works by the author under discussion and secondary works that might be useful to those wishing to pursue the subject further. In this supplement, the eighteenth in the series, we treat a number of classic authors from previous centuries, including Charlotte Dacre, Ann Hawkshaw, Thomas Heywood, and Mark Pattison. For various reasons, these have yet to be treated in this series, although each of them is an important and "classic" writer. For the most part, this supplement centers on modern or contemporary writers from various genres and traditions. Few of them have had little sustained attention from critics, although they are well known. Gregory Burke, Seamus Deane, Len Deighton, Carol Ann Duffy, Eamon Grennan, Jen Hadfield, Rachel Ingalls, Andrea Levy, William McIlvanney, Helen Oyeyemi, Stephen Poliakoff, Kathleen Raine, Fiona Sampson, and Colin Thubron have all been written about in the review pages of newspapers and magazines, often at length, and their work has acquired a following, but their careers have yet to attract significant scholarship. That will certainly follow, but the articles included in this volume constitute a beginning of sorts, an attempt to map out the particular universe of each writer.

Our belief, as always, is that general readers will discover in these pages a number of authors who will continue to speak to them for years to come. These articles represent a considerable effort by each critic, who has done a significant amount of research on the life and times of the author at hand, looking for the contours, the lay of the intellectual landscape in each case. The close reading of individual works are designed to stimulate ideas and prompt further reading. Overall, I believe we have managed to assemble an extremely interesting and varied group of writers in this supplement, and my hope that readers will agree.

—JAY PARINI

Contributors

Debbie Bark. Dr. Debbie Bark is a scholar of the nineteenth century, working at the University of Reading and for the Open University. Her research specialism is nineteenth-century poetry, particularly the Manchester poetic revival of the 1830s and 1840s. Her most recent research recovered the work of Ann Hawkshaw, combining close textual analysis with biographical, contextual and intertextual research to make the first coordinated reading of Hawkshaw's poetry, published in four collections between 1842 and 1871. ANN HAWKSHAW

Zoë Brigley Thompson. Zoë Brigley Thompson is a Visiting Research Fellow at Northampton University, England. Most recently, she edited the Routledge volume, *Feminism Literature and Rape Narratives* (2010). She has written on contemporary poetry for *Orbis Litterarum* and the *Journal of International Women's Studies,* and reviews for *Contemporary Women's Writing, English Studies* and ABES. She has received an Eric Gregory Award (2003) and the English Association's Poetry Fellows' Award (2007). Her debut poetry collection, *The Secret* (Bloodaxe, 2007) was a Poetry Book Society recommended title and was long-listed for the Dylan Thomas Award. JEN HADFIELD

Oliver S. Buckton. Oliver S. Buckton was born in London, England, and educated at Cambridge and Cornell Universities. He is a professor of English at Florida Atlantic University in Boca Raton, where he teaches British literature, film, and literary theory. He is the author of *Secret Selves: Confession and Same-Sex Desire in Victorian Autobiography* (University of North Carolina Press, 1998), and *Cruising with Robert Louis Stevenson: Travel, Narrative, and the Colonial Body* (Ohio University Press, 2007). A longtime enthusiast of spy fiction, he is currently researching a book-length project on the British spy novel from 1900 to the present. LEN DEIGHTON

Ashley J. Cross. Ashley J. Cross is an Associate Professor of English at Manhattan College in the Bronx, where she teaches courses in nineteenth-century British literature, women's literature, literary theory, and writing. She has published articles on the Shelleys, Mary Robinson, Coleridge, and Aphra Behn in *ELH, Women's Writing, Studies in Romanticism, Fellow Romantics* (edited by Beth Lau) and the *MLA Approaches to Teaching Oroonoko.* She has also written essays on Mary Robinson and Anna Seward for Scribner's *British Writers* series. Her current work focuses on dialogues between male and female Romantic writers. CHARLOTTE DACRE

Katherine Firth. Dr. Katherine Firth is International Visiting Scholar at the School of Culture and Communications at the University of Melbourne and Visiting Research Fellow at Trinity College, Melbourne. She has previously published on aspects of nineteenth- and twentieth-century poetry, particularly in relation to music, and is currently working on collaborations between poets, composers and performers in the early twentieth century. KATHLEEN RAINE

Christopher Kydd. Christopher Kydd is currently researching a thesis examining the transatlantic dimensions of contemporary Scottish crime fiction at the University of Dundee, where he is also involved in teaching modules in literature and film studies. His research interests include crime fiction of all kinds, twen-

CONTRIBUTORS

tieth-century Scottish fiction, genre theory, transnational studies, film noir, the novels of Alasdair Gray, and the films of the Coen brothers and Billy Wilder. WILLIAM McILVANNEY

Joseph Lennon. Joseph Lennon is Director of Irish Studies and Associate Professor of English at Villanova University. He earned a Ph.D. at the University of Connecticut in 2000, M.A. degrees at Boston College (Irish Studies) and Northern Illinois University (English), and a B.A. from Knox College. His book *Irish Orientalism: A Literary and Intellectual History* (Syracuse University Press, 2004) won the Donald J. Murphy Prize for Distinguished First Book from the American Conference for Irish Studies. His debut volume of poetry, *Fell Hunger,* was published by Salmon Press (2010). EAMON GRENNAN

Gail Low. Gail Low teaches book history and contemporary literatures in English at the University of Dundee. She co-edited *A Black British Canon* (Palgrave Macmillan, 2006) with Marion Wynne Davies and is the author of *Publishing the Postcolonial* (Routledge, 2010) and *White Skins/Black Masks* (Routledge, 1996). HELEN OYEYEMI

Maureen Manier. Maureen Manier attended the University of Notre Dame where she spent her junior year studying literature in Dublin. During that year she studied modern Irish poetry with Seamus Deane and completed an independent study project under his direction. She is now vice president of marketing and communications for Riley Children's Foundation in Indianapolis. SEAMUS DEANE

Steven Matthews. Steven Matthews is Professor of English at Oxford Brookes University, UK. He is author of *Irish Poetry: Politics, History, Negotiation. The Evolving Debate, 1969 to the Present* (Macmillan, 1997); *Yeats as Precursor* (Macmillan in 2000); and *Les Murray* (Manchester University Press, *Contemporary World Writers* Series, 2001). He has contributed the volume on Modernism to the *Contexts* series

(Bloomsbury Academic) of which he is founding editor. (2004). He is also editor of the *Sourcebooks* series for Palgrave, where his *Modernism* appeared in 2008. He is completing a study of influence and the Renaissance in T. S. Eliot's poetry for Oxford University Press (2012). FIONA SAMPSON

Abby Mims. Abby Mims' fiction and essays have been featured in *The Santa Monica Review, Other Voices, Swink,* in the 2006 Emerging Voices show at the Beverly Hills Library, as well as several anthologies, including *Cassette From My Ex* and *Woman's Best Friend: Women Writers on the Dogs in Their Lives.* She has an MFA from University of California at Irvine and is currently at work on a collection of essays and a novel. COLIN THUBRON

Niall Munro. Niall Munro works primarily in the field of American Literature, in the areas of poetry and drama. His recent doctoral research examined the queer modernist aesthetic of the poet Hart Crane, and he is currently at work on studies of the American avant-garde theater practitioner Joseph Chaikin, and of the Federal Theatre Project. He teaches at Oxford Brookes University in the UK. STEPHEN POLIAKOFF

Nissa Parmar. Nissa Parmar is writing a doctoral thesis that identifies and analyzes an American strain of poetry which includes the work of Walt Whitman, Emily Dickinson, William Carlos Williams, Adrienne Rich, Marilyn Chin, and Sherman Alexie. She has taught English and Humanities in a variety of academic settings and currently works as an adjunct instructor at the college level. CAROL ANN DUFFY

Philip Parry. Philip Parry teaches English and Drama at the University of St. Andrews in Scotland. He specialises in academic aspects of playwriting, acting, and dramaturgical theory in Shakespeare, and in contemporary British and American theater. GREGORY BURKE

Sayanti Ganguly Puckett. Sayanti Ganguly Puckett received her doctorate in seventeenth-

CONTRIBUTORS

century British and nineteenth-century colonial literature from Oklahoma State University in 2009. She is now an Assistant Professor in the English department at Johnson County Community College in Kansas. She is currently working on a book on the libertine "babus" of nineteenth-century Calcutta. THOMAS HEYWOOD

Yumna Siddiqi. Yumna Siddiqi is an Associate Professor of English at Middlebury College, where she specializes in postcolonial South Asian, African and Caribbean literature, postcolonial theory, diaspora and migration studies, literary theory, nineteenth- and twentieth-century British literature, and gender studies. Her book *Anxieties of Empire and the Fiction of Intrigue* (Columbia University Press, 2008) explores the contradictions of postcolonial modernity in turn of the nineteenth- and turn of the twentieth-century fiction of detection and espionage. She has published articles on postcolonial literature and culture in *Cultural Critique,* *Victorian Literature and Culture, Renaissance Drama, Alif,* and *South Asia Research.* ANDREA LEVY

Christopher Vilmar. Christopher Vilmar is Assistant Professor of English at Salisbury University, where he teaches widely in British literature and culture. He has written on Samuel Johnson, John Arbuthnot, and Mark Pattison. His current research includes a monograph on Johnson and eighteenth-century satire as well as co-editing (with Adam Rounce) the poetry volume of the forthcoming *Wiley-Blackwell Encyclopedia of British Literature, 1660-1789.* MARK PATTISON

Julie Wakeman-Linn. Julie Wakeman-Linn is an instructor at Montgomery College, and editor of the *Potomac Review.* She is the author of short stories and nonfiction, and received a Pushcart Prize nomination in 2010. She is currently at work on two novels. RACHEL INGALLS

BRITISH WRITERS

GREGORY BURKE

(1968—)

Philip Parry

GREGORY BURKE, BORN in Dunfermline, in Scotland, in 1968, was late arriving as a dramatist but has quickly made up for lost time. *Gagarin Way* (2001)—though an immediate and overwhelming success that within weeks of its first night had significantly changed the face of contemporary Scottish theater—did not appear on stage until its author was thirty-three years old, nor did it grow out of any preestablished interest in drama. Instead, according to Burke's self-deprecating retelling of events, it was the result of a happy accident. Bored with temporary jobs and poor wages, he had wanted to prove his worth by writing a novel, but, finding description difficult and dialogue easy, he thought of supplying scripts for television or film instead. However, having invented four characters who spend all their time talking politics in a single room (his description is deliberately unflattering), he felt that the only alternative left to fall back upon was traditional theater.

But happy accidents have happy outcomes. Just four published stage-plays later—*The Straits* (2004), *On Tour* (2005), *Black Watch* (2007), and *Hoors* (2009)—Burke has eclipsed (whether permanently or not is an open question) his more productive and longer-established contemporaries: David Harrower (1966–), Anthony Neilson (1967–), even perhaps the famously precocious and hugely prolific David Greig (1969–). Indeed, among modern Scottish writers of his generation only Irvine Welsh (1958–), not primarily a dramatist, is more immediately recognizable. Moreover Burke is not merely hugely successful but is successful in ways that have earned him a rare and deserved combination of popular acclaim and critical respect. *Black Watch*, for example, appeals to a wide range of audiences, not all of whom will agree about what they have

seen, but it is also a radical and innovative piece of work—perhaps a pageant, certainly not a conventional play—that, properly considered, may prompt even the most reluctant theorist to redefine theater. And, whether or not Burke is judged to be a political dramatist of the left or of the right, all of his plays raise issues that in a period of severe economic recession confront us urgently. In the United Kingdom, for example, both national and local-council funding of theater is widespread and taken for granted but is now, at the time of writing and for the foreseeable future, under threat. "When it comes to the allocation of scarce resources," Burke asserted presciently in a *Guardian* interview seven years before the banking crisis hit the Western world, "there are a lot more deserving cases than theatre" (July 6, 2002). Theater is expensive, resources are scarce, choices will have to be made; Burke's views are not unusual, but it is unusual for a playwright to express them so boldly or with such persistence. "People ask me why I write plays," he told Anna Burnside in a 2009 interview (*Sunday Times*, April 26, 2009). "I get commissioned to write them and I do it for money" was his explanation.

The economic aspects of theater are worth stressing. Plays in performance are always the products of costly interactions between individuals (actors, writers, members of the audience) and organizations (theater companies, production teams, managements, agents, fund-raisers, sponsors). A symbol of these interactions is the way in which the Faber first edition of *Gagarin Way* doubles, as is often the case with Faber editions of new plays, as a set of program notes. When you walked into the Traverse Theatre in Edinburgh in July 2001 to collect your ticket for this much-applauded play by a rising Scottish talent, you were able to buy a copy of the text at a generous discount, bound in with which were nine pages of conventional program-matter that related quite specifically to the production that you were about to see: a cast list, advertising material about the play's sponsors, a brief note on the author's life and an authorial preface, cast and crew biographies, a list of the actors who workshopped the play prior to rehearsal, a couple of pages of acknowledgements and commercial sponsorship details, and even thanks to the soap company that supplied the wardrobe department with cleaning products. Much of this material, detailing financial and practical arrangements that have to be in place if any professional production is to proceed, is of a kind that students of theater conspire to ignore as they exalt art above economics. Yet Burke's preface and the greater part of *Gagarin Way* itself insist that we remember the economic basis of all human activity. Prepared three months before the play's first performance, the preface presents a list of themes and interests and also a style of writing, a mixture of self-defensive flippancy and underlying seriousness, that is characteristic of Burke whenever he is discussing his own work.

LIFE

Burke's father was a dockyard worker at the naval shipyard in Rosyth, three miles from Dunfermline. This service background shaped Burke's early life and adolescence in profound ways. Between 1979 and 1984 the family was stationed at the British naval base in Gibraltar. There in 1982 was assembled a fleet of ships, a twentieth-century armada-in-reverse, to take troops out to recapture the Falkland Islands, a British crown protectorate in the South Atlantic that had been invaded by Argentina. This task was swiftly accomplished with relatively few British casualties, and it became a defining moment in the political life of the United Kingdom's first female prime minister, Margaret Thatcher. (A figure not mentioned in Burke's plays yet a pregnant absence; a woman dominant in a traditionally male role, Thatcher held office from

1979 until 1990.) Burke's return to Fife, and his recovery of the local accent that he had lost during his time in Gibraltar, coincided with a second major episode in Thatcher's political life, the miners' strike that lasted for nearly a year in 1984–1985. She provocatively linked this strike to the Falkland conflict by boasting in Parliament that, having defeated the enemies without, she would now defeat the enemies within.

After having been taught locally in schools in Rosyth, Gibraltar, and Dunfermline, Burke entered the University of Stirling, a new Scottish university situated about forty miles from Dunfermline, where he read politics. His time there was unhappy. For reasons that have only recently emerged, he left without completing his degree and under a cloud that waited twenty years to pour down upon him its burden of rain. In 2009, riding on the back of the international success of *Black Watch*, Stirling University offered him an honorary doctorate but found itself embroiled in controversy when newspapers reported that while he was an undergraduate he had been disciplined—though not expelled—for an attack on a seventeen-year-old male student. Urged to apologize, Burke was reported in the *Sunday Times* as offering the following explanation:

> I got banned from campus for a fight … I'm not going to apologise for that. Coming from Dunfermline, if someone looked at you squint, you went across and battered them. […] If somebody was wide with you, you fought them. University was one of the first places where I encountered people who weren't like that. They might have been looking at you because they liked what you had on. Whereas I still thought: what are you looking at? That was a culture shock for me.
>
> (quoted in Stuart MacDonald, 2009)

In many ways this is an illuminating statement that casts light on class and character elements in his plays, but it did little to stem opposition to the proposed honor. Shortly afterward, to spare the university embarrassment, Burke withdrew his acceptance of the degree, as the BBC reported on May 1, by an uncomfortable coincidence the day on which *Hoors*, his most recent stage play, received its world premiere at the Traverse.

Having dropped out of university Burke became, among other things, a dishwasher. But he also did something much more positive. In 1998, having written an early version of *Gagarin Way* that he kept by him for a year, he sent it to John Tiffany, a young director who was at that time literary adviser to the Traverse Theatre in Edinburgh. Tiffany liked it, put it through a work-shopping session, and encouraged Burke to revise it. Trimmed and tightened, it emerged in 2001 to enormous acclaim at the Edinburgh Fringe in a coproduction between the Traverse and the London-based Royal National Theatre Studio. This was the beginning of Burke's short journey toward unparalleled success. (There is a vivid account of the impact of *Gagarin Way* upon Burke's life in an article that he published in the *Guardian* newspaper on April 12, 2003.)

BACKGROUND

The kingdom of Fife (an ancient and officially redundant title, though commonly used and more attractive than the "unitary council area" of modern administrative jargon) is the setting of three of Burke's five plays and is the spiritual homeland of all of them. This might seem surprising if one contrasts his plays' postindustrial roughness with Fife's largely pastoral image in modern advertising, but it is also a divided county: to the northwest and northeast there are farms and fishing villages and the university city of St. Andrews—very much not the Fife that Burke records with such precision—but from Glenrothes southward and toward the west is historic coal-mining territory with a proud tradition of militant trade unionism. This last has expressed itself in hostility toward free-market capitalism and the United States of America and in sympathetic support for socialism and the former Soviet Union: all of which is indicated in the play's title and explained in the body of its text. This militancy exhibited itself with special forcefulness twice in the twentieth century: in the General Strike in 1926, when Fife miners were among the last to return to work, and fifty-eight years later during the national coal miners' strike in 1984–1985. The defeat of this protracted but ill-judged strike (see Eddie's condemnation of it in *Gagarin Way*, p. 69) left the National Union of Miners divided and crippled and led indirectly to the extinction of coal-mining in Fife and its replacement by new industries—in finance and Internet technology and light engineering—that were designed to absorb out-of-work miners. (Val McDermid's *A Darker Domain*, which appeared in 2008, is a thriller set both in the present and in 1984 in Coaltown of East Wemyss. McDermid, a Fifer who grew up in a mining community, gives a vivid picture of how divisive and destructive the strike was at a local level.)

Parallel to the loss of the coal industry was the transfer to private hands of the dockyard at Rosyth in 1987 and the closure of the naval base, with a substantial loss of civilian jobs, in 1994. These things were the cost-cutting consequences of the collapse of the Soviet Union, the end of the cold war, and the advent of the so-called peace dividend. Politicians applauded an opportunity to cut the defense budget while wringing their hands over the loss of jobs in heavy industry that would inevitably follow. Eddie's judgment is unequivocally bleak. "I've not been up the town for ages," Tom tells him, to which Eddie replies: "You're no missing anything. The alpha males are still out in force. The gene pool's still as shallow. (*Beat.*) It's no the same though ... no sailors tay fight since they shut the yard ... fucking peace dividend ... cameras everywhere ... it's pish" (*Gagarin Way*, p. 19).

Most of Burke's plays are involved in one way or another with these issues. *Gagarin Way* applauds the Fife socialist tradition, celebrates the spirit that underpinned the miners' strike, but also shows the debilitating impact on male pride of the loss of the county's traditional industries. Light industry, because it provides jobs that are as suitable for women as for men, is not a complete answer to the problems of long-term male unemployment. Eddie, a bit like Burke himself in this respect, makes a joke of things:

> I used to live way [with] a lassie like. (*Beat.*) Well ... I say lived way her ... more ponced off her really ay. (*Beat.*) It's tough when your salaries arenay [are not] compatible. (*Beat.*) I didnay object to her be-

ing the main breadwinner like ... she was the old-fashioned one. I thought she woulday, ken [would have, you understand] ... fucking applauded my willingness tay abdicate fay [from] the traditional male role ... but she couldnay understand why I didnay want equality.

(p. 17)

Issues of masculine loss of self-respect remain. "Ponced off" is a revealing verb; for a man to live off his wife's earnings makes those earnings immoral by turning her into a prostitute and him into a pimp. Eight years later, in *Hoors*, Tony tells Nikki that "a man's got to ponce off someone" when he is trying both to seduce her and to find out what work she does (p. 61). Women, he adds, are now outdrinking men, thus robbing them of the last activity in which male dominance remains.

GAGARIN WAY

Granted Burke's personal history, the political and historical background to which *Gagarin Way* so frequently alludes, and its violent and murderous plot, one might have expected a very different kind of play. Instead one gets a comedy of manners, and not especially bad manners, in which all four of the play's characters, two of whom will murder the other two, participate in verbal comedic routines that have their origins in music hall. Thus, while recovering from concussion, Frank—whose name means "free," who may have achieved through insight a measure of personal freedom, but who is nonetheless bound at this point both by his job and by Gary and Eddie—asks a question. There then follows an extended verbal exchange (from which the following extract omits stage directions to bring out the pattern of the dialogue more clearly). It might also be worth pointing out, since some people find it disconcerting, that Burke's frequent and routine obscenities, though sexual in origin, are almost never sexual in their application:

EDDIE: Where are you from?

FRANK: Leven.

GARY: Leven?

TOM: Leven. Fife.

EDDIE: You're kidding me on ay?

GARY: Did he say Leven?

EDDIE: He said Leven.

GARY: Fucking Leven.

EDDIE: The cunt.

GARY: He cannay be fay [from] Leven.

TOM: That's what he said.

EDDIE: I'm gonnay fucking kill the cunt if he's fay Leven. You're fucking dead if you're fay Leven.

GARY: He doesnay sound like he's fay Leven. You dinnay sound like you're fay Leven.

FRANK: Well I wouldn't ... I haven't lived here for ...

EDDIE: Let me kill him.

FRANK: ... for years.

(pp. 54–55)

Generally speaking, whenever this type of patterned speech emerges it is Eddie, the play's consummate wordsmith, who has the last word. And it is he, too, who ends the play as a whole: "We better get a move on. We've got tay be back in here in two hours. We dinnay want tay be fucking late. *Curtain*" (p. 92). Curtain, but also curtains. In real life the story could not possibly end here: there would be bodies to dispose of, blood to wash away, police enquiries to combat. But the play—for no play, when all is said and done, is simply a transcription of reality—just ends, but does so in a puzzling half-echo of the final words and last stage direction of Samuel Beckett's *Waiting for Godot*.

Eddie is exceptionally articulate. Is he, then, Burke's spokesman? Hardly, although Eddie's verbal facility and his self-conscious art of speech do link him both to the play's author and to its principal victim, the university-educated Frank. Indeed Frank's spirited defense of himself as standing in no need of defense earns Eddie's admiration and prompts a sense of kinship.

Moreover Frank's main point, that revolution simply cannot get started in a society where everyone is built into the very structure that revolution would need to overturn, has already been enthusiastically exemplified by Eddie's endorsement of designer labels and Big Macs. Eddie, wonderfully seductive while he remains trapped on stage, is someone you would take great care to avoid in real life. He is also utterly apolitical: for him violence is at best a hobby or an experiment. For good or ill, since it is hard to decide whether purposive or purposeless torture is the more sinister, he merely flirts with Gary's view that violence can be an acceptable part of a carefully planned political course of action. Eddie tells Tom: "I thought ... seen [seeing] as how I'm a bit more mature now, seen as how I've advanced way beyond the point ay [of] thinking going home to kick the loved ones in the puss is the path to spiritual contentment, I thought I should maybe try something more idealistic, something way a point [...] violence way a reason" (p. 41).

Those who cannot engage with the play's humor (and it is not a taste for every palate) will think this merely gross. But that is to miss quite a bit of what matters; the words here are genuinely witty in the way in which they mix linguistic registers as they move from "puss" (slang for face or mouth) to "spiritual contentment." Our pleasure, though, should not deafen us to the fact that Eddie is a hyperintelligent but emotionally pinched psychopath. Fifty pages later the joke that Burke is here setting up with considerable care comes to its gory conclusion. "You're too fucking emotionally involved," Eddie tells Gary, deficient emotional involvement being one of the classic symptoms of a psychopathic personality:

(*Stabs Tom.*) That's a big fucking weakness. (*Stabs Tom.*) You end up relying on cunts. (*Stabs Tom.*) This cunt couldnay be relied on. (*Stabs Tom.*) You get rid of everything you cannay rely on. (*Stabs Tom.*)

(p. 91)

So is Tom—the play's innocent abroad, the boy who has stumbled into a man's world—Burke's spokesman? Hardly, though like the writer-interviewer of *Black Watch* he is one of Burke's

highly ironical versions of himself. Tom, with his degree in politics from Stirling (notably both the university and the degree-course that Burke dropped out of), has impeccable credentials—a father who is a former shipwright and a grandfather who was a miner—but his own contribution to political awareness is to have written an undergraduate dissertation on working-class militancy in Lumphinnans between the wars, based on interviews with former miners and union men, in which it is clear, though not quite clear to Tom, that he has been taken for a ride. He is in favor of a blending of conservative and socialist politics that seeks to preserve the strength of both traditions: probably not the syndicalism that Gary mentions approvingly but the Third Way associated with the academic sociologist Anthony Giddens (1938–) and his disciple, Tony Blair (British prime minister from 1997–2008). But this serves only to unite Gary and Frank in foul-mouthed condemnation of him.

Is Gary, who thinks that the kidnapping and killing of Frank will send a message to the media and beyond, Burke's spokesman? But to be a spokesman you have to be able to speak, and to pass on a message you need greater verbal skill than Gary possesses. In this area even Tom surpasses him, as his analysis of the note that Gary plans to pin to Frank's corpse makes embarrassingly clear. Or is Frank, who thinks that in a world where everyone is complicit there is no one who will take responsibility for receiving messages, Burke's spokesman? Much depends upon whether one thinks that Frank is right. Gary by the end of the play certainly thinks so. Frank's unintended death—a murder, not a political assassination; stabbed not shot—"doesnay mean anything [...] It's just murder [...] It means nothing" (p. 89).

But what of the play? Does it mean anything? Or is it, as some have suggested, merely an unwitting tribute to moral uprootedness and political indifference? In particular is it one of those plays which is up-to-date one moment and behind-the-times the next? When it transferred to the Cottesloe stage at the National Theatre complex in London in September 2001, critics who had reviewed it in Edinburgh were able to give it a second airing, while those who had not were able to see what all the fuss had been about. But only for a short while. On September 11, 2001, a dust storm greater than any new play can raise rolled in from across the Atlantic. Some critics suggested that *Gagarin Way* had simply been overtaken by events and that Frank's claim that nobody has anything to overthrow because we all draw benefit from what we oppose was proved wrong. Most prominent among these was Michael Billington, who in a review of the play's London production for the *Guardian* in October 2001 wrote that "the world has totally changed since Burke wrote his play: even the idea that the multinationals are impervious has been shattered." Looking back, however, it is not clear what point Billington is making, unless perhaps he is saying that post–Twin Towers at least we know who our enemies are. But, several years later and with the War on Terror as unfocused as ever, that is not a very comforting observation nor an obvious dismissal of *Gagarin Way*. More significantly, perhaps, in a mood of growing financial pessimism and shared economic impotence, reviewers—in particular, Roger Cox and Ariadne Cass-Maran in 2009—greeted recent revivals of the play by claiming it to be more relevant than ever.

THE STRAITS

One consequence of the exceptional level of success of *Gagarin Way* both at home and abroad was that Burke was awarded a Pearson Television Bursary, which attached him to the Royal National Theatre studio in London. This move enabled him to keep in touch with John Tiffany, who had become associate director of Paines Plough, a London-based company founded in 1974 to encourage new theater writing. (The company's artistic director was Vicky Featherstone, who in 2004 would become inaugural director of the National Theatre of Scotland.) One result was a forty-minute radio play, *Occy Eyes*, for BBC Scotland in 2003 and a project to convert it into a full-length stage-play. This expanded version—retitled *The Straits*, directed by Tiffany, and cosponsored by theaters in Hamp-

stead and Plymouth—was to be given its first performance in the Traverse in August 2003 as part of the Edinburgh Fringe.

In the light of what we now know it seems best to judge *The Straits*, a study of an isolated military community under stress, as a milestone, both for its author and its director, on the road to *Black Watch*. However, in 2003, a year before *Black Watch* was on anybody's horizon, it was Burke's eagerly awaited second play. Although it was well received, in part owing to Tiffany's vigorous staging of it, some critics felt it to be a less than fully dynamic follow-up to *Gagarin Way*. Yet this second play has considerable merits, some of them of a kind that are not immediately associated with Burke. At the level on which it is most obviously successful it tells the story of four adolescents, children of dockyard workers and servicemen, idling away their summer on a British overseas naval base. Until they are old enough to enlist, Doink (who is English) and Jock (who is Scottish) hunt octopuses, which they sell to local restaurants. They are joined by Darren and Tracy, newcomers anxious to establish themselves: Tracy, who is seventeen, by dating sailors; Darren, her deeply insecure fifteen-year-old brother, by latching onto older boys whose attitudes and conduct he imitates. Finding a place and a space you can call your own in a hierarchy that allows your basic individuality to flourish are concerns, acutely felt by teenagers but by no means unique to them, that are at the center of Burke's interest.

Two things complicate what is in outline a very simple play. One is internal to it, a matter of characterization blossoming as plot; for it is Doink, although he is in many ways the weakest personality in the play, around whom the others revolve. By contrast Jock, despite his physical presence and fearlessness, is far from being a stereotypically assertive Scot proud of his country and protective of his non-English identity. Indeed, like Burke himself while on Gibraltar, he has lost his accent in an effort to blend in with his surroundings, a loss that parallels Darren's much more desperate act of assimilation later in the play. As a result Jock is both defined and demeaned by Doink, so much so that his principal attempt at preserving his difference merely proves how completely it has evaporated. "He's the only English kid to play for a spic team," Doink says (p. 35), carelessly including the Scots among the English yet provoking no protest from Jock by doing so.

Doink divides his world into an undiscriminating opposition between "us" (the English) and "them" (the spics); seeks to impose this opposition upon those around him; and does so with varying degrees of success that Burke sets down with insight and subtlety. Tracy uses the term only once and in a context that calls its propriety into question; Darren, by contrast, uses it often and unthinkingly; while Jock uses it sparingly, but with gathering frequency in the scenes where, pressured to show sympathy, he throws in his lot with Doink. It is a term that is applied to three quite distinct groups. First are the Spanish, whose government intermittently presses for restored sovereignty over Gibraltar. Then there are those who live, work, and vote in Gibraltar, most of whom are ethnically Spanish but who have adopted British forenames and consistently vote to retain their British status. They are quite brutally dismissed by Doink: "The spics might say they're British but they're only fuckin British cos this place belongs to us. It's us that puts the food in their fuckin mouths. They might all be called Albert an fuckin George an Montgomery an stuff but they're all fuckin spics when it comes to it" (pp. 11–12).

And finally there are the "Argies"—Spanish-speaking South Americans whose military forces have invaded the Falkland Islands. Doink is quick to spot what he thinks is a significant link between these groups: "If we let the Argies have the Falklands the Spanish could just walk in here an have this place" (p. 19). But this assertiveness is the product of insecurity rather than of insight; Doink's older brother is serving aboard HMS *Sheffield* in the Falklands, and toward him Doink is deeply subservient. As Jock tells Tracy: "His brother, yeah. He's a brilliant bloke. He'll do anythin. He's good at everythin. Football, swimmin, fightin. Doink ain't so good at stuff. Cept fightin. He's good at fightin" (p. 57). It is Doink's blaming of the Argentine "spics" for causing his brother's death that feeds the revenge that is sated indirectly, through Darren's killing of a "spic" who is hunting for octopus in a stretch of water off Gibraltar that Doink deems to be narrowly British.

The second complication is political. "There is no mention of politics in *Occy Eyes*, but political it certainly is," Burke wrote in the 2003 *Guardian* article "Funny Peculiar." Whether he was referring to his radio play or to its stage version is not clear but the relevance of his comments to *The Straits* is not in doubt. How he defines what he means by "politics" is crucial, for by doing so he points forward toward *Black Watch*, backward toward *Gagarin Way*, and shows what unites all three plays. The characters in *The Straits* are, he says in the 2003 article, "part of a working-class community who define themselves in terms of service to the crown." They form a community "where brothers, fathers and grandfathers join the same services, in some cases the same units, for generations, in exactly the same way that the old industrial communities handed down their trades and their politics from father to son. Communities like Portsmouth, Plymouth, Chatham and, in Scotland, Rosyth."

But is the play political in the sense that it contributes toward an enhanced understanding of the Falklands War itself? And, if it is, why is there "no mention of politics" in the printed play? The answer lies in part in the difference between text and performance. A printed script of *The Straits*, as has been the case with all of Burke's stage plays except *Black Watch*, was made available to audiences at the beginning of the play's run. But preperformance scripts, not surprisingly granted that they are printed before rehearsals are complete, give a reader very little sense of how plays are staged. Nowhere is this gap greater than in *The Straits*, where Tiffany's highly stylized production was grouped around a single all-purpose set that allowed actors to dive in and out of an onstage pool. This staging is quite different from what the headnote to scene 2 suggests Burke had in mind. And, as anyone who saw early performances of the play will scarcely forget, and as newspaper reviews bear out, there were also elaborate sequences of carefully choreographed movement, supplied by Steven Hoggett (who would later work on *Black Watch*), and a musical accompaniment that included the soundtrack of the Sex Pistols' *God Save the Queen* album. In an online audio discussion in November 2003, Aleks Sierz defends the play by repeatedly drawing attention to its choreographed movement and its soundtrack, which he thinks significant and effective. His argument is that *The Straits* has a much larger theme than its story of three boys losing their rag; that theme is British militarism, of which the play is critical; the elaborate dancelike routines are quasi-military exercises; the real parable is not the production's probing of teenage anxieties but its exposure of British imperialism. Sierz's final assessment is that Tiffany has managed to achieve a really good production that goes beyond what is written. Whether one accepts this judgment or not, and 2003 is rather late for an anti-Falklands play, it does raise important questions about the ownership of plays in performance. An excellent production that goes far beyond what is written is exactly how many spectators have characterized *Black Watch*.

ON TOUR

Why Burke's third play should have been swallowed up into silence is something of a puzzle, for it is certainly not an out-and-out disaster. Indeed were it a first play it would have been thought distinctly promising. But, after *Gagarin Way* and *The Straits*, being promising was clearly not enough. Yet to expect more was to expect too much: no dramatist, however gifted or however fortunate, delivers a finished masterpiece every time. Not even Shakespeare came close to doing that. That said, *On Tour* (2005) is not the equivalent of minor Shakespeare. But it is a second product of Burke's time working at the National Theatre Studio; unlike *The Straits*, however, the play was not directed by John Tiffany and it was not taken to the Traverse as part of the Edinburgh Fringe. Nonetheless its credentials are impeccable, since it was sponsored by the London-based English Stage Company (famed for its encouragement of new writing for

more than fifty years) and by Liverpool's Everyman Theatre. But, performed in London and Liverpool in October 2005, it was very scantily reviewed and has disappeared from sight. Another heist-gone-wrong play, and thus highly reminiscent of *Gagarin Way* but with no Scottish content at all, there does seem to be a lack of focus about the piece. Its three characters are from London, Manchester, and Liverpool, which sounds like the beginnings of a joke, and all of them are football (soccer) club supporters, but the play exists in a not-very-coherent relation to this footballing background. Perhaps the worst problem that it faces, however, is that it sounds like a slowed-down version of a David Mamet play, but it simply lacks the efficiency of the best Mamet dialogue, which, far from delaying or deferring or substituting for a play's action, is the principal medium through which its characters act.

THE NATIONAL THEATRE OF SCOTLAND

A good deal of Burke's success stems from his association with a single director, John Tiffany, and with a single company, the newly emergent National Theatre of Scotland (founded in September 2003 and active with stage production since 2006). Before the creation of NTS there were already two national theaters in that complicated constitutional entity usually referred to as Britain (with or without an accompanying Great) but known formally as the United Kingdom of Great Britain and Northern Ireland. Both of these theater organizations, however, were perceived to be English-based and Anglo-centric. One was the Royal Shakespeare Company (RSC), reconstituted in 1961 and based in Stratford-upon-Avon and London; the other was the (Royal) National Theatre (NT), more than seventy years in planning and housed since 1976 in a vast concrete box on London's left bank. Inevitably, with so much heavily subsidized theatrical activity strung out along the relatively short line that connects London and the densely populated industrial midlands, the more distant English counties and districts felt starved of theater, and the situation in Wales and to the north of the English-Scottish border was worse.

Scotland is a small country, with one tenth of the population of the United Kingdom as a whole, with a small theatrical establishment and with only a relatively recent tradition of play-making. But it is emphatically not England and, in a period of growing demands for political devolution and regional and national assemblies, conclusions were being drawn. Moreover by way of inspiration and example there was a further national theater within the British Isles but outside the United Kingdom. This was the Abbey Theatre in Dublin, in effect though not in name the national theater of the Republic of Ireland. Growing out of needs identified by William Butler Yeats and Lady Gregory when they set up a short-lived Irish Literary Theatre, the Abbey, given its letters patent in 1904, began to accept government subsidies in 1925, three years after the founding of the Irish Free State.

But what exactly is a national theater? Until fifty years ago the English answer, a tribute to one writer's dominance of the English theatrical scene, was that it is either a building in which Shakespeare's plays are performed or a company that performs them; indeed the origins both of RSC and of NT lay in proposals very early in the twentieth century to found a Shakespeare Memorial Theatre in Kensington. The Irish answer to the question, both before independence and for many years afterward, was different: what a national theater would celebrate was not a national bard but nationhood itself. This is a rousing answer but fraught with problems, for nations are controversial entities that can raise fierce and contradictory passions even among nationalists. One of the worst moments in the Abbey's history occurred in 1907 when, during a performance of John Millington Synge's *The Playboy of the Western World,* there was a noisy disturbance brought about by a reference to the heroine's "shift" or nightgown. Merely to mention such a late-Victorian unmentionable was to impugn the purity of Irish womanhood, a thing that no truly national Irish theater could ever contemplate doing. One thing, then, that Yeats's opponents thought that a national theater ought to do, perhaps the principal thing, was to uphold and promote a national moral self-image. That is surely very much what one would expect people to have said early in the twentieth century, and a considerable advantage of entering late into the field is that such sentiments are much less likely to be voiced early in the twenty-first. One need only compare the anger over a single word in 1907 with the remarkably widespread acceptance, with very little protest or even adverse comment, of what was until recently the heavily tabooed language that is used throughout *Gagarin Way* and *Black Watch* and is indeed common in all of Burke's plays.

Nobody can doubt that the NTS's founding committee did its homework thoroughly. English, Irish, Scandinavian, and other examples of national theaters were thoroughly considered and a plan for the new theater was constructed in reaction to them. To the disappointment of some individuals and organizations, but to the relief of many others, its remit was to be widely defined. Nonetheless its Scottishness and its commitment to taking theater to all parts of Scotland, even those places geographically or socially remote from the great theater venues, is a prominent part of its manifesto, as also is its commitment to ambitious theater projects. What the NTS would not do, however, would be to occupy a particular theater building, whether newly built or expensively restored. In part this decision was reached because its finances are modest, but, also, there was a desire to avoid the controversy that surrounded the building of the new parliament at Holyrood, which cost more than ten times its original estimate and dominated Scottish news headlines for several years.

The contrast between the expensively housed Scottish parliament and Scotland's peripatetic national theater was brought into sharp relief when in June 2007 three performances of *Black Watch* were commissioned by Alex Salmond, leader of the Scottish National Party, to mark his emergence as first minister. (They were performed about a quarter of a mile away from the parliament building in a University of Edinburgh sports hall.) It can scarcely have escaped Salmond's attention that he is the only politician shown in a favorable light in the play: in an extract from a genuine interview on BBC television he protests both against the war and against the deployment of Scottish troops by a British prime minister.

BLACK WATCH

Italicization matters. Where would you rather be? In Edinburgh, London, Los Angeles, or Sydney watching *Black Watch*? Or in Iraq serving with the Black Watch? And what would you rather pay? Twenty pounds for a ticket to get in? Or an arm and a leg for a ticket to get out? These are crudely framed questions, but they serve their purpose if they force us to consider carefully a quite common response to *Black Watch* in performance. Scarcely anybody who has seen the play live, regardless of their political position toward the Iraq war, has failed to register its immense power to move and to convince. A common reaction is to say that it makes one feel that one has been out "there"—where "there" means Camp Dogwood itself. And, as the BBC Scotland documentary—"*Black Watch*: A Soldier's Story" (included on the 2008 DVD edition of *Black Watch*)—clearly shows, even soldiers who have served with the regiment have been heard to make this point. But what these soldiers are saying is perfectly coherent: the performance reminds them, through the power of theatrical recreation, of a reality that they have already encountered at first hand. Wholly incoherent, locked away in an entirely separate realm of vanity and self-deception, are those who say these things without firsthand experience.

Burke is well aware of this point and wants us to be aware of it. The project attracted him, he said in a Scottish newspaper interview with Barry Didcock in 2007, because "it relates to me, it relates to Fife, it relates to people in my family who have been in the Black Watch. It relates to the history of the regiment, to something that's part of Scotland." That is certainly to play the local card strongly, and the positive response to the play within Fife, Perthshire, and Angus, the regiment's traditional recruiting grounds, suggests that the card has been played effectively. But, like most of us who go to see the play, Burke has no direct experience of what he is writing about. This makes him a close cousin to the wet-behind-the-ears Tom who interviews the ex-miners in Lumphinnans in *Gagarin Way*. To avoid such embarrassment Burke's ploy is to dramatize and embed his Writer fully within *Black Watch* itself as "a kind of left-wing do-good writer." This is his description of this character, given in the BBC documentary, but also the sign of an attitude from which he hopes to hold himself distant. Such wrong-footing of the outsider—whether the Writer, or Burke himself, or his audience—is a powerful element throughout *Black Watch*. "At first, I didnay want to day this," Cammy tells us as the play opens: "I didnay want to have tay explain myself tay people ay. […] I think people's minds are usually made up about you if you were in the army" (p. 3). There is a direct challenge here to his audience, for Cammy assumes that we, and the Writer who is our representative, are people of words and opinions and of minds-that-are-made-up but people also without relevant experience.

This challenge makes the opening of the play edgy, with an edginess that increases as the interview scenes multiply, until near the end of the play there is a scene, set in Fife, of shocking and only just-suppressed violence. In their initial interview Stewarty, the soldier brought back into the front line though medically unfit to serve, responds to the Writer's insensitively framed request:

CAMMY: What day you want tay know?

WRITER: What it was like in Iraq.

CAMMY: What it was fucking like?

STEWARTY: Go tay fucking Baghdad if you want tay ken what it's like.

(p. 7)

By the end of the play there is no doubting Stewarty's angry contempt for anyone—like Tom or the Writer, or like us—who tries to lay claim to understanding based solely upon research:

STEWARTY: Write it down way a broken arm though.

Stewarty grabs the Writer's arm.

CAMMY: Come on Stewarty, leave the boy alone.

STEWARTY: Let me break your arm and see if you can write it down way a broken arm.

CAMMY: Stewarty, come on tay fuck.

STEWARTY: If he wants tay ken about Iraq, he has tay feel some pain.

(p. 65)

There is a tension here not just between the Writer and Stewarty but between that other writer, who is the play's author, and the very institution that has made his play possible. In his Author's Note, one of three prefaces with which *Black Watch* is burdened, Burke says that one young actor (it seems to have been Ali Craig, who played Stewarty so memorably) told him that he was open to the possibility of joining the military, which Burke describes as "an institution that has refined its appeal to the male psyche's yearning for a strong identity" (p. vii).

The reference quite clearly is to the Black Watch, but it might equally well be a warning about the seductive nature of theater itself. Everyone seems to have fallen in love with this play and that, granted the nature of what we are being shown, ought to make us pause for thought. But still the bandwagon—or is it by now a juggernaut?—rolls on. In 2009 NTS proposed issuing an educational pack, comprising three copies of the DVD and some accompanying notes, so that the play could be studied in Scottish schools. The Educational Institute of Scotland, a teaching union that is opposed to recruitment visits by army units to schools, nonetheless welcomed the proposal on the grounds that the play does not present a falsely glamorous view of war. Indeed it does not, but it might be glamorous without being falsely glamorous, and in any case a play written to celebrate a famous fighting unit will be at best an ambiguous vehicle upon which to mount an antiwar message. Without denying the power of *Black Watch*, which in performance is every bit as overwhelming as it is popularly supposed to be, it is worth suggesting that its politics are not as obvious as some have strived to make them seem. On tour overseas, in the United States very markedly, it has been interpreted as a protest of the Iraq war or of war in general, but it also speaks up on behalf of an historic Scottish regi-

ment that the British government announced it would reform and reduce while at the same time dispatching it to Iraq to bear some of the worst of the fighting. A Scottish regiment shamelessly manipulated by a British government is an antithesis that matters within Scotland a very great deal.

Seeing *Black Watch* is obviously not the same experience as being in Camp Dogwood. Nonetheless there is an issue of authenticity that will not go away, for to have seen *Black Watch* in a live performance is indeed to have been "somewhere" and, moreover, somewhere special. Ideally one should experience the play first in a live performance, in a particular venue that has been modified for the purposes of production, and only subsequently refresh one's memory of it by reading it or by viewing the DVD; for these last are activities that can be endlessly repeated anywhere one chooses. But, however many times the play is revived, not everyone—as the inclusion of DVDs in the NTS Educational Pack obliquely testifies—will be able to see it live before reading or watching it. What, then, are the disadvantages of not having been able to experience it in the right order?

This is an important question that bears down particularly, perhaps even controversially, on the way in which *Black Watch*—or rather *The National Theatre of Scotland's "Black Watch"*—is presented in print. Most theater exists in a complicated and delicate relationship between text on the one hand and performance on the other. Which is the true play? Is it text, as literary critics often assert, or performance, as favored by theater critics? In creating a twenty-first-century performance of *Othello*, a play staged in Shakespeare's lifetime (1564–1616) but not printed until 1622, a director will read the text, will cast in the light of it, and will hand copies of a script to actors prior to rehearsal. So here text precedes performance, and performance is an interpretation of text. But someone in an audience watching *Othello* in 1604 would have had access only to what was shown on stage. He or she would have had to wait until 1622 to buy an individual printed copy of the play or until 1623 to buy it in a collected edition of

Shakespeare's works. In this case then, and from the perspective of the theatergoer, performance long precedes text. So is a play a text, and performance an interpretation of that text? Or is the play the performance itself? And, if so, what is the text?

Dramaturgical theorists have given a wide range of often contradictory answers to these questions. How does *Black Watch* fit into this argument? The first thing to note is that the play was given its official first performance on August 5, 2006. In this case, uniquely so far in Burke's career, Faber did not publish a copy of the text. (One was planned but was canceled because the text of the play was not sufficiently settled.) Instead, once it was recognized that the production was an immense success, a decision was reached to revive it the following year and take it on a world tour. For that revival a text was to be prepared that would acknowledge the distinctive nature of the play's creation, for essentially *Black Watch* was the product of the same team—author, director, and movement director—that had put together *The Straits*. The result is that in *Black Watch* movement and music are truly part of the play, no more readily detachable from it than the words themselves. Indeed, if you ask spectators who have seen the piece live, they are likely to remember at least three incidents none of which is principally verbal. The first ends the scene of an interview in a Fife public house when the baize on a pool table is ripped open and soldiers climb up through it. This is now one of the most talked about bits of the play, and (inevitably) its being talked about is what has drained away from it that element of surprise that made it talked about in the first place. The third moment, to step out of line briefly, is when Cammy relates the history of the Black Watch and, while doing so, is carried around by his friends and dressed and undressed in the various uniforms characteristic of its long history.

But the second of these moments is for many the most moving in the entire play. Not only does it dispense with words but there is the very radical suggestion that where real feelings are involved words themselves are never enough. It occurs when letters from home—words indeed, but words on paper—are distributed to the troops. They respond by articulating these letters publicly but silently through the power of gesture. As with the other examples the NTS text registers and explains what is happening by means of an unusual typographical convention, in which what are in effect stage directions (though of directorial rather than authorial origin) are printed between rules in a sans serif nonitalic font that is distinct from the authorial directions that are printed in ordinary italics:

....

> The sergeant enters with a bundle of airmail letters (blueys). Stewarty notices him and takes the letters. He opens one and starts reading it, the words giving him comfort. Another soldier enters and takes the remaining letters. Stewarty creates a subconscious sign-language which expresses the content of his letter. One by one the soldiers enter, take the bundle of letters and, finding the one addressed to them, repeat the process for themselves.

(p. 39)

....

Finally, once again suggesting that words are not enough, we are given a reference to the second illustration in the photographic section of the text. These things are done in order to bring the printed version of the play into line with performance; nonetheless how far a printed version of a play can be said to capture the play in its entirety remains an issue fundamental to an understanding of Gregory Burke's greatest success. But perhaps the problem is an unnecessary one caused by a void in our critical precepts. The series to which this essay belongs structures criticism both biographically and in terms of reading rather than watching, as its title (*British Writers*) indicates. In an essay on Gregory Burke, man and writer, the distinction between what Burke has done with pen and paper and what derives on stage from Tiffany or Hoggett or Featherstone or Davey Anderson (*Black Watch*'s musical director) will seem to be an important one. But from a different point of view—essentially a theatrical point of view that emphasizes the unity of performance in what is clearly a corporate and communal art form—making these distinctions is an irrelevance. What matters, and all that matters, are the results.

GREGORY BURKE

HOORS

Increasingly Gregory Burke is beginning to look like the victim of his own success. Since whatever he wrote after *Black Watch* was bound to be judged harshly, his instinct to try something different was wise but unavailing. Yet it is *Black Watch* that is the odd play out, for between *Gagarin Way* and *Hoors* (2009) there are distinct lines of affiliation. Here, from an interview included in a "learning resource pack" compiled by the Traverse for the use of Scottish schoolchildren, is Burke's account of his new play's origins:

> I began to write it in 2005 when I had come back to Scotland after a couple of years in London. There was this explosion of house building that had gone on in west Fife, it could be anywhere really, anywhere there are new build flats and houses, but it feels very transient and rootless. […] If you're from Dunfermline, like I am, to suddenly be confronted by the fact that your town is prosperous is very disturbing. I couldn't work out where the prosperity had come from. I was very suspicious that it might be an illusion.
>
> (Traverse Theatre education pack, p. 7)

Indeed it could be "anywhere really," for nowhere in the play's dialogue or stage directions is Dunfermline mentioned. The cover, however, is more forthright: "Small Town, Fife." This is picked up by the play's character Vicky—"Town this size, you can't help but bump into ghosts" (p. 36)—who also brands her plush domestic surroundings as "all an illusion" (p. 16). This is to be a play about escape and failure to escape, a movement from social and cultural imprisonment but also back into it.

How well do the play's vision and its plot coincide? Andy—a builder but not a university graduate (it is odd how this point is emphasized)—has died of a drug-induced heart attack brought on by a vigorous stag party in Amsterdam and an even more vigorous flight home. His fiancée (Vicky), her sister (Nikki), and his fiancée's former and future lovers (Tony and Stevie, more or less in that order) have assembled—somewhere in a small town in small-town Fife—to attend his funeral on what was meant to have been his wedding day. Not much happens, and nothing that does happen goes ac-

cording to plan: Tony pursues Nikki but ends up with Vicky and is impotent; Stevie pursues Vicky but ends up with Nikki, whom he disappoints for a reason even more embarrassing than Tony's. It is in part a battle of the sexes but principally a play about not getting on and not getting off. The women, who are in their twenties, seem to be wealthy, though how they have acquired their money is not clear. Nikki perhaps works for the Scottish government, or is a lap dancer, or does research and development for an aerospace company, or is a liar. Tony also seems to be rich, building car parks at airports and investing all of his energies, sexual and business, in the present, while ignoring the future.

Born amid the restrictions of Fife, movement is part of their breaking free: Tony has flown in from Dubai; Nicky has been shopping in the United States; Andy's corpse has arrived from Amsterdam. Where will they go next? Andy, of course, has made his final flight of freedom and will soon be going to ground. (Not quite: he is to be cremated.) Vicky, Nikki, and Tony have more meaningless traveling to do before they too come down to earth somewhere near Andy. But it is Stevie who shares the wisdom and the restricted horizons that are the inheritance of a character trapped by life and Fife:

> STEVIE: It's good to live somewhere crap too, though.
>
> NIKKI: It is?
>
> STEVIE: It's character-forming.
>
> NIKKI: Right.
>
> STEVIE: You live somewhere shit, like here, then any bairn's gonnay rebel against it. They're going to want to get out, want to be a success. They'll jump on the first milk float out at fifteen, and by the time they're thirty they'll be Bill Gates.
>
> NIKKI: I never thought of that.
>
> STEVIE: There's a lot to be said for staying in the one place.
>
> (p. 95)

This is brilliant in a way. Stevie has a really good argument, even perhaps a witty one, but throws it all away with his ineffective punch line. But if you are Stevie, a man whose cupboards and whose skeletons are suspiciously real, the best thing to be said for social immobility is that it helps the police keep track of you.

Hoors is a black comedy of what passes for courtship in a society where love is just a word, and lifelong marriage and fidelity between partners are not even pretend virtues, as conveyed in Vicky's sentiments about her fiancé's death: "No. I mean I'm really relieved I'm not having to get married. The spark had gone. The second wind had blown itself out. Would've been a huge mistake" (p. 25).

Until *Hoors* appeared Burke could have been characterized as a dramatist whose plays heavily privilege working-class men and their attitudes and practices. *Gagarin Way, On Tour,* and *Black Watch* are without women and even Tracy in *The Straits*, though she is more level-headed than either Doink or Darren, is not the pivot around whom the plot revolves. In this respect *Hoors* is decidedly different. Whether there are two or four "whores" in the play, Tony's and Steve's status as prostitutes is not in doubt. But they are amusing, and reviewers even of this play have suggested that Burke writes primarily for men and much less assuredly for women. (Is it, one might wonder, significant that Vicky's and Nikki's names rhyme? Or that all the names are diminutives?) Indeed, with his habit of self-deprecation, Burke may be slyly alluding to this potentially misogynistic element of his talent in Steve's description of watching television with his grandfather:

> We'd sit there, Saturday afternoon, some daft war film on, or a cowboy or something, John Wayne, and as soon as the first woman appeared on screen up he'd get. Big sigh. That's the picture finished he'd say, there's a woman in it. An' he'd turn it over. I used to say to him, what's wrong and he'd say, there's a woman in it. It's ruined, they're no' gonnay do anything now. Women spoil everything.
>
> (p. 40)

But in this play, with its grim message of drink, drugs, and pretending to be merry for tomorrow you die, it is the switched-on men who get switched off early. "*Vicky walks over to the coffin and looks at it,*" reads the final stage direction. "You only get a little bit of time," she says, and pauses for a beat. "Then it's all over" (p. 131).

CONCLUSION

Hoors is a much better play, much sharper and much funnier, than reviewers obsessed with its relationship to *Black Watch* have been prepared to admit. "It's one of the hazards of being part of the creative team that produced *Black Watch* that all of us are saddled with its legacy," Burke wrote in a diary item in the *Financial Times* (June 21, 2008). There is a positive and a negative here. The positive is obvious. As Tiffany notes, the production, and the kind of Scottish theater which it represents, is "bound to the time in which it is created" (p. xi). At some point then the production must be consigned to history, where it has an honorable part to play and from which, from time to time, it might emerge in productions other than NTS's own. But, with no other NTS production having achieved anything like its degree of success, *Black Watch*—its professional and amateur performance-rights withheld for the foreseeable future—remains firmly behind stable doors that are locked lest the horse bolt. Indeed July 2010 saw its return for yet another international tour, with some changes of cast where necessary but still in its initial NTS production.

Whatever happens to the National Theatre of Scotland as it struggles to survive in an increasingly hostile economic climate, it seems overwhelmingly likely that *Black Watch* will forever be a large part of its early history. One's hope, of course, is that, so far as both Burke and NTS are concerned, this is a history with a future.

Selected Bibliography

WORKS OF GREGORY BURKE

TEXTS
Gagarin Way. London: Faber 2001.
The Straits. London: Faber, 2003.
On Tour. London: Faber, 2005.

The National Theatre of Scotland's "Black Watch." London: Faber, 2007. (An edition of *Black Watch* dated 2006, which appears occasionally in catalogs, is a "ghost" that was canceled before publication.)

Hoors. London: Faber, 2009.

ARTICLES

"Funny Peculiar." *Guardian* (http://www.guardian.co.uk/stage/2003/apr/12/theatre.artsfeatures1), April 12, 2003.

"The Diary." *Financial Times,* June 21, 2008. (http://search.ft.com/search?sortBy=gadatetimearticle&page=2&queryText=%22Gregory+Burke%22).

OTHER MEDIA PRODUCTIONS AND RELATED WORK

DVD: *Black Watch.* John Williams Productions, 2008. (The BBC TV production of the play. Also includes "*Black Watch*: A Soldier's Story," a BBC Scotland documentary on the making of the play and its production.)

Radio plays: *Occy Eyes* (2003; the BBC Scotland radio play that was the precursor of *The Straits*) and *Shellshocked.*

Television play: *One Night in Emergency,* BBC Scotland, May 13, 2009. (Press release, http://www.bbc.co.uk/pressoffice/pressreleases/stories/2009/05_may/13/emergency.shtml)

Unpublished plays: The Chain Play (2001); Debt (2004); Liar (2006); Battery Farm (2010); The Party (nd).

BIOGRAPHICAL, CRITICAL, AND HISTORICAL BACKGROUND AND SOURCES

THEATER HISTORY

Burke's rise to prominence is so recent that most of the books in this section were published too early to take account of his work. They do, however, provide useful background reading for both British and Scottish theater.

Beauman, Sally. *The Royal Shakespeare Company: A History of Ten Decades.* Oxford: Oxford University Press, 1982.

Billington, Michael. *State of the Nation: British Theatre Since 1945.* London: Faber, 2007.

Eyre, Richard, and Nicholas Wright. *Changing Stages: A View of British Theatre in the Twentieth Century.* London: Bloomsbury, 2000.

Itzin, Catherine. *Stages in the Revolution: Political Theatre in Britain Since 1968.* London: Methuen, 1980.

Kavanagh, Peter. *The Story of the Abbey Theatre, from its Origins in 1899 to the Present.* New York: Devin-Adair, 1950.

Lane, David. *Contemporary British Drama.* Edinburgh: Edinburgh University Press, 2010.

MacLennan, Elizabeth. *The Moon Belongs to Everyone:*

Making Theatre with 7:84. London: Methuen, 1990. (A history of radical theater by one of the founders of 7:84 and 7:84 Scotland. Particularly strong, therefore, on Scottish political theater 1973–1988.)

Rebellato, Dan. *1956 and All That: The Making of Modern British Drama.* London: Routledge, 1999.

Scullion, Adrienne. "Theatre in Scotland in the 1990s and Beyond." In *The Cambridge History of British Theatre.* Vol. 3: *Since 1895.* Edited by Baz Kershaw. Cambridge, U.K., and London: Cambridge University Press, 2004. Pp. 47–84.

Shellard, Dominic. *British Theatre Since the War.* New Haven, Conn., and London: Yale University Press, 1999.

Sierz, Aleks. *In-Yer-Face Theatre: British Drama Today.* London: Faber, 2000.

Stevenson, Randall, and Gavin Wallace, eds. *Scottish Theatre Since the Seventies.* Edinburgh: Edinburgh University Press, 1996.

GENERAL PREVIEWS, REVIEWS, INTERVIEWS, AND ARTICLES

BBC News. "No Honour for Black Watch Writer." *BBC News,* May 1, 2009 (news.bbc.co.uk/1/hi/scotland/tayside_and_central/8029063.stm).

Didcock, Barry. "His Play *Black Watch* Has Become the First Cultural Landmark of the 21st Century: So What Inspired Gregory Burke to Take on the Army?" *Herald,* March 3, 2007 (http://www.heraldscotland.com/his-play-black-watch-has-become-the-first-cultural-landmark-of-the-21st-century-so-what-inspired-gregory-burke-to-take-on-the-army-1.836303).

"Guardian: Stage." Interview with Gregory Burke. *Guardian,* July 6, 2002 (http://www.guardian.co.uk/stage/2002/jul/06/whoswhoinbritishtheatre.features29).

Jeary, Louis. "Black Watch on the March" (http://www.ayoungertheatre.com/interview-black-watch/).

MacDonald, Stuart. "Outcry as University Honours 'Fight' Writer Gregory Burke." *Sunday Times,* April 25, 2009 (http://www.timesonline.co.uk/tol/news/uk/scotland/article6169283.ece).

National Theatre of Scotland. "*Black Watch,* Edinburgh 2006." Interview with Davey Anderson and Steven Hoggett (http://www.youtube.com/watch?v=GPxen1dgSKs).

National Theatre of Scotland. "Making the Music for *Black Watch.*" An interview with Davey Anderson (http://dexstar.egobots.com/content/default.asp?page=s667).

Ross, Peter. "Gregory Burke interview: Once more unto the breach." *Scotland on Sunday* (http://scotlandonsunday.scotsman.com/sos-review/Gregory-Burke-interview-Once-more.5182112.jp), April 19, 2009.

Sierz, Aleks. "Interview with Gregory Burke." At Sierz's website for his book *In-Yer-Face Theater* and related content (www.inyerface-theatre.com/archive9.html#9).

Waters, Darren. "*Gagarin Way*'s Edinburgh Success." *BBC*

News, August 10, 2001 (http://news.bbc.co.uk/2/hi/entertainment/1483836.stm).

REVIEWS OF *GAGARIN WAY*

Billington, Michael. "Moving Target." *Guardian* (http://www.guardian.co.uk/culture/2001/oct/06/artsfeatures), October 6, 2001.

Dunlop, Bill. *EdinburghGuide.com* (http://www.edinburghguide.com/festival/2009/edinburghfringe/gagarinway-3999), 2009.

Fisher, Philip. *The British Theatre Guide* (http://www.britishtheatreguide.info/reviews/gagarinway-rev.htm), 2001.

King, Alan. *Crackerjack* (http://www.crackerjack.co.uk/bristol/review/gagarin-way-ustinov-studio/theatre), 2009.

Latham, Peter. *The British Theatre Guide* (http://www.britishtheatreguide.info./otherresources/fringe/fringe01-09.httm#way), 2001.

Renton, Jennie. "Gregory Burke Interview." *Textualities,* 2005.

REVIEWS OF *THE STRAITS*

Encore Commentary. "Edinburgh Shrapnel." *Encore Theatre Magazine* (http://encoretheatremagazine.blogspot.com/Commentary.html#Edinburgh), September 23, 2003.

Henshaw, Amber. "Fringe Reviews: *The Straits*." *BBC News* (http://news.bbc.co.uk/1/hi/entertainment/3161263.stm), August 18, 2003.

Sierz, Aleks, Jane Edwardes, and Carole Woddis. "*The Straits*: Gregory Burke's Follow-up to *Gagarin Way* Sharply Divides Jane Edwardes, Aleks Sierz, and Carole Woddis. David Benedict Hosts." Audio discussion among theatre critics at *TheatreVoice* (http://www.theatrevoice.com/listen_now/player/?audioID=61), November 7, 2003.

REVIEW OF *ON TOUR*

Fisher, Philip. *The British Theatre Guide* (http://www.britishtheatreguide.info/reviews/ontour-rev.htm), 2005.

REVIEWS OF *BLACK WATCH*

Brown, Mark. *Socialist Review* (http://www.socialistreview.org.uk/article.php?articlenumber=10449), June 2008.

Featherstone, Vicky. *Scotland on Sunday* (http://news.scotsman.com/leaders/Wha39s-like-us—Vicky.3628195.jp), December 30, 2007.

National Theatre of Scotland. Details of 2010 tour (http://www.nationaltheatrescotland.com/content/default.asp?page=home_Black Watch 2010).

REVIEWS OF *HOORS*

Brown, Mark. "Scottish Playwright Gregory Burke's New Play Is Pleasurable Enough but Fails to Match His Majestic *Black Watch*." *Telegraph* (http://www.telegraph.co.uk/culture/theatre/regional-shows/5286458/Hoors-at-the-Edinburgh-Traverse-review.html), May 6, 2009.

Chadwick, Alan. "Gregory Burke's Next Step into the Fray." *Metro* (http://www.metro.co.uk/metrolife/636212-gregory-burkes-next-step-into-the-fray), April 28, 2009.

Ferguson, Euan. *Observer* (http://www.guardian.co.uk/stage/2009/may/10/hoors-gregory-burke-theatre), May 10, 2009.

Fisher, Mark. "Gregory Burke on His Black Watch follow-up." *Guardian* (http://www.guardian.co.uk/stage/2009/apr/20/gregory-burke-hoors-black-watch), April 20, 2009.

Ross, Peter. "Gregory Burke Interview: Once More into the Breach." *Scotland on Sunday* (http://scotlandonsunday.scotsman.com/sos-review/Gregory-Burke-interview-Once-more.5182112.jp), April 19, 2009.

Sloan, Billy. "*Black Watch* Playwright Gregory Burke on His Latest Dramas." *Sunday Mail*, May 15, 2009.

Traverse Theatre and Noëlle O'Donoghue. Learning Resource Pack (http://www.traverse.co.uk/downloads/Education%20Pack%20-%20Hoors.lowres.pdf), May 2009. (Contains an interview with Burke.)

ABOUT THE NATIONAL THEATRE OF SCOTLAND

Bell, Barbara. "Revisiting the National Theatre Debate: Once More, with Feeling …" In "Theatre in Scotland," *Edinburgh Review*, no. 105:5–13 (Edinburgh, 2000).

Harrower, David, and David Greig. "Why a New Scotland Must Have a Properly Funded Theatre." *Scotsman,* November 25, 1997, p. 15.

National Theatre of Scotland. Inaugural brochure (http://www.nationaltheatrescotland.com/inaugural brochure feb - june 06. pdf).

Savage, Roger. "A Scottish National Theatre?" In *Scottish Theatre Since the Seventies*. Edited by Randall Stevenson and Gavin Wallace. Edinburgh: Edinburgh University Press, 1996. Pp. 23–33.

Scott, Robert Dawson. "Scotland Expects More from National Theatre." *Caledonian Mercury* (http://entertainment.caledonianmercury.com/2010/06/23/scotland-expects-more-from-national-theatre/00759), June 23, 2010.

CHARLOTTE DACRE

(c. 1771—1825)

Ashley J. Cross

CHARLOTTE DACRE, MORE popularly known as "Rosa Matilda," was a risk taker. In the early nineteenth century, when middle-class British culture was increasingly invested in ideals of virtuous duty and a model of domesticity that curtailed female desire, Dacre dared to create female characters who hazard everything to satisfy their desires and who are markedly antidomestic. At a time when the excessive ornamentation of Della Cruscan writing had gone solidly out of style, Dacre wrote and published poems (*Hours of Solitude,* 1805) that not only embodied the florid theatricality of that late-eighteenth-century school but also reinvented its model of pseudonymous, erotic textual exchange. Though Matthew Lewis, responding to the cultural climate, had severely expurgated the salacious elements of his gothic novel *The Monk* (first published in 1796) for its fourth edition, Dacre dedicated to him her first novel, *Confessions of the Nun of St. Omer* (1805). While other writers (with the exception perhaps of Emily Brontë) steered clear of female passions in the early half of the nineteenth century, especially their physical, sexual nature, Dacre's novels addressed female desire directly. The characters of her most famous novel, *Zofloya* (1806) might have come, as Algernon Charles Swinburne suggested, straight out of the Marquis de Sade's work, but *The Libertine* (1807), with its French context and title, further exploited such radical and obscene connections. Though debates on the passions had lessened and sensibility had become more often a target of mockery, *The Passions* (1811) spends four volumes tracing out the intricate, powerful, and devastating effects of passion on her characters. Dacre, indeed, challenged early nineteenth-century models of propriety, womanhood, and desire in both her content and style. There was, however, no actual woman named

"Charlotte Dacre." "Charlotte Dacre" and "Rosa Matilda" were both fictional identities constructed by Charlotte King Byrne to enable her to explore the literary, sexual, and social limits of her day and to appeal to the unfulfilled desires of her bourgeois readers. Dacre was, in fact, quite conservative in her politics, but she was willing to risk her politics to portray the powerful passions that she saw driving human beings, especially women.

CHARLOTTE KING BYRNE

The biography of Charlotte King Byrne, the woman behind the pseudonyms, has only been pieced out at the start of the twentieth-first century—and still somewhat tentatively—primarily by Ann Jones and Adriana Craciun. Charlotte King was born to John "Jew" King (1753–1824, née Jacob Rey) and his first wife, Deborah, in either 1771 or 1772. Dacre's first volume of poems was a joint venture with her sister, Sophia King (Fortnum), in 1798. She began her newspaper writing career as "Rosa" when she published "To Him Who Says He Loved" in 1802 in *The Poetical Register and Repository of Fugitive Pieces.* As both Rosa Matilda and Charlotte Dacre, she became a prolific writer of popular poetry and novels. In addition to her voluminous verse for the *Morning Post* from 1804 to 1815, she published two volumes of sentimental poetry and four racy novels, most of the novels going into multiple editions and translated into foreign languages. Her sister also went on to write poetry and novels—of particular notice the anti-Godwinian *Waldorf; or, The Dangers of Philosophy* (1798).

Darting about in his yellow carriage, John King, Dacre's father, lived a fashionable life, with a home in Clarges Street, the future abode of Edward Bulwer Lytton. He made his living as a moneylender, banker, and writer, and he was a supporter of the arts, especially the theater and literature. His reputation for being a good entertainer and supporter of William Johnson Fox and Thomas Paine earned him the company of many of the radicals of his day, including Robert Merry, William Godwin, William Sheridan, and John Taylor. He also dealt with Percy Shelley, Lord Byron, and Mary Robinson (1758–1800), with whom he may have had an affair. In 1781, when Charlotte was about ten years old, he published an erotic correspondence, *Letters from Perdita to a Certain Israelite, and His Answers to Them*, in an attempt to capitalize on his intimacy with Robinson.

King offered his daughters a model of how an outsider could make his way in the world through the sheer power of his wits and cunning; he must also have presented an unconventional model in terms of sexual relations. His life was not easy; in addition to the alienation he must have experienced for his outsider status as a Jew in an anti-Semitic culture, he struggled financially and was involved in several lawsuits, including two different ones for sexual trespasses against women. Around 1785, at a time when divorce was not readily available, he divorced his wife and married a countess, Jane Rochefort Butler, the daughter of the first Earl of Belvedere. Given their father's divorce, his Jewishness, his financial dealings, his upward striving, his writing aspirations, and his radical connections, the King sisters' writing careers were bound to be controversial.

Charlotte's adult life was anything but conventional. In July 1815, she married the widower Nicholas Byrne, the owner and editor of the *Morning Post* from 1803 to 1833. It seems, however, that the Byrnes's relationship had started well before Nicholas's wife died, perhaps shortly after Charlotte began writing for the *Post*. Nonetheless, Byrne remained with his first wife until her death. By the time Charlotte and Nicholas married, they already had three children: William Pitt, 1806; Charles, 1807; and Maria, 1809, all baptized in 1811. The Byrnes showed

their political colors in naming their firstborn son after the prime minister who died the same year (Dacre also wrote an elegy to honor him), and these conservative politics came increasingly to shape Dacre's writing. Not much else is known of her life except that she died at age fifty-three at Lancaster Place, London, in 1825. The story does not end there, however; her husband was mysteriously assassinated in his office on November 2, 1872, possibly because of his Tory political views. While Byrne was alone, a masked man entered the office and stabbed him many times—a fitting end for the husband of a gothic novelist.

Dacre's work fascinates critics because of her exploration of passion, especially women's, and her authorial self-fashioning. Her writing inhabits a critical paradox: while her novels and poems purport to show the dangers of desire, warning women about the dangers of reading and of pursuing their passions, often through a moralistic ending, they also display the power of that passion and aim to seduce readers. That is, Dacre's writing embodies the very thing she critiques. Dacre's oeuvre, though relatively slight and compressed within a span of just over ten years, is intensely focused in its exploration of transgressive desire. Crossing boundaries of sex, race, class, and religion, Dacre explores the struggle (and mostly failure) of characters to manage their extreme desires and depicts the resulting psychological and physical effects. Her characters, attuned to the cadences of their bodily desires and seduced by the erotics of language, sacrifice themselves, but not for domesticity or marriage. Instead, they choose to follow their desires to the point of self-annihilation. However, this realization of passionate desire yields a moment of self-definition—a spiritual and physical moment that melds body, mind, heart, and soul, even if it is destructive.

TRIFLES OF HELICON

The full realization of passionate and destructive desire would wait for Dacre's mature work; it is apparent in nascent form, however, even in her first collection of poems, coauthored with her sister Sophia. The title *Trifles of Helicon* (1798) itself indicates the sisters' sense of their poetry as juvenilia, the work of young ladies demonstrating their accomplishments, but the King sisters clearly wanted their readers to be conscious of the disjunction between their youthful age and their passionate content. The writers assert their poetic authority by going to classical sources of poetic inspiration (Helicon and Parnassus) and modestly trivialize them by labeling them "trifles." These poems (the majority of which are labeled sonnets, though not one adheres to the sonnet convention of fourteen lines) include primarily apostrophes to states of being (sleep, oblivion, meditation, indifference, love), a pair of descriptive sketches ("Morning" and "Evening"), several ballads, two antiwar poems ("War" and the ironic "Peace"), and many poems spoken by women intensely conflicted about their desire for their lovers. Most of these poems were reprinted in the appendix to *Hours of Solitude* with a note claiming they had been written when she was between thirteen and fifteen, though she was actually closer to twenty-five when the volume was published, and thirty-three not twenty-three when she published *Hours*. These early poems prefigure her later work in their complex exploration of the psychology of desire—its motivations, its absences, its agonies and pleasures, and, especially, its unsustainability in this world. Partial to iambic quatrains (either pentameter or ballad), Dacre tries to represent the agitated, uncertain state of her speakers through her style; the poems are often a series of questions and oxymoronic phrases, full of dashes and exclamations that are meant to convey the speaker's overwrought state. Though manifested bodily and driven by the heart, these states are, for Dacre, primarily of the mind, a function of imagination. The giddy brain, drenched in passion, drives many of the speakers in these poems to the frenzy of madness, but it also frees them. At the end of "Edmund and Anna: A Legendary Tale," for example, the heroine Anna poisons herself at the exact moment her lover is executed and achieves a near-orgasmic moment of union that is spiritual and physical, transcendent and sexual, despite her lover's absence.

Though the poems in the volume alternate between the sisters, Charlotte's poems dominate as they both begin and end the volume, framing it in a gothic context and presenting the maddened woman as a figure for the woman poet. The opening poem serves to locate the scene of writing in a dramatically imagined seascape, a locale not of the sublime so much as a place of horror:

> Where the hoarse billows rush upon the shore
> Where shrieks some screech-owl's melancholy voice
> Where the bleak winds in loud defiance roar
> Where horror reigns—that spot shall be my choice.
>
> (p. 1)

The sounds here are so deafening one wonders if the speaker can even think, let alone write poetry. Nonetheless, this powerful assertion of location may be the only certainty the speaker has. Surprisingly, however, she turns for inspiration not to the male lover of so many of the poems, but to Laura. The poem thus shifts genre as it moves from the gothic landscape of horror to the romantic landscape of Petrarchan love poetry. Laura's appearance—as a vision, as a ghost, as a dream, we can't be sure—highlights how Dacre's poetry combines the gothic with the romantic and identifies the poet with the female lovers of her poems. The sustaining power of mental, if not bodily, union with another parallels the reciprocal sympathy necessary for creative production. Dacre's identification of several of these verses as poems of enthusiasm, in the headnotes, further connects the poet's creative receptivity with her heroine's sympathetic intensity. As a word that designates both emotional responsiveness (poetic fervor) and a revolutionary politics that Dacre went on to reject later in her life, it also links her poetry specifically to Charlotte Smith, the Della Cruscans, and the bluestocking coteries.

Whether poet or lover, the main figure in these poems is the "wretch distrest" (p. 5) as Dacre identifies the sleepless speaker in "The Invocation to Sleep," an implicit allusion to Smith's "poor wearied pilgrim" ("Sonnet IV: To the Moon") in her *Elegaic Sonnets* (1784). Smith's sonnets, in fact, haunt *Trifles*. While

CHARLOTTE DACRE

Dacre's poems are not localized in specific places but rather in states of mind, they develop, to an extreme extent, latent elements of Smith's poems: melancholy becomes gothic nightmare and obsession with death, Smith's unrealized gothic backdrop materializes in Dacre's settings and ghost lovers, while the desire to escape the conflicts of this world is physically and spiritually realized in repeated death scenes. Most significantly, Dacre's poems reframe Smith's concerns explicitly in terms of love and sex. As one example, Dacre's "Invocation to Sleep" models itself on Smith's "Sonnet XI: To Sleep," even borrowing some of Smith's specific diction. Like Smith's, Dacre's speaker, using Smith's exact language, calls in the second line for sleep to "strew thy poppies round my aching head" to give her "brightest visions" (p. 5). However, Dacre's poem remains intently focused on the single self, "the wretch distrest" and tormented by her passions. Whereas Smith presents the peaceful sleep of laborers to contrast her speaker's anxious state, Dacre (again borrowing Smith's images) focuses on the bodily effect sleep can provide by stopping "stormy passion" (p. 5). Her poem, however, offers no respite to passion's sleeplessness and no world outside the speaker's mind. As this specific imitation of Smith's sleep sonnet suggests, Dacre generates her poetic sensibility in these poems by taking Smith's melancholy to an extreme. In fact, Dacre's poems might be more likened to Smith's passionate Werther sonnets in which a lovesick Werther despairingly pursues, over the course of five sonnets, an obliteration of self in suicide, rather than the sonnets written in response to a natural setting that were to inspire William Wordsworth. What Dacre does, however, is make these expressions more specifically female and sexual; her characters' suicides are not acts of defeat but rather are acts of passionate choice.

Yet the *Trifles of Helicon* cannot be understood without appreciation of the Della Cruscan context that it invoked—a context that would have been immediately obvious to readers of the time. Della Cruscan verse was begun in Florence by a poetic coterie experimenting with erotic Italian verse forms. Robert Merry as Della Crusca introduced the craze to England on his return in 1787, when *The World* published his "The Adieu and Recall to Love." When Anna Matilda (Hannah Cowley) responded passionately to his poem with one of her own, a two-year erotic poetic exchange began that grew to embrace several other writers, including one of Dacre's favorites, Mary Robinson writing as Laura Maria. These textual sexual performances—what Jacqueline Labbe has aptly called "textual intercourse" in "The Anthologised Romance of Della Crusca and Anna Matilda" (par. 11)—conducted in a highly emotive and hyperbolic style, employed exactly the elements that Dacre wanted to exhibit in her own verse: the interconnection of love and pain in a cerebral sensuality. Coded sexuality, passionate exclamations, the sentimentality of tears, and the spiritual yet physical heart are all elements of this poetry. The fusion of physical, spiritual, intellectual, and sentimental that the Della Cruscans achieved through their eroticized textual exchanges became hallmarks of Dacre's poetry.

HOURS OF SOLITUDE

Hours of Solitude (1805), Dacre's second volume of poetry, extended this Della Cruscan sensibility into a fully developed erotic aesthetic. The volume addressed many of the same themes of the earlier volume, but it had greater literary pretensions, offered a more complex exploration of both male and female desire, and showed a more mature understanding of poetic form. The volume went into two editions within the year. Formally, Dacre's *Hours* contributes to the genre of the effusion, a lyric genre that many of the Romantic writers experimented with, including Samuel Taylor Coleridge, whose first volume of poems, *Poems on Various Subjects* (1796), included thirty-six poems labeled effusions. The term "effusion" belies the careful construction of the poems and suggests instead a more spontaneous emotional outpouring, meant to be a genuine, more informal utterance, a private moment expressed publicly. Dacre's mistaken attribution of her book's epigraph to John Milton, rather than to James Beattie's *The Minstrel; or, The*

Progress of Genius (1771), a Spenserian poem on the growth of a poet's mind, further underscores her desire to highlight the volume's literariness.

At the same time, however, Dacre capitalizes on her sexual appeal as "Rosa Matilda," including opposite the title page a sensual portrait under that name. The image—a young, beautiful woman, hair slightly tousled, seductively gazing forth with dark, limpid eyes and the trace of a smile, wearing a dress whose décolletage blurs fabric and white breast, and set against the backdrop of a garden landscape—is meant to titillate the reader. More in the manner of Joshua Reynolds' 1782 portrait of Mary Robinson than the bonneted Charlotte Smith of *Elegaic Sonnets*, the portrait alerts the reader to pleasures to come and conflates the eroticized female body with the poems. Dacre dedicates the volume to John Penn, Esq. (1760–1834), a grandson of William Penn, a fellow poet, and most likely Dacre's patron. The volume includes a subtly erotic but oddly obfuscating dedicatory poem to him, implying, as many of the other poems in the volume, an intimate exchange. This kind of suggestiveness was central to Dacre's poetic project. While the critics sought to mock her by dubbing the poems as Rosa Matilda effusions, as each of these gestures suggests, Dacre exploited this effusive identity to elicit her readers' interest and mark her poems' literary quality.

The poems themselves are quite varied, giving voice to a wide range of characters and perspectives, though the predominant tone is gothic and the main theme is female passion, both its danger and its power. *Hours* shares *Trifles'* fascination with suicide as an act of female agency and desire, passion as the defining characteristic of female subjectivity, and extremes of sensibility that intertwine mind and body. The title of the volume indicates its Romantic leanings and its investment in the imagination. Unlike earlier Romantic writers, such as Wordsworth, whose hours of solitude involve self-sustaining reflections on a natural scene, or Smith, whose meditations on the local scene become metaphors for the speaker's solitary state, however, Dacre's hours of solitude are spent tracing out the precipitous and volatile experience of desire—her speakers search for that acutely sympathetic lover, the other who reflects the self and who responds with sigh for sigh and tear for tear, and they spend their solitude bemoaning its loss or absence. In isolation, they obsess about their feelings, often experiencing imaginative visions. Like *Trifles,* this later volume is, literally and figuratively, haunted by dead lovers who lure their partners into an alternative world—much as John Keats's Porphyro melts into Madeline's dream in *The Eve of St. Agnes* (1820), but with a morbid twist.

The largest group of poems fits this description; these poems explore, either through the voice of a single speaker reflecting on his or her passion or through a dialogue between the speaker and his or her (often dead) lover, the extremes of passionate desire, both physical and spiritual, the hopes and betrayals of love, the impact of seduction especially on women, and the possibilities of erotic union, often expressed in the lover's choice of death. They range from the amusing and slightly silly "Fracas Between the Deities. Addressed to Mr. F——, an Enthusiastic Votary of the Shrine of Bacchus," in which Bacchus and Pallas Athene compete (complete with food fight) to prove whose model of desire is better, to the horrifically gothic "The Skeleton Priest; or, The Marriage of Death," in which the female lover's expression of desire leads to her horrific marriage with the reanimated skeleton of her lover's first wife. Some of these poems about seduction play out the issues allegorically, as in "The Triumph of Pleasure," in which Age and Pleasure compete to win Beauty's affections. They also include the Ossianic "Song of Melancholy" and "The Mistress to the Spirit of Her Lover" as well as the more Della Cruscan poems like "Lasso a me!" and "Alas Forgive Me!" or the orientalist battle in "The Moorish Combat." Even the unusual series of poems about personified natural elements ("Fog," "Will-o-Wisp," "Mildew," "Wind," "Frost," and "Thaw") rely on the language of visionary lovers; each element becomes embodied and seductive, even ghost-like, like many of the lovers in the more explicitly erotic poems. Deploying an early modern trope of orgasm as death, many of these poems portray lovers uniting, spiritually and sexually, in death. At its most extreme, consummation is an act of mating, literally, with death, as in, for example, "Death and the Lady," a rewriting of an eighteenth-century broadside ballad. Again and again, Dacre emphasizes the emaciating effects of desire. Lovers are cadaverous as desire threatens to become necrophiliac.

The poems explore both female and male passion as subjective states that determine identity and behavior. Paradoxically, however, lovers who desire the sympathetic other of the Della Cruscan exchange can only imagine a partner when they are themselves alone. Romantic unions are solely textual, intercourse mentally achieved. These love poems are most often written from a female perspective, so the reader experiences female desire subjectively, as in, for example "The Unfaithful Lover." In this poem, the speaker expresses her anger at her lover's fascination with another's "meretricious charms" (vol. 1, p. 37), hardening herself (she repeats the word "cold" four times and imagines herself as "flinty rock"), until she becomes almost corpse-like. Rather than choose virtue or self-sacrifice, she opts to dwell in this state of impassioned numbness, unhealed—an affirmation of self that suspends the self in its painful state. Several of the verses exploring states of passion are written in male voices that express an equally intense experience—for example, "The Lover's Vision." In a series of poems that self-consciously mimic the Della Cruscan erotic poetic exchanges, Dacre portrays male desire as a version of female. The supposed author of these poems, Azor (as Craciun points out, Rosa backward), mirrors Rosa in his emotions, language, and style but styles himself more explicitly a poet. He longs for a sympathetic response, but, as with many of these poems, his poems do not respond directly to another poem, making the poetic exchange one-sided. Azor, too, imagines his love in solitude, an identity and a sexual union achieved mentally, textually—the only means of achieving desire in these poems.

Such imaginative visions are a dominant trope of these poems and further mark them as Romantic poems, even if for Dacre these visions border on the destructively macabre. To see that such Romantic visions are part of the cultural discourse of the day one has only to think of Oothoon in William Blake's *Visions of the Daughters of Albion* (1793), the Poet's vision of the veiled maid in Percy Bysshe Shelley's *Alastor* (1816), John Keats's belle dame, or Samuel Taylor Coleridge's Geraldine and the Abyssinian maid of "Kubla Khan"—even perhaps Victor Frankenstein's dream of Elizabeth turning into the corpse of his dead mother fits this genre. Dacre's poems are, in a sense, gothic conversation poems in which the addressed lover remains physically absent but mentally present. In poem after poem, the speakers' hours of solitude allow them to carry on conversations with these phantasms, the externalization of their mental states in a visionary moment that reveals the mind's power to shape its own reality. For Dacre, this power is ambivalent and often double; the visions are troubled and inspiring, threatening and impassioned, transcendent and mortal, erotic and morbid, spiritual and embodied. In their most positive form, as in "The Mistress to the Spirit of Her Lover," they allow lovers to cross physical boundaries. In their most negative form, they produce monsters, as in "The Visions of Fancy" and "Aerial Corpse." Perhaps the most intriguing of these visionary, supernatural poems is "The Musing Maniac," a poem that first appeared as "The Spectre's Jubilee" in Dacre's earlier novel, *Confessions of the Nun of St. Omer.* The change in the title shifts from the novel's emphasis on death's dance to the speaker's disoriented state—a state the title suggests that is conducive to poetry. This extreme loss of identity, such that the speaker cannot locate herself in time or space and only can dance with death—here joyfully and carelessly—epitomizes Dacre's liminal visions.

In a poem written much later, published March 4, 1814, in the *Morning Post,* Dacre makes more explicit the significance of such visions, calling them "viewless spirits of the Air." For her, these omnipresent spirits produce the necessary and vital emotional response of "secret sympathy" and hold "O'er the thoughts, the heart and brain" a "magic influence." They embody the involuntary, intellectual power of passion and inhabit a pre-Romantic landscape. The poem's epigraph from *Paradise Lost,* book 1, connects Dacre's spiritual lovers to Milton's spirits, who "when they please / Can either sex assume, or both." For Dacre, to deny the existence of such spirits means never to have known solitude, never to have truly loved, never to have felt the extremes of passion, and, most significantly, never to have experienced the power of the imagination. Though her poems warn against the dangers of delusional passion, to fail to recognize this sympathetic, spiritual power is to fail to comprehend the transformative powers of imagination and the gender-bending boundary-crossing nature of love—the very basis of her aesthetic.

The previous writer who most embodies this aesthetic for Dacre is Mary Robinson; in *Hours,* Robinson functions as a muse figure, as a literary foremother, and as an erotic poetic double. Dacre and Robinson shared a concern with female desire and its repercussions, a desire to bridge mind and body, and an investment in sympathy as the basis of human identity and their poetic practices. Dacre literally calls Robinson back from the dead (in "To the Shade of Mary Robinson") to lead her, but Robinson's presence pervades this volume, from Dacre's use of pseudonyms to her themes and forms. In both of Dacre's poetry volumes, the frenzied female lovers recall Robinson's Sappho, who, overcome by her passion and the indifference of her lover, Phaon, commits suicide in the penultimate sonnet of Robinson's sequence. Robinson's description of Sappho as a poet of sensibility, whose poems are "the genuine effusions of a supremely enlightened soul, labouring to subdue a fatal enchantment" (*Sappho and Phaon,* 1796, p. 25), might well fit many of Dacre's speakers and certainly her model of the effusive poet. More generally, Dacre's women share a similar tumultuousness of desire with the lovelorn, emotional speakers of many of Robinson's poems, from earlier poems like "Ode to the Nightingale" (1791) and "Ode to Rapture" (1793) to Robinson's final poems in *Lyrical Tales* (1800). There are also numerous echoes to the volume of poetry that Maria Elizabeth Robinson published after her mother's

death, *The Wild Wreath* (1804), a collection of poems by many Romantic writers, but primarily Robinson. Many of these poems were published pseudonymously in the *Morning Post,* where Robinson was lead poet from December 1799 until her death at the end of 1800, and for which Dacre regularly wrote after 1804. The connections between Dacre's *Hours* and this volume are too many to enumerate here, and include work by other poets in the volume, especially Lewis and Merry, but of particular note is Robinson's "A Kiss," the precursor to Dacre's "The Kiss."

Dacre must have identified with Robinson. As a writer for the *Morning Post,* partial to the use of pseudonyms, as a woman who had three children out of wedlock with her married boss, as a poet of sensibility and passion, Dacre must have been highly aware of Robinson's writing career. In *Hours,* she seems intent on resurrecting Robinson as poet, muse, misunderstood woman, and sympathetic other. Intriguingly, Dacre's poem "To the Shade of Mary Robinson" repeats the spiritual conjuring of many of the love poems in this volume in the context of a same-sex dynamic. Elegiac and worshipful in its tone, the poem expresses Dacre's identification with Robinson as an intellectual, sexual woman whom the world did not appreciate. Though the speaker despairs in the first lines that she never met Robinson, the poem seeks to reanimate Robinson, now literally and figuratively visionary, by praising her, by protecting her from those who denigrated her, and by following her ghost through an imagined landscape in the final stanzas of the poem. Dacre represents herself as the ideal sympathetic other to Robinson's sensibility with "heart form'd to love thee— / An heart which responsive had beat to thine own" (vol. 1, p. 130). Using a similar botanic metaphor to describe poetic rivalry as Robinson's "Ode to the Snowdrop," Dacre both protects Robinson's fame and poetic skill and simultaneously asserts her own poetic authority—a double move that Robinson herself perfected in poems like "To the Poet Coleridge." Where Dacre's later novels try to enforce a moral to control the passions they set in play, Dacre's poem to Robinson, as the other poems in *Hours,* reveals that the sympathetic and passionate connection between two people, whose hearts beat as one, even across the bounds of death, is her real interest and the main source of her poetic authority.

As the poem to Robinson's ghost indicates, *Hours of Solitude* has a double project of defining relationships of passionate love and constructing a poetic philosophy that extends that of the Della Cruscans. This philosophy of love is embodied in "The Kiss," the most often cited of Dacre's poems from this volume and, in the opinion of the critic Jerome McGann, the embodiment of sentimental poetry. Marked as feminine, such poetry, McGann argues, represents true love as "a total intensity of the total person—mind, heart, and (here was the sticking point) body" ("My Brain Is Feminine," p. 31). Creating a textual sexuality, the kiss is a physical but imaginary act that blends body, mind and soul:

THE greatest bliss
Is in a kiss—
A kiss of love refin'd
When springs the soul
Without controul,
And blends the bliss with mind.

(vol. 1, p. 22)

Desire itself is not enough to produce "the fond delight" of true love, but the eye must beam "sentiment" (p. 23) to reach the "soul" (p. 22); and yet it is the body that speaks through sighs, and voluptuous eyes, and heartbeats. Dacre's "Kiss" sets out to enact the very blending that it articulates, turning the kiss itself into a figure for her poetry. Its short lines emulate impassioned breathing and separate physical responses onto individual lines. The poem lasts but a moment; it teases and exhilarates, its breathy brevity gone in a moment, like the kiss it mimics.

CONFESSIONS OF THE NUN OF ST. OMER

On April 25, 1806, the *Morning Post* published a short poem by Francisca Julia, "On Modern Female Writers," that constructs a canon of the most popular female novelists of the day, the ones to choose when one wants to "beguile the dull hours." It includes the "well-told light fic-

tions of [Mary] *Meeke*"; "*Charlotte Smith*'s plaintive hist'ry of woe"; Ann Radcliffe's romances that "harrow the soul, and amaze all our fancies"; Eliza Parsons, Anna Maria Bennet, and Rachel Hunter, in whom "treasures abound"; and Regina Maria Roche, Elizabeth Helme, and Elizabeth and Susannah Gunnings, in whose work "some beauties are found." The author saves for the highest praise Rosa Matilda's novels, which can "ravish our senses," underscoring her higher status by giving her the final line of the poem. The writer contrasts Rosa's emotional power with the "queer fiction" of male writers who "abuse female writers for mere contradiction." The poem thus valorizes Dacre's style and simultaneously asserts her ability to best male novel writers in the marketplace. Said with passionate gusto, the last line of the poem riffs on the contemporary anxiety about female reading and revels in the idea that a novel might overcome one's senses, that reading is a sexually charged experience— one that Dacre understood better than her male and female contemporaries. Dacre's writing ravishes her female readers, and that is exactly what they want.

No wonder Dacre's novels came to be associated with pornography. While they confronted her readers with many of the same themes as her poetry, they also made their sexual nature more explicit. They even more intensely focused on the work of the passions on the individual mind, tracing out the progress of her characters' emotional absorption, step by step, over several volumes. At a time when literary women writers came increasingly to worry about their propriety, when the gothic was increasingly framed as pornographic, Dacre wrote and published a series of novels that included female characters whose behaviors range from seduction and murder to incest, obsession, and suicide—none of these exactly appropriate behaviors for the proper lady. While radical women writers like Mary Wollstonecraft and Mary Robinson were ignored or vilified, Dacre's more conservative politics allowed her to continue to write on sexually active, though usually (self-)destructive, passionate women who pursued their desires.

As easy as it was for reviewers to write such novels off as disgusting and indecent, Dacre's interest in tracing the passions was part of an ongoing philosophical discussion at the end of the eighteenth century. Since Frances Hutcheson's *An Essay on the Nature and Conduct of the Passions and Affections* (1728), there had been greater interest in thinking through the relationship between reason and passion. In *A Treatise on Human Nature* (1739–1740), David Hume argued for the primacy of the passions as the motivating force behind human action, claiming that "reason is, and ought only to be, the slave of the passions" (cited in Baillie, p. 32). Adam Smith further developed a contextualized theory of sympathy in *Theory of Moral Sentiments* (1752). Perhaps most importantly for Dacre's work, Joanna Baillie's *Plays on the Passions* (1798) attempted dramatically "to trace them [the passions] in their rise and progress in the heart" (p. 91). Like these thinkers, Dacre was a philosopher of the passions, but she chose to explore them in the novel form, a form that allowed her to address more explicitly the subjective nature of those passions as they affected specific individuals.

Published just prior to *Hours*, Dacre's first novel, *Confessions of the Nun of St. Omer* (1805), a fictional memoir, explores the effects of a "fatal passion" (vol. 3, p. 180) on the first-person narrator, Cazire Arieni. Ever the victim, Cazire corresponds with her son, Dorvil Lindorf, from the convent of St. Omer, where she has interred herself after the gruesome deaths of her lover and husband. Willing to risk losing her son's love as the cost of telling her story, Cazire relays her physical, emotional, and intellectual struggle to understand and take control of her passion. The story, though set in luxurious Italy, takes place primarily in a garden or on a couch, locations of romantic seduction. The narrative traces out Cazire's intimate, sexual relationships with three different men: the hedonist, Godwinian philosopher Fribourg, a married man whom she passionately desires (her "fatal passion") but virtuously withstands at the beginning of the novel; the libertine Lindorf, who woos her with poetry and music after Fribourg returns to his wife, sets

her up as his mistress, impregnates her with his son, and then reveals that he is married; and the angelic, forgiving St. Elmer, who marries and loves her even after she becomes a fallen woman, only to have her revert to her initial passion for Fribourg on his reappearance at the end of the novel. The novel thus asks its reader to judge men's behavior and the philosophical principles that guide them. While Fribourg offers a model of free love that critiques the system of marriage, St. Elmer embodies a model that challenges the idea that sexuality defines a woman's identity. None of these relationships, however, is sustainable because of Cazire's self-division: Lindorf runs off in search of novel pleasures; St. Elmer ends up murdered by Fribourg in a duel; and Fribourg ends up, Werther-like, committing suicide, when Cazire rejects him for the dead St. Elmer.

At the end of the novel, Cazire defines her story as a "fatal warning to him [her son] of the delusions of passion, and a warning of the miseries which are entailed by neglecting the early formation of the heart and principles" (vol. 3, p. 192). It is also a warning to her own sex, especially those "wildly enthusiastic" (vol. 3, p. 190) like herself, to abide by their duties to father and husband. The facile closing moral, however, cannot undo the powerful language of passages like the following in which Cazire speaks her desire:

> He gazed on me, and drew me closer in his arms. Involuntarily my eyes met his. Their expression disarmed my soul, and I sunk unresisting on his breast.—In an instant his lips were fixed on mine— then they dwelt upon my bosom.—I sighed deeply. I was conscious but careless of my danger.—Tossed in a delirium of passion, every nerve in arms, I was indifferent to all but his transports—his breath of glowing ardour—his trembling agony, as he entwined me in his embrace—I was indifferent to virtue, to the world, to every thing but love and Fribourg.
>
> (vol. 3, p. 155)

Like the poem "The Kiss," this passage emphasizes sensual physicality. The reader is caught up in the passionate moment, feels the lover's look, touch, kiss, breath, succumbs with Cazire, giving up everything but love. Though Cazire's words point to her "careless" and "indifferent" state, the "danger "to her "virtue," the narrative, punctuated by dashes that mimic the speaker's escalating passion, instead emphasizes the value of the moment itself, the transformative, climactic, if transitory power of the kiss. One understands exactly Fribourg's argument when he asks Cazire, somewhat rhetorically: "Can it ever be a crime to love, think you?" (vol. 3, p. 135).

Though she comes to see herself as a monster, Cazire does not reform like other heroines, but in an attempt to control her desires, she incarcerates herself in a nunnery—ironically, the very place that was the source of her poor education earlier in the novel. This education, and in particular her novel reading, shapes her principles and drives her passions. Caught between an ineffectual, passive mother, who hopelessly waits for her husband's return, and a father willing to sacrifice his daughter's love to the whims of his overbearing mistress, Cazire indulges in every kind of inappropriate reading possible, supplied to her by a female servant from her father's library. Before she has even fallen for the sophistry of Fribourg or the eloquence of Lindorf, Cazire has been seduced by books, "enslaved with the brilliancy of the language and speciousness of the arguments" (vol. 1, p. 71). In a chapter titled "Dangerous Reading," she claims she has a "furor for dangerous reading" (vol. 1, p. 66), a word that makes explicit the connection between reading and sexuality. As Adriana Craciun argues, the word "furor," a medical term used to describe nymphomania (*furor uterinus*) in the eighteenth century, specifically linked women's sexuality to imagination. Again and again, Cazire emphasizes that her mind is out of control and takes the heart with it—a striking inversion of what one might expect.

The novel is obsessed with the dangers and pleasures of reading and language. Reading is clearly a seductive, often sexual, act; Lindorf wins Cazire by reading her his poetry; Fribourg seduces Cazire by reading Charlotte and Werther to her; and even the perfect St. Elmer convinces Cazire to marry him through letters. But writing is just one form of the seduction of discourse; the novel traces out in great detail Cazire's seduction by language more generally. Intimacy is created by conversation, and the novel explicitly links desire and intellectual exchange. Fribourg woos Cazire in the language of liberty, turning radical philosophical thought into an erotic discourse of seduction. Even the act of writing becomes erotically charged, because it takes its source from a passionate emotional response. Cazire only becomes a poet and tries to publish as a direct result of her passionate actions.

Cazire fulfills her sexual desire, but it also destroys her, suggesting the impossibility of inhabiting, except momentarily, a fully embodied female subjectivity. The novel warns against the dangers of conversation, philosophizing, and reading; the voracious nature of female desire; and the destructive cultural opposition between passion and marriage—but it also shows the failure of models of duty to thwart such desires. More in the Sturm-und-Drang style of Johann Wolfgang von Goethe's *Sorrows of Young Werther* (1774) than gothic, *Confessions* shares with all Dacre's novels an ambivalence about erotic desire by portraying and thus eliciting the very response it claims to be warding off. Even the title, which seemingly creates the religious context of the nun's confession, evokes the pornographic with its allusions to Denis Diderot's scandalous novel *The Nun* (1796; English trans. 1797) and Jean-Jacques Rousseau's equally subversive *Confessions* (1782, 1789). The dedication of Dacre's novel to Matthew Lewis furthered these connections. Moreover, Dacre claimed to have written this seductive novel at just eighteen—"from the feelings of the heart," she says in the book's dedicatory letter. Bourgeois readers could have their senses titillated, could experience Cazire's ravishment, and return to the safe middle-class world affirmed by her plight and the novel's moral. No wonder this novel went into almost three editions.

ZOFLOYA; OR, THE MOOR: A ROMANCE OF THE FIFTEENTH CENTURY

When Sarah Green, a contemporary of Dacre's and a sharp critic of the late-eighteenth- and early-nineteenth-century novel, called Dacre one of "the most licentious writers of romance of the time" (note to p. xii) in the preface to her parodic *Romance Readers and Romance Writers* (1810), she refers to *The Libertine* (1807), but she could also have been thinking about *Zofloya,* Dacre's second and best novel. Published in 1806, Dacre's novel took "wild"—a word she uses frequently to describe Victoria, the novel's protagonist—to a whole new level for a woman writer. Victoria's wildness is truly licentious—a matter of violent, uncontrolled passion and an unruly willfulness that does not submit to any moral authority but its own desire. Unlike the rational heroines of Romantic novels such as Marianne Dashwood or Elizabeth Bennett, Victoria does not become the proper lady, who directs her excessive sensibility into the correct channels; unlike other gothic heroines like Emily St. Aubert or Ellena Rosalba, she does not become the threatened heroine who finally resolves through rational means, moral integrity, and marriage the terrors that plague her. Instead, the novel presents a violent and impulsive woman who pursues her sexual desires to the point of destroying her husband (Berenza), his brother (Henriquez), his brother's fiancée (Lilla), and finally herself, by making a pact with a Moor (Zofloya), a servant to Henriquez, who turns out to be the Devil in disguise. Victoria is a character right out of Sade, and the plot an imitation of Matthew Lewis's *The Monk,* with this critical difference: the main character is a volatile female. In the course of the narrative, we are shown a young woman who is willing to commit three calculated murders, including that of her husband; have sex with her husband's brother while she is disguised as his virginal fiancée, Lilla; drive the brother to suicide when he realizes the truth; torture and kill that fiancée; and increasingly express her desire for a black servant, whom she frequently meets privately in isolated and sublime landscapes. She is also Venetian, aristocratic, and dark in contrast to the blond, blue-eyed, angelic Lilla with whom she is so starkly opposed. Victoria, thus, symbolically condenses many of the early-nineteenth-century middle-class social fears about women's increasing cultural authority. Her violent demise at the end of the novel—Zofloya, transformed into a monstrous Satan, "fierce,

gigantic and hideous to behold," casts her "headlong down the dreadful abyss" (quotations are from the 1997 Broadview edition, p. 254)—is thus overdetermined from the novel's start.

The novel tries to recontain the transgressive energies it sets forth with a closing moral about the dangers of "infernal influence" (p. 255) and the need for severe constraints on passion. However, the brevity of the moral and its simplistic religious language in a novel that—until the end, when Zofloya appears as Satan—emphasizes instead passionate drives and what Adriana Craciun defines as a pre-Nietzschean will-to-power undermines the gesture. Instead, through Victoria's agency and her transgressive sexual desires, the novel encodes bourgeois fantasies that are engendered by the very social and personal restrictions that bourgeois respectability imposes. Significantly, however, while Victoria may be a unique female character in the extreme violence of her passions and her willingness to pursue it at all costs, she is not unique in her sensibility or desire for self-actualization. Victoria may be increasingly masculinized over the course of the novel, but her desires originate in specifically female problems.

Critically, however, it is not just Victoria's hyperbolic behavior that makes this novel so transgressive. The transgression arises in the fusing of the sexual and violent with the equally fraught issues of race and class in the figure of Zofloya, the magnificent, seductively subservient black man whom Victoria, if unconsciously, desires. The novel is, after all, named after him and not Victoria. And though Victoria's libidinous desires are clearly established well before his entrance into the novel, his figure progressively dominates the text. Victoria's agency comes to depend on his expertise. Even if Zofloya is read allegorically as the projection of Victoria's desire, one cannot overlook the racial and class politics of presenting them in a spectacular black male body or the specter of miscegenation that Dacre raises by coding their exchanges in romantically charged and increasingly physical language. In the year before the abolition of slavery in Britain and in a context of slave revolts like that in Saint-

Domingue (the Haitian Revolution, 1791), the image of a black servant, whose knowledge of poisons and shape-shifting (knowledge shared with Lewis' Matilda) both enables a woman to sadistically destroy others and feeds his own brutal desire for vengeance, would have resonated powerfully in British imaginations. The novel puts in play two threats as doubles of each other: a woman in league and in lust with a black man and a black servant's potentially insurrectionary vengeance against his enslavement. The narrative offers a possible critique of the damaging effects of enslavement and simultaneously suggests the potentially threatening alliance of marginalized others. However, the fact that Dacre demonizes these subversive elements, in a stereotypical gesture of conservative backlash, by revealing Zofloya as Satan effectively returns the narrative to a racist Western fantasy of the rapacious, menacing other. The novel suggests that desire and domination are inextricably bound up with one another, each igniting the other, but it damps this conclusion by reducing desire to evil.

The dynamic is further complicated by the orientalist coding of Victoria's desire. Wrought to a fever pitch by her desire for Henriquez; her disdain for Berenza, her husband, who only marries her after she saves his life; and her hatred of Lilla, she has a dream vision of Zofloya before she even meets him:

> as if from the midst of them, she beheld advancing a Moor, of a noble and majestic form. He was clad in habit of white and gold; on his head he wore a white turban, which sparkled with emeralds, and was surmounted by a waving feather of green; his arms and legs, which were bare, were encircled with the finest oriental pearl; he wore a collar of gold round his throat, and his ears were decorated with gold rings of an enormous size.
>
> (p. 145)

The heavy-handed orientalist imagery presents Zofloya as a Moor of noble birth, like Othello, but primarily as a feminized object of Victoria's desire. The luxury of the description allows her to objectify him, so that in the second dream, when he offers to fulfill her fantasy, she readily promises herself to him.

Ironically, as she becomes darker, larger, and increasingly masculine, more and more like Zofloya, the less Victoria is her own agent and the more subject she is to Zofloya's sublime power. When she appears to Henriquez as Lilla under the effects of Zofloya's love potion, she takes on the form of the victim, the submissive heroine, but she still cannot become what she wants, the object of Henriquez' desire. Victoria's transformation here foreshadows her destruction; she is trapped, literally and figuratively. And this is confirmed in her commitment to Zofloya: "I am thine ever," she weeps (p. 231), and in the final pages of the novel, she gives herself to him "heart, and body, and soul" (p. 253) in a gesture that perverts the Della Cruscan romantic exchange. The novel tries to establish a power dynamic in which there are only two options—domination or submission, pleasure or pain, violence or violation, Victoria or Lilla. It instead exposes the interdependence of the terms; pleasure and pain are not alternatives but rather are bound together. That both Victoria and Lilla are destroyed, and in the same manner, at the end of the novel reveals their imbrication; it highlights the lack of complex subject positions for women in a society that vitiates female desire.

Given the volatile issues the novel sets in play, Stephanie Burley asks a key question about Dacre's authorship and her relation with her audience: "how can a woman who knows so much about desire, seduction and murder be a trustworthy producer of cultural capital?" (p. 198). The majority of reviewers were shocked by the novel, one going so far as to suggest that Dacre suffered from the "disease of maggots in the brain" (contemporary reviews reprinted in Craciun, *Zofloya*, p. 265). What seems most to have horrified critics was that a "lady, who used to write stimulating love verses in the newspapers," could write a "stimulating novel after the manner of the Monk—the same lust—the same infernal agents—the same voluptuous language" (contemporary reviews reprinted in Craciun, *Zofloya,* p. 262). The problem here, then, is a woman writing like a man, not about love, but about lust, and in the more dangerous form of the novel. Nonetheless, *Zofloya* was an extremely popular novel, enough so that it was published as a chapbook, *The Daemon of Venice: An Original Romance,* "By a Lady," in 1810 by Thomas Tegg (a publisher of cheap pornography), then republished in German in 1806, and in French in a four-volume edition in 1812.

Dacre clearly knew how to ravish her readers' senses, mixing together elements from the sentimental novel, the Jacobin novel, the oriental tale, French pornography, and the Romantic sublime to create an allusively hybrid text whose generic boundary crossings parallel those of her characters. As Craciun persuasively argues, Dacre's work, both in terms of content and style, does not fit either current portrayals of a distinct feminine Romanticism (rational, egalitarian, other-directed) or a female gothic of terror (beleaguered heroine who transforms male difference through love). Neither, however, does it fully correspond to the male horror gothic, with its focus on violation and morbid, graphic detail and an alienated, controlling male protagonist, because of its concern with female desire and agency. Far from imitating *The Monk,* Dacre's *Zofloya* subverts that text not only because it foregrounds a violent female victimizer but also because it combines that gothic with elements of other genres. Indeed, it has become commonplace to talk of *Zofloya* as blending Radcliffe's terror gothic with Lewis' horror gothic, to create as Kim Michasiw writes a "bold synthesis of [their] supposedly opposed Gothic forms" (p. viii). In revising the gothic, Dacre exploits her readers' need to experience, vicariously and surreptitiously, the very desires that middle-class culture demanded they publicly control. In the novel's closing scenes, a repetition of Ambrosio's death at the end of *The Monk,* Victoria is punished for her behavior, and yet one cannot forget the lovers of Dacre's *Hours* poems, ecstatic in death. *Zofloya*'s revelation as Satan, thus, provides Dacre with the means to make *Zofloya* safe reading; it allows her to disguise the erotic textuality with which she appeals to her readers, even as he is its primary source.

THE LIBERTINE

Perhaps because of *Zofloya* and its racy title, *The Libertine* (1807), Dacre's third novel, ran into three editions within the year of its publication and was translated into French in 1816, as *Angelo, comte d'Albini; ou, Les Dangers du vice.* Even more popular than her earlier novels, *The Libertine* still provoked the reviewers (with the exception of the *Morning Post*), who found it "absurd trash" written by a "fair libertine" and "weak enthusiast" (Green, p. xii), "worse than wild nonsense" (cited in Jones, p. 245), and written for the "depraved" and "warped" (cited in Craciun, *Fatal Women,* p. 114). The *Annual Review* critiqued Dacre's language as "sometimes ungrammatical, and often bombastic" but still "bold, stimulant and energetic." This reviewer saw libertinism as "the vice here traced from its polluted source through all its wild and capricious meanderings; the noxious current, blasting whatever it meets with, and accumulating in its course, at length with headlong fury, is itself precipitated into the gulph below" (p. 667). Surely a reference to *Zofloya*'s catapulting of Victoria into the abyss, the reviewer highlights the self-destructive, impulsively passionate nature of libertinism. Focusing on the tortuous relationship of a virtuous, intelligent, self-sacrificing woman (Gabrielle Montmorency) who is repeatedly seduced and abandoned by a selfish, feckless libertine, Count Angelo d'Albini, this novel offers another exploration of unrestrained passion, this time foregrounding male desire in order to critique the impulsiveness of male libertinism and to show how, in a patriarchal culture, it affects and thus shapes female desire and experience. Angelo continually means well, repents, and returns to the terminally loyal Gabrielle, only to again be drawn in by the superficial appearances and the impulses of desire. Passion for him is a kind of high-stakes game, very much like the gambling that ruins and nearly kills him and Gabrielle. Rewriting the fallen-woman narrative, Dacre constructs a double perspective—that of the fallen woman who, though playing the victim role of the sentimental heroine, refuses to stay home and passively accept her fate, who remains virtuous and strong, despite her sexual transgression; and that of the seducer, who, partly because of his limited education and primarily because of his unchecked passions, is driven by desire from woman to woman and becomes both victim to his desires and criminal in his actions. In the end, as in *Zofloya,* neither character—the virtuous woman nor the passion-driven man—survive. Even though Angelo finally realizes the value of Gabrielle, even though he repents, his initial crime, of seducing Gabrielle and refusing to marry her because she gives in to their desire, sets in motions a series of actions that lead to the destruction of everyone tainted by his desire. Dacre thus gives her readers, again, a world in which both options—virtue and impulsive desire—lead only to inexorable suffering and struggle. In contrast to *Zofloya,* however, the dominant emotions here are guilt, despair, and remorse. As in her earlier novels, the only escapes from such torments are death, madness, and a convent; any domestic felicity is transient and delusive.

Though some modern critics find this to be Dacre's best novel, especially in terms of its "labyrinthine" structure, it lacks the same narrative energy, dare one say passion, of the earlier novels, perhaps because the female character is too virtuous. Time after time, Gabrielle returns to Angelo, though she claims to be doing it primarily for her two children and not for love. Clearly, a virtuous heroine uniting excellence of mind with natural beauty, she is most interesting when she cross-dresses as a dark-skinned boy—Eugene—to pursue Angelo. In the fashion of Shakespeare's *Twelfth Night,* the novel sets in play, though to a lesser extreme than Zofloya, cross-racial, cross-class, and same-sex desire. The most erotic scene in the novel occurs when Angelo returns one night to find Gabrielle as Eugene, reading love poetry. Angelo is so drawn to Eugene that he cannot help caressing him and touching his hair, and he pledges his love to him. Later, however, Gabrielle becomes a figure of judgment and forgiveness, increasingly "angelic," a selfless martyr, who is at one point compared to a Madonna and who acts out of duty until it kills her. As the narrator tells us, "the female who desires to be happy must forgo all idle gratifications of vanity and of foolish egotism … the female who loves, and is beloved, may readily sacrifice these nothings at the shrine of reason"

(vol. 2, p. 156). Gabrielle does all this but does not gain happiness. Whereas Jane Austen's heroines learn the appropriate ladylike behavior to become marriageable, Dacre's heroines become marriageable only through their complete self-sacrifice, disembodiment, and death. With the exception of one small error, an error of passion, love, and ignorance, Dacre's Gabrielle and her daughter, Agnes, behave properly only to have it destroy them.

By contrast, Angelo's character engages for its thorough portrait of the libertine driven by his "slavish and degenerate" (vol. 3, p. 84) desires. In fact, if it were not so fatal to others, his continual susceptibility to each new woman who evokes his chivalric self-love would be comic. Not himself wicked, but of a weak character and indulgent background, Angelo cannot resist the lure of desire; he "requires continually the poignant and extraneous inducements of ever-varied novelty to prolong, or to renew it; his passion can only be kept alive by artifice, obstacles or perpetual interruption" (vol. 2, p. 56). Half-Italian and half-English, Angelo gets bored with virtuous domesticity; he wants theater, and the novel figures this desire, the "meretricious pleasures of guilt" (vol. 3, p. 46), as a kind of prostitution. The women he falls for appear to be the opposite of Gabrielle: Oriana, the vengeful, manipulative, and depraved murderer; Paulina, her beautiful, but mindless student and adopted sister; and Millborough, the upwardly mobile, greedy nurse, whose indulgences corrupt the son as well as the father. Significantly, all of these scheming and predatory women use their sexuality and their acting skills to seduce Angelo, and all of them have crossed class boundaries to achieve their power. Angelo's desire is thus doubly transgressive because it betrays Gabrielle's and it crosses class. But Gabrielle is only different in degree from these women; the narrative suggests that women must perform in order to achieve their desires. Moreover, it suggests that violent or virtuous, pursuing these desires will lead to destruction: Oriana is stabbed by a tyrant lover; Paulina runs off with another lover; Millborough is shunned by Parisian society and ends up incarcerated in a lunatic asylum; and

CHARLOTTE DACRE

Gabrielle ends up married but dead. Each relationship leaves Angelo increasingly debilitated, maniacal, and remorseful, until, like Cazire, he comes to recognize himself as the "monster" he is.

To be fair, Angelo does try to redeem himself after Gabrielle's death by searching out his children to fulfill her dying request, but, again, even at this point he cannot escape his passions. In increasingly religious language, the novel draws to a gothic climax, piling up incest, murder, domestic abuse, robbery, and suicide in the last few pages, to emphasize that the *"'sins of the father shall be visited upon the children'"* (vol. 4, p. 223). As in her earlier novels, Dacre underscores parental failure, suggesting both a genetic snowball effect and the dangers of overindulgence and improper education. Angelo may have repented, but his crimes have infected the younger generation: Agnes repeats her mother's sin, Felix repeats his father's, and Angelo's guilt becomes compounded in his interactions with them. Having almost committed incest, he locks his daughter away in a convent and murders her lover. Fleeing that crime, he is robbed by his disguised son and ends up giving evidence against him that condemns him to death. Shaped by the deleterious environments of their childhoods, Angelo's children, one mad in a convent, the other imprisoned and soon to die, embody the contaminating effects of his passion. Dacre, here, recycles and expands many elements from her earlier novels: Cazire becomes Agnes, Fribourg becomes Angelo, Lilla becomes Gabrielle, Victoria becomes Oriana/Millborough, but the novel leaves one deflated, not ravished. Though one may become caught up in the plot, without the first-person subjective experience of *Confessions* or the complexity of Victoria's character, Dacre's seductive textuality is overpowered by the relentless, moralistic hammering on Angelo's libertinism. One longs for Zofloya to return and toss them all into the abyss.

THE PASSIONS

In her last novel, *The Passions* (1811), Dacre recovers some of the emotional energy and intensity of *Zofloya*, by using the outdated epistolary style of earlier eighteenth-century novelists like Samuel Richardson and returning explicitly to debates about passion and female desire in particular. The passions she traces, here, are furious, vengeful passions. These passions are embodied in two characters, both of whose behaviors drive the novel's plot: a female one, Appollonia Zulmer, who seeks vengeance for having been spurned by the man she loved, and a male one, Count Darlowitz, who cannot control his illicit desires for another man's wife, Julia Montalban. The epistolary style effectively shifts the focus of the novel from the dramatic action of *The Libertine* to the emotions. Moving among the Swiss Alps, fashionable Vienna, rural Austria, dissolute Naples, and classical Rome, the landscape of *The Passions*, again, has gothic elements, but is more what Craciun terms "a psychological landscape" (*Fatal Women,* p. 144), a landscape created by the play of passion. If the novel gets mired in these emotional states, the epistolary form at least allows Dacre the freedom to return to her earlier use of textual eroticism to elicit her readers' interest. At the end of the novel, however, she breaks the epistolary genre and provides a long, third-person, prose conclusion in order to convey the tragic ending, the madness and death of Julia in the snow on her husband's doorstop—the kind of death scene that is Dacre's specialty. Perhaps avoiding the sexual content, the reviewers chose to focus, instead, on the "repulsive affectation of her style" and the "inflated extravagance of diction which deforms" the novel (cited in Summers, p. 70), but their use of the words "repulsive" and "deforms," two words used about Appollonia, a figure of demonic desire, reveals a displaced disgust that links Dacre and her character.

The novel consists of a series of letters among two married couples, two opposing advisors, and a single woman, the rejected Appollonia. Focusing on Appollonia's revenge on Wiemar for having repulsed her love, the letters investigate the central role of passion in shaping identity. Appollonia violently asserts her agency in response to what feels to her like a moment of self-erasure, and she puts her plot in motion by seducing Wiemar's wife, Julia. She activates Julia's desire through dangerous reading and an alternative gender philosophy that asserts the self-actualizing power of female passion. Julia expresses her newfound power in her adulterous desire for Darlowitz. If *The Passions* accentuates the dangers of these emotions, it does so to participate in current debates of the day, in particular over the definition of woman, of female desire, of adultery, and about the proper mode of education. Dacre pits male characters' versions of the ideal passive woman against Appollonia's erotic model and the economic model of Madame de Hautville (Appollonia's teacher). She asks her readers to watch the effects of female desire as it transforms the heroine Julia from a docile, obedient wife into a sexually desiring, emotionally tormented woman. She compares the educational ideal of the self-enclosed domestic community established in Vienna by the two couples and their families, with Appollonia's libidinous education of Julia.

The novel also returns to another central Dacrean theme: the dangers of reading and the tutelary relationship. The novel presents itself as a revision of Rousseau's *Julie; or, The New Heloise* (1761), the most famous story of the day about love between a teacher and student. Julia's name is certainly a reference to Rousseau's Julie. However, whereas Rousseau's novel shows a young woman able to achieve virtue in marriage and suppress—or at least appear to—her passionate premarital love, Dacre's novel inverts the narrative by making Julia's desire arise after marriage in order to reframe Rousseau's terms in the context of adultery. Unlike Julie's husband, Wolmar, however, Wiemar does not stand by his Julia. Moreover, though Dacre tries to contain the passions her novel sets in play with a quick moral at the end, she ends up countering Rousseau's idea that virtue and marriage will contain and rectify earlier passions. In fact, the only characters alive at the end of the novel are the men's advisor, the philosophic, rational Rozendorf, and the Rousseauistic, sublimely focused Wiemar; all the women are dead. Thus Dacre underscores the masculinist gender politics of

Rousseau's philosophies. *Passions* simultaneously shows the damaging impact of uncontrolled passion and points to its cause: as in *Zofloya,* a model of womanhood that seeks to contain, if not nullify, female desire within the constraints of marriage.

The novel's most engaging, subversive character, Appollonia, is modeled after Victoria Arieni; as in that novel, Dacre accentuates Appollonia's character by contrasting her with women described as her opposites and, in so doing, implicitly creates a mutual critique. Appollonia's aggressive behavior, practical philosophy, and violent rage challenge the model, constructed by the male characters, of the ideal woman—passive, dutiful, selfless, "formed for love … but [only] *love for him*" (vol. 1, p. 31). Like Victoria, Appollonia chooses violence as the means to achieve her desires; sexual desire is displaced into hatred of Wiemar. Like Medusa, with whom she identifies (vol. 2, p. 209), her "fierce and penetrating" gaze withers men (vol. 1, p. 27). What's more, she has the power to persuade others to her view, and she enters conversation freely and equally, causing all, especially women, to admire her. As Craciun argues, she represents the Burkean sublime in female form (*Fatal Women,* p. 139), something Wiemar loves in nature but not in women who are supposed to be beautiful "ornament[s] for the drawing room" (vol. 1, p. 30) or, in a more telling orientalist language, "the Houri's [sic] of the Mahomedan paradise" (vol. 1, p.121). What Appollonia represents instead is female independence: she transforms the debilitating and enslaving emotions of love into an affirmation of her own power over men. To her, men are "tools" (vol. 1, p. 55), and if she can't have Wiemar in love, she will have him through other means, by taking away his wife's desire, by making him experience the "horror" of rejection, which is the erasure of self. Literally, what she attempts to do is to make him change places with her; no longer the victim, she will victimize him. The novel, in a sense, opposes a Rousseauvian model of femininity with a Wollstonecraftian one, albeit in a perverted form; Wiemar clearly chooses the former, but the text does not completely devalue Appollonia's authority.

Passions also highlights the sexual power of language. Words, not deeds, cause havoc in this novel: there is no actual adultery. The emotional betrayal occurs in writing, in the love letters that pass back and forth and in Appollonia's homo-erotic reeducation of Julia. Dacre has, in fact, returned to an idea she introduced in *Confessions*—that reading, textuality, is itself an act of sexuality—a dangerous argument for Dacre to make and one that again implicates her texts in the very acts they supposedly condemn. In the final scenes of the novel, Julia deteriorates into madness and becomes a specter, one of the frenzied lovers of the *Hours,* torn between her love and her despair. Her two final gestures demonstrate the divided self she has become. In a moment of passion that becomes madness, she draws the head of Darlowitz and presses it to her bosom, claiming that there he still lives. But it is her husband's "threshold" upon which she seeks to die, and, in the cunning clarity of the mad-woman, she plots her escape, steals a knife, and after several tries escapes, like "some timid spirit new burst from the enchanter's spell" (vol. 4, p. 326), through the snowstorm (for pages), clad only in a nightdress, dragging herself along, tortured and in pain, only to die before gaining her husband's pardon. Julia thus comes to symbolize the cost of these passions: Appollonia's anger, Darlowitz's desire, Wiemar's self-absorption all serve to alienate her from herself. Neither feminine ideal nor feminine evil, Julia is literally driven mad, as the text reveals, through her character, the inseparability of the two terms. In its penultimate lines, the novel leaves the reader with a histrionic image of a grief-stricken, raving Wiemar holding the corpse of Julia in his arms, like Lear with his daughter Cordelia. In this tragic world, there is no consolation, except death or the arbitrary power of virtue, which supplies insufficient morals about "the danger of listening to the delusive blandishments of soph-istry; of yielding to the guilty violence of the Passions, or of swerving even in *thought* from the sacred line of virtue, and our duty" (vol. 4, p. 340).

DACRE'S PSEUDONYMS

To understand fully Dacre's project, we need to take into account the mode in which her works were presented to her contemporary readers. For Dacre, in fact, published all her writing under pseudonyms designed to control perceptions of her authorial persona and to place her work in literary traditions with which the early-nineteenth-century public was familiar. Calling herself "Rosa Matilda," she connected her writing to both the Della Cruscan poetic exchange in the newspapers of the 1780s and to Matthew Lewis' scandalous gothicism. The name "Rosa Matilda" refers specifically to Ambrosio's de-monic seducer in *The Monk,* who calls herself both Rosario and Matilda, and it foregrounds Dacre's interest in the violent, irrational elements of the male horror gothic. More in the manner of the 1830s penny dreadfuls and the later sensation fiction of Mary Elizabeth Braddon, Dacre's novels are full of violence, adultery, theft, murder, seduction, kidnapping, madness—gothic elements derived from Lewis that were to become the essence of Victorian thrillers. Yet "Rosa Mat-ilda" also recalls Anna Matilda, the public lover of Della Crusca, whose poetic romance in the pages of the era's popular newspaper, *The World,* had captured the public's attention.

Dacre could not, however, control the signifi-cations of "Rosa Matilda" as she might have wished. As the gothic was increasingly associ-ated with the obscene, her work as Rosa Matilda came to be falsely associated with Minerva Press and developed a pornographic resonance, despite her respectable publishers. The poetry's exces-sive emotion and theatricality, markers of femi-nine style, also were increasingly—and falsely—opposed to the masculine sincerity of Wordsworth and the biting satire of Lord Byron. As Lisa Wilson argues, the name "Rosa Matilda" came to represent a specific mode of hyperbolic writing, "defined as an excessively ornamented and sentimental style that was damned as manufac-tured and derivative by its association with writ-ing for the marketplace" (p. 403). The pseudonym took on a life of its own and became a deroga-tory label for feminine effusiveness. Reviewers referred to Dacre as Rosa Matilda to denigrate her writing; the poems were thus deemed the outbursts of a sexually experienced lover, not the craft of a serious poet. Even as late as 1842, Edgar Allan Poe could use this moniker to discredit rival women writers. Either excessively sexual or excessively emotional, "Rosa Matilda's" writing could be dismissed as second-rate.

As much a literary construct as Rosa Matilda, her other sobriquet, "Charlotte Dacre," reveals a third source of Dacre's writing: Romanticism. Dacre's poetry shares with Romantic poetry an interest in the power of imagination to shape its reality, an investment in authorship that conflates the speaker and author, and a belief in the importance of meditative solitude for a sustained sense of self. This name also had important literary connections. "Dacre," a Brythonic Celtic word meaning "trickling stream," connected her persona to nature. "Charlotte" alluded not only to Charlotte Smith, but also to Charlotte Corday, the assassin of the radical journalist Jean-Paul Marat (a violent woman like Dacre's characters), and Werther's Charlotte, the married woman who provokes the protagonist's emotional intensity and for whom he commits suicide, in Goethe's *Sorrows of Young Werther.* Though Dacre's work stressed the perverse manifestations of the imagination, it nonetheless also stressed imagination's power to shape perception and it derived its intensity from its representation of the impassioned mind. The name "Charlotte Dacre" was an attempt to martial the visionary power of Romantic poetry in the service of her gothic sensibility. Jointly, then, the pseudonyms enabled Rosa/Charlotte to engage in controversial, even pornographic, debates about sexuality and desire without repercussions to her personal identity. Persona and character reflected back on one another in a closed textual circuit, allowing Dacre to break the traditional identification between a woman's writing and her life, especially her sexual life, and to create the kind of exchangeability necessary for selling books in a consumer culture.

CONTEMPORARY RECEPTION

Contemporary reviewers found Dacre's work to be scandalous: with its dashes, exclamation points, italics, questions, melodramatic and oxymoronic epithets, personified feelings and synecdochic figures, her language suggested she was as excessive as her characters. In 1806, the *Annual Review* wrote of *Zofloya*:

> We are sorry to remark, that the "Monk" seems to have been made the model, as well of the style, as of the story. There is a voluptuousness of language and allusion, pervading these volumes, which we should have hoped, that the delicacy of a female pen would have refused to trace; and there is an exhibition of wantonness of harlotry, which we would have hoped, that the delicacy of the female mind, would have been shocked to imagine.
>
> (p. 542)

Other significant writers of the day had similar fears. In *Coelebs in Search of a Wife* (1808), one of the most popular didactic novels of the early nineteenth century, Hannah More imagined Dacre's writing as a danger to unwary young women, who should instead be reading Robert Southey or John Milton. More suggests that Rosa's style is seductive but insubstantial; it threatens to turn young women into consumers of sentimental novels and not into learners of domestic ideology, to cultivate their desires and not their reason.

Not all writers were as simply disapproving as More. Byron, for instance, borrowed from Dacre as well as criticizing her. In *English Bards and Scotch Reviewers* (1808), he sneered at her poetry as Della Cruscan and her prose as an imitation of Lewis' *The Monk*: "This lovely little Jessica, the daughter of the noted Jew K——, seems to be a follower of the Della Cruscan School, and has published two volumes of very respectable absurdities in rhyme, as times go; besides sundry novels in the style of the first edition of the Monk" (p. 58). For Byron, the Della Cruscan style of her verse marks Dacre as an ephemeral newspaper-writer, frivolous, flirtatious, excessively emotional, while the similarity of her novels to the first edition of *The Monk* shows them to verge on the salacious and pornographic. Despite his belittling of her ethnically, sexually, and poetically, however, Byron's very act of criticizing her in the same breath as Southey, Wordsworth, Coleridge, Walter Scott, and William Bowles belied his judgment and heightened the value of her writing. Byron had specific reasons to distance himself from Rosa Matilda, as he had mimicked her popular *Hours of Solitude* in his first volume of poems, *Hours of Idleness* (1807). He later disowned his more feminine early sentimental poetry and denigrated Dacre's poetry as "prose in masquerade" (p. 58), but, even after the critique in *English Bards,* his poetry kept getting tangled with hers. In April 1814, he expressed concern to his publisher about appearing too "Rosa-Matilda-ish," and his anonymous "Ode to Napoleon Buonaparte" published that month just prior to Dacre's "Irregular Lines on Napoleon Bonaparte" was mistaken for hers.

Percy Shelley was also highly aware of Dacre. In contrast to Byron, he was so intrigued with *Zofloya,* according to his biographer Thomas Medwin, that he rewrote and even borrowed parts of it in writing his early romances, *Zastrozzi* (1810) and *St. Irvyne; or, The Rosicrucian* (1811). These novels not only share *Zofloya*'s interest in transgressive desire but also repeat specific plot elements and rework Dacre's names. Moreover, Shelley's sister adopted the name Cazire, the heroine of Dacre's *Confessions,* for their jointly authored first volume of poems, *Original Poetry* (1810). The very fact that Dacre elicited such fervent responses from fellow writers indicates the impact of her writing. Combining the gothic, Della Cruscan, and Romantic, Dacre fashioned herself into a writer of seductive texts that had a formative effect on young Romantic poets such as Shelley—and Byron—even if they did not entirely approve of them. In whatever terms, Dacre's writing provoked extreme responses.

AFTERWORDS

"The Storm," a poem published January 9, 1815, in the *Morning Post,* might be read as a metaphor for the trajectory of Dacre's career, with its raising of tumultuous powers only to contain them through God's saving grace. Rejecting "Zephyr's soft sigh" (a trope of Della Cruscan poetry), Dacre turned to the "loud raging song" of storming passions in her novels. By the time she published

her last novel in 1811, she had had three children by Byrne, her then lover, and must have had some personal insight into the psychology of adultery as well as the passionate seductions of literary exchange. Though she had touted the importance of marriage in *The Libertine,* it was not until 1815, well after her last novel, that she and Byrne actually married.

Though she stopped writing novels in 1811, Dacre published poems under her Rosa Matilda pseudonym in the *Morning Post,* Byrne's paper, up until her marriage in 1815. Whether she was ultimately retreating from the passions that she had evoked in her novels is hard to say. With poems squeezed in among the daily fashionable events, Dacre wrote in a wide variety of moods and modes, including ballads, odes, the Greek-inspired meter called Anacreontics, occasional poems, love verses, and poems of sensibility on nature and the seasons. She also increasingly tried her hand at more overtly political poems, as the *Post* became a mouthpiece for King George IV's administration. The most intriguing group of these is a series of poems spoken by Napoleon Bonaparte in 1814–1815. In one of the last poems of this group, "Bonaparte and the Weird Sisters" (March 17, 1815), the title being an allusion to Shakespeare's *Macbeth,* Napoleon has a dialogue with the three fates who urge the anxious "tyrant" on "to death or glory." Startlingly portentous, as the emperor's defeat at the Battle of Waterloo was less than three months away, the poem was published on the day the Seventh Coalition mobilized against Napoleon. A jack-of-all poetic trades, Rosa Matilda had clearly reshaped herself to the *Post*'s political agenda. At the end of her career, she became a spokesperson for conservative politics and English nationalism. In 1822, she published the flattering long poem *George the Fourth,* praising his rule—ironic, given George's fraught relationship with Caroline. The final image of Dacre's life comes from the obituary in the *Times* for November 9, 1825; it notes that she died "after a long and painful illness, which her purity of heart and sublime greatness of soul enabled her patiently and piously to endure" (cited in Jones, p. 227). Dacre the risk-taker had been transformed into the pious, saintly married woman, living the deathbed scene of her characters.

Even in 1814, however, the *Modern Dunciad* still called her poetry "love and nonsense" and defined her in terms of passion and sexuality, subtly hinting at her intimacy with her female readers. Like Mary Robinson before her, she was "Rosa, the Sappho of the Morning Post" (Daniel, p. 32). As Rosa, Dacre embodied female desire, and the Sappho label underscores the tragic nature of that desire, identifying, with a whisper of homophobia, Dacre and her female characters. Dacre may have wanted to leave behind those passionate and violent explorations of love, but just as she never escaped her pseudonyms, she continues to be valued for the very thing she wanted to critique. Like the phantom lovers of her poems, who continue on after death, Dacre's history reminds us of the power of desire to speak its subject.

Selected Bibliography

WORKS OF CHARLOTTE DACRE

NOVELS

Confessions of the Nun of St. Omer. 3 vols. London: D. N. Shury for J. F. Hughes, 1805. Reprint, edited by Devendra P. Varma, New York: Arno Press, 1972. (Quotations in essay are taken from the reprinted edition.)

The Libertine. 4 vols. London: Cadell & Davies, 1807. Reprint, edited by Devendra P. Varma, New York: Arno Press, 1974. Reprint, edited by Gary Kelly, London: Pickering and Chatto, 2002. (Quotations in essay are taken from the reprinted edition.)

The Passions. 4 vols. London: Cadell & Davies, 1811. Reprint, edited by Devendra P. Varma, New York: Arno Press, 1974. (Quotations in essay are taken from the reprinted edition.)

Zofloya; or, The Moor: A Romance of the Fifteenth Century. 3 vols. London: Longman, Hurst, Rees, and Orm, 1806. Reprint, edited by Devendra P. Varma, New York: Arno Press, 1974. Reprint, edited by Adriana Craciun, Peterborough, Ont.: Broadview Press, 1997. Reprint, edited by Kim Michasiw, Oxford: Oxford University Press, 1997. (Quotations in essay are taken from the Broadview edition.)

POETRY

"Spirits of the Air." By Rosa Matilda. *Morning Post,* March 4, 1814.

"The Storm." By Rosa Matilda. *Morning Post,* January 9, 1815.

Trifles of Helicon. With Sophia King. London: James Ridgeway, 1798. Reprint, Breinigsville, Pa.: Gale ECCO Print Editions, 2010. (Quotations in essay are taken from the Gale ECCO edition.)

Hours of Solitude: A Collection of Original Poems, Now First Published. 2 vols. London: D. N. Shury, 1805. Reprint, edited by Donald Reiman, London: Garland, 1979. Reprint, online British Women Romantic Poets Project, University of California, Davis (http://digital.lib.ucdavis.edu/projects/bwrp/Works/DacrCHours1.htm), 2000. (Quotations in essay are taken from the online edition.)

George the Fourth. London: Hatchard, 1822.

WORKS IN TRANSLATION

Zofloya; ou, Le Maure: Histoire de XVeme siecle, traduit de l'anglais par Mme. De Viterne. 4 vols. Paris: Barba, 1812.

Angelo, comte d'Albini; ou, Les Dangers du vice, par Charlotte Dacre Byrne connue sous le nom de Rosa Matilda, traduit de l'anglais par Mme. Elisabeth de Bon. 3 vols. Paris: A. Bertrand, 1816. (*The Libertine.*)

OTHER WORKS ATTRIBUTED TO DACRE (AUTHORSHIP NOT DEFINITIVE)

The Daemon of Venice: An Original Romance: Tegg's Edition. London: Thomas Tegg, 1810.

The School for Friends: A Domestic Tale: By Miss Dacre. London: Thomas Tegg [n.d.]

CRITICAL AND BIOGRAPHICAL STUDIES

Baillie, Joanna. *Plays on the Passions.* Edited by Peter Duthie. Peterborough, Ont.: Broadview Press, 2001. (First published in 1798.)

Beauvais, Jennifer. "Domesticity and the Female Demon in Charlotte Dacre's *Zofloya* and Emily Brontë's *Wuthering Heights.*" *Romanticism on the Net,* no. 44 (http://www.erudit.org/revue/ron/2006/v/n44/013999ar.html?lang=en), November 2006.

Burley, Stephanie. "The Death of Zofloya; or, The Moor as Epistemological Limit." In *The Gothic Other: Racial and Social Constructions in the Literary Imagination.* Edited by Ruth Bienstock Anolik and Douglas L. Howard. Jefferson, N.C.: McFarland, 2004. Pp. 197–211.

Byron, George Gordon, Lord. *English Bards and Scotch Reviewers: A Satire.* 3rd ed. London: James Cawthorn, 1810.

Cass, Jeffrey. "Milton's Satan and Dacre's Zofloya: Orientalist Camp." *Questione Romantica: Rivista Interdiscipli-*

nare di Studi Romantici 12–13:65–75 (spring–autumn 2002).

Chaterjee, Ranita. "Charlotte Dacre's Nymphomaniacs and Demon Lovers: Teaching Female Masculinities." In *Masculinities in Text and Teaching*. Edited by Ben Knights. New York: Palgrave Macmillan, 2008. Pp. 75–89.

Craciun, Adriana. "'I hasten to be disembodied': Charlotte Dacre, the Demon Lover, and Representations of the Body." *European Romantic Review* 6:75–97 (1995).

———. Introduction to *Zofloya; or, The Moor, by Charlotte Dacre*. Peterborough, Ont.: Broadview Press, 1997. Pp. 9–32.

———. "Unnatural, Unsexed, Undead: Charlotte Dacre's Gothic Bodies." In her *Fatal Women of Romanticism*. Cambridge, U.K.: Cambridge University Press, 2003. Pp. 110–155.

Daniel, George. *The Modern Dunciad.* London: John Rodwell and Effingham Wilson, 1814.

Dunn, James A. "Charlotte Dacre and the Feminization of Violence." *Nineteenth-Century Literature* 53:307–327 (1998).

Erdman, David. "Byron's Mock Review of Rosa Matilda's Epic on the Prince Regent—A New Attribution." *Keats-Shelley Journal* 19:101–17 (1970).

Frank, Frederick S. Entries for Charlotte Dacre. *The First Gothics: A Critical Guide to the English Gothic Novel.* New York: Garland, 1987. Pp. 84–88.

Gamer, Michael. "Charlotte Dacre's *Zofloya:* Two New Editions." *Romantic Circles Review* (http://www.rc.umd.edu/reviews/zofloya.html), December 1998.

———. "Genre for the Prosecution: Pornography and the Gothic." *PMLA* 114, no. 5:1043–1054 (October 1999).

Green, Sarah. *Romance Readers and Romance Writers: A Satirical Novel.* London: T. Hookham, Jr., and E. T. Hookham, 1810. Reprint, Chawton House Library (http://www.chawton.org/library/novels/green_romance.html).

Haggerty, George E. "Mothers and Other Lovers: Gothic Fiction and the Erotics of Loss." *Eighteenth-Century Fiction* 16, no. 2:157–172 (January 2004).

Hoeveler, Diane Long. "Charlotte Dacre's *Zofloya:* A Case Study in Miscegenation as Sexual and Racial Nausea." *European Romantic Review* 7:411–22 (1997).

———. "Charlotte Dacre's Zofloya: The Gothic Demonization of the Jew." In *The Jews and British Romanticism: Politics, Religion, Culture*. Edited by Sheila A. Spector. New York: Palgrave Macmillan, 2005. Pp. 165–178.

———. "Hyperbolic Femininity: Jane Austen, 'Rosa Matilda,' and Mary Shelley." In her *Gothic Feminism: The Professionalization of the Gender from Charlotte Smith to the Brontës*. University Park, Pa.: Pennsylvania State University Press, 1998. Pp. 123–183.

Jones, Ann H. "Charlotte Dacre." In her *Ideas and Innovations: Best Sellers of Jane Austen's Age*. New York: AMS Press, 1986. Pp. 224–249.

Kelly, Gary. Introduction to *The Libertine*. In *Erotic Gothic*. Vol. 3 of *Varieties of Female Gothic*. London: Pickering and Chatto, 2002.

Labbe, Jacqueline M. "The Anthologised Romance of Della Crusca and Anna Matilda." *Romanticism on the Net*, no. 18 (http://www.erudit.org/revue/ron/2000/v/n18/005916ar.html?lang=en), May 2000.

McGann, Jerome J. "'My Brain Is Feminine': Byron and the Poetry of Deception." In *Byron: Augustan and Romantic*. Edited by Andrew Rutherford. Houndsmills, Basingstoke, U.K.: Macmillan, 1990. Pp. 26–51.

Mellor, Anne K. "Interracial Sexual Desire in Charlotte Dacre's *Zofloya.*" *European Romantic Review* 13:169–173. (2002).

Michasiw, Kim. Introduction to *Zofloya; or, The Moor*. New York: Oxford University Press, 1997. Pp. ix–xlii.

Miles, Robert. "Avatars of Matthew Lewis' *The Monk*: Ann Radcliffe's *The Italian,* and Charlotte Dacre's *Zofloya; or, The Moor.*" In his *Gothic Writing 1750–1820: A Genealogy.* London and New York: Routledge, 1993.

Moreno, Beatrice González. "Gothic Excess and Aesthetic Ambiguity in Charlotte Dacre's *Zofloya.*" *Women's Writing* 14, no. 3:419–434 (2007).

Mulvey-Roberts, Marie. Entry for Charlotte Dacre. In her *The Handbook of the Gothic*. 2nd ed. New York: New York University Press, 2009. Pp. 21–22.

Murillo, Cynthia. "Haunted Spaces and Powerful Places: Reconfiguring the Doppelganger in Charlotte Dacre's *Zofloya.*" *Studies in the Humanities* 32, no. 1:74–92 (June 2005).

Pearson, Jacqueline. *Women's Reading in Britain, 1750–1835: A Dangerous Recreation*. Cambridge, U.K.: Cambridge University Press, 1999.

Pollin, Burton. "Byron, Poe, and Miss Matilda." *Names* 16:390–414 (December 1968).

Reiman, Donald. Introduction to *Hours of Solitude,* by Charlotte Dacre. New York and London: Garland, 1967.

Review of *The Libertine,* by Charlotte Dacre. *Annual Review* 6:667–668 (1807). Reprinted in Corvey Women Writers, 1796–1834, on the Web (http://www2.shu.ac.uk/corvey/cw3/ContribPage.cfm?Contrib=195), November 1999.

Review of *Zofloya,* by Charlotte Dacre. *Annual Review* 5:542 (1806). Reprinted in Corvey Women Writers, 1796–1834, on the Web (http://www2.shu.ac.uk/corvey/cw3/ContribPage.cfm?Contrib=282), January 2000.

Review of *Zofloya,* by Charlotte Dacre. *New Annual Register* 27:372–373 (1806). Reprinted in Corvey Women Writers, 1796–1834, on the Web (http://www2.shu.ac.uk/corvey/cw3/ContribPage.cfm?Contrib=335), January 2000.

Robinson, Mary. *Sappho and Phaon.* London: S. Gosnell, 1796. Reprint, online British Women Romantic Poets Project, University of California, Davis (http://digital.lib.ucdavis.edu/projects/bwrp/Works/RobiMSapph.htm), 2000.

Schotland, Sarah D. "The Slave's Revenge: The Terror in Charlotte Dacre's *Zofloya*." *Western Journal of Black Studies* 33, no. 2:123–131 (summer 2009).

Summers, Montague. "Byron's 'Lovely Rosa.'" In his *Essays in Petto*. London: Fortune Press, 1928. Reprint, Freeport, N.Y.: Books for Libraries, 1967.

———. Introduction to *Zofloya,* by Charlotte Dacre. London: Fortune Press, 1928.

Thomson, Douglass H. "Charlotte Dacre [Rosa Matilda]." In *Gothic Writers: A Critical and Bibliographical Guide*. Edited by Douglass H. Thomson, Jack G. Voller, and Frederick S. Frank. Westport, Conn.: Greenwood Press, 2002. Pp. 99–103.

Varma, Devendra P. Introduction to *Confessions of the Nun of St. Omer*. New York: Arno Press, 1972.

———. Introduction to *The Libertine*. New York: Arno Press, 1974.

———. Introduction to *The Passions*. With a foreword by Sandra Knight-Roth. New York: Arno Press, 1974. Pp. ix–xvi.

———. Introduction to *Zofloya; or, The Moor: A Romance of the Fifteenth Century*. New York: Arno Press, 1974.

Wilson, Lisa M. "Female Pseudonymity and the Romantic Age of Personality: The Career of Charlotte King/Rosa Matilda/Charlotte Dacre." *European Romantic Review* 9:393–420 (1998).

SEAMUS DEANE

(1940—)

Maureen C. Manier

AS IRELAND'S PREMIER critic and a respected poet and author, Seamus Deane has spent his career concerned with the sources and effects of violence and the challenge of exploring a "culture which is neither wholly national nor colonial but a hybrid of both," as he maintains in *Celtic Revivals*, his 1985 collection of essays about Irish literature and culture (p. 11). Many critics of Irish literature have asserted that there is one dominant cultural theme in that literature, not to mention that they identify Irish literature as having begun with William Butler Yeats and James Joyce, Deane has spent his career disputing that claim and reweaving the strands of Irish literature from across the centuries. As he asserted in a 1991 National Public Radio interview about *Field Day Anthology of Irish Writing*, "There is no central tradition. There is no metaphysical ghost of Irishness haunting these pages." Concerned as he is with oversimplification, however, Deane does not deny that there is something distinctive to being Irish, something he describes as having produced an "imaginative intensity, a domestication of poetry into the fabric of daily lives" (*Celtic Revivals,* p. 25). That intensity is shared in Deane's criticism, poetry, and fiction as he examines and tells the stories that seek to give coherence to the incoherence that has come to define Irish experience. As Deane concludes about Ireland in the Field Day Anthology pamphlet *Heroic Styles: The Tradition of an Idea* (1984), "In a culture like ours, 'tradition' is not easily taken to be an established reality" (p. 6).

Deane was born in 1940 in Derry, Northern Ireland, into a Catholic nationalist family, but not a great deal is known about his childhood other than what he reveals in his poetry and in his semiautobiographical novel *Reading in the Dark* (1996). What is known is that Deane's educa-

tional journey began early when he attended the well-known St. Columb's College, where he became friends with his fellow student Seamus Heaney. He continued his education at Queen's University in Belfast in the 1950s and Pembroke College at Cambridge University, where he earned his PhD in 1963. His teaching career included several stints at American universities during the late 60s and 1970s, including as a Fulbright Fellow at Reed College in Oregon and Woodrow Wilson Fellow at the University of California at Berkeley. He also spent time as a visiting lecturer at Indiana University and the University of Notre Dame. He later became a professor at University College Dublin, a position he resigned to accept a chaired professorship in Irish studies at the University of Notre Dame in 1989, where he is now an emeritus professor. After years of holding prestigious academic positions, Deane also attained literary prominence when he published his first novel, *Reading in the Dark,* in 1996 to resounding accolades. The novel, which was short-listed for the United Kingdom's most vaunted literary prize, the Booker, tells the story of a Northern Irish family haunted by untold secrets and tragedies. In a 1997 interview with Ross Andrew of *Salon* magazine about the book, Deane spoke specifically about how his own life, and thus his career, was shaped by what is known in Ireland as "the Troubles":

> I don't suppose there was any point at which I ever felt that there was a visible gap between politics and my private life. The two things were always integrated. I learned that a political system, especially when it's a rancid one, as in Northern Ireland, has an effect on personal relationships—in fact, it spreads right through the whole society.

This impact can be found in the underlying political questions that dominate Deane's criticism, editing choices, poetry, and fiction.

SEAMUS DEANE

Amid a professional trek that veered between academia to poetry to fiction, Seamus Deane emerges as one of the most prominent Irish intellectuals of his time. He has plunged the depths of understanding the link between politics and aesthetics and has explored and revealed profound insights about an Ireland "still imprisoned within its colonial past" (*The Field Day Anthology of Irish Writing*, 1991, p. 681). As described in the *Yearbook of English Studies*, Deane can "reasonably be described as having decisively shaped Irish literary studies over the last quarter century" (McCarthy). Whatever direction his criticism takes, it is truly unique to Deane. While he might share some ground with other critics, there is always an intellectual peak that Deane climbs and from which he speaks that is distinctive and challenging. For those who have read his work or who have studied with him, his criticism, whether of literature, public life, or politics, is always acerbic, shrewd, and enlivened by a brisk if not always approachable wit.

MAJOR INTELLECTUAL INFLUENCES

At first, it might seem incongruent that Seamus Deane cites his major intellectual influences as Edmund Burke (1729–1797) and Theodor Adorno (1903–1969). Burke was ultimately remembered for his political conservatism, and Adorno was a major contributor to the heritage of Western Marxism. Yet their respective observations on the Enlightenment intersected with Deane's own view that "both the political Right and political Left blamed mythic thinking for the excesses of the Revolution," put forth in his 1988 study, *The French Revolution and Enlightenment in England* (p. 11). Mythic thinking is certainly something Deane often writes about as he draws connections between Irish political and literary history. Perhaps mythic thinking is the inevitability of Irish history, but it also serves as an obstruction. "Deane has a sense that Irish literary and political history is characterized by the experience of rupture, discontinuity, break and breakdown," Conor McCarthy has observed (p. 235). Deane's writing about Burke and the Enlightenment and his acknowledgment of Adorno's influence

reinforce Deane's intellectual ambitious and his commitment to making his criticism innovative in terms of both method and function. As he stated in his introduction to Burke in the *Field Day Anthology of Irish Writing*, Deane viewed Edmund Burke quite simply as "the most remarkable political philosopher of eighteenth-century Ireland" (p. 807). The Irish-born Burke became known first for his support of the American Revolution and later for his criticism of the French Revolution. Burke's departure from Ireland and subsequent role as a statesman philosopher in England did not diminish his continued struggle with the compatibility of colonialism and liberty. Although a Protestant himself, Burke issued frequent pleas on behalf of Irish Catholics in opposition of the Protestant ascendancy. His assertion was that Ireland could not succeed as a nation with the Protestant aristocratic faction "governing it against the interest of the many and for the interest of the few" (*Field Day Anthology,* vol. 1, p. 808). Burke's reflections intrigued and profoundly influenced Deane.

Edmund Burke viewed liberty as an essential right but only if it were a liberty connected with order. He believed that liberty could thrive under colonial rule except in those places where colonial rule escaped the rule of law. In light of this position, Burke sometimes found himself in the position of condemning colonialism—a seeming contradiction to the conservatism he most frequently espoused. However, as the historian John Richard Green observed about Burke in *History of the English People*:

> A nation was to him a great living society, so complex in its relations, and whose institutions were so interwoven with glorious events in the past, that to touch it rudely was a sacrilege. Its constitution was no artificial scheme of government, but an exquisite balance of social forces which was itself a natural outcome of its history and development. … To touch even an anomaly seemed to Burke to be risking the ruin of a complex structure of national order which it had cost centuries to build up.
>
> (vol. 10, p. 59)

Deane has found Burke's arguments both intellectually challenging and particularly relevant in considering the origins and perpetuation of Irish political strife; a situation which has led, he claims, to an essential lack of societal cohesion and stability. Therefore, not surprisingly, Dean is fascinated by Burke's assertions of traditions and history being at the core of a country's identity. What, then, would that line of thinking imply for Ireland, a country that even Deane refers to as a "strange country" (the title of Deane's 1997 book-length study of Irish writing since 1790). What Deane sees in Burke's writing is the core of the issue of what it means to be Irish. The traditions and history that Burke cites as the sacred center of a society do not exist in Ireland outside of the contexts of colonial constraint. Even since Ireland's own revolution, the political division of the country combined with the lack of a continuing linguistic tradition has continued to symbolize this absence of a wholeness that has dominated Irish society and literature through the centuries.

Burke's influence is evident as Deane explores the idea of tradition and its connection to national character in *Heroic Styles: The Tradition of an Idea* (1984). Writing about Irish literature, he points out that in the works of William Butler Yeats, James Joyce, and Padraig Pearse, there is a drive in Irish nationalism to restore "dignity and power to what had been humiliated and suppressed." At the heart of that humiliation is a sense of alienation from a colonized country and even from an imposed language that often leaves the Irish feeling unconnected to any country; Deane points out that this is true for Stephen Dedalus in *Portrait of an Artist as a Young Man* (1916) and also for its author, James Joyce, "Betrayed into alienation, he turns to art to enable him to overcome the treacheries which have victimized him" (*Heroic Styles*, p. 11). In Joyce, Yeats, and Pearse, Deane sees a conviction that "a community exists which must be recovered and restored" (*Heroic Styles,* p. 13). But, in the ultimate complexity, Deane believes that there is no "one" community to restore, no entirely common set of traditions and history on which to build. With this in mind, it is appropriate for Deane to conclude in *Heroic Styles* that "everything, including our politics and our literature, has to be rewritten—i.e. reread. That will enable

new writing, new politics, unblemished by Irishness, but securely Irish" (p. 18).

Deane's interest in Theodor Adorno, a German-born philosopher and social critic who lived almost two hundred years after Edmund Burke, might appear to stand in stark contrast to Deane's study of Burke. And yet there is an interesting thread that connects the two influences. For Adorno, the art object and the aesthetic experience of the art object contain a "truth-content," something "which is not exhausted either by the subjective intentions of its producers or by the subjective responses of its consumers" (quoted in Jarvis, p. 98). The critical theory espoused by Adorno and other neo-Marxist thinkers associated with the Frankfort School is based on the supposition that teaching about society can only be developed in the most tightly integrated connection of disciplines; above all, economics, psychology, history, and philosophy. For Burke, the truth-content of society is found in its historical anchor. Adorno also looks to history for answers, but with strikingly different results. "History is, for Adorno, a catastrophic process, a Splengenian narrative of decline and failure," says Conor McCarthy (p. 241).

DEANE'S LITERARY CRITICISM

Deane's critical work reflects this paradox: if history is at the heart of a nation, how can a nation dominated by colonialism have a heart that beats clearly and true? Rather, as he writes, "Nothing is more monotonous or despairing than the search for the essence which defines a nation" (*Celtic Revivals*). Deane finds Adorno's claims of history being a catastrophic process resonant with his own view of Irish history, except for an injection of optimism. It is this perspective that forms the basis for Dean's nationalist opinions, as he writes in *Strange Country*, "Thus, central to the nationalist position were the claims that (a) Ireland was a culturally distinct nation; (b) it had been mutilated beyond recognition by British colonialism; and (c) it could nevertheless rediscover its lost features and thereby recognize once more its true identity" (p. 53).

Looking at the body of Deane's work as a critic and then later as the general editor of the culminating anthology *Field Day Anthology of Irish Writing* reveals what could be called a prolonged mediation on the idea of national character. The choices and introductions in *Field Day*'s three volumes speak powerfully to readers as the project's volume editors try to translate what Deane often calls the "strange country" of Ireland to the rest of the world. In speaking about the anthology, Deane asserted that he and his associate editors shared the goal of avoiding a narrow interpretation of "literature." Instead, they sought to create a "meta narrative" in which the Irish culture struggled against and within a colonizing presence in the search to find and express its voice. That voice can be found in poetry, fiction, and drama, but being true to Ireland it is also found in political speeches and writings and in song. *Field Day* does not simply anthologize Irish writing; it celebrates all that Irish writers through the centuries have attempted to capture about the struggles and achievements of their country.

In the *Field Day Anthology* and other works Deane writes critically about many Irish writers. But it is in his comments about two of Ireland's most prominent twentieth-century writers that he explores the issues of nationalism that have intrigued Deane throughout his career.

In his *Field Day* introduction to Joyce, Deane points out that whether one considers Yeats, who took a revolutionary's approach to the issue of nationalism, or Joyce, who largely abandoned his national connections, both writers are responding to the same reality. For Joyce, in contrast to writers such as Yeats, the goal was not recovery but cleansing. As Deane writes, Joyce was a "lonely anarchist, a man who repudiated all that he had inherited and spent his life perfecting the ultimate weapon of destruction that would restore everything to its primal, unstructured essence" (*Field Day Anthology*, vol. 3, p. 1). Joyce experienced what had occurred in Irish society as a collapse that each individual must live through alone. Deane suggests that loneliness is at the heart of Joyce's 1914 short-story collection, *Dubliners*: "The paralysis that pervades the city and its inhabitants is like a plague generated from within. The city is closed; there are no exits, just struggles to escape" (*Field Day Anthology*, vol. 3, p. 2). For this reason, it is not surprising that he creates protagonists such as Stephen Dedalus and Leopold Bloom who are foreigners within their native cultures. Ultimately, Deane suggests, Joyce portrays a central truth about Ireland: that it stands as "a monument to a terrible history in a dream landscape" (*Field Day Anthology*, vol. 3, p. 1) rather than existing as a country with an identity to which its inhabitants can feel intrinsically connected. For Joyce, the act of rebellion was the act or writing.

Deane contrasts Joyce with William Butler Yeats, whom Deane identifies with a long line of European Romantic writers who focus on the theme of "regeneration." Ireland was always for Yeats a revolutionary country because in the oldest sense, in the tradition of Burke, it was a traditional one. As Deane writes in *Celtic Revivals*, Ireland is the only place in Europe where Yeats believes the aristocratic and peasant elements have a fair chance of surviving together: "Ireland was not only a special country. It was the one where the great battle must be won because it had been so totally lost elsewhere" (p. 39). Sadly, for Yeats as for Joyce their wars took place primarily within themselves. Consumed as they both were with writing their answers to their Irish experiences, they are ultimately unable to do so and both are, in some sense, as Yeats writes in "Sailing to Byzantium,"

sick with desire
And fastened to a dying animal
It knows not what it is; and gather me
Into the artifice of eternity.

Nothing shares Joyce's terrible history or Yeats's terrible beauty more directly than the autobiographies and memoirs about which Deane writes in his *Field Day Anthology* introduction in volume 3. What Deane suggests in his introduction is that the Irish authors included in this section are searching through the catalog of their own experiences as well as through an evaluation of historical events to better understand what gives their life shape and meaning. His premise is that in a colonial or neocolonial country like Ireland that search is often hampered and diverted by the sense of "otherness." The other can be identified as the colonial presence, but it is just as easily be described as being within each individual. With all the revelations found within the memoirs of writers such as Yeats, John Millington Synge, Kenneth Tynan, and George Bernard Shaw, "None of these autobiographies or memoirs can avoid the sense of a missing feature or energy" (*Field Day Anthology*, vol. 3, p. 383).

These themes recur again in Deane's introduction to "Political Writings and Speeches" later in the same volume. The featured essays and oratory range from the beginning to the end of the twentieth century, but always they return to one immutable truth: "For all the changes in structure and name that it has undergone, Ireland has remained imprisoned within its colonial past" (p. 681). In an earlier Field Day pamphlet, *Civilians and Barbarians* (1983), Deane characterizes that imprisonment as a battle between civilians and barbarians: "To become free and prosperous the Irish were evidently going to have to become English" (p. 5).

But perhaps Deane's critical understanding of Irish authors' quest is most poignantly shared in his analysis of the work of his former classmate and lifelong friend, the poet and Nobel Prize winner Seamus Heaney. He praises Heaney's evocative renderings of traditions, customs, and rural landscapes. But still, Deane believes, Heaney returns to what can only be described as an emptiness: "The quest for a center, for what he calls an 'omphalos,' is darkly stimulated by his recognition that the idea of a center is fictive" ("Powers of Earth and Visions of Air," p. 28). Deane suggests Heaney's poetry is an attempt to give voice to that "pure emptiness" (p. 29). His personal connections with Heaney as well as his critical acumen lead him to declare that Heaney's reading of Yeats is essentially a "reading of himself," particularly what he calls a "desire for foundedness" and the accompanying "fear of unfoundedness that might lurk beneath it" (p. 33). Heaney's challenge is the one all Irish authors, including Deane in his work as a poet and novelist, must face: "In one sense, it is the struggle to become a writer rather than an Irish writer. You can't be one without the other; yet to be too self-consciously Irish might rob one of the freedoms to be a writer, an author" (p. 33).

DEANE'S POETRY

Deane writes of a "fear of unfoundedness" in Heaney's work; Deane's poetry, meanwhile, is his vehicle to express his own fears. Three volumes stand as Deane's poetic oeuvre: *Gradual Wars* (1972), *Rumours* (1977), and *History Lessons* (1983). A volume of selected poems was published after *History Lessons* and also includes a few new poems and translations. Each volume represents an important step, but his poetry as a whole "earns its keep" in what the critic Tom Halpin describes as "the thinnest of margins between desolation and hope, paralysis and possibility" (p. 20). The same themes Deane contends with as a critic can be found in his poetry, only now they are viewed through the most personal themes of family, fear, loneliness, and love.

Gradual Wars has been described as primarily dealing with the sources and effects of violence. Published in 1972, near the beginning of Deane's academic career, the collection speaks powerfully to the violence that dominated these decades, as in the poem "After Derry, 30 January 1972":

> ... Death is our future
> And now is our past.
> There are new children
> In the gaunt houses
> Their eyes are fused.
> Youth has gone out
> Like a light ...
>
> (p. 15)

The critic Douglas Dunne suggests that although violence pervades this collection, the poems are at their most interesting when they address what violence does to people. In "Eleven," Deane touches upon the havoc violence causes to relationships.

> Now unless I feel
> Attrition as our strategy,
> I cannot edge nearer you.

Violence denatures
What was once fidelity.

Fidelity is a recurring theme in Deane's poetry and, later, in his first novel. He struggles with his own ability to be faithful as well as trusting others' loyalty. In "Something Faithless," he identifies his touch as faithless and can only wish that his touch could have the "fidelity of stone" (p. 27). He also visits the issue of fidelity, constancy, and vulnerability in the second poem in the collection, "Two," in which he asks those haunting questions that plague all lovers: "Would love / Never stop? Would it / Have everything?" (p. 27). But it is violence and how violence changes everything and everyone that finds its way into almost every poem in the collection—even if only in a fleeting image. In "Landscape into Art," Deane vividly describes how violence attacks like a biting wind: "In so affronted a landscape I find / Nothing to shelter my face" (p. 57). The search for relief from that type of violence leads the reader through poem seven in the "Fourteen Elegies" in the collection. The imagery of the poem implies scenes of ruin, "rats undermining the house," "police plunging like animals" (p. 17). As in "Landscape into Art," all the writer seeks is a place to find peace: "Peace is all I prayed / But with rigour, no hopelessness; / The room heard my breath" (p. 57).

The collection takes a few detours with poems written during Deane's experiences teaching in the United States. In "Smoke Signals in Oregon," Deane turns to Native American imagery to share the depth of his loneliness: "The ghost totem mounts in a pillar / Of vague faces; the First Faces; / Faceless; smoke signals for fright" (p. 36). He also writes about his experience of being "High in San Francisco," where "Night had gone. / Form had been driven from the room / In a mad exorcism" (p. 37). These poems and a few others in the collection divert the reader from the main focus of the collection, although their imagery of death, snakes, blood, and fire are reminders that violence is always close to the surface of the poet's consciousness.

The title poem of the collection is particularly eerie in its description of the intense loneliness of a life lived amid violence. The slow death caused by violence is presumed to be as much emotional as physical, as Deane compares it to the slow freeze of pipes "choked in ice." The intensity of the experience is known only by those who experience it, who together speak a common language: "This is the language / that bespeaks / Gradual Wars" (p. 53).

Several poems in *Gradual Wars* set the stage for Deane's next collection, *Rumours,* which contains reminiscences of childhood and particularly of his relationship with his father. These poems often communicate moments of longing for those times before the writer's realization of how violence was a permanent part of his life, as in "Great Times Once":

But I had great times once.
Remember that, and see
The child looking out of my face.

(p. 60)

Published five years after *Gradual Wars, Rumours* journeys back to Deane's childhood to capture many of the moments and emotions that later featured in his first novel, *Reading in the Dark.* The poem "A Schooling" harkens to his father's job as an electrician's assistant in the naval yard, a distant cry from what would be his son's academic journey.

He laid cables, rode the dour
Iron swell between his legs
And maybe thought what kind of son,
An aesthetician of this cold,
He had, in other warmth, begot.

(p. 11)

Father and son are separated by the different paths they travel. Deane runs from Derry to the comfort of academic pursuits, as he writes in "Scholar II," "I'll know the library in a city / Before I know there is a slum" (p. 43). The secrets that stand between Deane and his father are the chasm they cannot seem to cross. In "The Birthday Gift," Deane recalls an incident where he deliberately ruins his father's rose garden. Even decades later he longs for them to resolve what stands between them:

I wish he would speak.
Even my name
Would be something now.
Remember the boy
In the garden. Let your anger issue
At last in words.

(p. 15)

Even as Deane anticipates his father's death in "The Broken Border," he knows that they will never connect beyond the broken border, the "half-submerged circle of stones": "That even reliving it all with you, / must still be reliving it alone?" (p. 13). Similarly, in "The Birthday Gift," Deane knows his father's death is imminent as he looks at the blood in the Kleenex into which the father has spat. Still, all he can do is drive away, even as he knows his father will "be here, suddenly dying" (p. 15).

Rumours continues the discussion started in *Gradual Wars* about how Ireland's history and political strife dominate the poet's view of his world. As he writes in "Middle Kingdom," "History is your wall of pain" (p. 47). In "A Fable," Deane tells the story of a young man in Belfast leaping from a ladder through a pane of glass and then being shot. He describes the man as being like a "stricken deer," as if he is shocked by the moment of extraordinary violence. And, yet, what happens to the jumper and to so many others in Belfast seems like both a "question of Fate" and a "stricter question of hate" (p. 28). With an overwhelming sense of the ironic, Deane takes no sides between the killer or the killed. Rather, he sees them as ending with the same reality. There is still someone holding a gun; the bloodied violence continues.

With "Migration," Deane delivers a call for what he calls a "fifth season," a place that is at the core of his inheritance (p. 9). Throughout Deane's work, from criticism to poetry to fiction, he writes of that search for a national identity that for the Irish is so closely linked to personal identity. In this poem and throughout this collection he shares poetic expressions of that search. But nowhere is the search more directly stated than in this poem, which ends with the stunning phrase, "His tongue still undelivered, / waiting /

To be born in the word home" (p. 9). That search is also summarized in the poem "Return":

In this Irish past I swell
Like sound implicit in a bell ...
I am in Derry once again
Once more I turn to greet
Ground that flees from my feet.

(p. 28)

The fleeting ground, as the tongue undelivered, are powerful images of the absences—of words that are foreign rather than in their own language and of a country that is home and yet always somehow a "strange country."

History Lessons, Deane's third poetry collection, was published in 1983. This collection largely represents the pursuit of relief from the burden of history and its bloody explosion. Several of the poems contain harsh and evocative imagery of the world created by centuries of violence, including "Guerillas," in which Deane describes this world and the ensuing inescapable isolation; and "A World Without a Name."

In "History Lessons," Deane dives right into historical comparisons of the unrest of 1981 Ireland, which included the deaths of ten men from hunger strikes, with Russia during the overthrow of Tsar Nicholas II and the German Third Reich. Using the image of a boy running, the poem describes the relentless intensity of the Irish political reality:

... The city is no more. The lessons learned.
I will remember it always as a burning
In the heart of winter and a boy running.

(p. 10)

In contrast, "Breaking Wood" begins with the seemingly innocent imagery of a boy chopping wood in the shed. But, again, the moment changes instantly when a gust of wind and a missed stroke return him to a memory of his father. With those memories come a feeling of regret. Suddenly, the reader is back in the swirling intensity of Deane's imagery of the woodcutting scene, a reminder of the irrefutable reality of Irish life.

Deane's *Selected Poems* appeared in 1988. The collection pulls from his previous three poetry volumes as well as including several new poems and translations. As Tom Halpin writes in his review in the 1989 *Irish Literary Supplement*, collections imply that a writer is taking critical stock of his work and, even if unconsciously, suggesting how he would like the entirety of his work read.

Deane's poetry brings readers from his Derry childhood, through marriage, fatherhood, a life in academia, and journeys to the United States and the former Soviet Union. But always there is a resonance of what he often calls an "inheritance," which he references in "A World Without a Name." His skills sharpen through the volumes, and that is clearly illustrated in this collection, particularly in the selections from *History Lessons* such as "Send War in Our Time, O Lord" and "The Party Givers." Both these poems deal with the vulnerability associated with what Halpin calls, "the attrition of the individual reality" and the "terrorizing force of contemporary historical experience" (p. 20). In "The Party Givers," that transition between individual and political reality happens in a split second of chilling self-recognition. Those moments of clarification and renewal recur in others of Deane's poems such as in "Breaking Wood" or in "Daystar." There is nothing more powerful in Deane's work than that moment in which time stands still and emotional reality floods in.

One of the most compelling new poems included in this 1988 collection is "Reading *Paradise Lost* in Protestant Ulster 1984," included in the third volume of the Field Day Anthology of Irish writing. In this poem, Deane pulls from John Milton's great work rather than from history to draw connections: "From Milton's devils is the present crew / Of zombie soldiers and their spies" (p. 1379). There are even allusions to Burke's philosophy about the sacred bond between a people and their country: "None should break the union of this State / Which God and Man conspired to ordain." Making the parallel with *Paradise Lost,* this poem emotionally connects Ulster with the fall from paradise. It identifies a future at tremendous risk, with the children, the only hope, being lured by Belial, one of the crown princes of hell. The poem ends with a dramatic cry for salvation, "Rebels surround us, Lord. Ah, whence arose / This dark damnation, this how unrainbowed rain."

Deane's work stands as a whole as a testament of recognition and resilience regarding the violent backdrop against which it is set. It is this insistence that ensures that the poems "earn their keep." Their existence is positive; their unwillingness or even inability to find what could be characterized as anything that is unequivocally hopeful is what makes them completely authentic.

DEANE'S NOVEL

That same authenticity is one of the most distinguishing features of Deane's novel, *Reading in the Dark,* which appeared in 1996. This book, which has what the critic Julia O'Faolain describes as the "focused compression of poetry," begins and ends amid shadows on the steps in the unnamed narrator's boyhood home. Between those moments are a series of what the critic Anne Devlin suggests are like folktales that build a labyrinth, "a labyrinth of separate passages which in the end turns into one at the center" (p. 17). Trapped in the center of these passages are the narrator's mother and the secrets she and her husband—and eventually their son—hold.

Many critics have speculated on how closely *Reading in the Dark* aligns with Deane's life. The critic Terry Eagleton describes the novel as occupying "some transitional zone between fiction and autobiography" (p. 46). In a *Salon* online magazine interview from 1997 with Andrew Ross, Deane acknowledges that there is a good deal of autobiographical material in the book, what he calls "a conflation of two or three family histories, with my own family the most prominent among them." He also explains that the editor "dragged" the book out of him, calling it a "reluctant birth." That reluctance is not surprising, because whether it is a retelling or a reimagining, the novel takes readers into the painful reality of a haunted family. Throughout his career Deane has written about the impact of Ireland's violent history. In his novel readers experience at the closest personal level what Deane calls "the deforming aspects" of a political system based on various forms of coercion and betrayal. Hailing *Reading in the Dark* an artistic triumph, Eagleton calls it "an act of loving fidelity to the social landscapes of his childhood and a hard-headed refusal to idealise them."

The world of this novel is, as Eagleton describes it, "awash with rumours, haunting, metamorphoses and misinformation" (p. 46). The book opens with the protagonist encountering his mother on the stairs, where she tells him to stop because, as she explains, "There's something there between us" (p. 3). Those prophetic words define the novel's plot. What stands between the narrator and his mother are secrets of the deepest and even the most unholy nature. As Anne Devlin writes, "A law has been broken—a taboo older than the laws of consanguinity." As the story progresses, we realize that there are layers of secrets to be peeled back before the deepest secret, the most heinous of betrayals, is revealed.

The book follows the narrator from his days as a sometimes precocious boy in Derry to receiving his college degree, a first for his family. But the tale is far from innocent. Amid a few humorous memories, such as a priest's awkward attempts to relay the "facts of life," and a few bucolic childhood memories, such as playing with his brother in an old fort, are a series of chilling stories about secrets and hauntings that build upon each other to the final denouement that reveals what lurks at the story's core.

As the novel progresses, it appears every one in Derry has a secret: Mother, Father, Grandfather, Aunt Katie, Crazy Joe, and, ultimately and most tragically, the narrator. From the beginning, however, it is clear that one of the lynchpin secrets revolves around Eddie, the older brother of the narrator's father. Eddie had vanished years before on a fateful night when a big shoot-out had occurred between the Irish Republican Army and the police. Eddie's brothers frequently speculated about what happened. Had he died in the shoot-out and been dumped in a vat of whiskey by the police? Or had he possibly run away to Australia or America? But the narrator's father never participates in the discussions about Eddie or in any of his brothers' fanciful

conversations. Instead, he stays in the background or leaves the room. The narrator is left feeling confused by his father's reaction. He wishes the father would enter into the animated discussions and wonders why he couldn't or wouldn't do so. But even without the narrator's father engaging in the discussions, Eddie remains part of the family's lore, someone who is present even in his absence: "I felt like we lived in an empty space with a long cry from him ramifying through it. At other times, it appeared to be as cunning articulate as a labyrinth, closely designed, with someone sobbing at the heart of it" (p. 42).

The other story that threads through the novel involves the narrator's Aunt Katie. Katie, his mother's younger sister, married young, even before the narrator's mother. Her husband, Tony McIlhenny, deserted her while she was pregnant. The tale is that he had gone to America looking for work, never contacted Katie again, and years later had married and had children there. No one talks about what happened. Katie lives with her daughter Maeve until Maeve moves to England, and over time Katie became like a second mother to the narrator's family.

Once a great source for benign bedtime stories, Katie graduates to telling ghost stories as the narrator and his siblings grow older. One of her more eerie stories, about a brother and sister who were changelings, is recounted in the book. First, the children exchange coloring; later they change gender. The protagonist in the story, Brigid, knows she is being challenged by the devil. As the story progresses, the truth emerges that Brigid's family is cursed, as she continues to watch the children's changes until they disappear and Brigid goes completely insane. The haunting of Brigid sadly resembles Katie's own haunting by the unexplained mystery of her husband's disappearance. The explanations of what happened to Uncle Eddie and to Katie's husband never ring true, and it is clear there is more to be said about what happened in both instances.

In between the stories of disappearing uncles, changeling children, and the death of the narrator's young sister, Deane does write about moments of the narrator's life that intimate something more appealing, less somber. Having written an essay with what he later realizes are too many "big dictionary words," the narrator is drawn to a classmate's essay that his teacher selects to read. The essay deals with an evening in the classmate's life: "It was ordinary life—no rebellions or love affairs or dangerous flights across the hills at night. And yet I kept remembering that mother and son waiting in the Dutch interior of that essay, with the jug of milk and the butter on the table, while behind and above them were those wispy, shawly figures from the rebellion, sibilant above the great fire and below the aching, high wind" (p. 21).

As the critic Josephine Humphreys points out in her *New York Times* book review, the world of *Reading in the Dark* is alive and pungent for the narrator—a candle "stubby in its thick drapery of wax," the linoleum pattern "polished away to the point where it had the look of a faint memory, a long, chill pistol, blue-black and heavy" (pp. 27–28). No object is inanimate; rather everything is charged with what Humphreys calls "energy and significance" (p. 6). Chimneys breathe, shows watch, ice snores. Odors are exact and emotionally identifiable—such as the whiff of soap on the dead sister's pillow or the "police smell" that can awaken the narrator and leave him feeling breathless and apprehensive (p. 30). Everything that happens—every object, sound, vision, smell—leads us to the second part of the novel, to the final unpeeling of the layers that stand between the narrator and the secrets that truly haunt his family.

Part 2 of the novel opens with a scene of rats emerging from demolished air raid shelters. The rats are relentless, coming through bolt holes, a "king rat" even emerging from a burning heap of rats. The narrator is sickened by the scene and ominously imagines the remaining living rats, "breathing their vengeance in a dull, miasmic unison deep underground" (p. 80).

From that moment, the novel changes plot pace, and there seems to be a plodding yet decisive progression toward the truth. The father, previously a quiet if somewhat mournful figure, strikes the narrator after a policeman brings him home from a bullying incident. Clearly, for the father the presence of the policeman in his house

and then his son's reference to his Uncle Eddie stir up something violent in him that is startlingly close to the surface. The boy responds to being hit by cutting off his father's prized rose bushes. When confronted, he responds simply to his father, "Tomorrow, and the day after, and the day after that, and every other day that comes, you'll know" (p. 108). The father and his brothers pour concrete over where the rose bushes had once thrived, another moment of symbolism: "Walking on that concreted patch where the bushes had been was like walking on hot ground below which voices and roses were burning, burning" (p. 111). As with the rats, there is something burning under the surface of the cement, something waiting to burst forth.

When the narrator is sent to help his Aunt Katie with his maternal grandfather, who is extremely sick, he witnesses his mother leaving her father's sickroom and knows that something has forever changed as she moans and whispers Eddie's name. The secrets had begun with Eddie—and the narrator now knows there are secrets beyond what he had imagined. Eventually, he convinces his grandfather to reveal his secret to him. He learns that his grandfather had ordered Eddie's execution because he had been told that he was an informer. Only later did the grandfather discover that Eddie had been set up and was not an informer. Instead, the real informer was Tony McIlhenny, Aunt Katie's husband. By the time his grandfather had learned of the mistake, Eddie was dead and Tony McIlhenny had left the country.

What the narrator eventually learns from his mother is that this is not the only secret surrounding Eddie and Tony. That night in her father's sickroom the narrator's mother had learned the horror of Eddie's execution at her father's behest. But what her father never learned was that the narrator's mother had been the one who had tipped off Tony McIlhenny, the true informer. Later in the novel, the mother learns from Sergeant Burke, the same police officer who plays an intermittent role in her family's lives, that McIlhenny had been recruited by police to be an informer as revenge against a police officer who had been killed by nationalists. What the narrator's mother doesn't tell him is that McIlhenny had been her boyfriend before marrying Katie—something the narrator had learned from Katie herself. This leaves him wondering what role his mother's lingering feelings had played in her decision to urge him to leave. Not only had his mother kept this secret from his father but also from her sister, who had spent her life never knowing why her husband had deserted her and never knowing how upset McIlhenny was at having to leave his young pregnant wife. The narrator immediately realizes his life and his relationships with his parents are forever changed: "I could never talk to my father or my mother properly again" (p. 194).

Shortly after his grandfather's death, the narrator's father takes him and his brother Liam on a nostalgic walk and rowboat ride that leads him to tell his sons stories from his own childhood. He remembers happy times with his parents and his brother Eddie, visiting well-off relatives who had a pony and trap that they had ridden. But soon, as he stands by the church they had sometimes visited on Sundays, the father feels compelled to tell his sons his own secret, that he knows that Eddie wasn't killed in that shoot-out and that he knows instead he was an informer who had been killed by his "own people" (p. 139).

As the narrator listens to his father he realizes that the secrets that have been revealed have filled his life with more questions that will never be answered. He will never know how much his parents know about what happened or how much they have shared with each other. What he does know is that his father believes Eddie was an informer, and the narrator knows that he can never tell the father that Eddie wasn't, because it would destroy his parents' marriage and his mother's increasingly fragile emotional and mental health. Walking into their house that evening, the narrator is overwhelmed: "When we came into the kitchen, my mother looked up and the whole history of his family and her family and ourselves passed over her face in one intuitive waltz of welcome and then of pain" (p. 141).

The narrator longs for his mother to know all that he knows. And so he writes it down in English and then translates that into Irish. He destroys the English version and reads the Irish version to his father and mother—knowing full well that they did not understand Irish. Strangely, his mother seems to understand what he is speaking about, and that "truth" now stands both boldly and coldly between them.

The narrator realizes there is no longer a place for him at home, after several years of agonizing emotional distance, when he asks his mother what she would like for her birthday and she asks him to go away: "Then maybe I could look after your father properly for once, without your eyes on me" (p. 235). To stay loyal to his mother, the narrator finds he must be disloyal to his father. He keeps him at an emotional distance so he won't be tempted to tell him the full truth behind his family's secrets. The only way he can show his love for his parents is by leaving. Over time, he finds "to his pleasure and surprise" that the betrayals become confused and muddled for him: "Hauntings are, in their way, very specific. Everything has to be exact, even the vagueness" (p. 236).

The book concludes with the narrator leaving Derry and pursuing the education that his father had always dreamed of having. He knows his father is living through his accomplishments, and yet, because of all that stands between them, the narrator knows that he and his father can never be close. Similarly, although the narrator longs to comfort his mother, her only comfort is his absence. He returns infrequently to Derry, and even as his parents grow older he knows that his responsibility to them remains in keeping their secrets, even though it brings them no peace: "Looking at his mother and father grown old, he realizes that the truth that would ease them would also destroy them" (p. 243).

Paradoxically, when his mother suffers a stroke and is unable to speak, the narrator and his mother are finally able to be with each other again in their silence. When his father dies, he realizes that amid his mother's grief and even as the violence of the Troubles encroaches upon their Derry home, his mother and his father are finally free, as his mother sighs in her sleep and his father's coffin is taken to the cathedral before which "he so innocently lay" (p. 246).

Reading in the Dark operates on several levels. The political implications of the story are powerful. These families are pulled into intrigues involving murder, betrayal, and ruined lives that all stem from the tensions between the police establishment and nationalists. The tensions are introduced at the beginning of the novel with the uncles' tales about Uncle Eddie's fate. But elements of that tension creep into almost every subsequent chapter. The "brokenness" of the families is so evident to the narrator that he describes it as "a catastrophe you could live with only if you kept it quiet" (p. 202).

This "brokenness" is even apparent in the first novel the narrator reads, titled *The Shan Van Vocht*, a phonetic spelling for the Irish phrase that means "the poor old woman"—a traditional name for Ireland. The book is about the great rebellion of 1798 and is rife with a romantic mingling of love affairs and war. Even the boy's dreams of the future, inspired by the book, were tainted by the violence, he thinks about "some time in the future when the shooting and the hacking would be over, when what was left of life would be spent listening to the night wind wailing on graveyards and empty hillsides" (p. 20).

The most powerful reminder of the political tension is embodied in the form of police, always a dark force in the book, even referred to as the "black uniforms." As the critic Robert Boyers writes, "Sometimes in Deane's world, it seems the worst thing a decent person can do is talk to a policeman, as if to do so were to sell one's soul to the devil" (p. 34). When the narrator takes out a gun to show his friends, a local police informer "rats" on him. Soon his house is being ransacked, and then he, his brother Liam, and his father are in a police car and taken to a basement to be questioned for hours. Once in the police station the father and his sons are badly beaten. This incident causes nightmares for the narrator, who so vividly remembers the beating that "if a light flickered from the street beyond, the image of the police car would reappear and my hair would feel starched and my hands sweaty" (p. 30).

The character of Sergeant Burke is one of the strongest reminders of the political violence and betrayal that dominate the characters' lives. After throwing a stone at his car to get the policeman's attention to save himself from bullies, the narrator begins to learn from Burke that there is more to Eddie's story than he had previously heard, that somehow his mother knows more about the story than his father. Hearing this from Burke, he also knows that there is something inherently rotten at the core of this story, since that is what the police represent to this boy born in a Catholic nationalist family. Thinking about what it all means, the narrator feels the beginning of the hardening that will culminate later in the book: "My face felt as though it had set into a hard plaster mask, although I was crying inside, hard and dry, but crying."

Without the police there would have been no informer, no misunderstandings, no missing uncles, and no secrets that have caused a deepening breach in the narrator's family. Even Burke acknowledges this when he comes to speak to the narrator's mother: "Politics destroyed people's lives in this place, he said" (p. 100).

As the family's secrets unravel, their connection to their country's political strife is undeniable. The political disorder of Ireland is, as the critic Derek Hand explains, clearly viewed through this "small" story of the narrator's family: "Deane does not intentionally attempt to tell the 'big' story of Ireland or the north of Ireland; rather he focuses on a 'small' story through which larger issues may be viewed" (p. 20).

But as much as this story is connected to Ireland's political realities, it is also exploring what secrets can do to relationships and to a family. As the narrator's mother explains in describing the moral of a story: "People in small places make big mistakes. Not bigger than the mistakes of other people. But there is less room for big mistakes in small places" (p. 221). Ultimately, for the narrator's family the biggest mistake is that the secrets prevent them from ever being totally at ease, totally at home. As the critic Richard Eder writes in his review of the book, "Silence is the killer" (p. 2).

SEAMUS DEANE

A minor controversy erupted when *Reading in the Dark* was short-listed for the United Kingdom's 1996 Booker Prize: was the book fiction or memoir? Deane has ceded that the book contains many autobiographical details. But whether it is Deane or a "conflation" as he as suggested, the book's narrator is indisputably a potent memoirist. In *The Field Day Anthology of Irish Writing*, Deane introduces the section on autobiography and memoirs by suggesting: "Autobiography is not just concerned with the self; it is also concerned with the 'other,' the person or persons, events or places, that have helped to give the self definition" (p. 380). With the search for the factual truth, this book also seeks truths about the "other," about what makes us who we become. The narrator spends this novel looking back and retelling his story, peeling back the layers that bring him to that place where he can finally better understand not just his family but himself and the life he has had to live, knowing that he is a plague to the mother he loves.

As Josephine Humphreys suggests, the title of the novel implies that it is about "ways of knowing" (p. 6). There is hardly any light, literally and metaphorically, for the narrator to make out how things really are. And so he must continue to read in the dark, trying to discern the reality amid the shadowy secrets he finds as he turns every page.

It is no surprise that the narrator in Deane's novel escapes to his books and, ultimately, to the life of an academic, to a world that is at once both intellectually rich and emotionally safe. He can live within the books he loves much better than in the world into which he was born. Emotionally exiled by his mother and self-exiled from his father, the narrator has no choice but to leave Derry. As he melodramatically but accurately explains, he "looked at the Sacred Heart and thought [he] understood how Jesus felt, him with his breast open and the pierced blood-dripping muscle emblazoned there" (p. 226).

Richard Eder describes the "beauty of Deane's lament" being that it is not told as such. Rather, the narrator speaks with vitality, curiosity, and an "appetite for life" (p. 2). His family's

secrets devastate his life even as they give him a sense of purpose. He becomes the guardian of the secrets and, in so doing, the guardian of his family's future and his parents' survival.

Not all critics have praised Deane's novel for its sparse, if provocative, details. In his 1997 *New Republic* review, Robert Boyers wrote that he believed it to be difficult for readers to be interested "in characters who have few thoughts and little inclination to open themselves to sharp sensory experiences" (p. 35). Boyers argues that the book is "thin" and lacking in ideas and development. One of his specific criticisms is that while all the elements for deeper plot and character development are there, Deane chooses not to pursue them. Rather, he decided to "set things down as if they spoke for themselves" (p. 34). Boyers claims that Deane's characters are so "inured to the facts of their lives" that they are almost "constitutionally averse to development" (p. 34). What Boyers admires, however, is the tenacity of Deane's characters, which he admits can "seem almost wonderful" (p. 35).

Despite the overwhelming critical praise *Reading in the Dark* received, Boyers' concerns cannot be ignored. For all the lyrical vitality of the book, the characters are sketched rather than fully painted. We are only given a few characters' names and know only sporadic details about their lives, their views, their future, or even their present. The book ends without complete plot resolution. The only resolution is that the narrator believes that giving his mother some modicum of peace in her final years and allowing his parents to spend those years together was the best decision he could have made—not even necessarily believing it was right. As the reader can't help but do, so does the narrator wonder about the answers to the questions that linger as he reflects upon his parents: "I imagined that, in her silence, in the way she stroked his hand, smiled crookedly at him, let him brush her hair, bowing her head obediently for him, she had told him and won his understanding. I could believe now, as I never had when a child, that they were lovers" (p. 243).

Perhaps this book about mysteries ends only as it can, with revelations that ultimately change very little but what is known and what is unknown. As the *New Leader* critic Edward Conlon writes, the question at the heart of this novel is not these secrets but rather the deeper secrets of being Irish and "whether the Irish will be free of Ireland, with its violent hopes and seductive griefs" (p. 17). In 2010, the book was optioned by a Northern Ireland film company to have a script developed to make *Reading in the Dark* into a motion picture.

Knowing of Deane's own journey from Derry to the life of an academic, it is tempting to posit theories about the impact on his career and his personal outlook of the autobiographical elements from his novel. Throughout his career Deane has been known for extraordinary incisiveness and intensity. Popular at the universities at which he has taught, he has also occasionally been described by critics such as Conor Cruise O'Brien as "verging on the precious or the pompous" (p. 18). But knowing at least pieces of the past from which Deane came, it is appropriate to speculate as to whether Deane has dedicated his professional life to doing what he does so well in his first novel—imposing order and meaning upon disorder and violence. Whether in his historical reflections, criticism, poetry, or fiction, Deane routinely returns to the effort of understanding, even dissecting, the culture in which he was raised and lived his life. It is a culture that he believes to be at once beleaguered and remarkably tenacious. For Deane, through all his travels and literary explorations, his first major work of fiction finds him again posing the question that might best be described as his life's refrain: What does it mean to be Irish?

Selected Bibliography

WORKS OF SEAMUS DEANE

NOVELS AND SHORT STORIES
Reading in the Dark. London: Jonathan Cape, 1996. New York: Vintage, 1998.
"Ghost Stories." In *Granta: The First Twenty-one Years.* London: Granta, 2001.

POETRY
Gradual Wars. Shannon: Irish University Press, 1972.
Rumours. Dublin: Dolmen Press, 1977.
History Lessons. Dublin: Gallery Press, 1983.
Selected Poems. Oldcastle, County Meath, Ireland: Gallery, 1988.

OTHER WORKS
Civilians and Barbarians. Derry, Northern Ireland: Field Day Theatre Company, 1983. (Pamphlet.)
Heroic Styles: The Tradition of an Idea. Derry, Northern Ireland: Field Day Theatre Company, 1984.
Celtic Revivals. Faber and Faber: London, 1985.
The French Revolution and Enlightenment in England. Cambridge, Mass.: Harvard University Press, 1988.
The Field Day Anthology of Irish Writing. 3 vols. (As editor.) Derry, Northern Ireland: Field Day, 1991.
"Powers of Earth and Visions of Air." In *Seamus Heaney: The Shaping Spirit.* Edited by Catharine Malloy and Phyllis Carey. Newark: University of Delaware Press, 1996.
Strange Country: Modernity and Nationhood in Irish Writing Since 1790. Oxford: Oxford University Press, 1997.

CRITICAL AND BIOGRAPHICAL STUDIES
Adorno, Theodor. *Aesthetic Theory.* Translated by Robert Hullot-Kentor. Minneapolis: University of Minnesota Press, 1997.
Boyers, Robert. "Identity and Diffidence." *New Republic,* May 19, 1997, pp. 33–36.
Conlon, Edward. "Violent Griefs and Seductive Hopes." *New Leader,* September 8, 1997, pp. 16–17.
Deignan, Tom. Review of *Reading in the Dark. America* 177, no. 10:28 (October 11, 1997).
Devlin, Anne. "Growing Up in Ireland's Shadowlands." *Observer Review,* August 25, 1996, p. 17.
Dunn, Douglas. "The Speckled Hill, the Plover's Shore." *Encounter* 41, no. 6:70–76 (December 1973).
Eagleton, Terry. "The Bogside Bard." *New Statesman,* August 30, 1996, p. 46.
Eder, Richard. "Ghost Story." *Los Angeles Times,* May 11, 1997, p. 2.
Ewart, Gavin. "Accepting the Inevitable." *Times Literary Supplement,* November 25, 1977, p. 1381.
Flanagan, Thomas. "Family Secrets." *New York Review of Books,* October 22, 1997, pp. 54–55.
Green, John Richard. *History of the English People.* Vol. 10. Barcelona: Athena University Press, 2004.
Halpin, Tom. "The Razors of Perception." *Irish Literary Supplement* 8, no. 2:20 (fall 1989).
Hand, Derek. "The Endless Possibilities of Ordinary Life." *Irish Literary Supplement* 16, no. 1:19–20 (spring 1997).

Hughes, Eamon. "Tradition and Modernity." *Irish Literary Supplement* 16, no. 2:21 (fall 1997).

Humphreys, Josephine. "Ghosts." *New York Times Book Review*, May 4, 1997, p. 6.

Jarvis, Simon. *Adorno: A Critical Introduction.* New York: Routledge, 1998.

Keefe, J. T. "A Review of *History Lessons.*" *World Literature Today* 58, no. 4:608 (autumn 1984).

Kenner, Hugh. "There's Music in the Ould Sod Yet." *New York Times Book Review*, January 26, 1992, pp. 3, 23.

McCarthy, Conor. "Seamus Deane: Between Burke and Adorno." *Yearbook of English Studies* 35, no. 1:232–248 (January 2005).

McGonigle, Thomas. "Two Novels Look at Life in Northern Ireland." *Chicago Tribune Books*, June 8, 1997, p. 8.

O'Brien, Conor Cruise. "Cult of Blood." *Observer Review*, August 18, 1985, p. 18.

O'Faolain, Julia. "The Boy Who Wanted to Know." *Times Literary Supplement*, September 27, 1996, p. 22.

Parrinder, Patrick. "Celtic Revisionism." *London Review of Books,* July 24, 1986, pp. 16–17.

Ryan, Alan. "Effervescence." *London Review of Books*, November 9, 1989, pp. 10–11.

INTERVIEWS

Edwards, Bob. "Morning Edition." National Public Radio, December 12, 1991.

Ross, Andrew. "Irish Ghost Stories." *Salon* (http://www.salon.com/april97/reading970411.html), April 11, 1997.

LEN DEIGHTON

(1929—)

Oliver S. Buckton

IT IS ONE of the ironies of Len Deighton's long and varied literary career that he has been in some ways overshadowed by his own characters: in particular, by the anonymous narrator first introduced in *The Ipcress File* (1962), a working-class intelligence agent from Burnley who would also feature in five subsequent novels. The remarkable success of *The Ipcress File* brought Deighton fame as a novelist—particularly following the 1965 film adaptation starring Michael Caine as the newly christened Harry Palmer—yet the prominence of this work has also resulted in some distortions of the writer's career. For Len Deighton is far more than the author of *The Ipcress File*, indeed far more than a spy novelist. Unlike Ian Fleming, to whose career Deighton's stands in an intriguing contrast, Deighton has moved beyond his most famous character to excel in a variety of genres. Yet the popularity of Harry Palmer, as an antidote to the romantic glamorization of the spy in Fleming's James Bond, has given Deighton his most famous, if not necessarily most impressive, creation.

Leonard Cyril Deighton was born in central London on February 18, 1929. His parents were both in the service of Campbell Dodgson, Keeper of Prints and Drawings at the British Museum. As noted in a 1993 interview with Lisa See, Deighton "often tells people 'I was born in a house with 15 servants,' then adds that his mother was the cook and his father the chauffeur" (p. 56). His mother also cooked for Anna Wolkoff, the former White Russian fascist, and the young Len Deighton witnessed Wolkoff's arrest, at the behest of MI5, on espionage charges (Masters, p. 257). An ironic and subversive attitude toward class divisions, especially in Britain, is one of the characteristics of Deighton's writing, which has led some critics to group him with John Osbourne

(1929–1994) and Kingsley Amis (1922–1995) as part of the "angry young men" generation of British writers. In sharp contrast to the upper-class grooming of Bond's creator Ian Fleming—who attended Eton and Sandhurst—Deighton attended Marylebone Grammar School before being transferred to an emergency school during the Second World War. At the age of seventeen he was conscripted into the Royal Air Force, where he became a photographer, a role that included taking photographs of crime and accident scenes with investigative units. Following his discharge from the air force, Deighton attended St. Martin's School of Art in London, as the recipient of an ex-service grant. In 1952 he won a scholarship to the Royal College of Art in London, graduating in 1955. He took a position with the state airline, BOAC (British Overseas Airways Corporation; now British Airways), as a flight attendant (1956–1957) before launching a career as a designer and illustrator. Deighton worked on a variety of publicity assignments in London and New York, did drawings for various magazines including *Esquire*, and illustrated over two hundred book jackets for publishers including William Heinemann, Secker & Warburg, and Penguin Books. Deighton married Shirley Thompson, an illustrator, in 1960. In 1961 he published an innovative cartoon-style cookery strip in the *Daily Express*, which led to his influential and long-running "Cookstrip" in the *Observer*, beginning in 1962. Deighton's longstanding interest in cookery has resulted in several more substantial publications, one of which—*Len Deighton's Action Cookbook* (1965)—was rereleased in 2009 by Harper-Collins.

During an extended working vacation in the Dordogne region of France in 1960 Deighton began writing *The Ipcress File* for his own amusement. Deighton published this, his first novel, in 1962 with Hodder & Stoughton, and it was a serious contender for the British Crime Writer's Association's competition for the best crime novel of the year. This groundbreaking espionage novel—introducing an unnamed working-class narrator whose spycraft was in direct contrast to the glamorous jet-setting antics of James Bond—was followed by several others, including *Funeral in Berlin* (1964) and *Billion Dollar Brain* (1966). These later novels featured the same unnamed agent for WOOC(P), Deighton's fictionalized British intelligence department. These novels established Deighton in the front rank of spy novelists, along with Fleming and John le Carré. The influential film versions of several of these novels—beginning with *The Ipcress File* in 1965—established the protagonist's name as Harry Palmer, in an acclaimed role by the British actor Michael Caine (for convenience, this character will be referred to as Harry Palmer in discussing the novels as well as the films). Paradoxically, although promoted as an "anti-Bond" project, the films were produced by Harry Saltzman, who also produced the Bond movies. In later novels Deighton expanded his repertoire to include a wider range of characters and subtler discussions of psychology and relationships.

In addition to his spy fiction, Deighton has written extensively about World War II, in both fictional and nonfictional narratives. His own background in the RAF has contributed to the impressive authenticity of his accounts of aerial warfare in novels such as *Bomber* (1970, included by Anthony Burgess as one of the ninety-nine best novels published in English since 1939) and historical works such as *Fighter* (1977), his acclaimed account of the Battle of Britain. Deighton has blended his historical interest in World War II with his storytelling powers in *SS-GB* (1978), a novel that takes as its premise an imaginary occupation of Britain by Nazi Germany in 1941 Deighton's most important fictional protagonist since Harry Palmer has been Bernard Samson, a senior intelligence agent for "London Central," who has featured in three trilogies, the first of which—*Berlin Game* (1983), *Mexico Set*

(1984), and *London Match* (1985)—was televised by Granada Television in 1988, directed by Ken Grieve and Patrick Lau, and starring the British actor Ian Holm as Samson. Bearing some resemblances to John le Carré's hero George Smiley, Samson—as his longevity suggests—has provided the perfect vehicle for Deighton to explore the complexities, betrayals, and alienation of spying for the modern era. In between the first two Samson trilogies, Deighton published *Winter: A Berlin Family 1899–1945* (1987) that gave background on Samson's family, on other characters of significance in the Bernard Samson series, and on Germany before and during the war. His research and extensive knowledge of World War II has also produced several further works of nonfiction military history, including *Blitzkrieg: From the Rise of Hitler to the Fall of Dunkirk* (1979) and *Blood, Tears, and Folly: In the Darkest Hour of the Second World War* (1993). Several experts in the field have praised Deighton's historical works, including the leading British historian A. J. P. Taylor. Deighton has lived and worked in a variety of locations, including Ireland, Portugal, and Southern California. Yet London remains his imaginative home, and most of his works are based in London and the South of England. However, another key venue is Berlin, a city to which Deighton has made numerous visits. Both as a divided city (represented by the Berlin Wall) and as an inverted mirror image of London, the center of British intelligence operations, Berlin is a crucial location and symbol in Deighton's work. Indeed, critics have singled out Deighton's works as among the most powerful and authentic representations of Berlin in postwar European literature.

One of the most important and distinctive aspects of Deighton's work—whether fiction or nonfiction—is the vast amount of research on which his books are based. Deighton is renowned for meticulously researching the geographical, technical, and historical information deployed in his books, and this creates their distinctive aura of authenticity. In response to occasional criticisms of his books being "overresearched," Deighton again invokes the British social system: "All you need is a profound inferiority complex:

no training as a writer and growing up a victim of the English class system" (quoted in See, p. 58). Following the end of the cold war, later works by Deighton have been based in South America (*MAMista*, 1991) and Southern California (*Violent Ward*, 1993). Since the completion of his third Samson trilogy, *Faith, Hope, and Charity*, in 1996 Deighton's output has slowed considerably. Yet he remains one of the major figures of twentieth-century British fiction, having transformed both the spy novel and the historical novel with his powerful blend of technical expertise, meticulous research, and insight into the foibles of social classes and human character.

Because of the large volume of Deighton's output and the variety of genres in which he has published, the discussion of his works that follows will be divided into several categories, representing the main areas of his achievement. The majority of this essay will focus on Deighton's fiction, however some commentary is also offered on his nonfiction works and films based on his works.

ESPIONAGE FICTION

While Deighton has made significant contributions to several different fields of literature, his chief reputation and acclaim is undoubtedly that of a master of espionage fiction. Along with Ian Fleming (1909–1954) and John le Carré (1931–), Deighton is one of the foremost practitioners of the British spy novel in the postwar era. Following in the tradition of literary excellence established by earlier espionage novelists such as Joseph Conrad (*The Secret Agent,* 1907), Eric Ambler (*The Mask of Dimitrios,* 1939), and Graham Greene (*The Third Man,* 1950), Deighton broadened the appeal of the spy novel by introducing a working-class protagonist defined by a satirical sense of humor and a deep-seated antiestablishment attitude. While Fleming merits distinction as the creator of the most famous spy of the twentieth-century in James Bond, and le Carré has deservedly won acclaim for his serious and disillusioned portrayals of spycraft, Deighton made a niche for himself by writing from the

perspective of a working-class outsider, allowing his novels to achieve distinction as much for their social observations about class as for their details of espionage. Like le Carré, Deighton offers a frequently cynical perspective on the shadowy, often corrupt world of espionage, and casts doubt on the motives and morality of the modern spy organization. Yet while le Carré's cynicism is tinged with bleakness, even despair, Deighton's vision of the spy world is leavened by humor and a down-to-earth resignation to the contradictions and often futile efforts involved in modern surveillance and espionage. Harry Palmer's hostile relationship to the political establishment he serves is a leitmotif of the early novels, as exemplified by an exchange with Jean—his assistant and lover—in *Funeral in Berlin*:

> "Simmer down," I said. "It's not the role of this department to make political decisions. That's what we have Houses of Parliament for."
>
> "Which, coming from you," said Jean, "is very funny."
>
> "Why coming from me?"
>
> "Because when Parliament wakes up in the small hours of the morning bathed in sweat and screaming, you are what they are dreaming of." [...]
>
> I took no notice. "You only have the same sort of fear that everyone here has. That's why you are employed here. The moment we notice someone who isn't frightened that this set-up and all the other set-ups like it are a threat to democratic parliamentary systems—we fire him. The only way a department that pries can run is to admit of no elite which is immune from prying."
>
> (p. 251)

One recurring characteristic of Deighton's spy fiction—like le Carré's—is his fascination with betrayal, and Deighton has devoted entire works to the exploration of betrayal of one's country, one's spouse, one's friends, and oneself.

Deighton's spy fiction may be further grouped with reference to its two main protagonists. Deighton's original protagonist is the anonymous narrator of his first five spy novels: *The Ipcress File* (1962), *Horse Under Water* (1963), *Funeral in Berlin* (1964), *Billion Dollar Brain* (1966), and *An Expensive Place to Die* (1967). The same protagonist also features in a later novel, *Spy Story* (1974).

The anonymity of this protagonist is itself significant. It suggests a reaction against the iconic status of James Bond—whose appearance is famously accompanied by a self-naming, "My name is Bond"—by which Deighton implies that the spy world is anonymous, requiring a loss or concealment of identity rather than its brandishing. Identity for the spy is dependent on external markers, such as identity papers, rather than an inner sense of self. Yet despite being anonymous, Deighton's character has a highly distinctive persona. The chief traits of this character are an irreverent sense of humor, a deeply seated antiauthoritarian attitude, a passion for the good life represented by fine food and wine, an inclination for womanizing evidenced by his frequent philandering, and a professional pride that does not suffer the incompetence of his superiors gladly. For example in *The Ipcress File*, the narrator's first meeting with his superior, Colonel Ross, is described with characteristic antagonism:

> Ross, the man I had come to see, looked up from the writing that had held his undivided attention since three seconds after I had entered the room. Ross said, "Well now," and coughed nervously. Ross and I had come to an arrangement of some years' standing—we had decided to hate each other. Being English, this vitriolic relationship manifested itself in oriental politeness.
>
> (p. 5)

The narrator's shady past includes time in prison and several black marks on his military record, weaknesses which Ross and Dalby—his superiors in WOOC(P)—exploit to keep him in line. The flawed yet appealing character of the central narrator provides this group of novels with a coherence they would otherwise lack.

Despite the unity provided by the continuing narrator, the plots of Deighton's first four novels are actually quite disparate and eclectic. *The Ipcress File* deals with a plot to kidnap and brainwash leading British scientists, orchestrated by a man code-named Jay. These top scientists

either disappear or are returned in an incapacitated state, effectively useless. The title refers to the process—Induction of Psychoneuroses Under Stress—by which the scientists are rendered useless. Early in the novel, the protagonist (hereafter called "Harry Palmer") is transferred from the military intelligence unit under Col. Ross—where he had been seconded from the army—to the civilian intelligence unit under Major Dalby, an agency known only by the initials WOOC(P). Palmer's insubordinate attitude is no less evident in his relationship to Dalby than it was with Ross, as observable in a conversation soon after Palmer's transfer:

> "You are loving it here of course?" Dalby asked.
>
> "I have a clean mind and a pure heart. I get eight hours' sleep every night. I am a loyal, diligent employee and will attempt every day to be worthy of the trust my paternal employer puts in me."
>
> "I'll make the jokes," said Dalby [...]
>
> Dalby tightened a shoelace. "Think you can handle a tricky little special assignment?"
>
> "If it doesn't demand a classical education I might be able to grope around it."
>
> (p. 12)

The exchange concisely reflects Palmer's sarcastic attitude toward authority (his "paternal employer") as well as the chip on his shoulder regarding his lack of a "classical education," the benchmark of the upper-class elite.

Harry Palmer's efforts to unravel the mystery behind the disappearing scientists prove fruitless, despite the assistance of the narrator's friend in the police, Keightley. However, the discovery of a suspicious house in London in which a piece of audiotape is found, offers a significant lead to the conspiracy. The story then moves to the Taiwe Atol in the South Pacific, where the United States plans to detonate the world's first neutron bomb. The protagonist, having foiled a plot to sabotage this detonation and leak details of the bomb to the Soviets, is then held captive and tortured in what appears to be a foreign prison (in Hungary), an incarceration orchestrated by Jay himself. Yet on escaping from his captors, the narrator discovers that "they were holding me in a big house in London's Wood Green from the word go" (p. 254). Having suspected his former boss, Ross, of treason, the narrator uncovers the fact that the plan to sabotage the neutron bomb and betray secrets was actually arranged by Dalby, who is a Soviet double agent. Thus the novel introduces the theme of betrayal—of country and profession—by highly placed agents that will play a central role in Deighton's later spy fiction. In the course of this novel, Harry Palmer acquires an assistant, Jean, who becomes his love interest and "Dr. Watson role" (denoting one who allows the protagonist to explain his methods and discoveries for the reader's benefit; see Edward Milward-Oliver, 1987, p. 285).

The second "Harry Palmer" novel, *Horse Under Water*, sends Palmer to the coast of Portugal, in an effort to salvage a buried treasure at sea. Britain plans to use the profits from this treasure hunt to fund the liberationist army in Portugal, without being officially involved in the civil strife. In the course of his investigation, Palmer discovers a plot to produce and smuggle heroin, a large cache of the drug being the actual valuable contents of the sunken ship (hence the novel's title). In the course of the investigation the narrator discovers that the true treasure is a secret list of prominent British subjects who were willing to help the Third Reich, in the event of their victory in World War II, set up a puppet government in Britain. In destroying this drug cartel, Palmer also brings embarrassment to his own government but gains the approval of his new boss, Dalby's replacement, Dawlish. The drug cartel turns out to be connected to a Nazi organization that has survived following the German defeat in World War II, reflecting the lingering of the war and the Nazis in much of Deighton's work. This nautical adventure—reminiscent of Robert Louis Stevenson's and Joseph Conrad's maritime yarns—is the only one of the first four novels that was not made into a film.

The third novel featuring Harry Palmer, *Funeral in Berlin*, deals with an elaborate plot to export a leading Soviet scientist to Britain—for a price. Harry Palmer is sent to Berlin to negotiate the terms of the defection, which is arranged by Palmer's long-term Soviet adversary, Colonel Stok of the KGB. The actual defection is arranged by King (aka Johnny Vulkan), a German who acts more like an American. King plans a fake funeral in which the scientist will be placed in a coffin, allowing him to cross the border between East and West Berlin without inspection. The corpse will be given the false identity of Paul Allan Broum, and the papers establishing this identity are delivered. However, it turns out that Broum was actually a wealthy prisoner of a Nazi concentration camp in World War II and died there without an heir. After the war, the Allies determined that anyone proving he was Broum or his heir could claim the fortune, which is being held by a Swiss bank. Palmer eventually discovers that "King" (aka Vulkan) is in fact Broum—having concealed his identity since collaborating with the Nazis—but he lacked identity papers and so arranged the fake funeral of Broum solely to acquire such papers from the British. In this plot Broum uses Samantha Steele, who poses as an ally of Palmer but is actually an Israeli agent trying to track down war criminals. King is eventually killed and placed in the coffin intended for the scientist—and Palmer secures the fortune but not the scientist. The novel is the first by Deighton to make extensive use of Berlin as a setting—a city that will play an increasingly important role in his spy fiction. In *Billion Dollar Brain*, the fourth novel, Palmer becomes part of an organization run by a Texas billionaire, General Midwinter, run from a vast computer network known as the Brain. Midwinter, a fervent anti-Communist, is planning an anti-Soviet coup in Latvia, his ancestral homeland, which at the time of the story is part of the Soviet bloc. Midwinter's covert operation is run both in Europe—where he is training an army to invade Latvia and fight the Communists—and in Texas, which is the headquarters of his operation. The key to Midwinter's organization is a massive computer—the "Brain" of the title—which plans each move and issues coded instructions over the telephone to the operatives of the "Facts for Freedom" organization. Palmer's involvement begins when he is recruited by an American, Harvey Newbegin, to carry a packet from London to Finland—a packet containing eggs that contain a deadly virus that will be used by Midwinter's organization to wage biological warfare against the Soviets. Having switched them for a harmless pack of ordinary eggs, Palmer infiltrates the Midwinter organization as a British spy. His contact is Signe Laine, a beautiful young Finnish woman who is Harvey's girlfriend—though Newbegin will not leave his wife to live with her. In a subplot that typifies Deighton's ambivalent portrayal of women—an issue to be discussed later in this essay—Signe becomes Palmer's lover and then will attempt to kill him, although Palmer evades assassination and eventually foils the American's plot to destabilize Latvia. Harvey Newbegin is killed as he attempts to escape by train. Also indicative of Deighton's critical stance toward American cold-war paranoia, in this novel it is the American-sponsored anti-Communist organization, rather than the Soviet Union, that is portrayed as the chief enemy and threat to world peace.

Despite the diverse locations, plots, and chief concerns of these four novels, there is a certain unity to them that allows them to be considered as a group. Most importantly, the coherence of the four works is provided by Harry Palmer, a resolutely working-class figure, whose antiestablishment attitudes are embodied in his contempt for the products of public schools and Oxbridge and his disdain for the snobbery of his superiors. Notwithstanding this working-class background, Palmer has an expensive taste for luxury items, especially food and alcohol, though he remains distinct from the extravagant sophistication of Fleming's Bond (who first appeared in the 1953 novel *Casino Royale*). Palmer is as much concerned with securing his expenses as with catching foreign spies, and the financial concerns of Palmer are often highlighted. Palmer is well read, has a passion for studying history, is something of a gourmet (many references are made in the novel to his shopping for delicacies and to his culinary skills), and enjoys classical music. In many respects, Palmer is a web of contradictions—as is Deighton himself, who combines a passion for military history, machinery, and spycraft with a long-standing interest in cookery and art. As the first five novels progress, one comes to understand that some of Palmer's bluntness, blundering, and insubordination are a front: a deliberately constructed persona that distracts attention from his actual purpose and lures his enemies into a false sense of security. In particular, Palmer's insubordination allows numerous opportunities for sardonic banter with his superiors, which establishes the humorous and subversive tone of the narratives. In *Horse Under Water*, a conflict occurs when Palmer asks permission to take a pistol on his assignment to Portugal:

> There was a long silence, broken only by the sound of Dawlish blinking.
>
> "Pistol?" said Dawlish. "Are you going out of your mind?"
>
> "Just into my second childhood," I said.
>
> "That's right," said Dawlish, "they are nasty, noisy, dangerous toys. How would I feel if you jammed your finger in the mechanism or something?" […]
>
> He removed his glasses and began to polish them carefully. "You have a pistol of your own that I am not supposed to know about. Don't take it with you, there's a good chap."
>
> "Not a chance," I said, "I can't afford the ammunition."
>
> (pp. 34–35)

With superb economy, this exchange captures the paternalistic attitude of Palmer's employers and his own rebellious reaction to this treatment. Palmer's distrust of those in authority is not just a source of humor but rather it leads to some of his most important insights and is key to his successes as an agent. He rarely follows orders—at least not to the letter—and often disagrees with, or mocks, his bosses. One telling example is in *The Ipcress File* when—having been transferred to Dalby's civilian intelligence unit—he is approached by his former boss, Ross, who offers to sell Palmer a valuable file of information. Ross is short of funds and is attempting to divert money in this way from Dalby's more lucrative operation. In a comment that typifies his antiauthoritarian persona, Palmer refuses and snubs Ross's attempt to pull rank over him, stating, "You've got the nerve to sell something that doesn't belong to you to someone you don't like. Well you're right. That is the sort of business we're in" (p. 126).

Other striking features of Palmer include his comparatively humble tastes in some areas: where James Bond drives a vintage turbo-charged Bentley, for example, Palmer will be satisfied with a Humber or Sunbeam, costing less than £1000. Though he enjoys fine food—like Bond—he does not always dine at fine restaurants, but he is a keen cook and will settle for a sandwich from the local Wally's delicatessen. Stripping much of the glamour away from Fleming's world of Bond, Deighton portrays the cold war—as far as we can tell from Palmer's outlook—as dirty game in which neither side is much better than the other. In this respect, Deighton's is closer to John le Carré's cold-war vision in *The Spy Who Came In from the Cold* (1963). An important difference, however, is that Palmer's view of the cold war is infused with a humor lacking in le Carré's protagonist, Alec Leamas. Though Palmer works for British intelligence, he is often critical of his own organization and even more so of Britain's leading allies, the Americans. Though individual Americans are portrayed with respect and affection, the United States as a whole is satirized as a puzzling, ruthless, and self-indulgent superpower, an even greater risk than the Soviets to global security. This is nowhere more evident than in *The Ipcress File*, where an American major explains the tremendous destructive power of a nuclear explosion, and then "looked at his audience like he expected applause and went on to explain about ways in which it had become possible to dispense with tritium and with refrigeration, so making the bomb cheaper and easier to produce" (p. 157). The novel is also satirical of American military presence abroad, as "we fenced off a few questions about leaks in the UK, to persuade them that we didn't know what was happening. It wasn't difficult. Skip saw us off down to the little white-painted fence by means of which a consid-

erate army enabled him to feel he had never left New Jersey" (pp. 168–169).

Palmer appears in two further Deighton novels. In *An Expensive Place to Die* (1967), Deighton changes the formula in several significant respects. In the first place, the novel is set in Paris, somewhat outside the main battlegrounds of the cold war (such as Berlin and London) that provided the locations of the previous four novels. Where the narrator of the earlier novels has a grudging affection for London and Berlin, his view of Paris is bitter and cynical. While the central narrator remains recognizably the same as in the previous four novels, his point of view is less dominant in the novel as a whole: significant episodes in the novel are narrated from the point of view of Maria Chauvet—an attractive Parisian woman who is both lover and antagonist of Palmer. The plot revolves around a sinister figure, M. Datt, who runs a Maison de Passe on the Avenue Foch. Datt uses drugs and sex to extract confessions from important foreign dignitaries and spies, using the information to blackmail them. In fact Datt is a puppet of the great powers that use his ability to bring scientists together to avoid a third world war. The hero is administered with a LSD-based drug serum, but he is rescued by Maria, who is Datt's illegitimate daughter and the former wife of Chief Inspector Claude Loiseau, the French policeman. The plot also revolves around a conspiracy to conceal the devastating effects of nuclear fallout, which is leading apparently inexorably to the explosion of a Chinese hydrogen bomb. The anonymous narrator makes a final appearance in *Spy Story* (1974), though he is now employed under the name Patrick Armstrong for a war-game center, STUCEN, supervised by the American Col. Schlegel. The reader wonders: is this the unnamed narrator from the first five spy novels? There are clues that suggest he is the same man, such as when he meets Dawlish, with whom he worked previously. In this novel, the narrator becomes involved in a British attempt to sabotage German reunification talks in Copenhagen. In an echo of *Funeral in Berlin*, the narrator returns to field intelligence work in Copenhagen, leading an attempt to extract a Soviet defector, Admiral

Remoziva. However the defection of Remoziva is actually intended by the British to put pressure on his sister, in charge of the German reunification talks.

An important spy novel appearing between the two major groups of Deighton's espionage fiction is *XPD* (1981). In some ways a transitional work, this novel weaves together a complex plot set both during World War II and shortly after the election of Margaret Thatcher's Conservative Party in 1979. The novel also moves between London, Germany, Switzerland, and California, following the covert operations of British, U.S., and Soviet intelligence agencies, all of whom are interested in securing the missing "Hitler Minutes." These documents are the only record of a secret meeting between Hitler and Winston Churchill in June 1940, in which the two discussed peace terms that would have been highly advantageous to Germany. Initially concealed in the Kaiseroda Mine, two hundred miles from Berlin—along with a large part of the gold and monetary reserves of the Third Reich—the Hitler Minutes were stolen by a group of American soldiers in Patton's Third Army, known as the "Kaiseroda Raiders." These men—led by Charles Stein—have lived affluently on their ill-gotten gains, until the truth threatens to come out when a movie company plans to make a film about the Kaiseroda Mine. A struggle ensues for possession of the Hitler Minutes between agents of several powers, including the KGB agent Willi Kleiber, who ruthlessly pursues the documents, murdering anyone in his path. The novel also features a British secret agent, Boyd Stuart, who is unhappily married to the daughter of his boss, Sir Sydney Ryden. While Stuart has some of the freewheeling and antiauthoritarian traits of Palmer, he lacks the charm and humor of his precursor. The novel's greatest creation is Charles Stein, the obese, Falstaffian former U.S. officer who orchestrated the theft of Nazi gold and documents. Ill-prepared for the crisis that ensues, Stein is a fine example of Deighton's skill at creating morally ambivalent yet thoroughly human characters. In a brilliant denouement to the novel, Stein pursues Max Breslow—a minor Hollywood film producer who attempts to conceal his Nazi past—to the

film studio where production is under way for the film about the Kaiseroda Mine. Still concussed from an auto accident, Stein's hallucinations weave together the past and the present in a way that exemplifies Deighton's rich historical vision:

> A thousand Hitlers stood up and glared at Stein, raising their hands mockingly in mute salute to him.
>
> "Breslow!" Stein's voice was so loud that it made the thin hardboard walls of the dressing room rattle as they echoed back the sound of it. "Breslow!" It was more like a cry for help than a threat. "Breslow!" shouted Stein again. He was beginning to realize that Max Breslow controlled a thousand Fuhrers. It was Breslow he would have to finish off. Breslow had become the focal point of all Stein's anger, sadness, and frustration.
>
> (p. 400)

The novel's wide historical perspective and multiple, international locations prepare the ground for Deighton's second major achievement in spy fiction: the Bernard Samson series.

The second major group of Deighton's spy novels revolve around his protagonist Bernard Samson, a leading figure in London Central, the heart of British intelligence operations during the cold war. Samson—who was raised in Berlin by his father, Brian, also an intelligence agent serving as London Central's Berlin resident—is the hero and narrator of three trilogies: *Berlin Game* (1983), *Mexico Set* (1984), and *London Match* (1985); *Spy Hook* (1988), *Spy Line* (1989), *Spy Sinker* (1990); and *Faith* (1994), *Hope* (1995), and *Charity* (1996). Samson has a number of qualities in common with Harry Palmer—Deighton's original protagonist—and may be viewed as an evolution of this character, updating him to the 1980s and 1990s. However, there are also some significant differences, particular in Samson's attitudes toward intelligence work and in the complexity of his personal relationships. The first trilogy—collected as *Game, Set, and Match*—deals with the discovery by Samson of a leak at the highest levels within London Central. The plot begins as one of London's leading foreign agents behind the Iron Curtain—known as Brahms Four—is demanding a safe passage to the West because of increasing evidence of treachery in London. Samson grows suspicious of several of his senior colleagues in London Central, including the wunderkind Dicky Cruyer—recently promoted (instead of Samson himself) to the head of German networks—and Brett Rensselaer, the American who runs Brahms Four and his associated network. To complicate matters, Samson suspects Rensselaer of having an affair with his wife, Fiona, who also has a prominent position in London Central.

Another possible suspect as the "mole" is Frank Harrington, London Central's Berlin resident, who is nearing retirement. Samson's ultimate discovery—that the double agent is in fact his own wife—is not only personally devastating but casts him under much suspicion from London Central of treason in the following novels. *Mexico Set* deals with an attempt to recruit (or enroll) a KGB agent, Erich Stinnes, and exploit his knowledge of Soviet spy networks. *London Match* begins as, following the successful enrollment of Stinnes, Samson attempts to use his knowledge to penetrate and destroy a KGB network in a military research laboratory in Cambridge. The failure of the attempts to stake out this network lead to further suspicions of treachery in London Central, in which Samson—following the defection of his wife—is among the chief suspects.

Unlike Harry Palmer—a carefree bachelor—Samson is defined in many ways by his marriage to the upper-class, brilliant, and wealthy Fiona, and he is severely damaged—emotionally, psychologically, and professionally—by her betrayals. Samson is also marked by the frustration of his professional ambitions, after being passed over for promotion to head of the German desk. At frequent intervals in the *Game, Set, and Match* trilogy Samson's narration comments acerbically on the shameless self-promotion and incompetence of the German stations controller Dicky Cruyer who—like Rensselaer—suffers from an inferiority complex because of his lack of experience in the field. Cruyer takes center stage alongside Samson in *Mexico Set*, the second novel in the trilogy, as he accompanies Samson on the mission to woo Stinnes from the East. In a telling description, Samson unsparingly reveals

the pretension and self-importance of Dicky's character:

> It was Dicky's faded work suit, his cowboy boots and curly hair that had attracted the attention of the tough-looking lady immigration officer at Mexico City airport. It was only the first-class labels on his expensive baggage and the fast talking of Dicky's counselor friend from the embassy that saved him from the indignity of a body search. Dicky Cruyer was a curious mixture of scholarship and ruthless ambition, but he was insensitive and this was often his undoing. His insensitivity to people, place, and atmosphere could make him seem a clown instead of the cool sophisticate that was his own image of himself. But that didn't make him any less terrifying as friend or foe.
>
> (pp. 2–3)

The character of Bret Rensselaer is an interesting example of Deighton's ambivalence toward the United States. Rensselaer is an Anglophile working in British intelligence, but his national identity is frequently alluded to, often in a satirical context. He is described in *Berlin Game* as

> a dark-suited American in his middle fifties, with fair receding hair and a quick nervous smile. Bret was the sort of American who liked to be mistaken for an Englishman. Recruited into the service while at Oxford on a Rhodes scholarship, he'd become a dedicated Anglophile who'd served in many European stations before taking over as Deputy Controller of the European Economics desk, which later became the Economics Intelligence Committee and was now Bret's private empire.
>
> (p. 41)

The reference to Rensselaer's empire building within British intelligence evokes fears of the United States's displacement of Britain from the world stage as an imperial power. Significantly, Samson suspects Bret of having an affair with his wife Fiona—indicating that his (and perhaps Britain's) sense of insecurity has sexual as well as professional and political dimensions.

From the beginning of the trilogy, in *Berlin Game*, moreover, Deighton portrays an American failure to prevent the original construction of the wall: Samson's friend Werner Volkmann recalls, "There were Russian trucks, and lots of soldiers dumping rolls of barbed wire outside the Charité Hospital. We came back quite soon. Silas said the Americans would send in tanks and tear the wire down. Your dad said the same thing, didn't he?" Samson responds, "The people in Washington were too bloody frightened, Werner. The stupid bastards at the top thought the Russkies were going to move this way and take over the Western Sector of the city. They were *relieved* to see a wall going up" (p. 6). Samson's comment suggests an American betrayal of its European allies in the long-enduring division of Berlin. As the critic Jurgen Kamm has commented, "It is interesting to note that from a British perspective the blame is shifted to the Americans and consequently it is an ex-CIA man who in *Spy Line* supplies Samson (and the reader) with a detailed account of the Wall from its ramshackle beginnings to its technological and bureaucratic perfection in the late 1980s" (p. 69).

In 1987, in between the first two trilogies, Deighton published *Winter*, which fills in the background of Samson's family—including his father Brian, London Central's Berlin resident—and German history from the beginning of the twentieth-century through World War II. The second trilogy, *Spy Hook*, *Spy Line*, and *Spy Sinker*, furthers Deighton's exploration of treachery within British intelligence, as Samson is still suffering from the fallout of his wife's defection to the KGB. Samson discovers the disappearance of half a million dollars of departmental funds, and he seeks to discover whether it is embezzlement or the work of a KGB mole. Suspecting that he may have stumbled on another secret operation organized by his wife, Samson ends the novel on the run in Berlin. *Spy Line* finds Samson still hiding in Berlin, named as a traitor by London Central, although the British Secret Service knows his whereabouts and continues to pay his salary. He is allowed to return by London Central, with all charges dropped against him, and is then given an assignment in Vienna. Yet this assignment proves unexpectedly dangerous as he gets closer to the center of a web of treachery in the Secret Service. He travels to Czechoslovakia, where he discovers the sender is Fiona, who reveals she's been working for London Central all this time. It is suggested that Bernard had already reached that conclusion on

his own. In a disastrous confrontation on a rainy motorway clearing, a shootout ensues in which Fiona's sister Tessa is killed, along with Stinnes. The theme of betrayal continues, as Bernard questions whether he can trust those closest to him—his family, friends, and colleagues. There is a clear pattern in Deighton's world of espionage, in which simple answers are never easy to come by. Deighton changes his narrative architecture in the third novel, *Spy Sinker*, by dropping the first-person narrative of Samson to retell the whole series of events from Fiona's point of view, though in the third person.

The third trilogy, *Faith*, *Hope*, and *Charity*, was written after the cold war had ended, in 1993–1994. Like other writers of espionage fiction—most notably le Carré—Deighton faced a serious challenge to his main themes as a writer following the bringing down of the Berlin Wall—symbolic of the cold-war era—in 1989. However, *Faith* continues from the ending of *Spy Line*, in the summer of 1987. In these three volumes, Deighton attempts to provide resolution to his series and explore in more depth the complex psychology of his female protagonist, Fiona Samson. This book explores the long-term effects of the whole Samson saga on the key characters. Bernard is deep undercover in Magdeburg in 1987, helping the East German Christian church. In an effort to reclaim control of his career and his marriage, Bernard tries to bring over a Russian defector, "Verdi." However, Samson remains haunted by the shocking death of Fiona's sister Tessa by a motorway outside Berlin, and he tries to uncover the truth behind this tragedy. In *Hope*, Deighton brings together the personal and political fallout of betrayal, considering whether treachery in a marriage, let alone the spying game, can be forgiven. Finding an injured man on his doorstep one evening, Bernard discovers this leads to a series of events that starts to uncover the facts behind Tessa Kosinski's murder in Berlin. Samson's investigations reveal even more unsavory truths about his own department and the involvement of the veterans Silas Gaunt and Bret Rensselaer. Beginning in Poland in 1988, *Charity* has Bret Rensselaer—who had returned to the plot in *Spy Hook*, having apparently been killed at the end of *London Match*—back at the head of the department. Bernard becomes increasingly anxious that he will be accused of Tessa's murder unless he can unravel what actually happened. Other major characters from the previous trilogies who reappear are Gloria Kent and Silas Gaunt, a retired senior MI6 agent and distant relative of Fiona, who still wields considerable influence with London Central and holds weekend house parties to which he invites departmental staff. Bernard's discovery of a box at Frank Harrington's Berlin residence ultimately leads him to the truth about his wife's disappearance and her sister's death in Berlin.

Berlin is itself one of the main characters in the ten Bernard Sampson novels—including *Winter: A Berlin Family 1899–1945*, which follows the Winter family during the rise of Hitler and the Nazis. As such, the novel provides the background to the first trilogy, *Game, Set, and Match,* providing a backstory for Lisl Hennig, Bret Rensselaer, Werner Volkmann, and Bernard's own father, Brian, who is MI6's field agent in Berlin and then becomes the postwar Berlin resident. Berlin is an ideal setting for the cold-war novels, representing as it does the divisions and contradictions of the military and ideological struggles between East and West. In particular, Bernard Samson's character in many ways mirrors the fractured city in which he grew up. Overall, the Samson series of novels represents Deighton's most substantial contribution to the spy fiction genre, with its range of characters and settings. However, the early novels featuring the unnamed narrator and WOOC(P) were highly significant in changing the landscape of spy fiction in the 1960s.

A particularly noteworthy development of the Samson series is the greater amount of attention to personal and sexual relationships. Indeed, by having Fiona's betrayal of her husband run parallel to her apparent betrayal of her country, Deighton sets up rich and intriguing parallels between the worlds of political ideology and sexual desire. Deighton attempts to place the female spy in a more central position and to make gender issues a central concern of his saga. Yet,

ironically, this has led to some criticism of Deighton's female characters as relying on stereotypes. The critic Dudley Jones concedes that Deighton here explores "in more detail both the relationships between the main characters and ethical and political issues raised by espionage" yet criticizes "Deighton's weakness in portraying mature relationships between men and women" (pp. 106–107). Samson himself admits in *Berlin Game*, "I suppose I will never understand women. The trouble is that they all understand me; they understand me too damned well" (p. 12). It is perhaps unfortunate that Samson's self-confessed limitations have been ascribed to Deighton himself.

OTHER FICTION

Len Deighton's experience in the Royal Air Force immediately following World War II, has influenced his interest and expertise in military history. His war novels—beginning with *Bomber* in 1970—are meticulously researched and include authentic period atmosphere and technical detail about the machinery of war in World War II. While Deighton's fiction might at times seem biased toward the British and Allied side in the conflict, his novels show a profound awareness of the human suffering and tragedy on both "sides," and he portrays German characters with subtlety and sympathy. Deighton's masterpiece of war fiction is *Bomber,* subtitled *Events Relating to the Last Flight of an RAF Bomber over Germany on the Night of June 31st, 1943*. The documentary style and immense technical detail of the novel distinguish it from the majority of war novels, yet its fictional status is evident from the very title. Referring to the two main locations of the novel, Deighton reminds readers in an author's preface to the 2009 edition that he has invented the world depicted in its pages, despite its vividness and authenticity. The events of the novel take place in a single day and focus on the crews of the British RAF Lancaster heavy bombers—with such evocative nicknames as "Creaking Door" and "Joe for King"—that launch from Warley Fen airbase. The novel offers a powerful indictment of war, by dividing its focus between

LEN DEIGHTON

the crew of the British bombers and the residents of the fictional German town of Altgarten in the country's Ruhr region. The intended target of the bombing raid is the city of Krefeld, but as the result of an error in dropping the marker flares, the tons of high explosives and phosphorous incendiaries are mistakenly dropped on Altgarten. The novel examines the tragic effects of the raid on both the British pilots and crews—many of whom are killed during the raid—and the Altgarten residents—who are caught unaware by the raid and suffer helplessly as their town is destroyed. Another significant location in the novel is the coastal radar station Ermine, on the Dutch coast near Eindhoven, which is commanded by Oberleutnant August Bach; in an ironic twist, Bach evacuates his ten-year-old son and his fiancée from Krefeld to Altgarten, and then he tracks the heavy raid by RAF bombers as it mistakenly drops its bombs on Altgarten. Deighton's narrative powers are displayed to the full in weaving together the disparate tales of the British and German air forces and civilians, as their fates become enmeshed in a single day of war. With particular insight, Deighton traces the harmful effects of prolonged combat on the crew of "Joe for King":

> The eleventh trip was marked by more subtle defensive changes in the crew: a fatalism, a brutalizing, a callousness about the deaths of friends and a marked change in demeanour. Noisy men became quiet and reflective while the shy ones often became clamorous. This was the time at which the case histories of ulcers, deafness, and other stress-induced nervous diseases that were to follow the survivors through their later years, actually began. The crew of Joe for King were on their eleventh trip.
>
> (p. 280)

One of Deighton's most original war novels, *SS-GB*, published in 1978, belongs to an "alternative history" genre. The premise of *SS-GB* is that Britain has surrendered to Germany in 1941 and is now occupied by the Nazis. Winston Churchill has been executed by the Third Reich, and the king of England is a prisoner in the Tower of London. The protagonist—Detective Inspector Douglas Archer—is called in to investigate a murder in a flat in London's Shepherd's Market.

Accompanied by his long-serving assistant, Harry Woods, Archer uncovers a conspiracy behind the murder that leads to an involvement with British resistance against the German occupiers. Archer—in the difficult position of working for Scotland Yard being run by the Germans, as represented by Oskar Huth—discovers a plot by the SS to secure Britain's atomic research for its own research program, allowing Germany to defeat the United States in the world war that still rages. The key struggle unfolds between rival organizations within the German military—the SS and the Abwehr—as both seek to gain control of Britain's atomic research. The British resistance leader, George Mayhew, plays the two organizations off against each other, while exploiting the rivalry between Huth and his fellow SS officer Fritz Kellerman. A key aspect of the plot involves an attempt by the British resistance to free the king from prison and secure his escape to the United States, where he might serve as a British leader in exile. While it might also be classified as a spy story, *SS-GB*'s densely researched narrative of World War II Britain under German rule belongs more properly to Deighton's war fiction. The novel displays Deighton's great thoroughness in research, conveying the harsh conditions of wartime Britain, with his narrative gifts and inventive powers.

Deighton's novel excels in exploring the complex reactions of Britons under Nazi rule. The imaginary nature of the events allows Deighton the freedom to examine the conflicted attitudes of his hero, Douglas Archer. Required to work under the German SS Standartenfuhrer Huth, Douglas is appalled at the contrast between the well-heeled elegance of a party held by the antiquarian and art dealers, Garin and Shetland, and the miserable conditions of most Britons:

> It was like half-awakening from some terrible nightmare, thought Douglas. The long dresses of fine silks and hand embroidery, the carefully tailored evening suits of the men, and the impeccable clothes of the waiters, came as a shock after the cruel and cynical mood of defeat that prevailed beyond those wrought-iron gates and well-kept

gravel drive, and the neat lawn that was shiny and pink in the last evening light.

(p. 111)

Deighton's distinctive gift for describing physical action—combined with a skill at understatement that is almost anticlimactic—is also in evidence in the scene where the British resistance party, trying to bring the king out of the country, is attacked by a German fusillade:

> Douglas saw the light sweep across the King and the two men carrying him. They disappeared into a cloud of flying earth clods, as the machine-guns followed the beam of light. Douglas ran forward but he was downed by a flying tackle that knocked all the air out of his lungs. By the time he'd recovered it was all over. Bodies were strewn in every direction. The Germans had timed it to perfection; not more than a half-dozen men of this party of raiders had got down to the sea in safety. The mangled bodies of two dozen or more of their companions marked the pathway. Among the dead were Major Dodgson, Danny Barga and King George the Sixth, Emperor of India.

(pp. 389–390)

Another important entry in the catalogue of Deighton's war fiction is *Goodbye Mickey Mouse*, published in 1982. Where *Bomber* dealt with a single (imaginary) day of an RAF bomber fleet attacking Germany, *Goodbye Mickey Mouse* narrows its focus in a quite different way. The novel focuses on a U.S. airbase in East Anglia, England, telling the story of a group of American fighter pilots flying missions over Germany in 1943–1944. The narrative is told from several points of view, though using a third-person voice. The key protagonists are Captain Jamie Farebrother, a self-assured pilot who is estranged from his father (a colonel); and the cocky lieutenant Mickey Morse, fast becoming America's leading flying ace, with whom Farebrother forges an unlikely friendship. In addition to the multiple points of view, the novel impressively explores the self-contained community of the U.S. airbase, and examines with Deighton's scrupulous historical accuracy the impact of the Americans on the local civilians in Britain. As much social history as military history, *Goodbye Mickey Mouse* is also a portrait of a romance, involving the far-reaching consequences of Farebrother's love affair with

Victoria Cooper, a passionate young Englishwoman who works for a Cambridgeshire newspaper. In his 2009 preface to *Goodbye Mickey Mouse*, Deighton concedes, "*Goodbye Mickey Mouse* is a love story. Almost every fiction book I have written is to some extent a love story; I suppose I must be some sort of closet romantic" (p. ix).

NONFICTION

Aside from espionage, Deighton's most frequent and significant topic as a writer is World War II. The two interests clearly overlap in novels such as *SS-GB*, while much of Deighton's espionage fiction explores the cold war as a development from the political and ideological conflicts of World War II. In addition to his significant body of work as a war novelist, Deighton has contributed several impressive entries in the field of military history. Perhaps inevitably, there are important parallels between Deighton's narrative technique and style as a novelist and as a historian. Equally, the meticulous research he conducts prior to writing each novel suggests the scholarly methods of the historian. Perhaps more than other writers, Deighton's practice as a writer transfers remarkably well from fiction to nonfiction. Deighton was originally encouraged to write a work of history by the prominent British historian A. J. P. Taylor, and the result was *Fighter: The True Story of the Battle of Britain* (1977). Perhaps Deighton's most compelling readable work of nonfiction, *Fighter* deploys the same gift for combining a broad historical viewpoint with detailed characterizations of individuals involved in combat that stood out in *Bomber*, his masterpiece of war fiction. *Fighter* traces the Battle of Britain as a crucial component of the Germans' Operation Sea Lion, the planned invasion of Great Britain by Hitler's Germany, which required aerial supremacy over Britain as an imperative: "the Luftwaffe had a specific task: it must reduce the RAF morally and physically to a state where it could not deliver any significant attack upon the invasion units" (p. 7).

An account of the political and military decisions (and errors of judgment) that determined the outcome of the decisive aerial battle between the RAF and the Luftwaffe in the summer of 1940, *Fighter* offers fascinating insights into the British development of radar under Hugh Dowding, and the rival development of the Messerschmitt Bf 109 fighter and the British Spitfire, a rivalry that proved central to the Battle of Britain. Dowding, a key figure—first on the Air Council in his work regarding supply and research, then as commanding officer for the RAF Fighter Command—helped to develop the use of radar and modern aircraft such as the Spitfire, arguably the two keys to British victory. In a telling passage, Deighton draws attention to the parallels between fiction and nonfiction in developing character:

> In March 1936, as the Spitfire prototype took to the air for the first time, and the radar he had nursed into being made rapid strides, Dowding ended his job as Member for Research and Development (the supply part of his original task had been given to another member of the Air Council). With a neatness usually only found in the pages of fiction, Dowding was now appointed to prepare these weapons and take them to war. This appointment, to Commander in Chief of Fighter Command, was not due to any friends that Dowding had in the Air Ministry. On the contrary, plans were afoot to deprive Dowding of the promotion to Chief of Air Staff which had already been promised to him.
>
> (p. 40)

One of the fascinating subplots of *Fighter*—indeed it seems quite novelistic in structure—relates to the ironic twists of fate by which Dowding—along with his colleague, the New Zealander Major Keith Park—are consistently opposed and ridiculed by those higher up in the British Air Ministry despite the proven success of their tactics. This culminates in their ritual humiliation and dismissal, following the victory of Britain. The scene depicts a betrayal that equals any from Deighton's spy fiction:

> As the air assault against England dwindled into harassing daylight attacks and a night offensive, the RAF High Command acted more vindictively against the two men who had succeeded than did Goring against the men who had failed. Dowding and Park had committed an unforgivable sin in the eyes of the Air Ministry and their other critics: they had proved their theories right. In a manner more appropriate to the already obvious failure of Bomber

Command than to the remarkable achievements of Fighter Command, the Air Ministry called a meeting to discuss the Battle.

> (pp. 224–225)

This passage reveals a scenario familiar to readers of Deighton: the maverick and insubordinate protagonists pitted against an intractable and incompetent higher administration, a confrontation that could be taken from *The Ipcress File* or *Game, Set, and Match*. Both the betrayal by one's bosses, and the punishment for defying authority, are persistent Deighton themes. Whether in writing history or fiction, Deighton's vision is relentlessly antiestablishment.

Another controversial aspect of Deighton's nonfiction—and one that also marks novels such as *Bomber*—is the balance between opposing points of view. Specifically, Deighton gives almost as much weight and attention to the German Luftwaffe at its efforts to defeat Britain's RAF as to the RAF's ultimately successful defense of Britain from the Nazis. Deighton's narrative technique weaves together perspectives from the highest military commanders of both sides, to the men actually doing the fighting in the air. In this sense, Deighton's subtitle, *The True Story of the Battle of Britain,* is both justified and misleading: the story is true in that it is balanced and based on accounts from numerous perspectives. Yet this very multiplicity of views indicates that there is no one "true" story.

Deighton has also given extended treatment to World War II in subsequent works: in particular, *Blitzkrieg* (1979), which examines the Wehrmacht's plans for the invasion of Europe and provides much detail of battle formations and military weapons. A particular focus of this narrative is the infighting among the German High Command, revealing Deighton's wider knowledge of the Nazi state. The validity of Deighton's historical account is vouched for by no less a figure than the highly placed German general Walther Nehring, who had been General Heinz Guderian's chief of staff during the conflict. Nehring endorses the accuracy of Deighton's accounts in a foreword to a 2007 edition of the volume. In 1993, Deighton published his most in-depth account of World War II,

Blood, Tears, and Folly. This volume examines the middle years of the war in extraordinary detail, combining firsthand personal accounts with Deighton's broad historical vision of the major global war of the twentieth century, tracing its consequences in the cold war and the postwar economic and political crises that accompanied it.

No survey of Deighton's nonfiction would be complete without mention of his contribution to popular culinary literature. A sly reference to Deighton's cooking expertise occurs at the beginning of the film of *The Ipcress File,* when one of Deighton's "Cookstrips" (originally published in the *Observer* newspaper) is shown pinned to Harry Palmer's wall. As this image suggests, Deighton's recipes were part of the swinging bachelor London scene of the 1960s, and in particular his *Action Cook Book* sought to bring a certain macho panache to the art of cookery. At a time when—in Britain and the United States—cooking expertise was often viewed as the exclusive domain of women, Deighton's cookbooks challenged this gender bias, and indeed one of Harry Palmer's distinguishing traits is his skill in the kitchen. The message was clear: part of a spy's repertoire was being proficient at making an omelet, as well as consuming vodka martinis. Deighton's skills as an illustrator are also on display, as the *Action Cook Book* contains distinctive black and white illustrations derived from his "Cookstrips." Another significant contribution of Deighton was to broaden the somewhat provincial culinary horizons of the British middle-class, by focusing on the art of French cookery, seen as the basis for all haute cuisine. His pioneering cookbook *Où est le garlic* (1965) succeeded in cutting through the intimidating mystique surrounding French cookery, in an unpretentious and practical style. The success of this book, following Deighton's early Harry Palmer spy novels, offers proof that Deighton's reputation was not limited to espionage and that his versatility as a writer was accepted by a wide public.

FILMS

Film has played a significant role in Deighton's career, particularly his career as a writer of espionage fiction. Indeed, it has been the films based on his novels, as much as his books themselves, that cemented Len Deighton in the popular consciousness, especially in Britain and the United States. In particular, the three groundbreaking films of the 1960s *The Ipcress File, Funeral in Berlin,* and *Billion Dollar Brain*—left an indelible mark on the spy film genre and challenged the supremacy of James Bond as cinema's most iconic spy. Though perhaps lacking the global recognition of Bond, Harry Palmer—played in unforgettable style by Michael Caine—is no less emblematic of the postwar spy film than Sean Connery's Bond. While the novel *The Ipcress File* was successful, it was the film version in 1965 that made "Harry Palmer," Len Deighton, and Michael Caine household names. As the film and television critic Wesley Britton remarks in his 2005 study of spy books and film, *Beyond Bond,*

> The movie version of *The Ipcress File* had a wide influence on the spy milieu. The production team, while headed by Bond coproducer Harry Saltzman, consciously tried to create an "anti-Bond" approach to the genre to avoid overt imitation. For example, Palmer was no globe-trotter. Although he was captured and apparently tortured in Albania, the setting was actually a fake and Palmer never left the boroughs of Westminster and London.
>
> (p. 131)

The parallels between the Harry Palmer films and Bond movies are intriguing: not only did Harry Saltzman produce both, but the second Harry Palmer entry, the 1966 film *Funeral in Berlin,* was directed by Guy Hamilton, who also directed *Goldfinger* (1964) and would later direct further Bond films, *Diamonds Are Forever* (1971) and *Live and Let Die* (1973). Moreover the films shared several other production figures with the Bond films, including John Barry (music), Ken Adams (sets), and Peter Hunt (editing). Despite the "anti-Bond" spirit of Deighton's novels, the films made Harry Palmer the leading cinematic rival to 007. With his working-class background, heavy National Health spectacles, and often unkempt appearance, Caine's Harry Palmer is a far more down-to-earth spy than Bond, whose first appearance onscreen was in an elegant casino, dressed in a tuxedo, in *Dr. No* (1962).

The third film in the Palmer series, *Billion Dollar Brain* in 1967, was directed by Ken Russell, one of Britain's most original and iconoclastic filmmakers, bringing a 1960s avant-garde sensibility to the spy story. Some of Deighton's other ventures into filmmaking have been less successful, however. The adaptations of *Spy Story* in 1976 and *Only When I Larf* in 1968 were disappointments at the box office, while his screen adaptation of the play *Oh! What a Lovely War*—despite a stellar cast and top director in Richard Attenborough—was not to Deighton's liking. Indeed he subsequently had his name removed from the credits to the 1969 film.

The most prominent television adaptation of Deighton's work was the twelve-part miniseries *Game, Set, and Match*, directed by Ken Grieve and Patrick Lau, with a screenplay by John Howlett. The series had an outstanding cast, including Ian Holm as Bernard Samson and Mel Martin as Fiona Samson—and was broadcast starting in October 1988 over twelve weekly episodes. Yet despite the fidelity of the adaptation to Deighton's best-selling novels, the miniseries failed to achieve the ratings that ITV—Britain's leading commercial channel—had expected. Copies of the miniseries on VHS or DVD are hard to find.

CONCLUSION

Len Deighton was one of the writers instrumental in transforming the British spy novel in the postwar period, from a genre based on adventure fantasy to a form of historical realism. In contrast to Ian Fleming, Deighton—from his first novel, *The Ipcress File*—sought to bring a gritty realism and working-class sensibility to the world of espionage: a world that had long been associated with the fantasy of the upper classes. The detailed social observation contained in Deighton's spy fiction establishes him as a realist as much as a popular entertainer, and to this extent classifying Deighton as a "spy novelist" is a distortion of his actual achievement. Deighton deserves reevaluation as one of the major British writers of the postwar period, a true polymath whose output includes fiction, history, and cookbooks, as well

as a significant body of work as a designer and illustrator. There are few writers of the twentieth and twenty-first centuries who can equal either the volume or the diversity of Deighton's output. All the more remarkable is that this volume and diversity are matched by a consistently high quality of literary prose, distinguished by impeccable research, telling social observation, and an underlying tone of ironic, frequently acerbic, humor. It is this combination of dense historical and technical research with a human perspective of the excitement, contradictions, and horrors inherent in war and espionage that distinguish Deighton's unique contribution to postwar British literature.

Selected Bibliography

WORKS OF LEN DEIGHTON

NOVELS AND STORIES

The Ipcress File. London: Hodder and Stoughton, 1962; paperback ed., London: HarperCollins, 2005. (Quotations in text are from the 2005 edition.)

Horse Under Water. London: Jonathan Cape, 1963; paperback ed., London: HarperCollins, 2009. (Quotations in text are from the 2009 edition.)

Funeral in Berlin. London: Jonathan Cape, 1964; paperback ed., London: HarperCollins, 2009. (Quotations in text are from the 2009 edition.)

Billion Dollar Brain. London: Jonathan Cape, 1966; paperback ed., London: HarperCollins, 2009. (Quotations in text are from the 2009 edition.)

An Expensive Place to Die. London: Jonathan Cape, 1967.

Only When I Larf. London: Michael Joseph, 1968.

Bomber: Events Relating to the Last Flight of an RAF Bomber over Germany on the Night of June 31st, 1943. London: Jonathan Cape, 1970; paperback ed., London: HarperCollins, 2009. (Quotations in text are from the 2009 edition.)

Declarations of War. London: Jonathan Cape, 1971.

Close-Up. London: Jonathan Cape, 1972.

Spy Story. London: Jonathan Cape, 1974.

Yesterday's Spy. London: Jonathan Cape, 1975.

Twinkle, Twinkle, Little Spy. London: Jonathan Cape, 1976. (Published in the United States as *Catch a Falling Spy*.)

SS-GB. London: Jonathan Cape, 1978; paperback ed.,

London: HarperCollins, 2009. (Quotations in text are from the 2009 edition.)

XPD. London: Hutchinson, 1981; paperback ed., London: HarperCollins, 2009. (Quotations in text are from the 2009 edition.)

Goodbye Mickey Mouse. London: Hutchinson, 1982.

Berlin Game. London: Hutchinson, 1983; New York: Knopf, 1984. (Quotations in text are from the 1984 Knopf edition.)

Mexico Set. London: Hutchinson, 1984; New York: Knopf, 1985.

London Match. London: Hutchinson, 1985; New York: Knopf, 1986.

Winter: A Berlin Family 1899–1945. London: Hutchinson, 1987; New York: Knopf, 1988.

Spy Hook. London: Century Hutchinson, 1988.

Spy Line. London: Century Hutchinson, 1989.

Spy Sinker. London: Century Hutchinson, 1990.

MAMista. London: Century Hutchinson, 1991.

City of Gold. London: Century Hutchinson, 1992.

Violent Ward. London: HarperCollins, 1993.

Faith. London: HarperCollins, 1994.

Hope. London: HarperCollins, 1995.

Charity. London: HarperCollins, 1996.

"Sherlock Holmes and the Titanic Swindle." In *The Verdict of Us All*. Edited by Peter Lovesey. London: Allison & Busby, 2006. (Novella.)

NONFICTION

Len Deighton's Action Cook Book. London: Jonathan Cape, 1965. Rerelease, London: HarperCollins, 2009.

Où est le garlic; or, Len Deighton's French Cook Book. London: Penguin, 1965.

The Assassination of President Kennedy. Compiled and edited by Michael Rand, Howard Loxton, and Len Deighton. London: Jonathan Cape, 1963.

Len Deighton's London Dossier. Compiled and annotated by Len Deighton. London: Jonathan Cape, in association with Penguin, 1967.

Len Deighton's Continental Dossier. Compiled by Victor and Margaret Pettitt. London: Michael Joseph, in association with Wylton Dickson, 1968.

Fighter: The True Story of the Battle of Britain. London: Jonathan Cape, 1977; London: Vintage, 2008. (Quotations in text are from the 2008 edition.)

Airshipwreck. With Arnold Schwartzman. London: Jonathan Cape, 1978.

Basic French Cooking. Rev. and enl. from *Où est le garlic*. London: Jonathan Cape, 1979.

Blitzkrieg: From the Rise of Hitler to the Fall of Dunkirk. London: Jonathan Cape, 1979; London: Pimlico, 2007. (Quotations in text are from the 2007 edition.)

Battle of Britain. London: Jonathan Cape, 1980.

The Orient Flight LZ 127–Graf Zeppelin. With Fred. F. Blau. Westminster, Md.: German Philatelic Society, 1980.

The Egypt Flight LZ 127–Graf Zeppelin. With Fred. F. Blau. Westminster, Md.: German Philatelic Society, 1981.

ABC of French Food. London: Century, 1989.

Basic French Cookery Course. London: Century Hutchinson, 1990.

Blood, Tears, and Folly: In the Darkest Hour of the Second World War. London: Jonathan Cape, 1993. Reprinted as *Blood, Tears, and Folly: An Objective Look at World War II*. London: Vintage, 2007.

UNCREDITED SCREENPLAYS BY DEIGHTON

From Russia with Love. Early screenplay drafts by Deighton. EON, 1963.

Oh! What a Lovely War. Screenplay by Deighton. Directed by Richard Attenborough. Accord, U.K., 1969.

Never Say Never Again. Early screenplay drafts by Deighton. PSO, 1983.

FILMS AND TELEVISION ADAPTATIONS BASED ON DEIGHTON'S WORK

The Ipcress File. Screenplay by Bill Canaway and James Doran. Directed by Sidney J. Furie. Steven/Lowndes, 1965.

Billion Dollar Brain. Screenplay by John McGrath. Directed by Ken Russell. Lowndes Productions, 1967.

Funeral in Berlin. Screenplay by Evan Jones. Directed by Guy Hamilton. Lowdes Productions, 1966.

Only When I Larf. Screenplay by John Salmon. Directed by Basil Dearden. Beecord, 1968.

Spy Story. Directed by Lindsay Shontoff. Lindsay Shonteff Productions, 1976.

Game, Set, and Match. Directed by Ken Grieve and Patrick Lau. 12 episodes. Granada Television, 1988.

CRITICAL AND BIOGRAPHICAL STUDIES

Banks, Jeff, and Harry D. Dawson. "The Len Deighton Series." *Mystery Fancier* 3, no. 1:10–13 (1979).

Britton, Wesley. "From George Smiley to Bernard Samson: The Counter-Fleming Movement." *Beyond Bond: Spies in Fiction and Film*. Westport, Conn.: Prager, 2005. Pp. 123–145.

Brown, Geoffrey. "Len Deighton's Non-Fiction." *Book and Magazine Collector*, January 1991, pp. 4–10.

Denning, Michael. *Cover Stories: Narrative and Ideology in the British Spy Thriller*. London: Routledge & Kegan Paul, 1987.

Erisman, Fred. "Romantic Reality in the Spy Stories of Len Deighton." *Armchair Detective* 10:101–105 (April 1977).

Fitzgibbon, Constantine: "Len Deighton's Cold New View." *Spectator*, April 8, 1972, p. 546.

Gardner, Colin. "From Mimicry to Mockery: Cold War Hybridity in Evan Jones's *The Damned, Modesty Blaise,* and *Funeral in Berlin.*" *Media History* 12, no. 2:177–191 (2006).

Gwilliam, Graham, and Crispin Jackson. "Len Deighton: The Master Thriller Writer Turns Seventy." *Book and Magazine Collector*, March 1999, pp. 4–14.

Jones, Dudley. "The Great Game? The Spy Fiction of Len Deighton." *Spy Thrillers: From Buchan to Le Carré.* Edited by Clive Bloom. New York: St. Martin's, 1990. Pp. 100–112.

Kamm, Jurgen. "The Berlin Wall and Cold-War Espionage: Visions of a Divided Germany in the Novels of Len Deighton." In *The Berlin Wall: Representations and Perspectives.* Edited by Ernst Schurer, Manfred Keune, and Philip Jenkins. New York: Peter Lang, 1996. Pp. 61–73.

Lense, Edward. "They've Taken Away Your Name: Identity and Illusion in Len Deighton's Early Novels.*" Clues: A Journal of Detection* 12, no. 2:67–81 (1991).

Masters, Anthony. *Literary Agents: The Novelist as Spy.* Oxford: Blackwell, 1987.

Mews, Siegfreid. "The Spies Are Coming In from the Cold War: The Berlin Wall in the Espionage Novel." In *The Berlin Wall: Representations and Perspectives.* Edited by Ernst Schurer, Manfred Keune, and Philip Jenkins. New York: Peter Lang, 1996. Pp. 50–60.

Sauerberg, Lars. "Literature in Figures: An Essay on the Popularity of Thrillers." *International Review of Literary Studies* 38, no. 2:93–107 (1983).

———. *Secret Agents in Fiction: Ian Fleming, John le Carré, and Len Deighton.* New York: St. Martin's, 1984.

INTERVIEWS

Bragg, Melvyn: "Len Deighton: 'The Most Hard-Working Writer I've Met.'" *Listener*, December 22–29, 1977, p. 859.

Milward-Oliver, Edward. Interview with Len Deighton. In *The Len Deighton Companion.* London: Grafton, 1987. Pp. 11–25.

See, Lisa. Interview with Len Deighton. In *Writing for Your Life #2.* Edited by Sybil Steinberg. Wainscott, N.Y.: Pushcart Press, 1995. Pp. 55–60.

BIBLIOGRAPHIES AND COMPANIONS

Milward-Oliver, Edward. *Len Deighton: An Annotated Bibliography, 1954–1985.* Maidstone, U.K.: Sammler Press, 1985.

———. *The Len Deighton Companion.* London: Grafton, 1987.

CAROL ANN DUFFY

(1955—)

Nissa Parmar

THE AUTHOR CAROL Ann Duffy and her work are remarkable on a variety of fronts. Duffy has been the poet laureate of Great Britain since 2009, and her appointment to the position is especially notable as she is the first woman, the first Scot, and the first openly gay person to occupy the distinguished role. All of these firsts are particularly suggestive given that she is also the first British poet laureate of the twenty-first century. Her selection strongly indicates a new direction for British poetry, whose history has long been dominated by male writers possessing elite educational backgrounds and typically associated with conservative poetic traditions.

Despite the catalog of firsts, Duffy's appointment caused little of the controversy that might be anticipated by the breaking of so much new ground. If anything, many observers found it long overdue. She had also been nominated for the role in 1999 but was passed over in favor of Andrew Motion, an Oxford-educated poet who typifies the male-dominated tradition of British poetry. Some media sources suggested that Duffy's gender and mixed-race lesbian relationship with the prominent Scottish poet Jackie Kay might have made her appointment too controversial. However, Duffy's acclaim only grew as a result of being passed over initially.

By the time Motion stepped down from the role, Duffy, who had been proclaimed "the most popular living poet in Britain" in 2005 by the widely read British newspaper the *Guardian* (John Mullan, para. 11), was a clear favorite to take his place. Duffy's popularity is the result of her relatively rare (in contemporary poetry) ability to garner critical recognition while appealing to a broad audience of readers. She has received a lengthy list of prestigious awards both at home and abroad, and her poetry is part of the curriculum of many universities and secondary schools in the United Kingdom.

Her simultaneous critical and popular appeal highlights another feature of the poet's work—its contradictions, which have generated varied critical interpretations of work. However, these contradictions also enable Duffy and her poetry to act as bridge between diverse poetic audiences, high and popular culture, the personal and the political, and, most significantly, Great Britain's poetic past and its future.

Duffy was born on December 23, 1955, in Glasgow, Scotland, to Frank and May Duffy (formerly May Black), both of Irish descent. They moved to Stafford, England, when Duffy was seven. The poet would later explore her childhood emigration from Scotland to England in the collection *The Other Country* (1990). In England, her father worked for English Electric and was a member of his trade union, eventually entering local politics as a representative for the Labour Party. In his spare time, he coached a semiprofessional soccer team.

Duffy was raised as a Catholic and her religious background is evident in poems such as "Confession," which presents a critical view of the church. Though no longer conventionally religious, in various poems and interviews she has suggested that poetry might serve as an alternative to religion, observing, "poetry and prayer are very similar" (interview with Hephzibah Anderson, para. 16). The poet identifies herself as coming from a working-class background and both details and characters derived from this background frequently occur in her writing, bringing a largely unwritten about sector of the British population into the country's poetic mainstream.

In her early teens, Duffy realized that she wished to be a poet and pursued her goal ambitiously. She published her first small collection, the pamphlet *Fleshweathercock* (1973), by her late teens, although she now considers that book to be embarrassing early juvenilia. She attended college at Liverpool University, where she studied philosophy and became immersed in the Liverpool poetry scene. "Liverpool poetry," which experienced its height during the 1960s and 1970s, has had a significant and lasting impact on Duffy's writing. The scene was youth-oriented and informed by the Beat poetry scene of the United States and the work of its notables like Allen Ginsberg. It was democratic and held itself in opposition to the poetry establishment, blending popular and working-class culture with less accessible European-derived artistic movements like surrealism and symbolism. The Liverpool Poets presented their work in live performances that both they and their audiences considered on par with attendance of a pop music concert, emphasizing the entertainment value of poetry over its connections with academia and tradition.

Many of the Liverpool Poets were also musicians or artists. Some incorporated music into their poetic performances. Others, like Adrian Henri, who was one of the leaders of the scene, were visual artists whose writing and art were mutually informing and sometimes blended. Duffy and Henri lived together in Liverpool and collaboratively wrote Duffy's next pamphlet, *Beauty and the Beast* (1977). The collection is a poetic retelling of the fairy tale, which revises the ending to question the dichotomy between the beautiful and the beastly as well as the traditional depiction of gender roles in its namesake and other well-known fairy tales. Such a re-vision of traditional myths, fairy tales, and archetypes was a significant poetic strategy of the writers of the first wave of American feminism, who would also have a substantial impact on Duffy's writing.

"Re-vision" is, in fact, a term coined by the American feminist poet and cultural critic Adrienne Rich to describe the process of reviewing mythology and literature in order to rewrite it or write against longstanding cultural archetypes and stereotypes perpetuated through patriarchal literary traditions. Duffy's next pamphlet, *Fifth Last Song* (1982), is subtitled *Twenty-one Love Poems*, which is widely read as an allusion to Rich's small but groundbreaking collection of lesbian love poetry, *Twenty-one Love Poems* (1977). The collection was included at the heart of *The Dream of a Common Language* (1978), the apex of Rich's feminist poetry. However, Duffy's pamphlet is not particularly feminist in nature, and the poet herself has been ambivalent about the labeling associated with feminism through much of her career. In a 1988 interview, she explained, "I don't mind being called a feminist poet, but I wouldn't mind if I wasn't … I have never in my life sat down and thought 'I will write a feminist poem'" (McAllister, p. 7). However, the feminist strategy of rewriting fairy tales and myths would continue through her work, eventually culminating in an entire collection, *The World's Wife* (1999), which is part of what has been described as the overtly feminist phase of her career.

Duffy's ambivalence about being categorized as a "feminist" poet was possibly fostered by the difficulty of achieving success as a female poet in the male-dominated world of British poetry. The climate of this world was demonstrated by the less-than-flattering reaction of the prominent *Poetry Review*, the magazine published by the Poetry Society, in 1983 when Duffy won first prize for her poem "Whoever She Was" in the society's National Poetry Competition. The critic and poet Deryn Rees-Jones suggests the reaction of the magazine reflected its deference to traditional poetry and "is evidence also of the fact that the idea of a woman both being a poet and winning a competition was still a new phenomenon" (*Carol Ann Duffy*, p. 9). Duffy herself has suggested the poetry scene of her early career was not female friendly. During that period she found the traditionally inclined, older generation of male poets patronizing and was referred to as a poetess, a trivializing and old-fashioned designation for a female poet. With its feminine focus and surrealist elements, Duffy's "Whoever She Was"—whose speaker struggles with her identity after her children have gone—was quite different in both style and subject from the work of the previous generation of poets.

The poem was eventually published in *Standing Female Nude* (1985), Duffy's first full-length adult collection. She considers preceding pamphlets part of her juvenilia. However, all of the early works, especially those written under the Liverpool Poets' influence, would be critical in the development of her unique voice and aesthetic.

Through the rest of the 1980s and 1990s, Duffy evolved into a very public and very active poet, although she largely kept her personal life out of both her poetry and the press. In addition to gaining renown for performances of her own work, she published collections regularly, participated in various residencies, visited schools, worked with younger poets through Arvon Foundation courses, acted as the *Guardian* newspaper's poetry critic for a year, and won numerous awards. She also published in other genres and presented her work in various media. Duffy wrote a handful of plays, including *Take My Husband* (1982) and *Cavern of Dreams* (1984), which were both performed at the Liverpool Playhouse; *Loss*, first broadcast by BBC radio in 1986; and *Little Women, Big Boys*, first produced at the Almeida Theatre in London in 1986.

Carrying on in the tradition of the Liverpool Poets, Duffy has also continued to blend media. She has participated in various projects with links to the visual arts. The poem "Woman Seated on the Underground, 1941" was commissioned by the Tate Gallery and corresponds with the artist Henri Moore's drawings, while "Poem in Oils" was commissioned by John Willett for the Horsfield Exhibition in Dieppe, France. Both poems were republished in *Standing Female Nude*. In June 2010 Duffy co-curated an exhibition with the Tate Liverpool art museum titled *The Sculpture of Language*, which explores the way visual artists engage language. She also created a new sonnet for the exhibition. The poem, titled "POETRY," is presented interactively, allowing visitors to manipulate its words and participate in the poem's ongoing process of creation.

She has also brought her poetic prowess to musical ventures. Duffy translated the librettos of Mozart's *The Magic Flute* into English for Opera North (2003), furnished the lyrics for *Rapture*, a jazz album by Eliana Tomkins (2005), and created "The Manchester Carols" (2007), a musical retelling of the Christmas story for twenty-first-century audiences, with the composer Sasha Johnson Manning.

Duffy has a variety of editorial credits to her name as well. Two notable examples are *Answering Back: Living Poets Reply to the Poetry of the Past* (2007), for which Duffy invited contemporary poets to select a poem from the past and create a poem in response to it, and *I Wouldn't Thank You for a Valentine* (1992), an illustrated anthology created for young adult readers. The anthology represents an early example of Duffy's interest in children's literature, a genre she has written in increasingly since the birth of her daughter, Ella, in 1995. Since the start of the new millennium, she has produced a considerable volume of illustrated books and poetry for children. Duffy's forays across genres and media have gained her access to wider and wider audiences as well as the moniker "the superstar" of British poetry. While her work in other genres might have enhanced her notoriety, she is best known for her adult poetry and for being one of the preeminent voices of contemporary British poetry.

Duffy is widely considered a major voice and influence among what has been deemed the "New Generation" of British poetry. The group of poets described by this moniker is usually linked to the anthology *The New Poetry* (1993), the first major anthology of British and Irish poetry of the 1980s and 1990s. The anthology was controversial but significant, becoming a best seller and part of the curriculum in high schools and universities of Britain. The poetics of the New Generation is variously praised and derided, oftentimes for the very same qualities. Some feel the poetry is too evolved toward performance and therefore too accessible and too comedic in its leanings. While these critics see this poetic appraoch as too broad, others label this quality democratic and praise its wit and humor. Some opine the lack of the "universal" in the poetry, while others praise its diversity of voices. Duffy's own work has received parallel critical commentary.

In addition to the mixed reviews she has received in common with the New Generation poetry, Duffy's work has also been read in often contradictory ways. She is frequently identified as a postmodernist but is also linked with T. S. Eliot, the representative poet of high modernism, whom she once cited as a favorite poet. Her work has drawn comparisons to Philip Larkin, who is known for his traditional British style and use of conventional form, yet she has also been identified as his antithesis. Duffy herself sees the poet Larkin as the leader of the previous generation of poets, which she calls "the Larkin generation" and links with patriarchal values. Not surprisingly, given the comparisons to Larkin, she is considered a traditionalist; however, her work has also been deemed experimental by critics like Linda Kinnahan.

This apparent dichotomy of critical interpretations likely originates from the disparity between Duffy's use of traditional form and her novel themes and subjects. The poet frequently employs the lyric, the dramatic monologue, and the sonnet. The dramatic monologue, the form with which Duffy is most commonly associated, has a substantial British tradition in the work of Alfred Lord Tennyson, who helped to refine the form and spread its popularity during the Victorian era. Robert Browning and T. S. Eliot, an American expatriate to Britain, are also recognized for their work with it. The dramatic monologue has additionally proven an appealing vehicle for female poets since the Victorian era, allowing them to adopt voices other than their own and thereby negotiate and highlight the difficulties of writing as women in a male-dominated literary genre. Duffy has typically used the dramatic monologue to introduce voices either unexpected or underrepresented in poetry.

STANDING FEMALE NUDE

Duffy's first full-length adult poetry collection, *Standing Female Nude* (1985), came out to good reviews. Many of its poems are dramatic mono-

logues that present voices and perspectives not commonly found in British poetry, which has privileged the "universal" perspective associated with white, educated, male experience. Duffy does not aim for the idealized, and her speakers often expose harsh realities and even disturbing perspectives like that of the young violent youth in "Education for Leisure." These gritty and unflinching points of view are why her early work has been deemed social realist.

The plurality of Duffy's speakers reflects both her own working-class background and the dramatic shift in British culture that occurred as she was growing up. In the decades of the 1950s through the 1970s, the British government solicited emigration to meet the nation's labor force needs, introducing large numbers of Caribbean, Indian, and Pakistani citizens to the United Kingdom. Duffy's mother was herself a first-generation Irish immigrant to Scotland, and her entire family immigrated to England while Duffy was a girl. Duffy's personal experience as an immigrant and her upbringing concurrent with the introduction of new citizens and cultures to the United Kingdom likely contributed to her interest in voices outside the cultural mainstream.

Some of these voices are represented in "Comprehensive," a poem that presents a different speaker in each of its seven stanzas. The title refers to a comprehensive school, the British equivalent of an open-enrollment public high school or middle school, but it also suggests that the diversity of the young adult voices of the poem will provide a complete and inclusive or comprehensive depiction of its students. Some critics also read the poem as a challenge to the idea of comprehensive education, the one-size-fits-all model of many British public schools. A few of the speakers include an African immigrant, a white racist boy likely to end up on welfare, a Muslim girl, and an immigrant from India.

Some of themes of "Comprehensive" are further explored in "Head of English," which also has a school setting but is spoken by the lead teacher of English at a girls' school. The teacher describes the visit of a poet, who could very well be Duffy, given her school visits and residencies. The voice of the speaker reflects the conservative tradition of British poetry and its prominent role in school curriculum. The teacher's identification with the conservative past of English poetry is evident when she laments, "for not all poems, sadly, rhyme these days" and quotes the opening words, "Season of the mists" (p. 12), of the renowned English poet John Keat's (1795–1821) famous ode "To Autumn." She also teaches Rudyard Kipling (1865–1936), another long-popular British author. Because his works have been criticized for their decidedly colonial and imperialist perspectives, teaching Kipling to a class with English-as-a-second-language students, who would likely be from former British colonies depicted in his works, seems an insensitive and old-fashioned choice. Further demonstrating an unwillingness to change with the times and consider a contemporary poetry more reflective of the diverse readers and students of Great Britain, she tells students to open a window at the back of the room because, "We don't / want winds of change about the place" (p. 12).

The teacher comments that the visiting poet's work provides "insight to an outside view" (p. 12) and, once the presentation has finished, dismisses herself from the poet's presence, suggesting a dismissal of the poet's view and poetics. Effectively, the "head of English" and the poetic and academic tradition she represents conflate the perspective of educated, upper-class, white male writers like Keats and Kipling with the universal or inside view, while the socially reflective and contemporary female viewpoint of Duffy and the mixed-age, cultural, and economic perspectives of the speakers of her dramatic monologues like "Comprehensive" are "outside" views.

Despite Duffy's ambivalence toward using the term to define her poetry, it is difficult not to read the some of these outsider views as feminist. "A Clear Note" features three female speakers each representing a different generation of an Irish family that has immigrated to Scotland. In addition to this detail in common with Duffy's own family history, the second speaker has four sons and one daughter like Duffy's own mother. The poem highlights the sacrifices made by the grandmother and mother for their husbands and children. It exposes the difficulty, or "impossible seas," of the first two generations of women, including the gender-enforced silent suffering of the grandmother and the closeted power of the mother. However, it also highlights the strong female bonds between the three generations of women.

The granddaughter's monologue significantly suggests a change from the cycles of the past. She says of her generation of women, "For we swim with ease in all / possible seas and do not forget them" (p. 31). The line emphasizes the ambiguity of Duffy's feminism. On the one hand, the poem is designed to present the voices of women, the "them" of the line above, who have been overlooked by the literature and history of their time—a definite feminist strategy. However, the idea that the daughter is easily able to swim in "all possible seas" suggests a postfeminist idealism in which the struggles women faced in the past have disappeared and been replaced with ease and opportunity.

Another significant component of the poem is the use of the moon, which would become a recurring motif in Duffy's writing. In classical literature, the moon is typically associated with the feminine and female goddesses. It is also linked with the tides and change. In this poem, the grandmother of the first monologue wants the moon, a play on the colloquial expression for asking for the impossible, and says to her granddaughter, "one day / you must tell them I wanted the moon" (p. 28). The granddaughter, who might be read as Duffy, presents it to her in the final line of the poem. This symbolic closing reflects the way the poem itself fulfils the granddaughter's promise to not forget the women of the past and to share her grandmother's story. It further emphasizes the idea that the tides have changed, and the roles and opportunities available to women have altered.

"Standing Female Nude," the title poem of the collection, is written from a feminist perspective and addresses the historic absence of women's voices in the arts. The dramatic monologue presents the voice of an artist's model who turns the gaze of the artist and the arts consumer back on themselves. The situation of the poem is traditional, but its perspective is not. It depicts a male artist identified as Georges and a "genius," and thought by a number of critics to be Georges Braque, a significant modernist painter known for developing cubism with Picasso. He is painting a female model, who is of disadvantaged socioeconomic status and works as both an artist's model and a prostitute. By giving the model a voice, the poem makes her into a subject rather than a mere object to be transformed by the artist into "volume" and "space" (p. 46) for consumption by the public.

In the poem, the details of the model's life as well as the story behind the painting in progress are examined. Though both the artist and model are poor, he is concerned with his art while she is concerned with a more basic need, her next meal. When she asks him why he paints he answers, "Because / I have to. There's no choice. Don't talk" (p. 46). The lines suggest an idealized notion of art as a transaction between a higher creative force, sometimes identified as the Muse, and its chosen receptacle, the genius artist. Simultaneously, they emphasize the limited role his actual muse or subject has in this exchange, indicated when he silences her. However, the speaker's explanation of how the "image of a river-whore"—herself—will be "analytically" hung in a museum to be admired by "the bourgeoisie" (p. 46) suggests that art is as much about economics, social class, and perception as it is about inspiration and genius.

The finished painting will have nothing to do with the actual life of its model; thus, through her speaker, the poet makes an acerbic comment on art that is disconnected from social reality, which is opposite to the kind of art or poetry she herself produces. The painter's response to the model's question causes her to smile; it is clearly ironic to her. As a woman coming from an underprivileged socioeconomic background, the person who truly has "no choice" in this equation or social transaction is not the artist but the model who is working to feed herself. The disconnection of the artist and artwork from her social reality is emphasized in her final comment and the last line of the poem, "It does not look like me." While this might be literally true once she has been transformed through Braque's cubist ap-proach, it is, moreover, a comment that reemphasizes the idea that the art is not reflective of its subject's life nor is it a cultural product to which she can relate. This is of course in contrast to Duffy's own art, which conscientiously features the voices and lives of subjects from a variety of socioeconomic and cultural backgrounds and is accessibly and engagingly written.

SELLING MANHATTAN

Duffy's next collection, *Selling Manhattan* (1987), continued in much the same vein as her first. Dramatic monologues and diverse voices dominate the poems as Duffy explores the theme of foreignness. In some instances, "foreign" constitutes voices and subjects not traditional to poetry, like the serial murderer–rapist of "Psychopath," who could be the adult version of the young violent speaker of *Standing Female Nude's* "Education for Leisure" or the man forced through police brutality to confess to a crime he did not commit in "Yes, Officer."

In "Foreign," Duffy addresses more conventional concepts of the term but adopts a different poetic strategy. Rather than a dramatic monologue, the speaker of the poem is ambiguous, possibly the poet herself, and uses a second-person voice in order to speak directly to readers. The speaker demands that they "imagine" the experiences of an immigrant struggling to maintain his or her native tongue while learning the language of a new country, negotiating a new currency, and dealing with hate crimes. The title of the poem is double entendre. While the experiences of the immigrant in his or her new country might be foreign, an empathetic reflection on immigrant experience is likely equally foreign to many of the poem's readers.

In the title poem, "Selling Manhattan," Duffy again employs dramatic monologue. The title of the poem refers to the sale of the island of Manhattan by its Native American inhabitants to Dutch traders in 1626. There are a variety of historical anecdotes surrounding this event. The one the first speaker of the poem, the white trader, provides is that the island was purchased for "*twenty-four bucks' worth of glass beads*" and "*gaudy cloth*" (p. 34). From his language, it is clear the trader is from a more contemporary time than the actual historic event. While his language seems chronologically mixed, it suggests overall the speech of a rural white Southerner of limited education. The speaker of the majority of the poem is a Native American who also seems to be speaking from a more contemporary period. The development of both voices of the poem relies heavily on cliché and stereotype. While the poem is meant to be empathetic to the Native American speaker and is based on the 1988 collection *Touch the Earth: A Self-Portrait of Indian Existence,* edited by T. C. McLuhan (according to the acknowledgments at the start of the collection), it jumbles diverse aspects of distinct Native American cultures together. For example, the primary speaker is linked with salmon and buffalo, animals associated with two other regions of the United States and tribes far distant geographically and culturally from the Lenape tribe involved in the selling of Manhattan.

The poem is designed to privilege the voice of the Native American, who has substantially more stanzas and a more eloquent speaking style, and thereby interrogate the cultural values behind colonization and capitalism. However, it highlights what might be judged a fault of Duffy's first two mature collections: the use of dramatic monologue to give voice to experiences and persons that are, in this case especially, foreign to her. In this poem, the poet crosses the border from inclusiveness to appropriation. While the poem does attempt to vilify the trader and revere the Native American speaker's perspective and way of life, the poem relies on romantic and reductive clichés and a homogenizing of Native American experience and history.

The collection also features a series of love poems that examine both love and communication and anticipate her later collection of love poetry, *Rapture* (2005). In all of the poems, the lovers are separated and forced to conduct their relationship through various media. In the first, "Postcards," a third-person speaker narrates the love that blossoms through a series of postcards.

The artwork depicted on each card is as significant to the recipient as the brief written notes. "Correspondents" is a dramatic monologue whose speakers are participants in an illicit affair conducted entirely through letters and fantasy. The constraints of their actual lives—both are married, and they have different racial backgrounds—intensify the pleasure of the affair, which is forbidden according to social mores. "Telegrams" is also a correspondence between two lovers. Written in short phrases with the stopped endings and capital letters of an actual telegram, the two are unable to communicate clearly and the relationship falls apart by the poem's end. The final poem of the series records an attempted phone call of which little is revealed to the reader. All of the love poems highlight separation, a theme carried through the rest of the collection and linked with the theme of foreignness in poems like "Deportation."

THE OTHER COUNTRY

Her next collection, *The Other Country* (1990), offers a more refined and complex negotiation of the foreigner and outsider experience. In addition to giving voice to the voiceless in poetry, Duffy explores and connects various manifestations of what it means to be an outsider or foreigner, including her own personal experience. The collection opens with "Originally," a lyric poem that depicts Duffy's childhood move from Scotland to England. Because of the move, the speaker "lost a river, culture, speech, sense of first space / and the right place" (p. 7). However, that is not all she has lost, for "All childhood is an emigration" (p. 7). The details of lost language and place are those Duffy has in common with the emigrant voices in the monologues of the first two collections. The other losses depicted in the poem are those that occur as any child transitions to adulthood and out of the familiarity of his or her unique family culture to deal with the demands and social mores of broader society. The poem presents the experience of being an emigrant from one country to another and thereby both becoming and experiencing the foreign as they are commonly understood. It also overlaps this experience with another type of emigration, the move from childhood to adulthood. Linking these experiences makes the poem truly inclusive. All readers can relate to cultural changes involved in entering the foreign world of adulthood. Rather than simply giving voice to a variety of experiences, Duffy builds bridges to identify common experiences among the diverse readers of British society.

"Translating the English, 1989" presents complex questions about who and what define culture. In the poem, an outsider or emigrant voice attempts to characterize or translate mainstream British culture to visitors to the country. The title is followed by a quoted epigraph, "… and much of the poetry, alas, is lost in translation …," which establishes the ironic tone of the poem. One can almost imagine the speaker as a cab driver addressing visitors recently arrived from the airport. The grammatical structure of the speaker's language—for example the verb phrases "we are liking" and "we can be talking"—suggests that English is not his or her first language or that the English is in a dialect not traditional to England and the speaker has likely immigrated to the country. However, the speaker clearly views herself or himself as English, as the poem enthusiastically opens, "Welcome to my country!" (p. 11). Despite the English identification, the speaker's point of view might be considered "outsider" and therefore there is another level of translation occurring in the poem as the speaker attempts to discern what might be considered common or representative features of English culture.

The epigraph might also allude to the poem's form, which is effectively a free-verse barrage of phrases and items that would not be described as poetic by the average reader. Some of the phrases and items are associated with traditional British culture and tourism like "Daffodils," "Wordsworth," "Fish and chips," and "Queen Mum" (p. 11). These are interspersed with less-attractive realities of the society, "Vagrants," "the football hooligan," and "ten pint and plenty rape" (p. 11), a reference to the country's drinking culture and related social problems. Other phrases refer to

popular culture, like the tabloid newspaper *The Sun* and the television talk-show host Terry Wogan. The range of references and the style of the poem suggest various discourses—for example, literary, tourist-oriented, and popular media—which each present competing and often clashing views of English culture.

Some critics link the speaker's references to money—for example, "All this can be arranged for cash no questions" (p. 11)—to a commodification of Britain's culture and history and suggest that the poem is meant to comment on the consumerism-driven culture that evolved during the 1980s under Prime Minister Margaret Thatcher's leadership. Such critics see the short sentences as media-speak designed to parody the tabloid press and reflect on the nonrepresentational status of language. According to either interpretation, the provocative poem requires the reader to consider this translation of the country's culture in relation to his or her own experience or version of what defines it.

"Poet for Our Times" focuses specifically on the media. The title is intended to be ironic, because the speaker of this dramatic monologue is actually a writer for a tabloid-style "daily paper" and not a poet at all. However, the title phrase has become a moniker for Duffy as well. The speaker's high regard for his own attention-grabbing, "inches high" headlines, which he equates to "punchy haikus" (p. 15), is satirical. At the same time, the poem makes a serious comment on the status and survival of poetry in a contemporary culture dominated by competing media in which news and information are dumbed down into quickly consumable sound bites accompanied with a serving of sex. For example, the fourth stanza refers to the topless models found on "page three" in British tabloid papers. The poem's final line is a mishmash of phrases: "The instant tits and bottom line of art." It indicates that the sort of instant gratification provided by this type of media is what sells, but it might also offer a broader commentary on the dominantly male viewpoint and values of both media and capitalism.

Many aspects of the approach used by the journalist and self-proclaimed "poet for our

CAROL ANN DUFFY

times" are the very same for which Duffy has been criticized. Her work has been described as "journalistic poetics" and prose that is merely passed off as poetry, not unlike the writer's headlines, which he claims are haikus. Duffy's style has also been called "slapdash" and her poetry too facile. Some critics suggest that her work does not require a second reading or prolonged engagement—like the headlines for the stories in the paper in "Poet for Our Times"

Despite what some might consider commonalities between Duffy's work and mainstream media, the poem serves as a critique of a competing type of cultural discourse and also acts as a defense of her own work. In the fourth stanza, the speaker laments his era and yearns for "the sense of panic / you got a few years back" (p. 15), a period prior to the competing medium of television, which he believes was truly conducive to writing great headlines. This observation is a reworking of the suggestion by Britain's famous expatriate poet W. H. Auden that "every poet under fifty-five cherishes ... a secret grudge against Providence for not getting him born a little earlier" (from his foreword to Adrienne Rich's first collection, the 1951 volume *A Change of World*).

Auden was referring to the historic advantages of being a poet during the pinnacle of modernism, the same period the newsman longs for, as indicated with his wish to have been around when the *Titanic* sunk. With the poem and the Auden reference, Duffy seems to be suggesting to her critics, who might be looking to the poetry of a different era as a standard by which to judge more contemporary works, that times have changed and therefore poetry must also. This notion is emphasized with her prepositional shift in the title. Rather than a "poet of our time," which was perhaps an accomplishable task during the more culturally uniform modernist period, the contemporary writer will be a "poet for our times." As a poet for our times, the writer must compete and negotiate a wide variety of media and types of discourse. Additionally, she or he cannot hope to reflect the entire era but rather must be part of a plurality of poetic perspectives and voices.

MEAN TIME

Duffy's next collection, *Mean Time* (1993), won the Forward Poetry Prize and the Whitbread Poetry Award. Like *The Other Country*, it includes biographical elements. The collection, particularly the first half, is focused on the themes of time and memory, which also occur in the previous volume, particularly as related to childhood. Those themes are also a notable aspect of the work of her predecessor the popular British poet William Wordsworth (1770–1850). While Wordsworth fondly reflected on boyhood in his poems, however, Duffy's reflections are not idealized or romanticized. For example, "Stafford Afternoons" is a lyric poem from a first-person speaker, likely Duffy, who recounts running into the woods as a young girl and encountering a man who exposes himself to her; the girl narrowly escapes molestation.

The collection's title is suggestive of the bittersweet nature of memory and time. *Mean Time* can be heard as the word "meantime" broken apart to indicate mean or hard times. It can also suggest a waiting period, things done in limbo or in between significant events. Finally, "mean" is also a mathematical term for average, a meaning that reflects the way this collection aims more toward the universal than her previous works. As Duffy explains, "The events in the poem can happen to the average man or woman" (*Poetry Society Review*, p. 111). While the collection still contains dramatic monologues, they are less prevalent and less conspicuously from outsider voices. Instead, the volume features a number of lyric poems utilizing a second-person voice to address or draw the reader into the work, as in "The Good Teachers," "Beachcomber," and "Brothers," the last of which has details in common with Duffy's life. However, despite the increasingly personal nature of her work, the poems using the second-person voice suggest that the poet is attempting to move beyond the sometimes-solipsistic lyric "I" and the merely personal to directly engage her readers in a shared experience. In general, the collection aims to explore universal themes and experiences.

The opening poem, "The Captain of the 1964 *Top of the Form* Team," is a dramatic monologue from what might be considered an insider voice. The poem suggests Wordsworth with its reminiscing on boyhood, but it also connects back to questions about culture in Duffy's previous collection. The speaker, an adult man, recounts his schoolboy glories, but the narrative is broken up with interjections. Most take the form of answers he might have given as captain of his *Top of the Form* team. *Top of the Form* was a long-running radio quiz show for secondary students of Britain's top-tier schools. In addition to the answers, the final stanza is interrupted with wry observations about his current life with his wife and children. The disruptions create the same sort of intensified reader engagement that occurred in "Translating the English, 1989" and the cultural references also conjure British culture of 1964 similarly to the way some references locate "Translating the English, 1989" in the year of that title.

Also running through the poem is the phrase "my country," which recalls the repeated use of "our country" running through "Originally." In that poem, the phrase refers to Duffy's childhood and her previous country, Scotland. In this poem, "my country" refers to the speaker's childhood but might also suggest a longing for a period in which British culture was more uniform. For example, the third stanza ends with the sentence "My country." The fourth starts with, "I want it back." Read together, the sentences could have a xenophobic undertone. The reminiscing of the entire poem indicates that the speaker wants his teenage years back, but he also longs for a less culturally and socially complex time when he seemed to be "The one with all the answers" (p. 7).

The collection also includes a number of poems that feature Duffy's ongoing, postmodern interrogation of language and meaning. "The Cliché Kid" is a jumble of popular expressions sometimes mixed together, which make it impossible for the speaker to articulate his memories or problems to his doctor, presumably a therapist. The speaker's inability to express his thoughts and feelings is emphasized by the poem's form. Each of its six tercets trail off in ellipsis as the speaker does not finish any of the stanzas grammatically or logically. The poem offers a transition between the memory-oriented first section of the collection to an emphasis on action in the next section, as the poems continue to probe how language works. In "Away and See" the speaker of the poem advises the reader to measure language against experience and maintain a critical regard of language and its uses, an idea that is similarly articulated in the lyric poem "Moments of Grace."

Following *Mean Time*, Duffy produced an increasing quantity of work for children, including two plays that adapted the fairy tales of the Brothers Grimm—*Grimm Tales* (1996) and *More Grimm Tales* (1997)—and a book of children's poetry, *Meeting Midnight* (1999). She has continued to regularly produce works for children into the new millennium. Her growing reputation as a poet was also suggested by her involvement in an increasing number of editorial roles in the 1990s, including work on *Anvil New Poets 2* (1995) for which she was editor and *Penguin Modern Poets: Vol. 2* (1995), which she edited along with Vicki Feaver and the renowned Irish poet Eavan Boland. Although she participated in the book's publication as an editor, Duffy was publicly critical of the fact that the *Penguin Modern Poets* was divided into two volumes separating male and female poets.

THE WORLD'S WIFE

With its entirely female perspective, Duffy's next full-length collection, *The World's Wife* (1999), might be considered an ironic response to the gender segregation of the *Penguin Poets* editions. The collection is regarded by many as blatantly feminist and returns to what have become two Duffy trademarks: dramatic monologue and the reworking of fairy tales and myths. Virtually every poem of the volume is a dramatic monologue, and all are from the perspective of females. In spite of what might be considered its gender-biased leanings, the collection has proved her most popular. It was the first to draw mass audiences and continues to be her best-selling work.

This may be because of its successful blending of traditional literary and historic works and figures with popular-culture sensibilities. Duffy borrows or invents characters associated with works of high culture and makes them readily accessible to a variety of readers. Some, like Demeter and Delilah, are famous characters of myth and the Bible. Many more are the wives of real historic figures or writers, such as Mrs. Darwin, Anne Hathaway, and Frau Freud, or the wives of famous male characters from literature, like Mrs. Faust, Mrs. Quasimodo, and Mrs. Midas. While some characters are purely products of her imagination, like Queen Kong and Mrs. Quasimodo, others have actual real or fictional predecessors. In these instances, the poet is not attempting to render an accurate depiction or likeness. Instead, Duffy creates personalities and voices for each character, allowing them to retell well-known history, myth, and literature from a woman's point of view, and their monologues often point out the failings of the male side of humanity.

In many ways, her approach is a return to first-wave feminist writing strategies. Duffy also frequently employs contemporary details and language that are not chronologically accurate for the settings or eras from which her speakers come. This suggests that Duffy is updating these myths and stories for a contemporary audience and a new time. The nature of the modern details and the language, which is straightforward and includes slang expressions, indicates that Duffy democratically intends the updates for a broad audience of readers. The poems feature many traits of performance poetry, like an emphasis on rhyme and rhythm and readily accessible content. In this sense, the poems live up to the criticism that her work does not require more than one reading. The playfulness and humor of the collection also embody the double-edged critical description of her work as children's poetry for adults. However, the qualities for which her work has been criticized are also likely the same ones that continue to draw such large audiences to the collection.

The opening poem, "Little Red-Cap," features the monologue of the fairy-tale character Little Red Riding Hood, although it has details in common with Duffy's own biography. It begins, "At childhood's end," represented in the poem as the end of town and the beginning of the woods, which is where Little Red-Cap first encounters the wolf. He is reading his poetry aloud. Red-Cap is sixteen, young, and inexperienced. The woods themselves represent potential danger, adult experience, and the unknown. In "Stafford Afternoons" from the previous collection, the woods at the edge of town are where the speaker of that poem encounters the pervert and potential child molester.

Despite the obvious risks, Little Red-Cap intentionally catches the wolf's attention, allows him to buy her her first drink, and follows him deep into the woods. She loses her innocence on multiple levels, evidenced, for example, in capturing and feeding a live white dove to the wolf and, over the next ten years, gains a great deal of personal experience as well as poetic knowledge. In this way, the character is similar to Duffy herself, who met the leader of the Liverpool Poets, Adrian Henri, at around the same age as Little Red-Cap ran off with the wolf. Duffy also ended up following Henri to Liverpool, where she enrolled in university and eventually moved in with him.

Eventually, Little Red-Cap becomes aware of the limitations and repetitions of the wolf's or male/patriarchal poetry. She takes an ax to the wolf, and inside his body she finds her grandmother's bones. The recovery of the bones, which had been swallowed up and concealed by the male wolf, serves as a metaphor to describe the purpose of the rest of the collection. The poems attempt to reveal or uncover women and their stories and perspectives, which have been concealed or swallowed up in male-dominated traditions of literature and history.

Though the opening poem might be somewhat autobiographical and offer a context or explanation for the female focus of the rest of the collection, the poems that follow are a return to pure invention. The exception, perhaps, is "Mrs. Beast." The poem's speaker is a character in common with her early rewriting of *Beauty and the Beast* with Adrian Henri and is an avid poker player like Duffy herself. The poem comes near the end of the collection and, like "Little Red-Cap," offers an explanation for the poems. The purpose of this and other poems of *The World's Wife* is to make the reader revisit and possibly rethink or reinterpret the social and cultural constructs that are presented in canonized history and fiction.

This version of the fairy tale is entirely from Mrs. Beast's point of view, and the Beast is actually presented as an alternative to a man, particularly to the princes of classic fairy tales, who she explains are typically "bastards." The poem celebrates the tough, wealthy, beautiful members of Mrs. Beast's poker club, for whom she has a clear sapphic admiration, and mourns the loss of women real and fictional who are "unable to win" and come to a tragic end like Marilyn Monroe, Bessie Smith, and Rapunzel. These women and characters are ghosts that stand behind each of the players—perhaps looking on enviously at their game, perhaps haunting them. However, the poem makes clear that they and the living women like them, whom the speaker describes as lost, captive, and less fortunate than the poker players, are all in some way victims of men specifically and the patriarchy more broadly. The closing line, "Let the less-loving one be me," provides the final explanation of what defines the difference between the players and other women. Other women are too caring and emotional, while the women at the table exert more emotional control, evidenced in their poker playing as well as their relationships.

The players, the speaker in particular, have adopted many of the qualities typically ascribed to men by first-wave feminists, for example emotional reserve and sexual dominance. In a reversal of traditional social scenarios, Mr. Beast shyly waits on the women as they play, quietly keeping his distance from their female bonding. Because the female characters of this poem adopt and celebrate classically male traits, the poem cannot easily be read as feminist, a categorization with which Duffy expressed frustration in 1988 while addressing the limitations of women poets: "For quite a long time even into this decade we've been allowed certain areas of subject matter, like children, what bastards men are, looms … But I haven't got any children and I don't define myself entirely as a woman: I'm not interested in weaving" (McAllister, p. 72). Clearly, Duffy's frame of reference has shifted substantially since making this statement. For example, she has identified the birth of her daughter in 1995 as a life-changing event, and "what bastards men are" is specifically addressed by Mrs. Beast. However, the poem also explores concepts of female identity. Like Duffy, Mrs. Beast does not seem to define herself entirely as a woman, and both are interested in expanding what defines a woman. For this reason, poems like "Little Red-Cap" and "Mrs. Beast" and possibly the entire collection are not satisfactorily described with the label "feminist" and are more accurately regarded as postfeminist.

In fact, the poem "Penelope," spoken by Odysseus's wife, specifically deviates from the original story in a key detail. In the well-known myth, the heroine kept her suitors at bay while waiting for her husband's return by weaving a burial shroud for her husband, which she would undo each night in order to protract the project. In Duffy's version of the myth, Penelope is depicted as a needlepointer rather than a weaver. This seems a purposeful attempt to distance herself from first-wave feminism, which the poet specifically identifies with weaving. However, rather than working on a burial shroud, Duffy's Penelope embroiders her own myths, making herself the center of the work and developing new mythologies parallel to the construction and ideology of the entire collection and feminist ideology more broadly.

Duffy's approach to feminism, which draws on some aspects of first-wave feminism while distancing herself and her work from other aspects of that social movement, might reflect the limitations of what some contemporary women writers see as feminism's narrow focus. Critics have suggested that the "other," nonhuman characters of Duffy's poetry like Beast and Queen Kong might have been created to broaden the discussion of both gender roles and human sexuality beyond traditional binaries of male/female and gay/straight.

FEMININE GOSPELS

Like *Mean Time, Feminine Gospels* (2002) offers a multilayered title. Gospels are best known as the four books of the Bible written about the life, death, resurrection, and teachings of Christ, although the word "gospel" originally derives from the Greek meaning "good tidings" or "message." The word also has the conventional meaning of something taken as the truth or final word. In *Feminine Gospels*, Duffy plays ironically on all of these definitions.

The collection could be divided into four sections, similar in this way to the biblical Gospels. While Duffy's "gospels" have little to do with the life of Christ, she does make some connections to Christianity. "The Virgin's Memo," "written" by Mary to her son, is a partial list of items the world and humanity could do without—for example, acne and jellyfish. Some entries are noted as "illegible" or "untranslatable." The poem is meant to draw attention to what has been left out or overlooked in both the Bible and history. The reader realizes that none of her suggestions were implemented, which highlights the limited roles of women in the Bible and leads to the question: why is there is no gospel by a woman, or a "feminine gospel"? Like *The World's Wife*, this collection further meditates on the gaps in history and literature where women are absent.

That said, Duffy's are not necessarily feminist gospels. While the book is entirely oriented around women and their experiences and perspectives, the endings of the poems are often left open or conclude badly for the female characters, suggesting a certain ambiguity about the female subject and experience. Duffy also plays on the idea of the gospel as the truth. While some reviewers have labeled the poems new myths and allegories, many poems, particularly those of the first section, read more like tall tales, a word employed in the opening poem, "The Long Queen."

Similarly to "Little Red-Cap," which offered an explanation of the themes of the rest of the collection, the opening poem of *The World's Wife*, "The Long Queen," presents the title character, who rules over all things feminine. The poems that follow draw on many aspects of female experience, sometimes exploring and developing clichés, like "The Woman Who Shopped," about a woman whose love of shopping eclipses every other aspect of her life until she becomes a department store. Others, like "Tall," about a woman who grows in stature until she outgrows both the world and humankind, and "Loud," about a woman whose voice becomes impossibly loud in reaction to the news, also examine a quality of the heroine that has become extreme. All three poems are examples of the tall tales that dominate the first part of the collection. These heroines do not follow the typical path of the protagonists of myth, who complete remarkable deeds and thereby gain recognition. Instead, their exaggerated obsessions and qualities isolate them from society. In "Tall," the woman's sudden growth begins as a gift, but continues to extremes, until she stands far out in space, howling as she looks back down to earth. The unpleasant endings of the tall tales make the moral of Duffy's poems in this section ambiguous, although the use of extremes and exaggeration might be meant to call modern female stereotypes or new female myths into question.

The second section of the book is dominated by the theme of the unheard voices and histories of women. "Sub" is a dramatic monologue in which the female speaker recounts the varied glories of her past. Most are sports related but drumming with the Beatles and participating in the first moon landing are also among her alleged accomplishments. In most cases, the speaker came on as a substitute for one of the men who actually participated in the historic and popular culture events she details, hence the title of the poem. In the final stanza, it becomes clear her accounts are imagined. The poem ends with a colon followed by a blank that discredits her previous descriptions.

The ending suggests she has nothing to say about her life as a woman or experiences as a mother and grandmother. All of the events in which she has claimed involvement are in fields traditionally dominated by men: sports, rock and roll, and the space program. The poem highlights that history has traditionally privileged public, male achievements as significant and domestic and female accomplishments such as motherhood and family life as insignificant, a viewpoint to which the speaker herself seems to ascribe.

The poem is followed by the previously discussed "The Virgin's Memo," which comments on the lack of female presence in Christianity, and "Anon," which plays on definitions of the word "anon." The term is an abbreviation of "anonymous" and is also defined as "shortly" or "later." The poem meditates on the anonymous female writer and women made anonymous through history or circumstances as well as the idea that things could change later or eventually.

Anon seems to come in the next poem, the lengthy "The Laughter of Stafford Girls' High," which also acts as the third section of the collection. In the poem, a single surreptitiously passed note containing a joke escalates into a long-term laughing epidemic that eventually closes down the traditional girls' school, much to the joy of its students and relief of its staff. The poem may have been inspired by an actual laughter epidemic that occurred at a girls' school in Tanzania in 1962, but the school's name is the same as the secondary school Duffy herself attended. The poem presents a smaller world of women and girls within the larger female world of the collection, and it also features a microcosmic shift that has significant implications in the female macrocosm of the entire collection.

Among the other poems, the setting, wordplay, and rhyme seem to set the poem apart as possibly more fitting in one of Duffy's children's collections, but the themes are largely adult. A major theme of the poem is the love between women, an arena the characters of the poem found impossible to explore prior to the laughing outbreak. The teachers initially try to suppress the laughter and carry on teaching the male-dominated curriculum—all the historic figures from the lessons are male, as are all the authors quoted and taught. The male orientation of the curriculum is emphasized particularly in Miss Nadimbaba's class, where the students recite the names of poets laureate, an entirely male list prior to Duffy's appointment to the position in 2009. Despite the teacher's efforts to carry on, the

laughter eventually overcomes the curriculum, and each teacher puts in her resignation to pursue her own personal ambition.

In most cases, these pursuits are successful. Two teachers realize their unrequited love for each other, while Miss Nadimbaba becomes a poet herself rather than merely quoting William Butler Yeats and teaching canonized male poets. One leaves her husband on a trekking journey that ends with her in the arms of the sea, while another teacher invites a student on a journey to climb Mount Everest.

The two climbers fall in their attempt, but they do so in each other's arms, suggesting that, while the effort to reach the summit may not have been successful, the attempt created a strong bond of female camaraderie. The mountain climbers recall Adrienne Rich's "Phantasia for Elvira Shatayev" from *The Dream of a Common Language*. The poem, based on an actual incident, presents an account of a women's climbing team that perished while climbing Lenin Peak and similarly celebrates the team's female bonds and their summit attempt rather than mourning their deaths.

The largely positive conclusion of "The Laughter of Stafford Girls' High" sets the tone for the final section of the collection, which attempts to rectify some of the social and historical imbalances presented in the previous sections. The lyric poem "White Writing" begins to fill the gap of women's perspectives and voices exposed in the second section by offering itself as replacement for the lack of prayers, news, poems, and so forth written about the poem's addressee, "you." Read biographically, "you" might be Duffy's long-term partner of the period, Jackie Kay, but it could also suggest women readers generally. "The Light Gatherer" seems to be a personal lyric celebrating the poet's daughter, and "The Cord" also explores the bonds between mothers and daughters. The collection concludes with the elegiac "Death and the Moon." While somber, the poem returns to the symbol of the moon, a recurring motif through this collection and in many of Duffy's previous works that suggests female power and influence.

CAROL ANN DUFFY

RAPTURE

Rapture (2005), a collection of love poems, won the T. S. Eliot Prize. It was praised by the judges as a rare achievement of great poetry with commercial appeal. More than a third of the poems in the collection are written in fourteen lines and therefore suggest sonnets. The poems also follow an overall trajectory or narrative of early love and its enchantments, straining love, and finally lost love, and some critics speculate the collection was inspired by Duffy's relationship with Jackie Kay. In its heavy use of the sonnet and overarching narrative, *Rapture* might readily be compared with Adrienne Rich's *Twenty-one Love Poems*, which has been identified as a modern sonnet sequence and to which Duffy clearly alluded in the subtitle to her early pamphlet *Fifth Last Song*. However, Shakespeare is English literature's most prominent penman of sonnet sequences, and his influence can clearly be seen in poems like "Hour," which riffs on the Bard's syntax and some of his themes.

Unlike Rich's or Shakespeare's work, which depicts same-sex love, the poems of this collection are not clearly homoerotic. Duffy has penned erotic lesbian poems before—for example "Oppenheim's Cup and Saucer" and "Girlfriends." However, in this collection, the speaker's beloved is so depersonalized that one critic has suggested the lover is not a person at all but poetry itself, comparing the collection to a thesis or treatise on the tradition of love poetry rather than a personal foray into the genre. Only the most subtle allusions to lesbian love occur in a few poems. Most works are scrupulously general, emphasizing the speaker's experience of love over the presence and experience of the beloved. In fact, the lover is absent from many of the poems, as the speaker either anticipates or recalls their experiences rather than actively engaging in them in the poem. This might be an intentional strategy to suggest the difficulty of capturing actual love in poetry, or the absence of a specific lover might be intended to create universal love poetry open to readers of any gender or sexual orientation.

The poems of the collection are formal, at times almost self-consciously so. In addition to the large number of sonnets, Duffy employs couplets and tercets. Even most of the free-verse poems are structured around a pattern of repetition or rhyme—for example, "Give" and "Chinatown." Like many contemporary poets working with traditional forms, Duffy does not follow the rules of rhyme, meter, and stanza patterns for the sonnet or the rules of rhyme for the tercet exactly. However, all poems suggest careful crafting and adherence to pattern either traditional or invented. They also incorporate clear allusions to English and Irish poetic predecessors like Shakespeare, who is quoted at the start of the collection and whose style and language informs some poems, and Louis Mac-Neice, whose well-known poem "Snow" is quoted in a poem with the same title. However, the earthy metaphors and blatant sensuality of many of the poems are more suggestive of a non-Anglo tradition of love poetry, specifically the work of the Chilean Pablo Neruda, who also wrote what he identified as a sonnet sequence, *Cien Sonetos de Amor* (*One Hundred Love Sonnets*; 1960). Duffy has cited the work of Neruda and other non-English poets as influential in her early development.

In addition to these influences, a number of the poems are peppered with words and phrases that will seem familiar to many readers. Rather than using the popular expressions and common language with which Duffy's work is associated, the poet has borrowed and reworked images and language from a variety of classic love poems. This technique is most obvious in "The Love Poem," which intersperses Duffy's lines with phrases from famous poems by writers including Shakespeare, Christopher Marlowe, and Elizabeth Barrett Browning.

Despite borrowing phrases and language from the past, contemporary references invade some poems like "Text," about the inadequacy of love texts sent with a mobile phone, and "Quick-draw," which compares the phone calls between lovers to an Old West gunfight.

As a whole, the collection provides a contemporary reflection on love and the ways in which it is captured and communicated, updating a classical tradition for the sensibilities of a modern audience. As a whole, it is representative of Duffy's oeuvre, which uses traditional forms to engage poetry's past together with language and details of common contemporary experience to bring British poetry into the new millennium and draw wider and more diverse audiences to the genre.

Selected Bibliography

WORKS OF CAROL ANN DUFFY

POETRY

Fleshweathercock and Other Poems. Surrey, U.K.: Outposts, 1973.

Beauty and the Beast. With Adrian Henri. Liverpool: Carol Ann Duffy and Adrian Henri, 1977.

Fifth Last Song: Twenty-one Love Poems. Liverpool: Headland, 1982.

Standing Female Nude. London: Anvil Press, 1985. (The citations in this essay come from the Anvil 2009 edition.)

Thrown Voices. London: Turret Books, 1986. (Most of the poems in this pamphlet were republished in *Selling Manhattan*.)

Selling Manhattan. London: Anvil Press, 1987. (The citations in this essay come from the Anvil 2009 edition.)

The Other Country. London: Anvil Press, 1990. (The citations in this essay come from the Anvil 2009 edition.)

William and the Ex-Prime Minister. London: Anvil Press, 1992. (Pamphlet.)

Mean Time. London: Anvil Press, 1993. (The citations in this essay come from the Anvil 2009 edition.)

Selected Poems. London: Penguin, 1994.

The World's Wife. London: Anvil Press, 1999. (The citations in this essay come from the Picador 2000 edition.)

Feminine Gospels. London: Picador, 2002.

New Selected Poems. London: Picador, 2004.

Rapture. London: Picador, 2005.

Love Poems. London: Picador, 2010. (A selection of previously published love poetry drawn from various collections.)

WORKS FOR CHILDREN

Grimm Tales. London: Faber and Faber, 1996. (Adapted from Grimm's fairy tales by Duffy and dramatized by Tim Supple.)

More Grimm Tales. London: Faber and Faber, 1997. (Adapted from Grimm's fairy tales by Duffy and dramatized by Tim Supple.)

Meeting Midnight. London: Faber and Faber, 1999. (Poetry.)

The Oldest Girl in the World. London: Faber and Faber, 2000. (Poetry.)

Queen Munch and Queen Nibble. Illustrated by Lydia Monks. London: Macmillan Children's Books, 2002.

Underwater Farmyard. Illustrated by Joel Stewart. London: Macmillan Children's Books, 2002.

The Skipping-Rope Snake. Illustrated by Lydia Monks. London: Macmillan Children's Books, 2003.

The Stolen Childhood. London: Puffin, 2003. (Original fairy tales.)

The Good Child's Guide to Rock 'n' Roll. London: Faber and Faber, 2003. (Poetry.)

Beasts and Beauties. London: Faber and Faber, 2004. (European fairy tales adapted by Duffy and dramatized by Melly Still and Tim Supple.)

Doris the Giant. Illustrated by Annabel Hudson. London: Puffin, 2004.

Another Night Before Christmas. Illustrated by Marc Boutavant. London: John Murray, 2005. (Retelling of Clement Moore's classic Christmas poem.)

Moon Zoo. Illustrated by Joel Stewart. London: Macmillan, 2005.

The Lost Happy Endings. Illustrated by Jane Ray. London: Penguin, 2006.

The Hat. London: Faber and Faber, 2007.

The Tear Thief. Illustrated by Nicoletta Ceccoli. Cambridge, Mass.: Barefoot Books, 2007.

New & Collected Poetry for Children. London: Faber and Faber, 2009.

The Princess's Blankets. Illustrated by Catherine Hyde. Dorking, U.K.: Templar, 2009.

DRAMATIC WORKS

Take My Husband. First production: Liverpool, Liverpool Playhouse, 1982.

Cavern of Dreams. First production: Liverpool, Liverpool Playhouse, 1984.

Little Women, Big Boys. First production: London, Almeida Theatre, 1986.

Loss. First production: BBC Radio, 1986.

MUSICAL WORKS

Rapture. Music and performance by Eliana Tomkins. Jazz7, 2005.

The Manchester Carols. Music by Sasha Johnson Manning. Performed by the Manchester Carollers, the Northern Chamber Orchestra, and Richard Tanner. Faber Music, 2007.

VOLUMES EDITED

I Wouldn't Thank You for a Valentine. Illustrated by Trisha Rafferty. London: Viking, 1992.

Anvil New Poets 2. London: Anvil Press Poetry, 1995.

Penguin Modern Poets: Vol. 2. Coedited with Eavan Boland and Vicki Feaver. London: Penguin, 1995.

Stopping for Death: Poems of Death and Loss. Illustrated by Trisha Rafferty. London: Viking, 1996.

Time's Tidings: Greeting the 21st Century. London: Anvil Press, 1999.

Hand in Hand: An Anthology of Love Poems. London: Picador, 2001.

Overheard on a Saltmarsh: Poets' Favourite Poems. London: Young Picador, 2003.

Out of Fashion: An Anthology of Poems. London: Faber and Faber, 2004.

Answering Back: Living Poets Reply to the Poetry of the Past. London: Picador, 2007.

To the Moon: An Anthology of Lunar Poems. London: Picador, 2009.

Duffy's papers, collected from 1985 to 1999, are held at the Manuscript, Archives, and Rare Book Library, Emory University Libraries (http://marbl.library.emory.edu/findingaids/search_results?q=findingaids/content&id=duffy834_10491).

CRITICAL AND BIOGRAPHICAL STUDIES

Brittan, Simon. "Language and Structure in the Poetry of Carol Ann Duffy." *Thumbscrew* 1, no. 1:58–64 (winter 1994–1995).

Forbes, Peter. "Profile: Carol Ann Duffy." *Guardian Review,* August 31, 2002, pp. 2–24.

Kinnahan, Linda. "'Look for the Doing Words': Carol Ann Duffy and Questions of Convention." *Contemporary British Poetry: Essays in Theory and Criticism.* Edited by James Acheson and Romana Huk. Albany: State University of New York Press, 1996.

———. *Lyric Interventions: Feminism, Experimental Poetry, and Contemporary Discourse.* Iowa City: University of Iowa Press, 2004.

Michelis, Angelica, and Antony Rowland, eds. *The Poetry of Carol Ann Duffy: "Choosing Tough Words."* Manchester, U.K.: Manchester University Press, 2003.

"New Generation Poets: A Poetry Review Special Issue." *Poetry Society Review,* 84, no. 1 (spring 1994).

Ozlem, Aydin. *Speaking from the Margins: The Voice of the Other in the Poetry of Carol Ann Duffy and Jackie Kay.* Palo Alto, Calif.: Academica Press, 2010.

Rees-Jones, Deryn. *Carol Ann Duffy.* Plymouth, U.K.: Northcote House, 1999.

REVIEWS AND INTERVIEWS

Anderson, Hephzibah. "Christmas Carol." *Observer,* December 4, 2005 (http://www.guardian.co.uk/books/2005/dec/04/poetry.features).

Campbell, Siobhán. "In Search of Rapture." *Poetry of Ireland Review* 85:85–90 (2006).

"Carol Ann Duffy." *BBC Poetry* (http://www.bbc.co.uk/poetryseason/poets/carol_ann_duffy.shtml). (Includes biography and audio and video interviews.)

McAllister, Andrew. "Interview with Andrew McAllister." *Bete Noire,* no. 6:69–77 (winter 1988).

Mullan, John. "What Are Our Poets Writing About?" *Guardian,* October 5, 2005 (http://www.guardian.co.uk/books/2005/oct/05/poetry.forwardprizeforpoetry2005).

Winterson, Jeanette. "Carol Ann Duffy" (http://www.jeanettewinterson.com/pages/content/index.asp?PageID=350). (Interview.)

EAMON GRENNAN

(1941—)

Joseph Lennon

THE POETRY OF Eamon Grennan charges the reader to intimately examine our world. Born and raised in Dublin, Grennan has spent his most of his adult life based in the northeastern United States, where he taught English at Vassar College, but he has regularly returned to Ireland. His poetry has a buoyant lyricism that attends to formal detail, and yet each poem also tells a story in blank verse—the story of the passing moment that the speaker faces, whether he is watching a child at play, a woman at a window, or a bee dying. Grennan has forged a resonant poetics not bound by ideology, word play, or contemporary aesthetics, but by artful sentences, clear vision, and emotional honesty.

Although Grennan has said that all lyric poetry is elegy, his own poems resist both the memorial and the anecdotal. His poems generally have a narrative spine that is delivered in the service of a mediation or realization. Although the speakers of his poems tend to be observers, the language of the poems tends to become involved in the event of their own telling. Epistemological and aesthetic questions have backlit Grennan's poems throughout his career, but rarely are his poems laden with abstract and existential theory: they are grounded in the immediate, the particular—the world noticed. He has achieved critical acclaim and literary success as a poet, having published nine distinct collections of poetry, two critical studies and two volumes of translation and having won the Academy of American Poets's Lenore Marshall Poetry Prize in 2003 for *Still Life with Waterfall,* published by Graywolf Press in 2002 (first published in Ireland by Gallery Press in 2001). Generally considered a major contemporary poet, Grennan writes in a way that brings us into natural and domestic scenes, both Irish and American, as well as into deeper understandings of masterworks of European art.

CHILDHOOD AND BOARDING SCHOOL

Born in Harold's Cross, in the southwest of Dublin, on November 13, 1941, Eamon is the eldest child of Thomas P. and Evelyn Grennan. A sister (Deirdre, born in 1942) and two brothers (Thomas, born in 1944, and Dermot, born in 1947) were born in the years through World War II and beyond. The family lived in the solidly middle-class southern suburb of Harold's Cross. Thomas Grennan (1910–1981) had a position as a vocational school inspector and in such a capacity traveled often throughout the Republic of Ireland. Grennan's paternal grandfather had been a county secretary, and that family lived in Navan, County Meath. After finishing school, Thomas entered the national seminary at Saint Patrick's College, Maynooth, but left to teach instead in County Tipperary. At age thirty, he met and married Evelyn Yourell (born in Kildare, then living in Dublin), three years his junior, and they settled in Harold's Cross. Her family had lived in and around Dublin for several generations, and Evelyn (1913–1991) had been raised in a family of tradespeople.

The neighborhood that they moved to belonged to the Harold's Cross parish, but the area was not strictly Catholic; Protestant and Jewish families also lived nearby. Grennan's parents kept a stable home environment. The solidness of their family life is illustrated in the fact that the family lived in the same house, on Clareville Road (as evoked in "Wet Morning, Clareville Road" in *So It Goes,* 1982), throughout his childhood. His mother was the center of their home life, and the community centered around the Church of the

Holy Rosary parish. Grennan, like many boys of the parish, served as an altar boy at Mass and other Catholic ceremonies. His father's job as a vocational school inspector caused him to travel, often three or four days a week, until he received a promotion to a desk job as deputy chief inspector of technical and vocational education in the Department of Education. His father was taciturn, except perhaps when drinking in the company of friends, and his mother appeared to Grennan as the lighthearted spirit of the home. Although there were occasions when his father's drinking led to problems in the home, his parents generally created a peaceable home life.

Grennan has written poems that remember both of them, close yet at some distance, poems such as "Vermeer, My Mother, and Me" in *Still Life with Waterfall* or "A Gentle Art," dedicated to his mother in his first book, *Wildly for Days* (1983). In the latter poem he recalls her teaching him how to build a fire, which alights and comes into its own "Like a child grown up, growing strange" (p. 29). At the sight of gulls in the United States in "Walking to Work" (*What Light There Is*, 1987), similarly, the poet recalls his father watching gulls take scraps of food from him in a frenzy.

In these poems, distance and intimacy harmonize in his remembrance, as in later poems such as "Walk, Night Falling, Memory of My Father" (from *As If It Matters,* 1991), "Birthday Walk with Father" (from *So It Goes,* 1995), or "Rome, the Pantheon" (from *Out of Breath,* 2007), in the last of which he recalls his father's wonder at the Pantheon "no common moment for that / man of sober nerve, sense of dread, on edge / until an early beer would settle him" (p. 40). The poems express a sense of being in loving proximity with his parents but often without mutual comprehension.

Although both parents were members of their nearby public library, literature had no real presence in their house except for popular novels and works of history and biography. His father did instill in his children, however, a keen interest in education, and the four Grennan children were successful students. His father had studied science, and many of the books to be found in the house were scientific. Without any particular scientific bent, Grennan as a child became an observer of the worlds around him, natural and personal, and he grew up as a watchful member of the family. When Grennan discovered reading for pleasure and escape at a young age at the local library, another world opened to him. At first he read comic books and children's stories, but when he went away at age thirteen to boarding school more complex literature intrigued him.

Grennan spent five years at Mount Saint Joseph's Cistercian College, in Roscrea, County Tipperary—76 miles (122 kilometers) southwest of Dublin, in the south midlands of Ireland. The distance from Dublin was not merely physical— the young Grennan had moved to a rural world, with a monastery on the extensive grounds (some 360 acres), and his time there transformed him. Grennan has written that his time at Cistercian College was "maybe the single most 'shaping' early experience in becoming an individual" (from an unpublished manuscript, "Autobiographical Sketch: God Help Us"). There he developed, what he has called (in an interview with Ben Howard) "a kind of sacramental twitch built into [his] way of seeing" and discovered the seeds of his future literary vocation.

The students at the boarding school were generally from a privileged class, being the sons of merchants, prosperous farmers, and Dublin professionals, but they did not seem to consider themselves rich, nor did the large estate feel like a privileged place, at least not to Grennan, in part because of the regimented Catholic austerity there. Grennan did not have extra money, but, he has noted, neither did he have wants unmet. The "spiritual reality" of the place appealed to him as he developed through courses an interest in the Romantic-era writers, particularly William Wordsworth and the essayists Charles Lamb and William Hazlitt ("Autobiographical Sketch"). Their carefully crafted syntax and Romantic idioms, particularly of solitude, nature, and desire, have had a lasting resonance with Grennan. Actual nature, as well, began to fascinate him, especially during his summer breaks.

Many of his summer days were spent on the beach, in Dublin, or on holiday trips to seaside towns. More influential trips, however, seem to have been the family's early long visits to Carraroe, County Galway, a village in the Gaeltacht (Irish-speaking area) in the western province of Connaught, which his father came to know by inspecting its school. In the late 1940s and early 1950s, the family often stayed there for a month or more during the summer to practice the Irish they had learned at school. His mother did not speak the language, but his father did, and he wanted the children to be able to speak Irish, even if haltingly. In the west, Gaelic culture, its language, music, and poetry, entered his intellectual life, but it is the landscape of western Ireland that appears more frequently in his poetry. Grennan had greater enthusiasm for the natural world he discovered there, and animal and plant metaphors tend to bespeak politics more than the other way around (as in "Sea Dog" in *As If It Matters*). His early summers in the rural west of Ireland provided him with a vivid contrast to a suburban life of streets, buses, and tram stations, as well as the ordered estate of Cistercian College—they offered an unkempt, unordered existence that amazed the young man and have continued to amaze the mature poet. Vivid details of thistles, cowpies, and night animals have long been a focus of his poetry, as the titles of many of his poems demonstrate—"Cows," "Ants," "Skunk," "Towards Dusk the Porcupine," and dozens of others.

During the terms at Cistercian College, he grew aware of the distinctions between home and away, a dominant theme that has also developed in his poetry (and in much of the literature of the Irish diaspora). Reading was respected at the college and in Irish culture, as were sports. For five years he played rugby and excelled in his English courses. He first read many classics of literature, including the works of William Shakespeare, to which he would later devote himself as a graduate student. *Portrait of the Artist as Young Man* (1916), James Joyce's semiautobiographical novel, framed literary aspirations for Grennan, as it had for many Irish writers. The Cistercian monks at Mount Saint Joseph Abbey, perhaps unlike Joyce's Jesuits at Clongowes, fostered a meditative atmosphere at the college and nursed the seeds of observation, writing, and study that grew within Grennan. The monks at Roscrea are semicloistered and have farmed their nearby land since 1878, but they have also run Cistercian College since 1905—and seemingly in a less severe manner that what Joyce depicts in *Portrait*. Yet, Grennan's memories are not entirely idyllic. In a draft of his "Autobiographical Sketch," Grennan commented,

> Proximity to the monastery, to the example of monks in the field, in the cloister, in the classroom, as disciplinarian deans of the school—monks as curious men, as tyrants, as people—all this expanded an awareness of the "spiritual life"—as did the weekly High Mass in the monastery, not to mention daily mass in the chapel at 6:30 each morning, after a cold wash in the washrooms and the hurrying from the dorms through the chilly corridors to the incense-and-furniture-polish-scented chapel, and the rosary at nights before late study hall and bed at 9:30 or 10.

The college and the abbey have as their motto *Insideat coelis animo sed corpore terris*: "While conscious of earthly needs, we seek the things of heaven." For his first years, Grennan seems to have been taken with the religious life, but it was not long before the young man began to seek more earthly fulfillment. He writes in the "Autobiographical Sketch":

> After one of the annual retreats, when I was maybe 15 or 16, I told the retreat priest, a redemptorist or a Dominican, that I wanted to be a priest, probably a missionary priest. He told me to talk to my parents and think it over. I thought it over, but didn't to talk to my parents about it. It was overtaken in the next couple of years by the world, the flesh, and girls.

Desire, a subsequently major theme in Grennan's work, found its first and juvenile expression in his journals and letters to young women he knew from Dublin or on whom he had developed crushes during break. From a young age, Grennan articulated desire in order to better understand it.

This writing occurred alongside his introduction to literary study. At Cistercian College, his teachers—among them Augustine (Gus) Martin and Liam Maher—inculcated within him a deep respect for literature and learning. Grennan particularly admired Martin, who was six years Grennan's senior and shared the same birthday, November 13. Martin had been a prominent graduate of Cistercian College and returned there to teach for Grennan's final two years before taking a post as a professor at University College, Dublin (UCD), where he influenced generations of Irish students and writers. Every aspiring literature student at the boarding school would have known when Martin arrived to teach that he had placed first in the nation's Leaving Certificate in English in 1953, only two years before Grennan himself enrolled. Martin was an important influencing force for Grennan, whose own star had begun to rise. The students had elected Grennan to be a house captain, and he was also elected captain of the rugby team—two positions, ironically, that Martin had held. Yet literary study became Martin's lasting influence on Grennan, and he encouraged the student to pursue it as a vocation.

Grennan's early taste of distinction had merged the physical, social, scholastic, and literary. His time at Cistercian College also helped him learn how to be alone. "It was an instruction in solitude as well as loneliness (and maybe it was responsible for the discovery of the difference between the two)," he says in the "Autobiographical Sketch." The college both put a stamp on his perspective and helped him envision his later craft.

DUBLIN AND ABROAD IN THE 1960S

After he graduated from Cistercian College in 1960, Grennan immediately enrolled in University College, Dublin, where he studied English and Italian, earning his bachelor's degree with first-class honors in 1963 and (instead of taking a teaching job in Uganda, which he had briefly considered) then taking a master's in English soon after, in 1964. These were busy and heady days for Grennan, as he began to write poetry and stories even as he was involved in his first romances. He lived at home with his parents, his sister, and his youngest brother as he became involved in Dublin's literary culture. He met many young writers his own age in the environ-

ments of UCD and Trinity College, including Derek Mahon, Michael Hartnett, Paul Durcan, and Eavan Boland (with whom he would later have a short-lived engagement). In his "Autobiographical Sketch," Grennan notes that he edited a literary magazine, *St. Stephens*, which Joyce had worked on, acted a little in small productions, studied hard for exams, drank and argued in pubs, and fell in love several times. The professors who most impressed him at UCD—Denis Donoghue, Roger McHugh, John Jordan, and Gioia Gaidoni—opened some doors for him after college. Upon graduating with an MA, he accepted a six-month Italian government scholarship in Rome, which Gaidoni had helped him secure.

Rome opened a new world to Grennan, who enjoyed a bohemian-style existence during the mid-1960s as he connected with a larger literary world. In Rome, he spent time with the poet and fellow Cistercian College graduate Desmond O'Grady, who was immersed in the literary culture there, having worked as an aid to Ezra Pound (1885–1972). In "Autobiographical Sketch," he describes this time as "wild and often happy days and nights in the city, between Campo dei Fiori and its evocative statue of the martyred Giordano Bruno (whose works I was reading) [and my room on the other side of town?] Too much drinking, too much of the appetite for living itself being satisfied." In Rome, in 1964–1965, Grennan also briefly met the American poet Charles Wright (1935–), who was staying in Rome after completing a Fulbright scholarship and translating Italian poetry. This seems to have been Grennan's first meeting with an American poet, but at the time Grennan was not aspiring to write poetry but, rather, short stories. He wrote some but never sought to publish them; art and its fixing of a single moment intrigued Grennan, as had, as a university student, the early lyrical poems of Pound, as well as the work of Wallace Stevens (1879–1955) and, to a lesser extent, T. S. Eliot (1885–1965).

The young Irishman had a full taste of Mediterranean culture, and his appetites were transformed—what had been primarily literary also became architectural and visual as he began to study the interplay between language, form, color, and light. Italian architecture, especially the baroque Roman churches of Francesco Borromini and the art in the Vatican galleries, as well as the historical layering present in Rome—contemporary art amid Roman ruins and Renaissance painting and sculpture—gave Grennan another, more peripatetic and less academic, education. Following his six-month scholarship, he moved to Brindisi at the southern end of the Roman Appian Way, to teach English at the Italian air force base for three months. He had hoped to write there, while reading James Joyce's *Ulysses* (1920) and Walter Jackson Bate's award-winning biography *John Keats* (1963), but his writerly life did not then unfold. Grennan described this time in his unpublished autobiographical essay as "a life complicated in emotional terms to the extreme. Whatever writing that took place took second place to these fierce entanglements of the emotional life," one of which was with the young Irish poet Eavan Boland. Indeed, the first poems that Grennan published in *Wildly for Days* (1983) continued to vacillate between beauty, joy, fear, desire, responsibility, and loss, but by that time he had found a way to bring these emotions to the page.

In July 1965, Grennan went with Desmond O'Grady and other, mainly expatriate, friends to visit the Two Worlds Festival in Spoleto, founded by the twentieth-century composer Gian Carlo Menotti, in order to meet the poet Ezra Pound. Among the friends was a young Italian divorcée, who was about Grennan's age and with whom he had struck up a close relationship. Grennan had been greatly taken with Pound's earlier poetry when he was a student at UCD. Meeting Pound had become almost a rite of passage of young poets. O'Grady introduced Grennan, then twenty-four years old, to Pound, the storied modernist, whose opera *Le Testament*, based on a poem of Francois Villon (1431–1463) was being performed at the festival. The thirty-year-old O'Grady, as Pound's sometime literary secretary in Rome, also served as his conduit to the younger poets. Grennan returned that July to Dublin, where he and Boland resumed their at-times-stormy relationship—"we were so young; I

was all at sea," he later described the time (personal correspondence, December 21, 2010). But he was not to remain in Dublin. He had applied and been accepted into in the English PhD program at Harvard University (among his chief recommenders were Denis Donoghue and Father Thomas Dunning, another important UCD influence on his literary studies), and Grennan took the chance and moved to Cambridge, Massachusetts.

Living on Cambridge Street with another Irish student and friend, Dara McCormack, Grennan focused on his studies and made close friendships, as with Joseph Butwin, a professor at the University of Washington to whom Grennan dedicated "Breaking Point" in *As if It Matters*; during part of this year, Derek Mahon also lived in the Cambridge Street apartment with Grennan. Grennan was passionate about poetry's attempt to illuminate, evoke, and capture reality.

His courses at Harvard with the young professors Anne Ferry, David Kalstone, and Neil Rudenstein focused his attention on the close details of poetry and New Criticism. He became enamored of the work of Wallace Stevens and other modern American writers, but Grennan had no time for creative writing at Harvard. He wrote for coursework and exams, as well as maintaining a correspondence with Boland back in Dublin. His intellectual life then focused on understanding literary traditions and the nature of literary creation. Perhaps because he had studied something of British and Irish traditions theretofore in Ireland, literary history, particularly American, British, and Irish poetry, have seemed closely related to him as a continuance, rather than as competing or exclusionary national literatures.

Grennan, age twenty-five, returned to Dublin in 1966 at the close of the academic year in order to teach for a year at UCD and figure out his personal relationships. He lived on Raglan Road, made famous by the Irish poet Patrick Kavanagh. For Grennan, these were difficult times; his father had become ill with tuberculosis, and he was uncertain if he would remain in Dublin or return to Massachusetts. That November was also the time of the great flood of Florence, in which millions of works of art were damaged or ruined. The times were tense, and mounting student protests around Europe, as well as the continuing war in Vietnam, charged the atmosphere. Grennan returned to the United States and Harvard a year later in the fall of 1967, with a new scholarship, his father recovered, and his engagement broken.

He returned to his old house on Cambridge Street at Harvard, and for the next two years he dove into his studies, taking courses, doing his preliminary exams, and preparing a dissertation topic. He had another relationship that led again to a short-lived engagement, but he mostly devoted himself to his studies and to literature. Questions of how to best understand the relationship between art and reality began to concern Grennan as he studied Shakespeare's works alongside existential and aesthetic philosophy, particularly that of the Danish thinker Søren Kierkegaard (1813–1855). He looked to Renaissance aesthetics and historiography to see how they might shed light on Shakespeare. He also began keeping a journal in the spring of 1969, which he has kept ever since (and which are housed in Emory University in Atlanta). Later that year he made his way back to Italy, to Florence in the wake of the destructive flooding of the Arno River, in which tens of thousands of books, manuscripts, and works of art had been damaged or destroyed. Grennan remembers attempting to check out books at the Florence National Library and having a clerk instead bring a note back instead of the book, with only the word *alluvion-ato* written on it—victim of the flood.

The vivid colors (many newly restored) and lifelike figures of Italian Renaissance painters struck Grennan, who went often to cathedrals to view the works of masters such as Masaccio (1401–1428) and Pontormo (1494–1557), both of whom developed dimensionality in figurative painting in their religious and classical works. Grennan began to consider how art structures the world, whether aesthetic representation creates order or reveals decay and disorder. Such questions have endured for Grennan throughout his career, as a poem from his first full-length American volume, *What Light There Is and Other Poems* (1989) reveals: in "Winn's Blackbird" the voice in the poem comments and observes an artist arrange and paint a dead blackbird. The paradox that art breathes life and endures while its makers or subjects may die and disappear recurs in other forms within Grennan's oeuvre, as in "The Cave Painters" (from *As If It Matters*), who "leave something / upright and bright behind them in the dark" (p. 50). So too endures the tension between the faith that art will outlast the matrix of its creation and its creator. But the thinking through of these ideas—and recognition of an existential reality that many works, as with those lost in the Florence flood, do not survive—might be dated to when he returned to Italy, taking daily notes in his journal and continuing his art education. Certainly these two preoccupations endure throughout Grennan's work: the fleeting and pure experience of existence and humanity's attempt to convey it. His work, particularly his later work, however, evinces a joy in serendipity and the balance often found within nature, as in a 2010 prose poem, "A Walk on Long Beach Island." But Grennan still had not turned to writing poems in 1969 to convey a moment, to express the world with language—or to "word the world," as he put it in a 2006 interview with William Walsh (p. 137).

Throughout that fall Grennan walked the streets of Florence, visiting museums, cathedrals, and libraries; it was a time of both expectation and disillusion in which he began to question his dedication to scholarship. He instead began to build a new life in which he wrestled with how to express the tensions he found in art, in literature, and in Shakespeare. He worked devotedly for a time, researching his dissertation and amassing many shoeboxes filled with note cards, but as he moved along, his topic narrowed and a life of scholarship began to lose its luster. The lived example of Ezra Pound, whom he met twice again through Desmond O'Grady, must have inspired Grennan (as well as alerted him to the dangers of zealous political convictions). He worked in the National Library of Florence and began to focus on aesthetic considerations and trim the archival research aspect of his project.

Living alone in Florence, he had had some hopes of reviving a relationship begun in Cambridge with a friend who had since moved to Germany, but again it came to nothing.

On a visit to Rome to see O'Grady, his life opened in another unexpected way; he met there his future wife, Joan Perkins, then Joan Baltaxe, whose "light and life, her dramatic energy" attracted Grennan as he came often to dinner parties at her house ("Autobiographical Sketch"). She was then married to a British forestry expert working for the United Nations Food and Agriculture Organization at its agency in Rome, who then spent much time away from home in the Middle East and North Africa. She lived with their two young boys, David and Peter, outside Rome in a house on the Appia Antica, the famous Roman end of the old Appian Way. She and Grennan became friends. Although she had a family, Grennan noted, "the life ignited between us as thoroughly real as it was possible to be." Soon after meeting her, Grennan also began to sketch poems, which he kept private for years. His year changed after he met Joan Baltaxe, and instead of heading to the library, he began visiting Rome, taking trips to Venice, and enjoying a fuller life while beginning a new apprenticeship in poetry. He spent time too with the Anglo-Irish poet Patrick Creagh and his wife, Ursula, on their farm in the Chianti country near Sienna. The intensity of his life and his emotional turbulence did not slacken, and he took daily notes in his journal, which had become his "rope over the streamsurge" (personal correspondence, August 4, 2010). Writing became a refuge and a place to work out his emotional life and develop a steady voice.

Not long afterward, in the winter of 1970, Grennan nearly died. One night in his studio apartment, in the San Frediano quarter of Florence, the old coke stove in his apartment leaked carbon monoxide, knocking him unconscious until it burned itself out. Because coke, a form of coal, burns warmly but gives off little smoke, it was commonly used. At times older stoves leaked the odorless and colorless gas and killed people during the shut-in winter months. Grennan went to bed one cold night and did not wake for thirty-six hours. When he eventually did, sickened and soiled, he had no strength, was cold and unsure of what had happened. He showered, dressed, and went outside to find a newspaper with the date. He describes the event in a revised version of his "Autobiographical Sketch":

> I had lost a whole day in this drugged sleep, my dreams full of Vietnam violence and memories of trying to wrench open the windows. On the paper, front page, when I got out and checked the date, the day, was a photo of a man and wife who had been that previous night monoxided to death. I climbed Giotto's [Bell] Tower, then went for dinner to a restaurant near the [Santa Maria del] Carmine [church]. As I ate I felt things dripping into my pasta and found out I was copiously crying, while a man with an accordion played some Italian popular tune.

He called Joan Baltaxe and related all to his new confidante. Confronting his own death (and realizing his own luck in being alive) must have sharpened his interest in existential philosophy and turned a page in his emotional and creative life.

A CAREER IN THE STATES

The 1960s had ended, and Grennan left Florence in the first half of 1970, planning to return to Harvard in the fall to work toward finishing his degree. Joan Baltaxe also returned to the United States that year, separating from her husband and living with her mother in Lansdale, Pennsylvania. Many of Grennan's friends had graduated from Harvard, and he too was nearing the end of his time there, although his dissertation remained a large and unwieldy project. He had ambitions to understand how Shakespeare conceived of the world and thus represented it. In the dissertation he explored how the shape of Shakespeare's first four history plays were determined by agendas, whereas the second and more famous tetralogy, consisting of the *Henry IV* plays, *Henry V*, and *Richard II*, contained colliding forces upon which Shakespeare did not impose a more ordered structure. He worked for months on a long chapter on *King Lear* and how Shakespeare's sense of a competing providence and fortune underwrote the drama, rather than a clear historical narrative or agenda. Grennan grew interested in questions about "the collision of aesthetic and existential categories," studying Kierkegaard (personal correspondence, August 4, 2010). He wrestled with conundrums of representation, subjectivity, and experience—whether art is an escape from experience or a way into it, and whether creating art could unify a fragmented self or further divide the self against its creation. Elements of Kierkegaard's thought endures in the aesthetics Grennan has come to create for himself, which often turn on the fleeting nature of existence and the subjectivity of beauty.

Many poems throughout his corpus question the act of representation itself. In a early poem titled "Something After All," written in 1980 and included in his first volume, *Wildly for Days*, the poet wrestles with whether art captures a view of the world or creates its vision of the world. The poet, who sits in the house of his recently deceased father ("now my mother's house") on Clareville Road, wonders "Will the mirror tell me what I have become[?]" and then imagines another poet viewing the gentle day:

[...] *It is,*
He says to himself or dreams he says,
How it is. The day endures in his breath,
In the light pooling his eyes; shadows live
Like cats in the back garden, and the doors
On the sunny side of the street are shining,
If I can believe my eyes, like new leaves.

(p. 23)

The poem closes with the poet's idle question of belief in what he sees and sense of wonder—"If I can believe my eyes." Notably the poem seems to beg us to reconsider the idiomatic phrase, as well as the cliché, "the sunny side of the street." As he noted in a 2000 interview with Ben Howard, his poems often work to "revive the cliché, make love to the dead metaphor." The question hanging is whether the vision is real or merely an aesthetic creation assembled to signify new growth after the death of speaker's father. Artistic creation both mirrors and remakes the world in fidelity to perception of reality—as such, it remains elusive and mutable.

In the winter of 1970–1971 Grennan's personal world was radically changing. He interviewed for a job in the Bronx at Lehman College, part of the City University of New York, which he was offered and he accepted. Teaching, which came to him naturally, had become a joy; he enjoyed the classroom and exploring texts with students. At Harvard he had worked as a teaching assistant, and even before then he had taught his own courses in Ireland at University College, Dublin. But by the fall of 1971, he began to teach full-time. Over that summer, he had moved to Greenwich Village in New York City, where he rented a small apartment. He continued to write poetry and work on his dissertation that year in the Village, but most of his energies went toward his teaching.

That year he also continued to see Joan Baltaxe, during which time she and her husband divorced. The following summer Grennan and Baltaxe, with her two boys, moved in together in Pleasantville, a small town north of the city, where Grennan busily worked on his dissertation. Later in the summer when he had completed ostensibly half of the proposed project (the part on the two tetralogies; he had presumed he would have to do the other half on the comedies), he met with his advisor, Walter Kaiser, who told him he had done enough—his dissertation was finished. The history play chapters were complete in themselves. Grennan went out and celebrated, and the dissertation was catalogued in 1973 under the title "History and Historia: A Reading of Shakespeare's History Plays." Grennan and Joan Perkins were married in a quiet Unitarian ceremony on November 4, 1972, amid friends; her two boys, David and Peter, then nine and ten years old, were the only relations to attend. Ten months later (September 9, 1973), their daughter, Kate, was born in Pleasantville. In the following year, Grennan continued to teach at Lehman while his wife began to teach high school in Poughkeepsie. Grennan became friends with another budding poet at Lehman, Billy Collins (1941–), whose first book of poetry, *Pokerface,* came out in 1977. Friendship and mutual encouragement has existed throughout their careers.

A calmer life outside New York agreed with Grennan, and when, in 1974, he was invited to apply to Vassar College in Poughkeepsie, he did so and was offered a position. The family moved up to Poughkeepsie that summer—three children and one on the way. At Vassar, Grennan taught a range of freshman courses and upper-level courses on Chaucer, Shakespeare, Milton, and Irish literature; he quickly began to publish critical essays on Shakespeare and, in a few years, on Irish literature, as well as some poetry. Before Vassar, Grennan only wrote small poems, "antics," he called them, which he would date and present to his wife every year on her birthday. His first poetry publication came in 1974, when he published "Suburban Wake" in the first issue of the short-lived *Sunbury: A Poetry Magazine.* This was followed by poems in other new journals such as *Ploughshares* (begun in 1971) and the *Journal of Irish Literature* (1972–1993).

Their son Conor was born in October 1974. Grennan's children appear in some of his best-known poems, including "Two Climbing" and "Two Gathering," the first and last poems of *As If It Matters.* On a side note, around then Grennan also discovered that one of his great-grandfathers had died and been buried in Catskill, New York, north of Poughkeepsie on the Hudson River, close to where Conor had been born. This discovered connection to his adopted homeland stuck with Grennan, an ancestral fact of the Irish diaspora, of which he had become a part without ever considering himself an emigrant. Grennan has long insisted that, although he lives in the United States as a registered alien, he is not American but retains his Irish citizenship. Such dual consciousness, being at home in both Ireland and America, is common to the generation of Irish writers who first came over in the 1970s or later, often tagged the "new Irish." The Irish-born poet Eamonn Wall—who has lived in the United States since 1982, teaches Irish studies at the University of Missouri–St. Louis, and frequently returns to Ireland—has described this generation not as exiles nor emigrants, but as commuters who never fully assimilate. Since his first arrival in the United States, Grennan too has consistently, usually once or twice a year,

returned to Ireland. But his main home has been in Poughkeepsie, New York, since 1974.

Ensconced at Vassar, Grennan began to develop his scholarship, partly in order to receive tenure and promotion. A year after his arrival at Vassar, he placed his first academic article, a study of Shakespearean influence on John Keats' "Ode to a Nightingale," prominently in the *Modern Language Quarterly.* His next article focused squarely on Shakespeare, reexamining some arguments about *As You Like It,* and was published in 1977 in another prominent journal, *English Literary Renaissance.* He also mined his dissertation and published articles about Shakespeare's *King John* (1978 in *Shakespeare Studies*), *Henry V* (1979 in *Papers on Language and Literature*), and *The Comedy of Errors* (1980 in *Philological Quarterly*). His arguments about the nature of Shakespeare's history plays and Shakespeare's representations of nature and custom have stood up over time—and in their backbone are questions about how to represent reality in text. His essay on "The Women's Voices in *Othello*: Speech, Song, Silence" (in *Shakespeare Quarterly* in autumn 1987) also hits another nerve that may vibrate in his work as a poet: how the language spoken by the female characters responds simply to what happens in the play and reveals an emotionally truer reality, one that differs from the reality that the male voices inhabit with their various power reflexes, calculations, and agendas. He also published a scholarly article in 1982 on Edmund Spenser's troubling images of sixteenth and seventeenth-century Ireland—by this time, his academic interests had begun to also drift across the Irish Sea.

Alongside these articles, he began to write and publish essays about Irish writing, first in 1978 with an overview in *Éire-Ireland* about Irish writing in the years 1977–1978. He followed this in 1979 with an important essay on W. B. Yeats, "Careless Father: Yeats and His Juniors," also in *Éire-Ireland.* In the essay (collected in *Facing the Music: Irish Poetry in the Twentieth Century*), Grennan discusses Yeats's posthumously published poem "Under Ben Bulben," which contains what Grennan calls his "majesterial injunction" (p. 133) to succeeding generations of Irish poets.

Yeats exhorted "Irish poets" to learn their trade and "cast your mind on other days" in the poem, published just six days after his death in 1939. Grennan argues that Yeats's injunction regarding aesthetics differed greatly from those of later poets, and he examines the works of Irish poets who succeeded him: Austin Clarke (1896–1974), Patrick Kavanagh (1904–1967), Louis MacNeice (1907–1963), and Denis Devlin (1908–1959). In the last two sentences of his essay, Grennan jumps forward in time: "The present world, with all its taxing, complex, and original demands would compel fresh responses. Neither metrically nor otherwise would they be likely to walk in their father's footsteps" (p. 143). And, this is exactly what Grennan had begun to do in his own writing, basing his poetics more on Kavanagh's model than on Yeats's, and being greatly informed by American writers.

FIRST POEMS

As a way to expand his own inner life, Grennan began to develop his "antics" into poetry, relying on his journal writing in which he recorded questions, musings, nature sightings, and day-to-day events. His and Joan's home life was bustling with four children, a dog, and a cat, and their social life was vibrant with friends often visiting and his wife throwing dinner parties. Amid these whirls of activity, Grennan carved out a core space in which he would write and record his inner life, working on his poetry and continuing his journal writing from his Harvard days. In these first poems, he explores daily life with formal precision and emotional clarity, and the voice is calm and observant even when the subjects are not. His first published poems are unlike the early poems of most published poets because Grennan did not publish anything but mature work.

In the mid-1970s Grennan settled into a pattern of annual migration back to Ireland from Poughkeepsie; he and Joan and their two younger children (the older boys' father lived in Rome and they mostly summered with him) would travel to Ireland after the academic year ended and stay for the summer. The places in his poems reflect this, ranging from Poughkeepsie to Ireland in most every volume. Amid their full lives in mid-1970s, Grennan increasingly began to look for writing time. He began to listen to a voice from, as he put it, "the romantic cellar of my psyche, a little crying out for more" ("Autobiographical Sketch"). After that voice had consumed Grennan for a time, and more in mind than flesh, he began to pay attention to how desire gave an erotic charge to his poetry. He has consistently interlaced desire within his poetry, in the seams of the domestic and the natural. Grennan noted in the interview with Ben Howard, in discussing the poem "Wet Morning, Clareville Road," "You can't have poems, you can't have art, without the erotic, it seems to me, and the nerve that is often pushing the narrative, whether covert or overt, is an erotic nerve [...]—the sexual nerve running through things—that, of course, is the life force." As Tom D'Evelyn commented in a review of Grennan's 2010 volume, *Out of Sight,* "Like other contemplatives, Eros is [Grennan's] theme: the Eros born of lack and surplus." Desire and the erotic is a major aspect of Grennan's poetry, but it may be, in fact, one of the elements that has been least recognized.

Having taken an unpaid leave from Vassar College in the summer of 1977, Grennan and his family lived in County Wexford (except for the two older boys, who went to live with their father). He began there to write the poems that would be published in his first volume, *Wildly for Days.* The first poem he wrote for the volume, "Speech," was written in response to a poem written by a friend. This exchange had prodded Grennan to find ways of representing his inner life through images of nature, of finding equivalencies for desire, jealousy, and tenderness. This "first poem" introduces several themes and tenors that continue throughout his oeuvre. As Grennan notes in his "Autobiographical Sketch," that summer when he began to write poetry in earnest he felt "the constant presence of desire, poems full of it whatever their subject, went hand in hand that summer of 1977." His first finished poem, "Speech," opens "Like learning a strange tongue" and develops a long simile that compares the poet's approach to a new language with an owl's hunting of a field mouse. The comparison subtly addresses the allure and danger of human desire:

> The brown fieldmouse
> Fast asleep
> In the hushed, unruffled
> Cradle of your beak.

(*Wildly for Days*, p. 41)

The quality of alertness throughout the poem, as well as phrases such as "moods by heart" (p. 41), point to the desire with which he wrestled. But the tenor of the ultimate metaphor, of a hunting owl, resonates the danger of an affair and perhaps its threat to home life, particularly to the smallest ones in the nest.

For the next year until the summer of 1978 Grennan and his wife lived in Ireland with their two young children Kate and Conor. They went primarily because Grennan needed to publish more before he went up for tenure; the unpaid leave, partly supported by grant by the American Council of Learned Societies, in effect, gave him an extra year of time, until 1982, before he was obliged to apply for tenure and a permanent position at Vassar. They stayed in the Coastguard House in Ballymoney, County Wexford, about forty-five miles south of Dublin, as well as spending some time in Renvyle, County Galway. The first poem in his *Wildly for Days*, and in all subsequent collected volumes, is "Facts of Life, Ballymoney," which was first published in the "New Irish Writing" section in *The Irish Press* in 1978. The poem dates from then and begins with the lines:

> I would like to let things be:
> The rain comes down on the roof
> The small birds come to the feeder
> The waves come slowly up the strand.
>
> Three sounds to measure
> My hour here at the window:
> The slow swish of the sea
> The squeak of hungry birds
> The quick ticking of rain.

(*Wildly for Days*, p. 11)

The tripling of images in lines that interlock alliteration and consonance resonates with much

medieval and early modern Irish-language poetry—signally his heritage as an Irish poet. Paradoxically, that year of leave in Ireland is when Grennan began to seriously study American poetry, especially Robert Frost (1874–1963), William Carlos Williams (1883–1963), Elizabeth Bishop (a Vassar graduate; 1911–1979), Robert Creely (1926–2005), James Wright (1927–1980), and Gary Snyder (1930–). Illustrating these two traditions, Grennan's "Facts of Life" gradually moves from a lyrical opening into narrative blank-verse lines that ultimately bring the speaker into the poem. Lines convey the beauty of the scene before the speaker, who is watching the herring-gulls fish and notes:

> They are killing cuttlefish out there,
> One at a time without fuss.
> With a brisk little shake of the head
> They rinse their lethal beaks.

This harsh and existential "fact of life," what Grennan has called "Darwinian violence" (in the interview with Howard), also runs as a theme throughout his volumes. This introductory poem seems to announce that his art will not look away from what is painful in the world—that the poems will pursue the real, whether fleeting, sentimental, or ugly, and will find language to convey it.

The academic year 1977–1978 that he spent in Ireland also was important for Grennan in that he and his family first went to a cottage in Renvyle, County Galway, that he eventually bought and to which he has returned nearly every summer since. The rural landscape surrounding the house has entered scores of poems over the years, poems that are collected in the limited-edition volume *Renvyle, Winter* (2003). On that first stay there, Grennan dove into American poetry and reimmersed himself in the works of contemporary Irish poets: John Montague (1929–), Thomas Kinsella (1928–), Seamus Heaney (1939–), Derek Mahon (1941–), and Eiléan ní Chuilleanáin (1942–). He was consciously trying to reenter the Dublin literary scene, but he already had a foot in America; this, in part, kept him, for years, from receiving much critical recognition in Ireland. That year changed the course of his future writing, however, and perhaps his sense of his writing from two traditions. Over the next few years he began to place poems in more prominent publications in Ireland, such as the *Irish Press*, *Irish Times*, *Irish University Review*, and *Poetry Ireland*.

In the late summer of 1978, Grennan returned to Poughkeepsie revived, with a new sense of purpose for his writing and hopes for a new start to his home life. Over the next few years he worked, helped raise his children, and kept up his social life. But his marriage grew frayed, partly due to a separate emotional relationship, the aftereffects of which appeared in his poems for years. He continued to publish scholarly articles, yet poetry writing began to become more central to him, although he had not yet produced a book. His writing served as a sort of meditation in language for him, in which he would reflect on desire, family life, and nature. Tenure weighed heavily on his mind in 1979, and he resolved to continue to put his oars into the currents of poetry and poetry criticism, rather than continue developing his Shakespearean scholarship. In the fall of 1980 he took another leave and returned to Rome, this time without his family, in order to reconnect with friends there and to write. Although he had never been greatly productive in Italy as a writer, Italy nourished him. He lived for a couple of months in Venice and wrote some essays and many poems, many of which would appear later. He returned home to Poughkeepsie for a month at Christmas, but he had begun to realize that tensions in his marriage would not resolve.

In February 1981, he traveled back to Ireland, planning to live in the Renvyle cottage for six months. His father had developed cancer at this time, and Grennan spent the next few months between Dublin and Renvyle, visiting his family and witnessing the death of his father that March, as Grennan turned forty. The pain of his father's death understandably hobbled his mother and family for months during which he remained with his mother in Dublin. When the volume *Wildly for Days* appeared in 1983, it was dedicated to the memory of Grennan's father as well as to the memory of the poet George Palmer, an old friend of Grennan's from Cambridge, who wrote under the name George Anthony and had died in 1976. Palmer and his wife Phoebe had a house in Monhegan Island in Maine, where Grennan had sometimes been their guest. Palmer had given Grennan a pair of binoculars in 1976, shortly before he died. This gift got him started on bird-watching and fostered his love of birds (poems referencing birds appear in every volume of Grennan's poetry). In a poem dedicated to Palmer, "In Mount Auburn Cemetery," birds dip "their wings in air" over his grave, and "A kingfisher pauses over water" (p. 28).

Some of the most poignant poems in *Wildly* reference death: his father's in "Something After All," "Common Theme," and "End of Winter"; the poet James Wright's death in 1980 in the poem by his name; and anonymous children in a graveyard "Gravechild, Renvyle." Accompanying these poems about human death, real and metaphoric, is "Lying Low," which opens "The dead rabbit's / Raspberry belly / Gapes like a mouth" and offers a grisly meditation on a body being eaten by insects "Who inhabit the red tent / Of his ribs, the radiant / Open house of his heart" (p. 47). Many of the poems also signal the changes happening in Grennan's life around the turn of the decade.

Later that summer of 1981, Grennan went with his wife, family, and widowed mother to the Yeats Summer School in Sligo, Ireland, where he had been invited to lecture. Many of the poems in his first few volumes, such as "Muse, Maybe" in *Wildly for Days*, struggle with questions of desire and others merely invoke it, as in "Fall," "Morning, Looking Out," "By the Hudson," and "Night Driving in the Desert." In the fall of 1981, he returned to teaching at Vassar, and to a shaken home life. By the winter of 1982, he and his wife had all but separated, amid much regret and sorrow, emotions that reappear in various forms in Grennan's art for years. Poems convey the guilt and sadness Grennan felt over his absence from his children in poems such as "Wife" and "Mother and Child," written well before the trouble in his marriage. Poems about leave-takings, albeit temporary, with his children when they were younger in some ways prefigure the sorrow of the divorce poems and point to

Grennan's emotions at the time. Poems such as "Daughter Waiting for School Bus" and "Taking My Son to School" empathetically signal the ends of their earlier childhoods, while other poems reference the breakup of the marriage in 1982.

This first volume introduces many of the themes and stylistic modes that would continue to appear in Grennan's work: nature and its "Darwinian violence"; familial life (and death) along with its emotional trials; desire and its enticements and entanglements; poignant moments and the transience of life. This volume also introduces Grennan's first ekphrastic poems: "In the National Gallery, London" (dedicated to Derek Mahon), "Cavalier and Smiling Girl," and "Raeburn's Skater." These poems, as well as Grennan's skill at evoking scenes, have led readers, reviewers, and scholars to tag his work as painterly, which he has accepted, even titling his most painterly volume *Still Life with Waterfall*. Grennan's poetry is consistently vibrant with visual imagery, but much of this seems driven by his fundamental interest in questions about the representation of reality and experience in art.

In early 1982 he received tenure, and at the same time his relationship with Joan Perkins broke entirely. Grennan moved into a small apartment just off Mansion Park in Poughkeepsie, wanting to be as close as he could to his children but to have a space of his own. At the same time a relationship more recently established with Rachel Kitzinger, a newly hired professor of classics, became closer, and eventually they became a couple, living in separate houses. After a year in Mansion Park, Grennan moved into a house on College Avenue in Poughkeepsie, a space large enough for the regular weekend visits of his two children. When Grennan and Kitzinger moved after that year into a house together on Wing Road in Poughkeepsie, his two children Kate and Conor, nearly teenagers, came to live with them. Eventually Kate moved to New Jersey to live with her mother, and a year later, Conor moved too so they could both attend high school there while living with her mother and her new partner. Grennan continued writing in these years during difficult divorce proceedings and had his first real taste of success, having his poems ap-

pear in more journals and giving some successful readings. Earlier, in fall 1981, an issue of *Irish University Review* had published five of his poems, including two poems set in Italy. Over the years, he had met Peter Fallon, an Irish poet and the founder and publisher of Gallery Press in Dublin. In 1982, he assembled the poems that Gallery would publish as *Wildly for Days*. The next year, *Ontario Review* published seven poems in the fall-winter issue of 1984, including "Winn's Blackbird" and several other family and ornithological poems later included in *What Light There Is and Other Poems* (1989).

These publications, as important as they were to his career, nonetheless did not match the prominence that his first *New Yorker* poem brought to his work in 1985. Publication in the *New Yorker* signaled that he was becoming known in the United States, even more so than in Ireland despite his not having had a book published in America. That poem, "Soul Music: The Derry Air," appeared in the January 14, 1985, issue of the *New Yorker* (p. 32). It reads as an "Irish" poem and unmistakably references sectarian "troubles" in Northern Ireland, with which Grennan was very aware, even if he had had little immediate contact with the violence and rarely offers overtly political comments in his poems. "Soul Music: The Derry Air" is often the first poem of Grennan's that Irish critics cite. It is a powerful poem that evokes everyday life amid the militarization of Derry in those years.

SUCCESS AS A POET

Between 1985 and 2010, Grennan published fifty-three poems in the *New Yorker*, becoming a regular contributor under the editorship of Alice Quinn and Howard Moss. He had published ten volumes of poetry as of the fall of 2010, some of which were published with different names in Ireland and America. He also had published a number of special printings and limited editions of suites of poems. He edited a book of criticism, *New Irish Writing*, with James Brophy in 1989, and in 1999 he published a critical study of Irish poetry that collects his essays on the topic, *Facing the Music: Irish Poetry in the Twentieth*

Century. He translated the work of the nineteenth-century Italian poet Giacomo Leopardi in a volume that was published in Dublin in 1995 and then by Princeton University Press in 1997; *Leopardi: Selected Poems* won the PEN Award for Poetry in Translation. With his partner Rachel Kitzinger he also translated the Sophocles play *Oedipus at Colonus,* in a volume published by Oxford University Press in 2005. He has contributed essays, reviews, and poems to dozens of literary journals and newspapers in North America, Ireland, and Europe.

Recognition has come gradually for Grennan, however, and after years of consistently writing well-received books. In early 1986, the divorce between Grennan and Joan Grennan was finalized. Later that year, on November 1, 1986, Rachel Kitzinger gave birth to Grennan's third child, Kira. They continued to live on Wing Road, teaching at Vassar. Grennan sent out poems to journals and magazines while Kitzinger edited the three-volume *Civilization of the Ancient Mediterranean World: Greece and Rome* with Michael Grant (1988). In the summer of 1987 Grennan spent the first of many three-week summer residencies at the MacDowell Colony in New Hampshire, from which a new set of poems emerged. He also continued his migration back to Ireland during the late 1980s, where Gallery Press put out his second full volume, *What Light There Is* in 1987, dedicated "To Rachel" and filled with poems about their life together. The following year, 1988, Grennan published his first book in the United States, a slim volume, *Twelve Poems,* in a limited run (150) with the small Occasional Works press in San Francisco, California. These two works, combined with *Wildly for Days,* came out together in 1989 in his first full-length American publication, *What Light There Is and Other Poems.* Shattering poems such as "Night-Piece" from this era reflect his divorce from a few years earlier, but much of the 1989 volume also points to new beginnings and hope.

In 1990 Edward Hirsch glowingly reviewed this volume in the *New Republic* and noted the steady voice of the poems, written over a decade:

Reading Eamon Grennan's poems as they have appeared one by one, in *The New Yorker* and else-

where, I have marveled at a lyric poet who seems amazingly content with daily life, with describing the pleasures and vicissitudes of the quotidian and the domestic, the homespun natural world, the mid-morning walk to work and the midafternoon hour spent at the second-story window. His quiet, well-crafted poems are painterly, sensible, shapely; they are eager, unrhetorical, straightforward, melodic. They are never extreme.

(p. 39)

Hirsch notices an element that runs throughout Grennan's work, that the poems are observant of detail; they do not shout and are well-crafted. He also discusses Grennan's sense of the "true precariousness" of things as they are in the world, which counterbalances the evenhanded voice that Grennan developed over years of writing about his own daily life.

With this volume, Grennan had arrived as a poet in the United States, gaining a "rousing welcome" from readers and listeners alike ("Grennan, Eamon" in *Contemporary Authors,* p. 105). Grennan returned to the MacDowell Colony in 1990 after finishing his teaching year, but his time there was interrupted when his mother grew seriously ill. She died on June 18, 1990, while he was en route to Dublin. The deaths of his parents were watershed moments in his life. His mother appears in a number of his poems throughout his volumes, but particularly in first section of *So It Goes* (1995): she is referenced in the poems "Outing," "Night Figure," "Heirloom," "Whistling in the Dark," "What Doesn't Happen," "Ghosts," and "Visiting Mount Jerome." The poems of *So It Goes* were begun in 1990, and the volume is dedicated to the memory of his mother and to the memory of a close friend, the Vassar classics professor James Day, to whom the poem "Two for the Road" is also dedicated.

Death had struck close to Grennan's life again when Day died in December 1990. Grennan discovered his friend's body on his kitchen floor when he entered, "As if all the clocks in the house / had stopped: iron silence, thickening of ice, / the air abruptly grown stone deaf" ("Two for the Road," from *So It Goes,* p. 17). The year 1990 marked the end of another period for Grennan at Vassar. The following semester he and Kitzinger took sabbatical leaves for the spring semester of 1991 and traveled to Ireland with Kira, who was then four years old. His older children, Kate (then seventeen) and Conor (sixteen) were finishing high school and living with their mother in Jersey City. With Kira, Grennan and Kitzinger stayed in Howth and sometimes visited the house in Renvyle. Grennan's relationship with Kitzinger has appeared in poems throughout these later volumes, some of which point to difficult times in their relationship. (From the evidence of such poems, it seems clear that for Grennan the active presence of desire in his own emotional life has never been a simple or singularly focused force.) But many of the poems point to the coexistence of passion and domestic love.

In particular, his second major U.S. publication, *As If It Matters*, dedicated "to Rachel," evokes their domestic lives in some of his most well-regarded poems, which include "Circlings," ("For Rachel and Kira"—about nursing) and "Kitchen Vision," which paints a picture of his life in miniature as reflected in "the electric / kettle's aluminum belly." (Grennan told Ben Howard: "I was going to call the poem 'Self-portrait in a convex kettle,'" as an allusion to John Ashbery's "Self-Portrait in a Convex Mirror," which in turn references the *Self-Portrait in a Convex Mirror* of the Italian mannerist painter Francesco Mazzola, known as "Parmigianino.") In evoking the ordinary, Grennan has presented himself in line with painters, and he alludes to several Dutch masters of the fifteenth to seventeenth centuries in the "Kitchen Vision"—Sandro Botticelli, Jan Steen, and Johannes Vermeer—"because I was trying to say something there about what art does, fixed in place and 'luminous in ordinary light,'" he told Howard. This sense of illuminating the ordinary increasingly became a concern for Grennan in the early 1990s.

After they returned to the United States in the fall of 1991, Grennan and Kitzinger resumed teaching at Vassar and raised Kira as Kate moved on to college and Conor finished high school. Grennan received a grant from the National Endowment of the Arts in 1991, which gave him more time to write and signaled the success of his first American volume. Grennan's next volume of poems, *As If It Matters,* came out first with Gallery Press in Ireland in the fall of 1991, and then with Graywolf Press, in Saint Paul, Minnesota in 1992.

The mountains in New Hampshire also began to appear in Grennan's poems in the early 1990s. Grennan continued going to the MacDowell Colony in June, going a total of four times between 1988 and 1996 and writing poems that would appear in *So It Goes* (1995) and *Relations: New and Selected Poems* (1998). His books had been positively reviewed, and in 1995 he was awarded the James Boatwright Poetry Prize from *Shenandoah* magazine. The same year he was awarded a Guggenheim Fellowship, allowing him time to write poems that would appear in *Relations* and *Still Life with Waterfall*, as well as to bring together his collected Irish essays, which he had steadily been writing since the late 1970s. Grennan also began in earnest another new project, which he had considered for some time: translating the major poems of the Italian Romantic Giacomo Leopardi (1798–1837), a poet he had been reading and quietly translating for years. Leopardi's poems are known for their treatments of landscape, mutability, and desire—all themes that repeatedly appear in Grennan's poems as well. Instead of bending the poems to fit with English rhymes, Grennan skillfully used assonance, consonance, and alliteration to lend music to the blank verse. Although in Italian the language of the poems dates from the early nineteenth century, Grennan often updated the language and expressions, as Leopardi had done in his own way and time. The collection first came out in Dublin with Dedalus Press in 1995, and two years later Princeton University Press released it in their prominent poetry in translation series. Later that year, Grennan won one of the most important prizes of his career for *Leopardi: Selected Poems*: the PEN Award for Poetry in Translation (1997). Also that year, he won the first of many Pushcart Prizes for his poetry, and his poems began to appear in anthologies.

In 1998 Graywolf brought out *Relations: New and Selected Poems*; and in 1999 Creighton University Press brought out *Facing the Music:*

Irish Poetry in the Twentieth Century, his collected essays written over the previous two decades. In Ireland the next year Gallery Press brought out a version of *Relations*, called *Selected and New Poems* (2000), which received positive reviews in the *Irish Times* and the *Times Literary Supplement*, among other periodicals—Grennan had finally become known outside his own poetry circles.

During his stays in the woods in the Monadnock Mountain region of southern New Hampshire in the 1990s, nature writing began to come even more to the forefront of his poetic vision, bringing his poetry into line with great North American nature writers such as Gary Snyder and Mary Oliver. His poetry, while it rarely rhymes, also remains close to an Irish tradition: it invokes Irish place and place-name poetry called *dinnseanchas* and its tradition of assonance, alliteration, and consonance—part of the music he has brought to the woods of New England.

In 2000 he began writing and submitting a series of poems all of which had ten taut lines—and eventually comprised *The Quick of It* (2004, 2005), his most experimental volume. He was also preparing his next volume, *Still Life with Waterfall*, which Gallery brought out in 2001 and Graywolf in 2002. He won three further Pushcart Prizes in 2001, 2002, and 2005 and gave readings across the United States and Ireland. Still, he found time to draft poems that would eventually be collected six years later in *Out of Breath* (2007). In the spring of 2002, he accepted a prestigious visiting chair for Irish writers, the Heimbold Chair, at Villanova University, where he taught two courses, gave readings around Philadelphia, and met with students. Indeed, Grennan saw himself primarily as a teacher, and secondarily as a poet, until around this time, when poetry began to take center stage in his career and life.

STILL LIFE *AND AFTER*

Grennan's art has often been tagged as painterly because of its evocative ability, and the way his poems have explored painting and aesthetics, but *Still Life with Waterfall* does so even more than others, invoking Vermeer (1632–1675), Andrea Montegna (1431–1506), Marc Chagall (1887–1985), and especially Pierre Bonnard (1867–1947). He brings together his naturalist eye with his sensibility about painting and the writing process most masterfully in the ultimate poem of *Still Life*: "Detail" (originally titled "Lesson"). The poem completes a series of images that runs throughout the volume (and his work), beginning with the opening poem, "At Work" (originally titled "Artist at Work"), in which a "marsh hawk is patrolling / possibility" (p. 3). Throughout the volume, Grennan references windows, at which he sits looking out on the natural world: watching bees try to get through the glass, as in "Up Against It" (originally "Desire"), or dying before its impossible barrier ("Windowgrave"). The window image also serves as a frame for the observer and a mirror for the artist, as other poems in the volume suggest ("Bonnard's Reflection" and "Bonnard's Mirror"). This last poem of the volume, "Detail," resolves at least a triad of tensions for Grennan (and perhaps the reader)—tensions that are all-persistent in these poems and elsewhere in Grennan's work—between a detached or an engaged observer of nature; between the creator and the process of creating art; and between natural beauty and nature's "Darwinian violence." The title invokes a "detail" of a painting and the first few lines remind us of the patrolling hawk in the volume's first poem, but here it catches some unexpected prey:

I was watching a robin fly after a finch—the smaller
  bird
chirping with excitement, the bigger, its breast blazing, silent
in light-winged earnest chase—when, out of nowhere
over the chimneys and the shivering front gardens,
flashes a sparrowhawk headlong, a light brown burn
scorching the air from which it simply plucks
like a ripe fruit the stopped robin[.]

(p. 67)

The poem concludes by comparing the sparrow hawk's hunt to the discovery process of writing, itself likened to viewing a painting:

[...] I began to understand
how a poem can happen: you have your eye on a
　small
elusive detail, pursuing its music, when a terrible
　truth
strikes and your heart cries out, being carried off.

Art and nature, creation and killing meld in this poem, one of Grennan's most well-known.

Around the time of the publication of *Still Life with Waterfall*, he signed up with the literary agent Alison Granucci to help coordinate his readings, the requests for which had grown. More importantly, later in 2003, his reputation was lifted into a more select circle when *Still Life with Waterfall* received the 2003 Lenore Marshall Poetry Prize from the American Academy of Poets, which came with a twenty-five-thousand-dollar award. In the citation for the prize, one of the judges, Robert Wrigley noted:

> Grennan would have us know—no, would have us see, feel, hear, taste, and smell—that the world, moment by ordinary or agonizing moment, lies chock-full with its own clarifications and rewards. That such rewards most often go unnoticed keeps the artists in business, so to speak, and if there is anything more likely to open us to the savor of life than poems like Grennan's, I can't imagine what it might be.
>
> (p. 40)

The prize along with the positive reception boosted Grennan's confidence in the quality of his work, which has often been intensely personal, and gave him a sense of how his work—as a poet who straddles Irish and American cultures—fit in "on the poetry map" (private correspondence, July 27, 2010).

In 2004, Grennan and Kitzinger took leaves from teaching and stayed on Long Beach Island in New Jersey. He used the time to produce new poems and prepare the manuscript of *The Quick of It* (2005). This volume more than others devotes itself to a sort of paradoxical representation of the fleeting. The volume is his most experimental in that he removed all titles from the ten-line poems, in part in order to heighten their immediacy and remove that which can fix a poem: its title, tag, or marker—often taken to sum up a poem. The second poem in the volume,

for instance, originally had the title "Rock Bottom," but on the page in the volume it begins, "So this is what it comes down to? Earth and sand" (p. 5). While he often has changed the titles of poems from original publication in a journal or magazine, he had never removed the titles entirely. These changes in *The Quick of It*, he explained to William Walsh in 2006, are a way to move away from "sign-posting," which may be helpful in a periodical publication, toward a more neutral presentation that resists summating the poem when it appears in a volume (p. 135). The poems without titles entirely appear then, as in the poems of Emily Dickinson, as lyrical fragments belonging to a larger work. Grennan commented to Walsh: "The whole issue of lyricism is about fragmentation, for me anyway. The moment. The fragment. Fracture. The things seen in passing. The notion that things halt, but only in our imagination for a half a second, and poetry is an attempt to slow things down a bit and hold on" (p. 129). Part of what Grennan is also discussing is the "many selves of the poet," which he explores more fully in his essay on Emily Dickinson, "'Identity to Seek': The Selves of Emily," published in *Green Mountains Review* in 2006.

In 2004 Grennan retired from teaching at Vassar College, but he has continued teaching graduate writing classes at New York University and Columbia University in New York City, and spending long summers in Renvyle. Freed up from regular teaching, Grennan worked with Kitzinger in translating the Sophocles play *Oedipus at Colonus* (2005) and revised the poems that would appear in *Out of Breath* (Gallery Press, 2007), which appeared with additional poems in the United States in 2008 as *Matter of Fact* (published by Graywolf). Grennan also has continued to write reviews and articles in the *Irish Times* and elsewhere, as well as essays on literary figures; in particular, he published two pieces for *Green Mountains Review*: one on Emily Dickinson (2006) and another on Wallace Stevens (2009). Graywolf issued Grennan's collection *Out of Sight* in 2010, containing another thirty new poems. As of that time, he had also begun to write more for the stage, adapting John

Millington Synge's book on the Aran Islands as a "dramatic recital for two voices," as well as another dramatic recital based on the Irish Famine of the mid-nineteenth century (private correspondence, December 21, 2010).

Grennan's poetry is intensely intimate and yet always welcoming. The poems thrive on the tension of blank verse between the syntax of a sentence and the breaks of lines. Some reviewers still seek to place Grennan in a stereotypical Irish tradition, but more are recognizing the particular poetics he inhabits, at once natural and created from a blend of Irish traditions, Italian (and more broadly, European) art, and American idioms. The critical work has mostly focused on his representations of art, silence, domesticity, nature, and transcendence—and all critical attention has praised his accomplishment. Grennan's poetics could be described as the poetics of immediacy. He gives great attention to detail, place, and moment, whether that moment is tranquil or violent, somber or expectant. His language heightens our attention and simultaneously relaxes the reader, helping us become receptive readers and viewers to the scene. The thwarted or submerged desire so present in his earlier work endures in his later work, but certainly in a more celebratory, and at times erotic, manner. Grennan's lines convey both the transient wonder of a passing moment and the enduring recognition of what is lost through decay, death, or ignorance. Grennan is a poet of America; he is a poet of Ireland. He is a poet of the lost and of the nascent. His poems celebrate, contemplate, and elegize his life's experiences and, by extension, our own.

Selected Bibliography

WORKS OF EAMON GRENNAN

Poetry Volumes

Wildly for Days. Dublin: Gallery Press, 1983.

What Light There Is. Dublin: Gallery Press, 1987.

What Light There Is and Other Poems. Berkeley, Calif.: North Point Press, 1989.

As If It Matters. Dublin: Gallery Press, 1991; St. Paul, Minn.: Graywolf Press, 1992.

So It Goes. Oldcastle, County Meath, Ireland: Gallery Press, 1995; St. Paul, Minn.: Graywolf Press, 1995.

Relations: New and Selected Poems. St. Paul, Minn.: Graywolf Press, 1998.

Selected and New Poems. Loughcrew, Ireland: Gallery Press, 2000.

Still Life with Waterfall. Loughcrew, Ireland: Gallery Press, 2001; St. Paul, Minn.: Graywolf, 2002.

The Quick of It. Oldcastle, County Meath, Ireland: Gallery Press, 2004; St. Paul, Minn.: Graywolf Press, 2005.

Out of Breath. Loughcrew, Ireland: Gallery Press, 2007.

Matter of Fact. St. Paul, Minn.: Graywolf Press, 2008.

Out of Sight: New and Selected Poems. St. Paul, Minn.: Graywolf Press, 2010.

Chapbooks and Limited Editions of Poetry

Twelve Poems. San Francisco: Occasional Works, 1988. (Limited edition.)

Provincetown Sketches. With Michael Peich. Westchester, Pa.: Aralia Press, 2000. (Limited edition.)

Renvyle, Winter. Philadelphia: Pointed Press, 2003. (Limited edition.)

In This World. With Tricia Treacy. Philadelphia: Pointed Press, 2003. (Limited edition.)

Critical Books

New Irish Writing: Essays in Memory of Raymond J. Porter. Edited by James D. Brophy and Eamon Grennan. Boston: G. K. Hall, 1989.

Facing the Music: Irish Poetry in the Twentieth Century. Omaha, Neb.: Creighton University Press, 1999.

Translations

Selected Poems of Giacomo Leopardi. Dublin: Dedalus, 1995. Reprinted as *Leopardi: Selected Poems*. Princeton, N.J.: Princeton University Press, 1997.

Oedipus at Colonus: Sophocles. With Rachel Kitzinger. New York: Oxford University Press, 2005.

Uncollected Essays and Scholarly Articles

"Keats's Contemptus Mundi: A Shakespearean Influence on the 'Ode to a Nightingale.'" *Modern Language Quarterly* 36:272–292 (1975).

"Telling the Trees from the Wood: Some Details of *As You Like It* Re-examined." *English Literary Renaissance* 7:197–206 (1977).

"Shakespeare's Satirical History: A Reading of *King John*." *Shakespeare Studies* 11:21–37 (1978).

"'This Story Shall the Good Man Tell His Son': *Henry V* and the Art of History." *Papers on Language and Literature* 15:370–382 (1979).

"Arm and Sleeve: Nature and Custom in *The Comedy of Errors.*" *Philological Quarterly* 59, no. 2:150–164 (1980).

"Dual Characterization: A Note on Chaucer's Use of 'But' in the Portrait of the Parson." *Chaucer Review* 16, no. 3:195–200 (1981–1982).

"Language and Politics: A Note on Some Metaphors in Spenser's *A View of the Present State of Ireland.*" *Spenser Studies* 3: 99–110 (1982).

"The Women's Voices in *Othello*: Speech, Song, Silence." *Shakespeare Quarterly* 38, no. 3:275–292 (autumn 1987).

"Fantasy Echo: Oracles, Enigmas." *Parnassus* 24, no. 2:333–349 (2000).

"'Only What Happens': Mulling over McGahern." *Irish University Review* 35, no. 1:13–27 (spring 2005).

"'Identity to Seek': The Selves of Emily." *Green Mountains Review* 19, no. 1:14–37 (2006).

"'Prologues to What Is Possible': Coming to (Some) Terms with Stevens Wallace Stevens" *Green Mountains Review* 22, no. 2:103–127 (2006).

CRITICAL STUDIES

Baker, Timothy. "'Something Secret and Still': Silence in the Poetry of Eamon Grennan." *Mosaic* 42, no. 4:45–62 (December 2009).

Fitzgerald-Hoyt, Mary. "Vermeer in Verse: Eamon Grennan's Domestic Interiors." *New Hibernia Review/Iris Eireannach Nua* 2, no. 1:121–131 (spring 1998).

Fleming, Deborah. "The 'Common Ground' of Eamon Grennan." *Eire-Ireland* 28, no. 4:133–149 (winter 1993).

Grand, Gordon. "Decaying Flesh and Human Transcendence in Eamon Grennan's Poetry." *Nua* 2, nos. 1–2:51–63 (autumn 1998).

"Grennan, Eamon." *Contemporary Authors, New Revision Series.* Vol. 86. Detroit: Gale, 2000. Pp. 104–105.

INTERVIEWS

Howard, Ben. "Interview: Eamon Grennan." *Cortland Review,* no. 12 *(http://www.cortlandreview.com/issue/12/grennan12.htm)*, August 2000.

MacCarthy, Catherine Phil. "The Shock of the Object." *Poetry Ireland Review,* no. 88:41–51 (December 2006).

Walsh, William. "When Language Fails: An Interview with Eamon Grennan." *Kenyon Review* 28, no. 3:125–139 (summer 2006).

Stap, Don. "Resident Alien: A Conversation with Eamon Grennan." *Florida Review* 34, no 1:16–30 (summer 2009).

SELECTED REVIEW ARTICLES

D'Evelyn, Tom. "Grennan's Latest Poetry Collection *Out of Sight.*" *Providence Journal,* August 23, 2010. Projo Arts Blog (http://artsblog.projo.com/2010/08/grennans-latest-poetry-collection-o.html).

Hirsch, Edward. "Available Light." *New Republic,* June 11, 1990, pp. 39–41.

O'Grady, Thomas. "Grappling with Proteus." *Irish Literary Supplement* 22, no. 1:14 (spring 2003).

Graham, Colin, "Small Profound Dramas." *Irish Times,* September 8, 2001, p. 70.

Sadoff, Ira. "'Flat Death': Irretrievable Loss in Three Contemporary Poets." *Kenyon Review* 31, no. 3:188–200 (summer 2009).

Wrigley, Robert. "2003 Lenore Marshall Poetry Prize." *Nation,* December 1, 2003, pp. 38–42.

JEN HADFIELD

(1978—)

Zoë Brigley Thompson

IN "THE POETICS of Devolution," the critic Alan Riach discusses how the creation of the Scottish Parliament in 1998 helped to redefine Scotland as an autonomous region of Britain with a burgeoning cultural and literary scene. Riach notes that Scottish poetry after devolution does not have to engage with Scottish nationalism as it once did; there is "room for dissent," and within the new "polyphony" of Scottish poetry, Riach lists the writer Jen Hadfield (p. 15). Hadfield is occasionally controversial in Scotland, because, being half-Canadian and half English, she brings to Scottish landscapes what the poet Tom Pow calls "an outsider's eye" (p. 112).

Hadfield is much admired by critics and other poets, however, for the genuine quality of her poetry, which takes sincere joy in her surroundings and in the rituals of ordinary people. The reviewer Stephen Burt suggests that though Hadfield tries to "sound worldly, even cosmopolitan," her poetry is particularly powerful because of the freshness of its childlike view of the world (p. 24). Pow recognizes this sense of novelty, too, but comments on the clarity and innovation of Hadfield's images, which "have the freshness of the haiku about them" (p. 111).

Hadfield is an innovator when it comes to recreating sensual experiences. She is also, however, an inventive creator in her use of form and language. The reviewer John Greening affirms that "she has a strong sense of shape in language—how to use spacing, lineation, margins" (p. 30). Rather than relying on traditional forms, Hadfield is interested in experimenting with poetry on the page, engaging with visually striking shapes as well as prose poetry and ritualistic anaphora. In addition, Hadfield's form is often driven by diction, and Burt suggests that "when Hadfield is not a poet of sight, she becomes a poet of sound" (p. 24). Hadfield explained to the interviewer Susan Mansfield that her experience of Shetland influences her poetic form, because in walking the island, she is "getting to know a place in such fine detail" that she becomes aware not only of the rhythms of walking, but of "speech rhythms" (online). Hadfield's unique mode of speech and use of language have led to her being compared to the Welsh poet Dylan Thomas, because Hadfield is likewise inventive in her use of adverbs and compound words—"a wormcast of ice" (p. 21), "porridge-white" (p. 25), and "noodle-legged" (p. 26) are a few examples from her 2008 collection *Nigh-No-Place.*

Hadfield avoids the confessional mode or anecdotal lyricism in her poetry. Burt notes that her writing is free from "inner dialogue or monologue," so her poetic voice is often completely devoted to the external world with only glimpses and hints of the speaker's biography (p. 24). Rather than focusing on her self, Hadfield "collects and cherishes impressions and things" (p. 24). Burt compares Hadfield's writing to the evocative landscapes of the novelist Joseph Conrad and to the Martian School of British poets of the 1970s and 1980s, the aim of which was to find new and unexpected metaphors to describe the ordinary world. Hadfield, in Burt's view, "wants above all to make us see, to register *sensibilia*," to convey sense experiences that are normally beyond the capacity of the human mind (p. 24).

LIFE

Like the poets Kate Clancy or Carol Ann Duffy, Hadfield is not uncomplicatedly defined as a Scottish writer. Hadfield was born in Cheshire,

England, to an English father and Canadian mother, Charles and Bonnie Hadfield, and she moved to Scotland as a teenager to study English language and literature at Edinburgh University graduating in 2000. Hadfield was tutored by the Scottish poet Robert Alan Jamieson, who introduced her to the Shetland Islands in the far north of Scotland, where he had grown up. In 2001, she completed an MLitt (master of letters) degree in creative writing at the University of Glasgow under Tom Leonard, a poet who, like Jamieson, writes in Scots dialect and is interested in questions of language and culture.

After graduation, Hadfield received a grant from the Scottish Arts Council that allowed her to live on the Shetland Islands for a year, where she finished writing her first collection of poetry, *Almanacs* (2005). During this year in Shetland, Hadfield began to explore connections between poetry and art, setting up the publishing venture Rogue Seeds. This press was established in order to create chapbooks and art texts. Hadfield has produced numerous limited edition pamphlets of her own work, including *Wet and Dry Flies to Rise a Ghost* (2002), the cover of which was embellished by a hand-tied fishing fly; *Marking* (2002), printed on tracing paper and bound concertina style; and *Fool Moon* (2002), bound with a length of nylon from fishing nets.

Although the Shetland Isles are Hadfield's spiritual home, she has also traveled elsewhere. When Hadfield received an Eric Gregory Award in 2003 (for a collection by poets under the age of thirty), she used it to fund a year's residence in Canada from 2005 to 2006, a journey that was to inspire some of the poems in her next full collection of poetry, *Nigh-No-Place* (2008). Also, thanks to a Dewars Arts Award from the Scottish Parliament, Hadfield traveled in Mexico in the winter of 2007–2008 to study folk art; her intention was to produce a collection of contemporary miniature landscapes of Shetland made from tin and found objects. These art objects would be companion pieces to some of the poems in her second poetry collection.

Nigh-No-Place was short-listed for the Forward Prize for Best Poetry Collection, it was made a U.K. Poetry Book Society Recommenda-

tion, and it won the prestigious T. S. Eliot Prize. Hadfield, however, is not altogether comfortable with fame or renown, and in 2006 she moved to the remote Shetland Islands with the intention of making the Isles her permanent home. Hadfield explained to Luke Leitch: "In Shetland ... where you might think someone would feel isolated, I feel connected and protected—and more willing to be connected and protected than I ever have in my life" (online). On her home of West Burra, which Hadfield describes as "a long, wriggly island connected to the Shetland mainland by low arched bridges," she is able to create a poetics that does not promote the cult of personality but rather devotes itself to the external world and human reactions to it ("Far North, Way Up High," p. 40).

ALMANACS

Written while she was based in Shetland, Hadfield's first collection, *Almanacs*, is inspired by the elemental routines of her remote island home. As the title suggests, the collection is bound up with the cycles of weather, astronomy, and the tides, as well as social rituals and the passing of time. The human and natural communities of Shetland dominate the poems, and there is a strong sense of the fragility of human beings pitted against powerful natural forces. For Hadfield, the danger inherent in the remote and windswept landscape is inspirational, because it reminds her of her own vulnerability:

> The cliffs are steep and their edges friable. The sea sweeps the rocks with unpredictable force and fetch. The wind can be so strong as to tear the roof off a bus shelter, or forcibly spin you through 180 degrees and frogmarch you in whichever direction it fancies. I freeze with fear relatively often, but this is something I value about my Shetland life: the need to respect weather, the cliffs and the sea, the fear keeping me safe.
>
> ("Far North, Way Up High," p. 40)

Hadfield admires the power and destructive strength of her natural surroundings not merely because of the spectacle that it provides, but because it reminds her that she is not invincible. Hadfield is, however, all too aware that the natural world, too, is under threat, and in the interview with Susan Mansfield she describes herself as having "this desperate feeling that it might be taken away for some reason" (online). Hadfield expresses this protective feeling toward nature in her poems, too. In "Glid" (a Shetland word meaning sunshine between showers), she describes taking a photograph of the glorious Scottish landscape as "precarious as a dandelion clock" (*Nigh-No-Place*, p. 37), and in the prose poem "The Wren," she commands: "You will love the land. You will love the land like a bairn [a child]" (p. 47).

The human relationship with the land is hugely significant in Hadfield's work, but she is also interested in people—not the modern subjects of cosmopolitan cities, but the folk who live in wild and primitive spaces. John Greening suggests that *Almanacs* has a "pagan energy," and there are a number of sequences in the book that focus on primitive cycles like the waning of the moon and the changing of the seasons (p. 30). Hadfield's almanacs are connected to the domestic workspaces of kitchen, farm, and garden. For Hadfield, though, everyday occurrences can take on profound meaning. Her poetic practice is summed up by the phrase that she uses to describe pot-making: "domestic orogenics" ("The Urge to Make," online). In this phrase, Hadfield links the safety and familiarity of domestic space to orogeny, the process of mountain making by the faulting and folding of the earth's crust. Domestic spaces are not necessary safe, then, but full of upheaval.

A sequence in *Almanacs* that emphasizes this domestic upheaval features poems on the changing seasons (distributed throughout the book). First is "Trespass/Saturnalia," based on a December festival in ancient Rome devoted to unrestrained merrymaking and the god Saturn. In Hadfield's version, a wounded woman is shown about to "cross / the barbed wire" (p. 66). The woman is bruised and battered, yet Hadfield describes her as a resurrected Green Knight. The reference is to the fourteenth-century Middle English romance, *Sir Gawain and the Green Knight*, in which a mysterious Green Knight challenges Sir Gawain at court, and despite being decapitated, the Green Knight cannot be killed. Like the Green Knight, the woman in Hadfield's poem is indomitable; she is described as bruised and fragile, but, in spite of her pain, she commits a courageous act of trespass.

"Trespass/Saturnalia" is a winter poem, but the other poems in the sequence focus on summer. "Lida Aerra/Joytime/June" takes place during the Anglo-Saxon month of Lida Aerra (in June and July), the mild month named after the Anglo-Saxon word *liðan*, to sail. The journey that Hadfield takes is back into her own childhood "milking rain from [her] tapering plaits" (p. 69). The act of coaxing rainwater from her soaked braids is compared to milking a cow, a metaphor that invokes fertility and fruitfulness. What emerges from the pastoral scene though is not a literal gravidity, but a poetic productivity. The speaker explains that "the hedgerow slopes / from my shoulders" and it is "a yoke to hang a poem and a pail" (p. 69). Through the yoking of the poet to the "hedgerow slopes," a poem is created and, like the pail of milk, it has the power to provide succor and enable growth. The conversation between poetry and nature is highlighted in the next seasonal poem, "Hooymaand/Hay Month/July," which refers to the Old Dutch hay month. Hadfield describes the passing of summer through the maturation of crops, as "wheat's green lingo / becomes a nanny English of rusks / and tsks" (p. 70). The wheat field is a language that, in its early stages, is "green" and fresh, but later it becomes "nanny English," and this phrase seems pejorative, because it recalls the derogatory term, a "nanny state" (a government based on regulatory and protectionist policies). This "nanny English" is not the language of poetry.

In "Hooymaand/Hay Month/July," however, the wounded but indomitable woman—the Green Knight of "Trespass/Saturnalia"—reappears. Again, she features as a stoic figure, when she "walks till there's holes in her corduroy" (p. 70). This is not a young woman, either; she is as "grey as the beard of a sage" and the seasonal change "makes her brood about her age" (p. 70). The woman's fragility is emphasized in the description of her "heart's moth clattering between underwires" (p. 70). An intimate picture is presented, as we see not only beneath the woman's clothes (the underwired brassiere), but inside her body. Her heart is as fragile as a moth, and the word "clattering" suggests that it is clumsy in its beating. This heart image appears again in "Thermidor," which is named after a month from the French Republican calendar (July to August). This month was named after the Greek word for heat, *thermas*, and in the warmth of summer, the narrator of "Thermidor" describes the indomitable woman about her work:

> her heart
> beat in her back—nudging
> her fragile T-shirt—
> a gecko
> on a scorching wall
>
> (p. 71)

As in "Hooymaand/Hay Month/July," the woman's heart is a diminutive creature: a lizard that clings to a wall while it suffers in the heat. The short lines linger over the evocative image, which is particularly ominous when one considers that the French *thermidor* can also refer to a period of change when the leaders of a political movement are replaced. Hadfield's narrative is not political, but it is a story about loss and the difficulty of coming to terms with losing an indomitable mentor, kinswoman, or friend.

The climax of this narrative comes in "Fructidor/September," which is inspired by another period in the French Republican calendar: the month of fruiting. In Hadfield's poem, however, this fruiting does not represent new life but, rather, decay and death. When the narrator touches the older woman's scalp, she describes how "blood overran my palm" (p. 72). This blood is not a source of horror but rather is described as a kind of gift:

> I was proud of it
> commonplace rare
> like home-made jam
>
> say medlar, rare fruit
> and rare word, common-place
> precious
>
> (p. 72)

Haiku-like in the precision of her images, Hadfield reverses the horrifying connotations of blood and makes it a familiar domestic object: jam to be bottled. She also emphasizes the uniqueness of the dying woman, using the word "medlar," which refers to a tree in the rose family and its fruit. Like the inimitable woman, the word "medlar" as well as the tree and fruit are rare, but it is also significant that medlar fruit are not fit to eat until they have begun to decay. For the dying woman, too, aging only makes her more glorious, like the image at the end of the poem of the cut creeper, which "died like a second sunset / in next door's tree" (p. 72). "Fructidor/September" brings an end to the seasonal cycle of poems, concluding with an elegy for a woman who may or may not be a real relation of Hadfield's. What is certain though is that the woman represents the zenith of domestic life: moments that are "commonplace rare" or "common-place / precious." Hadfield manages to use the seasons to map out the tragedy of loss and replace a more anecdotal account.

WRITING THE PHASES OF THE MOON

In writing about kin, Hadfield manages to avoid being obviously personal, and she uses the land as a means to convey her feelings. Burt has suggested that Hadfield has "a sometime gift for love poems" (p. 24), but Hadfield's love poetry does not include the dramatic telling of a romantic narrative; it is more concerned with working out how to overcome loss through a conversation with place. One typical sequence features four poems that take their titles from "the convention of naming full moons according to crops and seasonal tasks" (*Almanacs*, p. 79). "Full Walnut Moon" is marked by imagery of fecundity, decay, and later frost; "Fool Moon" and "Fool Moon Voices" suggest wintry scenes and harsh weather; while "Full Sheeptick Moon" is set at the height of summer. The poems also represent a movement from personal distress to a heightened awareness of the land.

"Full Walnut Moon" begins the sequence, suggesting that the moon "looks rotten / the way the night is cankered with trees" (p. 20). The branches of trees that stretch into the night sky become the veins of rot in an apple or moon, a comparison that evokes a powerful sense of disgust. Other portentous signs emerge from the landscape, such as a pheasant described as "Mars-red," yet the speaker never explains the distress that is redolent in the poem; she is only "compiling not transmitting / these garbled messages" (p. 20). A clue is given, though, in the final stanza of the poem, which suggests that a lost love is the answer to the ominous signs:

How's he doing then, your man?
My last loving ended
with his diesel engine's dwindling,
one hand on the door's frost brass
sensing the night hadn't done with me yet.

(p. 20)

The italicized question with its gossipy tone sounds like small talk: a question that a friend or neighbor might ask the speaker in passing. The response, though, is a kind of lament. The falling stresses placed at the end of the lines (in "ended" and "dwindling") signal a sense of loss, which is emphasized by the noise of the diesel engine that slowly fades as the lover travels away. The hand that touches the frost patterns raised like brass metalwork on the door is inside the house and belongs to the listener who is left behind. The question is whether the listener will remain indoors or go outside. What is clear, however, is that the landscape has a deep and abiding attraction for the narrator, and the rising stress on "yet" sounds a note of finality.

"Fool Moon" and "Fool Moon Voices" picks up where "Full Walnut Moon" left off, describing a harsh and fierce Scottish landscape that reflects the speaker's state of mind. The landscape is animated: "A trawler spins on its anchor. / The fishfarm begins to thrum" (p. 33). The ocean is a great live thing that spins boats like toys, and the fish farm pulsates with a life of its own. The constellation of Gemini (Hadfield mentions "Castor and Pollux") is made up of "burred / tick stars," evoking a universe where the stars are merely parasitic insects (p. 33). Ticking also relates to time, and it connects to one sense of the word "burr," which can denote a whirring

sound. More significantly though, there is the "Scottish burr," which refers to the trilling of the "r" sound in Scottish English. This animated and commanding universe is then peculiarly Scottish.

"Fool Moon Voices" develops this world, presenting a series of numbered, imagistic vignettes that place the speaker more directly in the landscapes of Shetland. The narrator is introduced to a young man, Tommy, with whom she has an affinity; his name is "a soft drum," echoing the later description of the narrator's own "gong heart" (p. 34). Contrasting with this human contact is elusive nature. When the sheep flee from the walkers, it is as inevitable as "foam" fleeing a "breaker" (p. 34); some events are unavoidable. Most significant of all, though, in this poem is the description of Fethaland, which is the northernmost point on the Shetland mainland:

Fethaland, the two oceans
are metres apart
and desperate for each other—

the greasy green feathers
of the North Sea, the reaching
brown kelps of the Atlantic.

(p. 35)

The sense of being in a space of "between-ness" occurs regularly in Hadfield's poems. In "Gigi in the Rockpools," Hadfield's narrator describes herself as "a rudder sinewed to these two winds" (p. 40). In "Fool Moon Voices," however, the North Sea and the Atlantic Ocean are described like lovers "desperate for each other," with the act of "reaching" emphasized by the break after the penultimate line. Such imagery is reminiscent of the missing lover who drove away in "Full Walnut Moon." The portrayal that follows, however, shifts us away from the human and back to nature; these are not human subjects desiring one another but rather are natural phenomena that, from a human standpoint, are revolting in color (green and brown) and texture ("greasy," "kelps"). Nature is a solace, then, but not merely because it is a beautiful subject for contemplation. In Hadfield's poetry, human distress is swallowed up by the magnificence of the Shetland landscape.

The final poem in the sequence, "Full Sheep-tick Moon," anchors this reading by offering a celebratory vision of Shetland's beauty and ugliness. Hadfield uses an epigraph from the poem "Feb" by Les Murray, which describes the "gifts" of an Australian summer, one of which is skin cancer or melanoma. Like Murray, Hadfield is aware that the full moon of summer brings not only great beauty but also annoyances and dangers: the "sheepticks" of the poem's title. The swallows on Shetland are things of beauty—Hadfield uses the image of a "black boomerang"— but they also come "loaded with ticks / and pearly winter weathers" (p. 51). Like most living creatures in nature, the swallows are infested with parasites and their presence on Shetland is temporary; as the winter draws in with its "pearly" cloud cover, they will migrate to warmer climates. This final poem is totally immersed in the natural world, and there is no sign of the earlier lost lover that haunted the other poems in the cycle. Instead, the main protagonist is nature itself with its squalls, tempests, chills, and summers.

THE SKERRYMAN AND OTHER MYTHICAL FIGURES

The Scotland that Hadfield writes about is not usually urban or modern. Pow suggests that she "make[s] Scotland seem exotic, almost free from history" (p. 112). This exoticism and antipolitical tendency is most redolent in Hadfield's poems related to myth, though she still manages to imbue these poems with a sense of the modern Scotland. In *Almanacs*, one such sequence is "Lorelei's Lore," which hinges on three mythical characters: Lorelei, the Skerryman, and Ghosty.

In her notes, Hadfield describes Lorelei as a "siren who lured sailors to their deaths on the Rhine," and she quotes Ira Gershwin's lyrics for the song "Lorelei" (p. 79). The story of Lorelei derives from the Lorelei rock on the eastern bank of the Rhine in Germany, and the name comes from the Old German words for "murmuring rock." The link to nature, and especially to rocks, is emphasized in the poem "Marking," when Lorelei describes how, touching lichen, she feels

"Stone and skin pressed warmer / than the Kama Sutra's Pressed Kiss" (p. 22), referring to a type of kissing described in the Kama Sutra, the ancient Hindu book of lovemaking. The desire of Lorelei, the siren, is "pressed" in the stones that touch like lips.

For Hadfield, human experience of desire and loss is often inextricable from the Shetland landscape. Take, for example, the poem "Crying Taing" (the title being a remote place in Shetland), where the narrator describes collecting bones from the peat bog "like almonds"; "like butterflies"; "like orchids, panpipes, fans" (p. 32). These bones may be animal or human, but the speaker uses them to reconstruct herself, collecting "a fragment / for every bone in my body" (p. 32). The narrator concludes by telling how she winds the reconstructed bones of her hands "round a panhandle, a pen" (p. 32). Out of the death and loss of the bone landscape comes poetry, though Hadfield's assertion of her status as a poet is humble, too; the hands that write a poem also prepare food or wash dishes. This self-conscious reference to being a poet reveals, though, that the heroine of "Lorelei's Lore" is a kind of alter ego for Hadfield herself. Lorelei is not unlike a poet, since she is a law maker described as "ruthless" in the back cover blurb, and poets too must make their own laws of form and substance. Lorelei, however, is also a purveyor of lore, a body of knowledge that is traditional and anecdotal, belonging to the folk.

The prose poem titled "Praise Poem" displays these two aspects of Lorelei, who is both a "ruthless" enforcer of law and a teller of folklore. The poem is not exactly a praise poem as it purports to be, which is unsurprising, since Hadfield has given an online workshop on anti-praise poems for the website of the British newspaper the *Guardian*. The narrator of "Praise Poem" describes how a lover or friend (the "you" that the poem addresses) closes her hands together "in the bud-coat of your palms" (p. 37). The visual image of the protecting hands, like the casing around a bud, suggests that the narrator's own palms are vulnerable and delicate. When Lorelei, however, is told that her hands are too soft to help with a job of building a wall, she asks sarcastically, "Will they [the hands] hatch a blue milk, magnolias?" (p. 37). Blue blood is traditionally a sign of royalty, and magnolias are delicate and beautiful flowers, but Lorelei questions why she should be special, why she should be excluded from work. Denying the protection of the friend or lover, Lorelei affirms that her fists are "hard under my shoulders" and her "feet are leafed arch to sole," comparing them to the tough flippers of seals which allow them to walk on land (p. 37). An italicized voice that must be her companion's describes Lorelei as *My hard woman*," and she makes the "you" of the poem "split my hands" until they are "lined with Shepherd's Warning" (p. 37). The phrase "Shepherd's Warning" refers to the British weather-lore rhyme: "Red sky at night: shepherd's delight. Red sky in morning: shepherd's warning." Lorelei demands that even she must live by the law of work and toil, and she figures this through symbols from folklore: the metaphor of blue blood, the associations of flowers, and weather lore.

Lorelei is the female aspect of Hadfield's mythic world, but the foil to Lorelei is the Skerryman who makes appearances throughout the sequence. The Skerryman derives from the Scottish phrase to "meet the skerryman," and he is an isolated figure living on a rock or island, a description that recalls Hadfield's choice to live on West Burra. For Shetlanders, however, to "meet the skerryman" can also mean to meet someone you did not expect, and the phrase is used as an evasive answer when the person being questioned does not want to reveal that person's name ("Who did you meet?" "I met the Skerryman"). In a note preceding "Lorelei's Lore," Hadfield expands on definitions of the Skerryman, providing a gloss that describes him as "the Green Man, a doleful Coyote, the Hanged Man (the martyr), the Devil (the challenge)" (p. 18). The Green Man is a figure associated with deities of nature, such as the ancient Greek god of shepherds, Pan. As a satyr god, Pan also relates to the tarot card symbol of the devil, which is often figured in tarot decks as half man, half goat. Coyote was a mischievous god in Native American traditions, and the symbol of the Hanged

Man relates to Norse mythology, especially the story of how Odin or Loki hung from the world tree, Yggdrasil, in order to gain the wisdom of the runes. Like Pan, Loki, Coyote, and the Devil, the Skerryman is a trickster, so in the prose poem "Tarantella," Hadfield depicts him dancing with a girl "threshing a sheaf of smoke, lanky and lovely as a liquorice bootlace" (p. 21). The Skerryman's link to nature and the land is emphasized by the image of threshing, and the sweetness of his seduction is obvious in the comparison with a licorice bootlace. Lorelei, who is narrating the poem, recognizes that the Skerryman, like her, is a purveyor of folklore; his advice on how to cure a sore throat is "*poultice, linctus, calamine. Macallans and lemon*" (p. 21). The Skerryman recommends the poultice cloth for an aching part of the body; linctus medicine for treating coughs; and lemon and Macallans, a type of Scottish whiskey. The Skerryman is established in this poem as a trickster and seducer as well as a transmitter of folk knowledge.

In addition to these mythical identities, Hadfield provides some more modern analogies for the Skerryman; she describes him as "the radio mast on Ronas Hill, the carcass of a stag on the beach at Skye: the discord that makes a pretty scene beautiful" (p. 18). The Skerryman represents glimpses of unconventional or unusual beauty that are not picturesque but magnificent. This splendid (but not quaint) beauty is specifically related to places in Shetland (Ronas and Skye), a landscape to which the Skerryman is intimately connected. In the prose poem "The Gannet and the Skerryman," Hadfield offers a creation myth, as the Skerryman is painfully released from the Shetland seabeds. The Gannet, a figure reminiscent of Ted Hughes's trickster in his 1970 collection, *Crow*, "snips open the seabed and lava elbows out to steam his skull, and piles out in triple chins, and kicks out—lava on lava until there crowns an island and a shivering mannie [man]: Skerryman, pushed prematurely from the hot earth's gut; sorrowful, shivering and basalt-black" (p. 36). The description of the lava is dominated by bodily imagery (elbows and chins), as it births the Skerryman, who is "premature," "sorrowful," and "shivering." Like other mythical tricksters, the Skerryman has little desire to exist in a human world. The compound "basalt-black" uses alliteration to emphasize the igneous color of the Skerryman and the hardness of his body made from volcanic rock. The Skerryman is bleakly handsome, and in the poem "Hey Hey Mister Blue," he prompts the question "What's beautiful?" (p. 56).

The title of "Hey Hey Mister Blue" is a reference to a popular song, "Mr. Blue Sky," released in 1978 by the band Electric Light Orchestra; the song personifies summer and asks "him" why he has to leave. The figure of Mr. Blue Sky is transposed by Hadfield onto the Skerryman, who is described as wearing a blue shirt that "makes everything like Indian summer" (p. 56). Lorelei is narrating the poem again, and she portrays the Skerryman as a trickster, a feckless seducer who loves and leaves her:

And Skerryman goes

right-o, time I was getting on

and moves your hand, and zips his fly, and antlered a silent Harrier zips the pale blue sky, trailing a streamer of ROAR.

(p. 56)

The prose-poem format of "Hey Hey Mister Blue" is interrupted by the Skerryman's voice right-justified on the page. His speech is colloquial and informal, not exactly what one would expect from a supernatural being, but it does tally with the trickster personality and it emphasizes his affinity with ordinary people: the folk. The description of the Skerryman moving Lorelei's hand is suggestive, as is the description of him zipping up the fly of his trousers. The Skerryman is also a seducer who comes and goes without warning; he is capricious like nature, but in a masculine mode, and this symbolism contradicts traditional personifications of nature as a fickle and unreliable woman. The moment of loss, though, is figured using urban rather than natural imagery, as the fly zipper becomes a Harrier jet in the blue sky. The feeling of loss is given gigantic proportions, and the disconcerting noise of the jet complements the jolting emotions of the encounter. The jet marks an intrusion on

Shetland from the modern world of engines, armies, and war, which contradicts the existence of the Skerryman, a creature of myth, folklore, and tall tales.

In contrast to the folkloric obsession in "Lorelei's Law," however, is another female character, Ghosty. In spite of her supernatural name, Ghosty is far more involved in modern, urban Scottish life than Lorelei or the Skerryman. Consequently, in "The King's Courtyard," Ghosty possesses the body of a woman cooking naan bread, a traditional South Asian food:

The city sky is baked in its own lights
and round and clay as tandoor,
but Ghosty, shredding the hot naan,
knows streetlamps are beautiful,
they *are*, oh *beautiful*, they star her face like butter.

(p. 19)

A tandoor is a round clay oven used in South Asia and the Middle East to make traditional tandoori food, and it indicates that Ghosty is entering the immigrant communities of urban Scotland. When Hadfield uses the tandoor oven as a metaphor for the city sky, her symbolism emphasizes the central place of immigrant communities in the modern Scottish metropolis. Even in this urban environment, too, Hadfield finds beauty; the description of the city as "baked in its own lights" recalls the light pollution of built-up areas. Ghosty finds beauty, though, even in the streetlamps, which are compared to stars, and their light, falling on Ghosty's face, is rich and delicious like butter. Ghosty represents another side to Hadfield's poetics, as she explores the beauty in metropolitan landscapes.

Ghosty is an urban creature. In the prose poem "A970," Hadfield refers to her as a "Francis Assisi for engines" (p. 31): that is, not a patron saint of animals but of the engine, the road, and the life of the traveler. The A970 is a road on Shetland that passes from its southernmost tip in Sumburgh to its most northern point in North Roe, and Ghosty travels the length of it, a "Girl Racer" and "darling of the Sumburgh road" (p. 31). Hadfield describes how "she splits the rock-candy of the cliff-road, spreading the speed limit through her prism" (p. 31). Ghosty is powerful enough to split rock, and the prism image suggests that she can change our perception of speed, like a ghostly road hog.

Even on Shetland, Ghosty is a creature of the modern and urban world, but the preoccupation with folklore appears again in the poem "Ghosty's Almanac," though the urban and social are still strong elements. The poem is written in prose, but its form is anaphoric: each paragraph begins with the question "How many ...?" Since the poem is an almanac, the passing of time is significant, yet it is also concerned with summing up the world as it is in a particular year. To make such a judgment, Ghosty begins with the seas ("How many seas?"), and she responds by imagining a polluted and sickening ocean evoked with rich, alliterative, onomatopoeic language: "Engines boiling water to black liquorice, the oily harbour at cracking point, the sea shrugging its itchy skins" (p. 58). Next she turns to the mountains, which, unlike the seas, still are pristine and remote: "Eaval, Dearg, a blue mountain, the Red Mountain pinned to the land like weird wild brooches" (p. 58). The image of the mountains as brooches personifies the land, but Ghosty is more concerned with the human communities on Shetland and her own experience of traveling through them. She considers what has given her courage and lust for life, asking, "How many pints? How many drams gave me the mythic wildness on an empty belly? How many gallons of Unleaded, the petrol cap like a black clover on the car's roof?" (p. 58). The petroleum that keeps the car running is equivalent to Ghosty's consumption of alcoholic drinks—she mentions a pint of beer and a dram, a Scottish word for a small quantity of whiskey—and the gas cap is a lucky four-leaf clover egging her on. Ghosty's reason for being is to roam, and this wanderlust is the source of the "mythic wildness," which is not induced by drinking alcohol on an empty stomach but rather by the desire to travel and explore the world.

While Lorelei and the Skerryman are static and deeply attached to Shetland, Ghosty. Ghosty offers a myth of modernity in Scotland: a world enriched by immigrant communities, by modern inventions like the engine, and by the possibilities of traveling the world. This desire is developed in Hadfield's next collection of poetry, *Nigh-No-Place*, which is dedicated to place to an even greater extent. Shetland is still significant in *Nigh-No-Place*, but it becomes a jumping-off place from which to explore the world.

NIGH-NO-PLACE

Nigh-No-Place is the title of Hadfield's second collection, published in 2008, and also of the poem that opens the book. *Nigh* is a Scottish word that means "near," "close to," or "almost." The place that Hadfield inhabits, then, as a poet is both a literal place close to nowhere (that is, Shetland or other wild spaces Hadfield has visited) and a philosophical space (almost nowhere or nothing). As Burt points out, Hadfield's "sensibility finds itself ... unquenchably attracted to the remote, the hardscrabble, the back-of-beyond" (p. 24). This poetics of the remote is summed up in the title poem, "Nigh-No-Place," which uses anaphora: the first fourteen lines beginning with the phrase "I will meet you," and the following ten lines opening with "I will bring you." What changes in the poem is a litany of place names from "Pity Me Wood" to "Booze, Alberta," but the move from a promise ("I will meet you") to an act of will ("I will bring you") is significant in light of the poem's epigraph from William Shakespeare's play *The Tempest*: "I prithee, let me bring thee where crabs grow; / And I with my long nails will dig thee pignuts ..." (*Nigh-No-Place*, p. 9). The character quoted, Caliban, is one of Shakespeare's most controversial creations; half monster and half man, he is forced into servitude by the magician Prospero. Like the Skerryman of Hadfield's *Almanacs*, Caliban is a trickster who is sorrowful about his life on a remote island. Though some critics have read Caliban as a colonial subject victimized by imperialism, the depiction in the play emphasizes his delight in plotting the murder of his master and the violation of Miranda, Prospero's daughter. Caliban is ambiguous, but he also has moments of intense eloquence in expressing his miserable condition. In quoting him, Hadfield lends the invitations of her own poem a sense of abjection, emphasized by the uncertainty of the final line: "Will you go with me?" (p. 10). The invitation in the poem that opens this collection is a summons to the reader to enter Hadfield's poetic world.

One of the new places that Hadfield invites the reader to visit in *Nigh-No-Place* is Canada. Hadfield traveled around Canada using funds from her Eric Gregory Award to visit family, and Burt suggests that she finds there "empty spaces and gloomy parallels to her own Scotland" (p. 24). Burt notes, too, that "rural Canada, like parts of Scotland, is nearly nowhere (thus the title), and yet such unpromising places (on either continent), once we notice their beauties, can make us more sensitive to what we see anywhere" (p. 24). Hadfield examines the literal parallels connecting Shetland and Canada in her 2010 essay "Far North, Way Up High"; she explains that the sixtieth parallel is the circle of latitude that "bisects Shetland, putting us at approximately the same latitude as the historic fur-trading port of Churchill on Hudson Bay," and she imagines "an irresponsible fantasy about the failing of the Greenland Pump, the faltering of the Gulf's systolic sweep from Cuba, the slow march of polar bears towards us over new sea ice" ("Far North, Way Up High," p. 40). Hadfield's daydream suggests that, if not physically connected, Canada and Shetland are parallel in Hadfield's mind.

In writing about Canada, Hadfield brings her shrewd eye for detail to a different space. While her poems about Shetland in *Almanacs* focused on the omnipotent powers of the weather and the cycles of the seasons, her writing about Canada emphasizes fecundity and fertility, and she highlights the reproductive capacities of nature. Most evocative is the long poem "The Mandolin of May," which describes a scene of lush springtime abundance. The mandolin of the title is significant, too, as physical reproduction is compared to the creative process of producing a poem.

The poem begins with Hadfield describing how "the garden bursts / open like a dropped melon," the surprise of the eruption being emphasized by the jolt in the line break from "bursts" to "open" (p. 16). The narrator describes herself in the banal act of carrying a chamber pot out into the yard, but even this action becomes sublime as the speaker notices the beauty of the scene around her: "Cottonseed roils and sinks slowly, / cladding the roof and catching on the gutter like curds" (p. 16). The fleecy cottonseed that covers the roof and blocks gutters is used to figure a scene of glutinous excess and proclivity. Faced with such a scene, the narrator considers her own fertility as a woman and a poet:

> I'm no great shakes at babies but I've been thinking more
> and more about mandolins, as the weeks go by. Crumpled notes
> would prang out of those paired strings, a salvage metal
> sound, like freight cars screeling over a crossing.
>
> (p. 16)

In colloquial terms ("no great shakes"), the narrator suggests that compensation for a lack or disinterest in human fertilty might be artistic creation as represented by the mandolin. The use of the mandolin as an artistic symbol recalls the nineteenth-century tradition of the *improvisatrice*, a term that describes a woman poet who improvises poetry and music (in the poems of the nineteenth-century British writer Letitia Landon, for example). Hadfield's poetry, however, is far from genteel, and her music is akin to the groaning of "salvage metal" or a train "screeling," a Scottish word that refers to a high-pitched, grating cry. The mandolin is also linked to fertility in Hadfield's symbology; she explains that "if I had a mandolin, I'd hug it to my belly like a watermelon" (p. 16), an image that connects the big belly of pregnancy to the explosive melon in the opening of the poem and the possibility of artistic creation through the mandolin. The symbolism of fruitfulness versus decay is likewise applied to poetry itself. Hadfield describes the frustration of artistic creation in "the same spoiled poem over and over again," which is

> mushy round the
> peach pit of the poem before. The same commas maul it, like
> fruitflies
>
> (p. 17)

Finding new inspiration is difficult, and the narrator expresses fear about the decay of poetic talent. This anxiety characterizes other poems set in Canada, such as "Still Life with the Very Devil," where ominous symbols question the longevity of poetic talent. A description of the "last clove of garlic," which "sprouts a yellow talon," is followed by the self-criticism, "All I'm good for is a rhyme in *r*" (p. 15). The garlic clove is the last one left, which suggests either that it is a remnant or that it is a scarce commodity almost used up. The sense of scarcity and scraps applies to the poetic talent, too, since the predatory bird talon is a visual match with the "rhyme in *r*." Altogether, this poem presents a picture of frustrated energies. Hadfield describes "the sink … plugged with duckstock" symbolizing blockage and excess (the rich and costly duck), while "dishes [are] stacked like vertebra," an image of inactivity—the dishes are waiting to be washed—and of fragility in figuring the precarious pile as a human backbone (p. 15). The final image recalls the reproductive, fertile imagery in "The Mandolin of May," which is here transferred to a domestic scene: "Under the broiler, / turned sausages ejaculate" (p. 15). The exploding fat of sausages on the grill is reminiscent of the exploding melon in "The Mandolin of May," though the use of the word "ejaculate" sexualizes the image and makes it darkly comic. The poem ends with an orgasmic motif, and in spite of the narrator's qualms, the act of writing about not being able to write has produced a poem.

Similarly, in "The Mandolin of May," the narrator does find inspiration through writing about the lack of inspiration. Related to fertility and poetic inspiration are images of fecundity and richness. Hadfield describes how, "with the white eye of a prophet, the salmon unravels but / swims upriver" (p. 17). The blank eye of the salmon can think of nothing but reproducing even though it knows that, upriver, it will breed and die in quick succession. This urge to reproduce is reflected in the narrator, too, as she identifies her bed as having "the fetid, residual warmth of a nest" (p. 17).

The human world of Canada is also full of death, however, and the figure of the grandmother, Grandmere, is related to resignation, stoicism, and toughness. The narrator describes how "Grandmere tonsures a tomato with a sharp little knife. She / saws around the withered stalk, excising the sunken socket" (p. 17). The comparison of the scalped tomato with a monk's tonsure humanizes the vegetable and makes the image more disturbing. This unease culminates in the use of the word "socket," which conjures the human body: the tomato as human eye ball and the stalk as its optic nerve. Grandmere is then a figure associated with tough endurance, which is emphasized when she shows the narrator "which fields are planted with corn" (p. 18). The narrator responds, "I don't see anything coming"—a reply that emphasizes a lack of fertility and new growth (p. 18). The reply might also relate to the narrator's own missing inspiration, however: ironically, a poem has been produced out of contemplation on a lack of productivity. "The Mandolin of May" journeys from being a self-conscious lament about the decay of poetic talent to a powerful commentary on the joy of fertility and the threat of death as they are exhibited in nature and traditional communities that are close to the land.

While the poems about Canada ponder the decay of poetic inspiration, Hadfield returns to the landscape of Shetland "to mind me what my poetry's for" (p. 35). At the "Daed-traa," the slack of the tide, Hadfield goes to the rock pool, which has "ventricles, just like us"; has "its theatre"; has "its cross-eyed beetling Lear" and "its billowing Monroe" (p. 35). In comparing the cosmos of the rock pool to human cultural institutions and icons (Shakespeare's *King Lear*, Marilyn Monroe), Hadfield is not suggesting that nature is a mirror for human worlds, but she tries to use familiar references to make sense of it, as one would on encountering any foreign culture. The natural world of Shetland may resemble its human counterpart, but it remains undeniably alien. In the prose poem "Snuskit" (a Shetland word to describe a sulky frame of mind), the speaker announces, "The shore is just not nice. Good" (p. 39). The narrator of "Snuskit" is not looking for the quaint beauty of pastoral scenes or manicured gardens but rather for the wild chaos and refuse of the Shetland coast: "the rubberduckery of the Atlantic"; "a bloated seal and sometimes skull, fishboxes and buoys, a cummerbund of rotting kelp" (p. 39). "Snuskit" inventories the beach refuse, elevating it at times (the kelp becoming a tuxedo sash), until it is not rubbish but treasure.

Like "Snuskit," the other Shetland poems in this sequence work as inventories that register the stark beauty of the Scottish landscape. The prose poem "Gish" (meaning "a channel of water"), for instance, considers the qualities of water in "hoof-shaped holes in a pasture"; "a leak from a washing machine"; "the black liquor that cooks out of mushrooms"; or the moisture on "the sound of breath like drowning" (p. 36). Water is a universal substance that exists on the land, in domestic devices for cleanliness, in food, and even in death: the image of drowning. While water is elevated in "Gish," the poem "Hüm (noun)" offers descriptions of the Shetland "twilight or gloaming" and the unpleasant bodily experience of being in the dark. Hadfield suggests that it is

to be abject; lick snot
and rain from the top lip
like a sick calf

(p. 38)

Another definition emphasizes the dangers that lurk in the darkness: "To cross the bull's field / in the dark" (p. 38); and an alternative reminds us of the decay in dark spaces, like the decaying byre or cow shed: "To pass in the dark / a byre like a rotten walnut" (p. 38). While water had a variety of associations (the land, cleanliness, food, and drowning), the darkness or "hüm" is only connected to sickness, death, and decay. In providing inventories of water and the dark, however, Hadfield conveys both the physical experience of living on Shetland and a sense of its routines and life cycles.

Human beings are at the mercy of such life cycles, as is shown in "Blashey-wadder," the title being a Shetland word to describe wet, unsettled weather. "Blashey-wadder" compares the power of urban and natural landscapes. Hadfield describes how "waterfalls blew right up off the cliff

/ in grand plumes like smoking chimneys," an image that works visually (water vapor and smoke) and compares the power of the waterfall to the power of fire and human industry (p. 31). Another significant description depicts the gritters' truck, which

rolled a blinking ball of orange light
ahead of it, like a dungbeetle
that had stolen the sun

(p. 31)

The mundane act of gritting (that is, sanding or salting the roads in winter) becomes mythical, since Hadfield refers to ancient Egyptian legends where scarab beetles were sacred because of their association with Khepri, the god of the rising sun. Like Khepri, the gritters roll the sun before them to bring about the dawn, offering possibilities for rebirth and renewal. The contemplation of the scene is interrupted, however, because the dog accompanying the narrator refuses to heel. Hadfield describes the dog "sniffing North addictively— / he saw we had it coming," and she tells how the dog predicts "more'n wet weak hail / on a bastard wind" (p. 31). In contrast to the rebirth signified by the beetle, the presence of the dog recalls the Egyptian god Anubis, a figure portrayed with the head of a jackal. Anubis was associated with the underworld and with the judgment of souls after death, and the dog takes on this kind of portentous role in warning the narrator of what storms are to come. The use of mythical allusion in "Blashey-wadder" links the Shetland landscape to something primitive and primal, as observations of the mundane become ur-moments of prophecy and revelation.

HADFIELD'S MENAGERIE

"Blashey-wadder" is one of many poems by Hadfield that focus on animals. Hannah Brooks-Motl sums up the energy of Hadfield's animal poetry most succinctly, when she describes how the poems "in more Hadfieldian terms, wriggle, cantor, and squirm" (online). Hadfield herself uses the extended metaphor of an animal for poetry in "Ashley Farm," which appears in *Almanacs*. In

"Ashley Farm," a "she" not an "it" confronts the reader, suggesting an equivalency between human beings and animals: "she looks up, a sure poem / with a skull like quartzrock" (*Almanacs*, p. 10). The animal/poem is confident with her solid quartz-rock skull, and she is a thing of beauty and bathos, as she "plays her tail xylophone / across byre bars" and "hooks her tail / in a high crozier, to shit" (p. 10). The animal/poem produces beautiful music out of the shed's bars, and, unlike a human being, she shows no shame in the act of defecating. Instead, there is something spiritual about her, as Hadfield mischievously compares the curl of her tail to a bishop's staff, a crozier.

The discussion of art and animals that began in *Almanacs* continues in *Nigh-No-Place* in the poem "Ladies and Gentlemen This Is a Horse as Magritte Might Paint Him." Magritte's horse, though, is not the confident creature of "Ashley Farm" but rather is a display presented for the audience implied in the poem's title. The horse is a sad spectacle "in blinkers and bridle and drugged of course," and Hadfield describes "the clapper seized in the brain's bell, / propped up on steel and the air's goodwill" (*Nigh-No-Place*, p. 28). In the way the animal is lacking in autonomy and independence, the depiction of Magritte's horse carries an implied criticism in its contrast with the unabashed and defiant creature in "Ashley Farm." Hadfield demands that representations of animals should not only be a lever for discussion of human desires and imaginings, but that they should treat animals with respect and dignity.

This kind of respectful writing is most evident in Hadfield's poems written for and about dogs, in which she describes a kinship between human beings and animals. Hadfield feels an affinity for animals that she describes in "Far North, Way Up High": "My breath comes in visible spurts. I'm feeling more mammal, weak and hot, insufficiently insulated. I see how little it would take to make me carrion" (p. 40). Living in extreme weather conditions and with few luxuries, Hadfield is aware of the struggle that animals have to make to survive. This sympathy is expressed again in "Self-Portrait as a Fortune-Telling Miracle Fish," where the narrator's

"daemon" is "a dogfish" or "a Starry Hound, a blunt and hungry hobo, / scrounging, starveling, sleeping on the go" (*Nigh-No-Place*, p. 42). Hadfield's sympathy for dogs emerges from a sense of shared struggle; like any living creature, human beings have to fight to survive and are vulnerable to sickness, accidents, and death.

The preoccupation with dogs began in *Almanacs*, where "Melodeon on the Road Home" uses an extended metaphor that compares the dog to a musical instrument, and "Orchid Dog" describes the joy that a dog takes in nature as it accompanies the narrator in exploring the Shetland landscape. Hadfield's poems in *Nigh-No-Place* elevate the dog, too, so in "Canis Minor," she associates them with the eternal symbols of stars. The dog is key to a better understanding of the world, though he remains crude and coarse: "He scours his butt and licks my elbow. / He falls back on his haunches like a telescope" (*Nigh-No-Place*, p. 13). As in "Melodeon on the Road Home," Hadfield finds a startling metaphor that describes the physicality of the dog and his importance as the poet's muse; here the dog is compared with a telescope, an instrument designed to aid the observation of remote objects.

Hadfield's dogs are not merely vehicles for poems about nature—they offer allegorical symbolism, too. In *Almanacs*, the epigraph of Hadfield's poem "Staple Island Swing" quotes Edwin Morgan's poem "A View of Things": "What I hate about love is its dog" (*Almanacs*, p. 12). Morgan plays upon the idea of the dog as a loyal companion never leaving its master's or mistress's side. In comparing love to a dog, Morgan implies that love is difficult to remove, and he evokes the emotional baggage that follows love. Hadfield finds Morgan's idea compelling, and she riffs on it in *Nigh-No-Place* in her own poem "Love's Dog": "What I hate about love is its me me me / What I love about love is its Eat-me/ Drink-me" (*Nigh-No-Place*, p. 50). What follows love could be selfishness ("me me me") or transformation ("Eat-me / Drink-me"— referring to the labels on the transformative potions that Alice drinks in Lewis Carroll's *Alice's Adventures in Wonderland*).

"Love's Dog" is a symbolic construct, a way of thinking about human love, but most moving is Hadfield's poem "In the Same Way," in which her affinity with animals and nature in general is mapped out with great sympathy and delicacy. Ostensibly, the poem describes the routines of a dog crying to be let in and out of the house; Hadfield repeats the phrase "so I open up" throughout the poem. There is, however, a greater significance to these rituals, which have a ghostly feeling, and the opening up is also an exploration of the power of nature. The animal itself represents a medium between the world of the domestic space and the wild natural world outside. Hadfield describes how the animal

cries at the kitchen door
with snailtracks of rain in her muscular fur
so I open up and she runs in singing

(p. 62)

Unlike human beings, the animal is at one with nature (shown in the visually striking image of rain as "snailtracks" in her fur) and with itself in the joyful image of singing. The animal is innocent of human self-doubt, and the narrator envies her lack of self-consciousness and her oneness with the world. Initially, the speaker of the poem opens the door to the pet, but later this becomes less clear; at one point it is the wind that cries at the kitchen door, and later the dog does not enter "but the wind does, / with rain, a squall of claws" (p. 62). This merging of the dog with a ghostly representative of nature lends ambiguity to the conclusion of the poem:

and the wind canters in
and she with a wild carol

and all the night hail
melted gleaming in her furs

(p. 62)

At the end of the poem, the "she" is the pet returning to the warmth of the house, but "she" is also nature itself: the wind that "canters in." In either case, the creature that enters is a thing of joy and beauty; the use of the word "carol" brings out its meaning as a song of praise, while the melting hail in the fur is a sensuous and decorous image. There is joy and sadness in Hadfield's writing about nature: a deep respect and admiration for its beauty, and a mournful sense of how far away human beings always are from being so at one with the world.

CONCLUSION

The landscapes and communities of Shetland dominate Hadfield's poetry. Hadfield explains that "the emotional fetch of Shetland's landscapes often exceed their scale" ("Far North, Way Up High," p. 40). A fetch can be an instance of fetching something or someone or it can be a trick or a ruse, and, in Hadfield's poetry, there is a sense that the place of Shetland is both a slippery adversary and a home of bleak magnificence. It is also connected to the emotional life of her narrators, though this is not simply another variation on pathetic fallacy. Instead, Hadfield contemplates the theater of nature and relates it to her own experience, almost as though nature itself was a foreign culture. As Burt suggests, "For her the world of the senses is the most important world, though it is only through our moods and our ideas that we do justice to that world" (p. 24).

This synthesis of mood and observation does not mean foregrounding the poet's personality by writing in a confessional or anecdotal manner. Hadfield's poetics are humble in their concentrated contemplation of the world around her, and she is always aware of the possibility of loss: the loss of loved ones, of home, and of nature. She sums up her poetics of humility and loss in the essay "From My Vow," which discusses Hadfield's research into Mexican ex-votos. The folk art of the ex-voto represents miracles in human lives enacted by saints or by god, and for Hadfield, the ex-voto is an apt analogy for poetry, because the gift of inspiration is miraculous. Such an analogy, Hadfield explains, "accounts for the nature of what I choose to call poetry" and this entails "the compulsion to faithfully record and renew the present tense in language which is more spoken than written, while suffering the continual losses of the present tense" ("From My Vow," online). Even as Hadfield records the happenings of nature or the routines of the folk, such events are disappearing into the past, never to be recovered. In her ex-voto, the poem "Our Lady of Isbister," Hadfield laments this loss as she longs for her life on Shetland to be never-ending and thanks some higher spiritual power for all her experiences: from the "wind driving spittlestrings" to "a whirlpool of Muscovey ducks" and "wet socks / slamdunked along the washing line" (*Nigh-No-Place*, p. 46). Hadfield concludes *Nigh-No-Place* by exulting Shetland as always, and the joy in her experience of the land is mapped across the page like the footprints of an explorer, voyager, wanderer:

> O send me another last life like this—
> This is bliss
>
> this
>
> no, this
>
> no, this
>
> (p. 46)

Selected Bibliography

WORKS OF JEN HADFIELD

POETRY

Fool Moon. Hale, Cheshire, U.K.: Rogue Seeds, 2002. (Bound with a length of nylon from unwound fishing nets.)

Marking. Hale, Cheshire, U.K.: Rogue Seeds, 2002. (Printed on tracing paper, bound concertina-style.)

Wet and Dry Flies to Rise a Ghost. Hale, Cheshire, U.K.: Rogue Seeds, 2002. (Hand-tied fishing fly attached to front cover.)

Heaventree New Poets 2. With Simon Turner and Anna Lea. Coventry, U.K.: Heaventree: 2004.

Almanacs. Tarset, U.K.: Bloodaxe, 2005.

Printer's Devil and the Little Bear. Clun, U.K.: Redlake Press/Rogue Seeds, 2006. (Limited edition of thirty: twenty-nine loose-leaf pages in Solander box.)

What Is the Song ... Lerwick, Scotland: Shetland Arts Trust, 2006.

Nigh-No-Place. Tarset, U.K.: Bloodaxe, 2008.

NONFICTION PROSE

"Jen Hadfield's Workshop." *Guardian* (http://www.guardian.co.uk/books/2006/apr/28/poetry), April 28, 2006.

"Far North, Way Up High." *Financial Times*, February 27, 2010, p. 40.

"From My Vow." *Edinburgh International Book Festival* (http://www.edbookfest.co.uk/uploads/article/Jen%20Hadfield%20From%20My%20Vow.pdf), 2010.

"The Urge to Make." *Verse Palace* (http://versepalace.wordpress.com/), May 31, 2010.

CRITICAL STUDIES AND ARTICLES

Bell, Kara Kellar. Review of *Almanacs*. *New Review* (http://www.laurahird.com/newreview/almanacs.html), 2005.

Bennett, Charles. "Current Literature 2004/5. New Writing: Poetry." *English Studies* 87, no. 6:679–691 (2006). (Review of *Almanacs*.)

Brooks-Motl, Hannah. "With My Little Eye." *Contemporary Poetry Review* (http://www.cprw.com/Misc/hatfield.htm), 2009.

Burt, Stephen. "Sound Sense." *Times Literary Supplement*, May 23, 2008, p. 24. (Review of *Nigh-No-Place*.)

Commane, Jane. "Strangely Wonderful and Often Incongruous." *Horizon Review* 1 (http://www.saltpublishing.com/horizon/issues/01/text/commane_jane_review.htm), 2008. (Review of *Nigh-No-Place*.)

Crown, Sarah. "All Fall Down." *Guardian* (http://www.guardian.co.uk/books/2006/mar/25/featuresreviews.guardianreview22), March 25, 2006. (Review of *Almanacs*.)

Crucefix, Martin. "Reviews." *Magma* 32 (http://www.poetrymagazines.org.uk/magazine/record.asp?id=18780#), 2005. (Review of *Almanacs*.)

Greening, John. Review of *Almanacs* by Jen Hadfield. *Times Literary Supplement*, July 1, 2005, pp. 30–31.

Knight, Stephen. "*Nigh-No-Place* by Jen Hadfield." *Independent* (http://www.independent.co.uk/arts-entertainment/books/reviews/nighnoplace-by-jen-hadfield-942338.html), September 28, 2008.

Leitch, Luke. "Jen Hadfield: A Jaunty Voice from the Isles." *Times* (http://entertainment.timesonline.co.uk/tol/arts_and_entertainment/books/poetry/article5511247.ece), January 14, 2009.

Leviston, Frances. "The Horse in Mid-Air." *Guardian* (http://www.guardian.co.uk/books/2008/feb/16/featuresreviews.guardianreview27/print), February 16, 2008. (Review of *Nigh-No-Place*.)

Lumsden, Roddy. "Roddy Lumsden Recommends Jen Hadfield." *Books from Scotland* (http://www.booksfromscotland.com/News/Roddy-Lumsdens-Blog/Jen-Hadfield) March 10, 2008.

Piette, Adam. Review of *Nigh-No-Place* by Jen Hadfield, *Between Cup and Lip* by Peter Manson, and *Collected*

Poems by Melvyn Peake. *Black Box Manifold* 1 (http://www.manifold.group.shef.ac.uk/issue1/piette.html), 2008.

———. "Nigh-No-Place." *European Journal of English Studies* 13, no. 2:241–245 (2009).

Pow, Tom. "Jen Hadfield, Jackie Kay, and Stewart Conn: Scotlands." *Scottish Studies Review* 7, no. 2:111–113 (2006).

Riach, Alan. "The Poetics of Devolution." In *The Edinburgh Companion to Contemporary Scottish Poetry*. Edited by Matt McGuire and Colin Nicholson. Edinburgh: Edinburgh University Press, 2009.

INTERVIEWS

Abe Books. "T. S. Eliot Prize Winner: Jen Hadfield." *Abe Books* (http://www.abebooks.com/books/jen-hadfield.shtml).

Arts and Ecology. "Jen Hadfield: The New Ecopoetics." *Arts and Ecology Magazine* (http://www.artsandecology.org.uk/magazine/features/jen-hadfield—ecopoetics).

Mansfield, Susan. "Jen Hadfield Interview: Northern Light." *Scotsman* (http://thescotsman.scotsman.com/14072/Jen-Hadfield-interview-Northern-light.5039185.jp), March 7, 2009.

Scottish Poetry Library. "Owl and Other Answers: An Interview with Jen Hadfield." *Our Sweet Old Etcetera …*, (http://scottishpoetrylibrary.wordpress.com/2009/07/23/owl-other-answers-an-interview-with-jen-hadfield/), July 23, 2009.

Van Winkle, Ryan. "November 5th: Jen Hadfield, Lise Sinclair, and Carry a Poem." *Scottish Poetry Library* (http://scottishpoetrylibrary.podomatic.com/player/web/2009-11-04T17_00_30-08_00), 2009.

ANN HAWKSHAW

(1812—1885)

Debbie Bark

ON MAY 1, 1885, the *Manchester Guardian* published an obituary for Lady Ann Hawkshaw, who had died the previous week at her London home: "We much regret to announce the death, which took place on Wednesday evening, at her residence, Belgrave Mansions, Grosvenor Gardens, London, of Ann, wife of Sir John Hawkshaw, F.R.S. Among many accomplished women who have made their home in Manchester during the past half century, none secured a deeper regard than the gifted lady whose death we now record." Clearly proud of her association with the city and her contribution to its cultural heritage, the newspaper traces Ann Hawkshaw's rise from a clergyman's daughter in rural Yorkshire to a writer who earned the respect of Manchester's literary community. Her first volume of poetry, the obituary notes, "attracted considerable attention and was very favourably received both in London and the provinces," while later works "showed much tenderness of feeling and beauty of expression." In privileging her talent as a poet over her status as the wife of a leading Victorian engineer, the 1885 obituary acknowledges Hawkshaw as a poet of some note: an accolade not repeated until the rediscovery of her work in the 1990s. Yet because of the time and place of her writing, there is much in Hawkshaw's four volumes of poetry, published between 1842 and 1871, to interest both casual reader and scholar.

On October 14, 1812, the Reverend James Jackson (1776–1849), dissenting Protestant minister of the Green Hammerton Independent Chapel in the West Riding of Yorkshire, and his wife, Mary, welcomed their second daughter into the world. Ann, their third child (Jane had been born in 1806 and James in 1809), would be followed by a further eleven children, although by the time Ann Jackson left home to be married in 1835, seven of these children had died, including Ann's beloved elder sister, Jane. James Jackson had come to Green Hammerton from Allerton Mauleverer, near Knaresborough, in 1794. He was ordained on November 5, 1801, and would go on to enjoy a forty-year tenure as Congregational minister of the parish. At the vanguard of a religious revolution, Jackson and his fellow clergymen offered rural Yorkshire an alternative to the established state church and oversaw the building of independent chapels in Green Hammerton and surrounding villages.

In the spring of 1806, the Reverend Jackson had married Mary Clarke, the daughter of an agricultural family who had owned land in Green Hammerton for over three hundred years. With Mary's parents living close by, the young Jackson children reveled in the attention of their grandparents and were free to explore the rural landscape during frequent walks and visits to neighbors. Ann's descriptions of Green Hammerton, recorded in later life in her short manuscript memoir, "Memories of My Childhood" (1856–1857), resonate with nostalgia for the rural idyll. "My native village," she recalls, "was one of the prettiest in the north of England," a "perfect picture of rural comfort and country beauty"— especially on those fine afternoons in summer or early autumn "when the heavy laden wagons were slowly coming up the road and the well fed cows were returning to their pastures after milking-time" (p. 3).

In this large clergyman's family, blessed with an abundance of life and yet touched by the reality of early death, Ann was raised under the strong and principled religious and moral influence of her father and grandfather, and the nurturing and encouraging eyes of a mother and grandmother who inspired Ann's love of reading, learning, and nature. In her memoir, Ann remembers her maternal grandmother with fondness, describing her as "a beautiful character" and admits to feeling for her "a love scarcely second to that I felt for my mother" (pp. 8–9). With her elder sister, Jane, Ann would sit sewing with her grandmother, listening attentively to her stories. Although their grandmother tended to "dwell on her long rambles over wild heaths and moors on a horse that no one but herself would mount" (p. 15), the girls would steer her toward their favorite subjects, for she "had a strong and energetic mind and could make clear and just views of life and duty." Ann grew to admire her grandmother's freethinking and religious independence, hearing how she "left the Church of England in whose communion she had been brought up, and joined the dissenters," because her "free mind turned with disgust from clergymen stained with vice of the most odious kinds, and her soul revolted at men who in meanness and dishonesty were below the peasants they professed to instruct" (p. 9).

"I was a very happy but a very idle child," recalls Hawkshaw in her memoir. "At six years old I could not read, nay did not know my letters and the only tears I remember to have shed were shed over the 'Reading Made Easy'—oh sad misnomer" (p. 13). Although slow to read, Ann nevertheless took great pleasure in listening to the rhymes and rhythms of Ann and Jane Taylor's recently published poetry for children. Under the guidance of her mother, Ann became part of that first generation of children to learn by rote the work of the Taylor sisters. "In my worst dunce days I could learn hymns and pieces of poetry from hearing them read over a few times," Ann recalls, "and never thought it a hardship to stand by my Mother's knee and while she plied her needle with a book open before her taught me one of Jane Taylor's little hymns for infant minds, or one of her 'Original Poems'" (p. 13). Before long, Ann became a competent, then voracious, independent reader: "When I did acquire the art of reading all my other amusements appeared tame in comparison … I became a devourer of books; suitable ones if they were to be had, unsuitable if no others were to be got" (p. 13).

While the value of reading, learning, and intellectual curiosity were instilled in Ann at home, at the age of fourteen she was sent away to school. "The first real sorrow I ever had, at least so I judge now, as it remains imprinted on my memory after thirty years have gone by … was leaving home for school" (p. 45), Hawkshaw recalls. From 1826, Ann was a boarder at the Moravian School in Little Gomersal, about forty miles distant from Green Hammerton. The Moravian Church had opened a day school for girls there in 1758, converting to a girls' boarding school in 1792.

At some time during the late 1820s, Ann met her future husband, John Hawkshaw. John had been born on April 9, 1811, the fifth child of the Leeds publican Henry Hawkshaw (1774–1813) and his wife, Sarah Carrington. Ann and John's paths most likely crossed during family visits to the village of Hampsthwaite, some fifteen miles west of Green Hammerton. Here, John's uncle on his mother's side and Ann's uncle on her father's were in business: Peter Carrington as a blacksmith, William Jackson as a farmer. Having left Leeds Grammar School at thirteen to take up a local engineering apprenticeship as pupil of the road surveyor Charles Fowler, John Hawkshaw had spent five years working on local turnpike schemes. In 1830, John moved to Liverpool as assistant to Alexander Nimmo, surveying a proposed railway connection from Liverpool to the Humber via Leeds. When Nimmo died in 1832, John decided to travel to South America, as engineer to the Bolivar Mining Association's copper mines at Aroa, Venezuela. By September 1834, John Hawkshaw was forced to return from Venezuela because of ill health, and on March 20, 1835, he and Ann Jackson were married, in the parish of Whixley, close to Green Hammerton.

At the time of their marriage, John was living in Liverpool, but by 1836, the Hawkshaws had relocated to Salford, where John took up an appointment with the Manchester and Bolton railway. As an engineer, John Hawkshaw flourished in Manchester, capitalizing on the expansion of the railway network across the northwest of England. For Ann, their Manchester years were defined by writing and motherhood. The poems in her first collection were crafted in the 1830s and early 1840s, during which time the first three of the Hawkshaws' six children were born: Mary Jane Jackson in 1838, Ada in 1840, and John Clarke in 1841.

"DIONYSIUS THE AREOPAGITE" WITH OTHER POEMS

"Dionysius the Areopagite" with Other Poems is a collection of twenty-two poems published in London and Manchester in November 1842 to some critical acclaim. Hawkshaw's debut onto the Manchester poetic scene coincided with a resurgence of poetic production in the city in the 1830s and 1840s, led by Samuel Bamford, John Bolton Rogerson, and John Critchley Prince. Manchester's poetic revival had been energized by burgeoning industrialization in the city and the widely held assumption that artistic expression had succumbed to a preoccupation with free enterprise. Although Hawkshaw was writing on the fringes of this group of established local poets, her *Dionysius* volume met with the approval of the most eminent of the Manchester group, Samuel Bamford (1788–1872), a weaver-poet erroneously jailed in 1819 for allegedly inciting a riot that led to the notorious Peterloo massacre. In the preface to his *Poems*, published in 1843, Bamford lists Hawkshaw alongside Rogerson, Prince, and others whose work had attracted the attention of Manchester's literary community and whose names were "destined for immortality."

Bamford particularly singles out the title poem of Hawkshaw's volume, "Dionysius the Areopagite," a long, narrative poem of some twenty-five hundred lines, organized into three parts, with each part divided into sections, and each section into verse paragraphs of varying lengths. The poem retells the biblical story of Dionysius the Areopagite, an elected member of the Areopagus in Athens, whose conversion to Christianity in light of St. Paul's teachings is briefly mentioned in the New Testament (Acts 17:34). Although the poem's opening sections are loosely based on the biblical account of St. Paul's teaching in Athens, the majority of the poem is an imaginative reconstruction of Dionysius' personal journey toward Christianity and his decision to choose the Christian faith over romantic love. Much of the poem is written as dialogue between Dionysius and the poem's other characters, namely Myra (his betrothed), Myra's father (a Stoic), and Corinna, their mutual friend whose clandestine conversion to Christianity by St. Paul prompts Dionysius to pronounce his Christian faith.

With Myra deeply suspicious of Christian teachings, Dionysius's decision to follow St. Paul means that he must break their engagement. Midway through the poem, after Dionysius and Myra separate, the setting shifts from Athens to Rome, to where Myra and Corinna have fled to avoid the plague that swept through Athens, decimating its population. Once in Rome, Corinna's Christian faith is exposed to the authorities, and after a summary trial, during which she refuses to renounce her faith, she is imprisoned and left to die. Corinna's conversion to Christianity, and her subsequent persecution, prompts the first of Hawkshaw's many debates with prominent contemporary historians in her work.

In this poem, the scriptural figure of Dionysius the Areopagite is a vehicle through which Hawkshaw explores doctrines of Protestantism, as she objectifies mid-nineteenth-century challenges to religious faith by looking back to the persecution of early Christians in the period shortly after the Crucifixion. By challenging the account of Christian persecution by the eighteenth-century historian Edward Gibbon in Gibbons's *The History of the Rise and Fall of the Roman Empire* (1776–1789), Hawkshaw uses the struggle between paganism and the emergent Christian church in Rome as a paradigm for a move away from High Church orthodoxy that she observes in mid-nineteenth-century Britain.

Although a religious poem, "Dionysius the Areopagite" is not a work of pious didacticism. True to her Protestant beliefs, Hawkshaw takes her poetic inspiration from the scriptures, but unlike the poetic reinforcement of ceremonial dogmas that defined the work of the Tractarian devotional poets of the period, Hawkshaw presents a practical religion anchored in the morality of the individual rather than in the ceremony of tradition. The poem's use of the spiritual journey has much in common with Thomas Moore's *The Epicurean* (1827), forerunner of Walter Pater's *Marius the Epicurean* (1885), particularly in its intertwining of faith and romantic love. Moreover, the introduction of female agency in the character of Corinna, and in Hawkshaw's polemic interjections as the poem's narrator, mark this out as an intriguing and substantial work.

In other poems in the collection, Hawkshaw reflects on the social consequences of Manchester's recent industrial development. The unprecedented expansion of the city in terms of population and manufacturing output, and the shifting emphasis away from a skilled workforce of traditional local handloom weavers to a mass of unskilled and low-paid mill operatives, brought in to meet the demands of a booming world market for cotton, had inevitably led to social division. Cotton production in the city had created a small class of wealthy men and a larger class of workers doomed to severe poverty. With John Hawkshaw at the forefront of industrial innovation in Manchester and the surrounding area, the Hawkshaws thrived in the city and, although not exclusively wealthy, were certainly well positioned in society. They mixed socially with many of Manchester's prominent names, such as the scientist John Dalton; the Radical manufacturer Richard Cobden, who, with John Bright, formed the Anti-Corn Law League in the city in 1838; and with Samuel Dukinfield Darbishire, solicitor to the Lancashire and Yorkshire railway and a leading Unitarian. The Darbishires became close family friends of the Hawkshaws, who often holidayed at their home at Pendyffryn. The Darbishires were great friends of the Reverend William Gaskell and his wife, Elizabeth, and through this connection John and Ann became acquainted with the Gaskells—a friendship that would continue after the Hawkshaws moved to London in 1850. The Gaskells' eldest daughter, Marianne, stayed with the Hawkshaws in their Belgravia home in the early 1860s and was visited there by her mother, Elizabeth, in 1862.

Ann Hawkshaw's connection to Elizabeth Gaskell, whose novels of social protest—*Mary Barton* (1848) and *North and South* (1855)—center on the human consequences of Manchester's industrial expansion during the 1830s and 1840s, extends to a shared concern over the city's preoccupation with capitalism and its consequences in terms of the spiritual and physical well-being of the population. Throughout this first collection of poetry, Hawkshaw shows concern for those unable to speak for themselves and draws attention to the practical, spiritual, and aesthetic challenges faced by her contemporaries. "Introductory Stanzas," which opens the *Dionysius* volume, excels in its representation of a particular moment in Manchester's literary history, as the city's aesthetic production competes with the forward motion of thrusting capitalism.

"Introductory Stanzas" begins by calling to mind poets of the past, in particular the popular Romantic poets Felicia Hemans and William Wordsworth, but suggests that their poetry lacks significance in an increasingly mechanized and capitalist society. Hawkshaw goes on to propose a new aesthetic and spiritual response to counter Manchester's all-consuming quest for either wealth or survival, which she, like Gaskell, observes on the city's streets:

> This is no time for song: there is a strife
> For wealth or for existence all around;
> And all the sweet amenities of life,
> And all the gentle harmonies of sound,
> Die like the flowers upon a beaten path,
> Or music midst the noise of toil and wrath.
>
> Oh! to awake once more the love of song,
> The love of nature, and of holier things
> Than crowd the visions of the busy throng:
> Alas! the dust is on the angel's wings,
> And those who woke the lyre in days gone by
> Wake it no more, or touch it with a sigh.

(p. iv)

In making clear her poetic ambition to "awake once more the love of song," Hawkshaw carves out a place for her own particular brand of poetry, in what is a remarkably self-confident debut onto Manchester's poetic scene.

Other poems in the collection, such as "The Mother to Her Starving Child," engage directly with social concerns. Spoken, as its title suggests, by a mother to her starving child, the personal and private moment of contemplation in Hawkshaw's poem is reflected out onto the very public concerns surrounding the Poor Law Amendment of 1834, in which outdoor relief for the able-bodied poor was abolished in favor of the workhouse. As with the child in Hawkshaw's poem, people starved to death on the streets, rather than apply for the poor relief that would divide families and condemn them to the workhouse.

The mother's opening appeal to her child to "sleep; I dread to see those eyes / To mine in silent grief appealing" (p. 170) moves into an imagined response to her child's wasted body if disease and not starvation had been the cause of the child's imminent death: "I might have born it if disease / Had changed thee thus, and only wept, / As others oft have wept before" (p. 171). Here, the reality and parental acceptance of nineteenth-century infant mortality through illness is set in opposition to death by malnourishment on England's streets. The mother imagines the consoling effect of memory were her child to be dying from disease and not hunger, configuring her imagined tears of sadness in terms of this consolation: "But they had only been such tears / As memory keeps for by-gone years, / Softening the heart like summer's showers, / That bend, but do not break its flowers" (p. 171). Here, the mother's visualization of mourning is written in the past tense, and in terms of a Wordsworthian notion of memory as a store of consolation, as Hawkshaw looks back to a time in which memory, and poetry expressed through the natural landscape, could offer relief. Whereas once the mother's tears may have been as balm, now, on the streets of Manchester in 1842, they corrode, falling like "burning drops to scorch my heart" (p. 172).

By tracing a move away from a Romantic sentimentalization of childhood death toward the more sober realities of the Poor Law Amendment through the image of a mother and her dying child, "The Mother to Her Starving Child" is a valuable addition to the poetry of social protest popularized by Caroline Norton ("A Voice from the Factories," 1836), Thomas Hood ("The Song of the Shirt," 1843), and Elizabeth Barrett Browning ("The Cry of the Children," 1843). In calling to mind a Romantic idealization of death and the consoling effect of memory, Hawkshaw expresses the inadequacy of such a response to a death that is both political and avoidable. In doing so, Hawkshaw marks the move away from the consoling balm of Romanticism toward a more sober Victorian poetic sensibility.

Hawkshaw's political voice comes to the fore once more in her support of the antislavery movement in the poems "Land of My Fathers," "Why Am I a Slave?" and "Sonnet—to America." In this group of poems, Hawkshaw celebrates Britain's moral supremacy postemancipation ("Land of My Fathers"), speaks movingly from the perspective of an individual plantation slave ("Why Am I a Slave?"), and draws attention to the anomaly of the United States resisting the abolition of slavery when its own Constitution sets out the principles of freedom of speech and freedom of religion in its First Amendment, in "Sonnet—to America":

Queen of the western world, upon thy brow
There is a spot of blood, a crimson stain
That dims thy greatness,—and it is in vain
Thy snowy sail on every sea to show;
Or through thy streets that streams of commerce flow,
Or that thy cities rise on every plain:
Though thou art loud when freedom is the strain,
Yet thou to heaven prefer'st a faithless vow;
Think not thy brightest deeds will weave a veil
To hide from God or man thy *one great crime*;
Wrongs that will turn the cheek of pity pale.
History shall write of thee in after time;
And future ages on one page shall see
The slave's unheeded prayer, the song of liberty!

Other prominent poems in the collection are "The Past" and "The Future"—companion poems of some length in which Hawkshaw is cast as a representative voice that speaks of the moment. The poems develop at length Hawkshaw's desire for an appreciation of the natural world and increased spiritual awareness, first raised in her "Introductory Stanzas." "The Past" and "The

Future" engage with some of the most challenging philosophical questions of the age, as Hawkshaw negotiates between a rationalization of man's pursuit of knowledge and her framework of Christian faith. In what would be the last moment before the evolutionary narratives of Robert Chambers's *Vestiges of the Natural History of Creation* (1844) and Charles Darwin's *On the Origin of Species* (1859) called into question the principles of natural theology, Hawkshaw uses these poems to engage in preevolutionary debates surrounding the reform of knowledge.

Writing in the tradition of natural theology, most probably informed by William Paley's *Natural Theology; or, Evidence of the Existence and Attributes of the Deity, Collected from the Appearances of Nature* (1802) and the more recent Bridgewater Treatises (1833–1840), Hawkshaw takes up the argument for design in these poems, in which evidence of God the Creator is enhanced, rather than demolished, by scientific observations of the natural world. Although embracing scientific knowledge and progress, Hawkshaw writes with a vocabulary of caution in these poems, lest, as she warns in "The Future," "the hand / Who built and furnished all the fair estate, / Be unremembered 'mid the works He planned" (p. 145). She urges her readers not to be seduced by scientific progress that questions God's agency and instead to celebrate the wonders of a God who, as she points out in "The Past,"

> spread
> The vault of heaven gave it a thousand hues,
> And strewed the very ground on which we tread
> With tinted cups, to hold the evening dews
>
> (p. 122)

and who has "spread the sky / With sparkling gems" (p. 128).

In "The Past" and "The Future," Ann's upbringing in a family of religious dissenters, and her position as the wife of an engineer whose work brought her into contact with some of the leading scientists and innovators of the day, come together in a narrative perspective that looks to accommodate intellectual and scientific progress with a deeply held faith. By reaffirming Christian theology, Hawkshaw resists a move toward rational explanations of the natural world and man's place within it. By upholding her belief in God the Creator and the preeminence of humanity, Ann Hawkshaw makes a notable contribution to mid-nineteenth-century assertions of faith.

POEMS FOR MY CHILDREN

At the time of publication of *Poems for My Children* in July 1847, the Hawkshaws were living in Broughton Lodge in the Manchester suburb of Higher Broughton, in a house built by John Hawkshaw on part of the old Zoological Gardens. There were now five young Hawkshaw children: Mary (aged nine), John Clarke (aged six), Henry (aged four), Editha (aged two), and Oliver (aged one). John and Ann's second child, Ada, had died of hydrocephalus in 1845, aged five. Despite her physical absence, Ada was still very much part of the family, as the inclusion of the poignant elegy "Ada" in this collection suggests. Five others of the twenty-seven poems in *Poems for My Children* are addressed to Hawkshaw's children by name, for instance, "Mary's Wish," "Editha" and "The Poor Fly—for My Little Harry," while seven more include dialogue between Ann and her children. In this way, Hawkshaw's first collection of poetry for children is positioned as a personal poetic offering that found its way to print, rather than a collection written with an external audience in mind. That said, *Poems for My Children* was published to be sold, and it includes several poems conveying obligatory lessons in mid-nineteenth-century middle-class morality and devotion, thus rendering the collection suitable for general consumption. Indeed, a number of poems from the collection were included in children's anthologies and educational readers in England and America between 1847 and 1913.

Many poems in the collection look to the natural world through the experience of the Hawkshaw children. The opening poem, "Spring Is Coming," resonates with images of hope and regeneration, prompted by the anticipation and certainty of the coming season:

For Spring is coming—and the flowers
Will waken as from sleep;
The birds will warble in the bowers,
In streams the fishes leap;
The butterflies will flutter past.
The bees begin their humming;
Cold winter does not ever last,
Spring, pleasant Spring, is coming!

(p. 2)

The three-stanza poem is accompanied by an illustration titled "Gathering Spring Flowers." With three children in the foreground, and the figure of a mother in the background, this is a likely representation of the eldest of the Hawkshaw children, Mary, John, and Henry, gathering flowers with Ann. Although this celebration of spring is somewhat undermined by the poem "Ada," which closes the collection, "Spring Is Coming" stands at the vanguard of Hawkshaw's appreciation of the natural world, which she seeks to nurture in her own children. Nature is the means by which a child, its world, and the God that created both can be known. In knowing God through the vibrancy of wondrous nature and not through staid, doctrinal theory, Hawkshaw guides her children and her readers toward moral and spiritual improvement through the example of God revealed in nature.

Although the majority of poems in the collection celebrate nature, others are set firmly in Manchester's urban landscape. Bearing in mind John Hawkshaw's position at the forefront of industrial expansion in Manchester, poems such as "Mary's Wish" and "The City Child's Complaint" suggest Ann's growing confidence in, and optimism toward, the city. Many poetic representations of industrial cities at this time uphold an antithesis between the nostalgic rural idyll and the spirit-sapping urban landscape. Yet Hawkshaw's poems reconfigure the city entirely in terms of what it offers, rather than what it takes away—even though the child in "The City Child's Complaint" begins by lamenting the absence of the natural landscape and wondering what can be learned without Nature as a teacher:

I never hear the wild bird's song,
Or see the graceful deer

Go trooping through the forest glades:
What can I learn from here?

(pp. 37–38)

In her reassuring response to the child, Hawkshaw places the edifying qualities of the city on a par with those of the natural landscape:

There is a voice can speak to thee,
Amid the works of men;
Speak, with a sound as loud and clear
As in the lonely glen.

Do not the works thou seest around
Spring from man's thoughtful mind,
And in *that*, is there nought of God, For thee, for all, to find?

(p. 38)

In looking for evidence of God in man's work, Hawkshaw is able to rationalize the changing physical landscape around her. Rather than lingering on the social consequences and grimy realities of industrial Manchester, as she does in her earlier poems, here Hawkshaw conceptualizes the physicality of Manchester's cityscape in terms of a manifestation of human intelligence, and this intelligence as a product of a good and loving God.

The series of five poems on British history in *Poems for My Children* anticipates Hawkshaw's ambitious survey of preconquest history, *Sonnets on Anglo-Saxon History*, which would be published seven years later, in 1854. Like the discrete yet interconnected snapshots of history conveyed through the sonnets in her later sequence, here Hawkshaw presents history to her children as individual "scenes"—moving chronologically from the "Scene in the Time of the Druids" through "Scene in the Time of the Romans," "A Scene in the Time of the Saxons," "Scene in the Time of the Normans," to "A Scene in the Time of the Crusades." Rather than being printed consecutively, the history poems are the third, seventh, fifteenth, twenty-second, and twenty-fifth of the collection's twenty-seven poems. In this way, Hawkshaw conveys a sense of distance and distinction between these periods in history, rather than blocking the poems together thematically as "the history poems." The effect of this infusion of history punctuating the personal interactions between mother and child that make up many of the poems in between is that history and the past are positioned as part of the present, with a relevance to day-to-day concerns.

Although *Poems for My Children* opens with an exultation of spring, "Cold winter does not ever last, / Spring, pleasant Spring, is coming!" ("Spring Is Coming," p. 2), by the end of the collection, the trope of regeneration is countered with the reality of loss as Ann addresses her young daughter Ada, who had died the previous spring:

Ada, the flowers of spring are blooming now;
The flowers we talked of in the wintry hours,
When at my feet thou sat'st, thy thoughtful brow
And fair face turned to mine; we talked of flowers,
Spring's sunny days, and birds amid the trees,
Themes that thy gentle heart could ever please.

And they are here; but thou art gone my child;
And even the sunshine seems a mournful thing
To my sad heart, that flattering hope beguiled,
To look with gladness to the coming spring:
For in those hours I had no secret dread;
Gazing on *thee*, I thought not of the dead.

(p. 108)

With the anticipation of spring now no more than a "flattering hope," Hawkshaw tells how in losing a daughter she has gained a "secret dread"— absent before her experience of Ada's death. In this new reality, spring is impotent, full of the empty hope of regeneration that cannot restore Ada to her. "Ada" offers an intensely personal insight into a mother's grief, with Hawkshaw taking her reader to Ada's graveside: "The snow was on the ground, the biting blast / Swept the bare earth when in the ground we laid / Thee, our first smitten flower" (p. 109). In drawing "Ada"—and *Poems for My Children*—to a close, Hawkshaw's tender yet uplifting expression of a mother's enduring love is anchored in the belief that she and Ada will meet again in heaven:

Therefore I will not say to thee farewell:
No, none shall fill thy place within my heart.
There love for thee, and thoughts of thee shall dwell

Until we meet again to never part.

(p. 110)

There is a prescience in Hawkshaw's reference to her "first smitten flower" that anticipates the deaths of more children. For by the end of 1856, Ann was to have buried her second child. During the family's summer holiday in Scotland, the youngest of the Hawkshaw children, Oliver, contracted typhoid fever and died. He was buried in the churchyard at Moulin, near Pitlochry. His sudden and unexpected death prompted Ann to write her brief memoir, "Memories of My Childhood," in which grief over the death of her second child awakens memories of her own childhood growing up in Green Hammerton. Likening her retreat into introspection with the opening dream sequence of John Bunyan's *The Pilgrim's Progress*, the preface to "Memories of My Childhood," written from the Hawkshaws' home in Eaton Place, London, reveals the catalyst for Hawkshaw's remembrances:

The isolation of soul made by sorrow has rendered me careless of what was passing around, the noise of the busy world without has been hushed ... the scenes of the present could not be seen through the midst of tears, while those of the past have risen up around me ... I have lived again in my childhood, my girlhood, my early married life; the fields where I played, the flowers that I planted, the companions I loved, all have been seen once more; I did not think the store-house of memory contained so many recollections of those early days and their simple pleasures. The past three months have been the saddest of my life ... Fallen for a while from the stirring scenes of existence, not compelled to mingle in the crowd by the calls of society, or the claims of affection, I have conversed with my own heart and communed with the past.

(p. 1)

Ann draws upon memory for consolation as she seeks solace in the past, as she internalizes an idea of childhood as a time of "simple pleasures" and innocence. The experience of losing Oliver leads Ann to reflect more broadly on what it means to be a mother. "It is a blessed but a fearful thing to be a Mother!" she exclaims. "Heaven with its splendours above her, the abyss with its terrors beneath her. Her life is multiplied but she must die many deaths." In her sorrow, Ann turns to God, as "He alone can know" a mother's grief, and "He alone can comfort" (p. 1), drawing strength from the certainty that she will meet Ada and Oliver again in heaven: "in your Mother's heart you both are cushioned, no years, no changes can deprive you of that home, not death, for that will reunite us" (pp. 1–2).

SONNETS ON ANGLO-SAXON HISTORY

In November 1854, Ann published her third volume of poetry, *Sonnets on Anglo-Saxon History*, using the London publisher John Chapman. As editor of the *Westminster Review*, Chapman championed the literary and political ambitions of a group of women intellectuals that included George Eliot, Harriet Martineau, and Bessie Rayner Parkes, making him an obvious choice of publisher for Hawkshaw's ambitious and notable sonnet sequence. In attempting a reworking of national history through the medium of the sonnet, in doing so in response to a poetic tradition appropriated by Wordsworth, her generation's leading male poet, and in openly challenging a tradition of historiography likewise gendered, Hawkshaw's sonnet sequence is a significant body of work that attracted a good deal of critical attention, being widely reviewed in both England and America.

The sequence of one hundred sonnets retells the history of Britain from the advent of its earliest inhabitants through to the Norman Conquest. In both form and broad subject matter, *Sonnets on Anglo-Saxon History* is Hawkshaw's response to Wordsworth's poetic survey of Church of England history, *Ecclesiastical Sketches*, first published in 1822. The sequence reflects Hawkshaw's Protestant, liberal perspective as stifling and corrupt organizational hierarchies are set against an individual's relationship with God, experienced through the natural world. Sections of the sequence are overtly anti-Catholic, while other sonnets make an implicit criticism of High Church ideology. Taking an eclectic range of subject matter, Hawkshaw expands and elaborates the historical framework on which Wordsworth based part 1 of his *Ecclesiastical Sketches*, broadening her remit to cover aspects of history

often overlooked by conventional narratives of church and state, such as the perspective of women and those oppressed by authority. Moreover, as each sonnet is faced on the page by a short prose extract—quotations from the work of prominent contemporary historians of the Anglo-Saxon period or from early-nineteenth-century translations of Anglo-Saxon texts—Hawkshaw draws attention to the practice of popular nineteenth-century historiography. Thus historians become as much the subject of Hawkshaw's work as the facts of history that they seek to convey.

Hawkshaw was clearly well read in Anglo-Saxon history. Her sources include Sharon Turner's landmark study, *The History of the Anglo-Saxons from the Earliest Period to the Norman Conquest*, published in four volumes between 1799 and 1805; Francis Palgrave's *History of the Anglo-Saxons* (1831); and J. M. Kemble's *The Saxons in England* (1849). The complete list of her sources reflects the availability of Anglo-Saxon texts in translation by the mid-nineteenth century, with Hawkshaw having access to many of the most popular historical works of the time. Other than Turner, Palgrave, and Kemble, Hawkshaw's primary sources include Asser's tenth-century *Life of Alfred*, Alfred the Great's translation of Bede, the English Historical Society's translation of *Bede's Ecclesiastical History* (1838), and the Bohn's Antiquarian library translations of *Bede's Ecclesiastical History* and *The Anglo-Saxon Chronicle* (1847).

The incorporation of historical sources into her sonnet sequence sees Hawkshaw once again interacting with historians—as she did with Gibbon in "Dionysius the Areopagite"—rather than simply citing them as a source. Instead she responds to, and challenges, the prominent Anglo-Saxon scholars of her day through her reflective and suggestive response to history and through the idiosyncratic formatting of her volume. In quoting her prose sources, sometimes verbatim, otherwise in précis, on the left-hand page facing each sonnet, Hawkshaw presents an implicit critique of traditional historiography. Different sources are often quoted together on the same page, and occasionally the reader is directed back to the historical text itself, with an instruction to "See *Sharon Turner's 'History of the Anglo-Saxons'*" (p. 68). By reworking the conventional historical narrative through a more intimate and personalized perspective in the facing sonnets, Hawkshaw makes a sustained challenge to traditions of historiography by noting its limitations and filling in the gaps.

For instance, Hawkshaw faces the sonnet "Canute the Great" with Turner's portrait of the king who, "from his warlike ability," is "surnamed the Brave; from his renown and empire, the Great; from his liberality, the Rich; and from his devotion, the Pious" (p. 154), followed by an extract from *The Anglo-Saxon Chronicle*:

> "1017. In this year King Canute obtained the whole realm of the English race. And he banished Edwy the Etheling, and afterwards commanded him to be slain, and Edwy, King of the Churls."

> "1029. This year King Canute gave to Christchurch, at Canterbury, the haven at Sandwich, and all the dues that arise thereof on either side of the haven."
>
> (p. 154)

By setting a contemporary historical account alongside a primary source, Hawkshaw shows how the earlier account of Canute's reign, defined in terms of his violent assassination of rivals and the pledging of gifts to the church, has been reworked by Turner into a celebratory narrative. Her own response to this in the opening lines of the sonnet is unequivocal: "Canute the Great!—the great in what? In crime? / I know no title that he hath to be / Ennobled thus by flattering history" (p. 155). Having pointed to the distorting prism of history that has elevated Canute so that "A massive figure through the mists of Time / He looms upon us," Hawkshaw revives *The Anglo-Saxon Chronicle*'s account of slain kings with an image of Canute's "stern red hand" and the suggestion that Canute "clutched" onto power with a "grasp death only could destroy" (p. 155).

In this sonnet Hawkshaw extends her criticism of contemporary historians to include those reading their historical accounts, cautioning against a teleological approach that looks to the past as a distant, simpler time: "'tis easy to forgive / Those whom we envy not; permit to live / Those whom we fear not to our height can

climb" (p. 155). Hawkshaw observes a tendency for modern observers to be blinded by the security of progress, to patronize the past rather than seeing in it a model for the present. Instead, she advocates an analytical reading of history that considers it in context and values it in present terms.

Aside from the idiosyncratic formatting, perhaps the most distinctive feature of the sequence is Hawkshaw's inclusion of female historical subjects. Although only eight of the one hundred sonnets have a female subject, with a further two acknowledging the female perspective, Hawkshaw's inclusion of women contrasts with the notable absence of female subjects in Wordsworth's *Ecclesiastical Sketches*, as she offers an alternative to historical narratives that habitually omit or marginalize women's contribution to British history. By taking up the imagined stories of Anglo-Saxon women such as the mothers of kings Egbert and Harold and the daughters of King Alfred, Hawkshaw finds freedom in the imaginative space of the sonnet to give her female subjects a voice. In many more of the sonnets a strong (female) narrative intervention implies a female perspective, which often challenges and counters the male historical narrative on the facing page.

The majority of Hawkshaw's female subjects in the sequence speak, as she puts words into the mouths of the silent women of history. Through these female speaking subjects, Hawkshaw reinforces her particular perspective on history by illustrating the enduring validity of individual spiritual and emotional experience, which constitutes the past and defines the present, but which is overlooked by conventional accounts of the Anglo-Saxon period. In "The Mother of Egbert" and "The Mother of Harold," for instance, Hawkshaw transforms the political bodies of exiled and slain kings into familial bodies through the imagined words of their mothers. While the prose extract facing "The Mother of Egbert" offers the usual factual historical narrative, noting that "Egbert was obliged to seek refuge in exile" (p. 84), the sonnet's octave tells of his "sad mother" (p. 85) lamenting his exile and murmuring "low her absent children's name" (p. 85). On the turn of the volta (the ninth line) her speech begins:

"My heart is dreary as my heart is lone,
For all are gone that made my pleasant cheer—
Some convent cells, and one the churchyard stone
Have covered up from life; and thou, so dear
Because the last, art now an exile gone,
And my eyes ne'er shall look thy face again upon."

(p. 85)

Here, Hawkshaw offers an alternative perspective to accounts of war and political subterfuge that mark out traditional history by writing the mother of Egbert into the historical narrative that omits her. By introducing the personal consequences of political deeds, Egbert is repositioned as a cherished son and brother, as well as the "sole king of the West-Saxons ... the most distinguished of all their monarchs before Alfred the Great" (p. 86) remembered by historians.

Unlike the mother of Egbert, the mother of Harold is included in historical accounts of the period. In the prose facing "The Mother of Harold," Hawkshaw notes that "it is said that Gyda, or Githa, the mother of Harold, offered to William the Conqueror the weight of her son's dead body in gold if he would give it her to bury, but that he refused" (p. 192). Hawkshaw follows this with a quote from the *Anglo-Saxon Chronicle*: "A.D. 1067. This year Harold's mother, Githa, and the wives of many good men with her, went to the Steep Holmes, and there abode some time; and afterwards went from thence over sea to St. Omer's" (p.192). With Githa remembered in history, Hawkshaw's sonnet initially reworks the historical narrative into verse, beginning with the perspective of the widowed wives of Harold's men,

Around that grief-struck woman silently
They stood, yet gave her not of words or tears,
For each one had her load of woes and fears,
Beneath whose weight she bent

(p. 193)

Hawkshaw goes on to extend the scope of traditional historiography by giving Githa a voice:

"I cannot bless the land where Harold fell,

And where the cup of woe to its last sip
The mother drained—nor will she curse where rest
Her children's graves, and where she once was blest."

(p. 193)

In the division of dialog between first and third person, Githa is both speaker and subject, unable to fulfill either the political expectation to "bless the land where Harold fell" or the familial expectation to "curse where rest[s]" his grave. Despite the historical certainty of Harold's defeat at the Battle of Hastings, his mother speaks of uncertainty, leaving open-ended a historical moment conventionally defined by its apparent finality, her female voice subverting the historical certainties of factual, male-dominated historical prose.

The trajectory of Hawkshaw's three-sonnet sequence to Ethelfleda and Ethelgiva, the daughters of King Alfred, encapsulates this move away from masculine historical narratives. Through Alfred's daughters Hawkshaw explores the relationship between public and private experience, critiquing the tendency to privilege the masculine qualities of a woman's public status over the domestic, private sphere of female experience. Over the course of the three sonnets, Hawkshaw moves away from the currency of traditional history, which favors heroic narratives, toward a more reflective and inclusive historical narrative that observes and values the essential femaleness of her Anglo-Saxon subjects.

CECIL'S OWN BOOK

There is a gap of some seventeen years before Hawkshaw publishes again, this time for private circulation. The events of the intervening years provided the inspiration for what would be Ann Hawkshaw's final collection of work. *Cecil's Own Book* (1871) comprises three short stories and ten poems and was written by Hawkshaw for Cecil Wedgwood, her young grandson who had been born in March 1863. Copies of the beautifully bound book, complete with line-drawn illustrations, seem to have been distributed among Ann's wider family, to friends, and to acquaintances. The circumstances of Cecil's birth are particularly pertinent to the themes addressed in the collection, which is dedicated to the memory of Cecil's mother, Ann's eldest daughter, Mary Jane Jackson Wedgwood.

At some time during the early 1850s, while the Hawkshaws were living in London, they had become acquainted with the Darwin-Wedgwood family. With Hensleigh Wedgwood and his daughter Frances (Snow) close friends with Elizabeth Gaskell, it is possible that Gaskell made the initial introduction of the Hawkshaws to the Wedgwoods and Darwins. In his account of a family holiday to Tunbridge Wells in 1857, Ann's eldest son, John Clarke, remembers how he, then sixteen, and his brother Henry, fourteen, had ridden to Tunbridge Wells on their ponies, "staying a night on the way at Mr. Darwin's house at Down. We took our night clothes and a comb and toothbrush rolled up on our saddles in front of us" (p. 43). Furthermore, Mary Pugh, who had been governess to the Hawkshaw children in the early 1850s, was later employed as a governess to the children of Charles and Emma Darwin. A somewhat melancholy character, Pugh was with the Darwins at Down House between 1857 and 1859, but kept in touch with the family and visited often—even after she had left her post. Although she was later certified mad and spent her last years in an asylum, Mary Pugh remained financially supported by her previous employers, with Charles Darwin paying £30 a year for her to have a holiday and John Hawkshaw paying her asylum fees.

By the early 1860s, the Hawkshaws' eldest children, John Clarke and Mary, were romantically involved with the siblings Cecily and Godfrey Wedgwood, the great-grandchildren of Josiah Wedgwood and Darwin's niece and nephew. Cecily and Mary had been at school together and were great friends. On June 24, 1862, Mary Hawkshaw and Godfrey Wedgwood were married at St. Peter's Church Pimlico. Mary became pregnant almost right away, yet by the following March, instead of joyfully anticipating the arrival of her first child, Mary was gravely ill with her mother by her side at the Wedgwoods' home in Hem Heath, Stafford. In a letter to her son Henry, dated March 27, 1863, Ann tells him that she is

"compelled to stay here" and that she "cannot leave poor Mary alone." The following day Cecil Wedgwood was born, and only fifteen days later Mary died from "puerperal mania" (postpartum psychosis). Losing their eldest daughter in this way was a terrible blow for the Hawkshaws, who had already buried two young children. One can only imagine Ann's distress at watching her beloved eldest child descend into madness.

In letters to her son Henry in the months following Mary's death, Ann speaks of her own illness, brought on by the trauma of losing her daughter: "This is only the second time since my illness that I have tried to write, so you must not be surprised at my singular penmanship; my hand does not seem much under the control of my will at present" (April 27, 1863); "I cannot write much for I am still very weak" (May 6, 1863). Although not mentioning Mary's death directly, Ann writes of the family's support of Godfrey Wedgwood, who "says he needs love so much now" (April 27, 1863) and who "clings more to us than ever; he has had baby [Cecil] photographed asleep in his cot, and dear Mary's dog Jack too" (May 6, 1863).

Under the watchful care of his father and grandparents, the young Cecil Wedgwood thrived. By the age of twenty-one he was a partner in Wedgwood's Etruria Works in Stoke-on-Trent, going on to become the first mayor of the town in 1910. Much of his early childhood was spent with his Hawkshaw relatives, particularly John and Ann at Hollycombe, their rambling West Sussex estate, which they had purchased in 1865. It was from here that Ann wrote *Cecil's Own Book*, undoubtedly to amuse her young grandson but also, as the book's dedication suggests, as a memorial to her daughter: "To the Memory of Mary, the Mother of Cecil."

As well as being the beneficiary of *Cecil's Own Book*, the young Cecil Wedgwood features in several of the collection's poems and short stories, in particular through Hawkshaw's characterizations of young, motherless boys in the stories "The Wonderful Adventures of Hassan the Younger, the Son of Hassan-el-Alfi the Camel Driver," "Little Prince Bepettedbyall," and "The Fairy Gift; or, The Iron Bracelet." In these,

ANN HAWKSHAW

Hawkshaw writes as a grandmother, weaving stories for her grandson in the style of the Arabian Nights, Charles Kingsley's *The Water-Babies* (1863), and Lewis Carroll's *Alice's Adventures in Wonderland* (1865). Just as in Hawkshaw's other collections, nature frames both poetry and prose in *Cecil's Own Book*. But unlike her other collections, God is absent in nature: not simply "unremembered 'mid the works He planned"—as Hawkshaw had predicted in her poem of 1842, "The Future"—but absent.

In her earlier writing, Hawkshaw operates in the tradition of natural theology, privileging man's response to nature as the reason for nature's being. By the time of writing *Cecil's Own Book*, however, man no longer interprets nature: nature speaks for itself, regardless of whether man is listening. In poems such as "The Selfish Toad," "The Discontented Stream," "The Ambitious Water-Lily," and "The Squirrel That Forgot That It Would Be Winter," animals and plants are engaged in a struggle for survival. They speak to each other, or to themselves, no longer satisfied with their place in the natural order, and look to act independently, against the expectation of their species.

Despite the whimsical tone and simple vocabulary of poems such as "The Squirrel That Forgot That It Would Be Winter," a serious evolutionary foreboding is evident. Competitive nature and the possibility of individual extinction are raised in these poems. "The Squirrel That Forgot That It Would Be Winter" tells the tale of Frisky the squirrel, who played all summer and quite forgot to gather up acorns for a winter's store. Faced with starvation he turns to his cousin Flosky, asking to share his ample reserves of food. But

When Flosky heard his cousin call,
He never said a word,
Pretending to be fast asleep,
And that he nothing heard.

(p. 65)

Only when "Grandpapa" (John Hawkshaw) "had put a heap / Of maize and barley" (p. 66) on the newly swept winter's lawn is the squirrel saved from starvation, confirming man as the site of benevolence rather than God in nature.

In Hawkshaw's earlier poems, each aspect of the natural world, from the tiniest drop of dew to the magnificence of the solar system, serves as evidence of a good and loving God. Yet in *Cecil's Own Book*, poems such as "The Ambitious Water-Lily" resonate with images of wasteful nature:

One by one the lily's petals
Browned and withered ere they spread,
And its leaves discoloured, shrivelled,
Sank within their muddy bed.

(p. 74)

Whether the death of Hawkshaw's beloved eldest daughter—like Darwin's own loss of his daughter Annie—raised the specter of wasteful nature to such an extent that she doubted the presence of God in the natural world can only be surmised. But there seems little doubt that having faced the death of three of her children, the comfort of life eternal spent with her children in heaven fades, leaving only earthly sadness. This sadness is most poignantly expressed in the final poem in *Cecil's Own Book*: "In Memoriam."

The end of Hawkshaw's poetic journey is marked by a poem that itself tells of a journey: a mother's journey through sadness and loss. "In Memoriam" is a touching elegy on childhood death from a mother's perspective, separated from the preceding poems and stories by an illustration depicting a small child with head bowed at the foot of a memorial stone in a churchyard. Among the branches of the churchyard trees are the words "In Memoriam" in a font resembling plant stems from which small shoots and blooms grow. From the final stanza of "In Memoriam" it is clear that the small child in the picture is Cecil, and the grave his mother's.

But the poem begins many years before, when Cecil's mother was herself a child, and when her own mother had been untouched by the all-pervading fear of loss—a fear that develops over the poem's eleven stanzas. Here the poem begins:

Once in a far-off northern home,
Five happy children played:

They ran beside the mountain streams,
And through the pine woods strayed,
Or watched the wild birds on the hills,
From morn to evening's shade.

One made a mill-wheel in a stream,
Another read a book—
Stretched on the sweet thyme-covered bank:
But oft away would look
To where his youngest brother fished
For minnows in the brook.

And ever by the brother's side
Kept the two sisters dear,
And borne upon the mountain breeze
Their laugh came soft and clear—
To where the mother sat—her heart
Had not then learned to fear.

(pp. 127–128)

Even though Hawkshaw narrates in the third person throughout "In Memoriam," the autobiographical subject matter combined with Hawkshaw's position of retrospection lends the poem an intensity of personal feeling. In setting her "happy children" in the hills and countryside surrounding their Manchester home, and in the mountains of Scotland where the family frequently holidayed, Hawkshaw draws on the memory of an idyllic rural landscape to represent an equally idyllic childhood. Here, within hearing distance of their mother, John Clarke occupies himself with a small-scale engineering project, making a "mill-wheel in a stream," while Henry reads a book and the youngest boy, Oliver, fishes for minnows, watched at the waters edge by his attentive elder sisters, Mary and Editha. Not until line 18 does the shadow of childhood death appear, in an allusion to the loss of Ada: "her heart / Had not then learned to fear."

Yet in reading on, it is clear that Hawkshaw had not "learned to fear" from the death of her first child:

For though within her distant grave,
One fair young sister slept,
Though softly still they breathed her name,
Though still the mother wept—
And hid deep in her heart of hearts,
That pure sweet memory kept.

Death is contented with that one:
Such was the mother's dream,
That bud of beauty, will it not
My other flowers redeem?"
Oh! foolish was that mother's thought,
Beside the mountain stream.

(p. 128)

Ada's continued presence in the busy Hawkshaw family, through the remembrances of her siblings, and in her mother's heart, calls to mind the concluding lines of "Ada" in *Poems for My Children*, in which Hawkshaw makes a posthumous promise to her daughter: "none shall fill thy place within my heart. / There love for thee, and thoughts of thee shall dwell" (p. 110). Indeed, rather than having learned to fear from Ada's death, Hawkshaw recalls her now seemingly naive hope that in losing one child, her "other flowers" would be redeemed. As she so poignantly acknowledges in the introduction to "Memories of My Childhood" in 1856, the experience of losing a child is part of the "blessed but … fearful thing" (p. 1) that defines motherhood. In retrospect, however, Hawkshaw knows that death was not content with one, nor two, but three of her children—far beyond the pact of motherhood that she had accepted.

Whether or not Hawkshaw's disillusionment with her earlier belief of redemption extends to her wider faith is not certain, but her allusion to foolishness suggests that she feels betrayed. As the following stanza shows, she is increasingly skeptical about the extent to which any comfort or reason can be found in the deaths of her young, innocent, and good children:

But then these young lives were so glad,
Their hearts so good and pure,
They filled one home so full of love,
It seemed it must endure:
For, to fill up such void on earth,
What solace, or what cure.

(p. 128)

Long gone is Hawkshaw's belief that she and her children will be reunited in heaven: long gone the security of God's goodness, revealed in death.

Stanzas on Oliver's illness and death follow next, his absence first apparent in the *"four"* children walking through the highland landscape of which they were all so fond:

> There came a change—through highland glen
> Walked quietly but *four*,
> Or talked with whispered words, within
> The heather covered bower,
> Or gathered for the sick boy's room,
> Green fern or autumn flower.
>
> (p. 129)

Oliver had lain ill for some five weeks with typhoid fever and peritonitis, and in remembering the last days of his life, Hawkshaw beatifies her son, recollecting his "fair brow and sunny hair" (p. 129) and how he bore his illness with fortitude, offering his mother comfort in the face of death:

> Upon his couch he lay,
> Patient and loving to the last:—
> And as he passed away,
> Giving sweet words of love to her
> Who wept in wild dismay!
>
> (p. 129)

Reuniting her son at last with the landscape he so loved, Hawkshaw buries Oliver in the Scottish highlands—no hint now of mother and child meeting again in heaven:

> Amid the scenes he loved so well,
> There is a little grave:
> The giant hills behind it tower,—
> Before it corn-fields wave,
> And there, with bitter tears, they lay
> To rest, their good and brave.
>
> (p. 129)

Hawkshaw's numerical countdown of untimely death calls to mind Wordsworth's "We Are Seven." And yet whereas the little girl of Wordsworth's poem holds on to the number seven in her imaginative state of family unity, Hawkshaw counts down, all too aware of the awful earthly reality of her children's physically diminishing numbers. The italicization of *"five," "four"* and then *"three"* inflects Hawkshaw's incredulity at their deaths as the poem progresses.

From her sadness at Ada's death in 1845, to the "wild dismay" of Oliver's in 1856, Hawk-shaw moves toward the "hideous dream" (p. 130) of losing her eldest daughter in 1863:

> Time passed—and then there were but *three*:
> Who wept in speechless woe,
> The young wife-mother, must she die!—
> Oh! God,—must this be so?
> It must be but a hideous dream!
> They could not let *her* go.
>
> Beside the village church, a cross
> Tells where that dear one sleeps:
> Her boy treads gently there,—and love,
> Untiring vigil keeps;
> And years go by, of good and ill,
> But still that mother weeps!
>
> (pp. 129–130)

In the death of this "young wife-mother," Hawkshaw's narrative of motherhood is doubly challenged. For not only has she lost another child, but a mother has also been lost. Mary's death takes Hawkshaw beyond her capacity to accept the wastefulness of early death, both as a mother herself and with Mary herself as a mother—and for the first time in the poem, Hawkshaw invokes God. Yet this is not the God of comfort, to whom Hawkshaw had previously turned, but God as an expletive—God as an expression of disbelief, rather than a statement of belief. Despite the hint of regeneration and hope implied in the shooting buds of the font used in the poem's title, hope is absent in the denouement of Hawkshaw's poetic remembrance. Rather than the hope of life eternal spent with her three children in heaven, the cumulative effect of their deaths has left Hawkshaw with only earthly sadness. The absence of biographical material between 1871 and Hawkshaw's death in 1885 leaves "In Memoriam" as Hawkshaw's final word.

CONCLUSION

The changing response to nature and death in Hawkshaw's poetry represents a loss of certainty in belief, rather than an absolute loss of faith. Even after her daughter Mary's death in 1863, the church continued to be central to Ann

Hawkshaw's life. Following Ann Hawkshaw's death from a stroke on April 29, 1885, the then Sir John Hawkshaw dedicated a stained glass window to his beloved wife in the parish church of St. Mary the Virgin, Bramshott, Hampshire, in sight of the Hawkshaws' Hollycombe estate. The window's pictorial images show a female likeness alongside Jesus and St. Peter, accompanied by brief biblical passages from the New Testament: one of these says, "God loveth a cheerful giver" (2 Corinthians 9:7). Two of the passages relate to Tabitha, said to have been raised from the dead by St. Peter: "This woman was full of good works" (Acts 9:36) and "When she saw Peter she sat up" (Acts 9:40). In light of Hawkshaw's changed perspective on death in "In Memoriam," it is notable that in death she is aligned with a woman who had been brought back to an earthly life rather than ascending to heaven. The composition of the dedicatory window suggests that both Sir John and Lady Hawkshaw acceded to the conventions of ceremonial Anglicanism, yet ended their lives reflecting on the worldly significance of death and their faith, rather than looking confidently on death and faith as the gateway to life eternal.

As the span of five decades between the first and last examples of Ann Hawkshaw's writing suggests, her poetry offers an exceptional insight into the changing political and religious landscape of the mid-nineteenth century. Conveyed through the perspective of a woman who began life in a large family of dissenters working the land in rural Yorkshire and who, by the time of her death, was titled, affluent, and moved in the most influential cultural and literary circles of the age, Hawkshaw's oeuvre has much to contribute to the field of nineteenth-century literary scholarship—as the growing interest in her life and work attests.

Selected Bibliography

WORKS OF ANN HAWKSHAW

POETRY
"Dionysius the Areopagite" with Other Poems. London: Jackson and Walford; Manchester, U.K.: Simms and Dinham, 1842.

Poems for My Children. London: Simpkin and Marshall; Manchester, U.K.: Simms and Dinham, 1847.

Sonnets on Anglo-Saxon History. London: John Chapman, 1854.

Cecil's Own Book. Printed for private circulation, 1871.

JOURNALS, CORRESPONDENCE, AND MANUSCRIPTS
"Memories of My Childhood." Manuscript, 1856–1857, from the private papers of Mrs. Diane Whitehead.

Letters from Ann Hawkshaw to Henry Hawkshaw, dated March 27, 1863; April 27, 1863; and May 6, 1863. From an original bundle of letters held at the Staffordshire and Stoke-on-Trent Archive Service, Staffordshire Records Office, reference D4347.

"The Diary of John Clarke Hawkshaw of Hollycombe: Volume 1," 1913. Unpublished document, transcribed from the manuscript notebooks by Martin Beaumont. Original manuscripts retained by John Clarke Hawkshaw's great-granddaughter, Dr. Christabel Barran.

REVIEWS, IN CHRONOLOGICAL ORDER
North of England Magazine, December 1842, pp.121–122. (Review of "Dionysius the Areopagite" with Other Poems.)

Gentleman's Magazine, January–June 1843, p. 621. (Review of "Dionysius the Areopagite" with Other Poems.)

Court Magazine and Monthly Critic, June 1843, pp. 60–61. (Review of "Dionysius the Areopagite" with Other Poems.)

Bamford, Samuel. "Preface." In his Poems. Manchester, U.K.: published by the author, 1843. (Discusses "Dionysius the Areopagite" with Other Poems.)

Athenaeum, January 15, 1848, p. 57. (Review of Poems for My Children.)

Manchester Guardian, November 8, 1854, p. 10. (Review of Sonnets on Anglo-Saxon History.)

Living Age, January 6, 1855, p. 142. (Review of Sonnets on Anglo-Saxon History.)

Athenaeum, January 20, 1855, pp. 76–77. (Review of Sonnets on Anglo-Saxon History.)

Monthly Christian Spectator, January–December 1855, p. 55. (Review of Sonnets on Anglo-Saxon History.)

Eclectic Review, July–December 1855, p. 376. (Review of Sonnets on Anglo-Saxon History.)

Manchester Guardian, May 1, 1885, p. 8. (Obituary.)

CRITICAL AND BIOGRAPHICAL STUDIES
Armstrong, Isobel. "'A Music of Thine Own': Women's

Poetry—An Expressive Tradition?" In her *Victorian Poetry: Poetry, Poetics, and Politics*. London: Routledge, 1993. Pp. 322–323.

———. "Msrepresentation: Codes of Affect and Politics in Nineteenth-Century Women's Poetry." In *Women's Poetry, Late Romantic to Late Victorian: Gender and Genre, 1830–1900*. Edited by Isobel Armstrong and Virginia Blain. Basingstoke, U.K.: Palgrave Macmillan, 1999. P. 7.

Armstrong, Isobel, Joseph Bristow, and Cath Sharrock, eds. *Nineteenth-Century Women Poets: An Oxford Anthology*. Oxford: Clarendon Press, 1996. Pp. 346–347.

Bark, Debbie. "Sight, Sound, and Silence: Representations of the Slave Body in Elizabeth Barrett Browning's 'The Runaway Slave at Pilgrim's Point,' Ann Hawkshaw's 'Why Am I a Slave?' and *My Bondage and My Freedom*, the Autobiographical Slave Narrative of Frederick Douglass." *Victorian Newsletter* 114:51–68 (fall 2008).

———. "Natural Theology and the Anxiety of Knowledge in the Writing of John and Ann Hawkshaw." Paper given at the British Society for Literature and Science Conference, University of Reading, March 2009.

———. "'Tis a hard thing to judge the past aright, / Harder to judge the present, though it be / Before our eyes in stern reality': A Victorian Woman's History of the Anglo-Saxons." Paper given at the joint British Association for Victorian Studies and North American Victorian Studies Association Conference, University of Cambridge, July 2009.

———. "The Poetry of Ann Hawkshaw, 1812–1885." PhD diss., University of Reading, 2009.

———. "'Written for Cecil Wedgwood': Post-Darwinian Foreboding and the Shadow of Personal Loss in Ann Hawkshaw's *Cecil's Own Book* (1871)." Seminar paper for the Science in the Humanities Seminar Series, Keele University, February 2010.

———. "Poetry of Social Conscience, Poetry of Transition: Ann Hawkshaw's 'The Mother to Her Starving Child' (1842)." Paper given at the Poetry, Politics, and Pictures in the Nineteenth Century Conference, University of Sheffield, March 2010.

———. "Reconfiguring the Urban Child: Ann Hawkshaw's *Poems for My Children* (1847)." *Leeds Working Papers in Victorian Studies*. Vol. 11: *Victorian Childhoods*. Leeds, U.K.: Leeds Center for Victorian Studies, 2010. Pp. 19–29.

Brown, Susan, Patricia Clements, and Isobel Grundy (The Orlando Project). "Ann Hawkshaw." *Orlando: Women's Writing in the British Isles from the Beginnings to the Present* (http://orlando.cambridge.org).

Davis, Glenn. "Artful Scholarship in Ann Hawkshaw's *Sonnets on Anglo-Saxon History*." Paper given at the Forty-second International Congress on Medieval Studies, Kalamazoo, Mich., May 2007.

———. "Memory and Dissent in Ann Hawkshaw's *Sonnets on Anglo-Saxon History*." Paper given at the British Women Writers Conference, University of Iowa, April 2009.

Evans, John. *Lancashire Authors and Orators: A Series of Literary Sketches of Some of the Principle Authors, Divines, Members of Parliament, etc., Connected with the County of Lancaster*. London: Houlston and Stoneman, 1850. Pp. 127–132.

Richards, Bernard. *English Poetry of the Victorian Period, 1830–1890*. 2nd ed. Harlow, U.K.: Longman, 2001. Pp. 216–217.

THOMAS HEYWOOD

(c. 1573—1641)

Sayanti Ganguly Puckett

THOMAS HEYWOOD WAS a well-known English playwright and actor whose career spanned the late Elizabethan and early Jacobean period. His place of birth is uncertain, although the county of Lincolnshire has most often been surmised and is suggested as well by his reference to a Sir George Saint Poole of Lincolnshire as "my countryman" (Cromwell, p. 7). Although the exact date of Thomas Heywood's birth remains unclear, it is probable that he was born between 1570 and December 1575; the scholar Richard Rowland states that he was almost surely born in 1573. Heywood's father, the Reverend Robert Heywood, was originally from a Cheshire family and probably moved to Lincolnshire with his wife, Elizabeth, sometime before Thomas Heywood's birth. Robert Heywood, who had graduated from Magdalene College in 1567, was the rector of Rothwell and of Ashby-cum-Fenby from 1575 to 1593. The Heywoods had ten children who were younger than Thomas Heywood, thus somewhat putting the family in financial instability.

In spite of being raised in financially straitened circumstances, Thomas Heywood did attend university, as is made evident by his sound knowledge of classical literature, which acted as a basis for at least five of his plays. In *Thomas Heywood: A Study in the Elizabethan Drama of Everyday Life,* Otelia Cromwell mentions that in his *An Apology for Actors,* Heywood writes of "the time of my residence in Cambridge, I have seen tragedyes, comedyes, historyes, pastorals, and shewes publickly acted, in which the graduates of good place and reputation have been specially parted" (p. 11). Scholars have conjectured about which college Heywood attended in Cambridge. In his 1658 edition of *An Apology for Actors,* republished as *The Actors' Vindication,* William Cartwright, a bookseller, wrote:

The Author of this ensuing Poem, not long before his Death, discovering how undeservedly our Quality lay under the envious and ignorant, made our Vindication his Subject, which he hath asserted with such Arguments of Reason and Learning, that the judicious will no doubt rest satisfied of the lawfulness and (indeed) necessity of it: the gentleman was a Fellow of Peter-house in Cambridge.

(quoted in Clark, p. 7)

Although Cartwright suggested Peterhouse, it is more likely that Heywood attended Emmanuel College from 1591 to 1593, since, as Otelia Cromwell suggests, Cartwright's faulty editing does not "inspire the reader's confidence in his unsupported statement" (p. 11). It is known, however, that Heywood's education at Emmanuel College was prematurely terminated when his father died in 1593. Heywood's quote about his short residence at Cambridge, however, is proof that he was interested in and exposed to the stage at an early age.

By 1594, Heywood had moved to London. He had not been trained for any particular line of work, and hence it is plausible that he moved to London directly looking for a means to make his way in the world. His first job was as an actor and playwright for Philip Henslowe, who was the manager of the Lord Admiral's Company. Heywood's biographer Frederick Boas notes a record of a payment of thirty shillings to Edward Allen in 1596 for the manuscript of one of Heywood's plays, probably the lost *War Without Blows and Love Without Strife.* Boas also notes that on March 25, 1598, Heywood contracted himself for two years as actor for no other manager but Henslowe, agreeing to pay Henslowe a penalty of forty pounds if he broke his contract. However, even though Heywood was contracted to Henslowe, no evidence suggests that Heywood held shares in the Lord Admiral's Company.

Otelia Cromwell surmises that between 1594 and 1596, Heywood wrote at least six plays for the Lord Admiral's Company. These were: *The Four Prentices of London, The First Part of Edward IV, The Golden Age, The Silver Age, The Brazen Age*, and *The Iron Age*. Evidence confirms that payments were made to Heywood for his plays during this period. In February 1598, for instance, he was given three pounds by Thomas Dowton for a play, and in December 1598 he received from Robert Shaw, Henslowe's agent, a sum of three pounds for another play that has since been lost.

Heywood's whereabouts from 1600 to 1602 are sketchy. His name does not appear in Henslowe's *Diary* and neither does it appear in a document signed by men belonging to the Lord Admiral's Company. It has been surmised that he might have been working for an unknown company or he might have traveled abroad, but none of these conjectures have been ascertained because of the lack of any historical record. Possibly during this time he was attached to the Earl of Derby's Company, which had performed his *Edward IV* some time between 1594 and 1599. This company, however, is not to be confused with the company of the same name that included William Shakespeare and later became the Lord Chamberlain's Men. The Shakespearean scholar E. K. Chambers noted that the Derby's Men who performed Heywood's play "was a second Earl of Derby's company organized possibly under the patronage of the successor of Fernando Stanley, the patron of Shakespeare's company, and playing frequently from 1594 to 1618 in the provinces" (quoted in Cromwell, p. 17).

Details about Heywood's private life are, like other biographical details, difficult to come by. Arthur Melville Clark, however, notes two records that perhaps give us some information about his marriages. The first record is from June 13, 1603, when a "Thomas Hayward" married an "Aenn Buttler" at St. Antholin's Church in London. The second record is in the register in St. James's in Clerkenwell. This records the marriage of Thomas Hayward to Jane Span on Janu-

ary 18 of 1632 or 1633 (Clark, p. 58). Although we are not entirely sure that this was indeed Thomas Heywood the playwright, these seem to be the two most probable entries that could pertain to the writer.

By 1601, a record in the Pipe rolls maintained by the English Exchequer of a payment made to him and William Kempe for plays to be acted during the Christmas season by the Earl of Worcester's Company (which performed at the Rose Theater) gives evidence that by that date Heywood was a member of Worcester's Men. At this company, Heywood again had dealings with Henslowe, who lent him two shillings and six pence for "a payre of sylke garters" (quoted in Boas, p. 14). The Earl of Worcester's Company presented at the Court on January 3, 1602, as well as on February 14, 1602.

When James I ascended the throne, the Earl of Worcester's Company became the Queen's Company in honor of its patron, Anne of Denmark. Heywood's name is third in a list of ten actors belonging to the Queen's Company, and he was one of the actors who took part in the coronation procession on March 15, 1604, dressed in red cloth that he had been given for this occasion. At Anne's death in 1619, he was given black cloth for his suit for the queen's funeral procession. Heywood played a significant part in the success of this company. He toured Norwich in 1617 with this company, and Henslowe's *Diary* notes that he was producing a play a month for an extended period during his attachment to this company. The Queen's Company performed not only at the Rose and the Curtain but also at the Red Bull and the Cockpit. They also gave some performances at the court and in the provinces. But, as the result of financial difficulties as well as problems caused by several lawsuits, the company's status began to dwindle in 1612, and its run ultimately came to an end in 1619 with Queen Anne's death. The last mention of Heywood in connection with the Red Bull is in an order on October 3, 1622, when he was instructed, along with some of his fellow actors, to repair the roads near the theater.

Heywood is not mentioned again as an actor after this period. Boas notes that thirty years after

Heywood's death Francis Kirkman, a bookseller, noted that Heywood "acted almost every day," but Boas suggests that this statement was a bit of an exaggeration (p. 15), and no records exist to indicate which plays he acted in or which parts were given to him. By Heywood's own admission, however, he continued his literary endeavors with much vigor, for, in his preface to *The English Traveller*, written in 1633, eight years before his death, he claims that there were two hundred plays in which he "either had an entire hand or at least a main finger" (Boas, p. 16). When Charles I came to the throne in 1625, a new troupe called Queen Henrietta's Company was formed. Although Heywood was not a member of Henrietta's Men, it is probable that he wrote for this company.

Heywood was appointed to the position of city poet in 1630, a post that he held for the next ten years. As city poet, he produced a number of pageants. In 1632, he produced *A Maidenhead Well Lost,* and when Queen Henrietta's Men revived Christopher Marlowe's *A Jew of Malta* in 1633, Heywood provided the prologue and the epilogue. In 1634, he collaborated with Richard Brome to write *The Late Lancashire Witches* for the King's Men. It was for the same company, and probably in the same year, that he wrote *A Challenge for Beauty. The Hierarchie of the Blessed Angells*, which contained a criticism of courtier poets such as William Davenant and Thomas Carew—who, Heywood felt, were writing plays only for an elite audience—was produced in 1635.

A prolific writer of plays, pageants, and pamphlets, who worked in a number of companies and served several patrons, Heywood was buried on August 16, 1641, in the churchyard of St. James's in Clerkenwell. Heywood was indeed a poet of London, and he celebrated the splendor of the city in not only the pageants he wrote in his official capacity as city poet but also in his refreshing and invigorating plays, many of them set in the city in which he lived and worked.

PLAYS OF DOMESTIC LIFE IN LONDON

Heywood was a poet of the city, and his plays present a vivid portrait of city life as Heywood knew it. His plays generally have realistic settings and convey a good idea of social customs and norms in his day. Twenty-four plays are now attributed to him. Of this number, *The Four Prentices of London, Edward the Fourth (Parts 1 and 2), If You Know Not Me You Know Nobody (Parts 1 and 2), The Wise Woman of Hogsdon, The Fair Maid of the Exchange, A Woman Killed with Kindness, Fortune by Land and Sea, The Fair Maid of the West (Parts 1 and 2), The English Traveller, The Captives,* and *The Late Lancashire Witches* present a portrait of contemporary London life. Lack of space prevents a discussion of all of these plays, but this essay will discuss some of the more well-known plays in some detail.

The years 1599–1600 have been cited as the probable dates for the writing of *The Four Prentices of London,* although it was published in 1615 with a preface addressed "To the Honest and High-Spirited Prentices, the Readers" and signed "Thomas Heywood." In his prefatory epistle, Heywood notes that it had been written about fifteen or sixteen years previously "in my infancy of judgment in this kind of Poetry and my first practice" (Boas, p. 26). The play begins with a pseudo-history: that of the Earl of Boulogne, which he is recounting to his daughter, Bella Franca. The earl has lost his wealth fighting for William the Conqueror. Consequently, he is residing in London and his four sons have been apprenticed to different trades. Godfrey is a mercer; Guy, a goldsmith; Charles, a haberdasher; Eustace, a grocer.

As the play progresses, the earl departs for the Holy Land, where he is going to take part in the First Crusade. The sons follow him after enlisting with Robert, Duke of Normandy, and Bella Franca, in disguise, follows her father and brothers. Unfortunately, the brothers are shipwrecked. Although separated, they are brought back together again by Fate when Charles and Eustace rescue the earl from banditti. In the meanwhile, they fall in love with the disguised Bella Franca because she reminds them of their sister. Godfrey and Guy find themselves in a quarrel, which is resolved by Robert of Normandy, while Tancred, an Italian prince, takes the sister under his protection. After several complications arising from cases of mistaken identity, they turn to focus on the fight for the Holy Land. Before the play ends, the brothers and the earl recognize each other, Bella Franca reveals her disguise, a French princess secures Guy, and the Christians win the battle.

The plot relies heavily on the failure of family members to recognize each other, and is, in this sense, quite implausible. Another improbability difficult to overlook pertains to the four brothers, who are relatively more believable as noble warriors than as apprentices in London. They combine chivalry with a working-class practicality that does not mesh as the play attempts to combine scenes from everyday life in London with high adventures by sea and land. The dialog lacks the lucid flow of Heywood's later plays and is repetitious and overwrought. The episodic structure of the play makes for choppy reading or performance, and it moves at a slow pace. In the London scenes, Heywood focuses on everyday life in Elizabethan England, and these scenes are more realistic than those set abroad. The play uses a "presenter" as well as a dumb show (that is, a part presented in pantomime), but it is marred by an immaturity that disappears from Heywood's later plays.

Heywood's play *Edward the Fourth* was printed in 1600, although it was entered in the Stationers' Register on August 28, 1599. This is a history play with diverse plots that are loosely connected. Part 1 deals with the Falconbridge Rebellion, and Edward's campaign in France is the basis for part 2. A chorus divides the two parts of the play. Edward is portrayed as being wise, brave, royal, commanding, and noble; he is quick to see through the treacheries of the constable of France and the Duke of Burgundy, and he joins forces with the king of France against the constable and the duke. In a play within the play, with the king of France as concealed audience, the treacheries are revealed, and the villains are disgraced. The second part deals with the rise of Richard III and the fall of Jane Shore, the king's mistress. The play highlights the turning of the wheel of fortune as Jane falls from favor and Richard rises to power. Mat-

thew Shore, Jane's husband, is also a prominent character in the second part of the play. The queen, whom Jane has wronged, tests Jane and finds her to be repentant, whereupon she forgives Jane. Eventually, Matthew overcomes his struggle to forgive his wife, and in the end they embrace and die, not from a sudden illness but instead from a desire to be rid of the world because of their protracted suffering.

Heywood portrays Edward as a noble and dignified king but also as a vulnerable one who is unable to protect his family. He strives to portray Jane Shore as a loyal and loving wife who is finally overtaken by circumstances she is too weak to control. But he also does not trivialize her sin, making her pay for it with her death. The theme of forgiveness is consistently emphasized, especially in the scenes between Jane and the queen. Heywood's treatment of the events is not historically accurate, but the play is noteworthy because instead of turning into a "revenge play," it remains intent on forgiveness and compassion. Although somewhat sentimental, the play is remarkable in its depiction of complicated and problematic domestic relationships.

Although missing a clown, the play contains doggerel and, at times, bears the mark of Heywood's characteristic humor. The events of the play are meant to arouse patriotic feelings in the audience, and Matthew Shore is presented in a manner that allows the playwright to exalt the characteristics of the hardworking middle-class to which Shore belongs. The play makes use of proverbs, biblical allusions, and popular sayings to emphasize the need for forgiveness. Even though the play is divided into two parts and is somewhat episodic, the figure of the king serves as an effective connection in this drama, which is, among other things, a kindly study of the wayward wife and the forgiving husband.

A Woman Killed with Kindness is probably Heywood's best-known play. A domestic tragedy, it was the first play that had Heywood's name on the title page when it was published in 1607. The late-nineteenth-century drama scholar Emil Koeppel pointed out that this play's main plot bears resemblance to the "fifty-eighth novel of the first book of [William] Painter's *Palace of Pleasure*," a popular collection of tales that had appeared in England in 1566 (quoted in Cromwell, p. 52). The play has a tragic main plot and a tragicomic subplot. The main plot deals with John Frankford and his wife, Anne Acton. Frankford invites a poor but attractive man called Wendoll to come live with them, and Wendoll returns the favor by seducing Anne. Frankford finds out about Wendoll's treachery from his servant, Nicholas. When he finds his wife in a compromising situation with Wendoll, he sends her away to one of his country estates but fully provides for her, thus justifying the title of the play. Anne is intensely remorseful and starves to death, but not before she receives her husband's forgiveness.

The subplot features Sir Francis Acton, Anne's brother, and Sir Charles Mountford, who undertake to engage in a contest of hawks and hounds that quickly disintegrates into a fight, as Mountford kills some of Acton's men. Mountford is imprisoned and is then reduced to poverty and physical labor in order to support himself and his chaste sister, Susan. He returns to prison over a borrowed sum of money, while Acton, falling in love with Susan, pays Mountford's debts. When Mountford learns to whom he owes his release, he offers Susan to Acton, who respects Mountford's as well as Susan's honor by marrying her.

The two plots are unified thematically; characters from the main plot enter into the subplot and vice versa. In her 1984 study of Heywood and his work, Barbara J. Baines notes that

> both plots present an act of passion that endangers or destroys an ideal state of contentment. Mountford's murderous rage and Anne's adultery represent the violation or loss of honor ... in both plots honor (developed as a masculine code in the subplot and as chastity in the main plot) is the context in which the theme of Christian charity and forgiveness is defined.
>
> (p. 81)

As with *Edward IV*, Heywood avoids turning this into a "revenge play," as Frankford shows Anne not only forgiveness but also charity in continuing to provide for her even after he banishes her. Yet Frankford's resolve to kill his wife with kindness and "his final acknowledgment of having

accomplished this morally questionable goal underscore the limitations of kindness or human charity in both plots" (Baines, p. 82). But, as this paradox makes clear, the theme of kindness and forgiveness remain the central focuses in the play, and Heywood expertly dramatizes the complexity of the domestic problems that face Anne, Frankford, and Wendoll, as well as Mountford, Susan, and Acton.

In terms of structure, both subplots begin with happiness and move on to grief before ending in compromise and resolution. Anne and Frankford begin as a happy couple, but their bliss is shattered by Anne's infidelity. The forgiveness and second marriage in death at the end of the play restores some of the felicity with which the play began. In the subplot, Susan and Mountford's happiness is dashed by the quarrel with Acton, but their reconciliation with Acton gives the subplot a happy ending. The motives that drive most of the characters, however, especially Anne, remain a mystery. It may be difficult for a modern audience to understand why she allowed Wendoll to seduce her. It is of course her infidelity that drives the main plot, and Barbara Baines suggests that "Heywood's treatment of Anne exemplifies the Renaissance assumption that women, however virtuous, are more susceptible to passion than are men. Anne's later reflection that she submitted to Wendoll 'for want of wit'—assuming wit here means reason—confirms this perspective" (Baines, p. 90). Wendoll himself is portrayed as a villain, a role he himself accepts when he likens himself to Judas, while Frankford is a figure of not only forgiveness but also virtuous resentment.

Heywood's skill at writing domestic tragedies featuring homely conflicts between husbands and wives becomes evident in this play. Scenes of temptation, seduction, repentance, and forgiveness are written in graceful verse that is well suited to communicate the complexity of the domestic lives of even ordinary people. Critics have sometimes denigrated Heywood for not possessing the poetic gift of some of his contemporaries, but the subject matter of his domestic tragedies were well suited to allow him to take advantage of the talents of versification and characterization that he possessed.

Fortune by Land and by Sea remained unpublished during Heywood's lifetime. It was first published in a 1655 edition that Clark calls "the most slovenly quarto of the Heywood cannon" (p. 50). The play is described as a tragicomedy and is attributed to Thomas Heywood and William Rowley, although it is more in Heywood's style than Rowley's. It was probably performed by Queen Anne's Company. The date of composition has generally been assumed to be 1609. This play bears similarities with *A Woman Killed with Kindness* insofar as it features a double plot that focuses on two different families. One plot of this play focuses on the Harding family and the other on the Forrest family.

The play begins with Frank Forrest's death at a tavern. He is murdered by Rainsforth, an influential man. Frank's brother, Young Forrest, takes revenge by killing Rainsforth, but he is forced to hide in the Hardings' garden. Old Harding is married to the virtuous but penniless Anne, but he threatens to disinherit Philip, his son, for marrying Susan Forrest, also virtuous but penniless. Anne discovers Young Forrest in the garden and is able to help him escape to her brother in Gravesend, who then sends Forrest on his adventures by sea, which wins Forrest his fortune. But the brother himself is captured by pirates, and when Old Harding hears of his financial losses caused by Anne's brother's supposed death, he himself dies before Philip is disinherited. Forrest captures the pirates, frees Anne's brother, and is granted a pardon. The play ends with the main characters coming together on stage for the festivities to celebrate the marriage of Anne to Young Forrest.

Although it has two plots, the play is remarkably well unified, except for the scene that presents the capture and execution of the pirates—nonetheless, a thrilling scene that audiences of Heywood's time would probably have found exciting. Young Forrest comes as close to an avenger as Heywood can manage, but he repents the killing of Rainsforth immediately and remains a virtuous character till the end. Anne and Susan, both without dowries, remain models

for perfect wives, allowing Heywood to make his point about what men should look for when choosing a bride. In Philip, we have the perfect son and husband. When reduced to the position of a servant in Old Harding's establishment, he laments not for himself but for his wife. Heywood sets high ethical standards for most of his characters in the play, and it gives Heywood the opportunity to show his audience how to be the perfect wife, husband, and son.

As the title suggests, Fate plays a significant part in rewarding the just, the loyal, and the virtuous by bringing them fortune, by land and by sea. The play exemplifies the difficulties that are faced by those in poverty, but it also shows the felicity that a change of fortune might bring about. Additionally, Baines rightfully notes that "this play, better than any other of the period, presents the custom of defending family honor through the private duel as the very real experience of ordinary men" (p. 66). The play is based on a well-worn theme: that of parental opposition to true love, and Otelia Cromwell also likens Philip's position as a menial in his father's house as a variation on the Cinderella story. Rich in realistic details and connecting at important points, this play illustrates Heywood's talents at the writing of domestic drama peopled by commendable characters who deserve the good fortunes that finally come to them. Realism, especially in the early scenes, blends perfectly with the high romance of the adventures by sea to make this an entertaining play.

The Fair Maid of the West; or, A Girl Worth Gold was published in 1631. It was entered in the Stationers' Register on June 16, 1631. Bess Bridges, the "girl worth gold," is a superb creation. She is a barmaid and a tanner's daughter, but she is feisty, spirited, and charming. She values and preserves her dignity and honor even though she is continuously surrounded by gallants at the tavern. Bess does, however, love a wealthy but deserving man named Spencer. During a quarrel over Bess, Spencer fatally injures an aristocratic but unpleasant man named Carrol, an unfortunate incident that forces Spencer to depart for the Azores. Spencer himself is injured in Fayal, but he sends his friend Goodlack to

England with a task: if Bess has been loyal to Spencer, she is to inherit his fortune; if not, Goodlack is to be the inheritor. On his voyage back, Goodlack hears that a man called Spencer has died, but this is, of course, not our hero. True to his name, Goodlack attempts to break Bess's faith in her lover, but he fails to do so, and he consequently joins the increasing ranks of men who admire her for her loyalty, dignity, spirit, and chastity. Bess herself travels to foreign lands and has adventures on the seas, even defeating a Spanish warship that has her Spencer on board. Bess, believing Spencer to be dead, thinks she sees his ghost, and Spencer is unable to recognize Bess in her captain's garb; hence the lovers are separated again. They finally come together at the court of Mullisheg, the king of Fez. Mullisheg, though initially coveting Bess, is finally awed and reformed by the force of her character, and the play ends with preparations for Bess and Spencer's marriage.

This is the story of the first part of *The Fair Maid of the West*. Barbara Baines describes the play as presenting the "ideal of honor in man and woman" and says that "what is particularly refreshing and truly human about Bess is that her virtue is not defined exclusively in terms of honesty (that is, chastity), but in terms of courage, chastity, industry, and Christian patience" (p. 44). Spencer, though playing a smaller role in the play, is a mate well-suited for Bess. He values Bess's honor and is an honorable, prudent, and intelligent man of courage and integrity. Although he has killed a man, he learns from his mistake and is essentially a pacifist.

Heywood adds humor to the play in the form of a bully named Roughman and his sidekick, Clem. Roughman acts as a foil to Spencer in his belief that honor consists in putting up a show of being a brave man and bragging about having taken part in many battles. Clem wishes to be considered an honorable man, but he remains a coward throughout the play. The contrast between the truly honorable hero and heroine of the play and Roughman and Clem consistently reminds the reader that honor, the main focus of the play, is determined by motivations and actions rather than words and appearances.

The play makes references to several well-known contemporary events, such as the Islands Voyage of 1597, in which England unsuccessfully sent an expedition to capture Spanish treasure in the Azores, and it also includes a dumb show that alludes to well-known contemporary courtiers. Part 1 of *The Fair Maid of the West* blends romance and realism and vividly evokes the atmosphere of Elizabethan life in London. This play is a comedy, but it is also a melodrama as well as a refreshing adventure drama. Its focus on issues such as the contrast between the West and the East, and between Christianity and Islam, brings up some interesting angles for modern theatergoers, and an adaptation of this play by Kevin Theis was staged by the CT20 Ensemble in Chicago in November 1994 and the American Shakespeare Center included this play in its fall 2010 repertoire.

Although part 2 of *The Fair Maid of the West* was also published in 1631, scholars generally agree that it was written about twenty-five years after the first. Bess, Spencer, Clem, and Roughman all appear in the second part of the play, which picks up where the first one left off. Honor still remains the thematic focus of the story, but in this second part we find ourselves in a darker, more complex world where the power of good seems to be weaker, where temptations are harder to resist, and where the virtuous are less able to engender reform in others. Yet, in the end, as with the first part, Heywood conveys the message that no matter how dark the world, honor is still found in love, courage, wisdom, and integrity.

In part 2, Mullisheg suffers a moral relapse and decides that he will possess Bess on her wedding night. He solicits Goodlack's help in achieving his evil design while his queen, Tota, enlists Roughman's help in her efforts to seduce Spencer. But Goodlack saves the day (or night) and arranges for a trick that ends in putting Mullisheg and Tota in bed together, each believing that they are with the English bride and groom. Under the cover of night, Bess, Goodlack, and Roughman escape to the ship; Spencer is left behind as a lookout, but he promises to join them aboard the ship soon. Unfortunately, plans go awry and Spencer is caught by the pasha Joffer, who lets

Spencer go when he witnesses Spencer's love for Bess—even though he will have to pay for Spencer's escape with his life. Spencer determines to say goodbye to Bess and return to Joffer so that Joffer's life will be spared; Bess consequently devises a plan of her own to save her husband's life. Bess offers her life in exchange for Spencer's; she wins over the king with her offer; and when the king learns of the bed trick, he forgives everyone and showers presents on Bess and Spencer.

The next section of the play takes place in Italy. After a shipwreck, Bess, Roughman, and Clem are washed ashore at Florence while Spencer finds himself in Ferrara, and Goodlack is in Mantua. Spencer and Goodlack eventually travel to Florence, where Bess is being courted by the Duke of Florence. A trick with a jewel that the duke had given to Bess results in causing Spencer to take an oath to avoid his own wife, and being an honorable man, Spencer keeps his oath despite the pain it causes. Bess requests the duke to transfer power over Spencer to her, which he does. Bess then proceeds to forgive Spencer, release him from his oath, and return his wife to him.

This play of intrigue turns largely on disguises, mistaken identities, and tricks. Deception plays a large part in bringing about the resolution at the end, and the characters, especially Bess, have to resort to craftiness in order to bring about the happy ending. The focus on sexual intrigues also compromises the honor of some of the male characters who now strive to defend their honor rather than gain new honors by adventurous exploits. Heywood communicates the focus on sexual intrigues through the use of sexual metaphors and clever wordplay. Additionally, the play features monologues focusing on the characters' future courses of action, which are reminiscent of similar monologues in *The English Traveller*, *The Wise Woman of Hogsdon*, and *A Woman Killed with Kindness*. Above all, the play remains noteworthy because of Bess's character. In her, Heywood portrays the ideal English girl who is chaste (in spite of the temptations of tavern life), independent, loyal, resourceful, humble, and charming.

THE TRAGICOMEDIES

Some of Heywood's plays that present portraits of contemporary life in London also fall into other categories, such as tragicomedies or comedies of intrigue. Some of his plays, such as *The English Traveller*, fall into both categories. According to the title page, *The English Traveller* had been "Publickely acted at the Cock-pit in Drury-lane: By her Majesties servants. Written by Thomas Heywood." It was entered into the Stationers' Register on July 15, 1633, and was likely performed in 1627. The date bears witness that this play was probably written late in Heywood's life. Also, the protest it includes against too much show on stage, probably motivated by the overwhelming splendor of masques and pageants as well as the voluptuous productions of other Jacobean plays, also point toward its having been written at a later date.

The English Traveller has some elements in common with *A Woman Killed with Kindness*, but, on the whole, it is a weaker play. The main plot focuses on Geraldine and the Wincotts. Geraldine returns from his grand tour and comes to stay with the Wincotts. Mrs. Wincott, Geraldine's old friend, promises to marry him once her elderly husband dies. But, they also decide that they will live honorably until they can be married. Geraldine's friend Dalavill appears to court Prudentilla, Mrs. Wincott's sister, but his interest actually lies in Mrs. Wincott. Dalavill hints to Geraldine's father that Geraldine's reputation is threatened by his affair with a married woman, and Geraldine's father extracts a promise from his son to avoid the Wincotts. Missing Geraldine, Wincott sends for him, but Geraldine hears Mrs. Wincott's and Dalavill's voice inside her bedroom and realizes that his beloved and his friend have become lovers. This realization ends in his decision to leave England, but he is forced to attend a farewell feast first. At the feast, Mrs. Wincott is overcome with shame, confesses to her husband, and dies. Free from her, Geraldine becomes Wincott's heir.

The subplot focuses on the Lionell house, which is next door to the Wincott house. While Old Lionell is away at sea, his son and the servant Reginald have converted the house into a brothel and are in debt. Old Lionell arrives unexpectedly, and Reginald concocts the story of the house being haunted. Old Lionell is further deceived into thinking that the allowance he had left them has been used to buy a neighboring house belonging to Ricott. Old Lionell's misunderstandings with Ricott lead to the realization that he has been tricked. But since the young Lionell and Reginald are repentant by this time, Old Lionell forgives them and agrees to go to Geraldine's farewell feast.

This play resembles *A Woman Killed with Kindness* in several ways: the betrayal by a friend, the illicit affair, the erring wife's shame, remorse, and death are all elements found in the earlier play. But Mrs. Wincott's death in *The English Traveller* is invested with less psychological and emotional complexity than Anne's in *A Woman Killed with Kindness*; Baines notes that her death is "a mere convenience for freeing Geraldine and Old Wincott from their commitments to an unworthy woman and elicits no more sympathy from them than it does from us" (p. 123). The audience does not feel sympathy for Geraldine or Old Wincott to the same extent that they do for Frankford because the playwright's attitude toward those characters is more cynical. Thus the themes and characters of this play are not as complex or invested with tragic proportions as those of the earlier play. The theme of deception and manipulation is common to both plays, but in this play Heywood takes a more satirical approach that spares Geraldine, Mrs. Wincott, and Wincott from experiencing the emotional intensity and betrayal felt by Anne and Frankford; it also spares the audience from feeling as intensely with Geraldine and Wincott as they had done with the main characters in *A Woman Killed with Kindness*.

Both plots are connected by the attention paid to sexual and filial relationships. This play is sort of a coming-of-age play where the young men learn to mature and reevaluate their priorities in life and their futures. Geraldine begins as a deluded young man whose education is completed by his rejection of a woman unworthy of him. But in comparison with Heywood's other plays with double plots, it remains comparatively lack-

ing in unity. At best the subplot provides a satirical counterfoil to the main plotline. It has been observed that this play greatly resembles the farces of Plautus; perhaps Heywood's greatest success in this play is the accomplished manner in which he has Anglicized his characters, setting, and atmosphere as well as his adoption of the prodigal son motif in the subplot.

A Challenge for Beauty was published in 1636, and was acted by the King's Company at the Blackfriars in the same year. It was probably written sometime between February 1634 and 1636. Of all Heywood's plays, this comes closest to the type of tragicomedy developed earlier in the century by the King's Men playwright John Fletcher. The main plot deals with the Spanish queen Isabella's assertion that no other woman alive can equal her in beauty and chastity. The hero, the Spanish lord Bonavida, nonetheless, finds Isabella's equal in England in the lady Hellena; he and Hellena exchange rings and carcanet (containing her picture), and before he returns to Spain he vows to her that they will never part. In Spain, when the queen finds the carcanet, Bonavida is imprisoned.

In the subplot, a Spanish lady, Petrocella, has a gallant named Valladaura. But Petrocella compares Valladaura to the English sea captain Ferrers and finds Valladaura's services inadequate. Ferrers is captured by the Turks and is sold to Valladaura, who treats him kindly. Ferrers, obliged to Valladaura, persuades Petrocella to marry Valladaura, but Valladaura, aware of the love between his beloved and his friend, tests Ferrers by making him pose as the groom on the wedding night after having him promise that he would not touch Petrocella. Valladaura means to surrender his wife to Ferrers by declaring that she has cuckolded him, but his plan backfires when Petrocella claims to have killed her husband, Valladaura. Valladaura bemoans his friend's death and explains his plan to test Ferrers before surrendering Petrocella to the sea captain. Finally, Petrocella and Ferrers's deception is joyfully revealed. In the meanwhile, after a number of twists and turns in the plot, Bonavida faces execution, which is interrupted by Hellena's plea for mercy. The queen grants his pardon, and all is resolved harmoniously.

The play highlights a Cavalier code of conduct and honor, but it also presents some independent and courageous women. As with *The English Traveller*, Heywood employs satire to highlight the weaknesses and limitations of the characters, which are so amplified that they seem almost laughable. In both plots, the characters are faced with a test: in the main plot, feminine virtue is tested, whereas in the subplot masculine honor and courage is put under trial. A pleasant parody, this is essentially a good-humored play that is a tribute to the new theatrical tradition brought into fashion by Francis Beaumont and John Fletcher.

COMEDIES OF INTRIGUE

In addition to part 2 of *The Fair Maid of the West*, Heywood wrote two more plays where the action turns on intrigue and deception. These comedies have complex plots and subplots and complicated stratagems are employed for plot movement as well as in the resolution. Plays like *A Maidenhead Well Lost*, *The Wise Woman of Hogsdon*, as well as part 2 of *The Fair Maid of the West* discussed above fall into this category.

A Maidenhead Well Lost was printed in 1634 but probably was written in 1632 or 1633. It was performed by the Queen's Company at the Cockpit Theatre in 1634. It is a comedy of sexual intrigue featuring aristocratic characters with slippery morals, probably inspired by Italian novellas, and is noticeably different from Heywood's other plays because it is lighter in tone and deviates from his usual focus on virtue and chastity. It does, however, share similarities with part 2 of *The Fair Maid of the West* in its use of the "bed trick." The particular treatment of honor in this play is reminiscent of Beaumont and Fletcher's work, especially their early collaboration *The Maid's Tragedy*, which was first performed around 1609 and printed in 1619.

Since this play is consistently less focused on chastity and honor, Heywood anticipates attacks from Puritans in his letter to the reader that prefaces the play, writing that "there is nothing herein contained, which doth deviate either from Modesty, or Good Manners ... Neither can this [play] be drawne within Criticall censure of that most honorable *Histriomastix*, whose uncharitable dome having damned all such to the flames of Hell, hath it selfe already suffered a most remarkable fire here upon earth" (quoted in Baines, p. 74). In the letter, Heywood alludes to the recent burning of *Histriomastix,* written by the Puritan William Prynne, an old enemy of Heywood's whose 1632 book contained an attack on the English stage.

The play opens with a revelation. Stroza, the villain, informs Julia, the daughter of the Duke of Milan, that her fiancé, the Prince of Parma, is having an affair with a lady, Laurette Although this is a lie, Julia believes it to be true and is particularly dismayed by it because she is pregnant. Stroza then confronts Parma and plants it in his mind that Julia's concern and jealousy are a façade to hide her own infidelity. Parma rejects Julia, and her father is forced to try to keep her honor intact by negotiating for a match with the Prince of Florence. Stroza's villainy continues when he abandons Julia's newborn child on a highway, where Parma finds it and begins to see the truth. By this time, Julia is engaged to Florence, but Florence is in love with Laurette, whom Julia had previously banished in her jealous rage. Florence finds Laurette in a forest and rescues her.

Florence finds himself unable to get out of his engagement to Julia, but he receives, just in time, an anonymous letter (from Parma) telling him Julia is unchaste. But since Florence has no real proof, he can do no more than announce that he will reject Julia and declare war on her country if he finds her unchaste on their wedding night. Stroza steps in again and substitutes Laurette on the wedding night; finding his partner a virgin, Florence gives her a ring and documents verifying their marriage settlement. In the morning, Julia is secreted back into Florence's bedroom while he sleeps, and Laurette returns to the forest with the ring and the document. The next morning, Laurette reveals the bed trick to Florence, who determines to expose Julia and Stroza—and successfully does so. Florence claims Laurette as his beloved, and Parma steps up, presents Julia with their son, and claims her for his wife.

Julia, who regrets having been overtaken by passion and consummating her relationship with Parma before their marriage, and who mourns for the loss of her valued chastity, is willing to accept punishment for any shame that her compromised status brings to her father. Julia's relationship with Parma does not seem to guarantee a happily married future for her, since the pairing is fraught with mutual jealousy and distrust. Parma realizes his mistake and is noble in his efforts to prevent Florence from marrying an unchaste woman. The Duke of Milan's sense of morality is ambiguous, evident in his attempt to preserve his own honor by foisting off his daughter on Florence as a virtuous lady. Laurette's actions, too, are ambiguous: In spite of being deeply attracted to Florence, she initially preserves her honor when he visits her several times. When Stroza approaches her with the plan for the substitute, she initially refuses, not because she is chaste, but because she wants to see Julia exposed. But ultimately she agrees, citing her love for Florence as her reason, although it is a reason that leaves the audience confused as to what her real motivations in agreeing to the bed trick actually are. Also confusing is Florence's attitude when the trick is discovered: although he makes much of the value of chastity throughout the play, he does not feel that Laurette has compromised herself in any way by consummating their relationship without marriage.

This is nonetheless, despite its contradictions, a "pleasant play" where everything ends happily. The play has only a single plot, compact and well-unified. Baines accurately notes that "the action involving the two couples is skillfully interwoven, and the auxiliary characters are integrated into the play's concern with masculine and feminine honor" (p. 78). Heywood offers a well-drawn portrayal of an Iago-like figure in Stroza, who skillfully manipulates power, passion, and jealousy to achieve his own ends.

MYTHOLOGICAL PLAYS

Heywood's knowledge of mythology is apparent from plays such as *The Ages, The Rape of Lucrece,* and *Love's Mistress; or, The Queen's Masque.* These mythological plays saw much success on the stage. *The Ages,* for instance, was performed by the King's and Queen's Men at the Red Bull and the Curtain in 1625. Additionally, these plays were remarkable because they, unlike many of Heywood's other plays, had magnificent settings that served as the backdrop for myths and legends from the Greek world.

The Ages is a five-part play comprising *The Golden Age, The Silver Age, The Brazen Age,* and *1 and 2 The Iron Age. The Golden Age* was published in 1611 and performed in 1625; *The Silver Age* and *The Brazen Age* in 1613; and the two parts of *The Iron Age* came out in 1632. Heywood's purpose in this play was to present the Greek myths and the story of the Trojan War. He begins, in *The Golden Age,* by presenting the struggle for power first between Saturn and Titan and then between Jupiter and Saturn. Jupiter is presented as more human than godlike, because he does not use his supernatural powers to achieve his ends. *The Golden Age* is Heywood's most erotic play, manifested in the amorous scenes between Jupiter and Calisto and Jupiter and Danae. It is not a very well-unified play, but in its use of masques, dances, a pastoral interlude, and abundant special effects it is certainly one of Heywood's most visually dazzling plays.

According to the title page, *The Silver Age* deals with Jupiter's love for Alcmena, Hercules' birth, and Proserpine's rape. Although the diversity of events covered in this play might make an audience wary that there will be no unity, Baines points out that "we can detect a degree of thematic substance and unity as the action of the various episodes reveals a divine ordering of events within a framework of justice" (p. 142). Jupiter plays a significant role in this part of the play, as in *The Golden Age,* and he arranges his amorous business with charm and ease, providing some comic relief. Jupiter describes his pursuit of Alcmena as a play within the play. Jove and Juno enter the play, and despite Juno's attempts to prevent his birth, Hercules is born to

Alcmena and triumphs over many obstacles set in his path by the jealous Juno. Ultimately Jove is able to establish order, and *The Silver Age* ends with the story of Proserpine's abduction and the resolution of the dispute.

The Brazen Age strikes a much less harmonious and felicitous note than the two earlier sections of *The Ages*. In this section, there is violence, deception, cunning, and death. The title page informs the audience that this play will deal with the death of the Centaur Nessus, with the tragedy of Meleager, and with the story of Jason and Medea as well as Hercules' labors and death. The fourth act has a comic interlude featuring Mars and Venus, but on the whole this play is not only darker but also less unified than the two preceding it. Families are torn apart, sexual jealousy is rampant, order is destroyed as the gods and men fight among each other. Poignancy is particularly heightened at the death of Hercules after he manages to overcome all manner of obstacles to accomplish his great labors.

1 The Iron Age begins the story of the siege of Troy, which is also the subject of *2 The Iron Age*. It pays special attention to Helen's abduction, the fight between Hector and Ajax, Achilles' slaying of Hector, Achilles' death at Paris's hands, and Ajax's death. As with *The Silver Age*, Heywood explores themes of sexual and familial ties. Helen is an important character in this section, and Heywood emphasizes the extent of her betrayal of her husband. Continuing with the focus on family, he spends much time in showing the manner in which she is accepted, loved, and valued in Troy, leading to the war. The fight between the cousins Hector and Ajax also emphasizes the theme of the breaking of family bonds. Through several other episodes, such as Hector's acquiescence about not fighting when informed of his wife's dream, Heywood keeps the theme of familial bonds in the forefront.

2 The Iron Age is divided into two parts, with the first three acts telling the story of the siege of Troy and the destruction of Priam's family and the second two acts presenting the fall of all the Greeks, except Ulysses. Although covering several mythological events, *2 The Iron Age* is surprisingly thematically unified. Out of all Heywood's plays, it is this which most closely follows the conventions of the revenge tragedy. Synon is the villain of the piece who thinks up the Trojan horse, convinces the Trojans to allow it inside their walls, and then basks in the violence that overtakes the sleeping Trojans. He only dies when he meets his match in the equally villainous Cethus. Pyrrhus's revenge on the women of Troy in order to retaliate for Polyxena's death also forms a significant portion of this play. Heywood himself seems to support the Trojan cause, and he portrays the Greeks as cunning, sly, opportunistic, ruthless, merciless, and violent. After the fall of Troy, revenge and deception continues in Clytemnestra's court; the pressing matter of family bonds, which were important in the preceding parts, is again resuscitated when Orestes is forced to decide whether to be loyal to his father or his mother. With the death of Orestes, only Ulysses is left to speak the epilogue of this play.

The world of *The Ages* gets progressively darker. In *2 Iron Age*, we find none of the idyllic pastoral world in which Jupiter played his amorous games. The lightness of *The Golden Age* is increasingly lost as the playwright takes us through *The Silver Age, The Brazen Age,* and finally through *The Iron Age*. On the whole, Heywood's achievement in deftly handling events of mythical proportions and weaving them into this play shows considerable skill. Arlene W. Weiner notes that "Heywood consolidates actions that takes place in many scattered passages in the narrative and eliminates hordes of minor characters and events, giving his version a relative shapeliness" (p. ix). Intertwining many stories and introducing many characters and themes, *The Ages* remains a fairly well unified and entertaining play.

LONG ESSAYS AND PAMPHLETS

In the last years of his life, Heywood wrote numerous pamphlets on contemporary subjects, which can be of interest to historians studying the age in which he lived. One of these was *The Rat-trap; or, The Jesuites Taken in Their Owne Net &c: Discovered in This Year of Jubilee, or*

Deliverance from the Romish Faction, 1641. This pamphlet begins as an attack on Jesuits but proceeds to become one on "those whose 'study is onely for blood, their Religion is Rebellion, their treaties are only treacheries, their plots are only powder-plots, their matches onely to out-match us'" (quoted in Clark, p. 196). Another was a satire titled *Machiavel, As He Lately Appeared to His Dear Sons,* also published in 1641 and written as an appeal to Parliament to protect itself from monopolists.

Probably the most famous of Heywood's long essays is *An Apology for Actors*, in which he presented a reasonable reply to Puritan attacks on the stage that he had served so diligently for so long—and in so doing, created an interesting historical document that provides much valuable information on the actors and acting conditions of Heywood's time. Heywood probably began working on this essay in about 1608, and Nicholas Okes published it in 1612. Heywood was using "apology" in the Greek sense here: he was not offering an excuse but was defending actors from Puritan attacks on them and their profession. The essay is prefaced by a dedication to the Earl of Worcester, but Heywood does not specifically name any Puritan attackers against whom he is defending his profession and colleagues. He mentions that he saw it fit to "stammer out my mind than not to speak at all," and Frederick Boas notes that Heywood, who had spent about sixteen years in the world of theater by 1612, was perhaps (excluding Shakespeare) the best person to undertake this defense.

The essay is divided roughly into three parts, characterized by Heywood's subtitle as "three briefe Treatises," although there is some overlapping: the first part deals with the "antiquity" of actors; the second part focuses on their "ancient dignity"; and finally Heywood addresses the "true use of their quality," "quality" being the term used during his time to refer to the acting profession. As with other writers who have defended the stage, Heywood too emphasizes the beneficial moral influence that the theater has on its audience, an issue that came under attack from Puritans who were quick to focus on the theater as a corrupting influence in society. The essay is loaded with classical references, as when Heywood points out that what inspired Hercules to complete his twelve labors was a play performed for him by the noblemen of Greece, in which they acted out the heroic deeds of his father, Jupiter.

In the section on the dignity of actors, Heywood references actors from the classical period as well as those who were acting during his own time, such as Richard Tarleton, Will Kempe, and Edward Alleyn. In this section, Heywood, in passing, identifies Thomas Kyd as the author of the late-sixteenth-century revenge play *A Spanish Tragedy*, which had previously been published anonymously. Heywood also refers to occasions when plays have elicited confessions of murders, as when a woman watching *The History of Friar Francis,* in which a woman is haunted by her murdered husband's ghost, confessed to having murdered her own husband some years ago.

Heywood writes eloquently about London as home to an illustrious theatrical scene, which strangers from foreign lands came to partake of. He takes pride in the London stage and asks if there is any other city where such enjoyable as well as edifying entertainments are offered nightly. Furthermore, he notes that the English language, which used to be a rough mish-mash, is increasingly becoming a refined and elegant tongue because of the efforts of playwrights who are attempting to give it a new sophistication in their works.

The passionate number of responses to *An Apology for Actors* can be used to gauge its achievement. In 1615, "A Refutation of the Apology for Actors" was written by J. G. and William Cartwright. *An Apology for Actors* marks Heywood as a passionate defender of plays, playwrights, actors, and the stage. This is hardly surprising given the fact that with the possible exclusion of Shakespeare, no other playwright had had as long an association with the London stage during the late Elizabethan and early Jacobean period as Heywood did.

MASQUES AND PAGEANTS

From 1630 to 1640, in his official capacity as city poet, Heywood produced a number of masques and pageants. celebrating the city of London and her inhabitants. These usually were spectacular shows with dazzling backgrounds and sumptuous costumes that were procured at a great expense. In the best-known of these, *Londoni's Jus Honorarium* (1631), there are shows on the water and Heywood presents London as a lady flanked by the other major cities of the realm such as Oxford, Lincoln, and York. Justice and Mercy ride before her and tributes are paid to London's haberdashers—the Company of Haberdashers commissioned the play—and its lord mayor. *Londoni's Jus Honorarium* was such a success that the next year the haberdashers again called upon Heywood, and in 1632 he produced *Londoni Artium & Scientiarum Scaturigo; or, London's Fountain of Arts and Sciences*. In 1633, Heywood produced *Londoni Emporia; or, London's Mercatura*, which was commissioned when Ralph Freeman became lord mayor.

In 1634, he wrote the masque *Love's Mistress*, which was produced by the Queen's Company to celebrate the king's birthday and was based on the mythological story of Cupid and Psyche. Inigo Jones provided the backdrops for this masque, which was acted by professional actors and presented in a private show before the king and the queen. Heywood's 1635 pageant, commissioned by another livery company of London, the Clothworker's Company, to celebrate the mayoralty of Christopher Clethrowe, was *Londoni Sinus Salutis; or, London's Harbour of Health and Happiness*, and it featured mythological gods such as Venus, Juno, Mars, and Pallas. The 1637 pageant was *Londoni Speculum; or, London's Mirror*, commissioned by the Haberdasher's Company. This also provided an elaborate show on water, with the appearance of St. Catherine being drawn in a chariot by two sea horses. In another show, London is presented as an impenetrable fort from which Bellona, the goddess of war, crowns the mayor as its chief general. The pageant for 1638 was *Porta Pietatis; or, The Port or Harbour of Piety*, written for the Company of Drapers. Heywood's final pageant, in 1639, was *Londoni Status Pacatus; or, London's Peaceable Estate*, also commissioned by the Draper's Company upon the mayoralty of Henry Garway.

In the civic and court masques and pageants, Heywood was able to give expression to his love for London and show himself as a patriotic son of the city in which he had arrived as a young boy after the sudden termination of his education. The masques and pageants allowed him to experiment with new literary forms, and his skill at them is evidenced by the fact that he was commissioned to produce masques and pageants on a yearly basis by different companies. In writing these pageants, Heywood successfully followed in the footsteps of writers such as George Peele, Thomas Dekker, Thomas Middleton, and John Webster.

CONCLUSION

Thomas Heywood's productivity was astounding. As mentioned earlier, by his own claim, he had either written or contributed to some 220 plays. Heywood was a playwright, actor, translator, pamphlet writer, and for a staunch defender of the stage. Ever the gentleman, in his plays he upheld honor, chastity, courage, and civic duty. He lived and worked in the city of London, and he painted contemporary life in that city in lively colors, emphasizing the dignity and potential of the ordinary Londoner. His career spanned almost fifty years, from the 1590s to the 1640s, one of the greatest eras of the English stage. In his introduction to *Thomas Heywood's Pageants: A Critical Edition* (1986), David M. Bergeron notes that "for better and sometimes for worse, Heywood was a writer, apparently relishing new or different literary forms, and impressive in his productivity and variety, embodying thereby the Renaissance delight in multiplicity" (p. 1). The light freshness of the comedies of intrigue, the depth of passion in plays of romantic love, the patriotism of the history plays, and the complexity of human emotions in the tragedies attest to his skill and versatility. Yet, until the late twentieth century, this great playwright of the late Elizabethan and early Jacobean period who was a driving force behind the theater of his time was a widely overlooked figure—with most critical reception being concentrated only on *A Woman Killed with Kindness* and *A Maidenhead*

Well Lost. But, given the wealth of information about contemporary life, stage, and living that is present in his plays, pageants, and pamphlets, it is not surprising that there has been a surge of modern interest in his work.

Selected Bibliography

WORKS OF THOMAS HEYWOOD

PLAY PRODUCTIONS

Edward IV, parts 1 and 2, London, Curtain theater(?), c. 1594–1599.

The Four Prentices of London, with The Conquest of Jerusalem (related to *Godfrey of Bologne,* part 2, c. 1594), London, Rose theater, c. 1594–1600.

The Fair Maid of the Exchange, doubtfully attributed to Heywood, London, unknown theater, 1594–1607.

The Fair Maid of the West, part 1, London, unknown theater, c. 1597–1610.

Sir Thomas More, probably by Anthony Munday, with revisions by Thomas Dekker, Henry Chettle, probably William Shakespeare, and perhaps Heywood, probably not produced until 1964, c. 1598.

War without Blows and Love without Suit (or *Strife*), London, Rose theater, early 1599.

Joan as Good as My Lady, London, Rose theater, 1599.

How a Man May Choose a Good Wife from a Bad, possibly by Heywood, Worcester's Men, c. 1601–1602.

Albere Galles (possibly the same play as *Nobody and Somebody*), by Heywood and Wentworth Smith, London, Rose theater, 1602.

The Royal King and the Loyal Subject, by Heywood and Smith (possibly the same play as *Marshal Osric*), London, Rose theater, autumn 1602.

Sir Thomas Wyatt (possibly incorporating *Lady Jane,* parts 1 and 2), by Heywood, Smith, Dekker, Chettle, and John Webster, London, Boar's Head or Rose theater, autumn 1602.

Christmas Comes but Once a Year, by Heywood, Dekker, Chettle, and Webster, London, Boar's Head or Rose theater, 1602.

The London Florentine, part 1, attributed to Heywood and Chettle, London, Rose theater(?), Christmas 1602.

The Blind Man Eats Many a Fly, London, Rose theater, early 1603.

A Woman Killed with Kindness, London, Rose theater, 1603.

If You Know Not Me You Know Nobody, parts 1 and 2, London, Boar's Head or Curtain theater, 1603–1605.

The Wise Woman of Hogsdon (possibly the same play as *How to Learn a Woman to Woo*), London, at Court, December 30, 1604).

The Bold Beauchamps, attributed to Heywood, London, unknown theater, c. 1606–1607.

The Rape of Lucrece, London, Red Bull theater, c. 1606–1608.

Fortune by Land and Sea, by Heywood and William Rowley, London, Red Bull theater, c. 1609.

The Golden Age, London, Red Bull theater, c. 1609–1611.

The Silver Age, London, Red Bull, Blackfriars, and Globe theaters(?), c. 1610–1612.

The Brazen Age, London, Red Bull theater (and possibly Blackfriars and Globe theaters?), c. 1610–1613.

The Iron Age, parts 1 and 2, London, Red Bull theater (and possibly Blackfriars and Globe theaters?), c. 1612–1613.

The Captives, London, Cockpit theater, autumn 1624.

The Escapes of Jupiter (or *Calisto*; scenes from *The Golden Age* and *The Silver Age*), London, unknown theater, c. 1625.

The English Traveller, London, Cockpit theater, c. 1625.

The Fair Maid of the West, part 2, London, Cockpit theater, c. 1630–1631.

London's Jus Honorarium, streets of London, October 29, 1631.

Londini Artium et Scientiarum Scaturigo, or London's Fountain of Arts and Sciences, streets of London, October 29, 1632.

A Maidenhead Well Lost, London, Cockpit theater, c. 1633.

Londini Emporia, streets of London, October 29, 1633.

Love's Mistress, London, Cockpit theater, 1634.

The Late Lancashire Witches, by Heywood and Richard Brome, London, Globe theater, 1634.

The Apprentice's Prize, attributed to Heywood and Brome, London, Blackfriars theater(?), c. 1634(?).

The Life and Death of Sir Martin Skink, attributed to Heywood and Brome, London, Blackfriars theater(?), c. 1634(?).

A Challenge for Beauty, London, Blackfriars and Globe theaters, c. 1634–1636.

Londini Sinus Salutis; or, London's Harbor of Health and Happiness, streets of London, October 29, 1635.

Londini Speculum; or, London's Mirror, streets of London, October 30, 1637.

Porta Pietatis; or, The Port of Piety, streets of London, October 29, 1638.

Londini Status Pacatus, or, London's Peaceable Estate, streets of London, October 29, 1639.

Love's Masterpiece, London, unknown theater, 1640.

BOOKS

Oenone and Paris, attributed to Heywood (London: Printed by R. Jones, 1594).

The First and Second Partes of King Edward the Fourth (London: Printed by J. Windet for J. Oxenbridge, 1599).

A Pleasant Conceited Comedie, Wherein Is Shewed How a Man May Chose a Good Wife from a Bad, possibly by Heywood (London: Printed by T. Creede for M. Lawe, 1602).

If You Know Not Me, You Know No Bodie; or, The Troubles of Queen Elizabeth (London: Printed by T. Purfoot for N. Butter, 1605).

The Second Part of If You Know Not Me, You Know No Bodie (London: Printed by T. Purfoot for N. Butter, 1606).

The Fayre Maid of the Exchange, doubtfully attributed to Heywood (London: Printed by V. Simmes for H. Rockit, 1607).

A Woman Kilde with Kindnesse (London: Printed by W. Jaggard, sold by J. Hodgets, 1607).

The Famous History of Sir T. Wyat: With the Coronation of Queen Mary (possibly incorporating *Lady Jane,* parts 1 and 2), by Heywood, Thomas Dekker, John Webster, Henry Chettle, and Wentworth Smith (London: Printed by E. Allde for T. Archer, 1607).

The Rape of Lucrece: A True Roman Tragedie (London: Printed by E. Allde for J. Busby, sold by N. Butter, 1608).

Troia Britanica; or, Great Britaines Troy: A Poem, attributed to Heywood (London: Printed by W. Jaggard, 1609).

The Golden Age (London: Printed by N. Okes for W. Barrenger, 1611).

An Apology for Actors: Containing Three Briefe Treatises (London: Printed by N. Okes, 1612).

The Silver Age (London: Printed by N. Okes, sold by B. Lightfoote, 1613).

The Brazen Age (London: Printed by N. Okes for S. Rand, 1613).

A Funerall Elegie, Upon the Death of Henry, Prince of Wales, attributed to Heywood (London: Printed by N. Okes for W. Welbie, 1613).

A Marriage Triumphe: Solemnized in an Epithalamium, [for] *the Count Palatine: And the Lady Elizabeth,* attributed to Heywood (London: Printed by N. Okes for E. Marchant, 1613).

The Foure Prentises of London (London: Printed by N. Okes for J. Wright, 1615).

[Gunaikeion]; or, Nine Bookes of Various History: Concerninge Women (London: Printed by A. Islip, 1624); republished as *The Generall History of Women* (London: Printed by W. H. for W. H., 1657).

A Funeral Elegie, upon the Death of King James (London: Printed by Eliot's Court Press for T. Harper, 1625).

Englands Elizabeth: Her Life and Troubles, During Her Minoritie, attributed to Heywood (London: Printed by J. Beale for P. Waterhouse, 1631).

The Fair Maid of the West, parts 1 and 2 (London: Printed by M. Flesher for R. Royston, 1631).

Londons Jus Honorarium: Exprest in Sundry Triumphs, at the Initiation of G. Whitmore, into the Maioralty (London: Printed by N. Okes, 1631).

The Iron Age, parts 1 and 2 (London: Printed by N. Okes, 1632).

Londini Artium & Scientiarum Scaturigo: Exprest in Sundry Triumphs, at the Initiation of N. Raynton into the Maior[al]*ty* (London: Printed by N. Okes, 1632).

The English Traveller (London: Printed by R. Raworth, 1633).

Londini Emporia; or, Londons Mercatura: At the Inaugauration of R. Freeman into the Maior[al]*ty* (London: Printed by N. Okes, 1633).

A Pleasant Comedy, Called A Mayden-Head Well Lost (London: Printed by N. Okes for J. Jackson & F. Church, 1634).

The Late Lancashire Witches. A Comedy, by Heywood and Richard Brome (London: Printed by T. Harper for B. Fisher, 1634).

The Hierarchie of the Blessed Angells, attributed to Heywood (London: Printed by A. Islip, 1635).

Philocothonista; or, The Drunkard, attributed to Heywood (London: Printed by R. Raworth, 1635).

Londini Sinus Salutis; or, Londons Harbour of Health: At the Initiation of C. Cletherowe, into the Maioralty (London: Printed for R. Raworth, 1635).

A True Discourse of the Two Infamous Upstart Prophets, R. Farnham and J. Bull Now Prisoners, with Their Examinations, attributed to Heywood (London: Printed by N. Okes for T. Lambert, 1636).

A Challenge for Beautie (London: Printed by R. Raworth, sold by J. Becket, 1636).

Loves Maistresse; or, The Queens Masque (London: Printed by R. Raworth for J. Crowch, sold by J. Emery, 1636).

The Royall King, and The Loyall Subject (London: Printed by N. & J. Okes for J. Becket, 1637).

Pleasant Dialogues and Dramma's, Selected Out of Lucian, Erasmus, Textor, Ovid, &c (London: Printed by R. Oulton for R. Hearne, sold by T. Slater, 1637).

A True Description of His Majesties Royall Ship (London: Printed by J. Okes for J. Aston, 1637).

Londini Speculum; or, Londons Mirror, at the Initiation of R. Fenn, into the Mairolty (London: Printed by J. Okes, 1637).

A Curtaine Lecture: As It Is Read by a Countery Farmers Wife to Her Good Man (London: Printed by R. Young for J. Aston, 1637).

The Phoenix of These Late Times; or, The Life of H. Welby (London: Printed by N. Okes, sold by R. Clotterbuck, 1637).

The Wise-Woman of Hogsdon: A Comedie (London: Printed by M. Parsons for H. Shephard, 1638).

Porta Pietatis; or, The Port or Harbour of Piety: At the

Initiation of Sir M. Abbot into the Majoralty (London: Printed by J. Okes, 1638).

A True Relation, of the Lives and Deaths of the Two English Pyrats, Purser, and Clinton (London: Printed by J. Okes, 1639).

Londini Status Pacatus; or, Londons Peaceable Estate: At the Innitiation of H. Garway, into the Majoralty (London: Printed by J. Okes, 1639).

The Exemplary Lives and Memorable Acts of Nine of the Most Worthy Women of the World (London: Printed by T. Cotes for R. Royston, 1640).

Fortune by Land and Sea: A Tragi-Comedy, by Heywood and William Rowley (London: Printed for John Sweeting & Robert Pollard, 1655).

EDITIONS

The Dramatic Works of Thomas Heywood. 6 vols. Edited by R. H. Shepherd (London: J. Pearson, 1874). Comprises *Edward IV,* parts 1 and 2; *If You Know Not Me You Know Nobody,* parts 1 and 2; *The Fair Maid of the Exchange*; *A Woman Killed with Kindness*; *The Four Prentices of London*; *The Fair Maid of the West*; *The Golden Age*; *The Silver Age*; *The Brazen Age*; *The Iron Age,* parts 1 and 2; *The English Traveller*; *A Maidenhead Well Lost*; *The Late Lancashire Witches*; *London's Jus Honorarium*; *Londini Sinus Salutis*; *Londini Speculum*; *A Challenge for Beauty*; *Love's Mistress*; *The Rape of Lucrece*; *Londini Porta Pietatis*; *The Wise Woman of Hogsdon*; *Londini Status Pacatus*; *The Royal King and the Loyal Subject*; *Pleasant Dialogues and Dramas*; and *Fortune by Land and Sea.*

The Captives. In *A Collection of Old English Plays.* Edited by A. H. Bullen. Vol. 4 (London: Privately printed, 1885).

If You Know Not Me You Know Nobody, parts 1 and 2. 2 vols. Edited by Madeleine Doran (London: Printed for the Malone Society at Oxford University Press, 1935).

The Rape of Lucrece. Edited by Alan Holaday (Urbana: University of Illinois Press, 1950).

The Captives. Edited by Arthur Brown (Oxford: Printed for the Malone Society at Oxford University, 1953).

A Woman Killed with Kindness. Edited by R. W. Van Fossen (London: Methuen, 1961; Cambridge, Mass.: Harvard University Press, 1961).

The Fair Maid of the Exchange, doubtfully attributed to Heywood (though not in this edition). Edited by Peter H. Davison (Oxford: Printed for the Malone Society at Oxford University Press, 1963).

The Fair Maid of the West, parts 1 and 2. Edited by Robert K. Turner, Jr. (Lincoln: University of Nebraska Press, 1967; London: Arnold, 1968).

The Escapes of Jupiter. Edited by Henry D. Janzen (Oxford:

Printed for the Malone Society at Oxford University Press, 1978).

The Late Lancashire Witches, by Heywood and Richard Brome. Edited by Laird H. Barber (New York and London: Garland, 1979).

Thomas Heywood's The Four Prentices of London: *A Critical, Old-Spelling Edition.* Edited by Mary Ann Weber Gasior (New York and London: Garland, 1980).

A Critical Edition of Fortune by Land and Sea *by Thomas Heywood and William Rowley.* Edited by Herman Doh (New York and London: Garland, 1980).

A Critical Edition of The Wise-Woman of Hogsdon. Edited by Michael H. Leonard (New York and London: Garland, 1980).

COLLECTED EDITIONS

The Dramatic Works of Thomas Heywood, Now First Collected with Illustrative Notes and a Memoir of the Author. New York: Russell & Russell, 1964.

Thomas Heywood's Pageants: A Critical Edition. Edited by David M. Bergeron. New York: Garland, 1986.

Thomas Heywood's Art of Love: The First Complete English Translation of Ovid's Ars Amatoria. Edited by M. L. Stapleton. Ann Arbor: University of Michigan Press, 2000.

BIOGRAPHICAL AND CRITICAL STUDIES

Baines, Barbara J. *Thomas Heywood.* Boston: Twayne, 1984.

Boas, Frederick. *Thomas Heywood.* London: Williams and Norgate, 1950.

Clark, Arthur Melville. *Thomas Heywood, Playwright and Miscellanist.* New York: Russell and Russell, 1958.

Courtland, Joseph. *A Cultural Studies Approach to Two Exotic Citizen Romances by Thomas Heywood.* New York: Peter Lang, 2001.

Cromwell Otelia. *Thomas Heywood: A Study in the Elizabethan Drama of Everyday Life.* 1928. Reprint, Hamden, Conn.: Archon Books, 1969.

Grivelet, Michel. *Thomas Heywood et le drame domestique elizabéthain.* Paris: Didier, 1957.

Johnson, Marilyn L. *Images of Women in the Works of Thomas Heywood.* Salzburg: Institut für Englische Sprache und Literatur, Universität Salzburg, 1974.

Rowland, Richard. *Thomas Heywood's Theatre, 1599–1639.* Surrey, U.K.: Ashgate, 2010.

Velte, Mowbray. *The Bourgeois Elements in the Dramas of Thomas Heywood.* New York: Haskell House, 1966.

Weiner, Arlene W. *Thomas Heywood's* The Iron Age. New York: Garland, 1979.

Wentworth, Michael D. *Thomas Heywood: A Reference Guide.* Boston: G. K. Hall, 1986.

RACHEL INGALLS

(1940—)

Julie Wakeman-Linn

IN 1986, WHEN the British Book Marketing Council named Rachel Ingalls' *Mrs. Caliban* as one of the twenty best post–World War II novels written by a living U.S. writer, American readers and critics discovered Ingalls, even though she had been writing for over fifteen years in England where she had a solid readership. The British Book Marketing Council list put Ingalls, an unknown in the United States, in the company of John Updike, Eudora Welty, and Thomas Pynchon. Since 1986, she has continued to write and be published, yet she has not been widely read. Ingalls is generally acclaimed to be a masterful storyteller.

Rachel Ingalls has written fifteen novellas, dozens of long short stories, and three novels. Her novel *The Man Who Was Left Behind* gained acclaim from the Great Britain Authors' Club in 1971, earning the group's First Novel Award. Her 1982 novel *Mrs. Caliban* was staged as a play at the Chicago Lifeline Theatre in spring 2010. In 2000, the story "Blessed Art Thou" (which first appeared in 1985) was made into an independent film produced by Edward Pressman that focused primarily on the monastic politics and played it for low comedy, "a burlesque of monastic life" (McCrory, p. 50).

Ingalls has been compared with American masters by reviewers such as William Packard, who writes, "In her best work, Ingalls is as monochromatic as Edgar Allan Poe, going straight to her target ... Her world view is more complex than Poe's: where Poe simply demonstrated the inevitable eruption of the dark powers, Ingalls has an alarming vision of the parasitical and parricidal relation between the present and the past" (p. 11). Yet another critic, Patrick Sullivan, states, "some of the best [stories in the 2005 collection *Times Like These*] may well remind readers of Shirley Jackson or Flannery O'Connor."

LIFE AND WORK: OVERVIEW

Rachel Ingalls was born May 13, 1940, in Boston, Massachusetts. Leaving high school, she traveled to Germany, where she lived and audited classes at the Universities of Gottingen, Munich, Erlangen, and Cologne. She returned to the United States, and after completing her BA in English at Radcliffe College in 1964, she immigrated to England and has remained there. All of her reported jobs circle around literature and the theater. She has rebuffed most interviews, but the general information is that she has worked as a theater dresser, a librarian, a publisher's reader, a film critic, and a ballet critic for *Tattler*.

Rachel Ingalls' writing resists categorization. The length of her narratives makes many of them novellas, which is certainly not a common postmodern form. In them, Ingalls delves into the family history of her characters, their lifestyles, and their psychoses. Penelope Power observes that "the stories are heavy with the sort of extraneous detail that is usually omitted from short stories" (p. 33). Ingalls establishes conflict immediately, but through multiple scenes she adds layers to her characters through richly detailed backstory and flashbacks. Anne Bernays in her review of *I See a Long Journey: Three Novellas* (1985), writes "Rachel Ingalls ... seems have found the ideal form in which to exercise her astonishing imagination." Ingalls including employs traditional techniques of setting, symbol and metaphor, and plot structures while also animating her fiction with fantastical or supernatural elements.

Her writing style has been labeled "American gothic"—Victoria Segal dubs her a "mistress of gothic horror," while Ed Park of the *Village Voice* calls her writing "gothic and ferocious"—although her work does not fit neatly into any one genre: the novel *Mrs. Caliban*, the story "Veterans" (from *Times Like These*), and others of Ingalls' works of fiction could easily be labeled science fiction or postapocalyptic or dystopian fiction. One collection, *The End of Tragedy*, is shelved under "Horror." Ingalls' novel *Mrs. Caliban* is often defined as a feminist work. David Cowart, writing in *Critique*, suggests other possibilities: "the novel subsumes or parodies several literary and cinematic genres, in both romance and realist modes. These include, beside the psychological novel, science fiction, fantasy, monster movies, and soap opera. Ingalls also invokes the spectrum from 'women's fiction' to feminist literature" (p. 77). Joyce Carol Oates places *Mrs. Caliban* in "fairy tale/wonder-tale mode" (p. 107) in a new "literary genre of "revisioned fairy tales (p. 98).

Ingalls often uses setting to escalate tension. Her stories are set in Greece (including the islands of Crete and Delos), an unnamed Amazon basin country, East Africa, or often in a vague but somehow familiar unnamed town. A review of *Times Like These* (2005) in *Publishers Weekly* adds, "Ingalls' command of her varied worlds—from bucolic small town to renegade postwar countryside—is impressive" (p. 45).

Ingalls does not usually set her stories in England; instead she often sets her stories in America. Ed Park, writing in the *Village Voice*, observes, "Ingalls … has lived in London since 1965, and it's as if she's merging a 40-year-old version of her native land with contemporary nightmares. The effect is unsettling, like visiting a town where all the letters have been rubbed off the signs. Everything feels fresh and ancient." Her characters are ordinary people, who lack self-awareness but who must confront their external and internal lives, often under the influence of psychological, surreal, or fantastical plot elements.

Ingalls' fiction employs metaphors like the ocean in *Mrs. Caliban* or a grandmother's ring in "Inheritance" (collected in *The Pearlkillers*, 1986) or the lion in *Binstead's Safari* (1983) that

function as symbols. Another device Ingalls uses often is foreshadowing; a character will express a sentiment that will be the key desire of another character, and that conflict will thwart the main character. In "On Ice," collected in *I See a Long Journey* (1985), the main character, Beverly, meets college acquaintances who disagree with her; she "hated it that others had discovered her secret, happy life" (p. 61). When she meets Martha Torrence, Beverly has stumbled into a group's insurance scam and is, paradoxically, trapped in *their* secret, happy life. Ingalls' characters often get want they wish for, but in unexpected, ironic ways.

Ingalls also reanimates classic plot patterns. Odysseus' return is tucked inside the story "No Love Lost" (from *Times Like These*), Beauty and the Beast is the shape of *Mrs. Caliban*, and in "Third Time Lucky," a fairy-tale maiden who is in need of rescue—isn't. Writing about the story collection that springs from Greek myths, *Days Like Today*, Margaret Walters writes, "Ingalls's precise, cool, ironic prose carries a sting in its tail."

MRS. CALIBAN

Mrs. Caliban (1982), as a novel, operates on many levels, offering a satirical attack on American marriage, the news media, the role of women, and the dangers of trying to defy convention when a housewife has an affair with a seven-foot frogman.

Dorothy is stuck in an empty marriage. She knows her husband, Fred, has had many affairs, but neither of them is willing to exert themselves out of their routine, their "similar litany" of daily "ritual" (p. 7) to divorce. Dorothy has another distraction; while she is doing housework and listening to the radio, "for the past three weeks she had been hearing things that couldn't possibly be real" (p. 8). Most of the messages are soothing her about her lost baby and her dead son, but she questions where they are real or not, whether she is going crazy or not. Then she hears a news report that a monster, a seven-foot-tall frogman who was captured from under the Gulf of Mexico, has escaped and is dangerous. She wonders if "the bulletin … was one of her special announcements" (p. 11). She thinks about protecting her little boy Scotty and next how her miscarriage has changed her marriage. She is about to go meet her friend Estelle when she hears another message, saying, "It's all right Dorothy. It's going to be all right" (p. 13). At the supermarket, the two women meet a food sample salesgirl whose "drooping gaze" (p. 15) makes her feel like she is from another planet; the description and image prepare the reader for the introduction of Aquarius the monsterman. While primarily discussing Estelle's lively love life, Estelle counsels that Dorothy should divorce Fred. Estelle, so many ways the opposite of Dorothy, is "perpetuating the dominant masculine culture" with her lovers and fashion shows, suggests the critic Rebecca Ann Bach (p. 2). Estelle must dress and behave so that others approve of her.

That evening, as Dorothy prepares dinner for her husband and a colleague he has unexpectedly brought home, "the screen door opened and a gigantic six-foot-seven-inch frog-like creature shouldered its way in … and stood stock-still in front of her" (p. 24). In her surprise and shock, she offers it a stalk of celery, even though she holds a knife. In his essay, "Mourning Monsters: Deception and Transformation in Rachel Ingalls's Fiction," Lee Upton writes, "Dorothy encounters her shadow self—a monster whose loneliness is stronger than 'hunger'" (p. 55). She feeds the monster and notices he is like a very large man. After a civilized exchange of "thank you" and "you're welcome," he says, "I need help" (p. 27), establishing his humanity. Aquarius has been named Larry by the lab technicians who held him captive. Dorothy hides Larry in a bedroom where Fred never goes, and Larry "caught both her hands in his and held them tenderly" (p. 29). The next day they begin having sex; Michael Dorris observes, "Larry … is both insatiable sex partner and fetus" (p. 7). Dorothy does not regret when Larry eats her prize apple cucumbers; instead she delights in feeding him, finding him sandals large enough, and buying him avocados, his favorite food. He is both lover and child for her.

Over the coming days and weeks, they converse about how different his underwater world is from southern California. Larry questions the need for following conventions, and the ingrained habits of everyday life, when he observes, "I like these things unrestricted. It isn't a matter of the rules of clothing. It's a question of freedom" (p. 32). Rebecca Bach observes that the novel allows Dorothy and the reader to "question the other binaries that structure culture: male-female, human-animal, white-black, clothed-naked" (p. 391). As they converse, Larry and Dorothy share as equals, making love, talking, "asking and answering questions" (p. 34). Larry even helps with the vacuuming.

Larry and Dorothy become bolder, driving out to the beach in the evenings and visiting deserted gardens and bamboo groves. Driving in an automobile, so ordinary in southern California culture, is another thematic layer in the novel. David Cowart comments, "The references to automobiles and driving … do more than authenticate the southern California setting: Cars traditionally suggest responsibility, a means of freedom, a potential danger to oneself and others" (p. 78). Larry takes this freedom and soon begins driving stolen cars he has hot-wired.

At the beach, Larry tries to explain his world to Dorothy, using the sound of the sea: "it's the sound of where I live … It's always there, like your heartbeats … Always, for our whole lives, we have music" (p. 44). Dorothy realizes how lonely Larry is; he answers "more than anything, more than hunger" (p. 45). And she recognizes it in herself as well. They plot how to return Larry to the Gulf of Mexico.

Dorothy thinks they ought to tell the world his version of events, and the story becomes a meditation on how a violent act is interpreted: Was it self-defense to escape the tortures of the lab? Ultimately how will Larry be perceived—as a human whose rights have been violated or as an animal who is not responsible? Larry takes her out of conventional ways of thinking and lets her consider other possible social realities. Bach observes, "Released into the world from a place not under the Western ideological sky, Larry opens up our culture for a rereading" (p. 391).

The world of southern California comes to the pair through television; some programs teach Larry about the human world, while the news broadcasts that they watch remind them that Larry is viewed as dangerous. The novel implicitly criticizes the news media as Larry observes, "You can't imagine what they've been saying about me … The monster this. The monster that" (p. 64). Larry wants to know if it is a common human trait to invent; Ingalls quietly reminds the reader of how humans lie about facts and lie to invent themselves.

As the two formulate their plan to return Larry to the ocean, he suggests that a baby would be an excellent hostage. This moment causes Dorothy to explain her loss of two children, but it also triggers a discussion of how babies are raised in U.S. culture. Larry is amazed that human offspring are helpless. Dorothy wonders if they could have a child. She states, "I'd be delighted if that happened," and goes on to postulate that their child, "born on American soil to an American mother—such a child could become President" (p. 66). Larry says he was labeled a different species at the lab and "a mixing of the species is said to produce a sterile offspring, isn't it?" Dorothy responds "They didn't like you and treated you shamefully. They'd want an excuse. For centuries people like that kept saying women didn't have souls" (p. 67). Dorothy now constructs her own ideas outside conventional thinking.

While Dorothy is as happy as a teenager in love, her friend Estelle's love life has gone wrong. Her two boyfriends were cheating on her as well. She accuses Dorothy: "You are just so unromantic … If we all only owned the things we needed! You don't understand the nature of desire (p. 77)." Dorothy answers, "I do. I do now" (p. 77).

She asks Larry about desire in his world, and his answer is simple: "When we want something, it's true. We don't want something we can't have and not like the thing we get instead" (p. 82). For Larry, obsession isn't a factor, only possession matters. At the beach, taking risks of being seen and caught, Dorothy is frightened. When Larry soothes her, she answers, "You're all I've got" (p. 84).

Estelle seeks Dorothy's friendship when her two teenage children's behave terribly. Her daughter is seeing an older man, someone Dorothy views as inappropriate and "unsuitable." The sexual politics behind her daughter's behavior are revealed when Estelle says, "She's trying to get back at me through this" (p. 90). Echoing a recurring theme in Ingalls' stories of sex as commerce, Estelle blames her divorce for her children's bad behavior, providing an ironic twist on her advice to Dorothy early in the novel.

In another instance of the novel's representation of sexual politics, Fred admits his current affair to Dorothy, wanting to protect her from the interfering anger of his sexual partner, who is "going to make a big scene" (p. 94). Dorothy finds she doesn't really care, thinking, "I have Larry. I can afford to be forgiving" (p. 94). Fred unilaterally wants their marriage to function again. She and Fred have sex while Larry is out driving.

In the morning comes the news that "Aquarius the Monsterman has struck again" (p. 96). Larry was attacked by a group of five young men, known to be "punks and troublemakers " (p. 97), even though in the news media they are portrayed as "the flower of our citizenry" (p. 96). Larry reports to Dorothy that they attacked him with broken bottles, so he killed them. In a plot coincidence, one of the young men is Estelle's son. In a discussion that hinges on the definition of truth, Larry questions why Dorothy's feelings about this self-defensive murder are different from her reaction about his murder in self-defense of the lab technicians who had been torturing him. Dorothy answers that it is worse that she knew the person. Larry responds, "To do a bad thing is the same from a stranger as from someone you know. Maybe it's worse from someone you know" (p. 101). His response is not softened or moderated by emotion. Dorothy's response is to worry about Estelle. Dorothy feels grief and anxiety about how and whether she will now comfort the woman who has helped her through the loss of her children. Dorothy "felt like crying; for Estelle at the moment and Estelle in the future, and for herself in the past when Scotty died" (p. 102).

Fred and she argue about Aquarius, whether he is real or a lab experiment gone wrong, whether the monster was inhumanely treated at the lab. Fred dismisses it as an "eight foot gorilla with web feet and bug eyes. A well developed frog? Not exactly an Ivy League type" (p. 103). Dorothy replies, "I've met plenty of Ivy-leaguers I'd call monsters" (p. 103). The humor lapses into irony as they have a quiet dinner. When Dorothy finally finds Estelle, the death of her son has changed her, "made her a different person" (p. 106). Dorothy remembers how in her own grief the medical profession offered nothing more than drugs and dismissive treatment and thereby made her into a victim, and through this reference the novel challenges and "jabs at other institutional power structures" (Bach, p. 395).

Dorothy and Larry head to the beach that evening for "a warm lovely night, full of promise and romance as she had dreamed about it in her teens and still promised, for her and for everyone else, too" (p. 115). They discover that Fred is having his latest affair with Estelle's teenage daughter. Dorothy is horrified and they flee, only to be followed by Fred and Estelle's daughter. In escaping, Dorothy drives too fast. Fred tries to run her off the road. Their cars bang together and Fred spins out of control, over the median and into another car. Dorothy sees those two "cars bursting into flames" (p. 121). Larry urges her to "keep going" (p. 121), and he slips away to the ocean. The novel closes very quietly. Dorothy settles Fred's estate, and she mourns Larry's absence at Fred's headstone. She returns to the beach in the evenings, watching for Larry. "One wave covering another like the knitting of threads, like the begetting of revenges, betrayals, memories, regrets" (p. 125). The phrase, "But he never came," is repeated (p. 125).

This ending has been criticized for its suddenness. Joyce Carol Oates argues the novel is "weakened by a hurried, rather sketchy denouement" (p. 107). Central strands are not resolved, including Estelle, Larry, and even Dorothy's future. Furthermore, the novel raises questions of how reliable Dorothy is as a narrator. Did she

only imagine Larry? She was hearing voices from the radio; Larry questions whether the pictures on TV are real. Perception isn't dependable in this world where science and the news media prove corrupt. Rebecca Bach observes that "just as we cannot know whether Larry is imaginary or a real actor in this world, we will never know the tenor of Dorothy's fate" (p. 3). Yet the ambiguity also points to Dorothy's growth from trapped woman to a woman freed from convention. Whether Larry is real or imagined is part of the novel's success. Cowart observes, "Interpreted symbolically, Larry gives expression to Dorothy's every secret fear, anger, and desire; his symbolic multivalence ultimately provides the most cogent argument for his being a fantasy and at the same time makes the novel such a tour de force" (p. 82).

Critics have also questioned which character is intended to be the "Caliban" of the title. Certainly Larry, "brutally tamed at the Institute, … is Shakespeare's Caliban in the twentieth century, an embodiment of nature as helpless victim of modern science," but also Dorothy, who is "Caliban's woman twice over; wife and servant to the moral monster, Fred, and lover of the physical monster, Larry" (Cowart, p. 79). So perhaps the closest reading of the novel reveals Dorothy as the most modern Caliban.

Several key ambivalent symbols are the ocean, garden, and automobiles. The ocean is a place of freedom for Larry and danger for Dorothy. It is his home, a place that is not racist, not obsessed with possessions and mating rituals, but a separate world. Dorothy initially compares the ocean to the beauty of a "lovely lighted aquarium" (p. 50); unlike an aquarium, which is an artificial environment, the ocean as "a world is not art. Dorothy thought about the living things that moved in that world: large, ruthless and hungry" (p. 50). Gardens and gardening reoccur throughout the novel. A minor character who is a touchstone for Dorothy, Mr. Mendoza, teaches her about gardening, and like the person she becomes at the end of the novel, he "has a mind of his own" (p. 97). Dorothy has begun to defy convention, first by harboring Larry and then by wanting her own version of truth and not the news media's. Larry and Dorothy walk in secluded gardens and a bamboo grove. Like the ocean, gardens are a place of freedom and danger. Larry runs freely over the grass, but he also kills his five young attackers in a garden, and Larry and Dorothy discover Fred with Estelle's daughter in a garden as well. The automobile frees Dorothy and Larry from the confines of her husband's house and gives Larry independence when he begins to steal cars to drive alone, but it also kills Fred and Estelle's daughter.

The novel tackles gender relations, racism, and many modern American institutions. John Updike observed, "I loved *Mrs. Caliban*, so deft and austere in its prose, so drolly casual in its fantasy … an impeccable parable, beautifully written from first paragraph to last" (quoted in Mehren).

BINSTEAD'S SAFARI

Binstead's Safari (1983) is a subtle novel that stacks social science against mythical transformation. Millie Binstead grows in self-awareness and has her own individual awakening against the African wilderness. As in *Mrs. Caliban*, the book's female protagonist, Millie, is trapped in a terrible marriage—with Stan, who belittles her, cheats on her, and demands she conform entirely to his wishes. Also like in *Mrs. Caliban*, a mystical figure from outside the wife's regular world, the "other," appears to help the woman free herself. Henry Lewis, the game warden/lion, is that figure.

Sexual relations as currency take a different turn here than in Ingalls' other works, as the lovers sacrifice human reality for a magical one. Ingalls structures the novel so that the female heroine is the primary actor in the romance. Alan Macdonald writes, "The spirit that informs the flight of heroines of romance is of a different order; innocence is what they want to escape, the innocence of men whose ideological project is, by the imposition of boundaries on the social world, to contain differences, domesticate them, flatten them out" (p. 166).

The novel makes several allusions to Ernest Hemingway's "The Short Happy Life of Francis Macomber," in which Francis dies, shot by his wife who can't allow his manhood to be fulfilled. MacDonald suggests that Henry Lewis, the mystical, powerful hero of Ingalls' story, actually "represents what Hemingway's buffalo represents—the spirit of nature."

The anthropologist and philanderer Stan Binstead takes his wife, Millie, with him on a business trip, even though he doesn't value her and in fact doesn't even want her to come. A small inheritance gives Millie the financial freedom to accompany Stan, first to London and then on to East Africa where he is researching an East African lion cult for an academic article. In London, while Stan ignores her and cheats on her nearly daily, Millie begins to enjoy life. She treats herself to new clothes, a new haircut, and visits to the theater and the opera.

Arriving in Africa for his big research project, Stan begins to diminish, and Millie blossoms. She surveys the landscape with interest and is generally delighted. They contract a safari company to take them into the bush so Stan can interview people. He develops troubling rashes and has nightmare dreams of his brother, who died in combat. The center of his study is "a theory about mythic character and the society that gives rise to it" (p. 24). Stan had been told of stories about "a man with supernatural powers in battle and medicine, and love. When he's in a tough situation, he can turn himself into a lion" (p. 25). As they prepare for the safari, Millie makes friends with the game guides, their wives, and some of the native workers. Stan can't understand how Millie is happy and cheerful, while he has "a sense of dread" (p. 44). Millie meets and becomes attracted to Henry Lewis, a well-respected game warden and expert on lions. He "was hypnotizing her … but what really captured and magnetized her attention was the fact that he seemed obsessed with her" (p. 52). Millie and Henry talk and shop together, and some Kenyan children tease her. Henry translates what they have said as "o Bwana Simba, what a beautiful bride you have" (p. 54). *Simba* means "lion" in Swahali, the first key foreshadowing of the novel. They laugh at the children's words, but then they go together to have tea, unable to resist their growing attraction. Stan attempts to make connections for his project, again leaving Millie alone which gives her time to be with Henry.

As he explores the countryside, Stan is part of a group that witnesses a lion attack that kills a woman and a child. At a party, Stan gets drunk, but Millie hears a cough and knows that it is Henry. They exchange gestures of love: she blows kisses and he mimics giving her his heart. On safari, Stan kills a cape buffalo, and it makes him feel strong and not fearful. He notices how beautiful Millie is, and he thinks he "has fallen in love with her again" (p. 89). Stan's research is floundering, because he misunderstands the local people whom he needs as sources, and his behavior drives them away. Millie and Henry meanwhile remain in regular communication via letter, even though he has returned to his district where he is game warden. Millie makes good friends of their guides, Nicholas and Ian and Ian's wife, Pippa. Ian tells Stan a ghost story he's heard "about a lion that lives among people and then goes back to the pride" (p. 100), to help with him with his stalled research. Stan gets closer to the cult of the lion idea, and the stories arise from villages in Henry Lewis' district. Stan thinks about lions and how "they were never afraid, never" (p. 116). Millie wills Henry's letters to come to her and they arrive as she wishes for them, evoking a supernatural bond between them. When she thought of Henry, "excitement and pleasure carried her" (p. 114), and she thinks she might be pregnant with Henry's child.

With her newly found self-assurance, Millie tells Stan she wants a divorce after this trip. Another sign of her personal growth is that Millie has been creating paintings that are praised by the safari group. As they all move deeper into the lion territory that is Henry's region, Stan tries to push Millie back into having sex with him, but she hits him and threatens to shoot him if he ever does it again. Her anger fades quickly, and Stan worries at the way her tone "had been leveled and controlled, dispassionate" (p. 142). The next morning Millie is up early and wanders about the camp. She hears a cough and then "is faced with a lion, a magnificent animal" (p. 145). Nicholas explains that a cough is the sound a lion makes.

Word comes that Henry has been murdered by poachers. Millie is distraught but is soothed with stories about how Henry "was greatly loved and greatly feared" (p. 149). Millie "wailed. 'I loved him so much … I feel like I've died'" (p. 150). She is reminded that "he loved you, too" (p. 150) by the man who had been carrying their letters.

A villager tells them that the people of the region are going to celebrate the bride who would come to join with their lion god. Stan and the guides are confused because it isn't clear whether Henry was perceived as their god figure or not. Nicholas isn't sure if the villagers mean the god is god of the lions or god of the local people. The safari group has found the cult that Stan is looking for, but Stan misses the point of Millie's connection to the ritual, and he crudely suspects human sacrifice of the bride. Stan and Millie finally discuss Henry, and Stan suspects Henry of manipulating the village into worshipping him and thinks "the whole business is a protection racket for poaching" (p. 153). Stan, in his misconceptions, nonetheless comes close to the truth when he states "if these cults start with a real person, this guy could be it" (p. 159).

The lion keeps appearing in the morning, always near Millie. She is drawn to the familiar cough, and the lion is drawn to her. Stan tells Millie and Nicholas that he suspects Lewis trained the lion as a way of tricking people to believe that he had special powers, and again he thinks the lion is part of poaching or some criminal activity. Things begin to unravel; Millie tells Stan she is pregnant. Stan questions Ian about Henry and why a lion would hang around a camp. He grasps at a crazy reason, claiming that the lion must be some sort of a "cookhouse pet" (p. 179). Ian tries to explain to Stan the respect Henry commanded, by saying that "he was a grand chap" but also a strange and intense man (p. 180). Stan's research is in full swing, and he takes pages and pages of notes. He also continues try to explain away the lion's appearance at the camp.

Millie's longing for Henry, and her attraction and pull to the lion, add to the story's mystery. The group tries to find the ceremony of the bride ritual, and as they proceed they find the outlying villages deserted. When they get to the village where the people have gathered, Millie is invited to play the bride in their ceremony. The people seem to recognize the necklace she wears. It is one that Henry gave her. The song they chant is "the story of the lion's bride" (p. 183). Stan argues that this is crazy—he came to prove a theory, and his wife can't be part of the cult: "this just can't be" (p. 184).

Stan's worldview, "his poetic world" is shaken up (p. 188). He may leave academia and study the lives of heroes like Henry Lewis, even though Stan still argues that Henry was "just an opportunistic explorer of black labor … a con man" (p. 190). At the same time, he can't believe how beautiful Millie has become and is awed by "her charm, her ease with strangers, her radiance toward the rest of the world and her ability to draw everyone to her" (p. 189). Stan has lost Millie, but he sees her clearly in almost the same terms used to describe Henry. Analyzing Stan's position in the novel, Alan MacDonald asserts: "As Stan is a professional reader, he is in one respect an appropriate figure for us to follow. His job as anthropologist is to read and interpret cultural signs. But here Stan is so bad at his work that his presence is unreliable" (p. 168).

The lion comes at dusk, and the group sees "Millie, like a shadow, move as though floating … She stayed where she was," and their shots drive the lion off (p. 191). Ian and Nicholas don't want to shoot this "lion of lions" (p. 193), but they plan to track it away from camp. They can't out-position the lion. Suddenly, however, "Millie walked toward it, her arms open" and "the lion struck, bolted, and was gone" (p. 192), leaving her dead. They bury Millie in the camp in the place that was her favorite spot to sit and paint. Two days later Stan is certain he sees the lion resting on Millie's grave, but no one else sees it and there are no tracks or broken grasses. Stan acknowledges that Millie "loved everything about this country and blossomed here" (p. 204). His self-delusions escalate as he comes to believe

that Millie walked out to the lion to save him. The poachers who killed Henry Lewis are found dead; oddly the poachers' injuries were caused by lion attack and the villagers. The nature and order of occurrence of the injuries is left vague; the narrative almost suggests it was a collaborative vengeance of lions and of villagers. Nicholas and Stan try to track the lion one more time, and only Nicholas comes back.

Ingalls sifts in humor and a nice dose of irony with her portrayal of Stan's inability to read the people he is trying to study—both Henry and the villagers—and she nicely balances the quietness of Millie and Henry's passion with the disintegration of Stan's blustery ego. The ending of the novel is again unclear, but it is more satisfying because the lovers have acted upon their own desires. MacDonald observes that "Millie's death is only outlined, not enlarged upon: its essential 'mystery' is left unexplained" (p. 168).

I SEE A LONG JOURNEY

In Ingalls' 1985 collection of three novellas, *I See a Long Journey*, the main characters desire to ascend, to know a purer, higher reality. Flora, a young rich wife; Beverly, a young fiancée; and Anselm, a young monk, all struggle against the conventions of their world and lose. Fantastical elements, including a child goddess and Gabriel the archangel as well as an ice maze, drive the plots. Irving Malin observes that the novellas "deal with the conflict between the mundane and the spiritual, social convention and the visionary gaze" (p. 164). The fable tone of the stories fits well with the fantasy-like or spiritual twists of the plots. Anne Bernays describes the settings as the "territory of fantasy and actual chaos, mingled and mixed" (p. 9). The magic realism of Anselm's gender switches brings to mind Virginia Woolf's *Orlando* (1928), the spiritual forces of the child goddess whom Flora encounters recalls the cave in E. M. Forster's *A Passage to India* (1924), and Beverly's ice maze is a physical and magical barrier of the sort associated with fictional fantasy locations such as Shangri-La or Brigadoon. A key theme is the "mysterious pattern in life—

ascent and descent, knowledge and ignorance" that shapes their outcomes, says Irving Malin (p. 164).

In the title story, "I See a Long Journey," Flora, the young rich wife who has made a careful marriage, essentially based on sexual commerce, struggles for more meaning in her life. Initially, Flora despises her husband's family. They are "like robots, attached to a master computer—they had no ideas, no lives" (p. 13). She is guided by her older husband, James, toward accepting the family conventions. In a masterful summary, Ingalls moves Flora to acceptance and temporary resignation. In an elegant description of Flora as a swan on the water, it is clear she has lost her identity to the family.

After her children are born, the potential for violence against the family is hinted at through an attempted abduction of a niece. Later, as Flora and James make plans to take a vacation that is more distant and removed from home than vacations they have taken in the past, James promises that they will be safe because Michael, his chauffeur and bodyguard, will protect them. Flora believes that "if Michael came along, nothing bad could happen" (p. 15). She believes Michael is the only innocent, loyal person attached to the family, and she begins to long to "put her arms around him" (p. 16).

In an unnamed Asian land, Flora's ambivalence about her marriage freezes her: "the more dissatisfied she'd become with her life, the more reluctant she was to make any changes" (p. 22). She enjoys the rituals of their vacation, managing the children, shopping, meeting other rich Americans. One of these other Americans tells her about a local "goddess," a girl trained in religious ritual, "one they train from childhood, like the Lama in Tibet" (p. 25). This chosen child was subject to "strict rules she's got to obey about everything, what she can eat and drink, all that. Oh, and she should never bleed" (p. 26). This conversation with another American wife about the goddess has details that are clearly parallels to Flora's married existence. The two women also discuss a previous goddess who ran away and got married, "an ex-goddess" (p. 26). Further developing the novella's theme of convention

and compliance, Flora admits doubts about the goddess but still insists upon seeing her.

Flora thinks about freedom and the compromises she has made; "most of her troubles," she decides, "had been caused by trying to switch from one set of conventions to another" (p. 31). But an attempted abduction of James and Flora frightens her, and her conclusion is that "it took a whole system of convention and ritual" (p. 39) to keep life safe. She hears that the ex-goddess, the convention breaker, has been stoned. Even while doubting the trappings and the costuming of, Flora visits the child goddess, who invites her to an audience to confide. Flora confesses her love for Michael. The child advises her to "ascend" and tells her that "true love is poor" (p. 45), which calls for Flora a complete rejection of James and his wealth and her careful choice. For his part in the discussion, Michael answers love—"it's deception" (p. 47). In a hurried climactic shoot-out during another abduction attempt, Flora is fatally injured. When she declares her love for Michael, he curses her and rejects her. Dying, Flora believes she must ascend. James merely says to Michael, "It's all right. She understands. Don't worry. After people die, they understand everything" (p. 48). The ending is satisfactory thematically but not dramatically. William Packard writes, "The placid style suddenly imperceptibly accelerates to a hallucinatory frenzy, erupting into melodrama in a dazzling shoot out climax … The effect is stunning, disquieting, awful" (1986, p. 3).

In the story "On Ice," civilization is defined by Ingalls with these requirements: belief in God, conformity to social sexual mores, and acceptance of fraud and abduction. Beverly is a young American woman about to marry her older German lover, Claus. Ingalls develops the character of Beverly through contrasts to Claus and to Beverly's acquaintance Angela. Although Beverly believes she is completely in love with Claus, they have different views of the world, beginning with their ideas about the details of their immediate experiences as they travel together and extending ultimately to their rules of civilization. The glacier they are visiting is "reminiscent of ordinary concrete" to Beverly, who is disappointed in it, while Claus "was mildly interested" (p. 57). They exchange presents on the trip only to be disappointed with the other's choice, and so they eventually swap the gifts. Even though she believes herself to be a mature woman because she is with the older Claus, their relationship and her self-appraisal are flawed. She criticizes other Americans who are staying at the same hotel as she and Claus, her acquaintances from college, dismissing them as rich and foolish. Evangelists from a group calling itself the Foundation of Light are visiting the area as well, and Beverly doesn't want them to know she is "falsely registered in a hotel as the wife of a foreign man ten years older" (p. 61). She values her "secret happy life" with him (p. 61). A long conversation with Claus reveals that they disagree on belief in God and on "what every civilized human being" believes (p. 70). The Fountain of Light group defines their purpose to Beverly as "a force of good in the world" (p. 66), saying that those who oppose them are "degenerate" (p. 74). But Tom, a Fountain of Light follower, attempts to seduce Beverly, and then he leaves her where she will be discovered by the characters who represent the real threat of the story.

Two old women offer to show her "the parts of the hotel you will never see," another secret life (p. 76). When she accidentally meets Martha Torrence, a woman whose funeral Beverly attended several years earlier, Martha explains how the members of the group have faked their own deaths to escape and live freely. They couldn't trust their families or their children, she says, and "so much in life is a matter of trust" (p. 80). The encounter leads Beverly to confront the flaw in her relationship with Claus, as exemplified by their presents: "We each chose for ourselves ... does either of us trust the other to choose" (p. 81). While Beverly is quietly contemplating her life and wanting to share it with Claus, Martha reveals the insurance scam that underpins the group's existence and how it is supported by the Fountain of Light. Martha explains that Beverly can never be released back to the world, because she would threaten the group's secret happy life. The glacier provides the barrier to escape, and if

anyone tries, they die on the wall of ice. The story ends with Martha urging Beverly to learn to play bridge, the most convention-bound of card games. Martha asks chillingly, "Are you ready?" (p. 86), because Beverly is giving up her entire life, family, Claus, freedom. She is "On Ice."

The final story, "Blessed Art Thou," a modern fable, again visits the themes of convention set versus the chaos of individual freedom, sexual commerce, and reality versus fantasy. The story's form, as William Packard has pointed out—like medieval *gesta* or French contes or fabliaux— echoes the tradition of Ovid and Boccaccio. The protagonist, Anselm, confesses his sexual intercourse with the Archangel Gabriel to the more liberal of the senior monks in the abbey where they all reside. Anselm believes that because of the experience "he could look deep into his own spirit and find a new and better self" (p. 90). He glories in the "joyfulness" he feels and asserts that "now ordinary life isn't any good" (p. 93). He, like Flora and Beverly, seeks to ascend.

Anselm's beatific postcoital vision is countered by the maneuvering of the Abbot Frederick and the two senior monks. The story's light dialogue brings a tone of bathos to the tale. The abbot shouts against "the gardener's boy," crying, "We will find the joker and throw him out" (p. 93), assuming that Anselm's encounter was with a real local boy. Frederick attacks Anselm's desire to ascend as "Delusion. Delusions of Grandeur" (p. 94). The modern voice and dialogue caps the moment when Frederick curses: "oh Christ." Anselm, focused, defiant, and self-righteous, declares, "You weren't chosen. I was" (p. 96). Anselm is confined to quarters.

The monks devolve into factions, one of which is led by the reactionary Adrian. Other monks begin to develop a sexual interest in Anselm's changes. He loses his beard, grows breasts, and is visibly pregnant. The abbey's doctor, Brother Duncan, examines Anselm and confirms that the monk is with child. In the abbot's office, Anselm, propped on pillows to support his back, argues, "Love conquers all ... I've had the proof. In fact, I am the proof" (p. 103).

Brother Adrian wants to burn Anselm at the stake. Duncan intervenes to protect him. The abbot is furious, calling it a "phantom pregnancy brought on by Anselm's overwhelming neurotic craving" and saying that he believes the infant will be "gristle and leftover pieces of stuff" (p. 105). In short—a monstrosity. The abbot is most angry at the threat that Anselm's transformation poses to his regime. He paces the room and says, "Years clawing my way up the ladder ... I worked like hell on this place" (p. 105). Frances, the liberal monk, argues that they can't harm Anselm, providing the story's first hint that violence will come to Anselm for his ascendance, for his independent, nonconformist thinking and behavior. The monastery whirls in its factions: those who pamper Anselm and want to touch his breasts and those who want him out. Adrian calls him the whore of Babylon and a blasphemy. The monks debate questions such as "what is man and what is woman" and "what is authority," often while getting drunk on the wine the monastery produces.

Turmoil increases as Anselm's pregnancy progresses. Adrian goes insane and is carried off. The doctor monk and Anselm debate whether authority is male. Duncan says that women are unworthy, while Anselm argues that "facts can change in an instant. That's what happened to me. It's like peacetime and wartime, like happiness and sorrow" (p. 123). Reading this interchange, the reader questions whether Anselm is deluded or whether this his reality. Does faith supersede fact? Can a patriarchal system add female influences?

Threats of violence from those who doubt Anselm's transformation are planned in a comic exchange of drunken monks that comes across sounding like the preparation for a gang fight. Of the ensuing debate about him, Anselm says, "I love these verbal tennis games ... They're just like theology" (p. 134). The senior monks decide to have Anselm committed to a mental ward, but Anselm hears of their plot and escapes the doctor, fleeing to a river to jump in and swim or drown—the ending is unclear.

William Packard comments that "the story builds to a final transfiguration ... but the entire tale is an allegory of what? Repression? Hypocrisy? Or true sanctity" (1986, p. 3). The best conclusion about the story may be to laugh at its impossibility, its comedy. Unlike the happy transformation of the title character in Virginia Woolf's *Orlando*, Anselm must die.

THE PEARLKILLERS

The novellas of *The Pearlkillers* (1986) are four tales of murder that begin in ordinary reality and progress to the grotesque. Jill Neville, in the *Sunday Times*, called *The Pearlkillers* "a swamp of violence and magic." The past threatens the present of the characters, and memory is key in the question: whose recollection provides the truth?

In the *New York Times Book Review,* Ursula Le Guin discusses the narrative technique and the blending of ordinary and fantastical. Thus Ingalls' style invites the reader, through accepting the story's ordinary details, to also accept its fantasy. Maurice Taylor's review in *Library Journal* highlights Ingalls' use of foreshadowing, saying that "each of Ingalls's four stories is chilled with enough foreboding to hold the reader" and offers "a final grim twist to satisfy" (p. 143). William Packard categorizes the character types and the pacing of *The Pearlkillers*: "her characters all bear the mark of Cain: they are innocents (no matter that some may be killers) who are swept along through tepid, flat circumstances until suddenly all hell breaks loose, and the Furies erupt to claim their prey" (p. 11).

In the story "Third Time Lucky," a young woman feels cursed and is only freed from it with the birth of her son. Lily's first husband was killed in Vietnam. She married again three years later, and her second husband was also killed in Vietnam. She refuses to marry again because "she was certain that if she tried to find happiness again, the same thing would happen a third time" (p. 10). She attends the Tutankhamen exhibit because it is "called the Curse of the Pharaohs" (p. 1).

Lily had been interested in Egypt since her childhood, when she heard an interview with an old lady who believed she had been a priestess of Isis in a former life. Lily had listened to the old lady's "quest for her true home with assurance and simplicity," and Lily wishes she herself knew so exactly "what you wanted and where you belonged" (p. 5). Lily has been facing pressure by her family and friends to finish her grieving and get on with life. It's another stab by Ingalls at conventionality: "People … believed that you ought to recover. They tried to cheer you up and they wanted you to be suffering the correct amount" (p. 3). To avoid them, Lily attends lectures and studies on Egypt; in an Egyptian context, like the old woman, Lily "felt that all these sights and objects were familiar to her in a way that her own life was not" (p. 6). When Lily meets Don, she agrees to marry him if he will take her to Egypt for their honeymoon, even though Lily thinks of Don as "boring … unexciting … sometimes irritating" (p. 11). They plan to get married in a registry office.

In the weeks leading up to the honeymoon, Lily begins to have a recurring dream of "standing in the sun, under that hot sky that was so blue and far away, and examining the foreign shapes of an unknown language" (p. 12). In Egypt, their relationship disconnects; Lily states, "I love it here," and Don responds, "And I love you" (p. 14). They join a tour group, which Ingalls uses to provide other perspectives: that of the tour guide, a troubled family, and another newlywed couple who fight. In contrast to these others, Lily finds that she is so happy, "she'd forgotten her irritation. She was glad to be with [Don] and have him holding her close" (p. 20). Her own happiness undermines her psychological state; that night she dreams of her first husband being mummified and ferried across the river, like the stories she has just heard about the pharaohs. In the dream, she screams and tries to reach him but fails. She awakens to Don kissing her in the dark, and they make love.

After a visit to the Valley of the Kings, Lily dreams "the same story but this time the man being prepared was her second husband" (p. 24). Echoing the way in which Lily's dreams blur the past and her memories, the tourists gossip about the way that the guide's version of the singing

statues at Karnack differs from their guidebook. A discussion ensues about the guide's personal history and to what extent it is "concocted" or true. Lily's questions about the old lady who believed herself to be a priestess of Isis go unanswered, and the quarrels among tourist couples multiply. Next Don and Lily fight about whether to go to Luxor or Abydos, but in their argument, their relationship's failure is nearly complete. Don first threatens to hit her and states, "You won't take anything from me, will you?" (p. 31). Lily agrees; she fears her curse, and in a paradox, "She also realized that although she couldn't accept his love, she wanted him to keep on caring" (p. 31). Don asks why she never talks about her first two husbands, and Lily pushes the question away, saying, "I don't remember," but she is thinking, "I remember everything—every room we were in, every place. Love does that … It was the only time I felt I was living" (p. 33). Don counters he wasn't the one to rescue her like a fairy-tale maiden "who had to have the spell broken" (p. 33). Lily sobs that "of course I love you" (p. 33).

The next day, when she pleads to go find the old lady's house, perhaps even stay behind in Egypt, Don threatens, "Don't push your luck, Lil" (p. 34). They have a calm day, and they visit the ruins of the Great Pyramid, but they begin to quarrel again. Don hisses, "The minute you get out of the bed, it's all gone. All I get is that silence" (p. 38). Climbing the pyramid, Lily "thought how pointless her whole life had turned out to be. It was no use trying to fight bad luck" (p. 39). They quarrel on the top of the pyramid; Don falls and dies. After the funeral, Lily embraces Don's mother and joins into his family. She is pregnant, and after the birth of her son, she worries that she is not a good mother, but "the only thing that she was sure of was that she loved her son" (p. 42). The story ends on a series of positive moments: Lily's divorced father reenters her life; her relationship with Don' family is strong; she doesn't dream her dreams but often remembers Egypt and the singing statues. The curse is finally lifted.

Isabel Raphael believes this story is the finest of the three; she comments, "Ms. Ingalls excels in suggestion, and the muted passions of 'Third Time Lucky' make a far greater impact than the bizarre violence of the other three pieces in the book."

In "People to People," after twenty years, four college friends unite, when a fifth insists the secrets of a botched college prank be revealed. Their immature taunting and hazing caused the death of another young man. They have all kept the secret, only telling a few details to their wives. They have all been divorced and remarried except Bill, who is newly married and for the first time. Now Bill, the friend most frightened, insists, "We wouldn't be worthy of God and His gifts to us if we continued to hide the truth" (p. 46). The other four friends gather to make a plan, and Herb acts as the unofficial leader because he is the only one outside the town. The four men fall into two factions: Joe and Herb, and Dave and Sherman. Joe first proposes murder by offhandedly remarking "I've still got my guns" (p. 48) from his military service. Dave and Sherman object to "this kind of talk" (p. 48). If Bill insists on going to the cops, they all fear jail terms and the ruin of their present lives. Herb insists that they decide and "we've all got to be together on it."

The tension of the impending conflict simmers while the next section of the story is a long flashback to the event twenty years earlier. They harass a richer, pretentious undergraduate whom they nickname Carmen. In their drunken stupor, they pitch Carmen off the roof. A noisy, raucous party adjacent to their dorm destroys the crime scene and provides their alibi. They are questioned, as is everyone in the quad of dorms, but they are never suspected. When Carmen's uncle and cousin come to get more answers, they speak to Herb. Herb explains that the party was wild and out of control; the uncle insists that the dead boy didn't drink. The uncle "held out his hand. Herb shook it" (p. 62). The handshake, a sign of honor between men, is a fraud, and Herb recognizes it. He thinks, "For the first time he realized he had destroyed part of his life; from that point onward all mention of the accident would call up the fabricated substitute: the safe, untrue, version" (p. 56). After the event, their friendship is

"broken." Herb had warned them all: "they'd never be able to let their guard down completely with anybody" (p. 57). Over the passage of time, they did tell their wives a modified version that focuses on the practical joke, blaming the alcohol. Marriage and other life responsibilities have diminished the event's importance, and it "had ceased to frighten them of the possible consequences" (p. 57).

As they meet and plan how to deal with Bill's decision to confess, Herb feels the most guilt, having spoken to Carmen's uncle, but he has also become the most determined to keep the event secret; "he had to be, forever afterwards, a man who was believed to be innocent" (p. 62). In a flashback to a discussion with his child's babysitter, Herb rationalizes his behavior, thinking the original event had only been manslaughter, but if it happened again, it would not be murder but self-defense. Herb, Sherman, Dave, and Joe arrange to meet Bill and his young wife, Nancy, in the model home of a new housing development. The men separate, and Herb and Joe take Bill and Nancy to talk. Bill will not back down from his desire to confess this "most important event" (p. 70) in his life. The other men argue that the death was not murder; Dave says to Bill, "Quit using that word. It was an accident. And nobody's going to know about it unless you tell" (p. 71). Bill and Nancy argue that the men must repent. They talk and drink and argue. Joe is ready to kill them. Herb agrees to take "Bill and Nancy for a little sightseeing" (p. 75). They work out the other details of their plan. Herb is now drunk enough to "be confident about carrying out any scheme successfully, but he had also reached the stage where he thought he was having important revelations about life" (p. 75). In this state of mind, after Joe shoots Bill, Herb shoots Nancy, Joe, Dave, and Sherman. He torches the model home and escapes. On the airplane he speaks to another young woman, much like his babysitter, about playing tennis; through the story the tennis match metaphor is hinted at and the dialogue feels like a fast volley. The young woman says she doesn't play in tournaments, only "people to people," and Herb responds, "That can be the most dangerous kind" (p. 81).

The novella has been criticized for its violence and its lack of character development. Le Guin argues that "the story is without real character, setting or action other than the interweaving and the final, abrupt undoing of the fatal connections between the five men" (p. 24). William Packard points to the core of the story in commenting, "It's as if the dislocated present were trying to extirpate the past" (p. 11).

The novella "Inheritance" has a lovely opening but in the last third descends to every grotesque available: vampire bats, forced lobotomies, suspected vampires, rape of slaves. The *Times* critic Isabel Raphael argued that "Inheritance" is the "least successful story" and "strays into the Gothic."

The story contrasts two families' gifts to Carla, which together amount to gifts of jewelry, lifestyle, and worldview. Carla has two losses—her marriage ends in divorce and her beloved paternal grandmother dies. In a flashback, the grandmother prepares to die by distributing her possessions. She says to Carla, "I don't like leaving things in a mess" (p. 83). When her grandmother offers Carla her choice of jewelry, Carla selects three items, including a ruby ring that replaces her wedding ring. The grandmother counsels Carla to wear and enjoy the items or give them away, saying, "What I don't want you to do is put everything in a drawer and save it. It's the same with life, the same with love. You've got to use it, enjoy it,—be happy with it. And if you lose it, so be it. Never mind" (p. 84). The grandmother dies, and Carla inherits enough money and stocks so she is free to travel, change her business, reshape her future. Declining an offer to visit her father and stepmother, she decides to find her mother's relatives, who are her great aunts. Her father says they are "rather strange people" (p. 86).

Arriving in the town, Carla gets lost and asks a mailman for directions to her great aunt Gisela's house. He answers, "Oh, the countess," and confirms, "That's what she calls herself" (p. 87). Carla is greeted by her aunt and a uniformed maid, Agnes. Over sandwiches and cakes, Gisela tells the family history of previous wealth, power of "the ancient, important and persecuted aristo-

cratic family" (p. 89), and she alludes to estates that were unavailable socially and politically in Soviet Eastern Europe.

During this scene, another aunt, Gerda, recognizes the lizard pin that Carla wears—even though the two sides of Carla's family have not been in communication. Gerda then explains her "photographic memory for jewels" and her desire to have been in the jewelry business, but she says her family wasn't the "kind that went into trade" and "the unfortunate family failing" (p. 91). Carla tries to restart the conversation, asking, what is the family failing? Gerda tells her, "We're pearlkillers" (p. 91). In this moment, as the discussion of pearls and their care unfolds, the narrator shows that Carla is vastly different from her aunts and from their attitudes toward family unity, toward servant's duties, and even toward possessions. An aunt named Ursula says, "Your mother betrayed her family" (p. 94), by marrying an outsider, a non-German. Carla is insulted and leaves. At the door, Agnes the servant apologizes for the aunts, saying, "They forget how to behave," and adding that the last time they left the house was for the engagement party of Carla's mother and "that was only to make a big scene" and "to refuse to go to the wedding" (p. 95).

Back in her motel room after the rude and unsettling meeting, Carla recollects memories of her mother, who after her divorce had checked into a motel room and committed suicide. Carla meets and quickly makes a happy alliance with her cousin Carl: "always … just when she was ready to throw in the towel, something nice turned up" (p. 96). Gisela calls and pleads with Carla to return so the aunt can finish her family history with the tale of Count Walter's treasure. Gisela insists that Carla must retrieve the treasure from Cousin Theo, who had absconded with it, offering Carl as escort. Carla demurs, but "Gisela overruled her," saying "I'm the one really doesn't have time … Just this one thing for your old aunt, little Carla" (p. 102). The next morning another phone call awakens Carla with the news that her aunts and Agnes have all died in a fire. Agnes is blamed, but no proof is offered.

The second part of the story has Carl and Carla chasing across Europe searching for Theo. Carla and Carl are now sleeping together; they discover that Theo is in South America, and he arranges their flights because, Carl says, he is "just dying to see you" (p. 106).

The story takes on fairy-tale qualities, with the pair taking a horse-drawn carriage ride from the edge of the South American city where they have gone to find Theo. Bats threaten the carriage, slapping into the windows, and then further grotesqueries begin when they reach Theo's house. The gatekeeper is "dwarfish" (p. 108). The aunts and uncles are so rich they are like "vampires" to their employees and to the native people of the area (p. 110). A pool is filled with fish that are like "piranhas" (p. 111). With each new exploration of the area, Carla begins to feel increasingly dizzy, and as the grotesqueries continue—leprosy, racist enslaving and raping of the South American employees—Carla thinks, "It was hard to believe that she was related to these people. They seemed grotesque" (p. 114). The xenophobic culture of the German family is illustrated with the expression of racist views of South American employees as "poor stock" (p. 115). The chronology of the novella becomes less clear; a haze of events propels the reader toward the ending. For example Carl has come to agree with Uncle Theo about the importance of "breeding" (p. 115). After a matter of only days, Carl has shifted to join the family in loyalty to their odd ideas. Before a ceremony to initiate Carl, Theo explains the necessity of the ritual lobotomizing of the family's employees and relates the women servants' supposed preference for having sex and bearing children with Theo and the German men. Carla tries to argue with Carl but gives up. Two of the aunts tell Carla that her initiation ceremony is also planned, "and you'll be wearing the family jewels. Including the treasure—they had such a time getting it away from Gisela" (p. 121). They dress her in a preternaturally white gown like a wedding dress, and they ply her with drink. Carla asks herself what she is "doing there at all, surrounded by these weird old women?" (p. 123), then they present her with the Treasure, which has been described to her as the largest pearl ever discovered. But inside the black velvet box, rather than a jewel of round luminescent beauty she finds the antithesis of pearl: "a large sunken blob of shriveled brown matter that resembled a piece of burned meat" (p. 124).

The ending leaves a drunken Carla saying, "Wonderful. Priceless," but the reader isn't sure whether Carla recognizes the irony. Critics split on the ending and the use of the pearl as metaphor. Harvey Pekar expressed disappointment in a *Washingon Post Book World* review. Ursula Le Guin, however, appreciated that the volume title is actually a factual condition, and she argues that the opening section of loving grandmother and granddaughter in "Inheritance" is a "pearl-like moment" (p. 24).

In the fourth of the novellas in *The Pearlkillers*, "Captain Hendrik's Story," Ingalls uses a familiar pattern: a man escapes with his life on an adventure that changes him for the worse. He returns to his normal, ordinary life only to have someone from the past come to demand money, protection. The man must kill the person to protect his present life. "Captain Hendrik's Story" includes thematic elements addressing what happens when a character challenges conformity, even conformity to an outlaw code. It also addresses the powerlessness of women, in its opening, although a woman plays a powerful part in the story later. The reviewer Isabel Raphael called the novella's plot "a contorted variation on a well worn theme," but Harvey Pekar, writing in the *Washingon Post Book World*, forgave the implausible story because of the strength of the novella as a whole.

TIMES LIKE THESE

The collection *Times Like These*, published by Graywolf Press in 2005, combines work from the story collection *Days Like Today* (2000) and new stories ("Somewhere Else," "The Archaeologist's Daughter," and "Last Act: The Madhouse"). These last three were also published in England under the title *Black Diamond* in 1992. The five stories that were published first in England as

Days Like Today spring from Greek myths; Amanda Craig observed in the *Times* that they are "re-working of classical myths in an examination of war and conflict." (All pages references will be to *Times Like These.*) The collection relies less on fantasy and supernatural elements than does Ingalls' other work and more on "psychological states where dreams, madness, and sanity converge," observed Patrick Sullivan (p. 50). The collection is much less violent than *The Pearl-killers,* but it is still about characters who lack self-awareness. These characters' lives are manipulated by others—in some cases by people very close to them, as in "Last Act: The Madhouse" and "The Archaeologist's Daughter."

Again Ingalls' intricate plotting draws both praise and criticism. A *Publisher's Weekly* review states that the collection has "elaborate plots and surprising if sometimes inconclusive resolutions." In tone the collection provides a different level of complexity on the cultural plane from her earliest work; her main characters are blind to circumstances around them, mothers manipulate, vague too-good-to-be-true offers trap a couple, a daughter cannot accept her father's infidelity even when it threatens her safety. Ingalls' irony and dark humor is also present; Penelope Power calls the stories "disturbing, surreal and sometimes comical" (p. 33).

The first story in the collection, "Last Act: The Madhouse," offers Italian opera as the extended metaphor by which to read this story, set in 1958 in small-town America. Ed Park labels it "an outrageous twist on the Cyrano story, the letters between William and his sweetheart are intercepted by his mother, who expertly forges both of their hands, sending mixed messages to pry them apart. And we haven't even come to the aria yet."

William, an only child of wealthy parents, loves his music and is an opera "specialist," studying its librettos, roles, arias, and customs. Opera is his reality. But trouble arrives as William begins a secret, forbidden affair with a younger, poorer girl named Jean. Ingalls tells their story with sly, backhanded humor that pokes fun at small-town morality.

Opera supplies the drama in William's life, and there is operatic foreshadowing—like the predictable hint of trouble in act 1—of the danger that his sexual activity creates, in the threat of how the town will treat a teenage boy and a teenage girl who get caught with a pregnancy. And indeed, Jean is next pregnant—like the plot of an opera, a predictable turn. The reader has been warned the town will attack, but it is the young couple's parents who attack. Like a chorus or a musical motif, the narrative repeats that the parents' live will be destroyed. William's mother interferes with the relationship and forges carefully placed letters to both Jean and William; coincidences abound; William is sent away and he willingly goes. These plot points function as the operatic counterpoint in the story. Act 2 of the story has Jean banished to a distant aunt, while William carries on with school and college. His father dies and then his mother. In sorting out his parents' house, William finds the letters his mother forged, and he goes mad. Jean has poisoned herself, William learns from her parents. In his madness, William is determined to find Jean, and he hires an unscrupulous detective to help. With full Ingalls irony, however, the girl they find isn't Jean and doesn't even look like her. William is nonetheless content and will marry the disabled and mentally handicapped girl the detective has produced. In one last but expected plot twist, Jean appears at the wedding, and William doesn't even recognize her.

"The Archaeologist's Daughter" has three sections: the first is set during the childhood of Beatrice Norbert, the motherless child of a famous and successful archaeologist; the second portrays her life as his adult daughter and how she helps with his work, caring for or curating his collection, making their home in Switzerland into a museum. The third section, after a transitional section about her father's mysterious death and burial, follows Beatrice as she settles his estate, reconnects with family and friends, and continues to search for answers about her father's death.

Beatrice is another of Ingalls' characters whose self-perception is not reliable; in the first part of the story we are told, "It never occurred to her that there might be girls in Paris who would think Cairo exciting and exotic, and who would long to go there. For her—at that age—wherever she was, was normal" (p. 42). Through school, she makes friends with an extended family, the Schuylers, who will provide her with a best friend, Claudia; a mother figure, Mrs. Schuyler; and ultimately her husband, Jack. In a Cairo shop with Claudia Schuyler, Beatrice sees a girl "who had the look neither of an Egyptian, nor a European" (p. 44). The old woman shopkeeper tells Beatrice, "That was your sister" (p. 44). Beatrice is an only child, her mother having died when she was young. Her friends and teachers all deny that her father was ever married to anyone else. Her school principal dismisses the story but also hints that "her father had been quite a ladies' man" (p. 45). Beatrice and her fatherdiscuss "the kinds of people who gossip," (p. 46), further dismissing the old woman's statement and establishing a key theme for the story—whose information can one trust?

The theme of the nature of secrets and gossip is reinforced through discussion Beatrice has with Claudia and later with her father. When she turns eighteen, Beatrice joins her father in his work. In the next section her father dies while he is in Baghdad. Beatrice first hears of his death by receiving an official letter of condolence. She begins to seek information about why he died and where he was buried. Her father's friends, the Hoffmans, help her find the gravesite, but they hint that "he might actually have been poisoned—that is murdered. There was a woman in the case: more than one woman. And that always made for danger" (p. 55). Beatrice dismisses the idea as "ridiculous" (p. 55). As she returns home, she begins to accept his death. To settle his estate, she recatalogs his library and prepares to "sell most of the Greek and Roman sculpture and the larger objects from ancient Egypt" (p. 61).

When Beatrice visits the Schuylers in Cairo, she meets Jack again, Claudia's brother, and they are soon engaged. The mystery of the "sister" in the shop resurfaces when Beatrice is invited to visit the people she saw—the girl, Ernestine, and her mother, Madame Cristo-Marquez, in their

home. The house, out of the edge of town, has always been rumored to be haunted: "Chanting. Wailing. Religious" (p. 67) is how Jack describes the goings-on. On the way there, Jack teases her and makes her laugh. As they approach the house, Beatrice remembers "a friend of hers in Switzerland—not a very close friend—had once accused her of being interested in the past because she was afraid of the future." Beatrice dismisses the comment again because "she loved the past because she was able to imagine it" and "now, all at once, she saw her own life, too, as it was and could become" (p. 67). The Cristo-Marquez house is practically straight from a tale by Edgar Allan Poe; inside, the narrow corridors with high ceilings make Beatrice feel "like being in some vast underground cave" (p. 68). Beatrice and Jack are escorted toward the sanctuary, which is like the "entrance to a tomb" (p. 70). They meet Madame Cristo-Marquez, who is "painted to resemble an ancient Egyptian queen"; her son, Hassan; and Ernestine. Hassan was the Egyptian buyer of her father's artifacts. She recognizes items from her father's collection; given their weight, she argues that they should be displayed on the ground floor, giving another layer of suspense to the story; the weight of the past might collapse on her as well.

Madame insists that Ernestine was also the daughter of Beatrice's father and that she herself was "the only love of his life" (p. 71). Beatrice is indignant but polite: "Mme. Cristo-Marquez was repulsive, outrageous, and offensive, but she was also ludicrous, pitiable, ill" (p. 71). Beatrice's balancing of good and bad impressions suggests maturity and a readiness for a happy future. Madame Cristo-Marquez continues, "in the end, he came to me … to seek his final resting place. He died of love" (p. 72). Beatrice, now more self-aware, recognizes this as more gossip by an unreliable character, yet, "A sense of her father's personality came to Beatrice so strongly that it was almost as if he were near her" (p. 72). Beatrice fights against the feeling, telling herself her father would have hated this irrational, theatrical woman. She argues that he died of food poisoning. Madame retorts, "Love is a poison," and she insists that "he has come home to me"

(p. 72). The sarcophagus in the room contains something, perhaps her father's body. She and Jack bid them good night and flee the room, only to encounter Madame Cristo-Marquez' son, Hassan. She asks him directly what was in the sarcophagus. He answers, "My father or your father—perhaps more than one person. Why should it make a difference to you?" (p. 73). Beatrice is appalled that Madame would "really go so far as to dig someone up," and Hassan answers, "Why not? It's what archaeologists do all the time … digging up the dead" (p. 73), Jack must push his way out and they run. Beatrice is frightened and relieved to be away, and Jack imitates their gestures and phrasing, repeating, "Love is a poison," which makes Beatrice laugh.

In "Somewhere Else," Alan and Beth own a travel agency, but their work owns them; they feel stuck in their marriage, and they themselves never travel. Beth says to a competing travel agent: "We both need a break … we just keep going and going" (p. 80). Beth's description of their lives shows that they have no family, no real friends, not even a neighborhood, because the office location at a mall means that "the mall was really the neighborhood where she lived" (p. 80). Beth tells the other agent, "The work is always just great. It's a substitute for everything else. I'm beginning to think it's my excuse for not living my life" (p. 81). They decide to go on a "too good to be true" trip, after a two-thousand-dollar offer comes in the mail.

As they prepare to leave for their trip to England, an additional offer comes to them for a special "Finborg weekend," and they rearrange their plans to extend their itinerary. After their trip to England, on the flight for the Finborg weekend, Beth dreams that the plane crashes and that Alan cannot get to her in the smoke and confusion. They arrive and join six other people for the journey to Finborg. They are loaded into horse-drawn carriages and given no explanations or itinerary details. After a long ride, they stop to water the horses, change carriages, and then continue. Another passenger wonders if it is "one of those mystery games" (p. 95). The stops, the rearranging of suitcases, and the changing of

seats continue; the narrative increases in speed with summaries of each stop; the passengers trade family stories, jokes, and travel-agent anecdotes; and they just keep on riding. Alan "began to lose heart. There was another trouble with traveling: everything was out of your hands" (p. 97). There is seemingly no ending to it; Alan fears "they were going to keep traveling, forever" (p. 98). Beth "never lost hope that if they continued to move ahead, somehow—all at once—they would reach the light. It would come upon them like a revelation of truth, a burst of sunlight" (p. 99). The story ends with Beth remembering their shared dream of dying in a plane crash. They are stuck in another ambiguous Ingalls ending.

"Correspondent" hovers close to the Cupid and Psyche myth and is a story in which, as Amanda Craig notes in her review for the London *Times*, "superstition, religion, convention and luck are all brought into play." Max, a famous war correspondent so highly esteemed as to be almost godlike, believes in the power of his lucky charms to keep him safe: "The less he believed in God, the more he valued the importance of what he wore into danger zones" (p. 109). When his wife, Joan, suspects she is about to be replaced with another woman, she steals his lucky charms and tricks him with a substitute, placing her trust in God, to whom she prays and pleads for Max's safety. Max is injured but escapes death, and as he is awakening after his surgery, he greets Joan with the words, "My beautiful wife" (p. 131). She explains that the lucky charms had been substituted by mistake. He answers that the substitution, the keys to the front door of their house, "pulled him through. They meant home" (p. 131). Joan nonetheless at the end of the story does not believe she can rely on God any more than on human love.

The fable-like "Fertility" evokes the mythical Greek wife Penelope and her faithfulness to Odysseus. A girl falls in love with a man and after he has gone to war, she bears his child. Her family, his mother, and the town all reject her and force her into prostitution. She suffers horribly, even hearing her own son, who has been abducted by his grandmother, taunt her and call her whore. The man returns years later and reclaims her and his child. The sweetness of the reunion is diluted in the story's ending, however; the narrative leaps twenty years into the future, where she and a friend discuss whether it was love or fertility that prompted him to reclaim her. "What is it that enables us to survive. Whom can we trust? What makes some turn to evil, and others to good?" asks Amanda Craig in her *Times* review, identifying the questions that Ingalls raises in this story and others.

The story "Veterans" uses the device of Oedipus at the crossroads to open and close the story of how two men are changed by war. Frank, a man whom the war frees from violence and a brutal childhood, saved Sherman's life. Sherman is described as "violent" by his doctors and is not at all rehabilitated by his wartime experience, believing that existence itself is essentially violent. Sherman seeks out Frank after the war, both resentful that he saved his life and resentful of the ease and peace of Frank's life. He moves in and thoroughly unsettles Frank's civilized domestic world, disgruntling his wife and alarming his children. In unusually heavy dialogue for Ingalls, the men discuss at length human nature versus animal nature, and the idea of survival of the fittest. The story, nearly a novella, stitches together—with metaphor, descriptions, and repeated events like the men's nightly drinking and storytelling—the themes of violence, human nature, and survival. Eventually Frank tires of him, and Irene launches an ultimatum that Frank must make him leave. After Sherman murders a distant relative of Frank's wife, and she comes into inheritance, he contemplates killing Frank and stealing his life—or even killing all of the family. Sherman's interior monologue has biblical overtones, and Irene, the wife, has similarities to the biblical Eve. Ultimately, Sherman takes the money Frank offers him and heads to the edge of town. In another of Ingalls' abrupt and vague endings, Sherman "hung in the twilight, undecided: breathing in and out, waiting for the long, languid swell of night to carry him into the darkness" (p. 201).

In "The Icon," curiosity and a desire for knowledge create a parallel between the paired characters of the story's grandfather and his grandson and the mythical Daedalus and his son, Icarus. In a large, extended, squabbling family gathered in their big summer house, the grandson Stratis "was the only one in the family who wasn't afraid of the old man" (p. 207). The old man "thought every one of them, except Stratis, was useless" (p. 208). There is an icon that the old man treasures and carries with him, and Stratis wonders about its significance, its value, and its origins. The old man only says that "it brought him good luck." He encourages Stratis to pick an occupation, to settle down and be disciplined. He tells him, "You don't have to have the shining object that's hanging just out of your reach" (p. 219). Stratis becomes more and more interested in the icon, questioning whether the grandfather stole it from a monastery and arguing with him about whether it should be returned. After a symbolic storm, Stratis and the icon disappear. The next thing the old man hears is that Stratis was badly injured in a fight in a Greek airport and that he died returning the icon to two priests. "The young were natural betrayers," the old man thinks, Daedalus-like, mulling over his disappointments and his losses at the end of the story. "Particularly young men: that was a fact of life. They were always moving forward too fast to keep up with the old ties" (p. 185). The story is a study in religion and belief and how patience struggles against immaturity.

In the long work "No Love Lost," a man struggles in a chaotic postwar society, hinting at but not mirroring Odysseus's battles with monsters, gods, and bad suitors. The story provides a Penelope figure who is diametrically opposed to the original loyal, faithful wife of Greek myth. "No Love Lost" contains a level of Christian allegory: after the war, the main character, whose left hand has been amputated, becomes a carpenter. His unscrupulous wife, however, takes charge of their livelihood; she trains their children to be thieves, and she cheats everyone around her, including an old woman who has been placed in her care.

Outside the town is an abandoned quarry that has become a dumping ground for the lawless of this society to get rid of their enemies, spouses, troublemakers. The quarry offers the protagonist a site for reverie on his childhood, for reflections on the dangers then versus the real dangers now in his life, and comparisons emerge in the narration between his own happy childhood and his children's miserable, hopeless childhood.

When the narrator catches his wife with her lover, an aid worker, they throw him into the quarry. But at the bottom of the quarry, in a surprising, positive twist, he finds children helping other people, and he meets a pregnant woman named Maria. In her *Hudson Review* essay, Susan Balée points out, "Readers looking for allegories will see that the narrator is a carpenter; he falls in love with a pregnant woman named Maria who is linked to an older maternal figure named Anna" (p. 693). He escapes, kills the wife and her lover, and rescues Maria and Anna. "He wanted peace; and to begin life again, with Maria" (p. 302). After another summer, his luck begins to improve. He has explained away the disappearance of his wife and the aid worker, regular supplies of foodstuffs are coming his way, and hope is returning as people find ways to work through cooperative exchanges and bartering. By the next spring, a fair comes to town, and he is able to treat his family to an outing. Visiting the gallery of artificial terror called the House of Horrors, his hope is restored. He thinks, "Having lived through so many horrors … was a kind of protection" against fear. He concludes "the answer wasn't that no one knew the difference between the true and the false; they knew. But they still needed magic" (p. 316).

Thus even in a world struggling against chaos, where instincts for survival destroy moral behavior, people need the magic of hope and a belief in luck to recover. Key themes of the story are moral degradation, hope in the face of disaster, the role luck plays in our understanding of ourselves, and how childhood shapes a person. In these five stories, the plot lines and patterns may be familiar, but, Victoria Segal notes, "These might be ancient themes, but Ingalls breathes new life into them."

BEFORE MRS. CALIBAN

Theft (1970), Ingalls' first novella, is a retelling of the crucifixion of Christ told from the perspective of the two thieves in a modern setting. Jake and Seth, two friends who are also related by marriage, get by, working, drinking, avoiding politics. They are both day laborers but times are so difficult that Seth still has trouble earning enough to feed his children and his wife. Desperately hungry, Seth steals a loaf of bread and is arrested. In the same afternoon Jake is also arrested but for stealing a horse. Seth considers that Jake is a kind of leader, with a kind of public reputation but he was "very relaxed when he toted things off" (p. 12).

In jail the two friends chat about life, family, and wives with Homer, their Greek jailor. The novella is not specific with setting, but it does make a reference to "fighting for our racial equality" (p. 6). That same afternoon a big political riot occurs, and some young activists are also jailed; observing them, Seth and Jake scoff that they are playing at politics. The young activists are bailed out by rich uncles and fathers, but Seth, who is poor and not about to be rescued, thinks, "That's what they come to jail for, to get right down to real life, to the truth, and if you're looking there, that's where you'll find it" (p. 51). Joining them in jail is a religious fanatic. This man is described as "an animal in a sack … gawky skinny, dressed in rags and covered in dirt" (p. 58), evoking an image of the Old Testament figure of John the Baptist, and he screams biblical references, including quotes from the New Testament. The fanatic prompts Seth and Jake to discuss political activism, idealism, and God. Jake admits that Seth has "that instinctive certainty of what's right and what's wrong" (p. 68). The novella skips the trial and goes right to the punishment, which "usually takes three hours" (p. 87), like the crucifixion of Christ. The hours, which may be a day or two, preceding their crucifixion are not clear. Dying, Seth "knew now all the things you need in life have to be stolen from somewhere, from the earth or from other people—food, water, warmth, you need them to live. But they can be taken from you" (p. 89).

Who is the good thief and who is the bad? Both are good thieves in that Seth dies peacefully, seeing the peace on the fanatic's face and agony which indicates regret, on Jake's. But Jake is also the good thief for his understanding of human nature and for his genuine love for both Seth and his own wife. This early work contains many of Ingalls' usual themes about individual survival in a chaotic world, the nature of personal truth, and the fact that being unconventional is usually fatal.

Ingalls' 1973 collection *Mediterranean Cruise* contains the novellas "Early Morning Sightseer," "St. George and the Nightclub," and "Something to Write Home About." (These three novellas were reprinted along with the 1974 story "The Man Who Was Left Behind" and "Theft" in a collection titled *Something to Write Home About,* published by Harvard Common Press in 1988. All page references are to that 1988 edition.)

"Early Morning Sightseer" is the story of two young men, friends in college, who are traveling together in Greece. The opening of the story mysteriously withholds who they are and why they are traveling, but it fits with the first-person narration by Barnes, who, while revealing information to the reader, will grow to self-awareness, self-assurance, and independence from his companion, Richard Tilney.

Rick Tilney is rich, spoiled, and misanthropic. The story opens with him criticizing the Greeks, their taxi drivers, the other tourists they meet. Barnes, nicknamed Barney by Tilney, is from Indiana and is not wealthy. We later learn that the two young men are together to help Tilney overcome the death of Diane, Tilney's fiancée, who died in a high-speed car accident. Barney thinks about how they are in a mythic land, and he also thinks about "the great myth of her and him" (p. 152).

Barney becomes fed up with Tilney's "damned romantic agony and suicide notes and spoiled brat grand gestures" (p. 156). Barney is furious both because he doesn't know if Tilney slept with Diane and because he doesn't know why she was going a hundred miles an hour when she crashed Tilney's Porsche into a oncoming car, killing a man and woman and two children as well as herself (p. 156).

The two young men argue throughout their car trip to Delphi. Barney ignores Tilney while contemplating the architecture. He seeks to understand it because "it wasn't really a question of art or aesthetics; I was sure that somehow it all had to do with religion, that at a certain point you could achieve a kind of revelation, like breaking the sound barrier, and from then on you would have special certainly that it would never forsake you" (p. 166). Ingalls' first-person narration reveals in layers Barney's character and the way he is changing. After he has begun to understand art for himself, Barney expresses his growing impatience with Tilney—"If only he would stop acting" (p. 168)—and also asserts that he had known and loved Diane first.

They climb to the temple of Athena, with Tilney verbally attacking the other people they encounter. It is part of his personality to vilify other cultures, to poke fun at history; "he had a set piece on the French, about how good propagandists had kept alive a myth about France being the head of the civilized world" (p. 176). Tilney "trotted this rigamarole out," says Barney, and "he could do it with any country. He could also do it for America, of course." Barney challenges him about "some of things you've been doing recently—getting drunk and yelling at people, acting crazy or let's say something quite simple like being rude," but he also acknowledges that a troop of lawyers would likely "materialize out of nowhere" to keep Rick out of jail (p. 183). Tilney's response is that "they should have a fight some day" (p. 184).

They reach the top, and Barney thinks about Diane and his New England education and "how fast everything had seemed and how special and different and sophisticated and rich" (p. 188). Barney considers Tilney with "his maniac jokes, his clothes and his car and its speed and his easiness and arrogance" (p. 189). Then Barney finds himself strangely homesick for Indiana; even though he is in "this beautiful place which I had been longing to see, and it was perfect ... yet it filled me with even more longing." Soaking up the hot sunlight, the beautiful sculptures, Barney "kept wondering about my life and what I was looking for, and looking out at the sea made me yearn to know what it was" (p. 189). His self-awareness has begun. He wanders away from Tilney and listens to other ordinary tourists, and "there was no sudden revelation, just the beauty and the peace of the place and the sound of the birds, the talk and the sunlight, which all combined to make me happy" (p. 193). In a comic turn, Barney overhears a tourist wishing for a Sara Lee cruller, and he smiles: "I could see the rest of my life, the possibility and the strength of it … I would know how to live it" (p. 193). His liberation from the sophisticated sarcasm of Tilney is nearly complete.

Almost as if Tilney can read Barney's mind and knows he is losing his disciple, Tilney starts verbally taunting him: "Undergraduate sinks without a trace in wine dark sea … Dramatic duel between the good old classic art of self defense and insidious inscrutable karate methods" (p. 197). As Tilney pretends to throw Barney off the edge of the cliff, they come perilously close to falling. Barney can't end it: "There were one or two basic moves I could make to break out of the hold he had me in," he says, "but if I used them he'd flip straight over the wall" (p. 198). Unlike Tilney, Barney is aware of real potential consequences. Tilney releases him and laughs. Barney walks down the hill, with Tilney following and calling his name. At the bottom, Barney hits Tilney in the face, three times—until he is satisfied with his punch. They return to their hotel, and Barney leaves Greece, telling Tilney he is going to Indiana. Over their remaining years of college, Barney avoids Tilney. In the years after graduation, Barney hears of another engagement and another suspicious accident involving Tilney, which kills the fiancée again. When he encounters Tilney in a bar eight years later, Barney barely speaks to him. He questions the past—"memory is strange"—and thinks "the hardest thing to remember is the truth about yourself" (p. 209). He remembers his complete happiness in Greece and how Tilney tried to kill him.

The story "St. George and the Nightclub" rests on cultural miscommunications and missteps. In Greece, Don and Jeanie are on an extended holiday, trying to resolve the problems in their marriage caused by his infidelity. Wandering the shops, Don wants to buy an icon, not of a Greek figure or an Orthodox Christian saint but of St. George and the Dragon, an iconic figure of English Christianity. It is the first of many miscommunications and cultural missteps. Later in the evening, they meet up with two other couples, including a newlywed American couple, Linda and Rocky Butterworth. During an evening spent together in a nightclub, Don shows that he knows some of the customs, like not applauding a sole dancer who "was clearly happy" and not performing (p. 227), but not others, like remembering to check the bar tab for accuracy. On the walk back to the hotel, Rocky engages Don in conversation and asks for advice because the honeymoon isn't going well. The adulterer Don talks Rocky through what women look like naked, what things to try with her. He rejoins his wife in the hotel lobby, and in a lovely moment so true to Ingalls' style, the reader understands that Jeanie is not going to forgive Don and their marriage is over: "She looked in our direction when we came in, and stood up. The difference there is in a face when someone is glad to see you—not even the posture of the body is the same" (p. 235). Next Don and Jeanie argue over Rocky and Linda; glossing over the fight, Don argues they are in Greece and it's beautiful, it's "a shame not to enjoy everything. But of course people can never enjoy enough, or at the right times, and certainly nobody ever learns" (p. 239). He tries to grab Jeanie and she knocks him away. Don cracks his head and nose on a windowsill. A comedy of trying to be understood in Greek and find medical help ensues.

The next day at dinner, they are discussing their son and their now-impending divorce. Don realizes he can read Jeanie's body language: "There are so many different attitudes, like different lives in a face and a body," he concludes. "How long it takes to know them all. And you never do" (p, 254). As they talk, they realize that several policemen have entered the hotel. Don learns that the American man has killed his wife: Rocky couldn't read Linda and inadvertently strangled her. Rocky quietly shoots himself offstage as the story is ending. Resting with Jeanie, Don thinks, "My nose was broken, my head was breaking up, my life was all broken up." He only now reads his wife in this moment of crisis. He tells her about Butterworth, and she cries, but Don holds his wife "close and carefully, by the waist and the shoulders" (p. 262).

The story explores the sadness in miscommunication and the way that connection to another person depends on accurate knowledge and reading of that person. The first-person narration of a man at first exploring unfamiliar surroundings and then exploring himself and his failures ends on a slight upbeat note. The pain medication begins to work, and at the end, he sleeps.

In "Something to Write Home About," John and Amy Larsen are touring the Greek isles, and John hopes that this trip will bring happiness to his wife and their marriage. Amy, suffering from an unnamed mental condition, is obsessed with postcards, finding them and mailing them. Every postcard is addressed to the same name and place. In contrast to other American couples, John and Amy seem immature, more like students; their interactions also reveal Amy's hypersensitivity. John watches for signs of her distress and carefully arranges the details of hotels and transportation to protect her frame of mind. "She was looking happy and was calm enough" (p. 270), he notes, but in their rented car, she screams for him to stop because she forgot to mail her postcards. He asks her to calm down and kisses her nose three times, another ritual. As he drives he considers that research has offered ways to overcome obsessive behavior, ideas that "could probably stop you washing your hand fifty times a day, but then you'd start something else, like picking your nose. Or worrying about postcards" (p. 272). As they tour the sites, he tries to distract her and also assures her that "it isn't inherited," raising more questions about her condition. At the Parthenon, "he wanted to talk to her and realized he couldn't" (p. 280). He has controlled all the details of the trip to satisfy Amy's needs, and in the beautiful setting, all alone, "he thought for the first time in a long while that everything was going to be all right" (p. 280). In a museum he

considers "the business of classical things" and that their beauty invokes their human creators. The experience created a memory "he would never forget as long as he lived and it would always make him feel good just to think about it" (p. 282). Buoyed on a sense of well-being, he risks telling Amy that "as long as you don't get worried about anything, everything will be okay" (p. 284). She answers without any confidence, "I hope so" (p. 284). After more shopping and sightseeing through John's careful care of her moods, Amy cries, "I love you so much sometimes it makes me want to throw up" (p. 288), indicating her dependence on him is growing stronger.

In a hotel lobby, however, Amy has another outburst when she cannot immediately find a rack of postcards. In a brief exchange the story reveals that Amy's mother, hospitalized and unable to read or understand the postcards, is their sole recipient. The postcards pile up, filled with Amy's descriptions of all the details of their trip, written to a woman who would not comprehend any of it. John thinks, *"It's going to be all right … This is Amy … the only person who's ever understood me … and it's just got to be all right"* (p. 295), but he begins "to sweat." In bittersweet irony, John will continue to try and Amy will still be obsessed.

The Man Who Was Left Behind is a novel from 1970 that was Ingalls' second major work; after its first U.S. publication (where it appeared with *Theft*), it was published by Faber in 1974 and has been included in several other collections, including the 1988 volume *Something to Write Home About*. (All pages references are to the 1988 edition.)

In *The Man Who Was Left Behind*, Mr. Mackenzie spends much of his time sitting in a park, with its scrubby grass and flaking paint, because it "suggested the thought of the tropics and of Mexico" (p. 94). Mackenzie, his wife, his daughter and her fiancé, and his son, Jim, had earlier traveled to Mexico to celebrate his retirement. He had enjoyed the "strange things about Mexico—you accepted it as natural" (p. 96). A tourist office employee at one point says of the Mexican Indians, "They have this inborn fatalism—they figure you die when your number comes up, so they never take any trouble to avoid accidents" (p. 96). Mackenzie is the last of the group to get sick, and so he stays behind while his family goes off to a nightclub, where they all die in a terrible fire. He returns home, sells off the house he has lived in since childhood, and moves into a small downtown apartment. He begins to drink heavily until he finds the park. His doctor and his housekeeper, Bessie, try to encourage him to eat well, to sleep better, to drink less. But in the park, things change: "Now was different. Now was better. He learned by himself during the first four days of sitting in the park" (p. 106).

Mackenzie rallies sufficiently to think about his will: with no family alive, who should he leave his substantial wealth to? The story reveals that Mackenzie also had a second, younger son, Ben, who had been his favorite. In the Korean War, Ben had been injured and returned a triple amputee. Mackenzie had urged Ben to be strong, but Ben had replied, "I can stand anything. Don't mind the pain. Don't care about hurt … Anything but this" (p. 114). That night Ben had dragged himself from his bed and committed suicide.

Passing time one day, Mackenzie goes to the library and checks out a copy of a book that turns out to be by the Greek historian Xenophon and that describes an "ideal Stoic philosopher" (p. 117). He walks to his old home and frightens the new owners by staring. The police and his doctor are called; Mackenzie remembers the details of Ben's death, how deliberate it was.

He returns to the park bench, "concentrated on the tree, and went out into Mexico" (p. 122). The three African American hoboes who are residing there, Elmie, Jumbo, and Spats, begin to speak with him, and "they accepted him and he discovered that he could tolerate being with them for hours or days, whereas he could not bear to be long in the immediate company of anyone else" (p. 124). Over time he decides how to settle his affairs—he will leave money to Bessie, to a former daughter-in-law (the first wife of his son, Jim), and to disabled veterans, as well as designating funds to build a library to house his books. Then fall becomes winter, the hoboes move on, and Mackenzie thinks, "It would be months

before the tree in the park regained its tropical look" (p. 145). He loses touch with reality while he reads Xenophon's description of Greek battles and the soldiers left behind to die in the cold. Bessie and the doctor discover him as he is dying, "one lone Greek in the middle of the great Persian plains" (p. 147).

The story is again that of an ordinary man who must cope with extraordinary losses. He finds some peace in the company of other men who have nothing, just like himself.

CONCLUSION

Ingalls is widely praised for her technical mastery. William Packard says in his 1986 review, "Ingalls is a superlative writer, careful in her craft and awesome in her effects." She rejects some modern devices, including present tense and minimalism, but, as Anne Bernays points out, she uses "architectural plots, the surprise narrative spin" (p. 9). Her narrative structure has been criticized for using contrived plotting and for the speed of her denouements (Pekar). Reviewing *Times Like These*, *Kirkus Review* called the end of the story "Veterans" "inconclusive," and the end of *Mrs. Caliban* likewise leaves questions unanswered. Although Ingalls seeds in plot development with foreshadowing, and she allows the story to linger at key conversations, still some of her endings rush the reader.

Ingalls maintains a balance between realism and the supernatural, using "allegory, fantasy, and grotesquerie" (Pekar, p. 6). Carla in "Inheritance" (from *The Pearlkillers*) is swept away by the weight of family tradition and history. Dorothy, in *Mrs. Caliban,* seeks happiness while she and the Caliban of the title, Larry, confront American social expectations, institutions, and mores. Rebecca Bach calls *Mrs. Caliban* a "dialogue that enables a critique of the institutions of American reality in the voice of the marginalized." Nearly all of Ingalls' main characters are outsiders in their society.

Throughout her impressive body of work, Ingalls' themes focus on the individual's struggles with questions of freedom in the face of convention or conformity and of survival in a chaotic world. A further thread throughout her work is the idea of struggle with gender roles or sexual commerce. Lee Upton notes, "Both novels are structured on deceptions in which sexual relations perform as exchange systems: romantic partners function like circulating currency" (p. 56). Many of the novellas and stories hinge on this struggle as well.

Her titles—*Days Like Today, Times Like These, I See a Long Journey, Something to Write Home About*—strike the reader as ordinary or banal, but the psychological complexity and the plot twists belie that interpretation. Ingalls' characters must wrestle with their past and try to live in their present.

Selected Bibliography

WORKS BY RACHEL INGALLS

Theft. London: Faber, 1970.

Theft and *The Man Who Was Left Behind.* Boston: Gambit, 1970.

Mediterranean Cruise. Boston: Gambit, 1973. (Novella; volume also contains "Early Morning Sightseer," "St. George and the Nightclub," and "Something to Write Home About.")

The Man Who Was Left Behind and Other Stories. London: Faber, 1974.

Mrs. Caliban. London: Faber, 1982; Boston: Gambit, 1983.

Binstead's Safari. London: Faber, 1983; New York: Simon & Schuster, 1988.

I See a Long Journey: Three Novellas. New York: Simon & Schuster 1985. U.K. edition, *Three of a Kind.* London: Faber, 1985. (Contains the novellas "I See a Long Journey," " On Ice," and "Blessed Art Thou.")

The Pearlkillers. London: Faber, 1986; New York: Simon & Schuster, 1986. (Contains the novellas "Third Time Lucky," "People to People," "Inheritance," and "Captain Hendrik's Story.")

The End of Tragedy. London: Faber, 1987. (Contains "Friends in the Country," "An Artist's Life," "In the Act," and "The End of Tragedy.")

Something to Write Home About. Harvard, Mass.: Harvard Common Press, 1988. (Contains "Theft," "The Man Who Was Left Behind," "St. George and the Nightclub," and "Something to Write Home About.")

Be My Guest: Two Novellas. New York: Turtle Bay Books, 1992. (Contains "Sis and Bud" and "Be My Guest.")

Days Like Today. London: Faber, 2000. (Stories.)

Times Like These. Saint Paul, Minn.: Graywolf Press, 2005. (Stories; published in the U.K. under the title *Black Diamond*.)

CRITICAL AND BIOGRAPHICAL STUDIES

REVIEWS

"*Be My Guest.*" *Publishers Weekly,* March 30, 1992, p. 87.

Bernays, Anne. "Brother Anselm, in a Family Way." *New York Times Book Review,* August 31, 1986, p. 9.

"*Binstead's Safari.*" *Time,* April 11, 1988, p. 74. (Review.)

Craig, Amanda. "Mistress of Her Subtle Craft." *Times* (London, England), January 27, 2000, p. 41.

———. "Things That Go Crash: *Black Diamond.*" *Independent,* July 4, 1992.

Dobyns, Stephen. "Waiter, There's an Ear in My Stew." *New York Times Book Review,* March 5, 1989. (Review of *The End of Tragedy.*)

Dorris, Michael. "Love with the Proper Amphibian." *New York Times.* December 28, 1986, p. 7. (Review of *Mrs. Caliban.*)

"*The End of Tragedy.*" *Time,* February 20, 1989, p. 101. (Review.)

"Ingalls, Rachel: *Times Like These: Stories.*" *Kirkus Reviews,* August 15, 2005, p. 874.

Innes, Charlotte. "Ingalls Askew." *Los Angeles Times,* July 5, 1992, p. 11. (Review of *Be My Guest.*)

Kakutani, Michiko. "Books of the Times: Well-Turned Twists on Well-Known Tales." *New York Times,* June 26, 1992. (Review of *Be My Guest.*)

Kemp, Peter. "Books: Let Down Murky, Twisted Ways; Reviews of *Tales of Natural and Unnatural Castastrophes* by Patricia Highsmith and *The End of Tragedy* by Rachel Ingalls." *Sunday Times,* November 8, 1987.

Leber, Michele. "Ingalls, Rachel: *Times Like These.*" *Booklist,* September 15, 2005, p. 32.

Le Guin, Ursula K. "Fatal Connections." *New York Times Book Review,* November 5, 1987, p. 24. (Review of *The Pearlkillers.*)

Lehman-Haupt, Christopher. "Books of the Times: Death Without the Sting in *The End of Tragedy.*" *New York Times,* February 23, 1989.

McCrory, Moy. "Sound, Action, and Light Reading: Paperbacks." *Times,* May 15, 1993, p. 50.

Mehren, Elizabeth. "Obscure U.S. Author Begins Storybook Life, Her Third Book, *Mrs. Caliban,* Hailed as One of the Top 20 Post WWII American Novels." *Los Angeles Times,* April 2, 1986, p. 1.

Nathan, Paul. "A Feel for Film." *Publishers Weekly,* January 13, 1997, p. 24.

Neville, Jill. "Books: Manipulators and Moralisers: Reviews of New Fiction." *Sunday Times,* May 4, 1986.

Packard, William. *"I See a Long Journey: Three Novellas* by Rachel Ingalls." *Los Angeles Times Book Review,* September 7, 1986, p. 3.

———. *"The Pearlkillers: Four Novellas* by Rachel Ingalls." *Los Angeles Times Book Review,* August 16, 1987, p. 11.

Park, Ed. "They Never Forget: Scream, Too: A Nightmare Maker's Latest Collection Applies a Steady Stream of Shocks." *Village Voice,* December 20, 2005.

Pekar, Harvey. "Elegant Nightmares." *Washington Post Book World,* September 6, 1987, p. 6.

Power, Penelope. "Ingalls, Rachel: *Times Like These: Stories.*" *Kliatt* 40, no. 2:33 (March 2006).

Prose, Francine. "The Objects of Their Obsessions: Stories of Greek Icons, Italian Opera, and Their Darkness Within." *Washington Post Book World,* November 13, 2005, p. 7.

Raphael, Isabel. "Books: Terrible Beauty of Passover: Review of Three Novels." *Times,* April 17, 1986.

Rubin, Merle. "Bookshelf: The Extraordinary in Ordinary Life." *Wall Street Journal,* July 27, 1992, p. A7.

Segal, Victoria. "Paperback Fiction: Books." *Times,* April 27, 2002.

Sokolov, Raymond. "Bookshelf: Dorothy and the Frogman." *Wall Street Journal,* March 15, 1988, p. 1.

———. "Bookshelf: Sleight of Hand: Rachel Ingalls' Tales of the Macabre." *Wall Street Journal,* January 17, 1989.

Spivack, Charlotte. "Fantasy Lives." *Women's Review of Books,* July–August 1987, pp. 27–28.

"Times Like These." *Publishers Weekly,* September 19, 2005, p. 45.

Sullivan, Patrick. *"Times Like These."* *Library Journal,* October 15, 2005, p. 50.

Taylor, Maurice. *"Binstead's Safari."* *Library Journal* 113, no. 2:75 February 1, 1988.

———. *"The End of Tragedy: Four Novellas."* *Library Journal* 114, no. 3:176 August 1987.

———. *"The Pearlkillers."* *Library Journal* 112, no. 13:142 (1987).

Walters, Margaret. "Thoroughly Modern Myths: Books." *Sunday Times,* January 16, 2000.

Williamson, Barbara Fisher. "In Short: Fiction: Book Review Desk." *New York Times Book Review,* April 17, 1988.

CRITICAL ANALYSES

Bach, Rebecca Ann. "*Mrs. Caliban*: A Feminist Postmodernist Tempest?" *Critique* 41, no. 4:391–402 (2000).

Balée, Susan. "Textual Pleasures and Pet Peeves." *Hudson Review* 58, no. 4:689–699 (2006).

Cowart, David. "Fantasy and Reality in *Mrs. Caliban.*" *Critique* 30, no. 2:77 (1989).

MacDonald, Alan. "Re-writing Hemingway: Rachel Ingalls' *Binstead's Safari.*" *Critique: Studies in Contemporary Fiction* 34, no. 3:165 (spring 1993).

Malin, Irving. "I SEE A LONG SHADOW *(Book)*." *Studies in Short Fiction* 25, no. 2:164 (1988).

Oates, Joyce Carol. "In Olden Times, When Wishing Was Having? Classic and Contemporary Fairy Tales." *Kenyon Review* n.s. 19, nos. 3–4:98–110 (summer–autumn 1997).

Upton, Lee. "Mourning Monsters: Deception and Transformation in Rachel Ingalls's Fiction." *Critique* 33, no. 1:53 (1991).

ANDREA LEVY

(1956—)

Yumna Siddiqi

ANDREA LEVY RECALLED in a 2010 interview that when she first began to write fiction in the 1980s, she was struck by the absence of literature about the experiences of black British people. In her novels, Levy brings the everyday lives of Afro-Caribbean people in the United Kingdom to center stage. She draws upon her own experiences to convey what it is like to grow up English yet be regarded as an outsider. It is with the double consciousness of being both black and British that Levy has tackled a wide range of black British experience in her novels. She fashions vivid characters and portrays their everyday lives, lives that are shaped by slavery, racism, empire, colonialism, war, postcolonial migration, and the tensions of being black and British. Her narrators, for the most part girls and women, tell stories about their families and communities in Britain and Jamaica. With empathy and a strong vein of humor, Levy conveys the challenges they face as they lay claim to their place in British society. Her novels have won her top literary honors: the Orange Prize, the Whitbread Award, the Commonwealth Writer's Prize, and an Arts Council Award. Her 2010 novel *The Long Song* was short-listed for the Man Booker Prize, and her 2004 novel *Small Island* was made into a television series by the BBC.

CULTURAL BACKGROUND

Black people have lived in Britain since the sixteenth century, when they were enslaved and transported from Africa. Following the abolition of slavery in 1833 in Britain, small communities of black people formed in the port cities of Cardiff, Liverpool, and London. The beginning of modern Afro-Caribbean immigration to Britain can be traced to the arrival of the S.S. *Empire Windrush* at the English port of Tilbury on June 22, 1948, bringing 492 men and women from the British colonies of Jamaica and Trinidad. Many of these voyagers and those who migrated after them had fought for Britain in World War II. When they returned home to the Caribbean, they were unable to find work. In Britain, however, the government was actively recruiting workers to fill a postwar labor shortage. Cheap fares were available to people under British rule in the Caribbean who wished to come to England. Many of those who arrived took up jobs in public transportation and in the National Health Service. Between 1955 and the passage of the restrictive Commonwealth Immigrants Act in 1962, roughly a quarter of a million people from the Caribbean emigrated to Britain.

Andrea Levy's father was part of this exodus of Jamaicans. He arrived on the *Empire Windrush* in 1948, and her mother followed six months later. In the essay "This Is My England," Levy writes of her father's expectations: "Far from the idea that he was travelling to a foreign place, he was travelling to the centre of his country, and as such he would slip-in and fit-in immediately. Jamaica, he thought, was just Britain in the sun." They both were in for a shock: rather than being welcomed, they struggled. "They suffered bad housing—by no means the plight of black people alone in those post-war days: the signs in windows read 'no niggers, no dogs, no Irish.' My dad faced incredible hostility when looking for somewhere to live because of the colour of his skin. He had a job with the post office. My mum, a trained teacher in Jamaica, had to sew to make a living here." They stayed and raised their son and three daughters on a council estate in North London. Andrea Levy, the youngest of their children, was born in 1956. After studying textile design and weaving at Middlesex Polytechnic in London, she worked for the BBC and Royal Opera House costume departments. Her first three novels, *Every Light in the House Burnin'* (1994), *Never Far from Nowhere* (1996), and *Fruit of the Lemon* (1999) reflect the experiences of her family.

While she may have felt that she was writing in isolation when she began to take creative writing courses in her thirties, Andrea Levy was in fact part of a growing confraternity of black writers in the United Kingdom. A brief overview of black British culture is helpful in contextualizing Levy's fiction. The phrase "black British" is commonly used to denote British people of Caribbean, South Asian, and African ancestry. Within this wider group one can identify a distinctive Afro-Caribbean British cultural formation. Just before and after World War II, a first wave of writers, among them E. R. Braithwaite, C. L. R. James, James Berry, Sam Selvon, George Lamming, Wilson Harris, and Kamau Braithwaite, came to Britain from the Caribbean. They wrote about their colonized homelands (*Minty Alley* [1936] by C. L. R. James; *In the Castle of My Skin* [1970] by George Lamming) and also about the experience of migration to Britain (*The Lonely Londoners* [1956] by Sam Selvon; *To Sir with Love* [1959] by E. R. Braithwaite). In 1966, influenced by the civil rights movement in the United States, the Afro-Caribbean writers Kamau Brathwaite and Andrew Salkey and the publisher John La Rose spearheaded the radically inclined Caribbean Arts Movement, a cultural movement that was expressly concerned with black identity and politics, and also with fostering third-world solidarity. In the 1970s, a new generation of black writers, poets, and reggae artists who had been born and had grown up in Britain emerged, among them the poet Linton Kwesi Johnson. These writers and poets voiced the anger of an entire generation of British-born young black people who were marginalized and discriminated against by the mainstream of British society. In 1981, two days of rioting in Brixton left three hundred people injured, and later that year there were so-called race riots again in Brixton, as well as in Manchester, the west London district of

Southall, and the Toxteth neighborhood of Liverpool—the first of such riots to occur since the Notting Hill riot of 1958. The mainstream of British society and the state began to recognize that black British people were deprived of equal educational and employment opportunities when Lord Scarman, in his report on the Brixton riots, said that "complex political, social and economic factors" created a "disposition towards violent protest." At the same time, he blamed poor police tactics and racial disadvantage rather than historical and institutional racism.

In his important study of race, class, and nation in Britain in the 1970s and 1980s, *There Ain't No Black in the Union Jack* (1991), Paul Gilroy argues that "the oscillation between black as problem and black as victim has become, today, the principle mechanism through which 'race' is pushed outside of history and into the realm of natural, inevitable events" (p. 11). He makes the case that thinkers on the left as well as the right tend either to ignore questions of race and racism, or they essentialize race and fail to explain race and racism in historical terms.

Even as the frustration of young black people in Britain with racism and with economic and social marginalization came to a head in the 1980s, exacerbated by the socially conservative free-market ideology of Thatcherism, black cultural expression burgeoned and new spaces for it opened up. In a landmark essay titled "New Ethnicities," presented at the Black Film/British Cinema conference at the Institute of Contemporary Arts in 1988, Stuart Hall identifies two overlapping and interwoven moments in black cultural politics. One refers to a period when the various marginalized ethnic groups began to organize and agitate politically, using the term "black" to reference the community as a whole. According to Hall, this was a moment when progressive Asian and Afro-Caribbean Britons attempted to mount a unified front against the exclusionary and marginalizing tendencies of white aesthetic and cultural practices, one that perhaps played into a naive notion of an essential black subject. This is not to say that black Britons were ever a homogenous group, but the thrust in cultural politics at this time was for recognition, and this meant that relatively little attention was paid to differences and tensions within black communities.

The chief aim of activists of this moment was to make a place at the table for black culture and experience. To this end, the cultural politics and strategies of this moment were focused on challenging the exclusion and marginalization of black artists while also contesting stereotypical and fetishistic images of black people and introducing positive black imagery. In 1982, the first International Book Fair of Radical Black and Third World Books took place in London, hosting readings, public discussions, concerts, plays and theater, and offering a wide variety of bookstalls. BBC Channel 4, started in 1982, had the mandate of providing programming to minority groups. The Black Audio Film Collective was formed in 1982 in London, producing thought-provoking documentary and experimental films about black experience such as *Handsworth Songs* (1986) and *Twilight City* (1989). Other collectives such as Sankofa, Ceddo, and ReTake also emerged in the early and mid-1980s. The photographic arts organization Autograph ABP was formed in 1988 to promote and educate the public about cultural identity and human rights. Afro-Caribbean music—styles such as ska, reggae, roots, and dub—entered the mainstream of British culture. In the field of literature, black British writers of different ethnicities came to prominence: for instance, Grace Nichols, born in Guyana, won the Commonwealth Poetry Prize in 1983; the British Indian novelist Salman Rushdie won the Booker Prize for *Midnight's Children* in 1981; the Nigerian Wole Soyinka won the Nobel Prize for literature in 1986; and Ben Okri of Nigeria won the Booker Prize in 1991 for *The Famished Road*.

According to Stuart Hall, adjacent and slightly later to this moment of cultural recognition and contestation, but also interwoven with it, was a second one, most marked in the late 1980s and after, when cultural practitioners tackled the varied and often fractured construction of black identities. No longer was the notion of a unitary black subject viable; rather, artists and critics explored the ways in which black identity was constructed and how this construction was inflected by gender, sexuality, class, and ethnicity. The complex nature of black identity in England was explored in 1980s films such as *My Beautiful Laundrette* (1985) and *Sammie and Rosie Get Laid* (1987), both based on screenplays by Hanif Kureishi. Kwame Kwei-Armah's 2003 play *Elmina's Kitchen,* the first play by a black British playwright to be staged in the West End, captures these complexities and tensions admirably.

Andrea Levy's novels for the most part reflect the preoccupations of writers, filmmakers, and artists of the first moment—the recognition and valorization of black British culture—although she occasionally explores the varieties of black experience and identity. Her first three novels have young female protagonists who grow up in London, but they are at times not regarded as truly English by their peers, and they are themselves very conscious of their parents' lack of conformity to English cultural norms. For these protagonists, to come of age is to assert their Englishness and to come to terms with their cultural roots. Two other currents in black British writing are reflected in Andrea Levy's novels: the representation of diasporic identity and experience, and the depiction of Britain as a multiracial and multicultural society. Paul Gilroy argues in *The Black Atlantic* (1993) that the triangular trade produced a diasporic formation of black people that spanned the West Coast of Africa, Europe, and the East Coast of America, a "black Atlantic." Travel between the Caribbean and England can be seen as part of this pattern of movement. Three of Levy's novels explore different kinds of transatlantic movement. In *Fruit of the Lemon,* the young protagonist travels to Jamaica and reestablishes ties with her extended family in her parents' homeland. In *Small Island,* Gilbert and Hortense travel to London from Jamaica in the first wave of postwar migration. In *The Long Song,* Levy explores the life of a woman who is born a slave in Jamaica. Levy also explores how these movements give England a strongly multiracial and multicultural inflection. Because of the history of colonialism, Caribbean and British cultures are too strongly intermingled and mutually constitutive to be thought of as distinct, yet the challenges of bridging the differences between black British people, white British people, black Jamaicans, settler white Jamaicans, other minorities, and all those in between, persist, and Levy gently satirizes these challenges in her fiction. In this regard her fiction is similar to that of other black British writers such as Zadie Smith and Hanif Kureishi.

The first three of Andrea Levy's novels are strongly autobiographical. Each novel is about a Jamaican family in North London, and in each, many of the particulars closely parallel those of her own family and their circumstances, as she recounts them in interviews. The protagonists are girls and young women who describe in realistic detail their family and friends, their homes and schools, and episodes in their lives. Andrea Levy's realism is not that of nineteenth-century writers who employ a detached, omniscient, objective point of view to represent a social milieu; rather, her first-person narrators have strong voices and an angular perspective on the mainstream of society. The novels are about childhood and coming-of-age as a young black woman in an urban, white working-class milieu. As such, the novels can be seen as examples of the subgenre of postcolonial bildungsroman. The somewhat naive, fresh perspectives of the young protagonists throw into relief the ideologies of race, class, gender, and nationhood that shape their milieus.

EVERY LIGHT IN THE HOUSE BURNIN'

"My dad once drank six cups of tea and ate six buttered rolls." With these words Angela Jacobs, the narrator of Andrea Levy's first novel, begins her story, describing an especially mortifying moment with her family. She is on her first family holiday, at a motorway café where their bus has made a stop. The children hopefully make requests; her father looks at the prices on the menu, jangles the change in his pocket, and orders tea and a roll for each of them. When Angela, her brother, sisters, and mother all say they aren't hungry, he methodically drinks all the cups of tea and eats all the rolls. He holds the bus up. Surely every reader recalls similar mo-

ments of helpless annoyance and humiliation in the company of one's family in public, and is hooked. *Every Light in the House Burnin'* (1994) is Angela Jacobs's account of growing up in North London with her parents, immigrants from Jamaica, and her brother and two sisters. Levy alternates chapters about Angela's childhood with chapters about her attempts as an adult to help her mother care for Angela's father as he develops cancer and grows increasingly ill and weak. This braided structure conveys the complexity of the bonds that hold her to her family—bonds of chagrin but also of love and anguish.

The chapters in which Angela recalls her childhood have a strongly ethnographic flavor, conveying the texture of everyday life in a North London working-glass Caribbean immigrant family. She describes each member of her family in sections subtitled "MY DAD," "MY MUM," "MY BROTHER," and "MY SISTERS," providing sketches of each as well as relating an incident that conveys something of the person's character and his or her relationship with Angela. The simplicity of the subtitles recalls a naive schoolgirl's essay, yet the vividness with which the characters and episodes are described reveals the narrator's shrewdness and keen eye. Her father and mother receive the most complex and full treatment in the novel. In her initial sketch of him, the narrator considers whether to describe her father "as a young man with neatly greased-back wavy hair" or as a "pot bellied middle-aged man who spent hours in front of the mirror trying to conceal his grey hairs," then she recalls her father's rage when she refused to go to school: "His face was contorted with anger—red and round." The narrator's physical descriptions also convey something of his character: his vanity, his quick temper. Angela knows her father works in a post office, she but knows little else about his working life. At home, he watches television, especially football. He does no cooking or cleaning, but he does all the ironing and makes the bed with a fastidiousness that he applies to his personal dress. Her mother also looms large in Angela's portrait of her family and her childhood, although she is a less mysterious figure. Describing her as tall, with thick wavy hair, a large, wise nose, thick lips, and light skin, Angela alludes to her ambiguous racial identification in Jamaica. On Sundays her mother dresses in her best clothes and takes a scrubbed and similarly dressed-up Angela to church with her.

The experience of immigration clearly shapes her parents' lives, a fact that Angela conveys in her portrait of them. Of her father's past, the narrator tells us that he arrived on the *Empire Windrush* in 1948. She knows little else about his past.

> He never talked about his family or his life in Jamaica. He seemed to exist only in one plane of time—the present. There is an old photo of him—grainy black and white, that shows him dressed in an immaculate tailored suit with wide baggy trousers, wearing a shirt with a collar held by a pin, and a proper tie. His hair is short and well groomed. He is standing by a chair in the grounds of what looks to be a beautiful house. The photo looks like my dad as a "Great Gatsby"–type millionaire.
>
> (p. 3)

When Angela questions him, he is evasive or rebuffs her outright. She is left with different images of him that she shares with us and that she cannot reconcile. She is shocked to discover when she is twenty-five that her father has an identical twin brother—who has just died. He is a Caribbean immigrant who has severed his ties to his past and to his family. She also recounts her mother's experience as an immigrant who, though she is a qualified and experienced teacher of young children, is not able to work in her field unless she retrains, and is forced to take in sewing. The narrator describes her mother's struggle to obtain English credentials—she first retrains as a teacher, and then, while she works and raises her children, does an Open University degree. As it does for many people, immigration for Beryl Jacobs means moving down the professional ladder, although she is ultimately able to take advantage of the public education system to become "an educated woman" in English terms.

Like Angela, her brother and sisters are London born and bred, and in her portraits of them, the narrator evocatively conveys the ordinary dramas of sibling relationships, the feel of life in a British public housing estate, and the cadences of youth culture in 1960s London. Her brother John—a know-it-all and irrepressible tease—gets into trouble with their parents for telling her the facts of life. Her teenage sisters live in a different world, in their room crammed with perfumes, hairsprays, creams, jars of make-up, clothes and jewellery. These ordinary teenage girls listen to records of Aretha Franklin, Ray Charles, Dionne Warwick, and the Yardbirds. Angela and John play games with the other children in the "yard," the shared compound outside. Yvonne and Patricia go to pop music concerts in mini-skirts. The entire family watches television, jockeying for the programs they favor.

Even as Angela conveys the ordinary idiosyncrasies of her family, she also relates how as an immigrant family they are "different." Her sense of this difference is expressed in two ways. On one hand, she perceives the cultural norms and the style of her family as different from her peers'; on the other hand, she becomes aware that her peers perceive her and her family as different, and they sometimes express racist views. A striking and mildly comical instance of her own sense of her family's difference is found in chapter 5, "THE HOLIDAY." Even during the journey, her family stands out: unable to carry it easily, her father decides to transport an enormous blue suitcase to the coach station on his head, causing people to turn and point. At the holiday resort, their father prevents the family from drinking anything but Coke. Her parents won't dance, her brother and sisters join other teenagers, and Angela is left thinking, "S'not fair … They have all the fun" (p. 81). Left one day alone with her father, she persuades him to go to the beach, where he lies dressed in his gray suit, in a small patch of shade. He tells her, "You shouldn't sit in the sun too long. You want to turn red like those—English people. You shouldn't sit in the sun." Angela protests, saying, "Everybody else—" "Cha," her father insists before she can finish, "We're not like everybody else" (p. 84). His daughters find their father deeply embarrassing because he makes no effort to blend in. Nor does he compromise his view of romantic and sexual behavior. When a boy walks Angela home, they are met at the door by her irate father, who shouts at the boy to get away and not come back. Furious and upset, Angela rounds on him, "You don't know anything!"

The feeling that her family is different is reinforced in a far more negative way when Angela and her brother contend with the prejudices of their friends and neighbors in the yard. A mild form of this prejudice is evident when Angela asks her friend Sonia over. Served a meal of spiced stew and beans, Sonia insists that her mouth is burning and that she doesn't feel well. When Sonia's mother questions Angela about what they eat, and whether they fry bananas, Angela is evasive. This latent sense of the Jacobs' difference becomes much more vicious when the children have a fight in the course of a game. Suddenly, Angela and Johnny find their friends chanting racial epitheths and saying they should go back to the jungle. When her parents insist that they are from England and no different from other children, Angela blurts out that they are different—they are colored. A détente occurs two days later, but the episode underscores how quickly racist violence can erupt.

The narrator juxtaposes descriptions of her childhood with accounts of her father's illness and her joint attempts with her mother to get adequate care for him. He grows frailer and more listless, but her mother won't tell him that he has lung cancer, convinced that he will simply give up. Conferring with each other, mother and daughter consult doctors and navigate the National Health Service. As their father declines, and contends with pain and humiliation, they look desperately for an alternative to hospital care and try to move him to a hospice, but they are foiled by bureaucratic regulations. The narrator conveys the frustration and anguish of negotiating an often unresponsive National Health Service. When her father's death comes, it is something of a relief—for everyone.

While it is not clear whether the forces that foil them are institutional racism or simply the unresponsiveness of a large health care bureaucracy, Angela must assert herself, somewhat to the surprise of the doctors she meets, to get the care she wants for her father. Her laying claim to her Englishness becomes literally a matter of life and death.

NEVER FAR FROM NOWHERE

While Levy's second novel, *Never Far from Nowhere* (1996), is about different characters, and is set in the 1970s, it is in some ways a sequel to *Every Light in the House Burnin'*. The two narrators, Vivienne and Olive, are sisters, children of Caribbean immigrants who grow up in public housing in Finsbury Park, North London. The novel is structured as a series of alternating chapters narrated by each sister in turn, so that their voices and experiences are braided but distinct. Vivienne and Olive take very different paths to young adulthood. Vivienne, the younger sister, does well in school, goes to a sixth-form college, does A-levels, and goes to an art college. Olive, three years older, drops out of school, becomes involved with a politically progressive working-class man, becomes pregnant, gets married and has a child, and finds herself on the street after her husband leaves her and her mother fights with her. Vivienne, who is light-skinned, disavows her Caribbean roots. Olive is fiercely proud of her black identity and sneers at Vivienne for denying hers. The novel points to some of the very different kinds of identification and circumstances of black British people that Stuart Hall speaks of in "New Ethnicities."

The novel is, like *Every Light in the House Burnin'*, as much about growing up in a working-class urban milieu as it is about being black in Britain. Vivienne spends her time with her friend Carol at a local youth club, goes to the pub, is encouraged by her teachers to do A-levels, and goes to the sixth form. She becomes involved with a dreamy, kind boy named Eddie, a want-to-but-will-never-be musician who doesn't look beyond his working-class horizons. Against her mother's wishes, Vivienne enrolls in an art college and moves in with a wealthy white student. Olive meets Peter at a club and listens to him talk about workers' rights and the exploitation of black people; she begins to have sex with him and becomes pregnant. He moves into her mother's house, because they cannot afford their own place. Things begin to go sour between them as she is exhausted and isolated taking care of their little girl, and he becomes less and less caring. He cannot find better-paying work, and they feel trapped in her mother's flat. He eventually leaves Olive and moves in with another woman. Angry and bitter, Olive refuses to allow him to see their daughter. She struggles to get housing from the council and is eventually successful. Poignantly and vividly sketched, this is the unruly stuff of ordinary life.

Because the novel is about teenagers and adults, when racial identification and racism do enter the picture, their manifestations are much more powerful than in *Every Light in the House Burnin'*. Olive tells us that her mother tried to believe that she was not black, and repeatedly spoke ill of black people. The reader is made aware at the outset that attitudes about race are likely to scar the sisters in one way or another. Darker than her sister, Olive furiously insists at the end of the novel that Vivienne has had it easy, although she doesn't spell out fully the politics of race that might be at play. Vivienne is not immediately identified by other people as black because she is light-skinned. She must contend with the racism of her peers when, for example, a black teenage boy who speaks to her is beaten up. A brawl ensues, and she is told that the white boy who instigated the fight, her friend's boyfriend, "couldn't stand that coon talking to one of his women" (p. 94). Even though she reacts angrily to this revelation, she later denies her Jamaican ancestry, telling her boyfriend Eddie, for instance, that her parents are from Mauritius. The novel traces her coming to terms with being black and British. At the very end of the novel, Vivienne says to a fellow passenger, when she is asked where she is from, that her parents are from Jamaica but she is English.

Much more invidious than the tacit racism of their mother or the overt racism of Vivienne's friends is the institutional racism portrayed in the novel—here seen in the attitude of the police. At the brawl she unwittingly precipitates, Vivienne sees pure hatred in the eyes of a young policeman who evicts her from the pub. The police are clearly not friendly guardians, although the degree to which the policeman in this scene is racist is not clear. Much more extreme than Vivienne's experience is the virulent racism that Olive faces in an encounter with the police. She is driving a borrowed car when she is pulled over for driving without her lights on. In the exchange that follows, the policeman makes racist sexual gibes, and when she tells him to fuck off, he plants marijuana in her bag and then charges her with drug possession. Later, discovering she doesn't have the means to fight the charge, Olive pays the fine—and gets a criminal record.

Olive's difficulties do not arise simply from the racial prejudice that she faces, however. Levy presents a complex picture of her character and circumstances: her disaffection at school, her frustration at a dull job, her conflict with her mother, her deteriorating relationship with her husband, and her struggle to take care of her baby. She also suggests in her depiction of Peter that a certain kind of leftist politics does not seriously engage with feminism or antiracism. Although he is a champion of the working masses, Peter becomes so thoughtless of Olive as to kick her and tell her to "Shut that fucking baby up!" when Amy cries at night (p. 98). Olive's own lack of direction and confidence exacerbate her difficulties. At the end of the novel, Olive says that she wants to move with Amy to Jamaica, and she gives vent to her resentment at Vivienne's success. She attacks her sister for being spoiled, and for not having had to face the difficulties Olive has had. Vivienne retorts that it was Olive's life, and her choice. Her mother cautions her that life in Jamaica is hard, and she pleads with her to follow Vivienne's example and to get an education and a good job in Britain. The reader sees the logic of both of these attitudes to Olive's predicament but, having followed Levy's nuanced portrayals of the sisters' lives, knows the complexity of the forces and character traits that have taken them where they are.

Levy also introduces another vital aspect of immigrant life in Britain: the implications of upward mobility and attitudes about social class. When Vivienne enters the sixth form and when she goes to art college, she finds herself among students who are wealthy and privileged. When Eddie and Olive fraternize with Vivienne's classmates, the contrast between their working-class milieu and Vivienne's new friends' cultural and hard capital is striking. Eddie, when he meets her college friends, enjoys amplifying his cockney charm, but Vivienne is mortified by his lack of finesse and also mortified because he guilelessly calls her bluff: that she is from a middle-class family in Islington. When tensions between them come to a head, and he says to her, "I can't be all clever and arty. I'm me. So is that good enough for you or not?" she replies that it isn't, thinking, "The choice had become my old life or new" (p. 268). For Vivienne, it is ultimately the inclusions and exclusions that constitute social class that are significant, as much as those of race.

A TASTE OF LEMON

Andrea Levy's third novel, *Fruit of the Lemon* (1999), straddles Britain and Jamaica. The protagonist and first-person narrator Faith Jackson is in her early twenties and has, like the protagonists of the first two novels, grown up in North London, the child of parents from Jamaica. She has moved into a shared house and started a job in the costume department of the BBC. She foots her way carefully through the quagmire of tacit racism at work and is drawn to her very English public-school roommate Simon. She and Simon witness a National Front attack on a black bookshop owner; soon after that event, she realizes that Simon and another roommate are lovers, and that they turn the attack into a joke. Faith consequently spirals into a depression. Her parents in the meanwhile have been planning to return to live in Jamaica, now that she and her brother are adults. When they are contacted by Simon and find Faith unwell and listless in bed, they persuade her to travel to Jamaica, thinking it might help her. Her mother tells her, "Child, everyone should know where they come from" (p. 162).

The second half of the novel recounts Faith's sojourn in Jamaica and her growing acquaintance

with where she comes from: the place but, even more importantly, also her extended family and their history. When she arrives in Kingston, she is immediately beguiled by a young man who offers to find her bag and then disappears with her five dollars. She is consoled and advised by a matronly fellow passenger, who remarks upon her innocence. Clearly Faith is an outsider. As she meets her relatives—her aunt Coral; her cousin Vincent; his wife, Gloria; their son Jonathan; her cousin Constance—she comes to feel part of large diasporic family, one that has spread from Jamaica to England as well as to the United States. Her aunt Coral tells her stories about the family: about herself, her mother and aunt, her father, her grandparents and cousins; about their work, their marriages, their migrations, their everyday lives. Listening to these stories, and learning about her patrimony, becomes a means of healing herself. At the end of the novel, Faith claims this patrimony as the source of her strength:

> Let those bully boys walk behind me in the playground. Let them tell me, You're a darkie. Faith's a darkie. I am the granddaughter of Grace and William Campbell. I am the great-grandchild of Cecelia Hilton. I am descended from Katherine whose mother was a slave. I am the cousin of Afria. I am the niece of Coral Thompson and the daughter of Wade and Mildred Jackson. Let them say what they like. Because I am the bastard child of Empire and I will have my day.
>
> (p. 327)

SMALL ISLAND

Levy's fourth novel, *Small Island* (2004), was a breakthrough volume that won international acclaim and garnered for her the Commonwealth Writer's Prize, the Orange Prize for fiction, and the Whitbread Novel Prize. Set during the period of World War II and the years before and after the voyage of the *Empire Windrush*, the novel brings alive through different voices the period when immigrants from the Caribbean arrived in Britain and struggled to remake their lives. The novel is composed of the interwoven first-person narratives of four people: Queenie, a white, working-class English woman; Bernard, her white, middle-class husband; Gilbert, a black RAF officer from Jamaica who returns to England on the *Windrush*; and Gilbert's bride, Hortense, who follows him there from Kingston, hoping to find work as a teacher. The novel pivots around 1948: the year of Gilbert and Hortense's move to England, their entry as lodgers into Queenie's home, and the return of Bernard, who has disappeared after being posted to India. The different numbered chapters are titled with the names of the four different narrators, and marked "1948," "Before," and "After," depending on when they are set. This structure makes the year of the *Empire Windrush*'s arrival a pivotal moment, to which other events lead up, and from which they follow. *Small Island*, like her earlier novels, has a strong autobiographical vein: Levy named Gilbert and Hortense after her parents, whose trajectories of immigration the fictional characters follow. The novel moves back and forth across time and space, traversing Jamaica, England, and India and going into the characters' pasts. It shows the global linkages between people and places in the British Empire, here in the phase of its formal demise. It shows also how, as a consequence of historical turns and twists, Britain has become a multiracial and multicultural society. Even more so than Levy's earlier novels, *Small Island* explores the complexities of gender, class, race, and imperialism, showing the intersecting and overlapping pressures of each on British identity.

"I thought I'd visited Africa." So Queenie Buxton begins the prologue to *Small Island*, describing how as a child she visits the British Empire Exhibition of 1924 with her family. The prologue thus introduces the theme of Britain's imperial career and the racial imaginary that this has produced. At a display of an African village, she encounters an African man:

> A monkey man sweating a smell of moth balls. Blacker than when you smudge your face with a sooty cork. The droplets of sweat on his forehead glistened and shone like jewels. His lips were brown, not pink like they should be, and they bulged with air like bicycle tyres. His hair was woolly as a black shorn sheep. His nose, squashed flat, had two nostrils as big as train tunnels.
>
> (p. 5)

Queenie draws on many similes and metaphors as she stretches to describe someone she perceives as completely different. "Monkey," "jewels," "bicycle tyres," "train tunnels"—this is the language of a child drawing on the vocabulary of her immediate world, rather than, one might argue, the language of racism. When her companions tease her and urge her to kiss him, the man offers to shake hands, and Queenie does. In this gesture of amity across a vast gulf, a gulf marked by political violence, economic exploitation, and cultural degradation, the novel envisions the possibility of a personal rapprochement. In its subsequent pages, the novel traces not only the possibilities but also the difficulties of such a rapprochement.

If young Queenie, the daughter of a butcher and raised on a farm, is almost completely ignorant of the remote peoples and cultures of the British Empire, Hortense and Gilbert, raised in Jamaica, have been schooled in the culture of the mother country, and taught to think of it as a second home. The body of the novel begins in 1948 with Hortense's arrival in London. She follows Gilbert, who had traveled on the *Empire Windrush* six months before, after a marriage of convenience: she has provided the money for his passage, so that she might follow him to London. There she finds herself lodged in a single room with Gilbert in Queenie's shabby house. "All I saw were dark broken walls. A broken chair that rested one uneven leg on the Holy Bible. A window with a torn curtain ... Three steps would take me to one side of the room. Four steps would take me to the other" (p. 17). She repeatedly asks Gilbert, "Is this the way the English live?" If Queenie has no sense of Africa, Hortense is bewildered by how different a war-ravaged England is from the storybook England that she has been raised in Jamaica to revere.

As Hortense recounts her childhood and the events that lead up to her departure for England, we see the complex ideologies of race and empire as they are articulated in Jamaica—in middle-class households and in schools. Notions of white racial and English cultural superiority prevail. She describes her childhood as an illegitimate child, born to a dark-skinned girl from the country and taken in by the middle-class cousins of her prosperous and widely respected father. Hortense has a strong sense of her superiority as a light-skinned girl: "I grew to look as my father did. My complexion was as light as honey. I was not the bitter chocolate hue of Alberta and her mother. With such a countenance there was a chance for a golden life for I" (p. 32). Hortense uncritically accepts white supremacist thinking and expects to benefit from it. Hortense trains as and begins to work as a teacher, where her belief that all things English are superior is strengthened by the Anglocentric schooling she receives. She soon comes up against the barriers of race and class in pursuing her dream to teach in a Church of England school in Kingston: "[The headmaster's] conclusion … was that my breeding was not legitimate enough for him to consider me worthy of standing in their elegant classrooms before their high-class girls" (p. 71). Frustrated by the experience of working in the "scruffy" classrooms of a parish school in Jamaica, and with her head full of rosy pictures of England, Hortense betrays her friend Celia's secret, that her mother is mad, to Gilbert, Celia's fiancé— and takes her place, traveling to England in her stead. Once there, when she tries to get a job at a school, she is told that her Jamaican credentials and experience have no value in England. Hortense's beliefs not only about England's physical beauty but also about its cultural embrace of its colonies and its recognition of merit without racial prejudice against educated, well-spoken Caribbeans are shattered when she begins to look for work in England. She resolves to work as a seamstress until she is able to obtain the credentials she needs to teach—as did Andrea Levy's mother, also a teacher, when she arrived in England in 1948.

Gilbert too experiences firsthand the contradictions of imperial ideology and the barriers of racism when he comes to England. He too is perplexed when he is stationed in England after joining the RAF:

> But for me I had just one question—let me ask the Mother Country just this one simple question: how come England did not know me? … And here is Lady Havealot, living in her big house with her ancestors' pictures crowding the walls … Ask her to tell you about the people of Jamaica. Does she see that small boy standing tall in a classroom where sunlight draws lines across the room, speaking of England, of canals, of Parliament and the greatest laws ever passed? Or might she, with some authority, from a friend she knew or a book she'd read, tell you of savages, jungles and swinging through trees?
>
> (p. 118)

Gilbert points to the profound asymmetry of imperial perspectives. He is educated in Jamaica to view Britain as the center of the earth, and Jamaica as a dear child of the mother country, and is disconcerted and vexed to find that English people either know nothing of Jamaica or think of it as a remote and barbaric outpost. He is also disappointed in how he is treated in the RAF. He comes to England expecting to be trained as a wireless operator and air-gunner or flight engineer, but he is instead put to work as a driver. He soon encounters Jim Crow policies, with which he is familiar from a stint of training in Virginia, when he is asked to pick up parts from an American airbus. By contrast, the racism of Britons seems moderate.

It is in the course of his service that he meets Queenie Bligh, after he brings her shell-shocked father-in-law, Arthur, back to her. When they become friends and he goes to a movie theater with her and Arthur, and she sits next to him in a theater full of American GIs, violence explodes— and Arthur is shot by mistake. While this is Gilbert's most dramatic and tragic experience of racism, it is not the only one; Gilbert too has difficulty finding the work he should in Britain when he returns on the *Windrush*, and he is explicitly denied jobs because of his race. He finally finds employment as a driver for the postal service, his hopes of becoming a lawyer dampened.

Queenie is the one white character who seems relatively free of racist prejudice even as a child, as we have seen. She is also more free-thinking in her attitudes toward class and gender. She balks at the prospect of being a beaten-down daughter and wife on a farm, destined to serve the needs of men, and she escapes to the home and patronage of a middle-class aunt who owns a sweet shop in London. There she finds middle-class expectations oppressive as well: she has elocution and deportment lessons twice a week from Mrs. Waterfall. Her aunt encourages her, "Just do it love ... She'll see you married to a prince" (p. 206). The "prince" whom she enchants is Bernard Bligh, who is so reserved that she thinks, "But, crikey, he lived in Earls Court with his father, he was a clerk at Lloyds Bank, and he liked fresh air. Surely after four months there was more to know about him then that?" (p. 211). When her aunt suddenly dies of a stroke, she agrees to marry Bernard rather than return to her family's farm. She finds her self trapped in a home with a man she does not love, unable to become pregnant, when the war comes. In Queenie's story, Andrea Levy explores the oppressive social codes and stark options of both working-class and middle-class women. The war, when it begins, feels like a time of liberation for Queenie, rescuing her from her dull domestic incarceration. When Bernard leaves to fight in India, and then disappears, she takes in boarders regardless of their race, sex, class, or profession, much to the disapproval of her neighbors. Her lodgers include Gilbert and Hortense.

Bernard is the least likeable of the principle characters: we know from Queenie's narrative that he is priggish, dull, cowardly, racist, sexist, and a snob. Levy's skill in developing character is at its greatest in her treatment of Bernard. When we read his first-person account of his service in India, we are presented with his perspective: his foolishness, inhumanity, and spinelessness come through even as he recounts his service in the army and imprisonment for dereliction of duty (he has failed to remain guard at his post when a fire breaks out), his tryst with a young prostitute, and his return to England but inability to face Queenie. In her portrait of Bernard, Levy takes us inside his prejudices and the lack of independence and courage that make him act on these prejudices. In this, he is very different from Gilbert, Hortense, and Queenie, all strong and courageous characters who struggle against external forces. Bernard's story also takes us to the last years of British rule in India and the unrest that will soon bring it to an end. The narrative speaks both to the reach of the British Empire and resistance to it.

The ending of the novel brings both couples into a confrontation, and a forced rapprochement. The ending also confronts squarely questions of race, identity, gender, and the future of Britain. Queenie becomes pregnant after a serviceman, Michael, is billeted at her house and has a brief affair with her. The reader, but none of the characters, know that Michael is Hortense's cousin from Jamaica, whom she loved, and who has died in action after his affair with Queenie. Some months later, Bernard, whom Queenie believes dead, returns and finds Hortense and Gilbert living in their house. As tensions between him and the other characters increase, Queenie's baby is born. Queenie's baby embodies the possibility of thinking against and beyond race; it heralds the future of England. But in the England of the day, he will be marked as an outsider, and perhaps hated by Bernard, which is why Queenie pleads with Hortense and Gilbert and persuades them to take her baby and raise him as their child.

THE LONG SONG

Andrea Levy has said that she felt she could not do justice to Afro-Caribbean experience without tackling a theme that she had until then avoided: plantation slavery in Jamaica. She had been chary of it because slavery was "upsetting, miserable, not a pleasant subject" and she didn't want to write a "misery fest" (interview with Pamela Johnson). Her interest in tackling the subject grew after reading *Domestic Manners and Social Customs of the White, Coloured, and Negro Populations of the West Indies,* an 1834 account by a white Englishwoman, Mrs. Carmichael, an apologist for slavery. Levy found that between the lines, she was able to discern something of the lives of people who attempted to make the most of their circumstances and were not simply victims of plantation slavery. She set about creating characters who, despite their abject conditions of servitude, had genuine lives. The novel chronicles the life of July, a slave girl who lives on a sugar plantation called Amity during the last years of slavery; the Baptist rebellion of 1831;

the abolition of slavery in 1834; and the tumultuous years after. Levy explains, "I wanted to show the slaves living a life, show them doing their job … They are real people. Some of them are better dressed than others and they have their rivalries" (interview with Pam Johnson). Andrea Levy's greatest achievement in *The Long Song* is to paint with a varied palette a rich portrait of a community of slaves and their owners, vividly rendering their moments of anguish, extreme physical duress, rage, mirth, and joy—indeed the full panoply of human emotions.

The novel has a frame tale: the ostensible story of its creation. Thomas Kinsman, who appears as a character briefly late in the novel, tells us in the first person how his mother pestered him to listen to her account so that he would then be able to pass it on to his daughters, but he was so busy and preoccupied that he was unable to give her his full attention; he therefore convinced her to write her story down herself, with the assurance that he would use his skills as a professional printer to edit and publish it. According to this fiction of its origin, what was supposed to be an oral tale for the family becomes a written narrative that could be circulated in print. This introductory frame imparts to the story that follows the aura of historical authenticity and prospective public knowledge. It also casts the novel as a family story, one that its narrator intended be passed down through generations. Finally, the frame tale also serves to introduce the reader to the narrator of the tale: a strong-willed elderly woman who resides with her son in Jamaica, and whose own voice surfaces in her chronicle every now and then as she remarks on her son's family or speaks about the writing of the story. For the most part, though, she tells the story in the third person. As her story unfolds, we realize that the narrator is telling her own story, which is the story of Miss July. Through this framing of the story and fracturing of the narrative perspective between a first-person narrator talking about her writing (and her conscious manipulation) of the story and a third-person narrator telling the story in the third person of July, her younger self, and her milieu, Levy foregrounds the blurring of boundaries between fic-

tion, autobiography, and chronicle. The novel claims to be all of these. Andrea Levy responds to the challenge of writing about slavery by crosshatching the personal and the historical, the public and the private, and the imagined and real.

The use of different kinds of humor is key to Levy's efforts to give the slaves in her novel a full and complex humanity. In her opening paragraph, the narrator is direct and abrasive. She bluntly describes and at the same time makes light of the rape that leads to July's inception. Defending herself against her son's charge that her beginning is "too indelicate," she asserts, "Please pardon me, but your storyteller is a woman possessed of a forthright tongue and little ink" (p. 7). The narrator then mocks the codes of decorousness that govern writing about colonial Jamaica, seen in books that "find you meandering through the puff and twaddle of a white lady's mind" (p. 8). The narrator soon gives us the experience of just such a lady, Caroline Mortimer, the sister of John Howarth, the owner of Amity. She uses slapstick to represent the slaves that Caroline meets not as victims but as omnipresent, unruly, and uncooperative occupants of her new home. "And yet, for all these house slaves that swirled around her every day, Caroline found the summoning of any of them to do her bidding a toilsome task for which she had no skill. They just stared on her entranced, like children upon Bonfire Night before the pinwheel starts to spin" (p. 27). The slaves repeatedly play tricks on their owners, steal from them, and make fun of them. Describing their indirect modes of resistance in a tart tone, the narrator imparts a note of comedy to the slave's harsh lives on the plantation.

This is not to suggest that the narrator glosses over the brutal conditions in which the slaves work and live. The novel relates in detail the hard labor of both field and house slaves and the punishments and routine violence that are meted out to them. Andrea Levy visited a plantation in the Caribbean so that she would better grasp and be able to convey its layout and workings. She comments, "The vastness of it was amazing to me, just to see the relationship where the works were to the fields, where the great house was to the slave village, how the cane came through, where the river was, how it all worked" (Johnson interview). She describes Kitty, July's mother and other field slaves, cutting cane, transporting it to the sugar works, and transporting manure to the cane fields. She also describes the somewhat easier labor of house slaves such as July, who cook and clean, fetch and carry, and pander to their owners' whims. The absolute condition of this labor is force and unfreedom. The slaves are objectified in other ways: they are bought and sold, and separated from their kin; when Caroline encounters Kitty carrying baby July, and takes a fancy to her, John Howarth takes her away from Kitty and gives her to Caroline to keep. The slaves are also imprisoned and tortured; in the years when Caroline takes over the plantation after Howarth's death, she has a dungeon constructed for slaves that even she is appalled by when she finally visits it.

The violence that is the absolute condition of plantation slavery is most starkly depicted in the section of the novel about the Baptist rebellion of 1831. In this part, the narrator's tone loses some of its jocular humor, as she describes the grotesque scenes of violence on the island, but she renders as farce the puffed-up attitude of the planters as they torture and kill the rebel slaves and other women and children. The narrator also draws on the narrative codes of melodrama when she describes John Howarth's suicide, with July and a manumitted slave named Nimrod hiding under his bed, the hysterics of Caroline, and the overseer Tam Dewar's subsequent pursuit of Nimrod and July. In a sensational finale, Tam Dewar shoots Nimrod; Kitty saves her daughter, and with her bare hands mauls Tam Dewar to death; she is caught and hanged.

In addition to depicting the difficult conditions of their lives, Levy portrays the consciousness of the slaves at Amity as complex and contradictory. She portrays the slaves' extreme awareness of racial classifications: mulattos, quadroons, and so forth, and their implicit conformity to the logic of a racist identification even though it dehumanizes them. She sketches their rivalries and betrayals of each other. She also adroitly conveys the complexity of their

relationships with their owners. July is Caroline's slave and maid but also her companion and counselor—for instance, identifying some slaves who claim they are ill as fit to work. Nonetheless, she is tortured in the stocks by Caroline after the Baptist rebellion, as the narrator tells us: "Should I paint a scene so you may conceive of how often the sizzle of the sun's heat fried July's skin to blisters and scorched her mouth so dry that she did not have spittle nor breath to shoo away any creatures or beings that came to plague her within those long nights?" (p. 146). Her relationship to her owners becomes even more complex when Robert Goodwin arrives to oversee the plantation and falls in love with July. Goodwin marries Caroline and at the same time sets July up in a room below the house, where he visits her every afternoon; he eventually has a child with her. July is at once cherished lover, mother, slave, companion, friend, and rival in the triangular relationship that develops with Caroline and Robert.

The relatively stable life of planters and slaves turns upside down as the plantation system is transformed after the Abolition of Slavery Act comes into effect. Historically, the emancipation of slaves in Jamaica was followed by a period when they were required to work for their former owners for forty-one hours a week and were permitted to engage in trade or cultivate the land on which they lived for the remaining part of the week. Levy describes how, after he fails to persuade the freed slaves of Amity to cut the cane when Goodwin requires them to, his supposed liberalism crumbles. He turns to violence, razing their huts and plots with the help of his white neighbors, and killing their animals. Most of the slaves leave Amity and set up a small community beyond its boundary. This also marks a turning point in his relationship with July. When Caroline and July find him trying to harvest the cane himself, his reason snaps and he bears down on July with an ax, but he is stayed by his wife. He and Caroline soon return to England, stealing July's child and taking her with them.

The novel returns at the end to a question with which it began: the line between, fiction, biography, and history, and the power and responsibility of the storyteller. The narrator and her son tussle over how she is to conclude the story of her life. There are parts of each of their lives that neither wants to tell, raking refuge in fiction and silence. The narrator at first fashions a "happily-ever-after" middle age for July as a prosperous vendor of preserves, and then "our July did grow so rich and old and happy upon her wit, that she did purchase a little boarding house." The narrator is ridiculed by her son, who reminds her how he met her thin and destitute in a courtroom, charged with stealing a chicken. The narrator withdraws her happy fabrication but will not speak of the thirty-odd years of starvation and misery she spent in the impoverished settlement outside Amity. We then are given another story: that of Thomas Kinsman, born to July in the turbulent period of the Baptist rebellion and given up by her to an English preacher and his wife; their return to England; and his education, apprenticeship as with a printer, and his life there. Kinsman inherits the press from his appreciative employer. Then Kinsman's story too has a gap:

> For reasons that must be gleaned only from the pulsing vein upon his head as it throbs and wriggles, Thomas Kinsman does not care to summon that time … No protestation will have him continue his tale until he has departed from the shores of England. No pleading, nor complaint will start the story again before three silent years have passed and Thomas Kinsman is, once again, back upon the island of Jamaica.
>
> (p. 301)

The narrator and the characters assert their power to be silent about parts of their lives. His story continues with his success in Jamaica as a printer and his presence as a juror in the courtroom where Miss July is charged with stealing a chicken. He recalls an essay Jane Kinsman wrote long ago about July, a slave girl, who abandoned her son outside their home. And now the dots are joined together, and the story reaches its end: he invites the thief, Miss July, his mother, and the narrator of the novel, into his home.

CONCLUSION

In an essay titled "This Is My England," Andrea Levy unequivocally asserts her own Englishness:

"I am English. Born and bred, as the saying goes … England is the only society I truly know and sometimes understand. I don't look as the English did in the England of the 30s or before, but being English is my birthright. England is my home." With these words, Andrea Levy gives voice to generations of black people who have made England their home. Tracing the intertwined imperial histories that have led to postcolonial migration to the metropole, Andrea Levy explodes the mythology perpetuated in the skinhead chant "There ain't no black in the Union Jack." Her novels express in fictional form the sentiment behind the antiracist, proimmigrant slogan heard in the streets of Britain, "We are here because you were there." She charts the key experiences—slavery, colonialism, immigration, diasporic linkings—that have shaped black British people. Every one of her novels ends with a small or large gesture of reconciliation or of hope for the future, expressing the hopefulness of her vision. Like her characters, she asserts unequivocally, "This is my England."

Selected Bibliography

WORKS OF ANDREA LEVY
Every Light in the House Burnin'. London: Headline, 1994. (Novel.)

Never Far from Nowhere. London: Headline, 1996. (Novel.)

Fruit of the Lemon. London: Headline, 1999. (Novel.)

"This Is My England." *Guardian*, February 19, 2000. (Essay.)

Small Island. New York: Picador, 2004. (Novel.)

The Long Song. London: Headline, 2010. (Novel.)

BIOGRAPHICAL AND CRITICAL STUDIES
Allardice, Lisa. "The *Guardian* Profile: Andrea Levy." *Guardian*, January 21, 2005.

Johnson, Pam. Interview with Andrea Levy. *Words Unlimited* (http://wordsunlimited.typepad.com/words_unlimited/2010/09/andrea-levy.html), September 27, 2010.

Renzetti, Elizabeth. "Andrea Levy: She Couldn't Remain Silent on Slavery Any Longer." *Globe and Mail* (http://www.theglobeandmail.com/news/arts/andrea-levy-shecouldnt-remain-silent-on-slavery-any-longer/arti cle1540982/), April 20, 2010. (Interview.)

GENERAL BACKGROUND AND WORKS CITED

Bennett, Louise. "Colonisation in Reverse." In *Writing Black Britain, 1948–1998: An Interdisciplinary Anthology.* Edited by James Proctor. Manchester, U.K., and New York: Manchester University Press, 2000. P. 16.

Dawson, Ashley. *Mongrel Nation: Diasporic Culture and the Making of Postcolonial Britain.* Ann Arbor: Michigan University Press, 2007.

Donnell, Alison, ed. *Companion to Black British Culture.* London and New York: Routledge, 2002.

Fry, Peter. *Staying Power: The History of Black People in Britain.* London: Pluto Press, 1984.

Gilroy, Paul. *There Ain't No Black in the Union Jack.* Chicago: Chicago University Press, 1991.

————. *The Black Atlantic.* Cambridge, Mass.: Harvard University Press, 1993.

Hall, Stuart. "New Ethnicities." Reprinted in *Stuart Hall: Critical Dialogues in Cultural Studies.* Edited by David Morley and Kuan-Hsing Chen. London: Routledge, 1996. Pp. 441–449.

Stein, Mark. *Black British Literature: Novels of Transformation.* Columbus: Ohio State University Press, 2004.

Scarman, George Leslie. *The Scarman Report: The Brixton Disorders, 10–12 April 1981.* Harmondsworth, Middlesex, U.K.: Penguin, 1983. Quoted in Q&A, BBC (http://news.bbc.co.uk/2/hi/programmes/bbc_parliament/3631579.stm).

Wambu, Onyekachi. "Black British Literature Since Windrush." *BBC British History In-Depth* (http://www.bbc.co.uk/history/british/modern/literature_01.shtml), November 5, 2009.

WILLIAM McILVANNEY

(1936—)

Christopher Kydd

WILLIAM MCILVANNEY'S REMARKABLE oeuvre spans more than five decades and encompasses novels, short stories, poetry, and essays. It shoulders an artistic and political weightiness and yet remains subject to an enduring popular appeal in both Scotland and further afield. McIlvanney is a significant writer in two main respects.

First, his work fills something of a void in the development of Scottish literature in the twentieth century, not only in terms of simply the historical juncture at which it emerges but in aesthetic terms, as well. In both senses, McIlvanney's work bridges the gap between the two widely celebrated "renaissances" in Scottish literary activity in the twentieth century. From the early to the mid-twentieth century, the Scottish literary scene had been dominated by the Scottish literary renaissance, a movement headed by the controversial modernist poet Hugh MacDiarmid and characterized by linguistic experimentation, serious literary ambition, and the use of myth. While displaying faint echoes of this earlier movement, McIlvanney's work motions forward, too, influencing, anticipating, and indeed participating in the later Scottish cultural renaissance, a resurgence in Scottish fiction throughout the 1980s and 1990s that is best represented by the work of celebrated writers such as Alasdair Gray and James Kelman. Various other earlier literary traditions also provide suitable contexts in which to understand and appreciate McIlvanney's work, although they might not necessarily provide a direct influence on it. In terms of Scottish writing, these traditions would certainly include the anti–"Kailyard school" novels of the early twentieth century (*kailyard* being Scots for a cottage garden or cabbage patch)—novels such as George Douglas Brown's *The House with the Green Shutters* (1901) and John MacDougall Hay's *Gillespie* (1914), which brutally rejected the stereotypes of quaint, idealized Scottish life found in the short-winded popular vignettes being produced at the turn of the century by writers such as J. M. Barrie. Another body of Scottish writing that is likewise relevant to McIlvanney's work is the social realist, urban working-class novels of the 1930s and 1940s by writers including George Blake, James Barke, Lewis Grassic Gibbon, and Edward Gaitens. This is not to mention the impressive range of non-Scottish literary traditions alongside which McIlvanney's work should be understood. It is worth pointing out, of course, that he subverts and reworks these traditions as much as he draws upon them.

The other main and very much related reason that McIlvanney should be regarded as a major figure in twentieth-century Scottish literature is for his incisive, pioneering representation of working-class life and the challenges it faced throughout the twentieth century. McIlvanney has argued that working-class characters and communities are traditionally excluded or marginalized in classical literature. In his 1991 essay collection, *Surviving the Shipwreck,* he explains that it was his ambition for his novel *Docherty* (1975) to overturn this cultural imbalance:

> I wanted to write a book that would create a kind of literary genealogy for the people I came from, the people whose memorials were parish registers. Since their history was largely silence, I would be constructing a communal fabric of myth ... *Docherty* is essentially an attempt to democratise traditional culture, to give working-class life the vote in the literature of heroism.
>
> (pp. 223, 231)

Although it is especially well-realized in *Docherty*, this ambition is largely applicable to

McIlvanney's work in general. He recognizes that the bare details of the kind provided by parish registers (baptisms, marriages, and funerals) are not enough for adequately representing a large and important section of society. It might be said that McIlvanney earnestly pays his respects to his people by furnishing them with the kind of imaginative representation they deserve within a sphere from which they are traditionally excluded. His depiction, moreover, is not some misguided, idealized version of working-class life. Rather, McIlvanney's work provides a remarkably rigorous and insightful engagement with a variety of powerful ambivalences involved in the representation of working-class Scottish communities. As Keith Dixon points out, "McIlvanney's exploration of what he himself calls the 'heroism' of working-class communities taking the brunt of contemporary and past economic recessions … has shown that there is still room for a dynamic and subversive realism in the contemporary British novel" (p. 197).

This article opens with a biographical section about McIlvanney, followed by four further sections devoted to extensive study of his primary texts. In some ways, it seems a shame to divide up McIlvanney's work for the purposes for description and analysis, because it is fruitful to regard it as a single cohesive body of work. Nearly all of his novels and short stories use the same setting of a large industrial borough on the west coast of Scotland called Graithnock, a fictionalized version of McIlvanney's hometown of Kilmarnock. His fiction also tends to involve an ensemble of recurring, closely related characters. Beyond specific textual connections of this kind, moreover, there are many affinities of theme, style, and subject matter that stretch across all of his novels, short stories, essays, and poetry.

THE LIFE AND TIMES OF WILLIAM MCILVANNEY

William McIlvanney was born on November 25, 1936, in Kilmarnock, Ayrshire, to William Angus McIlvanney, a coal miner, and Helen Montgomery McIlvanney. He was born into a family with two brothers, Neil and Hugh, and one sister,

Betty. His elder brother, Hugh McIlvanney (born in 1933), is a celebrated sports journalist who has reported for an impressive number of national newspapers throughout his career and is often referred to as the "boxing bard of Scotland" because of his proficiency in writing about that particular sport. After passing his "eleven plus" qualifying examination, William McIlvanney went to the local senior secondary school, Kilmarnock Academy, where he had the opportunity to study Latin and Greek. The first of his family to enter further education, he went on to study English literature at the University of Glasgow in 1956. After graduating from university with an MA in 1959, McIlvanney trained as a teacher and taught English literature at secondary schools in Ayrshire between 1960 and 1975, during which time he had his first few literary works published. Since the success of his novel *Docherty* in 1975, he has been able to sustain himself as a full-time writer, slowly but consistently producing works of a very high standard ever since. During this time, he has also taught creative writing as a writer in residence at the University of Strathclyde and the University of Aberdeen, and he has written numerous newspaper pieces, the best of which are collected in his excellent and thought-provoking anthology of essays, *Surviving the Shipwreck* (1991). Most of his novels have won prestigious literary awards, including the Geoffrey Faber Memorial Prize for *Remedy Is None* (1966), the Whitbread Novel Award for *Docherty*, the Crime Writers' Association Silver Dagger Awards for the first two Laidlaw novels (in 1977 and 1983), and the Saltire Society Scottish Book of the Year Award for *The Kiln* (1996).

The details of McIlvanney's life provide more than mere perfunctory padding to a study of his literature. There are tantalizing autobiographical dimensions involved somewhere in all of his major works. The basic autobiographical details given above, moreover, provide a helpful snapshot of the wider historical, political, geographical, and cultural contexts that are relevant to his work. It is impossible not to recognize the relevance, for instance, of his origins in a heavily industrialized working-class area in the 1930s as the son of a coal miner. Following the Wall Street crash of 1929, the 1930s were a time of global economic depression and great hardship in general. In the United Kingdom, this hardship was felt especially in industrial working-class areas like the West of Scotland where McIlvanney grew up. Manufacturing areas throughout Scotland, Wales, and the north of England that were dependent on traditional heavy industries such as steel-making, ship-building, and coal-mining suffered the brunt of the recession. They were not shored up by government support, leading to mass unemployment. During his formative years, then, McIlvanney was a firsthand witness to intense conditions of economic hardship and social injustice. These early experiences seem to have played a key role in the development of the interventionist socialism that underpins his literary works, especially the novels he wrote in the late 1970s and the 1980s. For Scotland, these decades represented another period of economic hardship, which was made worse by the radical right-wing economic policies of Margaret Thatcher's Conservative government, which included the deregulation of the marketplace, monetarism, anti–Trade Union legislation, privatization, and the revoking of the more progressive tax system that had been in place. In *Modern Scotland: 1914–2000,* the historian Richard Finlay points out the ways that the political and socioeconomic conditions of Scotland in the 1980s closely mirrored those of the 1930s:

> In popular Scottish mythology, the eighties match the thirties as the Devil's decade. Living memory has designated this era as the "Thatcher Years," and the images of this period in Scotland are overwhelmingly dominated by dole queues, factory closures, political strife, and a bleakness which was captured in much of the literature of the time. The contrast with the popular perception of the eighties in much of the south—that it was a time of extravagance, self-indulgence and affluence—could not be greater. Long-term mass unemployment, poverty and an uncaring government were common to both the eighties and the inter-war era.
>
> (pp. 341–342)

McIlvanney was vocal in his opposition to the policies of the Thatcher government, which he argued were inimical to Scottish life. Addressing the Scottish National Party conference in 1987,

he said: "Under this government, it is not only the quality of our individual lives that is threatened. It is our communal sense of our own identity […] Margaret Thatcher is not just a perpetrator of bad policies. She is a cultural vandal" (collected in *Surviving the Shipwreck,* p. 246). In line with this argument, McIlvanney's literary works are underpinned by a celebration of the communal over the individual and the endorsement of a social system based on cooperation rather than competition.

Other biographical details about McIlvanney foreground the appropriate cultural contexts of his work. The representation of academia in his novels, for instance, reveals profound ambivalences about his experiences of university. His character Detective Inspector Jack Laidlaw, who dropped out of university after one year, tells a colleague, "University failed me […] I took acres of fertile ignorance up to that place. And they started to pour preconceptions all over it. Like forty tons of cement. No thanks" (p. 178). It is difficult not to imagine at least a slight autobiographical dimension to remarks like these. Even McIlvanney's more positive remarks about his university education attribute little sense of achievement or prestige to the experience: "What a degree has done for me is a very simple thing—it has meant that having gone there—gone through the process, entered the fortress of academe—I was not intimidated by it," he said in an interview in the 1990s. "If I had *not* gone there, I would have had a kind of inferiority complex, as a lot of working-class people do" (in Isobel Murray, ed., 1996, p. 134). Indeed, throughout McIlvanney's work, a clash emerges between academia, with its connotations of being middle-class, elitist, and divorced from the demands of the "real world," and working-class life, with its more populist, down-to-earth, and physical connotations. (This split is perhaps reconciled by the time of McIlvanney's campus novel, *Weekend,* which appeared in 2006.) McIlvanney's more personal experiences also emerge throughout his work. It seems likely that the sudden death of his father when he was still fairly young is an experience that he gives to his protagonist in *Remedy Is None.* McIlvanney's experiences as a teacher leave their mark on his novels, too, most obviously in *The Kiln* but also perhaps in the childhood scenes from *Docherty* and the depiction of Laidlaw's late brother Scott, who was a teacher, in *Strange Loyalties* (1991). The influence of McIlvanney's own brother Hugh can perhaps be detected in the extensive physical descriptions of the bare-knuckle boxing match that forms the centerpiece of *The Big Man* (1985). While it is important not to overplay the biographical dimensions involved, there are so many intriguing links between McIlvanney's life and his work that it seems prudent to acknowledge them and to recognize that they may contribute to the keen sense of verisimilitude for which the author is justly celebrated.

EARLY FICTION (1960S–1970S)

McIlvanney's first two novels tend to be dismissed or neglected in critical discussions of his work. Alan McGillivray's opinion of these novels is fairly representative of the critical field: "In reading *Remedy Is None* [1966], and its successor, *A Gift from Nessus* [1968], we must be struck by a sense that these are not the stuff of an enduring reputation" (p. 15). Most of the key aspects of style, themes, and concerns of McIlvanney's work, however, are firmly established in these novels, especially in *Remedy Is None*, which will therefore be covered more extensively here. The key critical debates of McIlvanney's work are likewise initiated in these novels. For these reasons and, crucially, because of the fact that they are well-written and compelling novels in their own right, it is important not to overlook these early works.

Remedy Is None follows the story of a sensitive intellectual working-class Glaswegian student named Charlie Grant as he comes to terms with his father's tragic death, a death he blames on his mother and her new husband. The antagonisms between working-class life and high literary culture play a key role in the novel. It teems with stylistic dexterity and classical literary allusion, applying this to a contemporary working-class context in which this kind of discourse would certainly not be expected and

indeed might not even be welcome. The title, for instance, refers to a line from the poem "The Lament for the Makaris" by the medieval Scottish poet William Dunbar, and the narrative closely mirrors that of *Hamlet*. *Remedy Is None* opens with Charlie daydreaming through an English lecture, in which the lecturer is dissecting *Romeo and Juliet* in a somewhat pretentious and contrived manner: "Of course, it is hoped that Juliet will marry Count Paris. But in reciprocating Romeo's love she helps to create the microcosm of sanity and love within the macrocosmic hate and senseless conflict of Verona" (p. 4). During the lecture, Charlie's working-class friends Jim and Andy (perhaps the down-to-earth equivalents of Rosencrantz and Guildenstern in the novel's *Hamlet* schema) alleviate the monotony by engaging in spontaneous lowbrow banter. This contrasts well with the lecturer's strained intellectual jokes, which typically result in "dutiful laughter" (p. 3). This dynamic between different social classes is continued throughout the novel, exemplified by the difference between Charlie's warm recollections of a genuinely hilarious family anecdote about his uncle Hughie trying to crack an egg lengthwise against a scene in which Charlie's materialistic mother and her new husband host a bourgeois dinner party in which middle-class couples show off their vacation slides. In contrast to the qualities of spontaneity, informality, and human warmth central to the anecdote about uncle Hughie, the partygoers strive to demonstrate a sophisticated sense of humor by telling long-winded jokes and throwing divisive put-downs at one another, at best resulting in a "sprinkling of forced laughter" (p. 62). The implication of this relation between different social classes is a returning theme in McIlvanney's work generally and is especially well-executed in *Docherty*.

Charlie is also finding it difficult to pay attention to the lecture because he is worrying that his girlfriend, Mary, might be pregnant, giving rise to further worries about how they will be able to afford to raise a child: "Stuff Romeo, Charlie thought. He thought he had problems. He didn't know the half of it" (p. 6). Through the specific ways that it clashes working-class life against traditional literary allusion, the novel highlights and works against the ingrained bias in canonical literature to center on the dramatic emotional upheavals of characters in positions of privilege and wealth at the expense of engaging with the important everyday problems faced by less privileged characters who better represent the majority of the population. The university setting of the opening scene gives further resonance to this reading. As McIlvanney points out, "When I arrived at university as a first generation university student, I became progressively dismayed at how much 'literature' seemed neither for nor about most of the people I knew outside" (*Surviving the Shipwreck,* p. 185). In *Remedy Is None*, then, the disruption that sets the narrative in motion is not an interruption to an otherwise contented and satisfactory lifestyle, as is often the case in literary works, but an interruption to an already emotionally troubled and economically demanding way of life. The narrative disruption comes after the lecture, in the form of a sparsely worded telegram that Charlie receives: "FATHER DYING. COME HOME AT ONCE. JOHN" (p. 10). This message is a modified version of the telegram that Stephen Dedalus receives about his mother in James Joyce's *Ulysses* (1922). This allusion gestures toward a precedent of high literary discourse and classical mythology being applied to the everyday lives of ordinary people. Later passages in the novel even make use of a vaguely Joycean interior monologue technique, such as in a scene in which Charlie drunkenly has sex with a stranger at a party: "A cabal of giggles. Love in a forest of coats. Teeth parting to admit a tongue. Breasts tauten in their harness. Belly shivers. A handful of silk skin. A mouthful of cold crombie" (p. 158). The accumulation of such fragmentary and grammatically unsound sentences, which clash discrete images and sensations against one another, creates a striking impressionistic effect. Such passages defy standard characterizations of McIlvanney's work as traditional or realist, a critical commonplace illustrated well by Beth Dickson's discussion of "his typical narrative style, a relaxed naturalism" (p. 56). Admittedly, however, stylistic experimentation of this kind becomes far less pronounced in McIlvanney's later novels, emerging in more nuanced forms.

For the most part, *Remedy Is None* can be read as a kind of elegy, a prose equivalent of elegiac poems by McIlvanney's Northern Irish contemporary Seamus Heaney. Like several of Heaney's elegies, such as "Mid-Term Break" (1966), McIlvanney's novel presents the aftermath of a death with an inventive originality, encouraging the reader to think about and experience death and mourning in unfamiliar ways. The description of Charlie's father's funeral is a particularly compelling instance of the novel's thoughtful, incisive, and sometimes painful considerations of death:

> There was a vagueness about the whole thing, as if it didn't relate to anyone personally, but was merely a dismissal of anonymous remains. The minister's inaccurate and generalized eulogy typified it. This was a service dedicated to some uncertain and idealized image of a man that bore no resemblance to Charlie's father [...] Did they know what he had been and what he had been made into before he filled a box? Were they prepared simply to accept it as the way things were? Their faces showed nothing. They stood in their dark clothes like sentries barring the way to honesty, guardians of indifference and pretence.
>
> (pp. 37–38)

As a ceremony intended to mark the end of a person's life, it might be expected that a funeral would act as a forum either for a cathartic outpouring of grief at the loss of that person or for a nostalgic recollection of memories related to them. In the funeral scene from *Remedy Is None*, however, such expectations are not fulfilled. Instead, Charlie finds himself confronted with an overwhelming sense of injustice and a violent inarticulate rage about the circumstances of his father's death. His interpretation of his father's funeral is perhaps more of a symptom of these volatile feelings than a cause of them. The above passage is also a fitting illustration of McIlvanney's characteristic prose style. Charlie's inner world of thoughts and feelings is subtly conveyed through free indirect discourse, which is never used in an intimidating or pretentious way. Despite the use of heightened language and imagery, contributing to an eloquent "literary" style in general, there is also a raw and simple sincerity about the writing. The blunt image of his father's body becoming merely the filling for a box, for instance, overturns the traditional funereal language of spirituality, emphasizing the corporeal and emptying out any ceremonial connotations of the word "coffin" by describing it as a box.

Overall, then, *Remedy Is None* is a fascinating account of a young man's struggle to come to terms with his father's death in the face of what he sees as the increasing indifference of the world around him, which is reflected in his encounters with bourgeois materialism, academia, religion, and bureaucracy. The novel does not shy away from representing Charlie's more problematic responses to his crisis, condemning them where appropriate, but always in the spirit of respect and understanding. Charlie's need to see his father properly honored can perhaps be read in parallel to McIlvanney's overarching ambition to give Scottish working-class life the imaginative representation that it deserves.

In terms of content and style, *A Gift from Nessus* (1968) seems a natural successor to *Remedy Is None*. It follows the changing fortunes of Eddie Cameron, a disheveled sales representative for an electrical goods company, as he fiddles his accounts to scrape out a living and embarks on an ill-fated extramarital affair with a schoolteacher. Like McIlvanney's first novel, *A Gift from Nessus* is about a character reaching an existential crisis point. Faced with a loveless marriage and a spiritually unrewarding job, Cameron spends the novel confronting unbearable decisions about whether or not to end his affair and whether or not to change his career to something that would be more satisfying but that would be unable to fulfill his wife's aspirations toward a middle-class suburban lifestyle. Like *Remedy Is None*, *A Gift from Nessus* is also a novel that transposes the main components of classical tragedy to a contemporary setting. Indeed, Arthur Miller's play *Death of a Salesman* (1949) might be taken as a kind of literary predecessor for *A Gift from Nessus*. In *The Scottish Novel* (1978), Francis Russell Hart is particularly complimentary about *A Gift from Nessus*, comparing it

favorably to the work of esteemed Scottish novelists such as James Kennaway and Robin Jenkins and arguing that it easily surpassed *Remedy Is None*. While the writing is indeed more considered in the second novel, however, there is also an important sense of continuity and similarity between the novels. *A Gift from Nessus* maintains the warmth, the spontaneous wit, and understated qualities of suspense of its predecessor, once again embedding these engaging and populist tropes in a serious novel that strives to articulate aspects of working-class life in the West of Scotland in an even-handed way.

These qualities continue in McIlvanney's third novel, *Docherty,* in 1975. As the length of time between the novels perhaps indicates, however, this work heralds a change in direction for the novelist. *Docherty* is a dense, multilayered, and ambitious novel. It is also McIlvanney's first and only fully fledged historical novel. It charts the changing circumstances of several generations of the Docherty family starting in 1903 and taking place over about a quarter of a century, as their community comes to terms with aspects of modernity that threaten their way of life, such as deindustrialization, capitalism, international conflict, bourgeois individualism, and the rise of global political ideologies. The novel initially focuses on the Docherty family's pater familias, a coal miner named Tam Docherty, and then the story follows Tam's youngest son, Conn. Tam is a striking character. He is a key figure in both his family and his community: "Tam was very much liked and they would have liked him more if they had known what more in him there was to like. But he was largely in shadow. Forbidding and indistinct attitudes relating to the Church and working-class life and conditions of labour obscured the clear contours of his nature, like clouds of vaguely thunderous potential" (p. 34).

Tam is a heroic and dignified character who is caught in extremely demanding circumstances, but he can also be violent, uncommunicative, unpredictable, and self-destructive. He provides McIlvanney's most nuanced and convincing engagement with the stock character type of "the Scottish hard man," a figure who might be seen as a Scottish equivalent of such American archetypes as the frontier hero or the hard-boiled investigator. Critics have often seen Tam's violence and his unreconstructed masculinity as deeply problematic, especially in light of his being presented as a kind of hero. In the most incisive critical interpretation of the novel, however, K. M. Newton argues that such interpretations of the violence and masculinity are based on contemporary middle-class assumptions that have no place in Tam's prewar working-class community:

> In *Docherty* fighting is not represented as a mindless giving way to destructive impulses. From a conventional middle-class perspective such violence and fighting can only be condemned as a form of atavistic behaviour, but the novel sees it as being inseparable from an ethic of honor that one associates with traditional or pre-capitalist societies and which one finds embodied in Norse sagas, Arthurian legends, and traditional westerns of the John Ford type. In this working-class society to be a "man" is very important.
>
> (p. 106)

Tam represents a construction of a traditional Scottish masculinity in crisis that might become increasingly irrelevant over the span of the novel and certainly by the time of the novel's publication, but he is entirely appropriate to his time and place. Indeed, he should even be considered an admirable character when he is understood in light of the shared values and assumptions of his society.

The latter part of *Docherty* is concerned with the development of Tam's youngest son, Conn, who is intelligent enough to attend the local senior school and to gain qualifications that would offer him an alternative to becoming a coal miner like his father. As several critics have pointed out, D. H. Lawrence's novel *Sons and Lovers* (1913) is an obvious point of comparison in this regard. Instead of striving to escape the apparent horrors of working-class life and a career in the pit, as Lawrence's protagonist does, however, Conn is deeply ambivalent about taking such a route, seeing it as a betrayal of his family and an abandonment of all the shared values and assumptions that his community have instilled in him:

He knew his father's contempt for the way they had to live and his reverence for education. But against that went Conn's sense of the irrelevance of school, its denial of the worth of his father and his family, the falsity of its judgements, the rarified atmosphere of its terminology. It was quite a wordless feeling, but all the stronger for that.

(p. 112)

This tension within Conn is similar to the tension experienced by another character in a classic Scottish novel, Chris Guthrie, in Lewis Grassic Gibbon's *Sunset Song* (1932), when she considers the "two Chrisses" within her: the Scottish Chris of the land and hard work and the English Chris of manners, education, and culture. In *Docherty*, the tension is best explored in terms of language. Conn is drawn to Scots, associated with working-class life, over Standard English, associated with middle-class life. When Conn uses the mode of speech most natural to him to tell a teacher, "Ah fell an' bumped ma heid in the sheuch, sur," the teacher ironically replies, "That, Docherty, is impertinence. You will translate, please, into the mother-tongue" (p. 109). McIlvanney's inventive use of linguistic conflict as a means of negotiating complex situations involving social class, constructions of identity, and underlying structures of power was first introduced in *Remedy Is None*. In one scene, Charlie's lawyer tells him: "I would prefer you to speak in English. You've been to university. Presumably, you're reasonably articulate. I see no need for this ... linguistic affectation ... juries are recruited primarily from the middle classes. And they tend to judge people by the way they speak" (p. 218). After being castigated by his teacher, the young Conn writes down a list of Scots words and their Standard English translations down the other side, including *sheuch* ("gutter"), *brace* ("mantelpiece"), *gomeril* ("foolish man"), *wabbit* ("tired"), *tumshie* ("turnip"), and *breeks* ("troosers") (pp. 112–113). This last example is revealing because even Conn's "translation" remains in Scots, rather than the Standard English "trousers," indicating how natural and spontaneous the language is to him. The chapter ends with his class-based tension resolving itself linguistically: "Conn despaired of English. Suddenly, with the desperation of a man trying to amputate his own infected arm, he savagely scored out all the English equivalents" (p. 113). A similar tension perhaps exists in McIlvanney himself, who writes his dialogue in Scots but tends to use a Standard English narrative voice, unlike later writers such as James Kelman or Irvine Welsh, who write entirely in Scots. McIlvanney explains his reasoning behind this decision:

> I spoke Scots until I was five, and I went to primary school, and I was taught English—what I resent is that I was taught English to the *suppression* of Scots … I just think that you have to confront what is truly happening and inhabit that, rather than conceptually trying to force things back to a time which has gone.
> (quoted in Isobel Murray, ed., p. 137)

It was exactly this kind of move into the perspective of the present moment that McIlvanney took after *Docherty*, though in a thematic rather than a linguistic way. In contrast to this very dense and challenging historical novel, his subsequent work surprised critics and readers. It was an urban crime thriller titled *Laidlaw* (1977) that astutely dissected contemporary Glasgow in a very bold and immediate way.

THE LAIDLAW NOVELS

Laidlaw was one of the first Scottish novels to use the crime genre seriously and certainly the first crime novel to treat Scotland as more than a superficial backdrop. In *Laidlaw*, and its sequels *The Papers of Tony Veitch* (1983) and *Strange Loyalties* (1991), McIlvanney uses the mood and the conventions of the American hard-boiled mode to engage with Scottish culture meaningfully, recognizing the potential for a fusion between this very urban, masculine, and vernacular form of crime fiction and recent Scottish literary traditions. McIlvanney's sophisticated contribution to the crime genre has left a lasting legacy in Scotland, as this kind of literary fusion can still be seen today in the work of internationally best-selling Scottish crime writers such as Ian Rankin, Val McDermid, and Christopher Brookmyre.

Laidlaw introduces one of McIlvanney's most remarkable and genuinely heroic characters, a working-class Glaswegian police officer named Detective Inspector Jack Laidlaw. Like all the famous American hard-boiled investigators from Sam Spade to Dirty Harry, Laidlaw is tough, uncompromising, streetwise, laconic, and wittily sarcastic. He is, however, different from the generic archetype in several ways. He is a depressive intellectual who takes a philosophical approach to his job, deeply questioning every aspect of the process, including the ideological basis of how and why crime is investigated and punished. "One of the things I'm in this job to do is learn," he says in *The Papers of Tony Veitch*. "Not just how to catch criminals but who they really are, and maybe why. I'm not some guard-dog. Trained to answer whistles. Chase whoever I'm sent after. I'm not just suspicious of the people I'm chasing. I'm suspicious of the people I'm chasing them *for*" (p. 68).

In distinction to many traditional fictional detectives, he sees police work as more than just protecting bourgeois property values and containing a deviant criminal minority. With such an attitude to his job, he naturally causes friction and makes enemies within the police force. Unlike many of the hackneyed maverick cops that dominate the twentieth-century police procedural, however, Laidlaw privileges humanity and compassion over getting results: "The essence of his nature was the desire to be kind. His anger came from the bafflement of that desire, because he hated to think that his kindness might be abused" (*Papers of Tony Veitch*, p. 214). Whereas the rugged individualist investigators of the hard-boiled mode can usually be expected to confidently impose their own brand of justice upon criminals and corrupt city-dwellers, Laidlaw is as likely to upbraid his colleagues for not treating the criminals with the respect and understanding they deserve. He must settle for trying to live with his crippling doubts about his profession as healthily as he can. Of all of McIlvanney's characters, Laidlaw is perhaps the one who has the most to say about negotiating the myriad problems facing contemporary society.

In the first of the three Laidlaw novels, the protagonist is called upon to investigate the rape and murder of a young Glaswegian girl named

Jennifer Lawson by a young, mentally disturbed, closet homosexual named Tommy Bryson. The novel takes the traditional "whodunit" formula apart by revealing the murderer from the very first page, before it has even introduced the detective. The opening of the novel is stylistically striking because it uses an unusual second-person narrative voice to represent the thoughts and feelings of the murderer as he flees from the scene in a state of utter panic and mental disintegration: "Running was a strange thing. The sound was your feet slapping the pavement. The lights of passing cars batted your eyeballs. Your arms came up unevenly in front of you, reaching from nowhere, separate from you and from each other" (p. 5). This fairly simple but nonetheless fascinating device immediately creates a sense of empathy with the character, preventing him from becoming a dehumanized criminal other, as killers tend to be presented in popular crime fiction. In accordance with the novel's representation of Tommy, Laidlaw insists on reminding himself and his colleagues of the criminal's humanity throughout the investigation, no matter what he has done:

> Other people can afford to write "monster" across this and consign it to limbo. I suppose society can't afford to do anything else, or it wouldn't work. They've got to pretend that things like this aren't really done by people … This murder is a very human message. But it's in code. We have to try and crack the code. But what we're looking for is a part of us.
>
> (p. 72)

This notion that the murder is "part of us" plays into the image, common in American hard-boiled crime fiction, that every member of an unjust society is, in some sense, complicit in its crimes. In the hard-boiled mode, this vision of societal injustice is typically explored in terms of the uneven distribution of wealth across the city, exemplified by Philip Marlowe's investigations involving both the idle, indifferent rich and the disaffected, exploited poor in Raymond Chandler's novels. It is given its best expression in *Laidlaw*, however, in the novel's representation of the widespread homophobia in the hyper-masculine world of working-class Scotland.

Throughout the novel, homophobic attitudes of varying degrees are encountered in nearly every aspect of the investigation, permeating the victim's community, the Glaswegian criminals that become involved, and even the police force. It is suggested that Tommy had been driven to a point of complete psychological breakdown, and eventually been pushed to his horrific criminal act, because of the ingrained homophobic assumptions and prejudices of his society: "Finding himself becoming one thing, [Tommy] had rushed to prove himself another. Harry thought he understood the pressures that had made him make the attempt. They were a kind of absolution, as far as he was concerned. A lot of people had been present at that murder. Why should one person answer for it?" (p. 113). The Laidlaw novels repeatedly give voice to challenging ideas of this kind, making them a radical force within the traditionally conservative detective genre.

Having well established the character of Laidlaw and already subtly subverted the crime novel formula in *Laidlaw*, McIlvanney goes on in *The Papers of Tony Veitch* to use the same setup but widens the net even further in its development of the genre. The second Laidlaw novel stretches the expectations of crime fiction, both in terms of its intertwining of multiple complex narratives and in terms of the social, political, and psychological insight of its investigations into crime, class, gender, ideology, and power. *The Papers of Tony Veitch* opens with Laidlaw being requested to visit the deathbed of a homeless alcoholic named Wee Eck, whose final words indicate that he has been poisoned. Laidlaw's colleagues are largely indifferent and keen to declare it an accidental death. Laidlaw accuses them of letting Eck's lowly position in society inhibit their responsibility to him:

> "So Wee Eck. If the law works for them, it should work for him. If he'd died in a penthouse, let's hear you say the same. You know the life he had. Its patron saint was Torquemada. So the least he deserves is that we should care about his death enough to understand it"
>
> "When did you join the vigilantes, Jack?"

"Never. I'm not witch-hunting whoever did it. I just think some understanding is owed. The only healthy climate is the truth."

Harkness said, "So how do we get there, great white hunter?"

Laidlaw laughed.

(pp. 68–69)

The novel contains many such lines about responsibility in the face of indifference, echoing Charlie's sentiments about his father's death in *Remedy Is None*. Here, Laidlaw makes a clear distinction between himself and the hard-hitting renegade cops of derivative crime fiction when he argues that he is not advocating vigilantism but merely trying to bring compassion and understanding to the job. McIlvanney's work in general, however, avoids any sense of pomposity and self-indulgence in its expression of such high-minded sentiments. Here, the image of the great mythical, self-righteous quest of the detective is gently lampooned by Harkness's jibe and Laidlaw's appreciation of it. This line goes hand in hand with McIlvanney's celebration of working-class Glasgow as an unpretentious place where there is "no problem finding someone to deflate you" (p. 145).

The third and final Laidlaw novel, *Strange Loyalties*, is the most intelligent and most satisfying of the three. It is a departure from the first two novels and even further removed from the conventions of the crime genre. The most conspicuous distinction between it and its predecessors is the move from the third-person narrative voice to a first-person voice. In *Strange Loyalties*, the reader is given direct access to Laidlaw's thoughts and feelings. It is a striking narrative voice, often reminiscent of the witty and baroque hard-boiled narration of Chandler's Marlowe novels but also faintly echoic of Joycean interior monologue: "I didn't want this day. Who sent for it? Try the next house. I burrowed into the pillow. It was no use. A sleepless pillow. What was it they called that? Transferred epithet? My teachers. They taught me everything I don't need to know" (p. 3). Partly because of this kind of narrative voice, the mood is more intense and claustrophobic than the first two Laidlaw novels,

since the reader is trapped inside the consciousness of a rundown, guilt-ridden, and obsessive character.

The narrative also contributes to this mood. The novel follows Laidlaw, on leave from police work, as he carries out an unofficial investigation into the accidental death of his brother Scott, who has drunkenly walked out into the road in front of a car: "Nobody had said 'crime.' But that dying seemed to me as unjust, as indicative of meaninglessness as any I had known. And I had known many. For he had been so rich in potential, so much alive, so undeserving—aren't we all?—of a meaningless death" (p. 7). *Strange Loyalties* carries echoes of *Remedy Is None* in terms of its innovative and unfamiliar treatment of death. The inventiveness of this treatment partly arises from the novel's representation of very personal and painful mourning within a genre that routinely deals with corpses that serve little more purpose than to initiate a puzzle. The novel uses the investigative structure of the crime novel, involving interviews, interrogations, and the interpretation of evidence, but Laidlaw's very human and personal investigation is far more existential than one would expect of the genre: "But where did the accident begin? That's what I want to know. In the middle of the road? At the kerb? In the pub before he went out? In the fact that he drank too much? In the reasons why he drank too much?" (p. 18). Through the investigation, Laidlaw encounters a large cast of characters and uncovers ingrained injustice and indifference on an overwhelming scale, discovering nasty skeletons in the plushest of cupboards. The intricacies of the meandering episodic plot cannot be adequately conveyed in a study of this kind. One remarkable passage in the novel, however, stands out as being especially worthy of critical attention. This passage is Laidlaw's description of one of his brother's paintings:

It was a big canvas dominated by a kitchen window. In the foreground on the draining board there were dishes, pans, cooking utensils. Through the window was a fantastic cityscape of bleak places and deprived people and cranes and furnaces ... I remember a man's face seeming liquid in the glow of his own blowtorch, as if he were melting down himself. The whole thing was rendered in great naturalistic detail, down to recognisably working-class faces below the bonnets, but the total effect was a nightmare vision. On the left of the kitchen window, like an inappropriate inset scale on some mad map, was a small, square picture. It was painted in sugary colours in vivid contrast to the scene outside. It showed an idealised highland glen with heather and a cottage pluming smoke from the chimney and a shepherd and his dog heading towards it. Scott had called his painting "Scotland."

(p. 26)

Scott's painting provides a neat encapsulation of McIlvanney's overarching project to give contemporary working-class Scotland an honest, imaginative representation. The clash between the inauthentic, sentimental, "sugary" painting within the painting and the harsh realities of the "nightmare vision" outside the window is an especially appropriate image for the Laidlaw novels. Both Scottish fiction and British detective fiction have, to some extent, been dominated by disingenuous images of an idyllic rural life devoid of any real social problems, an imbalance that the Laidlaw novels powerfully redress.

LATER FICTION (1980S AND AFTER)

The tropes, themes, and concerns of McIlvanney's early novels are still discernible in the noncrime fiction that he has produced since the 1980s, but *The Big Man* (1985), *Walking Wounded* (1989), *The Kiln* (1996), and *Weekend* (2006) demonstrate a great deal more diversity in form, narrative, and subject matter than the other groupings of texts used in this article. It is around this point in McIlvanney's career that his focus on the class struggles of men gradually gives way, though is by no means abandoned, to more rounded novels that accommodate a wider variety of perspectives.

The Big Man can be seen as a kind of meeting point between the various groupings of McIlvanney's work. Coming in the midst of his Laidlaw novels, it continues to show the influence of the American hard-boiled tradition while maintaining the working-class masculine emphasis of his earlier novels and engaging with wider existential concerns. The novel follows the story of an unemployed man named Dan Scoular as he

is drawn into the dangerous world of illegal bare-knuckle boxing in order to provide for his family. Although the hard-boiled tradition is usually associated with private investigators, many hard-boiled narratives also concern ordinary people reluctantly drawn into criminal activity because of harsh economic circumstances. There are clear echoes of Ernest Hemingway's proto-hard-boiled short story "The Killers" (1927), though in terms of narrative rather than prose style. The novel opens with an extensive description of Dan's fictional community of Thornbank, a small town near McIlvanney's usual setting of Graithnock. After describing various admirable members of Thornbank, the omniscient narrator describes how Dan has somehow acquired a faintly mythic status within his community solely because of his physical prowess: "His place in the local pantheon was more mysterious. He was young for such elevation, thirty-three. His most frequently commented on talent was simple one. He could knock people unconscious very quickly, frequently with just one punch" (p. 14). The use of the word "pantheon" in this context is interesting. It is a rather grandiose term typically used to refer to the great heroes of mythology and literature but here it refers to a working-class man from small-town Scotland whose "talent" is violence. In some ways, then, Dan's inclusion in a "pantheon" is in keeping with McIlvanney's earlier novels in their project to democratize literature. In this case, the question of heroism is made relevant to the ordinary people who make up the majority of the population. In the context of the contemporary setting of *The Big Man*, during the period in which Margaret Thatcher's Conservative government was in power, however, McIlvanney's use of the word "pantheon" seems partly sardonic.

Indeed, the relation between violence and an ethic of honor—which, as K. M. Newton points out, is a crucial consideration for *Docherty*—can be seen to have become far more compromised during the period in which *The Big Man* is set. Dan's working-class society is the offspring of Tam Docherty's community, but its communal sense of identity and purpose has been gradually corrupted by aspects of bourgeois individualism and capitalist enterprise, which came to the fore in the 1980s. As such, the nature of the violence in *The Big Man* is far more troubling and complicated than in *Docherty*. Dan learns that the brutal boxing match in which he is taking part is being organized by two warring factions of Glasgow's criminal underworld to settle a score between them. Cutty Dawson, a former boxing champion who has likewise fallen on hard times, has been chosen as his opponent. As the two men beat each other senseless with their bare fists for the entertainment of wealthy career criminals, the narrator articulates Dan's anxieties about the wider implications what they are doing: "Dan seemed to himself to be fighting all those working-class hardmen who had formed the pantheon of his youth, men who in thinking they defied the injustice of their lives had been acquiescing in it because they compounded the injustice by unloading their weakness on to someone else" (p. 207). The use of the word "pantheon" in this context is more overtly ironic than the earlier usage, suggesting a debasement of heroism and folk culture in the contemporary political climate and revealing Dan's sense of complicity in the entrenched societal injustice.

A film adaptation of *The Big Man* was made in 1990 (it was reedited and released in the United States under the title *Crossing the Line*), starring Liam Neeson as Dan and the Scottish comedian Billy Connolly as his fitness trainer Fast Frankie White. Although the film is entertaining in its own right, the project falls short of its source material because it does not find a satisfying cinematic means of articulating the dense introspection of the novel, naturally concentrating instead on the more physical aspects. Some of the novel's depth nevertheless finds oblique expression in Ennio Morricone's excellent film score.

McIlvanney's subsequent prose work, *Walking Wounded* (1989), a collection of short stories all set in Graithnock, naturally follows on from *The Big Man* in terms of its depiction of impoverished and disaffected characters confronted with a seemingly relentless recession. The text features twenty distinct short stories, which can be understood and appreciated in their own right, but there are symbolic and thematic links that run through the collection, contributing to a dynamic sense of place. Consequently, *Walking Wounded* might be regarded as a composite novel in the same vein as works such as James Joyce's *Dubliners* (1914) or Irvine Welsh's *Trainspotting* (1993). The individual stories in *Walking Wounded* are character sketches, rather than plot-driven, "twist-in-the-tail" narratives. They demonstrate the same qualities found throughout McIlvanney's work but often in a more concentrated form. While there are still moments of comedy, such as the absurd image of a middle-aged philanderer hiding from an irate husband in a child's Wendy House that occurs in "On the Sidelines," the humor is less warm and convivial than in the earlier novels. Indeed, as the title suggests, *Walking Wounded* is perhaps McIlvanney's bleakest work to date. This change in tone, of course, reflects the burgeoning disaffection felt in Scotland toward the end of the 1980s as a result of the recession and the policies of the Thatcher government. Several of the stories directly address the social problems of the day. One in particular is worth examining in more detail.

"Mick's Day" is a succinct portrait of one day in the life of a character who, like many working-class Scots at the time, is forced to suffer the harsh experiences of a life that depends on scraping out survival from an unemployment benefit. Its opening sentence is arresting: "It is Tuesday, not that it matters" (p. 95). This might seem like an offhand remark with which to begin a story, but it is the glibness of the statement that is revealing. The day of the week is of no consequence whatsoever for the main character, Mick, because, owing to his long-term unemployment, every day is the same. The casualness of the opening sentence suggests the extent to which he has grown accustomed to his circumstances. Indeed, "Mick's Day" establishes the character's life as a monotonous cycle of repetition. Mick sleeps late most days "to postpone having to confront the day" (p. 95). He spends the rest of the day scraping together food, speaking to the other unemployed men who gather in the local precinct, and visiting the public library. The reader is told that he used to go the job center more frequently, but he has become more despondent about the lack of work and now often avoids it: "It's a bit like having your own uselessness officially confirmed" (p. 98). Occasionally, he goes to the pub, which is "the focal point of his life" (p. 99), because it is there that he is treated with the most humanity and benevolence. Despite the warmth he encounters in the pub in conversation, offers of food, old clothes, and the opportunity of a few hours of gardening work, the story ends on a rather bitter note:

> But the more time that passes like this, the less capable Mick is likely to become of ever getting out of his present helpless condition. Time never merely passes. It defines us as it goes until we run out of potential to contradict what it tells us. Mick's situation is like a prison sentence without any crime committed. It is an indeterminate sentence. So far he has served four years.

(p. 100)

The present-tense, objective style of narration makes the short story seem like a piece of interventionist journalism rather than fiction, lending the subject matter a much-needed sense of urgency and relevance. "Mick's Day" provides a good example of the way that McIlvanney's work throughout the 1980s challenges the popular perceptions of Thatcherite Britain. It confronts the delusion that people became unemployed through choice or as a result of laziness, a misapprehension fostered by the prime minister in her famous comments about there being no such thing as society.

McIlvanney's 1996 novel, *The Kiln,* is a coming-of-age narrative that is more personal and less political than his earlier work. It concerns a character named Tom Docherty, who made a cameo appearance in *Strange Loyalties* as a friend of Jack Laidlaw and is the grandson of Tam Docherty from McIlvanney's earlier novel. *The Kiln* would appear to be the most "autobiographical" of McIlvanney's novels, since the major details of his own career path are replicated in that of his protagonist. Indeed, most of the contemporary reviews of the novel in the press made oblique allusions to James Joyce's semiautobiographical novel *A Portrait of the Artist as a Young Man* (1916). It is tempting then to

see Tom as a thinly veiled version of McIlvanney, providing an interesting extratextual frisson to the novel, but making assumptions about McIlvanney based on the experiences of his character is necessarily in the realm of speculation. A former teacher, Tom is a middle-aged writer living in Edinburgh reflecting back over the events of his life and the decisions that he has made, trying to discern how he ended up isolated and disillusioned. It is perhaps McIlvanney's most formally challenging novel, mostly because the narrative flits back and forth through time, offering little explanation and none of the conventional cues that allow the reader to determine the chronology of the story. The novel is not separated into chapters like the rest of McIlvanney's work, but it is instead presented as one continuous series of fragments from throughout Tom's life.

Tom's reminiscences are dominated by the summer of 1955, which, for him, symbolizes his passing from childhood into adulthood. This was the summer between Tom leaving school and starting university. Like McIlvanney, Tom is the first of his family to enter higher education. During this summer, Tom takes on work in the kiln of a local brickworks. Again, McIlvanney explores the tensions between working-class life and education as Tom finds himself caught between the two ways of life. These tensions are evident, for instance, in the letter that he imagines that he will receive:

> We regret to inform you that there has, of course, been a mistake in the matter of your being given a place at this university. We trust that this error has not inconvenienced you too much by, for example, giving you absurd fantasies concerning the possibility that learned men will waste their time on a working-class toerag from Graithnock. We do, however, hope that you will find in the future some activity more suited to your abilities, such as shovelling shit.

(p. 93)

While *The Kiln* revisits the kind of tensions explored through the character of Conn in *Docherty*, the depiction of working-class life differs from that in McIlvanney's earlier work. This may perhaps be a result of the novels' different historical settings, but here Tom encounters aspects of working-class life that are less hospitable than those found in McIlvanney's earlier novels: "In the kiln, he would think, you will find the very way you breathe threatened. The heat is too intense, as if you have entered an alien atmosphere ... This is not a place for poetry readings. Here it's all down to bodies and sweat and strength and manual skill" (pp. 194–195).

Continuing this development, McIlvanney's 2006 novel *Weekend* is fully immersed in the world of academia. In this and other ways, it is unlike any of McIlvanney's previous novels. Indeed, in a laudatory review in the *Guardian*, the Scottish novelist Irvine Welsh argued that *Weekend* is so fresh and different from McIlvanney's other work that it feels like a debut novel rather than the work of such a well-established author. Indeed, *Weekend* does not contribute to McIlvanney's usual fictional world, not being set in Graithnock and not featuring any of his stock of characters, even in cameo. It presents complex, intertwined narratives of a large ensemble of English literature students and lecturers from the University of Glasgow who participate in a study residency on the island of Cannamore off the west coast of Scotland, which is presumably a fictionalized version of Canna. Much of the novel's immediate exuberance results from the high drama and humor of the characters' drunken debauchery, sexual liaisons, and marital problems. McIlvanney demonstrates that he is capable of accommodating the ribald themes of popular fiction and that he can do so with verve and authenticity. However, there is also a level of literary experimentation in *Weekend* that marks it out from the rest of McIlvanney's work. It might be best understood as a work of metafiction. This term, literarily meaning "fiction about fiction," refers to literary works that are aware of their status as fiction and that draw attention to this awareness. *Weekend* deliberately reveals its own artifice in several ways. Interspersed throughout the novel are fragments from the three lectures that are delivered over the weekend that comprises the time frame of the novel. The first two lectures are devoted to Scottish novels: Robert Louis Stevenson's *The Strange Case of Dr Jekyll and Mr Hyde* (1886)

and J. M. Barrie's *Farewell, Miss Julie Logan* (1932). The final lecture, intended to tie up the weekend, is mostly about the Oedipus myth. There are often ironic and revealing juxtapositions between the discussions of these literary texts that appear in the novel and the events that are unfolding over the weekend. By embedding discussion of how people read and respond to works of fiction within its structure, *Weekend* continually second-guesses and comments on the reader's assumptions, making it an engaging and almost interactive work. The jaw-dropping revelation of the novel's narrator in the final sentence contributes to its playful manipulation of the artifice. Finally, a poem called "Sphinx," alluded to throughout the narrative, forms an appendix to the novel and is attributed to one of the main characters, Harry Beck. This poem is in fact one of McIlvanney's own poems, which first appeared in his 1988 collection *In Through the Head*.

POETRY

In terms of the critical and popular attention they receive, McIlvanney's celebrated novels are perhaps guilty of overshadowing his achievements in the field of poetry. Indeed, his three collections *The Longships in Harbour* (1970), *These Words: Weddings and After* (1984), and *In Through the Head* (1988) are now out-of-print and not readily available. Fortunately, the most accessible of the three, *In Through the Head*, reprints the complete text of *These Words* and most of *The Longships in Harbour* (of the original collection of thirty, only seven short poems are not anthologized in the later work: "Building Site," "Three Sketches, One Condition," "Goodbye Forsyth," "Contemporary Biography," "The Fashion Now Forbidding Mourning," "Men Who Sit Where Fires Are," and "Intimations"). The sheer number of poems and the vast range of subject material covered in McIlvanney's three collections precludes comprehensive analysis in an essay of this length. It seems important, however, to accommodate at least some consideration of his poetry here, since there are significant overlaps of content and style with his fiction.

It is perhaps revealing that two of the best poems in the 1970 collection *The Longships in Harbour* are elegies for members of his family. "Grandmother" is a moving account of a young McIlvanney being shocked to discover, in the aftermath of his grandmother's death, the quiet dignity of her hard life outside of the context in which he had previously known her. The long poem "Initiation," which opens *The Longships in Harbour*, is an intense and painful elegy about his father. It provides an interesting companion-piece to *Remedy Is None*. Like McIlvanney's debut novel, the first four stanzas of "Initiation" negotiate the problem of how to mourn and how to pay respect to the dead in a way that is sufficient. The poem becomes especially interesting, however, in the fifth stanza, when the narrator discusses his father's harsh experiences and the sacrifices that he made during the General Strike of 1926. He notes that having undergone poverty, starvation, and humiliation in an attempt to improve working conditions, it must surely be distressing for his father to see the values of his working-class society eroded by bourgeois materialism.

Published over a decade later, McIlvanney's second work of poetry, *These Words: Weddings and After*, is understandably very different. It is a single poem, consisting of about fifty pages, made up of different sequences all drawn together under the framing narrative of a wedding. All the sections overturn the expected, traditional ways of representing wedding ceremonies. Contrary to presenting images of marriage as a formal celebration of permanent romantic love, McIlvanney's work takes pains to bring out both the essential strangeness and the potential hypocrisy of the institution. Indeed, much of the poem's force arises from its mixing of the sacred and the profane. At times, McIlvanney makes very serious points about the nature of marriage and the language of wedding ceremonies, including his acerbic parody of the traditional wedding vows, in which the use of words such as "convention" and "platitudes" suggest that the language of the wedding ceremony has become so familiar that its meaning is no longer fully considered. McIlvanney's subversion encourages the reader

to consider the assumptions that are embedded in the ceremony, such as the residual misogyny and the unfeasible certainty demanded by the wording of the vows. As well as making serious points about the nature of weddings, the poem also introduces comically absurd moments into the solemn proceedings, such as the hilarious stanza about an uncle who fears that his flatulence might interrupt the ceremony.

McIlvanney's third collection, *In Through the Head*, organizes his earlier poems alongside new pieces in thematic sections. The more playful dimensions of his poetry that were introduced in *These Words: Weddings and After* are developed further in most of the new pieces. "Modernism," for instance, uses the jangling rhymes and rhythms of doggerel verse to produce a droll indictment of elitism in the work of the high literary modernists.

While there is also a certain playfulness in the unwieldy title "The Song Mickey Heard at the Bottom of His Pint in the Zodiac Bar," this poem actually provides a succinct articulation of a serious concern that is central to McIlvanney's work in general: namely, the way that working-class characters have been traditionally excluded from canonical literature. It is perhaps this sense of marginalization that has provided much of the driving force behind his novels as well as his poetry, compelling him to renegotiate the terms of literature in order to make it relevant to his people.

CONCLUSION

The work of William McIlvanney remains a dynamic presence in Scottish literature. Its influence is evident in the various formulations of urban, working-class life that dominate Scottish fiction, providing the bedrock for the experimental work of novelists such as James Kelman as well as for the crime fiction of popular writers like Ian Rankin. McIlvanney's writing is consistent in its passion, eloquence, and humor. His commitment to giving working-class Scottish communities the imaginative representation that they had previously been denied comes across best in his subtle appropriations of existing literary forms. His analyses of Scotland, working-class life, and literature itself are the most obvious points of critical attention in his oeuvre. However, his work reaches far beyond these relatively narrow concerns and raises multiple complex questions about how to live and how to make sense of the world. Perhaps the most fitting description of McIlvanney's contribution to literature, then, comes in the form of his own description of one of his characters: "The only motivation he could find for writing was the one with which he had started, a compulsion to try and understand the strangeness of things, a fascination with our hardly known selves" (*The Kiln*, p. 170).

Selected Bibliography

WORKS OF WILLIAM MCILVANNEY

NOVELS AND SHORT STORIES

Remedy Is None. London: Eyre & Spottiswoode, 1966. Reprint. Glasgow: Richard Drew, 1989. (Citations are to the 1989 edition.)

A Gift from Nessus. London: Eyre & Spottiswoode, 1968.

Docherty. London: Allen & Unwin, 1975. Reprint. Kent: Hodder and Stoughton, 1975. (Citations are to the 1975 edition.)

Laidlaw. London: Hodder and Stoughton, 1977. Reprint. New York: Pantheon, 1982. (Citations are to the 1982 edition.)

The Papers of Tony Veitch. London: Hodder and Stoughton, 1983. Reprint. London: Hodder and Stoughton, 1996. (The second Laidlaw novel; citations are to the 1996 edition.)

The Big Man. London: Hodder and Stoughton, 1985.

Walking Wounded. London: Hodder and Stoughton, 1989. Reprint. London: Hodder and Stoughton, 1990. (Collection of short stories; citations are to the 1990 edition.)

Strange Loyalties. London: Hodder and Stoughton, 1991. Reprint. London: Hodder and Stoughton, 1992. (The third Laidlaw novel; citations are to the 1992 edition.)

The Kiln. London: Hodder and Stoughton, 1996.

Weekend. London: Hodder and Stoughton, 2006.

POETRY

The Longships in Harbour. London: Eyre & Spottiswoode, 1970.

These Words: Weddings and After. Edinburgh: Mainstream, 1984. (Also features an essay about elitism in modernist literature titled "'The Sacred Wood' Revisited," which is reprinted in *Surviving the Shipwreck*.)

In Through the Head. Edinburgh: Mainstream, 1988. (Reprints most of *The Longships in Harbour* and all of *These Words: Weddings and After*.)

ESSAYS

"Growing Up in the West." In *Memoirs of a Modern Scotland*. Edited by Karl Miller. London: Faber and Faber, 1970. Pp. 168–178.

Surviving the Shipwreck. Edinburgh: Mainstream, 1991.

FILM BASED ON THE WORK OF MCILVANNEY

The Big Man. Screenplay by Don MacPherson. Directed by David Leland. Miramax, 1990.

CRITICAL AND BIOGRAPHICAL STUDIES

Bold, Alan. "Proletarian Romanticism: Sharp, Hind, McIlvanney." In *Modern Scottish Literature*. By Alan Bold. London: Longman, 1983. Pp. 233–241.

Craig, Carol. "On Men and Women in McIlvanney's Fiction." *Edinburgh Review* 73:42–49 (1986).

Denith, Simon. "'This Shitty Urban Machine Humanised': The Urban Crime Novel and the Novels of William McIlvanney." *In Watching the Detectives: Essays on Crime Fiction*. Edited by Ian A. Bell and Graham Daldry. Basingstoke, U.K.: Macmillan, 1990. Pp. 18–36.

Dickson, Beth. "Class and Being in the Novels of William McIlvanney." In *The Scottish Novel Since the Seventies*. Edited by Gavin Wallace and Randall Stevenson. Edinburgh: Edinburgh University Press, 1993. Pp. 54–70.

———. *William McIlvanney's "Laidlaw."* Glasgow: Association for Scottish Literary Studies, 1998.

Dixon, Keith. "'No Fairies. No Monsters. Just People': Resituating the Work of William McIlvanney." In *Studies in Scottish Fiction: 1945 to the Present*. Edited by Susanne Hagemann. Frankfurt: Peter Lang, 1996. Pp. 187–198.

Humm, Peter, and Paul Stigant. "The Masculine Fiction of William McIlvanney." In *Gender, Genre and Narrative Pleasure*. Edited by Derek Longhurst. London: Unwin Hyman, 1989. Pp. 84–101.

Idle, Jeremy. "McIlvanney, Masculinity, and Scottish Literature." *Scottish Affairs* 2:50–57 (1993).

Jones, Carole. "White Men on Their Backs." *International Journal of Scottish Literature*, no. 1:1–16 (autumn 2006).

McGillivray, Alan. "Natural Loyalties: The Work of William McIlvanney." *Laverock* 2:13–23 (1995).

McLuckie, Craig W. *Researching McIlvanney: A Critical and Bibliographic Introduction*. Frankfurt: Peter Lang, 1999.

Murray, Isobel, ed. "Plato in a Boiler Suit: William McIlvanney." In *Scottish Writers Talking: George Mackay Brown, Jessie Kesson, Norman MacCaig, William McIlvanney, David Toulmin, Interviewed by Isobel Murray and Bob Tait*. East Linton, Scotland: Tuckwell Press, 1996. Pp. 132–154.

Murray, Isobel, and Bob Tait. *Ten Modern Scottish Novels*. Aberdeen: Aberdeen University Press, 1984. (Chapter 9 is devoted to an extended discussion of *Docherty*.)

Newton, K. M. "William McIlvanney's *Docherty*: Last of the Old or Precursor of the New?" *Studies in Scottish Literature* 32:101–116 (2001).

Winston, Robert P. "Travellers and Tourists: Rules of Engagement in William McIlvanney's Detective Fiction." *Studies in Scottish Literature* 32:117–131 (2001).

OTHER WORKS CITED

Finlay, Richard. *Modern Scotland: 1914–2000*. London: Profile Books, 2004.

Hart, Francis Russell. *The Scottish Novel: A Critical Survey*. London: John Murray, 1978.

HELEN OYEYEMI

(1984—)

Gail Low

THE PLAYWRIGHT AND novelist Helen Oyeyemi was born in Nigeria on September 28, 1984, but emigrated with her parents to London when only four years of age. Brought up a Catholic, she is the eldest of three children; she has a younger sister and brother. Her parents were teachers in Nigeria, but as their educational qualifications were not recognized in Britain, her mother worked as a underground train driver while her father undertook a variety of jobs, including that of a security guard; the family lived in a two-bedroom apartment in a council estate (public housing development) in the London borough of Lewisham and spent summer holidays in Nigeria. Given the rough neighborhood she was raised in and her parents' anxieties about their daughter playing outside on the estate, Oyeyemi has described her childhood as one spent essentially indoors writing and reading, cocooned in her own imaginary world. She attended Notre Dame, a Roman Catholic high school in Southwark, London, but felt unsettled and alienated, and she suffered from bouts of depression. Oyeyemi took an overdose of sleeping pills and painkillers at age fifteen and, on her discharge, was referred to a psychiatrist. Finding the session unhelpful, she did not return. After secondary school, she attended Cardinal Vaughan Memorial School in Holland Park, London, to complete her GCE A-levels (a two-year pre-university course of study roughly equivalent to Advanced Placement credits); she had a more successful time there and was encouraged to write and to try for a place at Cambridge University.

When in her final year at school, she sent a short story titled "The Icarus Girl" to a London literary agent to obtain some advice about writing; on the strength of the submitted work, the agent in question, Robin Wade, wrote back to say that he wanted to represent her. Oyeyemi spent the next seven months writing the novel in secret, in addition to revising for her final-year examinations. She created a literary sensation when she was given a significant advance and a two-book deal with Bloomsbury Books soon after the end of her A-levels examinations, and at the tender age of seventeen. Oyeyemi read social and political sciences at Corpus Christi College at Cambridge University; her debut novel, *The Icarus Girl,* was published in 2005, when she was only a second-year university undergraduate, to overwhelming critical acclaim. Two short plays, *Juniper's Whitening and Victimese* (published together in one volume), and a novel, *The Opposite House,* written by Oyeyemi while she was still at Cambridge, appeared in 2005 and 2007 respectively. Some of the themes of the plays have fed into her second and third novels. After her graduation in 2006, Oyeyemi volunteered at a South African children's charity for children born with HIV before being admitted for the prestigious masters degree program in creative writing at Columbia University in New York; Oyeyemi was writing her third novel while enrolled in the writing program, and she ultimately chose not to complete the degree. *White Is for Witching* was published by Picador in 2009.

Thematically, Oyeyemi's novels have been preoccupied with identity—cultural, ethnic, sexual, and familial. Her work addresses the in-between spaces where self is constantly being articulated in conjunction with, but also against, significant others—for example, siblings, close friends, twins, or mothers and daughters. She is also conversant with the staples of the gothic form, and many of her books contain "haunted" houses, doubles, doppelgängers, and alter egos, and they also include characters who find their own person mirrored by, or through, others. These doubles, often twins, also offer a chance for Oyeyemi to explore the dialectics of subjectivity as a process of identity and separation. Oyeyemi's work is not afraid to explore difficult issues such as madness, hysteria, and anorexia from a specifically woman's viewpoint; she seems particularly interested in psychoanalytic and literary concepts of the uncanny, with their distinctive combination of the unfamiliar in the familiar, or the strange as also oddly familiar. Much like Oedipus, who discovers unwittingly his role in an unfolding tragedy that was already scripted for him, her protagonists find themselves in cultural, historical, or familial legacies or mythic stories that seem already to have produced a role for them to play, which they struggle against, sometimes unsuccessfully and to their own destruction. Her skillful manipulation of the gothic genre allows her to traverse a twilight world where one cultural reality meets another and where one belief system intersects with others. Oyeyemi's depiction of the ordinary and the domestic is often made mysterious, magical, and extraordinary through her fascination with the otherworldly domain of the spirits, ghosts that are part and parcel of African, Cuban, Caribbean, and European myths and fables. Above all, much like her literary heroine Emily Dickinson, Oyeyemi's fiction is written with a haunting emotional intensity, heightened by a lyricism and a synesthesic gift for rendering feelings, thoughts, and ideas in figurative language. Oyeyemi possesses a fearlessness regarding poetic allusion, ambiguity, and complexity that stretches the conventions of the novel form. She names Dickinson among her literary influences and ancestry, alongside Edgar Allan Poe, Joseph Sheridan Le Fanu, Charles Perrault, the Brothers Grimm, Hans Christian Anderson, Jorge Luis Borges, Ali Smith, Dorothy Parker, Anne Carson, and Carl Almquist in all of her work, but *White Is for Witching,* especially, is informed by knowledge of the literary gothic.

THE SPACE OF CHILDHOOD

Oyeyemi's first novel, *The Icarus Girl* (2005), starts out as a moving bildungsroman about a precocious only child with English and Nigerian ancestry. Jessamy Harrison (Jess) is a character marked by heightened sensitivity and a rich interior imaginative life, and whose estrangement from her school environment and difficulties with her parents is exacerbated by her feelings of cultural and personal displacement. Jess's mother, Sarah, who came to Britain to study, has married an Englishman and is comfortably settled as a writer in London, but she still retains a strong link with her Nigerian family and culture; Sarah Harrison is able to move easily between the two cultures, for example, adjusting between the "bargaining, bantering tone" of "Yoruba and broken English" that she uses to talk with a taxi driver in Lagos as a cultural insider and the "smooth English accent" that is used to converse with her husband and child (pp. 14–15). Eight-year-old Jessamy has grown up in London and thus views her mother's Nigerian culture with the eyes of an outsider, knowing very little of the cultural traditions or the language of the country and needing to ask her mother to translate words and customs. In Nigeria, she is called an *oyinbo*, or "somebody who has come from so far away that they are a stranger" (p. 17), or more pejoratively, a half-and-half child.

Yet Jess is not quite at home in London either. As a result of her academic abilities, she is put into a class that is made up of children a year older than she is. She is seen as a loner and "weird" (p. 86) among her peers and labeled a difficult child by her teachers. She is not like the "blond, dimpled Alison Carr" (p. 83), nor is she part of the bossy playground set presided over by Colleen McLain and Andrea Carney; Oyeyemi's novel here shows an acute appreciation of playground politics and behavior, and the cliques that rule them. The fact that Jessamy calls attention to select external signs and markers of belonging such as blond hair and pretty looks is meant to signal a shortfall in the way she looks. Her unease at school and at home erupts into physical symptoms: illnesses, febrile convulsions, fits, tantrums, screaming fits or truculent behavior, all of which she seems to have little ability to prevent or stop. As a result, she is made to see a psychologist. Oyeyemi's fascination with such bodily and symptomatic rebellions particularly against a conventional notion of normal girlish behavior in this novel will, in her subsequent two novels, crystallize around the concept of hysteria, as a distinctively feminine condition. However, in this debut novel, Jess is described as prone to "inevitable fever[s], the whites of her eyes tinged pink, her head lolling dejectedly on her pillow, her fingers limp as if the bones in them had evaporated" during which she is unable to talk but can only make "small sounds, like singing noises, broken songs" (p. 80). Jess also has a predisposition toward screaming fits when frustrated, and these need to run their own course; "no wonder my class think I'm weird," she thinks (p. 86). The behavior of Jess's friend, TillyTilly, would also come to be associated with such rebellions and transgression of acceptable norms, albeit in a more manipulative, direct and conscious manner.

When in Nigeria, Jess strikes up a friendship with a young barefoot Nigerian waif who seems to live in the derelict outbuildings of her grandfather's yard. Titiola, or TillyTilly as she is called by Jess, is bold and adventurous, and she encourages Jess to break into grandfather Gbenga Oyegbebi's locked study to play and then, later, talks her into exploring the gated and closed local fairground simply to amuse themselves on its rides. TillyTilly's fearlessness, her quick temper, and her untroubled conscience are in stark contrast to Jess's fearful and timid personality; Jess soon begins to envy her new friend's devil-may-care attitude, her power and ability to impose herself. Through association with her new friend, Jess imagines herself as "becoming different, becoming stronger, becoming more like Tilly" and better able to take on the world (p. 151). Yet through a series of incidents that serve to highlight TillyTilly's baser instincts—her unchecked anger and her propensity for revenge directed first at the classmate Colleen, then at the teacher Miss Patel, and then later at Jess's father—readers are made to sense, even before it is made explicit, that Jess's imaginary friend or alter ego may be more malevolent than she initially appears: perhaps a Hyde to Jess's normally placid Jekyll.

TillyTilly acts out, and makes real, Jess's bottled-up feelings of anger and frustration, "getting" anyone who has attempted to hurt Jess. But because TillyTilly has magical powers, she also turns into a dangerous figure. When Jess begins to find friends of her own, TillyTilly is envious and tries to scare her friends away. Soon Jess begins to fear TillyTilly's jealous moods and especially her attempts to lay claim to Jess for herself exclusively. When TillyTilly jumps inside Jess's skin, Jess is thrown into a nightmarish world without moorings, a place of extremes: cold and dark and also unbearably hot. Uncontrollable in her hysterical fit, TillyTilly as Jess is progressively vindictive. Jess grows gradually more uneasy, "scared of the ice that lingered in the touching, and of the glint in her hidden eyes" (p. 234); her imaginary and magical friend begins to take over her life, telling her secrets calculated to put a wedge between, for example, mother and daughter. TillyTilly informs Jess that she is half of a twin, and that Fern, her sister, died in childbirth and that Jess's feelings of missing something, of not quite being whole, must be laid at this door. As a result of her mother's silence on the matter, and by seeming to act normally and not to grieve for the dead twin, TillyTilly also hints that the death of Fern was perhaps her mother's fault. TillyTilly then claims Jess as a twin: "You have been so empty, Jessy, without your twin; you have no one to walk your three worlds with you. I know—I am the same. … But now I am Fern, I am your sister, and you are my twin" (p. 170).

TillyTilly can be read as Jess's double, or doppelganger, in a European gothic tradition, but Oyeyemi complicates the picture by locating both within a Yoruba cosmology of the *abiku* child, and in relation to Yoruba beliefs about twins, thus offering a version of a postcolonial gothic in which one belief system interpenetrates another, or in which one cultural reality casts light on the fissures and anomalies of another. *Abiku* translated from Yoruba literally means "one who is born, dies"; Douglas McCabe, writing in *Research in African Literatures*, explains that the term is applied specifically to spirit children who are born into the human world but who plan to return to the spiritual world only to be born again, thus repeating a cycle of death and birth, tragedy and tears, until they are "fettered" to this world by their human parents (p. 45). *Abiku* is predicated on an in-between state between life and death, between the human world and the world of the spirits. Sarah Harrison, shocked by her daughter's discovery of a secret that she has kept hidden, calls Jess an *abiku* child; "the spirits tell her things, *Fern* tells her things," Sarah moans, regretting that the traditional Yoruba customs were not observed with the stillborn death of her other daughter (p. 174). By being *abiku*, Jess occupies a position of dislocation and alterity within her own family; she is at once a member of it but also a stranger within it. Sarah's refusal to have an *ibeji* statue to placate and remember the lost twin, which stems from her disavowal of some of the religious practices and traditions of her Yoruba culture, results in a further severance and splitting that describe Jess's in-between, half-and-half state. Clearly, one thematic trajectory of the novel concerns the disavowal of cultural ancestry and of the past, and the need to come to terms with those factors in order to be made whole again. With the creation of the *ibeji* statue, Jess's dreamlike feverish wanderings in the "wilderness for the mind" (p. 318) that is one of the worlds that the *abiku* child roams is aided by a nameless, silent girl who lets Jess ride on her back when Jess is tired. When she finally is able to look at her helper at close range, Jess thinks initially that she is looking at herself, then she recognizes differences: the smallness of the girl's stature, the "beautiful details of baby hair growing in as fuzz at the start of the forehead" (p. 321). With such a realization comes a recognition of her relationship with her Yoruba twin; Jess, who has both an English and a Yoruba name, promises to share her name, thereby acknowledging the familial connection.

The novel is written in the third person but focalized very tightly through Jess's eyes. The relationship between Jess and her mother is particularly fraught, but because events are viewed essentially through Jess's perspective, it is difficult to determine if her view of her mother is an accurate portrayal or if it is filtered by the child's emotional states. Oyeyemi remarked in a 2006 interview with Isabel Taylor on how limited, "cramped and small," Jess's perspective is and noted that her heroine actually says remarkably little that is specific about either Nigerian or English culture. As a character, Jess lives almost completely in the interiority of her own imaginative life; questioned about the title of the novel, Oyeyemi alludes to the myth of Icarus and Daedalus; the mother is an example of a Daedalus figure, who, as a writer, is able to discipline and craft her imagination, while the daughter has an "uncontrollable imagination"; Jess's "wings lead her to a force she can't [easily] handle," Oyeyemi told Taylor. The narrative jettisoning of the first-person voice in favor of the third person is perhaps also a small reflection on the necessity of creating some distance from the lead character, in order to create an atmosphere in which readers are not likely to be too overwhelmed by Jess's perspective and thus able to see that the character can be confused and driven by her own needs and desires. The third-person voice also allows Oyeyemi to preserve a fine balance between the gothic and realist elements of the novel, thus preventing readers from simply labeling the main character as merely mad.

Critics have all noted the novel's concern with femininity as a divided, split, and multiple states of being and take the text as one that explores these truths albeit, as Jane Bryce suggests, "inflected by issues of exile, hybridity and metissage" (p. 50). In an interview with Aminatta Forna, Oyeyemi remarked on the surprise evolution of the novel from one essentially about "an eight year old girl and her imaginary friend" to a "saga of identity" grounded in gender and ethnicity (p. 56). In her interview with Taylor, Oyeyemi concedes that, in the writing of the story, she was somewhat taken aback that Jess's "biggest issue was the choice between being English and being Nigerian." Oyeyemi's preoccupation with twinning, the lost figure of Fern as well as the presence of TillyTilly, offers a metaphor of Jess's divided state, which can be restored or made whole through the acknowledgement of what was marginalized or repressed. The novel offers a rich seam for this kind of interpretative work, which reads TillyTilly's hauntings as a past that returns again and again to trouble the present simply by virtue of the fact of its repression. TillyTilly's remarks about dispossession and unbelonging— "Land chopped in little pieces;" "Nothing, now, there is no one ... There is no homeland ... our blood ... split like water ... I'm a witness; twins should know what each other suffer!" (pp. 249–250)—can be read as referring also to Nigeria, thus broadening the context of such spectral hauntings. Thus the critic Madeleine Hron discovers in the trope to the twin, in the deployment of the child and childhood within third-generation Nigerian novels, and in Oyeyemi's references to "the word 'half' in her text, stylistically intimating Jess's sense of incompleteness" (p. 37), an allusion to the different realities within changing postcoloniality of Nigeria itself and how the nation must negotiate the different challenges represented by Westernization, global capitalism, and its "pluricultural values, myths and traditions" (p. 30). The doppelganger and the use of the gothic form invites readings that focus on the issue of hauntings. The critic Pilar Cuder-Domínguez has written that the doppelganger coupling of Jess and TillyTilly functions as a "racial shadow"—"suggesting either the subject's feelings of inferiority, haunted by an essential lack in authenticity, or else the missing connections to homeland" (p. 279). Jane Bryce, writing specifically of Oyeyemi's employment of the gothic form, remarks that Jess's struggles to free herself from TillyTilly's possession is part and parcel of a migrant consciousness; migrants are "denied the right of 'belonging,'" she says, and "ghostly presences and hauntings are intrinsic to the diasporic condition" (p. 64). Yet Chinenye Okparanta's warning, cautioning against an all-too-easy slide into a belief that all will come good through the invocation of an imaginary homeland, needs to be heeded; pointing to the differences between Jess and her mother, Okparanta argues that the novel "destabilize[s] facile conceptions of an imaginary homeland by exposing the chasms that exits between the individuals and their attempts to reach this figurative 'home'" (p. 206).

FATES, SCRIPTS, AND PLAYERS

During her first year at Cambridge, Oyeyemi wrote two short experimental plays published together in 2005 as *Juniper's Whitening and Victimese*; *Juniper's Whitening* was performed at the Corpus Playroom in Cambridge in 2004. Oyeyemi considers herself a novelist primarily, and in interviews she has described these plays as simple vehicles for eliciting an immediate response from the audience. *Juniper's Whitening* resembles a Samuel Beckett drama or one of Harold Pinter's early plays. All the play's action takes place in one location and includes a very small cast of characters; very little backstory is offered, and readers and spectators have to make sense of the sometimes confusing and bewildering action that simply unfolds in front of them. There are three characters in *Juniper's Whitening*: Aleph, Beth, and Juniper. Aleph strangles Beth, who returns to life only to be murdered again by Aleph. The murderous action, and the small acts of kindness that greet the resurrected murdered woman, including the intense sparring and countersparring between Beth and Aleph, seem to be part of a repetitive cycle of activity. The script for Beth and Aleph's behavior seems already put in place; as Aleph says to Juniper, who asks why Aleph keeps killing Beth, "It all appears voluntary; me ... being kind to Beth, you staying, but it isn't really ... We're being forced; and just because it's unseen and only partly felt, you think it is unsafe to acknowledge it" (p. 18). In an anecdote of parental child abuse, Beth seems to suggest that her desire to inflict pain, and also her desire to die, is formed by and a result of the twisted past relationships she has had; Aleph's arrival in her life seems to be linked with her desire to die, to be reduced to the whitening of the bones alluded to in the play's title. The two women attempt to kill Aleph in order to break out of this compulsive repetition, but Aleph returns toward the end of the play in order to initiate another round of similar action, with Juniper as the Beth figure. If there is anything in the play that might offer the possibility of a different future, it is the suggestion of an "outside" that is beyond the claustrophobic walls of the room. In the play, this "outside" is both feared—Juniper is repeatedly told to come away from the curtained window or not to look outside—and hoped for by the characters. *Juniper's Whitening* ends ambivalently with a declaration by Juniper that she has lost the struggle against her fate but also with the sound of laughter and the glass of the window shattering. Because the act takes place literally off stage, we do not actually know the significance or meaning of the action, which might represent a freedom from the prison of the room or the death alluded to in the title.

Victimese traverses the same terrain as *Juniper's Whitening*; it concerns a girl who does not see herself as a victim even when she quite clearly suffers from depression, feels trapped in her room, and has tried to commit suicide. Eve thinks that by relying on herself alone she can achieve a measure of independence and autonomy from others and thus not have to face the chance of disappointment. Eve decides to celebrate not her birthday but her "deathday" (p. 49), and she invites a small group of friends, including her sister, to mark the occasion. They humor the quirkiness of her request. The conversations that take place during the celebrations enable an unusual level of emotional honesty to be reached among its participants; each shares their deepest fears or a special moment of real anxiety. Eve reveals to the gathering that her strategy of self-harm is based in the need to remind herself of her stated goal of self-sufficiency and emotional distanglement. Yet outside the room a mysterious woman waits for Eve. One does not know if this woman is real, but she is referred to by Eve as her "nemesis," a probable source of harm or hurt as is suggested by others in their description of her as a lady with eyes like "frost tipped with light; ice melting with a glow stabbing through it" (p. 54), and of someone "incidentally beautiful, and purposefully cruel" (p. 73). Because Eve is celebrating her deathday, the nemesis is more likely associated with darkness and death. This lady, perhaps a concrete manifestation of Eve's fate, awaits to receive Eve outside her room. The room is slowly but gradually imagined as a prison (Eve's one-room apartment is again quite literary the only stage for the action that occurs), but we do not know if Eve survives her decision to venture outside this space. Yet the emotional honesty of her last hours, and also those of her friends, brings very little catharsis.

Themes in *Juniper's Whitening and Victimese* were more fully developed in *The Opposite House* and *White Is for Witching*. All three published texts are concerned with life as a narrative or script in which roles have already been preestablished through complex interpersonal relations that make each character react to others in a predetermined ways, or though a version of fate. *Juniper's Whitening and Victimese*, along with *White Is for Witching,* also play out the difficulties of coming to terms with or evading those allotted roles. All three texts are also preoccupied with death and they transgress a realist format, showing Oyeyemi as a writer who is not afraid to be enigmatic or to end her work on an unresolved note. Their dialogue, particularly in the case of *Victimese*, hint of how easily Oyeyemi moves between ideas and their concrete embodiment.

THE SOMEWHEREHOUSE

Oyeyemi's ambitious second novel, *The Opposite House* (2007), contains two different stories and worlds within its covers, each acting as a counterpoint or echo for the other. The main story concerns the tale of a black jazz singer of Cuban descent, Maja Carmen Carrera, who is brought up in London and details her relationship with family and friends. Maja's parents are exiled from Castro's Cuba; her father is an intellectual and academic, while her teacher mother, Chabella, is a fervent Santero, whose rituals and religious practices are also summarily dismissed by her staunchly rational husband. Maja also has a precocious younger brother, Tomás, who has difficulties at his school. Transplanted from Cuba to London via Germany, Maja faces cultural, linguistic, and personal dislocations, and the way she comes to terms with them lies at the heart of the novel and gives the book its contemporary topicality. Maja, who narrates her own story in the first person, speaks of the pain of separation where skin, culture, and language—"the inherited magical magic spells that make your skin real"—fail to knit together, thus spelling a kind of death: "unless your skin and your language touch each other without interruption, there is no word to make you understand that it matters that you live" (p. 185). Maja is not the only figure who straddles two or more cultures or who feels disowned by the country into which she was born. Aaron, Maja's lover, is a white Ghanaian who speaks English "crammed with tonality" (p. 22) and who still identifies strongly with the country of his birth despite settling more recently in London; Aaron can speak Ewe, and he does so when he mentors some Ghanaian students. Amy Eleni, Maja's best friend, takes her "Cypriot heritage seriously" (p. 34) even when she looks like any other English girl. Belonging is movingly described as enabling one to connect with and make sense of the world; otherwise, language and signs are empty ciphers and possess little life or meaning. Magalys, who was one of Maja's first playmates in Cuba before Maja emigrated, describes her residency in London as unsettling when they meet up as adults there; she complains that English places do not seem "real": "Lines are just lines, and letters are just letters," she says, "You can't touch the meaning behind them the way you can when you're home and you look at a map and you see, instead of a place-name, a stretch of road or an orchard, or an ice-cream parlour around the corner" (p. 167).

At the start of the novel, Maja discovers that she is pregnant; Maja's experience of pregnancy is one of the loss of bodily control as her food intake, sleep patterns, and even singing voice, change. The threatened miscarriage, and the imagined relationship she has with her unborn child, add to Maja's experiences of displacement; the sense of a self that is also some other being interpenetrates all aspects of the narrative. Yet alienation is not the only outcome; the possibility of another life, in the form of Maja's son, allows the novel to imagine a future that connects the legacy of the past with that of the future. Pregnancy brings a more optimistic note to the story, as her condition reminds Maja that there is a connection with the past and future to be forged despite broken ties and fragmented legacies. One

does not need to go backward but can look forward to a future; as the novel records, lost tongues and lives may stay lost, but new lives and tongues can grow, "no one need be maimed" (p. 235).

The second story in this two-hander novel concerns the lives of Yemaya, or Aya, the mother of the Yoruba deities, or orishas, who were brought over in the minds and imaginations of West African slaves when they were transported to Cuba to work on the sugar plantations. As Maja informs us, the orishas came on the ships of "black gold," "hidden in the unseen smack, smack, smack of the next man's head on the ship's boards as he tried to damage his brain and decrease his market value" (p. 24). The Cuban religion called Santeria was created out of the spiritual beliefs and practices that emerged when West African slaves transported to Cuba were forced to convert to Catholicism; Santeria is a syncretic fusion in which Yoruba rituals, deities, and cosmology mix with Catholic religion and traditions. In order to preserve their West African religious cultures, slaves "masked" their own gods in the faces and clothes of Catholic saints and identified certain West African orishas as Catholic saints. African gods such as Obatalá, the father of all mankind; Eshu, or Elegguá, the messenger; Oggun, the god of iron; Oshún, the goddess of love and beauty; and Yemajá, the mother of all gods, associated with the sea and the life-giving properties of water, mutated or were transformed, respectively, in Santeria into Our Lady of Ransom; St Anthony of Padua, the Holy Child of Prague or Achota (Christ); St Peter or the archangel Michael; Our Lady of Charity or La Caridád de Cobré, and Our Lady of Regla, the patron saint of Cuba, although other incarnations of these orishas are associated with other Catholic saints. Just as each Yoruba deity is traditionally able to take on more than one manifestation, each particular manifestation might lead to an association with a different Catholic saint.

In this mythic halfway "somewherehouse" that functions as a counterpoint to Maja's London, the story of the deities' confused and at times reluctant transformation is alluded to humorously and also with pathos. Aya's mother, reincarnated as the Proserpine, echoing the Greco-Roman figure associated with a seasonal cycle of death and rebirth, abandons the West African custom of wearing wooden masks on feast days. Eshu complains about being called Elegua and (mis)taken for Jesus, or the Holy Child of Atocha, who is "rosy-cheeked and dimpled and couldn't drink as much palm wine" (p. 112) as the original Yoruba deity traditionally would have. Ochun (Oshun), the goddess of beauty and love, "suffered secret agonies over the drab garb that her counterpart, Our Lady of Mercy, wore in portraits" (p. 113). Ochun, who leaves Aya's house in her costume of five bright silk scarves, later reappears in the form of the soft-spoken Amy, who smells of wild honey and suffers from anorexia nervosa. The Kayodes, who may be the three gods of the Dahomey branch of the family, who turn up in the boat to Cuba by mistake, are also transported from West Africa and live in the same "somewherehouse" as Yemaya/Aya. The Kayodes keep to themselves and refuse to change; they do not talk with anyone outside their own group, and they will not eat any of the Afro-Cuban food that is cooked for them. However enticing the aromas of these meals are, "born in Aya's pans" like "holy smoke," the threesome refuse to draw sustenance from the new cuisine and slowly starve to death, growing "too weak even to talk to each other" (p. 245).

The Opposite House, which takes its title from Emily Dickinson's poem of the same name, describes the intermingling of two different kinds of stories: the quasi-realist story of Maja's black singer in London and the more lyrical story of the transformation of Yemaya or Aya's family in Santeria religious traditions and practices. The "somewherehouse" is a magical place whose reality is constructed in the world of myths and whose linguistic register is more poetic, allusive, and relies more on metaphoric associations than does the prosaic language that forms the bedrock of the main realist narrative. The arresting opening chapter of *The Opposite House* not only sets up the novel's theme of migration, change, and multiplicity but provides the novel's compelling

image of a many-roomed labyrinthine fairy-tale house containing two different main exits and entries—one leading into the "ragged hum of a city after dark" but the other opening out to a place that is always "floridly day": the "tattered jester" Lagos, with its "striped flag and cooking-smell cheer" (p. 1). Its occupants have to become shape-shifters in order to survive. The more realist and the mythic stories are interconnected, however. Maja's pregnancy, for example, forms one of the many points of contact with the tale of the somewherehouse; her counterpart, Yemaya, is also a (divine) mother and a deity associated with fertility. Names such as Maja and Amy Eleni, and the names of Maya's parents—at times called Papi and Mami—are names also used in the second narrative, albeit with minor modifications: Maja's middle name is Carmen, the name also of her mother and grandmother. Maja echoes Aya, or Yemaya, just as her middle name calls to mind her grandmother and mother. Aya's parents are called Papa and Mama (though the latter mutates into Prosperine). The realist character Amy Eleni suffers from hysteria in a similar manner to Amy (or Oshun) of Aya's story. The deliberate counterpointing of houses and stories reference two different tales but they can be read as versions—opposites—of one another.

The structure of the novel underscores such a reading, because Oyeyemi's narration alternates the religious and fabular story, with the more domestic and realist plot set in metropolitan London. Transitions between stories happen suddenly and without warning or chapter division. There is also no meta-narration that acts as a framing device for the two stories, to provide readers with a reassuring overview or map of events. Yemaya's association with water and the sea is transformed into Maja's obsession with the leaking ceiling inside and the rain outside Aaron's flat. Maja tells us that her world seems cast adrift on water, it "whirls" and sloshes with the relentless drip of rain and with the bathroom leak, along with her tears and the movement of the amniotic fluid in which her unborn "sons swims as he sleeps" (p. 233). The temporal structure of *The Opposite House* is equally complex insofar as it moves without warning between the causal time and progression of the realist narrative, the analeptic backward time of the characters' memories, and the transcendent time of fable, religious epiphany, or fantasy. These effects make the alternating stories blend and bleed into one another; the result is a dizzying, vertiginous tale in which characters and stories are seemingly and confusingly protean and have a multiplicity of identity. Furthermore, Oyeyemi's rhetorical style, which echoes some of Emily Dickinson's sudden moves between the concrete image and the abstract idea, is markedly lyrical and poetic in relation to the fabular world of the Yoruba deities. Oyeyemi's language works associatively; moving between language worlds is less about translation per se than it is about creative semantics, as words are giving new meanings and life by these associations. For example, in the opening pages of the novel, the pain of dislocation is described as an "ache," a "bone-deep pain," but it in Yoruba, *ache* is also power or energy that connects all; in the context of both Maja and Yemaya's lives, "*ache* is blood ... fleeing and returning ... red momentum. *Ache* is, *ache* is is is, kin to fear—a frayed pause near the end of a thread where the cloth matters too much to fail. The kind of need that takes you across water on nothing but bare feet" (p. 3). The critic Brenda Cooper has called Oyeyemi's novel "an extended poem" of "disconnected words, worlds and layers of [at times] unintelligible connections" that is deliberately resistant to been pinned down to "fixed meanings" (p. 110) and her story a "narrative gymnastics of migrating metamorphosing gods and mortals" (p. 120).

MAD WOMEN ...

In Amy Eleni, in Maja, and in the Yoruba deity Ochun as Amy, *The Opposite House* introduces the idea of the woman as hysteric, which in an interview with Gráinne Lyons, Oyeyemi has called the manifestation of a "specifically female inner turmoil" (p. 15). Hysteria as a psychoanalytic concept, from Jean-Martin Charcot to Josef Breuer to Sigmund Freud, refers to the displacement of mental and psychological trauma or psychosexual disturbance into physical symp-

toms; in general, hysteria is predicated on the assumption that what the mind cannot admit into consciousness returns as unexplained physiological symptoms. Feminist psychoanalysts such as Hélène Cixous see in the expression of bodily symptoms what the conscious and rational mind cannot admit in patriarchal culture, hysteric symptoms are thus an unconscious language written and spoken by the body. Instead of pathologizing the hysteric, Cixous elevates the hysteric into a "threshold figure for women's liberation and as a form of resistance to patriarchy" (discussed in Ragland-Sullivan, p. 165). Oyeyemi's understanding of the hysteric as a distinctively feminine ailment also reads these bodily symptoms as, if not strictly the unconscious speaking, indicative also of a rebellion against what is acceptable norms or standards for feminine behavior. Hysterics in Oyeyemi's *The Opposite House* signal oppositional alter egos; in an interview with Michel Martin, she alluded to her hysterics as "messy and screamy and shouty," saying that they are reactions against the socialization of femininity: "parts of yourself that you need to tuck away" in order to fit into a version of respectable femininity as well-mannered, quiet, lovely and passive. In *The Opposite House,* Maja describes her hysteric not as an alter-ego as such but rather as part of her "store" (p. 30); her fantasies, her refusal to eat, is part of an anger that expresses itself not in the "screaming and fainting and clinging to walls" of the nineteenth century but as "a numbness of skin that demands cutting" (p. 71). While hysteria in the novel is the "trauma speak[ing] itself to excess," the "revelation" that women "refuse to be consoled" for "biscuit-tin discipline" (p. 35), it is also not necessarily life-affirming. As Maja's father says in the novel, "Suffering isn't [necessarily or always] transformative" (p. 76) but may lead to suicide and self-destruction.

Oyeyemi's interest in madness, hysteria, and self-destruction also carries through into her third novel. In a 2009 interview with the London *Times* writer Ben Machell, Oyeyemi says that madness in women is something of an obsession in her work—"how it can manifest itself, what it means, what pressures forces someone into these behaviours." *White Is for Witching* tells of the troubled life of a young girl, Miranda Silver (Miri), who suffers from "pica," an eating disorder that compels her to eat pieces of chalk or nonfood substitutes such as plastic or onyx chips. While Miri suffers from pica before the death of her mother, Lily, her condition—and the physical and psychological damage that result from and inform her illness—is compounded by Lily's death at a relatively impressionable age, when Miri is only sixteen. Miri's difficulty in consuming real food means that she slowly but surely starves herself, reducing her body to a pale shadow of her earlier self. The character's eating disorder is inherited from the women in her maternal line, who, at the start of the novel, are all deceased but within the context of this gothic novel exist as spectral traces of themselves in the house that they have all previously lived in. Miri slowly transforms herself into a ghost by literally starving herself. Her character also sees visions, and these sometimes take the form of images of her dead relatives, visions that later turn out to have been images of herself. Miri's fragile mental state coupled with such visions mean that we are never really sure whether these are simply hallucinations or whether Miri's madness lies in her ability to see visions that others cannot see. The novel also seems at times to suggest that Miri's insanity is a product of how her story is tangled up with the ghost of other stories, including those that are the product of memories, fairy tales, texts, and fables. Thus, in the quarrel between Miri and her twin brother that occurs toward the end of the novel, over the use of the winter apples that are baked into a pie, the apples are precisely of the same poisoned red and white variety used in the wicked queen's entrapment of Snow White in the fairy tales of the Brothers Grimm.

In the novel, Miri herself seems to be cast alternately as victim of loneliness that she brings upon herself and also of a fate that she cannot seem to dodge; within the novel, Miri's character seems predetermined by those roles linked with the darker protagonists and villains of fables and fairy tales. Miri, for example, is associated with vampiric figures; Oyeyemi has admitted to reading *Dracula* prior to the writing of *White Is for Witching*, describing Miri to Ben Machell as "a girl who eats chalk, but probably with a desire to eat something else." The link between Miri and vampires occurs very early, with the relating of Miri's childhood memory of her great grandmother, Anna Good, trying to rub blood on her lips. The recollection is narrated with a lightness of touch, because Miri likens her great-grandmother's strange behavior to that of a mythic, Christ-like heraldic pelican of the medieval period that was thought to feed her young on her own blood; Miri also puts these actions down to the great-grandmother's mental breakdown. But the incident is made memorable because Lily, Miri's mother, attempts to disavow the event—characterizing it as a false memory and angrily accusing Miri of making up stories.

The association of Miri with vampires is built up gradually but associatively in the text, although it is never declared outright. Miri dresses in black; her habits are more nocturnal than diurnal; she is linked with the "goodlady," or described as the goodlady herself. The "goodlady" is initially characterized as a protector of the family and then, later, as a sinister composite of the maternal line of the Silver family; the goodlady controls and protects her own to the exclusion of others, and she is linked with the soucouyant in Caribbean folklore, who sucks blood from her victims. Later, Ore as Miri's lover recounts describes the headiness, hypnotic quality, and intensity of their relationship, how disturbed their nights in bed were together, and how drained and tired Ore felt when with Miri. Because of Miri's difficulties with food, Ore may eat perhaps less than she describes: her obsession with food when not in the presence of her lover is a strategy for survival. Despite her gorging on food when not in the presence of Miri, Ore is reduced to a shadow of her physical self; she is described by another student as gradually "disappearing." When not with Miri, Ore also seems to acknowledge her gradual physical deterioration. Yet full recognition of her condition is deferred for a future time when she is alone; then only would she "look for wounds" (p. 185) on her body. In *White Is for Witching*, then, one cannot be sure if readers should read Miri as a vampire in the tradition of gothic tales or if readers are meant to see Miri as an extremely troubled young woman; in this, the ambivalence of *White Is for Witching* regarding its lead character is reminiscent of Henry James's 1898 novella, *The Turn of the Screw.*

... AND HOUSES

Akin to many gothic tales, and perhaps uncannily like Edgar Allan Poe's 1839 story "The Fall of the House of Usher," *White Is for Witching* is set in an old house. This house, which has passed down through the generations, is located near the cliffs of Dover and is the residence of a twin brother and sister, Eliot and Miranda Silver. The outline of the plot echoes Poe's story, in that Oyeyemi's 29 Barton Road is visited by another figure on the invitation of one of the siblings, who is friends with, and emotionally attached to, the visitor. Much like the house of Poe's story, 29 Barton Road is also depicted in the novel as a sentient being; some of the description of the exterior of the house, initially at least, references Poe's house even by virtue of being its opposite. As with Poe's House of Usher, windows are noted, but instead of being depicted as being vacant and eye-like, 29 Barton Road has windows that "were funny square eyes, friendly, [and] tired," even of they "didn't look as if they were there to let air or light in" (p. 17). The grounds of the house, described by the very young Eliot Silver, might seem bucolic—the landscape contains apple trees and hedges of wild flowers—yet the steps leading up to the house contain lumps of flint, "each a piece of knife to cut your knee open should you slip," and a graveyard lies in the vicinity (p. 17). In the eyes of the young Silver siblings, it was a cool and "wicked" and "magical" house (p. 18). Yet as the novel progresses, the description of the house and its rooms changes. The house seems to have a life of its own; the lit windows of the house, to which Miri returns after a spell at a psychiatric unit, is described as a malevolent smile in the gloom. The house imprisons the housekeepers' little girl in the old cast-iron elevator; it has rooms full of

secret memories and corridors that seem to lead nowhere. In a note slipped to Miri, the housekeeper's children warn that there is more to the house than meets the eye: "extra floors," the young girls write, "with lots of people on them. They are looking people" (p. 57). Miri's friend also experiences the house as evil; "the light in the house was subterranean, as if the place had been built out of mildew" (p. 205), Ore reports, and even the trees take on sinister aspect, depositing a poisoned apple on her pillow.

What is perhaps most striking in this partial reworking of the House of Usher is that the 29 Barton Road house is given its own voice in the tale. *White Is for Witching*, which starts where the story ends, namely in Miri's disappearance and probable death, is narrated in the first person by three different voices, each of which represent three different significant others in Miri's life. The first voice is that of Ore, a young black female student with whom Miri has a love affair when they are together as undergraduates at Cambridge. The second voice is that of Eliot, Miri's twin brother, whose relationship with his sister is close but strained, as both siblings feel an intimate connection and yet also a need to separate and develop personalities and identities that are distinct from each other. Miri and Eliot's relationship is also subtly eroticized in the novel; imagined as "born in love with each other" (p. 44) and the narrative seems to suggest that Eliot had secretly stalked his sister in Cambridge when he was supposed to be in South Africa. The final voice belongs to that of the house; at first, the reader may greet this voice with incredulity, but the voice is increasingly strident and emerges as a sinister character with the novel's progression. In effect, the house takes the role of writing the script of Miri's life and guiding her to see herself as an inheritor of the maternal madness that is identified with the Silver family line. When Miri falls asleep in a hammock, she finds herself in a world much like Alice in Lewis Carroll's stories—emerging from the trapdoor in the house into a room which contains a long table set with enticing dishes that is presided over by a capricious Red Queen–like figure who turns out to be her mother. Seated around the table are two other dinner guests, her grandmother and her great-grandmother, but they appear to have padlocks "placed over their parted mouths, boring through the top lip and closing at the bottom"; the horror of such mutilation is evident in the manner in which their tongues writhe (p. 127). Outside the house, an aerial bombardment seems to be taking place, and the "air was full of the smell of burning" and screaming (p. 126), but inside the room of this nightmare house, Miri sees disembodied brown fingers, which appear twitching in the holes of the concrete walls; these belong to Jalil, an acquaintance from school for whom she conceives a very brief and passing fancy. She feels responsible for the presence of his "ruptured nerve endings," as if she had dealt the blows in a fit of "inattention," "not unlike watching someone else take her hand and guide it." "It's safe in here," the mother declares. "Us Silver girls together" (pp. 128–129).

The house is ruthless in protecting its own and in excluding all that it decides are threats. When Jennifer, Lily's mother, decides to run away from her family, the house imprisons her in one of its endless store of hidden rooms. The house at 29 Barton Road also animates inanimate objects such as the dressmaker's mannequin, and it brings spectral shapes into life as puppets in its macabre shows. Furthermore, it also seems to exhibit xenophobic tendencies, targeting non-English people. It tries to eject the Iranian and Nigerian help whom Miri's father hires to help with his bed-and-breakfast operation, and it rejects the black guests who turn up as clients. The house succeeds in scaring the Iranian family by imprisoning their daughter in the elevator, and it scoffs at the attempts by the Nigerian housekeeper, Sade, to create her own spells in self-defense: "Juju is not enough to protect you. Everything you have I will turn against you. I'll turn sugar bitter for you. I'll take your very shield and crack it on your head … *White* is for witching, Sade goodbye" (p. 175). The black hotel guests are kept prisoners in their own beds for three days, "curved around the bed like fitted sheets with their faces crusting over" (p. 139). Ore, who arrives at 29 Barton Road as Miri's lesbian lover, is a young, feisty, and much-loved black girl who was adopted into a working-class

family and who can hold her own among her conservative cousins, who taunt her with fascistic comments; she also stand up to the buildings, textbooks, furniture, and august personages of Cambridge who whisper "*You don't belong here*" (p. 157). In temperament, Ore is resilient; her favorite story is that of the girl who manages to kill the fearsome soucouyant. Yet Ore finds her match in the house at 29 Barton Road because Miri is too intimately linked with the house and its goodlady to be separated from the house and its evil spells. When Ore tries to release Miri from the villainous form that her lover has been made to inhabit, Miri asks to be put back. "Don't become her [the soucouyant]," Ore says, but her pleas fall on deaf ears. Miri is drawn back to the orbit of the house and punished because she let the black lover leave. *White Is for Witching*, set as it is in a Dover that functions as the last frontier for unwanted outsiders who wash up against its shore, uses the metaphor of the xenophobic house to explore questions of incomers, whether those immigrants be Kosovan refugees, legal Eastern European workers who move to Britain or the illegal migrants who work in low-paid service jobs to prop up the tourist industry or found dead in the trucks used to traffic people illegally into the country or incarcerated in detention centers, choosing suicide instead of deportation. The Dover of the novel is a place of violence between and within communities; as Sade remarks, Dover is the "key to a locked gate, throughout both world wars and even before. It's still fighting" (p. 107).

Yet ultimately, the novel's world tells a metafictional story, an homage to and a story about the writing of uncanny gothic tales. The novel is narrated through three separate voices, with different ways of seeing, that weave and blend into each other. The alleged unreliability of any one of the narrative voices made by 29 Barton Road hints at readers' dilemma. Not only is it a question of trust but one of imaginative literary re-creation through words; as the house remarks, "Our talk depends upon the fact that you weren't there and you don't know what happened" (p. 226). Eliot's innocence is put in doubt with the house's revelation that he had been stalking his sister in Cambridge; Ore's account of Miri as being a soucouyant may reflect her own confusion as she tries to fit her lover into these Caribbean gothic tales. Miri's shape-shifting—from young girl, to Lily, to the goodlady, to paper drawings, to vampire and soucouyant—makes it difficult for the reader to decide the truth of the tale. What the novel amounts to is a labyrinth of stories of other stories and texts, a hallucinatory "psychomantium," a mirrored chamber. Miri's room, also called a "psychomantium," is where things and people "appear as they really are. Visions are called from a point inside the mirror, from a point inside the mind" (p. 33). The concept of the psychomantium perfectly embodies the spirit of the house and also its unsettling voice; it describes the novel's interface between the real world and the surreal, gothic, or uncanny one by externalizing the imagination.

Oyeyemi's method of working and her literary style has been characterized by Brenda Cooper as being generated through the links brought about by the sounds of words; thus Cooper describes *The Opposite House* as a "narrative labyrinth" or an "extend poem" (p. 110) One can also argue that Oyeyemi's characteristic tendency to work associatively not only through sound (as Cooper implies), but also through images and stories generated by other texts, renders her a writer who is acutely conscious of writing as a poetic and intertextual web. As a novelist, Oyeyemi's stylistic innovations move her work outside the boundaries of the realist novel even when she does not abandon those boundaries altogether. In the pursuit of the literary gothic, Oyeyemi perhaps has found the perfect vehicle that enables her to address the vital, volatile, psychological and imaginative states that are concealed between the cracks of everyday life in the world we live in.

Selected Bibliography

WORKS OF HELEN OYEYEMI

The Icarus Girl. London: Bloomsbury, 2005.

Juniper's Whitening and Victimese. London: Methuen Drama Series, 2005.

The Opposite House. London: Bloomsbury, 2007.

White Is for Witching. London: Picador, 2009.

CRITICAL STUDIES

Bryce, Jane. "'Half and Half Children': Third-Generation Women Writers and the New Nigerian Novel." *Research in African Literatures* 39, no. 2:49–67 (2008).

Cooper, Brenda. "The Middle Passage of the Gods and the New Diaspora: Helen Oyeyemi's *The Opposite House.*" *Research in African Literatures* 40, no. 4:108–121 (2009).

Cuder-Dominguex, Pilar. "Double Consciousness in the Work of Helen Oyeyemi and Diana Evans." *Women: A Cultural Review* 20, no. 3:277–286 (2009).

De La Torre, Miguel A. *Santería: The Beliefs and Rituals of a Growing Religion in America.* Grand Rapids, Mich.: Eerdmans, 2004.

Hron, Madelaine. "Ora na-azu nwa: The Figure of the Child in Third-Generation Nigerian Novels." *Research in African Literatures* 39, no. 2:27–48 (2008).

McCabe, Douglas. "Histories of Errancy: Oral Yoruba Abiku Texts and Soyinka's 'Abiku.'" *Research in African Literatures* 33, no. 1:45–76 (2002).

Gonzalez-Wippler, Migene. *Santería: The Religion.* New York: Harmony, 1989.

Okparanta, Chinenye. "Negotiating the Boundaries of Nation, Language, and Race in Helen Oyeyemi's *The Icarus Girl* and Edwidge Danticat's *The Farming of Bones.*" *Journal of African Literature Association* 2, no. 2:188–208 (2008).

Ragland-Sullivan, Ellie. "Hysteria." In *Feminism and Psychoanalysis: A Critical Dictionary.* Edited by Elizabeth Wright. Oxford: Blackwell, 1992. Pp. 163–166.

INTERVIEWS

Brace, Marianne. "Helen Oyeyemi: Purveyor of Myths Turns Her Focus to Cuban Deities." *Independent* (http://www.independent.co.uk/arts-entertainment/books/features/helen-oyeyemi-purveyor-of-myths-turns-her-focus-to-cuban-deities-449273.html), May 18, 2007.

Forna, Aminatta. "New Writing and Nigeria: Chimamanda Ngozi Adichie and Helen Oyeyemi in Conversation." *Wasafiri* 47:50–57 (spring 2006).

Lyons, Gráinne. "Helen Oyeyemi." *Aesthetica*, August–September 2007, p. 15.

Machell, Ben. "Helen Oyeyemi: The *Times* Interview." *Times* (http://entertainment.timesonline.co.uk/tol/arts_and_entertainment/books/article6344159.ece), May 23, 2009.

Martin, Michel. "Oyeyemi's *Opposite House.*" National

Public Radio (http://www.npr.org/templates/story/story.php?storyId=11384738), June 27, 2007.

Pan Macmillan. "An Interview with Helen Oyeyemi" (http://www.panmacmillan.com/displayPage.asp?PageID=7113). (Page includes a video of Oyeyemi reading an extract from *White Is for Witching*.)

Sethi, Anita. "I Didn't Know I Was Writing a Novel: Helen Oyeyemi." *Guardian*

Taylor, Isabel. "Interview with Helen Oyeyemi." *Albion* (http://www.zyworld.com/albionmagazineonline/books5_fiction.htm), winter 2006.

MARK PATTISON

(1813—1884)

Christopher Vilmar

IF A MEMBER of the nineteenth-century English reading public were to find themselves suddenly transported to the present, they would be surprised to find that Mark Pattison is remembered, when he is remembered at all, as a leading candidate for the original model of the failed scholar Edward Casaubon in George Eliot's *Middlemarch* (1872). In his own time, Pattison was widely regarded as the greatest scholar in England. His writing appeared regularly in popular journals and newspapers, and he was a leading expert on university reform and the history of religion and classical scholarship. Near the end of his life, as rector of Lincoln College, Oxford, Pattison was the living embodiment of the scholarly life: retired, erudite, and devoted to constant study, yet known for his sparkling conversational wit as well as the characteristically taut, tart phrasing of his written style. Politically, he was a Liberal, devoted to such causes as the education and enfranchisement of women and suspected of religious disbelief. Yet even in Victorian England these associations did little to diminish the respect in which he was held. On his death, as far away as America the *Proceedings of the American Academy of Arts and Sciences* regarded him in memoriam as "Oxford's most erudite scholar, and most competent critic in many branches of learning" (p. 539).

Pattison's rise to such eminence, however, is the story of a painfully slow progression from relative obscurity to positions of greater importance and influence. Along the way he met with many obstacles, including the insanity of his father and his troubled marriage to a woman twenty-seven years younger than himself, Emilia Frances Strong. And as his *Memoirs* (1885) reveal, Pattison possessed a tendency toward bitter and invidious self-reproach that could tarnish even those things which looked to the outside like spectacular success.

As Pattison himself announces on the first page of his *Memoirs*, "I have really no history but a mental history" (p. 1). Though not strictly true, his life was dominated by Oxford University, especially his residence at two colleges, Oriel and Lincoln. His mind also took shape from its encounter with a few luminous contemporaries, especially two men, John Henry Newman and Benjamin Jowett. And even when his marriage furnished material for several novels, most notably Eliot's *Middlemarch*, it was figured as an intellectual as much as an emotional or physical incompatibility. In all of these instances it is Pattison the scholar who figures most prominently in the account. Dinah Birch has described the contradictory tendencies that presided over his scholarly work: "The morose and fastidious Pattison embodies the most scrupulous development of scholarship, but he also represents the seeds of its self-destructive decadence" (p. 211). Pattison's attainments as a scholar are much debated, in fact, and it is difficult to obtain a correct assessment of his career without engaging with the wide range of his scholarly output. By his own admission he never finished the work he set out for himself, and assessing his achievements can only be undertaken by a careful consideration of his entire intellectual life as it winds from his Yorkshire childhood through many essays and reviews to the outpouring of books during his final years.

YOUTH AND OXFORD

Mark Pattison was born on October 10, 1813, in the village of Hornby in Yorkshire. His father, Mark James Pattison, was curate of the parish, and his mother, Jane Winn, was the heiress of a banker. The elder Pattison graduated from Brasenose College, Oxford, where, despite Pattison's negative opinion of his father's learning in the *Memoirs*, he read classical languages with enough facility and sensitivity to educate his son privately and to coach him for his entrance exams at Oxford. His religion was strongly Evangelical, and he was not unlike the stereotypes of nineteenth-century Anglican priests satirized by novelists like Anthony Trollope: little better than an entrenched, smugly satisfied Protestant prejudice. The Pattison children—whose numbers were increased over time by another son, born twenty-one years after Mark, and ten daughters born between those dates—played in the nearby castle of the Duke of Leeds, where their father possessed some influence. As a child Mark became intimate with the duke's second son, Lord Conyers Osborne, whom he idolized when the latter was home on vacation from Eton for being able to "do everything I could do, only ten times better, and write Latin verses fast without a false quantity" (*Memoirs*, p. 20). Pattison was himself educated at home. This was common, especially for the children of educated clergymen, and it is worth noting that even as a boy Pattison did not envy his friend's rank but rather his facility in Latin.

The elder Pattison hoped that his connections with the Duke of Leeds would bring him further preferment in the Church. Though preferment came, in 1825, it was from elsewhere, and Pattison was made rector of nearby Hauxwell, also in Yorkshire. Though Pattison only lived there for seven years before his matriculation at Oxford, Hauxwell remained a formative memory, and he returned there often on his vacations. He had few friends and preferred to roam alone through the countryside, where he delighted in discovering its beauties, studying its birds and insects, shooting, and indulging his lifelong passion of fly-fishing.

Almost from infancy Pattison had been intended for Oxford, where his father expected him to become a fellow. In 1830 his father took him to visit the university, where the two consulted with various parties, including his childhood friend Lord Conyers at Christ Church, about his prospects. It was eventually decided that Pattison would attend Oriel, at the time the most eminent of the university's colleges. A room was not expected to become available until 1832, and during the two years Pattison spent back at Hauxwell he read widely but with little comprehension or direction. The few books that he read carefully and with some intellectual profit are mentioned in the *Memoirs*, including Gilbert White's *Natural History and Antiquities of Selborne* (1769–1787), Prideaux John Selby's *Illustrations of British Ornithology* (1825–1834), George Montagu's *Ornithological Dictionary* (1802), and James Rennie's *The Natural History of Insects* (1829) and *Insect Architecture* (1830). Pattison later described his reading of William Wordsworth's *Prelude*, first published in 1850, as a story parallel to his own mental development, especially the transition from a boyish interest in nature to the mature study of poetry. The opening sentence of Rennie's *Insect Architecture* is as relevant to the youthful fascination with the natural world as to the later scholarly attention to the details of literary history: "It can never be too strongly impressed upon a mind anxious for the acquisition of knowledge, that the commonest things by which we are surrounded are deserving of minute and careful attention" (p. 1).

When Pattison finally received his acceptance letter from Oxford, the entire family was swept up in the excitement. He went up to Oriel in the spring of 1832, accompanied by his father. Two ideas dominate those parts of the *Memoirs* that recount his years as an undergraduate. First, his social awkwardness, which was partly caused by his solitary and isolated youth, and second, his disappointment at the low level of academic attainment that prevailed among the fellows and students even at a prestigious college like Oriel. The two partly exacerbated one another. Pattison could not imagine that students came up to the university for any reason other than serious study, and therefore felt ill at ease around the majority who had not. Pattison's father was "fond of repeating the sentence in the Eton Latin grammar—'Concessi Cantabrigiam ad capiendum ingenii cultum' [I went to Cambridge to acquire cultivation of mind]." Pattison continues, "This was the proverb which presided over my whole college life" (*Memoirs*, p. 22). The father echoes this sentiment in one of his first letters to Pattison at Oxford, when he puts his library at the son's command, claiming that it "cannot be more usefully and honourably employed than in enriching and storing a mind, the cultivation of which has been the nearest object of my heart for eighteen years" (*Memoirs*, p. 109). The cast of mind that remembered this sentence after so many years helps to explain why Pattison struggled socially and only made friends once he had improved his academic standing.

In 1830 John Henry Newman, Hurrell Froude, and Robert Wilberforce had been Oriel's tutors, and their presence heightened the college's intellectual standing. Reforms earlier in the nineteenth century had made the standard of instruction at Oriel perhaps the highest in Oxford. Yet when Pattison arrived in 1832, these three eminences had been replaced by less capable men. In 1833, when Pattison moved into rooms on the same staircase and directly opposite Newman's, he had little contact with the older fellow.

Pattison was disappointed with the teaching at Oxford, which even as a student he knew to have been often lifted or cribbed directly from the footnotes of the standard editions of the classical texts he was reading. He spent four unprofitable terms in this atmosphere, but during the vacation of 1833 he devised a plan for his own education. Having decided that his Oxford tuition had done little to improve his understanding, Pattison laid out a "scheme of self-education" meant to eradicate his false or prejudicial ideas; it was, as he later put it, "the first stirrings of anything like intellectual life within me" (*Memoirs*, p. 120). At this time, too, Pattison began to keep a journal of his reading, a habit he would continue with few intermissions throughout his life.

As Pattison would later reminiscence, this plan was ambitious but impractical. Though Pattison already loved the thrill of discovery and the process of working out his own thoughts, these habits were too labor-intensive to be of real use in preparing for Oxford's exams. Most students hired private coaches to help them prepare for exams, working up a basic understanding of the fundamental texts of the Christian religion as well as literature, mathematics, and physics in classical authors like the Greek playwrights, Euclid, and Aristotle. Pattison later hired a tutor himself, choosing one of the fellows of Oriel, C. P. Eden. Eden did not help Pattison cram but instead engaged him in serious conversations designed to probe and question what he had read. Though attractive to Pattison, this method was not designed to supply him with quick answers for the exam. He scored a second on his exam in 1836, rather than the first that, he hoped, would help him to become an Oxford fellow and spend his life studying within college walls.

Another event, unmentioned in the *Memoirs* but perhaps of still greater influence on Pattison's academic performance, was his father's insanity in 1834. The elder Pattison was placed in an asylum at Acomb, near York and not far from the family home. In 1835 the father was released but judged not safe to be at home, and Mark missed a term in order to care for him in York. For the rest of his life, the elder Pattison suffered from violent mood swings, sometimes shutting himself in his room and at others verbally abusing his wife and daughters. In later years, when his daughters followed their brother into high-church Tractarianism, he would ask visitors, "Will you take your dinner with the Papists in the dining room, or with the poor persecuted Protestant here?" (quoted in Sparrow, p. 35). He was paranoid, refused to allow his daughters to marry, and on occasion preached against his own family in the pulpit. Only those two daughters who were closest to Mark, Eleanor and Rachel, dared break their father's prohibitions to marry, and he disinherited them when he died in 1865.

TRACTARIAN AND FELLOW OF LINCOLN

Pattison's father was convinced that his son was too liberal to be a devout Christian, and therefore unfit to take orders in the Anglican church—a necessity if Pattison was to hold an Oxford fellowship for more than seven years. The father encouraged his son to pursue law instead. Pattison persuaded his father to allow him to remain in Oxford, where he competed unsuccessfully for fellowships at four colleges over the next two years. During 1837 he began to spend time socially with Newman and the other Tractarians, and by December, when he informed his parents that he intended to seek Anglican orders, he was living with other like-minded graduates in a house rented by E. B. Pusey on St. Aldates Street in the heart of Oxford. His father may have disliked the Catholic tendencies of his son's associates, but he could no longer doubt his sincerity.

Tractarianism, or the Oxford movement, had begun in Pattison's own college, Oriel. Newman, John Keble, E. B. Pusey, and Hurrell Froude were its key figures. In his famous Assize Sermon of 1833, Keble argued that the Church of England suffered under too much state control. And in a series of "Tracts for the Times," these men sought renewal by returning the English church to the apostolic and catholic foundations of Christianity. These reforms had an academic component, in the revision of the outdated curriculum of the university; this aspect may have been a key attraction for Pattison. For the time, much of the intellectual excitement of Oxford was found in these controversies, and by 1838 Pattison was, as he would later characterize it, rushing headlong into the whirlpool of Tractarianism.

In 1839, Pattison competed for a fellowship at Lincoln College, for which he was qualified by his Yorkshire birth. Lincoln was not a distinguished college, and its fellows were typical of the old, unreformed Oxford; further, they were rigidly opposed to the Oxford Movement. Pattison had fortunately moved out of the house on St. Aldates mere weeks before putting himself in for the fellowship, and he was still surprised to find that he won it. As he himself was later to describe the event in the *Memoirs*, "No moment in all my life has ever been so sweet." More than his own dreams were realized; as he continues in the *Memoirs*, "The joy at Hauxwell equaled my own" (p. 183).

Pattison's embrace of Tractarian tenets further estranged him from his father. When returning to his beloved home at Hauxwell became difficult on account of his father's illness and their religious disagreements, Pattison visited less frequently. The rest of the family felt the pain of their estrangement. His sisters sought relief from their father's oppressiveness by writing to Pattison often. He sent them Tractarian materials and supervised their reading and education by letter. When they too became caught up in the movement, their father responded with increased hostility. His sisters visited him in Oxford, where they looked on their older brother with adoration and, perhaps, envy. His beloved sister Rachel recalled one of her visits to him in a letter: "I have been full of O[xford] all day—I see you step across yr room I often think I never saw you walk so but in O[xford] I felt I was in your home when I saw that step, in that home which had combined to form you—it was so elastic—so vigorous so characteristic" (quoted in Sparrow, p. 38).

Part of this vigor and sense of belonging in Oxford was undoubtedly due to Pattison's first achievements in scholarship. His early publications were done in association with the Oxford movement, under the influence and direction of Newman. Pattison translated the commentary on the Book of Matthew in St. Thomas Aquinas' *Aurea Catena*, a large enterprise in four volumes edited by Newman. This book, an anthology of commentary that Aquinas compiled out of the writings of the early church fathers (c. 100–500 BCE), presented a special challenge to Pattison. Aquinas does not give references for the source of his passages, so Pattison spent much of 1839 laboriously searching out these sources in various editions scattered throughout the Bodleian Library. He became an acknowledged expert on patristic bibliography, admired for his skill at sleuthing out references and consulted as an authority on the Bodleian's holdings of patristic texts. He also published several essays in the *Christian Remembrancer*, a high-church publication sympathetic to Tractarian views. Pattison would publish almost exclusively with the *Christian Remembrancer* until 1853, writing reviews and essays on a wide variety of subjects including Gregory of Tours, Church poetry, and John Stuart Mill's political theory. One of his earliest essays, however, was on early British poetry in the high-church journal *British Critic*. Later, in 1845, he published the lives of Stephen Langton and St. Edmund in another series edited by Newman, *Lives of the English Saints*, A.D. *51–1250*.

At the end of 1844, the heads of the Oxford colleges considered imposing a test on fellows that would require them to subscribe to a rigidly Protestant interpretation of the Thirty-nine Articles of the Anglican *Book of Common Prayer*. Pattison decided that, if such a test were imposed, he would be forced to resign, but the proposal was never ratified. Instead, Newman left the Church of England for the Roman Catholic Church on October 9, 1845. This conversion caused a shock among English Christians, and it was widely thought that Pattison would follow him. But he did not; a story is told that were it not for a missed train or coach, which gave him time to reconsider, he would have.

The actual reasons are less romantic and more involved. Almost from birth Pattison had been raised to be a fellow in an Oxford college, which mandated that he remain in the Church of England. And in 1842, he was offered a tutorship in Lincoln. He threw himself into the work, and over the next decade he directed all of his attention to raising the tutorial standards at Lincoln. Instead of playing whist and drinking port after dinner with the other fellows, Pattison began to meet individually with students. Along with fellows at other colleges—for instance, Benjamin Jowett at Balliol—Pattison was responsible for inventing the tutorial system that remains foundational to undergraduate teaching at Oxford. This unremitting toil was instrumental in raising the intellectual prestige of the college. As a result Pattison accumulated power and influence in Lincoln, governing students, fellows, servants, and even the head until his sway within the walls was almost absolute.

Pattison also discovered during travel abroad that Catholicism on the Continent was as narrowly prejudiced and uninformed as Anglicanism back home. H. S. Jones has argued persuasively that Pattison's skepticism had been growing for some time before 1845. Pattison himself mentions his devotion to scholarship as a major deter-

rent to conversion to Roman Catholicism. The mental habits of the scholar led Pattison to doubt Christianity, and his doubts culminated in his decision in 1846 to side with reason and the skeptical temper against blind allegiance to any religious creed or dogma. Though religious ideas and patterns remained prominent in his thought for some time, for the rest of his life Pattison remained solidly liberal in matters of politics and rational in matters of religious belief. Neither of these convictions led to action; he neither went into politics nor forsook his clerical orders and therefore his fellowship. Instead he remained basically aloof from actual politics and gradually but steadily moved toward religious agnosticism. This combination of collegiate success, greater understanding of Catholic practices, and growing skepticism all led Pattison to resist the charismatic example of Newman's conversion.

Even as Pattison drifted toward secular rationalism, however, he continued to publish on religious subjects in high-church journals. He regularly wrote for the *Christian Remembrancer* until 1853. But during this period his essays and reviews began to cover a wider range of subjects than his earlier focus on church history at the height of his involvement in Tractarianism. Only some of his essays during this period were on overtly Christian subjects, such as his essays on "Church Poetry" and "The Oxford Bede." Others, like "Wordsworth's Diary in France," "Slave-Grown Sugar," and "Mill's Political Economy," show Pattison becoming interested in the issues and debates of the time, both at home in England and abroad on the European continent and around the world. The review of Mill was especially important. Pattison considered the publication of Mill's *Principles of Political Economy* (1848) as an event of major importance in Oxford intellectual life, a decisive move away from the Tractarian obsession with spiritual matters toward more practical, earthly concerns. Politics, especially when they intersected with proposed reforms in university funding and organization, remained a key interest that occupied Pattison throughout his career.

Pattison also began to deliver sermons from both the college and university pulpits. Four of the sermons found in his collected *Sermons* (1885) date from the period 1847–1851. Like all of his sermons, of which some survive in manuscript, they deal less with religious or theological truths than with the character of the intellectual life. These sermons are less traditional exhortations to piety than orations urging students to build character through laborious study. Pattison felt that deliberate, disciplined, and steady application to intellectual subjects would give students a kind of mental discipline useful beyond the walls of the university.

In 1847 Pattison fell into a depression, and his spirits became so low that he was barely able to meet his tutorial obligations. In 1848, however, T. H. Green, of Balliol College, nominated Pattison as an examiner for the literature section of the university honors exam. Pattison found that the other examiners were inferior to him in scholarship, and he was able to perform his duties with great success. Reports of his outstanding abilities as an examiner thrust Pattison into prominence as one of the finest young tutors at Oxford. It also made him aware, perhaps for the first time, that he might aspire to roles of greater influence and leadership in the university at large.

The moment was propitious for such thoughts. After Newman's conversion, university reform became an urgent national priority, much debated in parliamentary and public forums. In the *Memoirs*, Pattison writes that, "in the first rush of intellectual freedom, we were carried beyond all bounds, sought to change everything, questioned everything, and were impatient to throw the whole cargo of tradition overboard" (p. 239). He gave testimony to the 1850 Royal Commission of Inquiry, set up to investigate whether the universities needed to be reformed in order to meet the changing needs of an industrial, imperial nation. Pattison's thoughts were viewed as being especially valuable because he was one of the few Liberals to defend the existing tutorial system. He restricted his comments to the nature of teaching, arguing that life within a college ought to be life in common between tutor and student because the "insensible action of the teacher's character on the pupil's is the most valuable part of any education" (quoted in Jones, p. 182).

Though he later considered this impetuous drive toward reformation a mistake, Pattison became caught up in the attempt to replace the old Tory Oxford, which had changed little in centuries, with an institution demonstrably more modern and better suited to serve British society. As he mentions in the *Memoirs*, he had held the worst of the old traditions in disdain as an arriving student. And his own work in Lincoln, which had become stultified by its entrenchment in those old traditions, gave him a sense of the kinds of changes an enterprising man could bring about. These kinds of speculation had occupied Pattison for several years when John Radford, rector of Lincoln, died in the autumn of 1851, necessitating the election of a new head of the college.

RECTORSHIP LOST AND WON

The story of the lost election stands as one of the pivotal events in Pattison's life and in his *Memoirs*. When Radford died, there were eleven fellows in Lincoln, but two were abroad and therefore barred from voting by college statute. Pattison's stature in the college made him an obvious candidate, but several other fellows also put themselves forward as possible candidates. Pattison led a liberal voting bloc of three fellows, which with his own vote gave him four backers. The conservative faction in the college soon realized that they would lose if they divided their support among their own candidates, and they quickly resolved to put forward the elder William Kay as their choice, and they too had four votes. The swing vote belonged to J. L. R. Kettle, a lawyer who held a fellowship but was not in residence at the college. Kettle had hoped to nominate Richard Michell, who was vice principal of Magdalen Hall and a former fellow of Lincoln, though one disbarred by college statute from being eligible to be rector. Michell backed Kay, and Pattison strongly opposed what he saw as the malign if indirect influence of Michell over the college. He therefore threw himself into the struggle of academic politics necessary to get himself elected.

Because Kettle was in favor of university reform, Pattison initially secured his vote. Michell, however, had Kay send several letters, each of which professed slightly different principles depending on the known sentiments of the recipient. When Kettle received one of these letters, he was reluctantly persuaded to change his mind and back Kay. Kettle informed Pattison of his defection to the other party the day before the election. After a brief and unsuccessful attempt to win back the necessary vote, Pattison and his party moved swiftly to block the election of Kay. They settled on James Thompson, an inferior man but one of the original candidates proposed by the reactionary old guard. The liberals then persuaded Washbourne West, the bursar of the college, to remember his original promise to back Thompson; he was persuaded and supplied them with the necessary majority. In due course the next morning, on November 13, 1851, Thompson was elected rector of Lincoln College by a majority of five to two, with two of the conservative fellows abstaining in disgust at what they considered the underhanded tactics being employed.

Because the election coincided with the Royal Commission proceedings on university reform, it gained more notoriety than it might perhaps have done at another time. Various Lincoln fellows sought to have the election overturned by appealing to, or seeking redress from, university authorities; Kettle published a pamphlet that described in muckraking detail the double-dealing that led to the election of Thompson. Many thought that all of these machinations were in poor taste and that making such knowledge public violated the secrecy necessary to shield the inner workings of the college from outside scrutiny and censure. Even Pattison and his colleagues took advantage of the controversy generated to cast about for a possible replacement for Thompson, indiscreetly deserting the very man they had elected.

Yet Pattison paid a far greater price than mere public disgrace or censure. His single-minded devotion to the prestige and management of his college made his failure to be elected rector seem like total failure. Such thoughts brought forth his immense capacities for melancholy self-laceration. As he put it in the *Memoirs*, "In a single night the college was extinguished for the all the purposes for which I had labored … My mental forces were paralysed by the shock; a blank, dumb despair filled me; a chronic heartache took possession of me, perceptible even through sleep. As consciousness gradually returned in the morning, it was only to bring with it a livelier sense of the cruelty of the situation" (p. 290).

Pattison tried to return to his tutorial responsibilities, but in such a desultory and inefficient way that Thompson was forced to remove him from the tutorship four years later. Pattison tutored students from other colleges for money; Jowett was especially keen to send Balliol undergraduates to him. Pattison also began to take long vacations in the north of England and Scotland, walking and fishing for months on end. He explored Germany on foot, and took pride in discovering out-of-the-way corners of the countryside unknown to guidebooks. During many summers, Pattison took a curacy in some rural parish, handling pastoral responsibilities for the absent clergyman and obtaining both a supplemental income and a space in which to work away from Lincoln, which remained a source of resentment and unhappiness for many years. But this mere fact should not be taken as evidence that his faith had recovered from its low ebb; actually, his agnosticism and doubt continued to grow during this time and has been supposed to have supplied much of the anguish he felt during the remainder of his life.

It was also during the aftermath of the election that Pattison began his literary career in earnest. During the 1840s he had published almost exclusively in high church organs, but in the 1850s he began writing for a broad public in journals with a large circulation. The first essay he wrote for the prestigious *Quarterly Review*, "The Diary of Casaubon" (1853), is pivotal. Pattison reviewed the recent publication of the seventeenth-century scholar's daily journals and memoirs, the *Ephemerides*, which had been made available by the Clarendon Press in 1850. Reading this journal, Pattison discovered something that reminded him of his own history, and in this review he began a career-defining shift away from high-church journalism toward a serious and sustained engagement with the history of classical scholarship and more broadly with intellectual history. Several longer essays for the same journal were directly related to this new direction of his studies, one on the French scholar Peter Daniel Huet and one on biographies of the French writer Michel de Montaigne. Further essays, on such subjects as "English Letter-Writers of the Eighteenth Century," "Calvin at Geneva," and "Antecedents of the Reformation," show Pattison continuing to explore the literary history of seventeenth- and eighteenth-century Europe.

For several years, between 1855 and 1858, Pattison also wrote annual reviews of new books and developments in subjects like theology, philosophy, history, biography, and travel literature for the *Westminster Review*. He occasionally returned to this kind of work during the 1860s. He wrote an influential chapter on "Oxford Studies," which was yet another return to the subject of educational reform at the university, and a perceptive essay on "The Present State of Theology in Germany," which admired the historical and critical character of German theology even as it presciently noted the rise of absolutism in German thought and culture during the middle of the nineteenth century. In 1858, Pattison became the *Times* correspondent in Berlin, sending home articles about new developments in German government, policies, and society. He also wrote a report on the state of German schools for the Newcastle Commission on Popular Education, which sought to compare and contrast the systems of elementary education in Germany and Britain. These various projects helped Pattison became a recognized authority on Germany, which introduced him to the modern textual scholarship and history of criticism that was being written in German at the time and greatly broadened his conception of what university life might and should be like.

Two essays from this period are of crucial importance. The first was Pattison's chapter in the most controversial book published during the reign of Victoria, *Essays and Reviews* (1860).

H. B. Wilson edited the volume, while Pattison supplied the intellectual vision. Pattison hoped that *Essays and Reviews* might become a quarterly or annual journal for the exploration and dissemination of liberal theological positions, but there was no financial support for these plans and it was finally published as a single book. The book generated immense criticism because of its attempts to consider Christianity as a historical phenomenon rather than a revealed and eternal truth. The seven contributors became known as the "Seven Against Christ." Pattison's essay, "Tendencies of Religious Thought in England, 1688–1750," was probably the least offensive to contemporary tastes because it was not driven by ideological or Church partisanship. Rather, it looked at a discrete period in the history of religious thought by placing it more firmly in its particular historical context.

The other article from this period that was central to Pattison's growth was his 1860 piece in the *Quarterly Review* on Jacob Bernays' biography of the great sixteenth-century French scholar Joseph Scaliger. Pattison was, in fact, already planning his own biography of Scaliger, and shortly after the publication of Bernays' book in 1855 Pattison began corresponding with him. The two scholars met soon after during one of Pattison's trips in Germany, and they sustained their correspondence and friendship until the death of Bernays in 1881. Their friendship was based on the mutual admiration of one another's learning; Bernays dedicated a book on Aristotle to Pattison and wrote to Pattison greatly admiring his book on Casaubon.

In 1861 there was another election for the rector of Lincoln College. Again nine fellows determined the outcome. The two rivals were Pattison and Michell, who was now eligible to seek election in his own right. The nature of the politicking is not able to be as clearly established as that of the 1851 election, but the votes were tallied and Pattison was elected. Many, including his old mentor Newman, wrote congratulating him, expressing the sense that this outcome to a large degree rectified the oversight of ten years earlier.

Unlike the fellows of Lincoln, who were required to be celibate, the rector was allowed to marry. Pattison courted and won Emily Francis Strong. She was twenty-seven years his junior, an age discrepancy not uncommon during Victorian England when men married relatively late. Her father was an Indian army officer who had returned to manage the London and County Bank office in Oxford, where Pattison banked; his family moved in Oxford society. The courtship was quick, and the couple married within eight months of Pattison's election.

MARRIAGE AND SCHOLARSHIP

The other pivotal event in Pattison's life, his marriage, is not mentioned in the *Memoirs*. As with the lost election in 1851, the marriage grew to be a source of immense regret and pain for Pattison. The general view used to be that the marriage went wrong almost from the outset, but more recent scholarship has found that its decline was in fact slow and protracted. Francis was in many ways a remarkable woman: she was of the high church party, a talented amateur painter, and very ambitious. Though Francis apparently never warmed to Pattison sexually, he later described the early years of their marriage as an idyllic union that made their later estrangement seem darker by contrast.

The marriage between the Pattisons inverts the pattern of intellectual courtship found in other famous couples like Abelard and Heloise. Instead of the tutorial igniting a smoldering, illicit passion between teacher and pupil, the licit but sexually frustrating union instead led to an exchange of intellectual tutelage. Indeed, their shared intellectual interests are the one aspect of their married life that Francis always mentioned with respect and deep satisfaction. As he did with other students throughout his life, Pattison advised Francis to take up a single subject and to master it thoroughly. She became an expert on art history in sixteenth-century France, an area that substantially overlapped with Pattison's work on the history of French classical scholarship during the same period. During her life she published several acclaimed books on the subject, including *The Renaissance of Art in France* (1879), and was an art critic for the influential journal *The Academy*. The Pattisons also shared political causes, promoting education and protection for working-class women, for example, and also advocating for the enfranchisement of women. Some accounts dwell on the contrast between the chic, vivacious wife and her wizened, acrimonious husband, but the two enjoyed entertaining friends and guests, almost in the manner of a salon, well past the first decade of their marriage.

In 1875, however, Francis revived a friendship with Sir Charles Dilke that had been made when the two were young students at the National Art Training School. This friendship merely exacerbated the marital estrangement that had begun when Francis started wintering abroad in 1867. Though these absences were undertaken because of ill health, there are obviously reasons to suspect that she welcomed them as a temporary respite from her marriage. Francis appears to have been dutiful and even affectionate in her attempts to care for Pattison, who also suffered from increasingly bad health due to intestinal disease. But he saw her time abroad as a studied neglect of him and a betrayal of their earlier intimacy, and over the years his letters to her grew increasingly bitter and sullen. He accused her of martyrdom toward the marriage, maintaining appearances while subverting and destroying his domestic tranquility. She did not respond in kind, but she did seek solace in other friends, especially Dilke. There is no evidence that this relationship was ever adulterous, but Dilke was increasingly a supportive friend and even a confidant. The two married, eventually, after Pattison's death.

Pattison saw the rectorship largely as a sinecure, and he was singularly inactive during the entirety of his tenure in that office. From the 1860s to the end of his life, Pattison seems to have lived almost entirely for his books and for learning. Like his hero Isaac Casaubon, Pattison felt that any intrusion on his academic leisure was a waste of his time, and in his diary he publishes resentful or remorseful comments about the need to handle ordinary college business.

During this period of intense study he published with increasing regularity and much greater ambition. Six books, some edited and some written solely by Pattison, belong to the fifteen-year period between 1868 and 1883, as do scores of essays and reviews.

Pattison's research continued to focus on the history of literature and classical scholarship. He published a series of essays in these related fields during the early 1860s: "Philanthropic Societies in the Reign of Queen Anne" (1860), "Classical Learning in France: The Great Printers Stephens" (1865), "F.-A. Wolf" (1865). He also wrote on theological and religious issues, including "Learning in the Church of England" (1862), "Life of Bishop Warburton" (1862), and "Mackay's Tübingen School" (1862). The mature method pursued in these essays might best be described as historical. That is, as in his essay on eighteenth-century religious thought in *Essays and Reviews*, Pattison spends relatively little time exploring philosophical subtleties or examining dogmas and opinions for their truth or falsehood. Rather, he finds the meaning and significance of people, books, and ideas in terms of their historical contexts.

His writing brought Pattison many connections among the elite of British society. He was elected to an exclusive and highly intellectual London club, the Athenaeum, in 1865. When in London he could meet there with leading writers and opinion makers from outside the universities as well as within, breakfasting with Matthew Arnold, for example, in 1878. He was active in many learned societies, including the Oxford Philological Society and the Society for the Promotion of Hellenic Studies, and served as a delegate to the Clarendon Press at Oxford University. One of his initiatives at the press was to establish a fund for the publication of learned works—that is, unprofitable but highly specialized and accomplished scientific and critical studies which were necessary for the advance of knowledge.

In 1868 Pattison published his most accomplished and sustained work on universities, *Suggestions on Academical Organization*. Though sometimes mischaracterized as a book wholly devoted to the promotion of scientific research at the expense of teaching, it actually sketches Pattison's ideal of those two activities as complementary. Pattison longed "to erect teaching and learning, inseparably united, into a life-profession" (*Suggestions*, p. 204). This position is a development rather than a repudiation of his ideas about the tutorial in 1850, when he was so caught up in his own success as a tutor in Lincoln that his ideas were necessarily parochial. In the later book Pattison takes more comprehensive views of the university, its mission, and its place in the larger culture. The expansion of his ideas was the result partly of long thinking on the subject and partly of greater contact and understanding of the German university system, which had founded the modern conception of the research university.

These *Suggestions* in effect redefine the tenor and nature of university life. Rather than continuing to prepare somewhat older boys for more exams, the university is expected to unite a more exacting kind of teaching with modern, scientific research in all fields. Pattison hoped that a learned tutor would act as an example and mentor for the student and guide him toward mental maturity by encouraging diligent, self-motivated application to a single field of study. Professors, on the other hand, would be endowed to do research, to accumulate and extend knowledge according to scientific principles in all fields. The title of the book suggests that its claims are modest, and Pattison describes its contents as mere "notes and hints" (p. 1) rather than practical outlines for reform, but contemporary reviewers largely praised the book as one of the most profound examples of its kind. Later criticism has almost unanimously considered it the most comprehensive and far-reaching call for the endowment of research in universities that was made in nineteenth-century Britain. Pattison became one of the leading proponents of "research," as it was called, and was persuaded to write an introductory "Review of the Situation" eight years later for a volume titled *On the Endowment of Research* (1876).

Pattison next edited two volumes of the eighteenth-century poet Alexander Pope's poems, the *Essay on Man* (1869) and the *Satires and Epistles* (1872). Both volumes were published by the Clarendon Press as part of a series intended for use in schools, and the text of the *Satires* is slightly bowdlerized as a result. The excised passages, however, are marked by asterisks, making it easier for prurient readers to track down the originals. Pattison introduces each volume with a lengthy essay. He is severe on what he sees as Pope's defects: he calls the *Essay* insufficiently philosophical and scientific, and the *Satires* unjust because they were written by someone whose objectivity was sacrificed to party loyalty. Yet in spite of these deficiencies Pattison argues that Pope possesses real intellectual interest as well as being a masterful poet, and Pattison ranks him alongside John Milton as one of the genuine and enduring classics of English poetry. Pattison defends Pope's poems against the Romantic assertion that the best poetry possesses an organic genius quite separate from its historical context, an idea foreign to the historical cast of Pattison's mind, and argues instead that Pope must be understood in relation to the occasions that called forth his best poems. And in his essay "Pope and His Editors" (1872), Pattison further develops this idea. He describes the task of editing English poetry as one of helping the average reader form a balanced judgment of particular poems that make frequent references to people and events more than a century old and therefore difficult to understand. In the notes to his volumes of the poems, Pattison pitches his information at both the student and the more discerning reader. His notes alternate between textbook explanations of unfamiliar names or subjects and scholarly remarks on some technical aspect of poetry form or allusion.

Pattison's next book, *Isaac Casaubon* (1875), is still the standard work in English on its subject and Pattison's magnum opus. Yet that this book should be his best, and not the book on Joseph Scaliger that he planned and gathered materials for over a thirty-year period, offers an interesting look at his scholarly methods. Of this project, only the review of Bernays' book on Scaliger plus several fragments published in his collected essays were ever completed. Instead, *Casaubon*

was the book he completed, not the life of Scaliger, and *Casaubon* is the fullest expression of Pattison's ideal of the scholarly life. Pattison admired above all Casaubon's industry, and he notes that not a day passes in Casaubon's *Ephemerides* where the seventeenth-century scholar does not write a line or two about his studies: "If anyone thinks that to write and read books is a life of idleness, let him look at Casaubon's diary" (*Casaubon*, p. 123).

It was the scale of Casaubon's ambition matched with this ceaseless appetite for work that Pattison felt defined the scholarly life. Pattison, too, worked very hard on *Casaubon*, drafting and revising it on and off for twenty years. Throughout the biographical narrative of Casaubon's life, Pattison occasionally interjects his own summary comments on the life of the mind: "It is well that we should be alive to the price at which knowledge must be purchased. Day by day, night by night, from the age of twenty upwards, Casaubon is at his books ... Reading is not an amusement filling the languid pauses between the hours of action; it is the one pursuit engrossing all the hours and the whole mind. The day, with part of the night added, is not long enough" (pp. 490–491). This ideal was one which Pattison himself strove to exemplify in his later years, which has led some scholars to view *Casaubon* as a veiled autobiography. Pattison's definition of learning was also quoted often: "Learning is a peculiar compound of memory, imagination, scientific habit, accurate observation, all concentrated, through a prolonged period, on the analysis of the remains of literature. The result of this sustained mental endeavour is not a book, but a man" (p. 489). In some sense, these words can be read as Pattison's final and most eloquent defense of the life he himself had tried to live ever since arriving in Oxford as a young student.

By describing the difficulties that scholars overcame with intense industry—in Victorian England, where work was highly valued—Pattison made even the remote figures of classical philology accessible and alive to the reading public. But the book did not sell well; Pattison claimed to have lost money on it. Yet if *Casaubon* failed to gain a mass readership, it nevertheless had an electrifying effect on the intellectual classes. Bernays wrote to praise it, and reviewers were unanimous in calling it an immense achievement. In the book's final pages, Pattison argued that such strenuous readers made the Victorian image of lazy Oxford dons irrelevant to the life of learning. And, as H. S. Jones has suggested, by claiming that learning deserved greater respect in the culture at large than it was ordinarily given, Pattison made countercultural claims that may have lent it a special charm for learned readers eager to defend their own working lives.

Two of Pattison's articles in 1876, "The Religion of Postivism" and "Philosophy in Oxford," show him more directly engaging in cultural criticism. In "The Religion of Positivism," he criticized what he saw as the excessive authoritarianism of positivism, the philosophical system elaborated by the French philosopher Auguste Comte. Briefly, Comte argued that human history was the record of progress from theology and metaphysics to science, and he called for positivist philosophers to take charge of social development by creating a "religion of mankind" that would encourage the advance toward scientific knowledge. Like John Stuart Mill and many other Victorian intellectuals, Pattison was as fascinated by the questions that positivism raised as he was unsure that its answers were satisfactory. He agreed that scientific knowledge should be pursued, but he felt that it should not be for social reasons but simply for the sake of discovering the truth. Likewise, in "Philosophy in Oxford," Pattison returned once again to what he saw as the university's lack of philosophical culture. Once again he deplored the theological and religious partisanship that prevented the university from disinterestedly pursuing philosophical knowledge and the stranglehold its examination system had over the promotion of free inquiry among students. The opinions expressed in these two essays, in addition to his idealization of scholarship in *Casaubon*, help explain why Pattison contrived to refuse the vice chancellorship of Oxford when it was offered to him in 1878. He was deliberately keeping himself free from administrative commitments in order to pursue his studies without interruption.

Yet Pattison should not be imagined during this period of his life as wholly secluded among his books. He remained an enthusiastic sportsman, and his daily routine included a requisite three-hour walk. He was also fond of, as Walter Pater reported, "romping with great girls among the gooseberry bushes" and talking only of "petticoats and croquet!" (quoted in Vivian Green, 1985, p. 26). Many of these young women, including the future novelists Mary Arnold (later Mrs. Humphry Ward) and Rhoda Broughton, enjoyed playing outdoor games with Pattison but also sought out his tutelage. He would often read aloud to his young female friends from poetry or novels, and he is known to have read from Eliot's *Middlemarch* to his companions on several occasions.

During the last half of the 1870s, Pattison studied and wrote about John Milton, author of the greatest English epic, *Paradise Lost* (1667–1674). His essay "Milton" appeared in 1875, and it was followed by his book *Milton* (1879). The book was part of Macmillan's English Men of Letters series, under the general editorship of Pattison's friend John Morley. The series was meant to introduce the interested but unscholarly public to the life and works of Milton. Pattison himself acknowledged that his book was less ambitious and less accomplished than his contemporary David Masson's magisterial six-volume biography of Milton (1858–1880), which remains a standard work on Milton. Some critics have felt that Pattison's biography is marred by excessive autobiographical allusions, especially in passages relating to Milton's failed marriage, which are felt to have been written directly out of Pattison's own experience as a husband. But the book remains informative and was considered one of the best installments of an uneven series; students and teachers alike used it as an introduction and reference to Milton through the end of the Second World War. Pattison also wrote the "Introduction" to Milton in the four-volume series *English Poets,* also published by Macmillan, and he edited Milton's sonnets in a slender volume in 1883. To this edition he added a preface that traces the literary history of the sonnet in English and establishes Milton's place in that history.

In the last years of his life, Pattison had a sexually chaste but emotionally intimate friendship with a young woman named Meta Bradley. The two met in 1879. She was some forty years younger than he. Her relationship with her own family, especially her father, was strained, and when she was introduced to Pattison she was eager to cultivate the acquaintance and to benefit from the social opportunities that the salon of eager admirers around him afforded to her. But above all she admired Pattison, and he returned her affection. In their letters, which began almost immediately, it is possible to trace the quick development of their friendship and the deepening of their ties to one another.

The two exchanged more than four hundred letters, the largest collection of Pattison's correspondence still in existence. In these letters it becomes clear that these two lonely, troubled people developed a close bond that sustained them and might under other circumstances have developed into passionate love. But eventually Oxford gossip and the demands of Victorian morality and propriety conspired not only to separate the two friends permanently but to inform Francis Pattison about the outward appearances of the friendship. From the time of their separation until Pattison's death the friendship between the two was conducted solely through the mail, but it diminished little either in strength or expression as a result. In June 1883, he wrote to her, "I do not suppose confidence was ever more perfect between any two people than it is between us," and she responded in kind: "I shall never cease to wonder at our strange and perfect friendship. I have two feelings about it—one that it is so beautiful that all the world ought to know of it—another that it is too sacred for anyone else to know of it" (in Green, 1957, p. 317).

Meta Bradley urged Pattison to write his *Memoirs*, which he did during the final eighteen months of his life. He responded to her suggestions, entreaties, and prompting by going back through his diaries and working diligently to turn them into a chronicle of his life and opinions. He was driven also by the sense that he had little time left. His niece, Jeannie Stirke, was persuaded to assist him, and she read old letters to him as a way of helping to fix the chronology of events and thoughts in his life. The text of the *Memoirs* was basically complete by Christmas Eve 1883, and on his deathbed less than a year later Pattison gave detailed instructions about the preparation of the manuscript for the press.

Pattison was affected by various digestive ailments throughout his life, and by his seventieth year his health began to fail more precipitously. He was visited a final time by Newman late in 1883. Pattison suspected this visit, as he had suspected regarding an earlier letter from Newman, of being a last attempt to bring about his conversation to Rome. During the visit, however, their talk seems to have turned mostly upon their long and strangely shared history, and when Newman left Pattison remained a skeptic. Francis Pattison returned home early in 1884 and was with her husband during the final months of his life. She ministered to him in his final illness, which she describes in horrible detail: "The terrible fits of terror with shrieks which went through the house ... Let not my last days be like his. The moral ruin is awful" (in Green, 1957, p. 323). Pattison died, in great pain, on July 30, 1884.

SUBSEQUENT REPUTATION

Though Pattison had in effect promised Meta Bradley the role of his literary executor, that task fell instead to his wife. The first order of business was to prepare the text of the *Memoirs* for the press. Francis Pattison was enraged to find that not only had Pattison left £5,000 to Meta Bradley in his will but that he had intended her to be the dedicatee of the *Memoirs*. She therefore added the caustic and dishonest preface of the volume, which denies that the text is dedicated to anyone. This was surely the spiteful act of a wife determined to exact vengeance on a supposed lover of her husband's. Francis Pattison also carefully excised every reference to Bradley in Pattison's journals.

The *Memoirs* are famously a mental history, and they have been quoted at some length on the early details of Pattison's life above. Pattison is stoic about his life, even its setbacks, but his minute and painstaking examination of his inner life charges the surface impression of stoicism with an underlying egotism and self-absorption that is almost completely at odds with it. Pattison also refuses to spare or even blunt his forcible judgments—on acquaintances, on Oxford, and especially on himself—which results in a book that is equally scathing and self-pitying. Yet the final pages are almost pure triumph. Pattison describes the development of his life work as a failure, but a noble one, which was inevitable given the enormous scope of his work—the never completed history of the French school of classical learning, an "ambitious plan" of which Pattison had "only executed fragments," including the book on Casaubon and various essays on French and German philologists and the fragments of his planned vindication of Scaliger from Jesuit smear and censure (*Memoirs*, p. 320). Yet Pattison famously exonerated himself, writing: "I am fairly entitled to say that, since the year 1851, I have lived wholly for study. There can be no vanity in making this confession, for, strange to say, in a university ostensibly endowed for the cultivation of science and letters, such a life is hardly regarded as a creditable one" (*Memoirs*, p. 331). The final lines of the book are given to Johann Wolfgang von Goethe, "Of that which a man desires in youth, of that he shall have in age as much as he will" (*Memoirs*, p. 334). Thus even at the close of his life and at the close of his *Memoirs*, Pattison takes pains to defend his conception of the intellectual life from what he saw as an entire culture that deprecated and devalued this conception. The *Memoirs* are not just an autobiography but an apology, a vindication of Pattison's spiritual integrity in the face of widespread, typically Victorian suspicion that religious skepticism had corrupted his character and led him into an idle or dissolute life.

On publication, the *Memoirs* were received by the public in strange, contradictory ways. Reading them seems to have been more or less obligatory, at least for intellectuals, as was disapproving of the character that Pattison revealed within. It was generally felt that Pattison should

have been still more stoic and spared his acid tongue. Yet later readers have largely felt that Pattison wrote his life as he lived it, in accordance to very high, and often disappointed, standards of truthfulness and integrity. A. D. Nuttall has spoken of "that special somber elegance of which [Pattison] was master" (p. 123). There is perhaps no book of Pattison's other than his *Casaubon* of which that judgment can be made with greater truth.

After his death several volumes of Pattison's other, more miscellaneous writings were published. Along with the *Memoirs*, Macmillan published a volume of his collected *Sermons* (1885), which received very good reviews, and were generally thought to vindicate Pattison's literary reputation much better than the *Memoirs* had. In 1889 two volumes of his collected essays were published by his former student and friend Henry Nettleship and bore the imprint of the Clarendon Press which Pattison had served with such distinction. The same press issued a second, corrected edition of his *Isaac Casaubon* in 1892, also edited by Nettleship and containing corrections by several of Pattison's former students, including Richard Christie and Ingram Bywater. It is part of Pattison's legacy that each of these loyal students became eminent scholars in their turn.

Pattison also formed the basis for a number of novelistic representations, none of which seems to have been meant as an absolutely faithful portrait of him. The first was undoubtedly the most important: George Eliot's *Middlemarch* (1872). Eliot knew both Pattisons intimately during the decade of their marriage prior to her novel's publication. But she began her novel earlier, and the character of Mr. Casaubon, thought by many to have been inspired by and even directly drawn from the example of Mark Pattison, was fleshed out before her acquaintance with them began. There are several points of connection between the two: Mr. Casaubon shares the name of the book that Pattison was writing during this period (though it did not appear until three years after *Middlemarch*), Mr. Casaubon also marries a woman twenty-seven years younger than himself, and Mr. Casaubon is also inordinately devoted to his studies. Yet the points of difference are still more important. Pattison, whatever his personal demerits, was no failed scholar as Mr. Casaubon was; and though he alienated the affections of his wife he retained a magnetism over young women until his death as proved by the example of Meta Bradley and his other young friends. Much profitless criticism has explored the nature of these connections and departures, but it is probably best to remember that great novels, no matter how closely their subjects seem to mirror some aspect of real life, are ultimately fictions that result from a complicated interplay of inspiration and craft. Francis Pattison, however, is known to have seen much of herself and her situation in the oppressed Dorothea, the woman who marries Casaubon and sacrifices herself to that union. It may be that this identification of herself with the fictional wife contributed in some way to the estrangement that occurred. Mark Pattison, on the other hand, seemed not to find the novel oppressive, and as mentioned above he read it aloud to groups of young women.

Other novels that have represented Pattison or the events of his life include W. H. Mallock's *The New Republic; or, Culture, Faith, and Philosophy in an English Country House* (1878), Rhoda Broughton's *Belinda* (1883), Mrs. Humphry Ward's *Robert Elsmere* (1888), Robert Liddell's *The Almond Tree* (1938), Ronald Knox's *Let Dons Delight* (1939), and C. P. Snow's *The Masters* (1951). It is probably not necessary to dwell on these individually, though it should be noted that each contributes in small but definable ways to building up a full portrait of Pattison's character in its unflattering as well as its more admirable respects. Yet the fascination that has drawn novelists back to Pattison is further evidence, if any were needed, that the adverse opinion of his contemporaries was balanced by the magnetism he has had on the imagination of those during his own time and those who have lived since his death.

To sum up the life of Pattison, which according to his memoirs was a mental life, it is necessary to return to the question that began this biography, asking what exactly it was that Patti-

son achieved. His scholarship, though highly regarded at the time, has not always been praised by later scholars. Anthony Grafton argues that Pattison understood the implications of the highly technical nineteenth-century German scholarship but was unwilling to apply himself to it and therefore wasted his talent writing for the popular press. Rudolf Pfeiffer, on the other hand, praises Pattison's capacity as a sensitive and scrupulous historian of European scholarship. He finds Pattison's *Casaubon* not quite up to the highest standards but considers several of Pattison's essays absolutely first-rate.

But if Pattison's achievement, as he himself suggested, was that of the reader, writer, *and* talker, with both men and women, the man who for thirty years "lived wholly for study," then he cannot be measured by his writings alone. Max Müller, the great Oriental scholar and a friend of Pattison's at Oxford, called him "the best read man at Oxford" and continued that "anywhere but at Oxford he would have grown into a Lessing" (vol. 2, p. 177). Contact between the two was conversational, and this fact when combined with Müller's assessment of Pattison points toward an important distinction. Pattison defined the life of the mind in terms of the scholarly *life*, so that writing books and essays placed a distant and much less essential second to ordering his days so that he was able to dedicate his time to the study of the past as found in books. In his life of Casaubon, Pattison described the most telling results of a scholarly life as the scholar himself rather than his books. And one of the most salient aspects of Pattison's life in this respect was his championing, alongside of Jowett and a few others, the tutorial system at Oxford. The tutorial ensures that each student will have opportunities for direct communication with their instructors, and these conversations are meant to allow eager young people to profit from the presence and example of scholars more learned and accomplished than themselves. Pattison lived during a time of transition to the present university environment, when academic specialization was beginning to replace the more general education and approach to learning of earlier generations. It was quickly becoming impossible even for specialists to maintain familiarity with any but the narrowest and most technical questions. The tutorial, on the other hand, allows for the direct contact of one mind with another. It thus seems entirely fitting that one of the most important articles that Pattison left as a monument to his life was the tutorial system, and as such it is perhaps a much more fitting tribute than articles or books to the ideal life of the mind that Mark Pattison sought to exemplify.

Selected Bibliography

WORKS OF PATTISON

BOOKS

Matthew. Translated and introduced by Pattison. Vol. 1 of *Catena Aurea: Commentary on the Four Gospels, Collected out of the Works of the Fathers by S. Thomas Aquinas.* Edited by John Henry Newman. 4 vols. Oxford: J. H. Parker, 1842.

Stephen Langton. In *Lives of the English Saints, A.D. 51–1250.* Edited by John Henry Newman. London: James Toovey, 1845.(Published anonymously.)

The Life of S. Edmund. In *Lives of the English Saints, A.D. 51–1250.* Edited by John Henry Newman. London: James Toovey, 1845.(Published anonymously.)

Suggestions on Academical Organization with Especial Reference to Oxford. Edinburgh: Edmonston and Douglas, 1868.

Pope's "Essay on Man." Edited by Mark Pattison. Oxford: Clarendon Press, 1869.

Pope's Satires and Epistles. Edited by Mark Pattison. Oxford: Clarendon Press, 1872.

Isaac Casaubon. London: Longmans, Green, 1875. 2nd ed. Oxford: Clarendon Press, 1892.

Milton. London: Macmillan, 1879.

The Sonnets of John Milton. Edited by Mark Pattison. London: Kegan Paul, Trench, 1883.

Memoirs. London: Macmillan, 1885.

COLLECTED WORKS

Sermons. London: Macmillan, 1885.

Essays by the Late Mark Pattison, Sometime Rector of Lincoln College. Edited by Henry Nettleship. 2 vols. Oxford: Clarendon Press, 1889.

PAPERS

Mark Pattison's manuscripts are held in collection at the Bodleian Library, Oxford, and Lincoln College, Oxford.

His correspondence with William Stebbing is included in the Times Collection, Harry Ransom Center, University of Texas at Austin.

ARTICLES, REVIEWS, AND BOOK CHAPTERS
(Note: only those of more than five pages are listed, which excludes many of Pattison's shorter reviews)

"Earliest English Poetry." *British Critic* 21:1–36 (1842).

"Miss Bremer's Novels." *Christian Remembrancer* 8:13–25 (1844).

"Gregory of Tours." *Christian Remembrancer* 9:66–85 (1845).

"Thiers's Consulate and Empire." *Christian Remembrancer* 10:105–132 (1845).

"Wordsworth's Diary in France." *Christian Remembrancer* 10:356–376 (1845).

"Church Poetry." *Christian Remembrancer* 11:96–112 (1846).

"The Oxford Bede." *Christian Remembrancer* 11:331–446 (1846).

"Slave-Grown Sugar." *Christian Remembrancer* 12:325–376 (1846).

"Hugh Miller's First Impressions of England." *Christian Remembrancer* 14:290–313 (1847).

"Mill's Political Economy." *Christian Remembrancer* 16:315–344 (1848).

"Lord Holland's Foreign Reminiscences." *Christian Remembrancer* 21:465–476 (1851).

"Thomas Moore's Life and Poems." *Christian Remembrancer* 25:289–327 (1853).

"Diary of Casaubon." *Quarterly Review* 93:462–500 (1853).

"English Letter-Writers of the Eighteenth Century." *Fraser's Magazine* 50:629–640 (1854).

"Theology and Philosophy." *Westminster Review* o.s. 63:206–227 (1855).

"Oxford Studies." In *Oxford Essays.* London: Parker, 1855. Pp. 251–310.

"Peter Daniel Huet—Life and Opinions." *Quarterly Review* 97:290–335 (1855).

"New Biographies of Montaigne." *Quarterly Review* 99:396–415 (1856).

"Theology and Philosophy." *Westminster Review* o.s. 67:246–262 (1857).

"The Present State of Theology in Germany." *Westminster Review* o.s. 67:327–363 (1857).

"Buckle's Civilisation in England." *Westminster Review* o.s. 68:375–399 (1857).

"History, Biography, Voyages and Travels." *Westminster Review* o.s. 68:568–585 (1857).

"The Birmingham Congress." *Fraser's Magazine* 56:619–626 (1857).

"History, Biography, Voyages and Travels." *Westminster Review* o.s. 69:272–290 (1858).

"History and Biography." *Westminster Review* o.s. 69:603–621 (1858).

"Calvin at Geneva." *Westminster Review* o.s. 70:1–29 (1858).

"The Calas Tragedy." *Westminster Review* o.s. 70:465–488 (1858).

"History and Biography." *Westminster Review* o.s. 70:587–606 (1858).

"Antecedents of the Reformation." *Fraser's Magazine* 59:114–120 (1859).

"Tendencies of Religious Thought in England, 1688–1750." In *Essays and Reviews*. Edited by H. B. Wilson. London: Parker, 1860. Pp. 254–329.

"Joseph Scaliger." *Quarterly Review* 108:34–81 (1860).

"Philanthropic Societies in the Reign of Queen Anne." *Fraser's Magazine* 61:576–582 (1860).

"Early Intercourse of England and Germany." *Westminster Review* o.s. 75:403–418 (1861).

"Popular Education in Prussia." *Westminster Review* o.s. 77:169–200 (1862).

"Learning in the Church of England." *National Review* 16:187–200 (1862).

"Life of Bishop Warburton." *National Review* 17:61–102 (1862).

"Mackay's Tübingen School." *Westminster Review* o.s. 80:510–531 (1862).

"Classical Learning in France:The Great Printers Stephens." *Quarterly Review* 117:323–364 (1865).

"F.-A. Wolf." *North British Review* o.s. 42:245–249 (1865).

"Theology and Philosophy." *Westminster Review* o.s. 90:507–529 (1868).

"What Measures Are Required for Further Improvement of the Universities of Oxford and Cambridge?" *Transactions of the National Association for the Promotion of Social Science* 12:385–90 (1868).

"Pope and His Editors." *British Quarterly Review* 55:413–446 (1872).

"The Arguments for a Future Life." *Papers of the Metaphysical Society*, no. 25 (1872).

"Milton." *Macmillan's Magazine* 31:380–387 (1875).

"A Chapter of University History." *Macmillan's Magazine* 32:237–246 and 308–313 (1875).

"Review of the Situation." In *Essays on the Endowment of Research*. Edited by C. Appleton. London: King, 1876. Pp. 3–25.

"The Religion of Postivism." *Contemporary Review* 27:593–614 (1876).

"Philosophy in Oxford." *Mind* 1:82–97 (1876).

"Address on Education." *Transactions for the National Association for the Promotion of Social Science* 21:44–68 (1876).

"The Age of Reason." *Fortnightly Review* o.s. 27:343–361 (1877).

"Books and Critics." *Fortnightly Review* o.s. 28:659–679 (1877).

"Double Truth." *Papers of the Metaphysical Society*, no. 74 (1878).

"Middle-Class Education." *New Quarterly Magazine* o.s. 13:737–751 (1880).

"Industrial Shortcomings." *Fortnightly Review* o.s. 34:737–751 (1880).

"Introduction to John Milton." In *The English Poets*. Edited by T. H. Ward. 4 vols. London: Macmillan, 1880. Vol. 2, pp. 293–305.

"The Thing That Might Be." *North American Review* 132:320–331 (1881).

"Etienne Dolet." *Fortnightly Review* o.s. 35:35–43 (1881).

SECONDARY SOURCES

Badger, Kingsbury. "Mark Pattison and the Victorian Scholar." *Modern Language Quarterly* 4:423–47 (1945).

Birch, Dinah. "The Scholar Husband." *Essays in Criticism* 54, no. 3:205–215 (July 2004).

Francis, Mark. "The Origins of Essays and Reviews: An Interpretation of Mark Pattison in the 1850s." *The Historical Journal* 17, no. 4:797–811 (December 1974).

Funakawa, Kazuhiko. "Newman and Pattison: The Predicament of a Secularized University." *Christian Higher Education* 2:213–228 (2003).

Grafton, Anthony. "Mark Pattison." *The American Scholar* 52, vol. 2:229–236 (spring 1983).

Grafton, Anthony. "The Messrs. Casaubon: Isaac Casaubon and Mark Pattison." In *Worlds Made by Words: Scholarship and Community in the Modern West*. Cambridge, Mass.: Harvard University Press, 2009. Pp. 216–230.

Green, V(ivian). H. H. *Oxford Common Room: A Study of Lincoln College and Mark Pattison*. London: Edward Arnold, 1957.

Green, Vivian. *Love in a Cool Climate: The Letters of Mark Pattison and Meta Bradley, 1879 1884*. Oxford: Clarendon Press, 1985.

Green, Vivian H. H. "Introduction." In *Memoirs of an Oxford Don*. Edited by Vivian H. H. Green. London: Cassell, 1988. Pp. 1–15.

Heyck, T. W. "From Men of Letters to Intellectuals: The Transformation of Intellectual Life in Nineteenth-Century England." *The Journal of British Studies* 20, no. 1:158–183 (autumn 1980).

Jones, H. S. *Intellect and Character in Victorian England: Mark Pattison and the Invention of the Don*. Cambridge, U.K.: Cambridge University Press, 2007.

Manton, Jo. "Introduction." In *Memoirs*. By Mark Pattison. Fontwell, Sussex, U.K.: Centaur Press, 1969. Pp. v–xxii.

Müller, Friedrich Max. *The Life and Letters of the Right Honourable Friedrich Max Müller*. Edited by Georgina Adelaide Müller. 2 vols. London: Longmans, Green, 1902.

Nimmo, Duncan. "Mark Pattison, Edward Casaubon, Isaac Casaubon, and George Eliot." *Proceedings of the Leeds Philosophical and Literary Society, Literary and Historical Section* 17:79–100 (1979).

————. "Learning Against Religion, Learning As Religion: Mark Pattison and the Victorian Crisis of Faith." *Religion and Humanism: Studies in Church History* 17:311–324 (1981).

————. "Mark Pattison and the Dilemma of University Examinations." *Days of Judgment: Science, Examinations and the Organization of Knowledge in Late Victorian England*. Edited by Roy McLeod. Driffield, N. Humberside, U.K.: Nafferton Books, 1982.

Nuttall, A. D. *Dead from the Waist Down: Scholars and Scholarship in Literature and the Popular Imagination*. New Haven, Conn.: Yale University Press, 2003.

O'Boyle, Lenore. "Learning for Its Own Sake: The German University as Nineteenth-Century Model." *Comparative Studies in Society and History* 25, no. 1:3–25 (January 1983).

Pfeiffer, Rudolf. *History of Classical Scholarship from 1300 to 1850*. Oxford: Clarendon Press, 1976.

Roll-Hansen, Diderik. "Matthew Arnold and the Academy: A Note on English Criticism in the Eighteen-Seventies." *Proceedings of the Modern Language Associate* 68, no. 3:384–396 (Jun. 1953).

Sparrow, John. *Mark Pattison and the Idea of a University*. Cambridge, U.K.: Cambridge University Press, 1967.

STEPHEN POLIAKOFF

(1952—)

Niall Munro

STEPHEN POLIAKOFF WOULD like to be remembered. Much of his work, whether on stage, television, or in the cinema, is designed with this concept in mind: that the images should be sufficiently powerful to act upon the imagination of his audience and work against the prevailing culture of momentary glimpses and half-heard stories. His dramas may have shifted their geographical centers from inner-city shopping malls to millionaires' mansions, via casinos and do–it–yourself stores—he has always been interested in creating atmospheres—but they have maintained binding interests: in family, for instance, and in science and technology. Poliakoff claims that his best pieces of work do not have clear messages, but this does not mean they are not full of insight and intellect. He has been labeled a moralist, an immoralist, a political writer, and a writer who has no interest in politics. He seems to be obsessed by youth and contemporaneity while at the same time reveling in historical detail. He does not adapt or direct anyone else's writing, and he has been able to take control of his work like no other British writer, leading him to be called the last *auteur* of television.

BIOGRAPHY AND EARLY WORK

Stephen Poliakoff was born in Holland Park in London on December 1, 1952, the second of four children. (His elder brother, Martyn, is now a well-known professor of chemistry at the University of Nottingham; his sister Lucinda is a doctor, and his youngest sister, Miranda, is a museum curator.) On his father's side, the family was Russian Jewish and descended from Hasidic rabbis. His father was born near Moscow, where Poliakoff's grandfather, Joseph, was an inventor. According to Poliakoff, Joseph was one of the first people in the world to record sound onto film. At the time of the Bolshevik Revolution in 1917, Joseph and his family lived in an apartment overlooking Red Square in Moscow, and Poliakoff's father, Alexander, witnessed an uprising from his nursery window. As a result of the revolution the family was forced for a time to live, close to starvation, in their dacha outside the city. After the revolution, Joseph was given the job of telephone examiner. He set up the first automated telephone exchange in Moscow and was given his own train to travel around the country inspecting the telecommunications network—circumstances dramatized in Poliakoff's 1984 play, *Breaking the Silence*. But when Joseph Stalin came to power in 1924, the family was forced to flee Russia for England. They took with them a set of golf clubs and a diamond hidden in a shoe—the golf clubs being an effective ploy to distract border guards from the diamond.

In London, Joseph set up a company called Multitone Electronics with Alexander, where he invented the first hospital pager and developed the technology for hearing aids. For a time, the company supplied hearing aids to Winston Churchill, but MI5 finally prevented it from servicing them in case there were Russian spies listening in on Churchill's conversations.

If Poliakoff's interest in technology and history comes from his father's side, his fascination with literature and performance is derived from the female members of his family. His paternal grandmother, who lived for many years in an attic room above the Poliakoff home, used to recount how she had once followed Leo Tolstoy down the street to see how many people would recognize him, and how she attended the first production of Anton Chekhov's *The Cherry Or-*

chard in 1904. On his mother's side, his Anglo-Jewish grandmother wrote plays, and his mother, Ina Montagu, trained as an actress. Although she only appeared in semiprofessional productions, Ina was fiercely keen for her son to succeed as a dramatist, even warning him when he was seventeen that his career was going nowhere.

After attending preparatory school in Kent, Poliakoff was sent to Westminster School in London, where he acted in productions of *The Tempest* and *Billy Budd* and wrote his first play, "Granny," "about adolescents being nasty to each other" ("Profile," *The Lost Prince* DVD extra). A theater critic from the London *Times* newspaper happened to attend the production, and as a result of the *Times'* favorable review, the resident dramatist of the Royal Court Theatre, Christopher Hampton, also went to see the play. Hampton subsequently arranged a meeting between Poliakoff and the theatrical agent Peggy Ramsey and persuaded the Royal Court to commission a play from the seventeen-year-old. The play, scheduled to be directed by Richard Eyre, was never produced.

In 1971, Poliakoff was invited to collaborate on a new piece with six other writers, including Howard Brenton, Trevor Griffiths, and David Hare. Inspired by a true story, *Lay By*, first performed at the Edinburgh Festival, explored the issue of rape from both the woman's and the rapist's perspectives, and it concluded with the naked and dead bodies of the woman, the rapist, and his partner all being brought onto the stage and then washed in blood. The play was composed by the writers scribbling lines with crayons on strips of wallpaper that everyone else could see, and Poliakoff contributed only a few lines to the final play. In addition, his youth and inexperience (he was nineteen) meant that he had to consult a dictionary for some of the sexual terms being used in the play. Given his later assertions of a need for total artistic control, it seems likely that Poliakoff's negative reaction to the project was a result of its collaborative nature. The experience was nonetheless useful for his development. "Naturalism was frowned upon at the time," he told Nicholas Wroe in an interview for the *Guardian*, "and the sort of heightened realism I felt I was gravitating towards wasn't part of their world. The others weren't terribly interested in evoking time and place or psychological character development, and that helped to define me, albeit in a negative way, because at least I realised what I was not."

Poliakoff took two years off after school to continue writing. Just before he entered Cambridge University to read history, Poliakoff enjoyed his first professional production at the Traverse Theatre in Edinburgh. *Day with My Sister* was commissioned by the artistic director of the theater, David Rudman, for £25, on the condition that it be directed by the playwright David Halliwell, so that Poliakoff—whom Rudman found quite arrogant—could be taught something about how a play was staged. When he reached university, Poliakoff continued writing and also founded a society called Feast that staged rehearsed readings of his work.

Poliakoff left Cambridge at the end of his second year, disillusioned by the poor quality of the teaching and attitude of the tutors, and ambitious to write more plays. *Pretty Boy* had been staged at the Royal Court in 1972, and after he returned to London, Poliakoff began writing for other theaters that encouraged new writing, such as the Bush and Hampstead Theatres; *Clever Soldiers*, Poliakoff's first major London production, was staged at Hampstead in 1974.

THE 1970S: YOUTH AND DISAFFECTION

The plays that Poliakoff wrote in the 1970s use the lives of young people to reflect general discontent within society. *Clever Soldiers* was set in 1914 but allowed its audience to consider the social upheaval of the 1910s in Britain in light of the troubles of the 1970s, when months of strikes culminated in the "Winter of Discontent" from November 1978 to March 1979. *Hitting Town*, meanwhile, used a taboo subject to explore the effect of social and political crises upon the youth of the country.

Hitting Town, which premiered at the Bush Theatre in 1975, reveals the beginning of an incestuous relationship between Ralph and his sister Clare, who has recently broken up with her boyfriend. The tension of the play is sustained through the introduction of Nicola, a disillusioned young waitress, and the fact that Ralph was in Birmingham during the bombing campaign of the Irish Republican Army (IRA).

Hitting Town is a play that deals with the mood of the mid-1970s, says Poliakoff, "about people growing inward and private and lonely, after the noise and frivolity of the sixties" (*Stephen Poliakoff, Plays: 1*, p. xi). While the shy figure of Nicola lets out her frustration by singing and screaming in public places, Ralph and Clare turn inward to the secure idea of family. One of the strengths of the play is the way in which their relationship is depicted not as unnatural but as the inevitable emotional need of one body for another.

Poliakoff wrote the play quickly in February 1975, not long after the IRA bombings of Birmingham and Guildford. He has explained that at the time he was living near the Selfridges department store in London, "where all the windows were blown out one day near Christmas, leaving pieces of decorations and clothes scattered all over Oxford Street. It was a time when, as you walked down the street, you expected cars to blow up in front of you" (*Stephen Poliakoff, Plays: 1*, pp. x–xi).

Poliakoff captures something of this intensity in the play, particularly through the volatile character of Ralph. He is always on edge, showing how much the recent trauma has affected him. His senses appear to have been heightened, as he is preternaturally aware of sound, yet seemingly unable to control his own voice and movements. As Bonnie Marranca has noted, Poliakoff's early dramas are reminiscent of Sam Shepard's work, and the way in which Ralph is caught here between paranoia and self-defense, willing to take violent action where necessary, is akin to some of Shepard's one-act plays of the 1960s.

RALPH: (*suddenly urgent*). Clare—What's the time? I said—WHAT'S THE TIME?

CLARE: I heard.

RALPH: Well answer.

CLARE: Don't shout.

RALPH: I'll shout if I like.

CLARE: I've no idea. Two, three? I've forgotten all about time now.

RALPH: (*very loud*) You see! I don't believe it. Listen. (*Very loud.*) Listen to that!

Silence. Both listen. There is distant muzak and a voice.

(*Very loud, excited.*) At this time! And it's still going on—

(*Moving over to the wall.*) Alone in his room. (*He suddenly shouts.*) Be quiet—or we're coming to get you.

He punches the wall savagely.

(*Stephen Poliakoff, Plays: 1*, p. 111)

Hitting Town is one of a clutch of early plays—like *City Sugar* (1975), *Shout Across the River* (1978), and *Strawberry Fields* (1976)—that are particularly vivid in their depiction of inner-city landscapes, what Poliakoff has referred to as "urban canyons" (*Stephen Poliakoff, Plays: 1*, p. xv), the result of ill-advised postwar rebuilding projects. Poliakoff has called *Hitting Town* a "private reaction to public bleakness" (Wroe interview), and at times during the play it seems as if the incestuous relationship might not have happened were it not for this complicit urban environment. Poliakoff has explained that "the entwining of character and the outer world so they are practically inseparable, is my chief objective" (*Stephen Poliakoff, Plays: 1*, p. xii), and he has identified his fascination with the urban environment as a reaction against his old-fashioned upbringing and his father's typically English lifestyle. Poliakoff returned to this relationship between architecture and emotion in a number of later works, most recently in the paired television dramas *Joe's Palace* and *Capturing Mary* (both 2007), in which the house where the dramas are set itself seems like a character.

Poliakoff has explained that *Hitting Town* is the only play to which he ever felt compelled to write a sequel. In the 1991 film *Close My Eyes,* which was awarded the Best Film prize at the *Evening Standard* British Film awards in 1992, Poliakoff transposed the action of *Hitting Town* to newly affluent mid-1980s London, particularly the financial district around Canary Wharf. In addition, he deepened the exploration of sexual freedoms and dangers. Richard, an urban planner, thinks nothing of having sex with numerous women, but he is disturbed to discover that his boss, Colin, another heterosexual male, has contracted AIDS. Richard believes that the AIDS epidemic legitimizes his relationship with his sister, Natalie, for like the characters in *Hitting Town*, he has the illusion that the relationship is a safe haven.

In 1976, the year after *Hitting Town* was produced, Poliakoff was appointed as the National Theatre's annual writer in residence and also won the *Evening Standard*'s Most Promising Playwright award for *City Sugar*, a companion piece to *Hitting Town* featuring Nicola and a disc jockey, Len Brazil. Brazil objects to the way in which young people allow themselves to be manipulated by the record companies, and in the play's latter stages he challenges Nicola, accusing her and her generation of being too passive.

In *American Days,* which premiered in 1979, Poliakoff reversed the dynamic, with the aspiring female pop star manipulating the record producer. Her frightening self-possession recalls Charlotte, from the earlier *Strawberry Fields* (1976), who distributes fascist propaganda leaflets and meets with supporters during the course of a murderous journey. Poliakoff says *Strawberry Fields* is one of his most popular plays, regularly performed internationally, and it is easy to see why its intense atmosphere, with taut dialogue reminiscent of Harold Pinter, might easily have resonance in any country suffering social or political disquiet, as Britain was in the mid-1970s. If this play marks a rare explicit foray into politics for Poliakoff, it also contains a number of his usual traits, such as a strong reaction to modernity, epitomized here by the concrete artery of the motorway and the cafés that punctuate the route. But these modern features form part of the fascists' message, as they yearn nostalgically for Britain's green and pleasant land. Charlotte's

youth and privileged upbringing seem to be totally at odds with her political message. As such, she is a typically complex Poliakoff creation: unpredictable, even objectionable, yet compelling.

In *Shout Across the River*, first produced in 1978, Poliakoff presents another startling young character. Suspended from school for disruptive behavior, Christine decides that she will give her agoraphobic mother "lessons" in life. In the latter stages of the play, Mrs. Forsythe becomes far more assertive and confident, challenging a teacher, and even seducing a schoolfriend who tried to pay Christine for sex. At the end of the play, Christine says that she will tell social services that Mrs. Forsythe has abused her, but she is so weak from having starved herself that she is unable to threaten her mother convincingly.

Once again, Poliakoff presents a highly unconventional family structure. Christine relegates her mother to the position of elder sister and takes on the maternal role, ordering Mrs. Forsythe and her brother Mike around, going grocery shopping, and even threatening to give her mother a bath. *Shout Across the River* is an excellent example of Poliakoff's "heightened realism," in which he provides the audience with certain recognizable characters or settings, but "then you dramatise the inner life, you dramatise the force of whatever the conflict is about and the internal blood pulsing through the characters spills out" (Middeke, 1994, p. 278). While the "shout across the river" suggests a cry of protest toward the government buildings and lawmakers situated on the north side of the Thames (historically the south of the Thames in London was renowned for dirty industry, asylums, and prisons), it is also a cry of personal pain. Though Poliakoff most evidently dramatizes Christine's "inner life," he is also exploring her mother's struggles. Indeed at times it seems as if there is a supranatural bond between them. In one scene the stage directions describe how *"from the moment [*Mrs. Forsythe*] enters,* Christine's energy begins to flow back, and build and build" (*Stephen Poliakoff, Plays: 1*, p. 264). Such an inexplicable, primitive force is a common feature in Poliakoff's works about families.

As in *Hitting Town* and *Close My Eyes*, young people in *Shout Across the River* need to escape from their daily lives. And yet they escape to an alternative, rather than improved, vision of the world. While Mike reads disaster novels and worries about global warming, Christine tries to negate her existence entirely by starving herself and living as much in the moment as possible, acknowledging that "tomorrow" will bring everything to an end, and refusing to talk about the past.

> MRS. FORSYTHE: Christ, you're so strong, Christine. It's almost unnatural. And you seem to be getting stronger all the time.
>
> *She looks at* CHRISTINE.
>
> And you said you weren't eating!
>
> CHRISTINE: I think you may be getting above yourself, you know. It's really time for your fourth lesson.
>
> MRS. FORSYTHE: But that's happened already, hasn't it?
>
> (*Startled.*)
>
> CHRISTINE *shakes her head slowly, slow music playing.*
>
> What does that shake of the head mean?
>
> *She pulls* CHRISTINE *to her.*
>
> That dress smells of mothballs. Your eyes look very blue tonight. (*She laughs.*) I suppose they've always been that blue. I'm just seeing them again.
>
> CHRISTINE (*smile*): I've got something to tell you. I'm not really your daughter at all—I adopted you. You're adopted.
>
> (*Stephen Poliakoff, Plays: 1,* p. 280)

Unable to fit into society, Christine embraces unnaturalness, turning conventional understandings of the world upside down. The final moments of the play, however, show some kind of reconciliation between the two women and suggest that Christine's efforts at self-destruction were intended to bring her and her mother to a point where they might start all over again.

At the end of the 1970s, Poliakoff was nearly thirty, so it was perhaps understandable that his attentions should turn away from disaffected youth toward wider, even international concerns. Nevertheless, youthful figures would continue to play key roles in many of his dramas. Poliakoff, who has two children with his wife, the screenwriter Sandy Welch, contends that children "see things very clearly and slightly apart" (Middeke, 1994, p. 276), and young people in his work are filters through which the adult world and particularly societal crisis and change can be perceived. In later works, they are litmuses for the way in which society is changing: in the film *Bloody Kids* (1980), a group of frustrated youths cause havoc in the city; in *The Summer Party* (1980), a boy named Mr. David is a performer who claims he can break ugly modern objects with his mind; and in *Sweet Panic* (1996), a child psychologist tries to understand the effect that the modern urban society is having upon the children she treats.

THE 1980S: EUROPE AND THE IMAGINATION

Poliakoff began to write about international concerns during the 1980s, but they were always considered in a personal as well as political context. In one of his finest pieces from this period, the 1980 television play *Caught on a Train*, he depicted a conflict that existed simultaneously between different generations, nations, and classes.

Caught on a Train has its origins in a real journey that Poliakoff took in 1978 from London to Vienna to see some of his plays being performed. The trip was a disaster because an elderly Viennese woman incorrectly thought that Poliakoff had taken her seat. Since he refused to give it up, the resentful woman made Poliakoff feel decidedly uncomfortable for the remainder of the journey.

The film begins in exactly the same way, as Peter, who has refused to relinquish his seat to the elderly Austrian woman, Frau Messner, becomes convinced that she is trying to find ways of taking revenge. When the train stops at Frankfurt, Peter agrees to accompany her to find something to eat, but when he returns late to the station and rushes to catch the train, he falls, muddies his trousers, and loses his rail ticket. The German police later find his appearance highly suspicious, and when he is found to have fused lights in the train by removing a flickering lightbulb—at Frau Messner's request—he is arrested. Peter is saved by Frau Messner's intervention, but in his fury he nearly assaults her. Just before the train arrives at Peter's destination, Frau Messner unexpectedly invites him to stay with her in Vienna, but he rejects her offer.

Caught on a Train is a touchstone for Poliakoff's career. Not only was it both critically acclaimed and successful with audiences, it also drew attention to his work nationally and internationally; the film was nominated for the Prix Italia and won the Single Play award at the 1980 British Academy of Film and Television Arts ceremony. The film also featured one of Poliakoff's recurring themes: "how we have cut ourselves off, again and again through the century both emotionally and intellectually from events in Europe" (*Stephen Poliakoff, Plays: 3*, p. x). This idea is made explicit in the 1998 play *Talk of the City*, in which Poliakoff explores how the BBC tried to isolate itself from the events in Nazi Germany, but it is perhaps more powerfully treated here through metaphor. Peter perceives a Europe that is still "other" to the Englishman: children are huddled at Frankfurt station in sleeping bags as if they are refugees from conflict, and when he brandishes his British passport, Peter expects that he will be given free passage anywhere. But like other writers before him, most prominently Tom Stoppard in his 1977 television play *Professional Foul*, Poliakoff shows how the position of the Englishman abroad has become just as precarious as that of any other foreigner. Border checks are places of great anxiety because of the increased threat of terrorism. The Baader-Meinhof Gang, an anticapitalist, anti-American terrorist group, waged a murderous campaign in West Germany throughout the 1970s and was particularly popular among young people. The fact that the train is full of youths, that one boy is taken off the train for having an illegal passport, and that Peter is accused by one of the German boys of being American, all serve to heighten the tension.

Peter is also made aware that his views of others are mere stereotypes. Although she acknowledges that "we Americans are meant to find it amazing over here" (*Stephen Poliakoff, Plays: 3*, p. 61), Lorraine, a young woman from the United States, hates Europe and can't wait to return home. Instead of the polarized reactions that might be associated with Nazi Germany, Frau Messner, who lived in Austria with her aristocratic family throughout the Nazi occupation, neither supported nor despised Hitler, telling Peter simply, "I took no part. I didn't care for it really" (*Stephen Poliakoff, Plays: 3*, p. 49). But Peter's inability to understand Europe goes deeper than mere cultural incomprehension:

The train has stopped.

FRAU MESSNER: You pretend to of course, you pretend. (*She is staring straight at him.*) But you don't really care about anything do you? (*She stares at his pale young face, as he stands holding his case.*) Except maybe success in your work. Becoming very successful. It's all you have. You don't *feel* anything else. *Nothing. You just can't feel anything else.* (*She looks at him.*) Can you?

Silence.

I wonder what will happen to you?
                              (*Stephen Poliakoff, Plays: 3*, p. 80)

The kind of passivity and negativity that existed in *City Sugar* and *Shout Across the River* has given way, Poliakoff suggests, to a moral negligence that might actually do damage to other people. Poliakoff has frequently said that he has tried to make his work feel ahead of the times and has suggested that "you don't really care" seems to sum up the 1980s—indeed he has declared that this film is a disguised comment upon the early days of Margaret Thatcher's government ("Director's Commentary," *Caught on a Train* DVD extra). Peter might in fact do well in the coming decade, for he is ambitious and understands the value of having money. By contrast, Frau Messner seems to Peter to be "like a member of a nearly extinct species" (*Stephen Poliakoff, Plays: 3*, p. 77), and yet it is she who wonders what will become of him. When Peter declines Frau Messner's invitation, he exhibits a failure of imagination—always a serious weakness in Poliakoff's eyes—placing his own need for success over the wishes of someone else. When Peter repeatedly asks her if she wants to know his name, Frau Messner says nothing, even closing her eyes as if to erase him from her memory; a highly ironic gesture toward a man who has spent most of the journey telling people that his only desire is to become famous.

Poliakoff continued to examine our perceptions of Europe in *Coming in to Land* (1986), a play he considers one of his most traditional in form. The play shows how a Polish woman attempts to make her way into Britain, first by a sham marriage to Neville, a lawyer, and then as an asylum seeker, claiming—falsely—that she was abused by the Polish police. When Neville is placed in a similar position to Peter, and interrogated, we understand that Poliakoff is challenging our expectations of Europe and suggesting that our proximity is not and must not just be geographical.

Poliakoff's own personal connections to Europe are made plain in the 1984 drama *Breaking the Silence*, which deals directly with what happened to his family in Russia in the 1920s. The play opens in 1920, soon after the Bolshevik Revolution. Nikolai Pesiakoff, his wife, Eugenia, son, Sasha, and their maid, Polya are sent to live in a railway carriage after their house is seized by the government. Nikolai is appointed by Verkoff, the commissar of labor, to the position of telephone examiner. But Nikolai has been working to discover a way of transferring sound onto silent film, and he neglects his official duties to concentrate on his experiments. Once his wife and maid realize what is happening, they falsify the documents he should have completed. After Stalin succeeds to power, Verkoff warns the family to leave the country, and Sasha, believing that his father would never leave his work, destroys some of his father's valuable equipment. When the family reaches the border, Nikolai is threatened with arrest for impersonating a government official, but Eugenia manages to convince the guards of Nikolai's position by reciting facts she had learned when falsifying the telephone documents, and the family begins their trip to England.

Poliakoff took two years to write the play—longer than his usual—because of the difficulty he had in distancing himself from the material. The sense of loss that pervades the play is derived from a fusion of the personal and political, for by having them exiled from Russia, Poliakoff makes the family stand for all displaced persons. If it had not been for the good fortune of having a friend in Verkoff (and a chance meeting with the commissar of labor really did save the Poliakoff family), the Pesiakoffs might have disappeared.

Eugenia unconvincingly consoles herself by telling Nikolai that "you did it though. I know you did. We know we existed" (*Stephen Poliakoff, Plays: 2*, p. 104). Nikolai's invention and his single-minded pursuit of his work comes to represent something true and pure in the midst of chaos and suffering, and Polya, Eugenia, and most surprisingly, Verkoff, all cling to it. However, Sasha's instinct for self-preservation, longing to conform, and failure of imagination result in the destruction of his father's equipment. He has, Verkoff tells him, "to be told what [he] ought to think" (*Stephen Poliakoff, Plays: 2*, p. 74), and Sasha's mindless act is ironically the one most representative of an authoritarian government that snuffs out difference and change whenever it appears. By contrast, the actual government official is unexpectedly a man of intelligence and imagination, who puts his own life at risk to save Nikolai and to allow him to continue his work.

Poliakoff has observed that the play was first performed during the cold war—a period of paranoia that Poliakoff explored in much more detail in his television play *Soft Targets* (1982), which deals with the fractious relationship between a Russian journalist and member of the British foreign office. *Breaking the Silence* not only painted sympathetic portraits of Russians but also "challenged some of the received opinions about the aftermath of the Russian Revolution" (*Stephen Poliakoff, Plays: 2*, p. x). In this sense it broke an historical silence, and began a pattern in Poliakoff's works of settings in which characters were on the fringes or within earshot of great historical change, a technique most effectively employed in *The Lost Prince*.

THE 1990S: SCIENCE, MODERNITY, AND CHANGE

Poliakoff has suggested that *Breaking the Silence* can be seen to form one third of a scientific trilogy, with *Playing with Trains* (1989) and *Blinded by the Sun* (1996) being the other parts. *Century* (1994) should also be considered in this light. Having criticized other writers for presenting scientists as eccentrics and untouchable geniuses, Poliakoff in *Century* and *Blinded by the Sun* features scientist characters who are entirely fallible and sympathetic human beings.

Century begins on New Year's Eve, 1899. Mr. Reisner is holding a party to celebrate the new century, despite the rest of the town agreeing to celebrate it at the end of 1900. His son Paul is about to move to London to work at a new medical institute. After some months, Paul is invited to work with the head of the institute, Professor Mandry. Paul learns of a potentially revolutionary discovery in the field of endocrinology by his friend Felix, and the two present the ideas to the professor. When Mandry does nothing to develop the research, Paul angrily demands an explanation, and he is temporarily suspended and then banned from the institute. He begins a relationship with Clara, a laboratory worker at the institute. Paul discovers that Mandry has been carrying out eugenics experiments, sterilizing some of the women in the City of Rubbish, a homeless settlement. Paul manages to have the institute closed, but Mandry reappears at Mr. Reisner's New Year's Eve party to try to persuade Paul to help him reopen the institute. Paul refuses to do so, and the film ends with the ringing in of the new century in January 1901.

Poliakoff has explained that in this film he "wanted to actually portray the moment when ... the modern world came into being" (*Stephen Poliakoff, Plays: 2*, p. xii), and in *Century* we are given insights into the impact of new technologies upon society such as the car and the telephone. As in his earlier film *She's Been Away* (1989), which showed how a woman who had been shut in mental institutions for over sixty

years coped with a move back to the outside world, it is the effect of radical change by which Poliakoff is most intrigued. Just as Paul adapts to his new lifestyle, so Poliakoff presents us—often in striking visual terms—with a London that is suffused by a new kind of sensuality. The park near the institute is full of "couples, intimate, in love, flirting, or conducting agonizing partings, hovering, close to sex, kissing and breaking apart, entwined together half masked by bushes" (*Stephen Poliakoff, Plays: 2*, p. 332). As would continue to be the case in *The Tribe* (1998), *Shooting the Past* (1999), and *Perfect Strangers* (2001), Poliakoff constantly investigates forms of sensuality, and in *Century* he intimates that the advent of the "modern world" was also the beginning of new expressions of sexuality.

The film uses a technique of juxtaposition in which images powerfully contradict each other, partly to make them memorable and partly as social commentary. When Paul visits the patron of the institute in a nearby tearoom, he first has to negotiate the smoke and dust of roadworks, and we also see him rushing past a group of ragged, dirty children. The next scene presents the patron in "a long incredibly ripe interior, the tearooms dripping with affluence as well as cakes" (*Stephen Poliakoff, Plays: 2*, p. 336). The fact that wealthy women are listening to a lecture about eugenics while indulging themselves portrays them in a very negative light. According to Poliakoff, "The contention of *Century* is that all the seeds of what happened later, were discernible in the first moments of the new epoch, in that very first year" (*Stephen Poliakoff, Plays: 2*, p. xiii). Just as these wealthy women are implicated in condoning the kind of eugenics research that would lead to the attempted extermination of the Jews and other minority groups in Nazi Germany, so too there is a lesson for viewers today. Set in 1900 and premiered on New Year's Eve 1993, Poliakoff's film encourages us to make connections between the former and latter stages of the twentieth century and reconsider our notions of "progress." Thus the City of Rubbish is deliberately reminiscent of the shantytowns of less developed countries, and the exploration of eugenics as practiced by Mandry are implicitly paralleled with the investigations in our own time with genetic engineering.

Poliakoff also seeks to dramatize the fin-de-siècle uncertainty. Discussing the confusion over whether the new century began in 1900 or 1901, Paul's sister Miriam suggests that if people are so unsure, perhaps 1900 doesn't really exist. This makes Poliakoff's contention that the tragedies of the century were to be found in 1900 even more resonant, and echoes other works by Poliakoff which try to isolate crucial moments when change was set into motion.

According to Poliakoff, writing in 1994, "The tension between most people's natural desire for continuity, and the extraordinary forward burst of technology that is about to hit all our lives, is very strong, very potent. We seem to be utterly helpless before this new onslaught, uncertain whether its effect will be benign or malevolent, unable to influence its progress in any way at all" (*Stephen Poliakoff, Plays: 2*, p. xiv). From an opening of tremendous hope and optimism, this is the position which *Century* reaches, for having seen the dark side of human endeavor greeted by some as progress, the characters are left "excited and worried and hopeful" (*Stephen Poliakoff, Plays: 2*, p. 403). Appropriately, Poliakoff ends his introduction to *Century* with a prediction that proved accurate: "it is this strange tension, hovering somewhere between hope and dread, that will I think dominate most of the work I'm about to do" (*Stephen Poliakoff, Plays: 2*, p. xiv).

Poliakoff has suggested that we tend to portray scientists "always as people who are *apart* from the society they belong to" (*Stephen Poliakoff, Plays: 2*, p. xiii). In *Blinded by the Sun* (1996), he presents personal conflicts absolutely in the context of larger sociopolitical themes: the clash between the academic and commercial worlds and the sacrifice of intellectual achievement for fame and financial gain.

Soon after Al, a chemistry lecturer at an English university, is unexpectedly promoted to the role of head of the department, he learns that Christopher, a fellow academic, has developed the first-ever sun battery, a nonpolluting supply of hydrogen to replace fossil fuels. After Christo-pher announces the discovery to the press, Al finds out that Christopher faked the results, and he is forced to declare the experiment a fraud. (Poliakoff got the idea from the claim made by two scientists in 1989 that they had succeeded in creating "cold fusion," only for it to prove impossible to repeat the experiment successfully.) Over the next few years, Al becomes a successful author of popular science books but also has a potentially revolutionary idea about how to turn household waste into gasoline, which he cannot develop himself. He is also forced to close the chemistry department, leaving his colleague Elinor no time to complete her research.

In this play, Poliakoff reenters some of the territory of his television play *Stronger than the Sun* (1977), where he presented the struggle of one nuclear plant worker to expose the cover-up of a small-scale accident. Frustrated by the lack of action by a political group and the media, she steals plutonium in order to prove how easy and dangerous it is to do so, and as a final act of protest, she kills herself in a bath contaminated with radioactivity. Both works highlight the pressures that exist within an institution like a nuclear plant or a university department. They are each in their own ways highly demanding environments and worlds that resist outside interference, even to the point of concealment for their own self-preservation:

ELINOR: I probably know you as well as anyone—and I'm telling you this is not the time to intervene. There will be a professional and scientific explanation, of that I'm certain.

AL: Will there?

ELINOR: I am convinced there will be. But if you blunder in now, with your flair for popularising things—

AL: Yes. I know I'm a hack, but that's not the point—

ELINOR: —you will generate all kinds of media coverage, naturally. And that will have a devastating effect on Christopher's reputation …

AL: And if it comes out that I had prior knowledge of the deception—

ELINOR: There has been no deception, Albie.

AL: And if it comes out I had proof and did nothing—

ELINOR: Yes?

AL: Then the whole department is finished. That doesn't matter?

ELINOR: I don't think you have a choice, Albie.
(*Blinded by the Sun & Sweet Panic*, p. 63)

At the heart of the play is the conflict between the academic and commercial worlds. Despite their rejection by his colleagues, Al's own successes suggest that the eventual financial problems that close the department might well have been avoided if his ideas for change had been implemented. But his success in peddling popular science books is regarded by his colleagues as a betrayal. While he maintains that "most work should be geared directly to the market-place" (*Blinded by the Sun & Sweet Panic*, p. 93), Elinor tells Al that he has used Christopher's fraud for his own ends, encouraging people to treat scientists as villains. Most damning of all, perhaps, is her accusation that Al is no longer a hack, but "slightly more dangerous. Somebody who reduces everything to their own level—and does it very effectively" (*Blinded by the Sun & Sweet Panic*, p. 92).

Elinor's observation is apt, for notwithstanding his abridgment of scientific facts, typified by his five-minute radio talks, in another scene Al even manages to sum up each of his friends in one sentence. In the final scene of the play, Al also maintains that his obsessive collecting of objects to remind him of key events in his life can help him explain why things happened they way they did. But Poliakoff presents the facile desire for reduction as a way of escaping from what Al calls the space of creation, "the dark tunnel you have to be in" (*Blinded by the Sun & Sweet Panic*, p. 116). Instead of grafting out the idea, as Elinor continues to do, he abandons it. And yet Poliakoff does not hold Elinor up as an ideal. Instead, he leaves the play on a disturbingly ambiguous note. Elinor dies without completing or publishing her research, a victim,

Poliakoff suggests, of a modern world that moves fast and doesn't seem to allow for careful deliberation.

Poliakoff dramatized the modern speed of change in two works from 1999: his play *Remember This* and the television miniseries *Shooting the Past*. *Remember This* explored our understanding of the value of what we record and retain as a culture. The protagonist, a keen user of home video cameras, finds that his videos have lost all their pictures. The discovery becomes an international sensation, and his son, who had been writing a thesis on nineteenth-century literature, is so affected by it that he abandons his PhD in order to make video art installations. In the latter stages of the play he argues that "nobody really has a history any more, because things are moving THAT FAST. The past simply becomes abstract" (*Remember This*, p. 100).

If Poliakoff agrees that because of modern technologies history has become more malleable, he certainly does not believe that it makes the past any less valuable. On the contrary, the 1999 miniseries *Shooting the Past* shows how photography, a very twentieth-century technology, can illuminate the lives of those entering the twenty-first. Rather than being dusty artifacts, photographs are almost living things, and their preservation is vital evidence of our humanity.

Poliakoff had dealt with how we preserve the past before in *Hidden City* (1988), his directorial debut. Characters use black-and-white film and photographs to piece together the story of a secret government project that went wrong and has since been kept secret. The film, which takes place in subterranean and concealed urban areas, has an almost magical premise: that these technologies, that we think we control and that produce such straightforward narratives, can actually hide alternative stories. This concept is an integral part of *Shooting the Past*.

Shooting the Past is set in an eighteenth-century mansion on the outskirts of London. The building has been bought by an American businessman, Christopher Anderson, with the intention of converting it into a business school. When Anderson arrives, he discovers that the photographic library that occupied the building is still there, despite assurances he had received from Oswald Bates that the collection had been sold. The head of the collection, Marilyn Truman, refuses to accept the situation until Anderson has seen the collection. She uses photographs to tell Anderson the story of a Jewish girl who survived the Holocaust, and Anderson agrees to give Marilyn time to find a buyer for the whole collection. Marilyn decides to follow a trail that Oswald—who has attempted suicide—has left, convinced that he has discovered something that can help them. In the denouement, Marilyn uses photographs to recount to Anderson a new history of his grandmother. Anderson subsequently arranges for an American collection to buy the whole library.

Shooting the Past deals fundamentally with how change, especially the change that comes with modernity, affects people in different ways. The closing of the picture library is every bit as devastating for the employees as the closing of her laboratory is for Elinor in *Blinded by the Sun*, or the move out of the institution is for Lillian in *She's Been Away*. The picture library is a typical location for Poliakoff, for even though the place holds over ten million different images from all over the globe, "Everything about the interior of the building suggests a contained orderly world, untouched by the outside" (*Shooting the Past*, p. 8). The collection also grants employees like Oswald the "chance to dream ... dream from looking at these pictures ... let the mind float—make connections between things, daydreams, nightdreams ... We have space, time ... no pressure ... the most valuable things on earth" (*Shooting the Past*, p. 103). The way in which the imagination can alter people is plain to see in the change that is wrought on Christopher Anderson. Because of the photographs, he becomes "a more emotional freer human being" (*Shooting the Past*, p. 135).

Oswald, on the other hand, is a victim of technological progress. His suicide attempt is all the more disturbing for the fact that it is left unexplained. Marilyn guesses that the great change Oswald saw coming led him to conclude that his career was over and that he was now a figure from a time that did not have computers and cell phones. Yet Marilyn also maintains he is a very modern person, with a mind that works extremely fast and absorbs everything. These contradictions enable Oswald to stick out, sufficiently nonconformist to break the rules. As Marilyn explains at the end of the film, "without the Oswalds of this world—we have no future. None of us. They can do things other people can't" (*Shooting the Past*, p. 137). Oswald is one of the archetypal figures within Poliakoff's oeuvre who, as the author himself says, resists "being dragged into the world of mass culture" ("Featurette," *Shooting the Past* DVD extra). Whatever their failings, these characters are to be admired for their peculiar form of courage.

It seems likely that Poliakoff saw something of himself in the rebellious Oswald, especially after his well-publicized dispute with young BBC executives over the length and form of the film. Coming out of a television culture that encouraged the author to express his or her vision in the single-television-play format, Poliakoff was used to having his dramas presented as he had written them. In his opinion, "The voice of the writer has been squashed and diminished over the years with the death or semi-death of the single play" (Robert Butler interview). When Poliakoff proposed *Shooting the Past* to the BBC, he was advised to cut out thirty-five minutes in order to quicken the drama's pace. Poliakoff refused, arguing that he was trying to slow television down and challenge the idea that an audience could only pay attention for a very limited period of time. The success of the piece with viewers, together with a clutch of international awards including the Prix Italia and the Royal Television Society Award, meant that Poliakoff was subsequently given a free hand by the BBC to cast and write with little interference. Poliakoff has never been shy to criticize the BBC—perhaps because he recognizes its value in an era with so many channels of varying quality—but this rather dysfunctional marriage between the writer and the corporation has nonetheless seen Poliakoff write six lengthy dramas and one short piece for it during the period 2001–2007.

THE 2000S: "A DETECTIVE PATROLLING THE ZEITGEIST"

If Poliakoff's plays and films have frequently featured a mystery to be solved, in the 2000s, his films turned both inward—to uncover, in *Perfect Strangers*, family secrets, and, in *The Lost Prince,* to dramatize the secret life of a member of the royal family—and also outward, to represent recent history (in *Friends & Crocodiles* and *Gideon's Daughter*), in order to take a second, more informed look at it.

Perfect Strangers (2001), which won the international Peabody Award for television broadcasting as well as the prize for Best Writer in the Serials and Single Drama category at the Royal Television Awards, explored the idea that there are at least three great stories in any family. It was inspired by Poliakoff's attendance at his own family reunion, where he knew only five percent of the other guests. Seen through the eyes of Daniel, the narrative of *Perfect Strangers* is punctuated by a tale of a young Jewish girl managing to escape persecution by constructing a new family tree and identity for herself; a story of three sisters, one of whom loses her lover in World War II and the other two who live out part of the war in the woods as wild children; and finally the story of Richard, whose mental illness leads to him being shunned by his closest relatives until he is killed in an accident.

In some respects, *Perfect Strangers* picks up where *Shooting the Past* ended. Just as Christopher Anderson discovers a new family history through the photographs in the collection, so Daniel and his father are both shown pictures by the family archivist that ultimately lead them to completely reassess the character and life of Daniel's grandfather. There may be mystery in the family's past, but the living family members also have secrets, which Daniel strives to uncover. At the end of the film he suggests that Richard's death was inevitable because of a pattern that recurs in the family, a kind of dislocating force that is not explicable by science and which had emerged before in the wild children. Poliakoff presents a paradox: that the closest possible institution we have can also be the one most likely to drive us apart.

Poliakoff has said that he often wondered whether he should write the miniseries *The Lost Prince*, which aired in 2003 and won three Emmy Awards, arguing that "the royal family is such a surreal and unnatural institution it is very difficult to write about them without either parodying the characters or showing contempt for them" (*The Lost Prince*, p. x). Nevertheless, this story seems a logical extension of his previous work in *Perfect Strangers*. The House of Windsor, despite its uniqueness, stands as a representative family, with the flaws and eccentricities of the British character writ large, and so fits Poliakoff's style of heightened realism, in which some events seem too absurd or unlikely to be true.

The Lost Prince dramatized the little-known life of Prince John, known as Johnnie, the youngest son of King George V and Queen Mary. Johnnie suffers from epilepsy and severe learning difficulties. After his father ascends to the throne, it is arranged for Johnnie to move with his nurse, Lalla, to Norfolk. Poliakoff uses Johnnie's isolation and the perspective of his elder brother George at a naval academy to dramatize the advent and turmoil of World War I. Toward the end of the film, Johnnie gives a successful recital in front of his family and the royal household, but after returning with his brother to Norfolk he has a severe epileptic seizure and dies.

The Lost Prince exemplifies Poliakoff's favorite type of historical storytelling: choosing characters who are on the edge of things and dramatizing their indirect perspective upon great events. It is a technique that he used in *Breaking the Silence* and that he returns to in *Glorious 39* (2009). The audience does not see any fighting, but the family's story is presented as equal in importance to the conflict at the front and in the trenches. In addition, Poliakoff captures moments that crystallize the tension and danger of the atmosphere. When Queen Mary is driving toward her country house, for instance, the car is stopped by a group of men with guns. She thinks that these are revolutionaries, but they turn out to be the members of Johnnie's household. The moment dramatizes both the extreme unease of the royal family at this time—the film also explores the difficult decision to change the royal name from Saxe-Coburg-Gotha to Windsor—and also, more subtly, the way in which Johnnie's difference might still be construed as a danger to the family's reputation.

Poliakoff has arranged the narrative (sometimes rearranging actual historical events) to map Johnnie's growth onto seismic world events: two of his worst epileptic seizures occur on the day of Edward's funeral and on the eve of the declaration of war with Germany. And yet as Britain seems to decline, Johnnie prospers, progressing in his learning sufficiently to give a recital. Johnnie's remarkable energy during this invented and deeply moving episode is in acute contrast to the broken and distraught figures he sees around him. It is precisely because the recital's vitality is a clear contradiction of the general mood of the family and household that it throws into such sharp relief the state of the country at large. Indeed at times it seems as if Poliakoff has appropriated the real Prince John to act as a kind of talisman for the survival of the country, and when it is saved, he disappears.

While viewers of *The Lost Prince* implicitly made connections between the outbreak of war in 1914 and the imminent war in Iraq in 2003, Poliakoff's next two films for BBC Television directly investigated the recent past. *Friends & Crocodiles* and *Gideon's Daughter* (both 2006) are joined through the character of William Sneath, a journalist who is friends both with Paul, one of the protagonists of the first film, and Gideon, the main figure in the second. The latter won another Peabody Award and also two Golden Globes for the acting of Bill Nighy as Gideon and Emily Blunt as Natasha.

These films in particular prove Poliakoff to be, as his character Al was described in *Blinded by the Sun*, "a detective patrolling the Zeitgeist" (*Blinded by the Sun & Sweet Panic*, p. 102), seeking to interrogate the trends of modern times. *Friends & Crocodiles* features venture capitalists and the dot-com bubble of the late 1990s, but it concentrates upon the obsessive relationship between Paul, a visionary designer, and Lizzie, his personal assistant. Even after Lizzie recognizes Paul's instinct toward self-destruction, and is acutely embarrassed when he fails to live up to

her expectations, she cannot erase him from her mind. At the conclusion of the story, when the vast company she was running implodes, she returns to Paul, acknowledging that his earlier warnings had been justified. The character of Paul is indebted to Poliakoff's earlier creation, the maverick entrepreneur Bill Galpin in *Playing with Trains* (1989). Both Galpin and Paul act in ways that alienate them from the outside world: Galpin is so self-righteous that he damages his relationships with his children, whereas Paul courts chaos, something that Lizzie, who represents ambition and order, cannot comprehend. As the story progresses through the decades, we see how Paul's former friends sacrifice their dreams to become successful in ways they would have reviled as young idealists. Paul, however, despite moments of terrible failure, stays true to his visionary spirit, coming to represent the crocodile, a creature which, it is said, survived the extinction of the dinosaurs.

Gideon's Daughter is, by contrast, a far more intimate portrait of a relationship between a public relations expert and his daughter Natasha. The very public mourning for Princess Diana in 1997 is played off against Gideon's own form of mourning for the loss of his daughter's affection. Poliakoff uses the relationship to show the hollowness of Gideon's job, and when he is employed by the New Labour government to advise on national celebrations for the millennium, we are also presented with a critical view of a culture driven by image, focus groups, and celebrity. Gideon's relationship with a woman unconcerned with this world, still in mourning for a son who was killed in an accident, puts him back in touch with an unmanufactured reality, and ultimately back in touch with his daughter.

Poliakoff's television films *Joe's Palace* and *Capturing Mary* (both 2007) form another pair of complementary pieces, both set in a London billionaire's house. *Joe's Palace* deals with urban alienation, but not the alienation of the earlier plays and films, since here the urban landscape is one of luxury. In *Capturing Mary*, Poliakoff pinpoints a moment in British history when society shifted radically from the conservative

1950s into the more liberated 1960s, leaving some of the characters behind.

The film *Glorious 39* (2009) fits into the Hitchcock thriller genre, but it also builds on Poliakoff's previous work. "After writing *Capturing Mary*, which was quite a dark story with a spooky, visceral centre, I felt that was quite an interesting area for me to build on. I've always liked thrillers and films that satisfy in a suspenseful way but that also have things carefully worked out and make psychological and emotional sense," Poliakoff has said (Mark Dudgeon interview, p. viii). If he used the tone of *Capturing Mary* as one starting point for *Glorious 39*, he drew on his previous play, *Talk of the City*, as inspiration for the film's content. In that piece, Poliakoff intimates that during 1937–1938, the BBC avoided reporting details from Germany that might have suggested the persecution of the Jews and was instead intent on preserving the tightly scripted content and even tone of the usual broadcasts. The BBC is supposed to be a politically neutral institution, but Poliakoff's play suggests that by not reporting the oppression the BBC did indeed occupy a political position, one that could be said to morally implicate it in the treatment of the Jews.

In *Glorious 39*, Poliakoff uses the lives of figures on the fringes of power to show how close Britain came to making a deal with Hitler in order to avoid war. It focuses upon Anne, the adopted daughter of a politician, Alexander Keyes. At a dinner, Hector, a politician, voices his concern that the government's appeasement of Hitler is merely encouraging the Nazis to invade more of Europe. Soon after this, Hector apparently commits suicide, but Anne and her boyfriend, Lawrence, are unconvinced. When Anne finds a gramophone recording of Hector being threatened, she is convinced that he has been murdered. She asks a friend to listen to the recording of another meeting, but shortly after she gives it to him, he, too, is dead. When Anne listens to the recording, she hears her brother helping to plan the murder of Hector. Anne realizes that she is being spied upon, and when she tries to meet Lawrence to give him the recording, she finds him murdered. Soon afterward, she realizes that

her father is also one of the appeasers. She is drugged and shut up in her aunt's house until one day she manages to escape.

Poliakoff has said that one of the driving forces behind his writing of the film was the realization that, if appeasement had been successful, his Jewish family might never have survived in Britain. His mother's side in particular would have been in danger, since they were prominent members of the Liberal party. The film, he says, like the historical record,

> shows how an apparently civilised surface can crack open to reveal the darkness incredibly quickly, as most recently happened in the former Yugoslavia. We never had to face up to our antisemitism after the war because of our brave and proud history—and it was brave and proud. But it was a damn close run thing, and the forces trying to do a deal were incredibly powerful. It really could have happened here.
>
> (Wroe interview)

Glorious 39 is a family drama that crosses over, dangerously, into the political sphere. Once again it features an outsider, the actress Anne, who is adopted by the aristocratic Keyes family. The difficult position that Anne places herself in is made even starker when she learns that her family were Romany gypsies, another group of people that the Nazis would try to annihilate. The conspiracy within the nation to appease Hitler is mirrored within the Keyes family, and family upheaval is presented as equally as terrifying as political conflict: Anne is eventually shut away to keep her quiet. Anne's moments of rage toward the end of the film seem to stand for the rage of the dispossessed and tortured, and they demonstrate both her power and her impotence, the injustice of her treatment and that of so many others during this period. But they also suggest the impossibility of changing history. Poliakoff indicates that at this moment "her tone is not hysterical [...] it is full of authority. But her voice is entirely different" as she speaks to her adoptive father, brother, and sister: "Why are you looking like that? I don't see why you should be surprised! I am not frightened of you fucking people! Remember I am the daughter of gypsies and it was bound to come out sooner or later—

what I 'really am'—that's what you think isn't it? Well, here it is!" (*Glorious 39*, p. 118).

Anne's outburst echoes Poliakoff's fascination from other works (Daniel's talk of patterns in *Perfect Strangers* and the way in which mother and daughter become symbiotically linked in *Shout Across the River*) with finding something indelible in the family. Her body reduced almost to nothing by starvation, Anne's expression of rage is a natural, elemental force; it is what remains after her aristocratic nurturing and the decorous façade of her adopted family have been stripped away. Yet one of the striking features of the film is the way in which the relationship between father and daughter is portrayed. Alexander is caught between love for his country and genuine love for his adopted daughter, speculating that "maybe there are two sorts of love. I don't want to be made to choose" (*Glorious 39*, p. 116). His constant promise throughout the film is that he will keep her safe, and her moments of anger are shocking to him because in her safety he felt he was also preserving something of their life together. Alexander, who is a typically complex, dark Poliakoff character, tells Anne how "everything *I* believe in, democracy, culture, art— (*He smiles.*) all those sorts of things, civilisation itself in fact my dear, will be destroyed if we get involved in this ruinous war" (*Glorious 39*, p. 115). Even though the implication is that Anne is being kept safe from her real self, she remains peculiarly representative of the aim of the appeasers, for they urgently want to preserve their own comfortable lives. Anne, who used a romanticized English heritage in her childhood games, and who reads Keats and Shakespeare to the family, represents that old world without realizing it.

The film's images are as striking as they are unexpected, designed to be remembered, and almost too absurd to be true: a group of young women sleeping in their petticoats after a huge ball just a few weeks before war was declared; the boys' choir singing to Anne and her aunt in the otherwise empty local church. These are replaced by similarly memorable images of terror: a huge bonfire of pets that residents were forced to have killed when they fled London, and a shed full of the corpses of the animals. As Po-

liakoff has suggested, these latter images powerfully suggest what might have happened to minority groups in Britain had the appeasers won, and of course what did occur in the concentration and death camps in central Europe.

CONCLUSION

When critics discuss Stephen Poliakoff, they invariably focus upon his concerns with history, particularly his attempts to show how we should value the past. He uses history to isolate and then reflect upon moments of great change, and he seems to take pleasure in how this recourse to history frequently allows him to assess what matters in the present, and even to make suggestions about where the future might take us. This impulse to locate modern life is also to be found in Poliakoff's interest in science, which has led him to question our crucial yet ambiguous relationship with technology and our understanding of progress.

The early dramas took place against the backdrop of a modern urban environment, which he saw as frequently hostile and oppressive and yet also strangely alluring, with its soundtrack of Muzak and differing shades of neon. While never losing that fascination for the urban, which allowed him to hone his skills in capturing the atmosphere of a time and place, Poliakoff's work has expanded to place audiences in touch with modern and contemporary international events, especially those of twentieth-century Europe. Even here though, the perspective presented is deliberately oblique.

Institutions have been important locations for his work—from a nuclear power station to a university, a photographic library to a royal household. But the institution of the family has been the most prominent, and the sparse and elemental qualities of his early plays were frequently complemented by the almost primitive forces that bound—and sometimes tore apart— the members of a family. Children have always been central figures in his drama because their tendency to question matches Poliakoff's own intense curiosity. That inquisitive nature has meant Poliakoff sometimes comes across as deeply skeptical of modern consumerism and the culture of celebrity, but he has also drawn attention to ways in which clinging to the past and the status quo can do far more harm than good.

By deliberately complicating his characters and introducing paradoxes into his scripts, Poliakoff shows that life is by no means straightforward, and it is therefore natural that a deep sense of irony pervades much of his writing. Poliakoff is often criticized for apparent contradictions within the style of his work: incisive dialogue can give way to hackneyed expression, and recent work has sometimes seemed to make its points too explicitly, rather than rely upon the strength of metaphor that was a hallmark of earlier pieces. On the other hand, the power of Poliakoff's style of heightened realism relies upon an embrace of both the startling and the familiar, and this style is reflected in his dialogue just as much as it is obvious in his imagery. Within a modern existence that is full of sound and fury, Poliakoff's concern is to produce work that, after the credits appear or the house lights brighten, remains in the minds and imaginations of his audience, signifying something unique.

Selected Bibliography

WORKS OF STEPHEN POLIAKOFF

COLLECTED PLAYS

Stephen Poliakoff, Plays: 1. London: Methuen Drama, 1989. (With an introduction by Poliakoff. Contains *Clever Soldiers, Hitting Town, City Sugar, American Days,* and *Strawberry Fields*.)

Stephen Poliakoff, Plays: 2. London: Methuen Drama, 1994. (With an introduction by Poliakoff. Contains *Breaking the Silence, Playing with Trains, She's Been Away,* and *Century*.)

Stephen Poliakoff, Plays: 3. London: Methuen Drama, 1998. (With an introduction by Poliakoff. Contains *Caught on a Train, Close My Eyes,* and *Coming in to Land*.)

INDIVIDUAL PLAYS (WITH DETAILS OF FIRST PRODUCTIONS)

1970s

Lay By (as cowriter). London: Calder & Boyars, 1971. First production: Edinburgh Festival, August 1971. This play was first published in *Plays and Players*, London: Hansom Books, 1971.

Clever Soldiers. In *Stephen Poliakoff, Plays: 1*. London: Methuen Drama, 1989. First production: Hampstead Theatre Club, London, November 21, 1974.

Hitting Town. In *Stephen Poliakoff, Plays: 1*. London: Methuen Drama, 1989. First published by Eyre Methuen in 1976, revised in 1978, and reprinted by Methuen London in 1982. Revised for the 1989 edition. First production: Bush Theatre, London, April 1975. The play was subsequently produced by Thames Television and televised by ITV as part of the "Plays for Britain" series on April 27, 1976.

City Sugar. In *Stephen Poliakoff, Plays: 1*. London: Methuen Drama, 1989. First published by Eyre Methuen in 1976, revised in 1978, and reprinted by Methuen London in 1982. Revised for the 1989 edition. First production: Bush Theatre, London, October 9, 1975. The play transferred to the Comedy Theatre, opening in March 1976. It was subsequently staged at the Phoenix Theatre, New York, in January 1978. The play was also produced by Scottish Television and televised by ITV in the "Sunday Drama" series on August 6, 1978.

Strawberry Fields. In *Stephen Poliakoff, Plays: 1*. London: Methuen Drama, 1989. First published by Eyre Methuen in 1977. Revised for the 1989 edition. First production: National Theatre company at the Young Vic, London, August 1976. The play transferred to the Cottesloe auditorium, National Theatre, London, and opened on March 31, 1977. It was subsequently staged at the Manhattan Theatre Club, New York, in May 1978.

Shout Across the River. In *Stephen Poliakoff, Plays: 1*. London: Methuen Drama, 1989. First published by Eyre Methuen in 1979. Revised for the 1989 edition. First production: Royal Shakespeare Company at the Warehouse Theatre, Croydon, September 21, 1978. It was subsequently staged at the Phoenix Theatre, New York, in December 1979.

American Days. In *Stephen Poliakoff, Plays: 1*. London: Methuen Drama, 1989. First production: ICA, London, June 12, 1979. The play was subsequently staged at the Manhattan Theatre Club, New York, in December 1980.

1980s

The Summer Party. London: Eyre Methuen, 1980. First production: Sheffield Crucible Theatre, Sheffield, March 12, 1980.

Favourite Nights. In *Favourite Nights & Caught on a Train*. London: Methuen London, 1982. First production: Lyric Hammersmith, London, November 2, 1981.

Breaking the Silence. In *Stephen Poliakoff, Plays: 2*. London: Methuen Drama, 1994. First published by Methuen London in 1984. First production: Royal Shakespeare Company, The Pit, Barbican Centre, London, October 31, 1984.

Coming in to Land. In *Stephen Poliakoff, Plays: 3*. London:

Methuen Drama, 1998. First published by Methuen London in 1986. First production: Lyttleton auditorium, National Theatre, London, December 18, 1986.

Playing with Trains. In *Stephen Poliakoff, Plays: 2.* London: Methuen Drama, 1994. First published by Methuen Drama in 1989. First production: Royal Shakespeare Company, The Pit, Barbican Centre, London, November 29, 1989. Poliakoff later adapted the play for a radio production on BBC Radio Four. It was broadcast in the "Saturday Play" series in two sixty-minute parts on March 20 and March 27, 2010.

1990s

Sienna Red. London: Methuen Drama, 1992. First production: Peter Hall Company, Liverpool Playhouse, Liverpool, April 15, 1992. The production then toured the U.K.

Sweet Panic. In *Blinded by the Sun & Sweet Panic.* London: Methuen Drama, 1996. First production: Hampstead Theatre, London, February 1, 1996. Stephen Poliakoff directed this production.

Blinded by the Sun. In *Blinded by the Sun & Sweet Panic.* London: Methuen Drama, 1996. First production: Cottesloe auditorium, National Theatre, August 28, 1996.

Talk of the City. London: Methuen, 1998. First production: Royal Shakespeare Company, Swan Theatre, Stratford-upon-Avon, April 22, 1998. Stephen Poliakoff directed this production.

Remember This. London: Methuen, 1999. First production: Lyttleton auditorium, National Theatre, London, October 8, 1999.

SCREENPLAYS (WITH DETAILS OF FIRST BROADCASTS OR PREMIERES)

1980s

Caught on a Train. In *Stephen Poliakoff, Plays: 3.* London: Methuen Drama, 1998. First published in *Favourite Nights & Caught on a Train.* London: Methuen London, 1982. Directed by Peter Duffell. First broadcast: BBC Two, October 31, 1980, as part of the "Playhouse" series.

Soft Targets. In *Runners & Soft Targets.* London: Methuen London, 1984. Directed by Charles Sturridge. Produced by Hanstoll Enterprises for Goldcrest. First broadcast: BBC One on October, 19, 1982 in the "Play for Today" series.

Runners. In *Runners & Soft Targets.* London: Methuen London, 1984. Directed by Charles Sturridge. Produced by Hanstoll Enterprises Production. Opened: August 1983 in the U.K. The film had a limited release and was subsequently shown on Channel Four in the U.K.

Hidden City. In *She's Been Away & Hidden City.* London: Methuen London, 1989. Directed by Stephen Poliakoff. Produced by FilmFour International. Opened: August 1987, Venice Film Festival.

She's Been Away. In *Stephen Poliakoff, Plays: 2.* London: Methuen, 1994. First published in *She's Been Away & Hidden City.* London: Methuen London, 1989. Directed by Peter Hall. Produced by BBC Television. First broadcast: BBC One, October 8, 1989, in the "Screen One" series.

1990s

Close My Eyes. In *Stephen Poliakoff, Plays: 3.* London: Methuen Drama, 1998. First published as *Close My Eyes.* London: Methuen, 1991. A Beambright Production for FilmFour International. Directed by Stephen Poliakoff. Opened: September 6, 1991, in the U.K.

Century. In *Stephen Poliakoff, Plays: 2.* London: Methuen Drama, 1994. Directed by Stephen Poliakoff. A BBC Films Production in association with Beambright. Opened: December 31, 1993, in the U.K.

Shooting the Past. London: Methuen, 1998. Directed by Stephen Poliakoff. Produced by Talkback Productions for BBC Television. First broadcast: BBC Two, January 10, 17, and 24, 1999.

2000s

Perfect Strangers. London: Methuen, 2001. Directed by Stephen Poliakoff. Produced by Talkback Productions for BBC Television. First broadcast: BBC Two, May 10, 17, and 24, 2001. (The series was broadcast in the United States as *Almost Strangers.*)

The Lost Prince. London: Methuen, 2003. Directed by Stephen Poliakoff. Produced by Talkback Productions for BBC Television. First broadcast: BBC One, January 19 and 26, 2003.

Friends & Crocodiles. In *Friends & Crocodiles and Gideon's Daughter.* London: Methuen, 2005. Directed by Stephen Poliakoff. Produced by Talkback Productions for BBC Television. First broadcast: BBC One, January 15, 2006.

Gideon's Daughter. In *Friends & Crocodiles and Gideon's Daughter.* London: Methuen, 2005. Directed by Stephen Poliakoff. Produced by Talkback Productions for BBC Television. First broadcast: BBC One, February 26, 2006.

Joe's Palace. In *Joe's Palace and Capturing Mary, also featuring A Real Summer.* London: Methuen, 2007. Directed by Stephen Poliakoff. Produced by Talkback-Thames for BBC Television and HBO Films. First broadcast: BBC One, November 4, 2007.

Capturing Mary. In *Joe's Palace and Capturing Mary, also featuring A Real Summer.* London: Methuen, 2007. Directed by Stephen Poliakoff. Produced by Talkback-Thames for BBC Television and HBO Films. First broadcast: BBC Two, November 12, 2007.

A Real Summer. In *Joe's Palace and Capturing Mary, also featuring A Real Summer.* London: Methuen, 2007. Directed by Stephen Poliakoff. Produced by BBC Television. First broadcast: BBC Two, November 10, 2007.

Glorious 39. London: Methuen, 2009. Directed by Stephen Poliakoff. Produced by BBC Films, the U.K. Film Council, Screen East Content Investment Fund, and Quickfire Films for Talkback Thames in association with Magic Light Pictures. Opened: November 20, 2009, in the U.K. The film premiered at the Toronto International Film Festival on September 14, 2009.

UNPUBLISHED WORKS (WITH DETAILS OF FIRST PRODUCTIONS, BROADCASTS, OR PREMIERES)

1960S AND 1970S

"Granny." First production: Westminster School, 1969.

Day with My Sister. First production: Traverse Theatre, Edinburgh, August, 1971.

Pretty Boy. First production: Royal Court, London, June 1972.

Berlin Days. First production: Little Theatre, London, 1973.

Sad Beat Up. First production: Little Theatre, London, 1974.

The Carnation Gang. First production: Bush Theatre, London, September 1974.

Heroes. First production: Royal Court, London, July 1975.

Stronger than the Sun. Directed by Michael Apted. Produced by BBC Television. First broadcast: BBC One, October 18, 1977, as part of the "Play for Today" series.

1980S AND 1990S

Bloody Kids. Directed by Stephen Frears. Produced by Black Lion Films and ATV. First broadcast: ITV, March 23, 1980.

Food of Love. Directed by Stephen Poliakoff. Produced by Intrinsica Films/MP Productions. Opened: October 19, 1997, Cherbourg-Octeville Festival of Irish and British Film.

The Tribe. Directed by Stephen Poliakoff. Produced by Deep City Films for BBC Films. First broadcast: BBC Two, June 21, 1998.

OTHER WORKS

Foreword to *The Lost Prince*. London: Methuen, 2003. Pp. vii–xi.

"Between the Lies." *Guardian*, October 25, 2003 (http://www.guardian.co.uk/stage/2003/oct/25/theatre1;). (Poliakoff explains how his distrust of market research inspired him to write *Sweet Panic*.)

Introduction to *Friends & Crocodiles and Gideon's Daughter*. London: Methuen. Pp. v–xxiii. (Poliakoff describes what television has meant to him over the years, and why he continues to write for it.)

Introduction to *Joe's Palace and Capturing Mary*. London: Methuen, 2007. Pp. vii–xiv.

CRITICAL AND BIOGRAPHICAL STUDIES

Cardwell, Sarah. "Style, Mood, and Engagement in *Perfect Strangers*." In *Style and Meaning: Studies in the Detailed Analysis of Film*. Edited by J. Gibbs and D. Pye. Manchester, U.K.: Manchester University Press, 2005. Pp. 179–194.

_____. "Patterns, Layers, and Values: Poliakoff's *The Lost Prince*." *Journal of British Cinema and Television* 3, no. 1:134–141 (May 2006). (This issue features a triptych of short essays on Poliakoff. See Holdsworth and Nelson below.)

Demastes, William W. "Stephen Poliakoff." In *British Playwrights 1956–1995: A Research and Production Sourcebook*. Edited by William H. Demastes. Westport, Conn.: Greenwood, 1996. Pp. 326–334.

Hogg, Christopher. "Re-evaluating the Archive in Stephen Poliakoff's *Shooting the Past*." *Journal of British Cinema and Television* 6, no. 3:437–451 (December 2009).

Holdsworth, Amy. "'Slow Television' and Stephen Poliakoff's *Shooting the Past*." *Journal of British Cinema and Television* 3, no. 1:128–133 (May 2006).

Jacobson, Howard. "It's Magnificent, but It's Nothing to Do with War." *Independent*, January 25, 2003 (http://www.independent.co.uk/opinion/commentators/howard-jacobson/its-magnificent-but-its-nothing-to-do-with-war-602832.html). (An article that reflects on the importance of *The Lost Prince*.)

Marranca, Bonnie. Mini-reviews of Methuen's New Theatrescripts. *Performing Arts Journal*, 2, no. 2:99–100 (autumn 1977).

Martin, Matthew. "Stephen Poliakoff's Drama for the Post-Scientific Age." *Theatre Journal* 45, no. 2:197–211 (May 1993).

Middeke, Martin. *Stephen Poliakoff: Drama und Dramaturgie in der abstrakten Gesellschaft*. Paderborn, Germany: Schöningh, 1994. (Contains an interview with Poliakoff in English, pp. 270–282.)

_____. "Fashion and the Media: Hyperreality in the Plays of Stephen Poliakoff." *Contemporary Drama in English*, vol. 2, *Centres and Margins*. Trier, Germany: Wissenschaftlicher Verlag Trier, 1995. Pp. 109–117.

Nelson, Robin. "Locating Poliakoff: An Auteur in Contemporary TV Drama." *Journal of British Cinema and Television* 3, no. 1:122–127 (May 2006).

_____. *Stephen Poliakoff on Stage and Screen*. London: Methuen, 2011.

Peacock, D. Keith. "The Fascination of Fascism: The Plays of Stephen Poliakoff." *Modern Drama* 27, no. 4:494–505 (1984).

Spurling, John. "Stephen Poliakoff." In *Contemporary Dramatists*. Edited by D. L. Kirkpatrick and James Vinson. London: St. James Press, 1988.

INTERVIEWS

Poliakoff frequently gives interviews, particularly to British newspapers, and many of these are available online. The

DVD editions of his work also contain interviews with him and his cast members, and almost all have his director's commentary.

"Director's Commentary." *Caught on a Train* DVD extra. London: BBC Worldwide, 2004.

"Featurette." *Shooting the Past* DVD extra. London: BBC Worldwide, 2004.

"Profile." *The Lost Prince* DVD extra. London: BBC Worldwide, 2006.

"A Brief History of Now: Stephen Poliakoff." *Time Shift*. Directed by Matthew Pelly.

Gideon's Daughter. DVD extra. Bristol, U.K.: BBC, 2005.

Butler, Robert. "Stephen Poliakoff: Obsessive Teller of Awkward Truths." *Independent*, May 6, 2001 (http://www.independent.co.uk/news/people/profiles/stephen-poliakoff-obsessive-teller-of-awkward-truths-683919.html).

Dudgeon, Mark. "Q and A with the Author." In *Glorious 39*. London: Methuen, 2009. Pp. vii–xviii.

Hari, Johann. "Stephen Poliakoff: A Prince of Drama Turns His Gaze." *Independent*, January 11, 2003 (http://www.independent.co.uk/news/people/profiles/stephen-poliakoff-a-prince-of-drama-turns-his-gaze-601550.html).

Hoggart, Paul. "Interview: Stephen Poliakoff." *Guardian*, October 29, 2007 (http://www.guardian.co.uk/media/2007/oct/29/mondaymediasection.bbc).

Johnston, Chris. "Honest Scientist (Batteries Not Included)." *Times Higher Education Supplement*, December 20, 1996 (http://www.timeshighereducation.co.uk/story.asp?storyCode=91913).

Patterson, Christina. "The Big Interview: Stephen Poliakoff." *Independent*, November 20, 2009 (http://www.independent.co.uk/arts-entertainment/interviews/poliakoff-original-work-takes-arrogance-1823814.htm).

Wroe, Nicholas. "A Life in Drama: Stephen Poliakoff." *Guardian*, November 28, 2009 (http://www.guardian.co.uk/culture/2009/nov/28/stephen-poliakoff-interview-nicholas-wroe).

KATHLEEN RAINE

(1908—2003)

Katherine Firth

KATHLEEN RAINE WAS a poet who focused on the spiritual power of the natural world and the passionate refusal of love. She came to prominence in the 1940s, publishing three collections of poetry: *Stone and Flower* (1943), *Living in Time* (1946), and *The Pythoness and Other Poems* (1949). As one of the leading poets of the decade, Raine was associated with a group of New Romantics, particularly Edwin Muir, Vernon Watkins, and David Gascoyne. Their work was distinctive in the use of mythology, religious imagery, and a belief in the visionary vocation of the poet. As a critic, Raine's *Defending Ancient Springs* (1967) discusses Watkins and Gascoyne who shared this vision, alongside a commitment to the power of the natural world and of the subconscious. *Defending Ancient Springs* champions writers who are committed to the sources and holy wells of inspiration, and the image of the "beck," "well," or "spring" recurs in her poetry as a symbol of reflection and new life.

Raine was an evocative regional poet who drew inspiration from the north of England and the Scottish Highlands. Although she lived in London for most of her professional life, the north was always a significant place of pilgrimage and her poetic home. Raine had vivid memories of visiting Northumberland with her family as a small child, where she claims her poetic vocation was first awakened. Like many children in World War I, Raine was sent away from her parents' home near London to the country, where it was believed she would be safer. Raine adored her years in the north country and was sorry to have to return to Ilford in Essex and her parent's home. After the failure of her second marriage, she moved to the Lake District. First she lived with the 1930s poet and anthologist Michael Roberts and his wife, Janet Adam Smith, the literary editor of the British Broadcasting Corporation magazine *The Listener,* which had published Raine's early poems; then she moved near the village of Martindale just on the other side of Ullswater. When she had to return to London to work in the early 1940s, her children lived with Raine's longtime friend Helen Sutherland at Cockley Moor a few miles away, until the end of World War II. Later, Gavin Maxwell's Scottish home in Sandaig, on the Glenelg Peninsular near the Isle of Skye, would replace the Lake District as a place of poetic power in her work.

Kathleen Raine was a writer of extraordinary productivity and longevity. She published thirteen collections of poems, more than twenty scholarly studies of other poets, and four volumes of autobiography. Raine was one of the few women poets to be published in the seminal 1930s journals *Experiment,* edited by William Empson, and *New Verse,* edited by Geoffrey Grigson. She continued to produce new poems, published in *Poetry (London), Agenda,* and the *Temenos Review*, into the twenty-first century.

The early collections were widely considered critical successes. *The Pythoness* was awarded the Edna St. Vincent Millay prize from the American Poetry Society. However, Raine later felt her first three collections were too much influenced by the surface erudition of poets like William Empson, rather than truly inspired. Raine was trained as a scientist at Cambridge University, where she focused on botany, zoology, and the emerging field of experimental psychology. This rigor impacts on her poems of the 1940s. The early poetry has a searing intensity, a clarity of language, and a compressed passion married to dense allusion. The intelligence and emotion of poems like "Seed" enable the reader to understand the seed as both a botanical object and an "eternity" of potential, both the "common meadows" and "that interior and holy tree" (Raine, *Collected Poems*, 2000, p. 19). In *The Year One* (1952), widely considered her best collection, Raine's poetry gains an incantatory power from its repetition and inversions. Poems like the "Millennial Hymn to Lord Shiva," published almost five decades later, display a looser grasp on language, favoring a mystical apprehension of the universe to the scientific gaze. Raine herself considered her style to have developed to be able to pack more meaning into "the arrangement of simple words," influenced by her study of the radical eighteenth-century visionary poet William Blake (1757–1827) and of Neoplatonism in general ("Kathleen Raine Writes," p. 59).

In 1952, Raine was awarded the Harriet Monroe Memorial Prize for poems published in *Poetry* magazine. The longstanding collaboration between Raine and the journal was confirmed by another *Poetry* award, the Oscar Blumenthal Prize, given a decade later, in 1961. *The Year One* won the 1953 Arts Council of Great Britain Poetry Prize award. The same year, she published a selection of poems by the Romantic poet and philosopher Samuel Taylor Coleridge, whose imaginative poems "Kubla Khan" (1816) and *The Rime of the Ancient Mariner* (1798) she considered particularly inspired. Twenty-one years later, Raine edited a similar selection of Percy Bysshe Shelley's poetry. From 1955, Raine was a research fellow at her alma mater, Girton College, Cambridge University. Her first *Collected Poems* was published in 1956, which she saw as a chance to "discard work that should never have been published" (*Collected Poems,* 2000, p. v). Raine contributed two articles to the 1957 celebration of Blake's bicentenary, *The Divine Vision,* alongside Northrop Frye and Walter De La Mare. In 1962, Raine extended her interest in Blake's illustrations as the A. W. Mellon lecturer at the National Gallery of Art in Washington, D.C.

The *Hollow Hill and Other Poems* (1965), whose title refers to the Stone Age fort and megalithic stone circle associated with Wandering Aengus in Ireland, came out just before

Defending Ancient Springs. Six Dreams and Other Poems (1968) continues Raine's interest in the subconscious, psychoanalysis, and visions, and it was published in the same year Raine produced her two-volume collection of essays on William Blake: *Blake and Tradition,* which made the lectures she had given in Washington six years earlier available in print. The next year, Raine coedited *Thomas Taylor the Platonist,* a volume of the selected writings of Taylor (1758–1835), who was an influential English Neoplatonist (a form of mysticism based on the teachings of the ancient Greek philosopher Plato, which considers on the soul as the basis of all existence). These prose collections help to define the theoretical underpinnings of Raine's poems.

In 1970, Raine's poetry was collected for number 17 in the Penguin Modern Poets series, which brought together W. S. Graham, Kathleen Raine, and David Gascoyne. Raine also published her study *William Blake,* her most popular work on the author, in 1970, and in the same year she was awarded the Society of Authors Cholmondeley Award.

The Lost Country, Raine's eighth collection of poems, was published in 1971 and won the W. H. Smith Literary Award. Raine had portrayed her idyllic childhood in the north of England as a kind of lost Paradise since her first poetry collection, but in the 1970s, this theme came to the forefront. In poems like "By the River Eden" and "Childhood," Raine realizes that "Never, never, never will I go home to be a child" (*Collected Poems,* 2000, p. 158). In 1973 Raine finally published the first volume of her autobiography, *Farewell Happy Fields,* which explores the same terrain in prose. Yet Eden refers in the poems of 1971 both to her childhood and to her friendship in the mid-1950s with Gavin Maxwell, as in the "Message to Gavin."

In 1973, Raine produced *On a Deserted Shore,* a long poem of 130 stanzas, which Raine wrote extremely quickly, in a period of about two weeks. In the poem, she meditated on the failure of her platonic love affair with the writer and naturalist Gavin Maxwell. The two had been close friends, and Raine had often visited Maxwell at his home in Sandaig, where he cared for a newly discovered species of otter he had collected on an expedition in southern Iraq (and that was named *Lutrogale perspicillata maxwelli* after him), an experience he wrote about in *A Reed Shaken by the Wind* (1959). For Raine, Maxwell was the love of her life, but Maxwell was, she later realized, never as invested in the relationship as she was. The issue seems to have been less that he was homosexual than that Raine was dedicated to an exclusive and romantic friendship, while he saw her merely as another of his many friends. After one of their many disagreements, in 1956, Raine cursed Maxwell, "Let Gavin suffer, in this place, as I am suffering now" (Botting, p. 218). Soon after, Raine was caring for the otter, Mijbil, at Sandaig when it escaped and was accidentally killed. This caused an irretrievable rift between the two. In 1960, Maxwell wrote his version of the story in the best seller *The Ring of Bright Water* (borrowing the title from a phrase in a poem of Raine's, "The Marriage of Psyche"), which was made into a film in 1969, the year Maxwell died of cancer. The ripples of their unhappy relationship persisted even beyond his death.

On a Deserted Shore is permeated by grief both for the loss of the relationship and Maxwell's death. At the same time, the poet looks to the "stones and flowers," the "seeds," and "vegetation" to console her and to bring new life. Raine's searing, honest, prose description of the relationship was published as the third of her autobiographies, *The Lion's Mouth* (1977), in which Raine describes her eventual acceptance of the fact that Maxwell had not needed her although she had needed him, and she conveys the image of Maxwell with his golden hair, his home in the north, his writerly ability, and his love for the natural world.

In 1972 Rain had published *Yeats, the Tarot, and the Golden Dawn*, her first academic book on the Irish poet W. B. Yeats (1865–1939). The book considered Yeats's interest in the symbolism of the fortune-telling cards and his involvement in establishing the magical Order of the Golden Dawn in London in the early twentieth century. *The Inner Journey of the Poet* (1976) studied both the inner journey of poets who had influenced her work and her own inner journey. *The Inner Journey* was the first of her books to be published by the new Golgonooza Press, set up two years earlier by Brian Keeble, an artist and writer who became her long-term collaborator and literary executor. Golgonooza is a city of imagination envisioned by Blake, "the total form of all human culture and civilization," past and present (Frye, p. 95).

At the turn of the decade, Raine made the connection between her metaphysical philosophy, her spiritual interests, and her poetic work even more clear. In 1979, Raine published three works on Blake: the U.K. edition of *Blake and Antiquity* (released by Routledge & Kegan Paul), *From Blake to "A Vision"* (tracing a line from Blake's allegorical, religious-political landscapes to Yeats' description of his experiments with automatic writing), and *Blake and the New Age*. Blake used the term "the New Age" in his preface to *Milton: A Poem* in 1809, but by 1979 the term was popularly understood to refer to a late-twentieth-century alternative spiritual subculture. This last volume in particular connected the historical writers with the new esoteric and spiritual movements with which Raine was becoming actively involved.

The next year, Raine helped found *Temenos* magazine, with the architect Keith Critchlow, the artist Brian Keeble, and the writer and translator Philip Sherrard. *Temenos* was intended to be a journal that would publish creative and critical works that acknowledged the significance of spirituality for society, and it ran until 1992. The *Temenos Review* was refounded in 1998 and continues today. In 1991 the Temenos Academy was founded, to support the work of the magazine with classes and lectures. The journal's patron is Charles, Prince of Wales, who was strongly influenced by Raine's philosophy. Throughout the 1980s, *Temenos* combated what the founders saw as the materialistic, technocratic ideology of the decade. The name *Temenos* comes from the Greek for a sacred grove, a sanctuary, a holy place. For the early psychoanalyst Carl Jung, the word also suggested a magic circle. Jung's understanding of the psyche was influential on

Raine's understanding of the world and on the construction of her poetry—particularly in her use of archetypes, symbols that are held in common by modern and ancient civilizations, and by Eastern and Western spiritualities.

In *The Oval Portrait and Other Poems* (1977), Raine turns the focus of her poetry from a twenty-year-old love affair to her family—the title poem describes a photograph of her mother. Her love for her family, particularly her deceased parents, became an important theme of her later poetry. Raine's next book of poems, *The Oracle in the Heart* (1980), suggested that the prophet (or oracle) within each person might speak difficult truths, that the emotions may be the route to a deeper, and hard won, self-understanding. In 1982, Raine published *The Human Face of God: William Blake and the Book of Job*, in which she closely analyzed the engravings Blake made for his late work, *Illustrations of the Book of Job* (1826). In *Yeats the Initiate* (1986), Raine further explored Yeats' involvement as an adept of the magical Order of the Golden Dawn and its influence on his poetry. Her 1987 poetry collection *The Presence* continued to explore the idea of the immanence of the spiritual in the natural world.

The 1980s were a period of reassessment for Raine. She published two retrospective collections. At the age of seventy-two, Raine reflected on forty-five years of poetry in *Collected Poems: 1935–1980* (1981). At the end of the decade, she bought out another collection of *Selected Poems* (1988). Raine was beginning to consider her literary reputation, choosing the poems she wanted kept in her canon. In 1991, Raine published the three earlier volumes of life writing as a single volume, *Autobiographies*. The title alludes to the 1926 *Autobiographies of William Butler Yeats*, in which the poet had described an inner spiritual and emotional journey rather than a chronologically detailed list of external events. The final volume of Raine's autobiography, *India Seen Afar* (1990), described her feeling of homecoming when she finally visited India, as a guest of the Indian government. Linked to the visit, Meena Rani's study of *The Poetry of Kathleen Raine: A Pursuit of Patterns*

was published in New Delhi in 1989. Raine would visit India a further three times. Her final work of Blake scholarship appeared in 1989, titled *Golgonooza, City of Imagination.*

Raine also continued to write new poems. In 1992 she published *Living with Mystery,* which was awarded the Queen's Gold Medal for poetry. Her final work of Yeats scholarship, *W. B. Yeats and the Learning of the Imagination,* was published in 1999, when she was over ninety.

In 2000, at the age of ninety-two, Raine again reshaped her *Collected Poems,* reducing eleven volumes of poetry to only 350 pages of verse. (All poetry citations in this essay are for this 2000 edition, hereafter referred to as *Poems.*) As in her earlier *Collected Poems,* Raine excluded love poems, poems about her experience of World War II which she considered "occasional," and poems from her period as a Roman Catholic (p. vi). At the turn of the new millennium, Raine was honored as a Commander of the Order of the British Empire and a Commandeur de L'Ordre des Arts et des Lettres from the Academie Française. Raine had made translations from the French of Paul Foulquié's 1947 volume *L'Existentialisme (Existentialism,* 1948) as well as novels by Denis de Rougemont and Honoré de Balzac in the 1940s and early 1950s. Raine's work had been available in France since 1978, when the translation of *Farewell Happy Fields* (as *Adieu, praries heureuses*) was extremely popular and won a prize for the best foreign book of the year. Raine's work has received more academic attention in France than in England, thanks to the work of François-Xavier Jaujard, Claire Garnier-Tardieu and Jacqueline Genet.

Raine also continued to lecture, and to contribute essays to collections including *Seeing God Everywhere: Essays on Nature and the Sacred* (2003) and *The Betrayal of Tradition: Essays on the Spiritual Crisis of Modernity* (2005), both of which were published posthumously. At the age of ninety-five, Raine was knocked down by a car as she walked to the postbox at the end of her street; she died on July 6, 2003. At the service of thanksgiving for her life, the eulogy was given by Prince Charles.

EARLY LIFE, FAREWELL HAPPY FIELDS

Kathleen Jessie Raine was born on June 14, 1908, to George and Jessie (née Wilkie) Raine. George Raine was a Methodist schoolteacher who had come from a poor coal-mining family in County Durham, one of the most deprived and polluted areas of England. Jessie Raine had also trained as a teacher. She came from a family of teachers whose roots were in Scotland, though Jessie herself was born in Cumberland in the north of England. Kathleen Raine's parents had met at Durham University while undertaking their teacher training, although as a married woman, her mother never worked as a teacher. Two years after their marriage, Kathleen Raine was born.

In the first volume of her autobiography, *Farewell Happy Fields* (1973), Raine depicts the earliest years of her life as a series of lost paradises. The title itself, and the epigraph that stands at the head of the book, come from *Paradise Lost*, most of which her mother knew by heart. Milton's epic poem recounts the Fall, when Adam and Eve were expelled from the Garden of Eden. This trope is used over and over again in Raine's writing, as each idyllic part of her childhood is lost to her, never to be regained. Yet it was the "first foretaste of exile that first awakened the poetic instinct in me," in the attempt to recapture inaccessible beauty through language (*Farewell*, p. 6).

The first paradise was that of her mother's womb, "a place of perfect happiness" (*Farewell*, p. 1). Her memory, or at least the recurring dream of her birth, is recounted as an expulsion from a warm, safe place with "beautiful fields of flowers bathed in living light," where Raine felt herself to belong utterly (p. 1). Flowers and sunlight would continue to be markers of happiness and belonging throughout Raine's poetry. The transition to the world outside the womb was terrifying, yet Raine's memories of infancy also consisted of family, light and flowers, plants, streams, and hills.

Raine's early childhood was in Essex, in a village just northeast of London, in the years before the First World War. When she was born, her father placed a rose in her hand. The rose became a personal symbol for creation and birth

in early poems like "Ex Nihilo" ("out of nothing") and "The Rose," and it was a symbol of memory and childhood in late poems such as "Nameless Rose" and "Petal of White Rose." Raine's childhood was initially an idyllic one, which she described later as a garden full of flowers and birdsong and love and poetry that she learned by heart.

From the age of four, Raine attended Miss Hutchinson's School, and then Highlands Elementary School. School in Essex was a rigid and repressive place, where canings were common. But Raine retained her vivid imagination and found pleasure in feeding Miss Hutchinson's school tortoise or playing in the school's great cedar of Lebanon tree with her friends—that is, in escaping to the natural world. However, with the coming of the war when Raine was six years old, she remembered seeing a zeppelin crash and the boys taught by her father being sent to fight. Since the Raines lived so close to London, their home was in danger of aerial bombardment, and so Kathleen Raine was evacuated to stay with her mother's adopted sister, Peggy Black, who was a schoolteacher in Bavington, Northumberland, a tiny and remote village just south of the Scottish border.

One of Raine's most significant early memories was a visit to Bavington with her mother. Raine had wanted, desperately, to be pushed in her pram to "the old Man of the Wannies": a rock formation that looks like a man's face on the Great Wanney Crag north of Sweethope Lough (which Raine spells in the Scottish way, "loch"; p. 9). This hill represented "a place not so much in the world as in the poem"; the "wild hills o' Wannie" is the name of a folk tune (p. 9). They did not walk as far as the hill that day, but Raine claims she discovered poetry by chanting over and over again the "mantra," "I want to go to the wild hills o' Wannie" (p. 9). "By incantation," she wrote more than sixty years later, "I tried to bring near the far bright beauty of the hills" (p. 9). Raine therefore claims that her mature spells, prayers, and invocations were versions of this mantra. The repetitions and magical language of "Leaving Martindale," "Love Spell," or "Millennial Hymn to Lord Shiva" are intended to "bring near" unattainable people, places and states of being. As a writer for whom the poetic world was always more important than the physical world, the ability to achieve this closeness in language may have been sufficiently real. Moreover, instead of seeing her evacuation as an exile, the young Raine considered her time with her aunt during the war a version of Paradise.

Raine's father had gained his MLitt (master of literature) for a study of William Wordsworth (1770–1850), the Romantic poet closely associated with the northern Lake District. Wordsworth's poems celebrated the beauty and power of the natural world and the spiritual and moral values inherent in nature. In poems like "Tintern Abbey" (1798) and *The Preludes* (1850), Wordsworth described his childhood and claimed that it was the natural world that was his "nurse" and tutor, who brought him up and made him a sensitive and ethical human being and, more importantly, a poet. Raine claimed a similar pantheistic (seeing spirituality in all the natural world), moral, and educational experience for herself in Northumberland.

Yet Raine's version of her childhood is less about memory than about forgetfulness, as Sarah Wardle points out. That is to say, rather than focusing on Wordsworth's famous phrase about poetry being "the spontaneous overflow of powerful feelings ... recollected in tranquillity" (from the preface to his *Lyrical Ballads*), Raine was more interested in his argument that "our birth is but a sleep and a forgetting" (as he described it in his poem "Intimations of Immortality"). However, in *Farewell Happy Fields*, Raine played down the role of her father's poetic studies and instead attributes her poetic apprenticeship to her mother. Her mother had inherited a large store of Scottish and border folk songs and ballads. These poems belonged to the countryside itself, were as much as part of Northumberland as the mountains and rivers, Raine believed. Even Jessie Raine's love of Milton was associated with the land; as a girl, Kathleen Raine's mother had wandered the northern moors reciting *Comus, Samson Agonistes,* and *Paradise Lost.*

Raine wrote about this period of her youth in the 1950s: particularly in her fourth poetry collection, *The Year One*; her first study of William Blake, in 1957; and *Coleridge,* in 1953, before returning to her childhood memories with extended intensity in *Farewell Happy Fields.*

CAMBRIDGE, THE LAND UNKNOWN

When Raine returned to Ilford after the war, she was ten years old. As the 1920s progressed, Ilford became more and more a "horrific" suburb of London and less and less an Essex village (Caesar, p. 135). Raine went on to enjoy botany at secondary school, seeing in it a natural extension of her love of flowers, plants, and the natural world.

Raine decided to study natural sciences (biology, chemistry, and physics) at Girton College, Cambridge University. Girton was the elder of only two colleges for women associated with the university. Women followed the same course and sat the same examinations as male members of the university, but they were not full members until after World War II. Cambridge in the 1930s was heavily influenced by scientific rationalism, not only in the sciences but also in literature. Spirituality, morals, and traditions were considered superstitious, and logic and science, which in the 1930s meant Darwinian evolution and Freudian psychology, were privileged. Communism was also strongly influential at the time, and a radical rethinking of marriage, property, and the purpose of art was being undertaken by lecturers and students.

Raine knew many of the young writers at Cambridge. She wrote for the magazine *Experiment* and was friends with members of the *Experiment* and "Heretic" literary groups: William Empson (the poet and critic later known for *Seven Types of Ambiguity,* 1930), Humphrey Jennings (one of the founders of the British documentary film movement), Herbert Read (a major anarchist poet), Malcolm Lowry (novelist of *Under the Volcano,* 1947), and Hugh Sykes Davies (author of the only surrealist novel written by an English author, *Petron,* 1935). Stunningly beautiful as a young woman, Raine was widely popular. On completing her studies, she was unwilling to return to Ilford and the traditional Methodism of her family. She and Sykes Davies formed a marriage of convenience in 1930, and they moved to London.

Raine and Sykes Davies were married for three years. Accounts of the marriage's failure conflict. Probably Sykes Davies' infidelity was a contributing factor, and certainly Raine ended it by moving in with the poet and social scientist Charles Madge. Philippa Bernard's 2009 biography, *No End to Snowdrops*, quotes correspondence from Raine to Madge at the time, describing Sykes Davies practicing with a pistol, threatening suicide, and trying to persuade Raine to return to him by telephone. In 1934, Raine and Madge had a daughter, Anna, and in 1935 the two began to find literary work rather than the traveling sales work that Raine had undertaken up to that point. Their second child, James, was born in 1936.

In 1937 Madge, along with Jennings and Tom Harrisson, founded Mass-Observation, a cultural research project of interviewing and observing ordinary people to find out what they did and what they thought. (Their work continues in its successor body, the influential Ispsos MORI social and market research company.) Madge and Raine married in December 1937, but by the next year the marriage had foundered. Raine felt constrained by marriage, and she found a way out through a torturous and entirely unrequited love for a married man, Alistair MacDonald. This kind of relationship allowed Raine freedom to experience a full flood of untrammeled feelings without the social and emotional constraints of marriage. Raine wrote to Madge that she preferred to have "no desires, no ties, no marriage, no love" (quoted in Bernard, p. 43). Madge began (or had already begun) an affair with Stephen Spender's wife, Inez; their first child was born in 1939, and they married in 1942.

After her second marriage broke down, Raine left London with her children to return to the north, and she began to write seriously again. She based herself near Penrith, in the Lake District, and became part of an artistic community there. Leaving her children in the north

with Helen Sutherland and returning to wartorn London, she met the Tamil poet and publisher Meary James Thurairajah Tambimuttu, who published her writing in his magazine *Poetry London,* and her first two collections were published under his imprint, Editions Poetry London.

Raine's continuing personal unhappiness prompted her search for alternative succor, which she found in the spiritual guidance of the Catholic Church. In the 1940s, a number of major writers had converted to Roman Catholicism, including Graham Greene, Muriel Spark, and Evelyn Waugh, while others had joined the catholic wing of the Anglican (Episcopal) church, including T. S. Eliot and W. H. Auden. Raine's essays on Eliot and Auden from this period are collected in *Defining the Times,* published in 2002. The church seemed to offer a link to spirituality, tradition, and hope after the failures of radical atheism, of the rationalism and communism seen in the Soviet Great Purge in 1937, and the trauma of the Second World War. Raine was received into the Catholic Church in 1944. At the end of the war, Raine was reunited with her children, and she became an active member of the postwar London literary scene.

COLLECTIONS FROM THE 1940S

Raine claimed she was a poet "who attempt[s] to write the same poem, many times, some versions being better than others" (*Poems,* p. v). Raine's first collection of poems, *Stone and Flower,* was published in 1943, during the Second World War (1939–1945). *Living in Time*, published in 1946, covers the rest of the war years. Her third collection was *The Pythoness* (1949). Over these three collections, similar themes, images, and references recur: mythology, the natural world, and the difficulties of the female role.

Raine's poems in these collections present three worlds: the peaceful countryside, the wartorn city of London, and a mythological or religious world in which the two can be brought together. The death in the "desert" of "our boys" in the "Libyan sand" of the Western Desert

Campaign of 1940–1942, is linked to the resurrected fertility gods Osiris, and Adonis in "Mourning in Spring 1943" (*Poems*, pp. 30–31). In the poems, even seemingly innocuous references to the "sky" or the "sun" are in fact reminders of the aerial war that was going on over much of Europe. These references can be literal, as in mention of "the R.A.F.'s young heroes," the pilots of the Royal Air Force, in "New Year, 1943" (*Poems*, p. 23). Yet in other poems, the references become mythological.

In a poem representative of her early, clever, poetic style, "Far-Darting Apollo," the sun god Apollo is likened to a member of Parliament, in a line reminiscent of Emily Dickinson's "Because I could not stop for Death." The politician casts a glance over the war memorial, the Cenotaph, before going to ride the "horses of the Apocalypse," Conquest, War, Famine, and Death (from Revelation 6.1–8) across the skies (*Poems*, p. 5). The seemingly lighthearted line, therefore, "The sun plays a game of darts in Spain," becomes a reference to the aerial bombardment of Guernica in Spain by the German air force in 1937; the same year the "Chinese War" (the Sino-Japanese war) broke out (p. 5). Apollo is the god of poetry, of daylight, of beauty, and of sport. "His hyacinth breath" suggests the sweet smell of the spring flower, but it also refers to the myth in which Apollo accidentally killed his beloved Hyacinth with a discus, so that "all his sports are games to kill" (p. 6).

In "Harvest," Raine uses Greek mythology to assert instead the life-protecting force of daylight. The Shield of Achilles, from Homer's *Iliad*, depicts the cosmos, and scenes of everyday life, farming, law courts, weddings, dancing, as well as battles. In this poem, daylight is the "shield" that protects "we," the people, from the nightly bombing raids, enabling us to become "the seed" and "the grass," a living part of the natural world (*Poems*, p. 8).

The natural world is most identified with the north in these collections, such as "In the Beck" (for her daughter), "The Hyacinth" (for her son), and "The Speech of Birds" (for Helen Sutherland). These poems relate Raine's grief at leaving the north but also her sense of loyalty to those she leaves behind, in poems such as "To My Mountain," "On Leaving Ullswater," and the following lines from "Leaving Martindale":

Shall I be true
As these hills bind me
As these skies find me,
As water weather me,
As leaves crown me?

(*Poems*, p. 16)

Both because of her religiously conservative childhood and her new interest in Roman Catholicism, many of Raine's wartime images are biblical. "See, see, Christ's blood streams in the firmament" and "Good Friday" use images of Christ's death on the cross as a metaphor for the suffering of England under the German bombing raids; while "Angelus" and "Messengers" use the biblical stories of angels bringing heavenly messages of hope and peace in Luke 1:26–38 and Luke 2.14, respectively.

In "The Healing Spring," Raine's images link healing and washing through the Pool at Bethesda (John 5.1–18) and other biblical images of purity and water (Revelation 21.6, Psalms 51). Yet "The Healing Spring" is a troubling poem, because the "spring" also seems to be a pagan well, and her healing seems to be a betrayal. She asks love to "forgive the happiness" that "seals my grief" (*Poems*, p. 24). In "The Healing Spring," the feminine and maternal instinct is no longer wanted and is in fact seen as a kind of illness that requires healing, so Raine writes that "the womb heals of its sons." This is partly on account of the *daimon*, the inspiring spirit, which requires her to destroy or mutilate her female body in "Invocation," her "uterus cut out," "rain stones inserted in my breasts," in order to bring the poem into the world (*Poems*, p. 4). Raine would repeatedly return to the idea that poetry required sacrifices, paid not only by the poet but by her family and loved ones. Even in her first collection, Raine described the terrifyingly high cost of poetry.

The poems of *Stone and Flower, Living in Time,* and *The Pythoness* return again and again to the tropes of mother, whore, and virgin. Raine considers the nexus between spiritual passion and sexual purity in "The Red Light" (as in "red light district," a place where prostitutes gather) and "Four Poems of Mary Magdalene" (traditionally portrayed as a scarlet woman). In "The Goddess," Raine makes no distinction between the Blessed Virgin Mary; Venus, the goddess of sexual love; Diana, the virgin huntress; and Eve, the mother of humankind. Virgins, mothers, and whores are one woman who "goes by many names" (*Poems*, p. 37). The three goddesses return in "The Transit of the Gods," in which Raine more explicitly connects herself to these women, "I who have been" these three goddesses (p. 50). In *The Pythoness*, a further aspect of womankind enters the frame—the daughter. Persephone, who was kidnapped by the god of the underworld, leaving a grieving mother, is evoked in "The Transit of the Gods"; and in "The Storm," Raine likens herself to Goneril, the "thankless child" of King Lear, who throws her father out of her house into the tempest.

In *The Pythoness*, the mental landscape begins to take precedence over the literal northern landscape. The poems also show a new focus on Eastern spiritualities: Raine considered India to be "the supreme civilization of the imagination" as well as "the country where I have felt 'Home at last!'" (*Poems*, p. vi). In "Mandala," Raine explores the circular design in Indian Buddhist and Hindu art, which is an aid to meditation and a representation of the sacred space of the cosmos. Gazing at the mandala, Raine both descends to the "possibility" of a "seed," the potentiality of existence, and rises up to the orbit of the "sun" and "stars." This double movement is mirrored in her understanding of her own identity in this poem: she is both the individual "I," and part of "the infinity" where all "selves" come together as one (p. 44). The poem has intricate sound patterns of internal half-rhymes that mirror the visual patterns of the mandala itself and also reflect the similarity for Raine of the mandala and the rose. The rose is associated with the Virgin Mary but also with the world rising out of nothing, as in Raine's poem "The Rose" from *Living in Time*.

Raine would later consider many of the poems in these first three volumes products of

"insincere religiosity" and "contrived, occasional poems" about war or love (p. vi). These subjects, she claimed, "impeded" her imagination (p. vi). In her first *Collected Poems* (1956) she excluded all but two of the poems from *Living in Time*, although she reinstated eleven for her 2000 *Collected Poems*.

SCHOLARSHIP, MAXWELL, AND THE LION'S MOUTH

Although Raine later viewed her conversion to Catholicism as a mistake, she felt it also provided her with a way out from the overwhelming and messy sexual relationships she had been embroiled in, and she would from then on pursue Platonic (ideal and nonsexual) relationships. The most significant of these was with Gavin Maxwell, whom she first met in 1949. In a number of ways, he seemed the ideal candidate for such a relationship: because he was a homosexual, the question of sex was irrelevant; he was also a writer, loved animals, his mother had come from near Bavington, and his home at Sandaig (called Camusfearna in his books) was truly in the north, in the Scottish Highlands, across the water from the isle of Skye.

During this period in her life, Raine was becoming ever more interested in scholarship as well as in spiritualism and theosophy. She returned to academia as a research fellow at her old college, Girton, in 1955. She began to produce articles, lectures, and eventually books of criticism, particularly on the poetry and philosophy of William Blake. In her research and publications, Raine focused on writers whom she saw as challenging the "confrontation of science and the imagination," who brought together ways of empirically and intuitively studying the world (*Golgonooza*, p. 9).

William Blake was an eighteenth-century visionary poet whose poems and paintings depict his personal and complex mythologies; in his radical prophetic poems like "The Marriage of Heaven and Hell" and "The Daughters of Albion" the contemporary ills of society, such as poverty and industrialization, are played out by giants, spirits, and angels, perhaps metaphorical, perhaps divinely revealed. In her lectures and criticism Raine discussed Blake's poetry, his paintings and etchings, and his aphorisms. However, in *Golgonooza*, she claimed that it is "the doctrines of Swedenborg that Blake's works embody and to which they lend poetry and eloquence" (p. 76). Emmanuel Swedenborg (1688–1772) was a visionary scientist and philosopher whose books disputed traditional aspects of Christian theology such as the three-person Trinity. Blake eventually came to reject many of Swedenborg's ideas, but he was strongly influenced by Swedenborg's claim to understand the world through visions rather than science and likewise Swedenborg's argument that spirit and matter, or spirit and bodies, are not separated.

Jerome McGann has described Raine's *Blake and Tradition*, from 1968, as "one of the four most important works yet written on Blake's ideas," superior because of her care for detail, her professionalism, and her rigorous attention to the occult influences of Blake's work (p. 48). However, McGann disagrees with Raine's conclusion that Blake was a Neoplatonist. *Blake and Tradition,* published in 1968, is Raine's most significant work of scholarship and was republished again in a shorter version as *Blake and Antiquity* in 1977—but her 1970 volume, *William Blake*, is perhaps more popular. Raine also discussed the poet she considered her master in essays such as "The Lapsed Soul" and "Little Girl Lost and Found" (collected in *The Divine Vision: Studies in the Art and Vision of William Blake,* 1957) and in books including *The Inner Journey of the Poet* (1976) and *Golgonooza, City of Imagination* (1991).

Raine clearly saw a reflection of her own poetic interests in Blake and Swedenborg, as she did later in Yeats and Gerard Manley Hopkins. Raine wrote a poetry of "oppositions" that struggles to become a poetry that brings things together into union (Jeffares, p. 24). This union takes place on a spiritual level: between Eastern and Western religions, between the imagination and science, and between male and female.

Raine's desire to bring opposites together means that she resists ideologies that emphasize separateness or distinctions: including feminism, communism, and scientism. Raine rejected the way in which these worldviews stress difference and opposition: female versus male, or the workers versus the middle classes; or the way the petals of a flower are categorized as being distinct from the stamen, pistils, stem, calyx, or leaf. Raine was reacting to her experiences of being a female scientist in socialist Cambridge in the 1930s, where even the study of literature had been dominated by the scientific and psychological approaches to literary criticism championed by I. A. Richards and F. R. Leavis (particularly in Richards' *Practical Criticism*, 1929), and William Empson's mathematical approach in *Seven Types of Ambiguity*. Instead, Raine's criticism is often intuitive, visionary, and keen to make connections across fields.

Raine points out (in *Golgonooza*) that W. B. Yeats was instrumental in producing the first mass-published versions of Blake's works in 1893, nearly a century after Blake's death. Raine creates a line of spiritual influence from Swedenborg through Blake to Yeats, citing Yeats' paper on "Swedenborg, Mediums, and the Desolate Places," his editing of Blake's "prophetic books," and his statement of his own mystical understanding, *A Vision* (1927). Raine was at the forefront of the early reconsideration of Yeats's "excluded knowledge" (*Yeats the Initiate*, p. 1): his thinking on alchemy, tarot, astrology, automatic writing, and séances. As well as *Yeats, the Tarot, and the Golden Dawn* (1972), Raine collected papers and lectures given over three decades on Yeats's philosophy in *Yeats the Initiate* (1990) and *W. B. Yeats and the Learning of the Imagination* (1999).

Many of Raine's books are collections of lectures, with little alteration from the original stand-alone format of each paper. Their purpose was often to introduce either the poetry or the spirituality to an audience that may not have been previously aware of it. This can lead to repetition between the chapters of her books, and between the books themselves, as Norman Jeffares has noted. Other books are collections of essays, frequently written some years, if not decades, before the books were published, so her view of contemporary scholarship can seem out of date. For example, in *W. B. Yeats and the Learning of the Imagination* (1999), Raine seems entirely ignorant of twenty years of Yeats scholarship, from M. C. Flannery's *Yeats and Magic* (1977) to R. F. Foster's first volume of his biography of Yeats, subtitled *The Apprentice Mage* (1997). The introduction to Raine's book complains, "Academia seems to understand Yeats no better now than did Yeats's contemporaries of the 'thirties" (*Imagination*, p. 3). Yet these words originally were written as part of "Hades Wrapped in a Cloud," an essay by Raines published in George Mills Harper's *Yeats and the Occult,* a seminal collection from 1975, which therefore predates these other works.

THE MAXWELL POEMS

The Year One (1952) is often considered Raine's best collection, with "Northumbrian Sequence" and "The Marriage of Psyche" as highlights. In this collection, Raine developed a freer style, in which the magic of her childhood Eden and the sense of homecoming in her relationship with Gavin Maxwell could be described. The title suggests a creation narrative, the first year of the world, as well as of her own world. "Northumbrian Sequence" begins, "Pure I was before the world began" (*Poems,* p. 61). The collection includes a "Love Spell" and "Amo Ergo Sum" ("I love, therefore I am," playing on Descartes' declaration that he knew he existed because he was able to think, *cogito ergo sum*). The title of the poem "The Marriage of Psyche" refers to the Greek myth of Psyche (who stands for the soul, or the mind) and Eros (the god of love). The first half of the poem praises "The House" of her beloved, a description of Sandaig; the second half, "The Ring," claims a spiritual and universal wedding: "He has married me with a ring, a ring of bright water" (*Poems,* p. 93).

The relationship with Maxwell only lasted for seven years, from 1949 to 1956. However, the two continued to meet or correspond intermittently until Maxwell's death in 1969. Moreover, the relationship proved to be the major influence on Raine's poems for another two decades, as well as being minutely described in the third volume of her autobiography. Raine's influence

is significant on Maxwell's widely popular otter books—*Ring of Bright Water, The Rocks Remain,* and *Raven Seek Thy Brother*—even though she is only referenced in the title of *Ring of Bright Water* (quoting her love poem for Maxwell) and her curse beneath the rowan tree, described in *Raven Seek Thy Brother* (1968).

In 1971 in *The Lost Country,* Raine published "An Answer to a Letter Asking Me for a Volume of My Early Poems." The letter, clearly from Maxwell, requested copies of "those poems of Paradise / I wrote in heart's blood for your sake" but merely recapitulated the "bitterness" of their relationship for both parties (*Poems,* p. 165). She also included her "Message to Gavin" in that volume, a poem in which Maxwell becomes a symbolic landscape. In part that landscape is integral to the Inner Hebrides, visible from the place where Sandaig stood before it burned down in 1968. Yet the landscape is also partly heavenly. Maxwell's death and their parting means he has left her and she has left him, and yet there is a possibility of being together hereafter "as star with distant star" (p. 168).

On a Deserted Shore is a single, book-length poem, in 130 short stanzas. Raine compared it to the elegy written by Alfred, Lord Tennyson, for his friend Arthur Hugh Hallam, who died young of a brain hemorrhage. Tennyson's poem, *In Memoriam A. H. H.* (1850), comprised 131 four-line stanzas, plus a prologue and epilogue. Formally as well as in its purpose, Raine's poem is clearly modeled on Tennyson's, particularly in the second half of the poem, where there are more four-lined rhyming stanzas. The vast and sparse landscape of the Scottish coast is evoked most effectively in the stanzas extracted for *The Bloodaxe Book of Contemporary Women Poets* (pp. 106–117). This section depicts the trajectory of the poem in miniature, from inconsolable darkness to a grieving contentment.

Raine's honesty and detail was painful not only to her but also to her friends, family, and friends of Maxwell's. A. S. Byatt, reviewing *The Lion's Mouth* in the *Times,* thought the work was marred by "messy and vulgar" feelings (p. 10). Yet Raine defended publishing *The Lion's Mouth, The Lost Country,* and *On a Deserted Shore* because the feelings depicted in it, however messy, were true. Although she considered her autobiographies as the history of an "inner world" (*Autobiographies*, p. 345), Raine had no "sense of my life being my own property" (*Autobiographies*, p. viii). Instead, even the most private aspects of her life belonged to the wider human story. To a certain extent, she seems to have seen her story as a cautionary tale.

LATE LIFE

After coming to terms with the failure of her relationship with Maxwell, and then with his death, Raine claimed that her "story" had finished (*Autobiographies*, p. ix). Regardless of her sense that her life story was over, Raine continued to publish, write, and lecture. Living in Chelsea, her flat became the "centre of a discreet counter-culture" (Fletcher, "Raine"). Raine maintained an active correspondence with artists, poets, critics, and public figures. She cared for her elderly parents, and also for the widow of Edwin Muir, in her own house for many years, as well as helping with the care of her grandchildren when her daughter Anna's marriage was in difficulties. Raine's father died in 1971 and her mother in 1973.

It was in this latter part of her career that she was awarded honorary doctorates from the University of Leicester in 1974 and from Durham University in 1979; the Queen's Gold Medal for Poetry in 1993; and the Commander of the British Empire in 2000. A special edition of the poetry journal *Agenda* was published in her honor in 1994.

In 1981, Raine was a founding member of the arts journal *Temenos*, acting as editor from its fourth issue until it folded in 1992, succeeded in 1998 by the *Temenos Academy Review* (edited first by Grevel Lindop and later by John Carey and James Harpur). *Temenos* was a vehicle for much of her own poetry and criticism, but it also published a range of internationally recognized poets and critics as well as writing from the Prince of Wales and from Rowan Williams (the poet and theologian who was later named archbishop of Canterbury).

In 1983, Raine traveled to India for the first time, as a guest of the Indian government, in order to give the inaugural lecture to the new Yeats Society annual congress. She returned to India in 1987, 1989, and 1997, as a result of a longstanding friendship with the society's president, Santosh Pall. Raine had acted as an examiner on Pall's doctoral thesis, on Yeats and sacred dance, at the University of Delhi..

While Raine believed herself increasingly embattled in her quest for deeper spiritual meaning in England, in India she felt she was "understood" (Bernard, p. 163). Indeed, the first, and only, book-length consideration of Raine's poetry in English is Meena Rani's study, *The Poetry of Kathleen Raine: A Pursuit of Patterns,* which was published in New Delhi in 1989,. The final volume of Raine's autobiography, *India Seen Afar* (1990), describes Raine's feeling of homecoming to a country whose religion had long interested her. India is a notable influence on the poems in Raine's final collection *Living with Mystery.* However, her family is the major focus in her last five collections, *The Oval Portrait, The Oracle in the Heart, The Presence, Living with Mystery* and the final section of her 2000 *Collected Poems.*

LATE POEMS

After her mother died, Raine published a series of memorial poems in collections from *The Oval Portrait* on: "The Oval Portrait: Jessie Wilkie, 1880–1973," "Card-Table," "Your Gift of Life Was Idleness ...," "The Leaf," "Her Room," "With a Wave of Her Old Hand...," "My Mother's Birthday," and "Jessie." In "The Oval Portrait," Raine considers her mother as a young woman, in her engagement photograph (a similar picture is reproduced in Bernard, plate 1). A portrait of George and Jessie Raine with Kathleen aged two (Bernard, plate 3) is described in "Her Room," as Raine writes of clearing out the medicines, ornaments, and books, along with the memories, after her mother's death. Unlike the bitterness and hard-won hope that permeate Raine's poems after the death of Maxwell, these poems are full of peace and sunlight. The pity in "My Mother's

Birthday" is not for the death of a woman who lived to be more than ninety but rather is for Jessie Raine's hard childhood.

The companion poem, "My Father's Birthday," describes Raine's distance from her austere father, and her father's distance from his wife, in resigned language that suggests understanding rather than anger. In her autobiography, Raine came to recognize that in many ways she was very like her father. Like him, she learned to speak and write in a foreign tongue, Standard English, rather than the dialect of home. Like him, she pursued a university education and studied poetry at a high level. Yet, unlike him, her faith became less and less that of an austere Methodist Protestantism, or rational scientific thought. Instead she moved first to Catholicism and then to a more pagan, pantheist, esoteric spirituality. Her later interest in the tarot, pagan rituals, and spiritualism distressed her father as much as her romantic entanglements did. Nonetheless, the two were bound by the warm memories of her childhood and by a mutual respect. Her mother's poetry, a woman's poetry that was learned by heart and led to an inner world of imagination, and was intrinsically linked to the landscape of the north, was more to Raine's taste, and it was increasingly this inheritance that Raine would claim.

In "Too Many Memories Confuse the Old," Raine ruefully recounts her forgetfulness as she has aged, mixing up the names of her grandson and son. But this loss of memory is described instead as a surfeit, and her child and grandchildren respond with laughter. Moreover, from *The Oracle in the Heart* and through *The Presence*, her poems return to the close attention to flowers of the earliest collections, in "Campanula," "Sweet Briar Fragrance," and "Blue Columbines." In "Ah god, I may not hate / Myself," Raine refuses self-loathing, because God loves her and has made her as she is, as a "seed" and "harvest," echoing the title of poems from *Stone and Flower* (*Poems*, p. 254).

In her last collection of poetry, *Living with Mystery* (1992), and in the new poems assembled in the final section of her 2000 *Collected Poems*, Raine integrates the influence of her visits to India, particularly in "A Head of Pavarti," "Prayer to the Lord Shiva," and "Millennial Hymn to Lord Shiva." Pavarti is a Hindu goddess, the consort of Shiva. The three poems thus make a triptych. The first poem depicts Pavarti as a portrait of a woman in love, perhaps similar to "The Oval Portrait." "Prayer to the Lord Shiva" depicts the god as the Destroyer who brings transformations. In the poem, Raine seeks safety and life in the heart of the destruction, "from the killer / Claim sanctuary / In death" (*Poems*, p. 322). The poem is tightly constructed, leading inexorably to "bliss," through the seeming paradoxes of short lines and full rhymes. The "Millennial Hymn to the Lord Shiva," by contrast, is in five sections over as many pages. Yet the incantatory quality, the repetition and end rhyme of that poem, recaptures some of the power of the "Spell" poems from *The Year One*. This poem, placed at the end of her *Collected Poems*, calls on the Destroyer to free the world from its unbelief, its environmental decay, its consumerism and attachment to soulless technological advances. As in her work for the Temenos Academy, and in all her collections of poems, Raine prays in this concluding work for a rediscovery of spiritual enlightenment found in the natural world and in relationships between people.

LATE AND POSTHUMOUS CRITICAL RECEPTION

Raine's critical reputation had waned by the end of the twentieth century, before her death in 2003. According to Maurice Harmon (1981, p. 123) and Mark Rudman (2002, p. 113), she is "legendary" but "overlooked." Although Raine was awarded a number of prestigious awards after 1990, she was already in her mid-eighties and more than four decades had passed since her best work was written. Her biography, *No End to Snowdrops* (2009), written by a friend and neighbor (the writer and antiquarian bookseller Philippa Bernard), was published by a minor publishing house, but it is a laudable book-length study that allows readers to contrast the external facts of Raine's life story with her memories. The only book-length study of Raine's poetry, published in New Delhi in 1989, is currently out of print. Her earlier work was published by Penguin, Longmans, Hamish Hamilton, Allen & Unwin, and Oxford University Press. Her later works were exclusively printed, or reprinted, by small independent art presses: Golgonooza Press, Enitharmon Press, and Green Books. Each of her collections has divided critics. *The Hollow Hill,* a slender collection from 1965, was nominated for the Poetry Book Society Choice award, and the *Times Literary Supplement* thought it was a remarkable work, but Ian Hamilton in the *London Magazine* found it "stale" (Bernard, p. 111).

Some of her critical collections were taken from public lectures, whose purpose was to introduce "newcomers" to the works of Yeats or Blake or to their esoteric influences (Jeffares, p. 24). Moreover, Raine's critical writing, in works like *Defending Ancient Springs* (1967) and *The Inner Journey of the Poet* (1976), is often as interested in her own poetic and spiritual journey as that of the writers she studies. They are therefore intended to explain what the works mean to her personally, rather than provide original scholarship. Many of her works were written and published in small journals or were left as manuscripts for many years. The bulk of Raine's Yeats scholarship, and her account of *Visiting Ezra Pound* (1999), were only brought to a wider audience some decades after they were first written. Raine's scholarship appeared at a far more leisurely rate than is possible for most professional academic publications, meaning that it often seemed out of date.

Raine infamously opposed the feminist movement. Although Raine was inspired to pursue a life as a professional writer by hearing Virginia Woolf give her famous lectures on the need for women writers to have independence and "a room of one's own," Raine requested not to be included in a number of works that she saw as having a feminist perspective, which meant that critical attention after the 1960s was often alienated.

Unusually for a woman poet, Raine was published and well received by 1930s and 1940s magazines and writers such as *Experiment, New Verses,* and *Poetry London.* Philip Larkin, John Betjeman, William Empson, Tambimuttu, and Michael Roberts all provided public support by publishing her work or by praising it in print. Raine was one of only two women to be published in *Experiment* and one of only a handful to be published in Geoffrey Grigson's defining 1930s anthologies. This has meant she was given consideration in studies such A. T. Tolley's chapter titled "Defending Ancient Springs," on Raine, Muir, and Watkins, in *Poets of the Forties* (1985)—he also mentions Anne Ridler and Denise Levertoff—and Adrian Caesar's *Dividing Lines* (1991). (Caesar discusses "very few women poets" [p. 8], and Raine is the only one to receive extensive treatment.)

In 1952, Evan Owen claimed that "in the nature of their very being, women cannot attain that degree of aloofness necessary to the production of the superlative in poetry" (p. 35). On the other hand, W. S. Merwin, writing only one year later, suggested that there had been "more than the expected twaddle" about Raine as "woman poet" (p. 467). However, Raine herself suggested that it is impossible for a "woman poet" to be a great genius like Plato, Dante, or Shakespeare (Dowson, p. 94). Raine's poetic and spiritual models were all male: Blake, Yeats, Milton, and the male Romantics Wordsworth, Coleridge, and Shelley. The contemporary writers she valued were also all men: T. S. Eliot, William Empson, Vernon Watkins, David Jones, Dylan Thomas, and Elias Canetti. Raine's *daimon,* her inspiration, is the Eternal Child, the *"puer eternus,"* not a female Muse ("Kathleen Raine Writes," p. 60).

Moreover, Raine struggled with her failure to fulfill the traditional roles of womanhood, a failure emblemized by her two unsuccessful marriages and her distance from her children and from her parents. Raine came to see herself as a "pythoness," an "Ancient Murderous Bitch Goddess" (Fletcher, "Raine"), a destroying witch. She saw this as the price of being a poet, but she was uncertain if her contribution to literature justified the cost. Nonetheless, Raine came to understand her poetry as an oral, matrilineal inheritance, and her work has been collected in the seminal women's poetry anthologies *The Bloodaxe Book of Contemporary Women Poets*

(1985) and *Modern Women Poets* (2005). She worked closely with female artists including Barbara Hepworth (who illustrated Raine's first poetry collection) and Winifred Nicholson.

Raine's reputation is perhaps more elevated in France than in England. A number of French critics have focused on Raine's sense of place, primarily thanks to the work of the scholar Claire Tardieu-Garnier, who has written extensively on Raine since 1984. Tardieu-Garnier's work highlights Raine's relationship to the sense of spiritual place, particularly in Raine's sense of "exile" from the "symbolic landscape" of Bavington. Raine is considered as a major English author in Christine Jordis, *Le Paysage et l'amour dans le roman anglais* (The Landscape and Love in the English Novel, 1994), where Raine's experiences in Bavington and County Durham are discussed as mirroring the experiences of novelists from the north of England including Charlotte Brontë (*Jane Eyre*, 1847) and D. H. Lawrence (*Lady Chatterley's Lover*, 1928). Raine's work has also been translated into Japanese, Hindi, and Spanish.

As a critic, Raine ceaselessly championed new approaches to reading the work of major writers, approaches that have since become mainstream. In her autobiographies, Raine reflected her own experience with unflinching candor. Raine's best work is honest, insightful, alive to the beauty of the natural world but able to harness the details of seed or vegetation to illuminate broader, deeper aspects of human emotion and belief. Over seven decades, Raine's poetry built up a subtle and sustained exploration of a constant core of themes. As a woman poet, she valued subversion over conformity, and the "perceptive dislocation" (Glendinning, 1977, p. 1533) that privileges the inner, poetic world. Her voice is therefore visionary and unique.

Selected Bibliography

WORKS OF KATHLEEN RAINE

POETRY

Stone and Flower. London: Editions Poetry London, 1943.
Living in Time. London: Editions Poetry London, 1946.
The Pythoness and Other Poems. London: Hamish Hamilton, 1949.
The Year One. London: Hamish Hamilton, 1952.
Selected Poems. London: Weekend Press, 1952.
Collected Poems. London: Hamish Hamilton, 1956.
The Hollow Hill and Other Poems, 1960–1964. London: Hamish Hamilton, 1965.
Six Dreams and Other Poems. London: Enitharmon Press, 1968.
Selected Poems: David Gascoyne, W. S. Graham, and Kathleen Raine. Penguin Modern Poets 17. Harmondsworth, U.K.: Penguin, 1970.
The Lost Country. London: Hamish Hamilton, 1971.
On a Deserted Shore. London: Hamish Hamilton, 1973. (Excerpts from this volume appear in *The Bloodaxe Book of Contemporary Women Poets,* edited by Jeni Couzyn, Newcastle-upon-Tyne, U.K.: Bloodaxe, 1985, pp. 106–117.)
The Oval Portrait and Other Poems. London: Hamish Hamilton, 1977.
The Oracle in the Heart and Other Poems, 1975–1978. London: Allen & Unwin, 1980.
Collected Poems 1935–1980, London: Allen & Unwin, 1981.
The Presence. Ipswich, U.K.: Golgonooza Press, 1987.
Selected Poems. Ipswich, U.K.: Golgonooza Press, 1988.
Living with Mystery. Ipswich, U.K.: Golgonooza Press, 1992.
Collected Poems, Ipswich, U.K.: Golgonooza Press, 2000. (This collection, referred to as *Poems,* is used for all poetry citations in the essay).

AUTOBIOGRAPHY

Farewell Happy Fields. London: Hamish Hamilton, 1973.
The Land Unknown. London: Hamish Hamilton, 1975.
The Lion's Mouth. London: Hamish Hamilton, 1977.
Autobiographies. London: Skoob Books, 1991. (Includes *Farewell Happy Fields, The Land Unknown,* and *The Lion's Mouth,* with a new preface.)
India Seen Afar. London: Green Books, 1990.
"Kathleen Raine Writes." In *The Bloodaxe Book of Women Poets: Eleven British Writers.* Edited by Jeni Couzyn. Newcastle-upon-Tyne, U.K.: Bloodaxe, 1985. P. 58-60.

CRITICISM

"Little Girl Lost and Found" and "The Lapsed Soul." In *The Divine Vision: Studies in the Poetry and Art of William Blake.* Edited by Vivian de Sola Pinto. London: Victor Gollancz, 1957. Pp. 19–63.
Defending Ancient Springs. Oxford: Oxford University Press, 1967.
Blake and Tradition. 2 vols. Princeton, N.J.: Princeton University Press, 1968. (The A. W. Mellon Lectures in

the Fine Arts, 1962, at the National Gallery of Art, Washington, D.C.; first published in England in 1969.)

William Blake. London: Thames & Hudson, 1970.

Blake and Antiquity. Princeton, N.J.: Princeton University Press, 1977; London: Routledge & Kegan Paul, 1979. (A shorter version of *Blake and Tradition.* A Routledge Classics edition, with a new introduction by Raine, was published in 2002.)

Yeats, the Tarot, and the Golden Dawn. Dublin: Dolmen Press, 1972.

David Jones: A Solitary Perfectionist. Ipswich, U.K.: Golgonooza Press, 1974.

The Inner Journey of the Poet. Ipswich, U.K.: Golgonooza Press, 1976.

David Jones and the Actually Loved and Known. Ipswich, U.K.: Golgonooza Press, 1978.

Blake and the New Age. London: Allen & Unwin, 1979.

From Blake to "A Vision." Dublin: Dolmen Press, 1979.

The Human Face of God: William Blake and the Book of Job. London: Thames & Hudson, 1982.

Yeats the Initiate: Writing on Certain Themes in the Work of W. B. Yeats, London: Allen & Unwin, 1986.

Golgonooza, City of Imagination: Last Studies in William Blake. Ipswich, U.K.: Golgonooza Press, 1991.

W. B. Yeats and the Learning of the Imagination. Ipswich, U.K.: Golgonooza Press, 1999.

Visiting Ezra Pound. London: Enitharmon Press, 1999.

Defining the Times: Essays on Auden and Eliot. London: Enitharmon Press, 2002. (Essays from the 1940s.)

"The Underlying Order: Nature and the Imagination." In *Seeing God Everywhere: Essays on Nature and the Sacred.* Edited by Barry MacDonald. Bloomington, Ind.: World Wisdom, 2003. Pp. 171–192.

"India and the Modern World." In *The Betrayal of Tradition: Essays on the Spiritual Crisis of Modernity.* Edited by Harry Oldmeadow. Bloomington, Ind.: World Wisdom, 2005. Pp. 45–54.

As Editor

William Blake. London: Longmans, Green & Co., 1951.

Coleridge. London: Longmans, Green & Co., 1953.

Thomas Taylor the Platonist. With George Mills Harper. London: Routledge & Kegan Paul, 1969.

Shelley. Harmondsworth, U.K.: Penguin, 1973.

Translations

Talk of the Devil. By Denis de Rougement. London: Eyre & Spottiswoode, 1945.

Cousin Bette. By Honoré de Balzac. London: Hamish Hamilton, 1948.

Existentialism. By Paul Foulquié, London: Dobson, 1948.

Lost Illusions. By Honoré de Balzac. London: John Lehmann, 1951.

Journals, Correspondence, and Manuscripts

Kathleen Raine's papers are held in collections at the British Library in London, the University of New York, Buffalo State College, and Girton College, Cambridge.

CRITICAL AND BIOGRAPHICAL STUDIES

Bernard, Philippa. *No End to Snowdrops: A Biography of Kathleen Raine.* London: Shepheard-Walwyn, 2009.

Botting, Douglas. *The Saga of Ring of Bright Water: The Enigma of Gavin Maxwell.* London: Neil Wilson, 2000.

Byatt, A. S. "In the Wild." *Times,* September 29, 1977, p. 10.

Caesar, Adrian. *Dividing Lines: Poetry, Class, and Ideology in the 1930s.* Manchester, U.K.: Manchester University Press, 1991.

Dowson, Jane. *Women's Poetry of the 1930s: A Critical Anthology.* London and New York: Routledge, 1996. Pp. 92–95.

Fletcher, Christopher. "Raine, Kathleen Jessie (1908–2003)." In *Oxford Dictionary of National Biography.* Edited by Colin Matthew and Brian Harrison. Oxford: Oxford University Press, 2007.; online edition, October, 2009.

Frye, Northrop. *Fearful Symmetry: A Study of William Blake.* Edited by Nicholas Halmi. Toronto: University of Toronto Press, 2004.

Glendinning Victoria. "A Diet of Honeydew." *Times Literary Supplement,* December 14, 1973, p. 1233.

———. "Abysses and Infinities." *Times Literary Supplement,* October 21 1977, p. 1533.

Harmon, Maurice. "Review." *Irish University Review* 11, no. 1:112–116 (spring 1981).

Jaujard, François Xavier, and Diane de Margerie, trans. *Adieu prairies heureuses.* Paris: Stock, 1978. (Translation of *Farewell Happy Fields,* winner of the 1979 Best Foreign Book of the Year [non-fiction] awarded by a group of directors of French publishing houses.)

Jeffares, A. Norman. "Idle Shadows of Eternity." *Times Literary Supplement,* February 4, 2000.

Jordis, Christine. *Le Paysage et l'amour dans le roman anglais* [The landscape and love in the English novel]. Paris: Seuil, 1994.

Justice, Donald. "Sacred and Secular." *Poetry,* October 1957, pp. 41–44.

McGann, Jerome. "Blake and a Tradition." *Poetry,* October 1970, pp. 45–49.

Merwin, W. S. "Four British Poets." *Kenyon Review* 15, no. 3:461–476 (summer 1953).

Montefiore, Janet. *Men and Women Writers of the 1930s: The Dangerous Flood of History.* London and New York: Routledge, 1996.

Owen, Evan. "The Poetry of Kathleen Raine." *Poetry,* April 1952, pp. 32–36.

Rani, Meena. *The Poetry of Kathleen Raine: A Pursuit of Patterns.* New Delhi: Wisdom Publications, 1989.

Rees-Jones, Deryn, ed. "Kathleen Raine." In *Modern Women Poets.* Newcastle-upon-Tyne: Bloodaxe, 2005. Pp. 93–95.

Rudman, Mark. "Kathleen Raine's Originality." *New England Review* 23, no. 2:123–125 (spring 2002).

Stanford, Derek. *The Freedom of Poetry: Studies in Contemporary Verse.* London: Falcon Press, 1947.

Tardieu-Garnier, Claire, with Jacqueline Genet. "Le mythe de l'Eden et la tradition néo-platonicienne dans la poésie de Kathleen Raine [The myth of Eden and the Neoplatonist tradition in the poetry of Kathleen Raine]." In *Poètes anglais contemporains: G. Hill, P. Larkin, K. Raine, R. S. Thomas, K. White.* Caen: Université de Caen Press, 1984. Pp. 120–141.

Tardieu-Garnier, Claire. "L'Exil dans *Farewell Happy Fields* de Kathleen Raine [Exile in *Farewell Happy Fields* by Kathleen Raine]." *Etudes britanniques contemporaines,* no. 14:41–50 (1998).

———. "Paysage symbolique et mémoire culturelle [Symbolic landscape and cultural memory]." In *Paysages et cultures: Regards littéraires et artistiques.* Edited by Gabriel R. Thibault. Vol. 1. Rouen: Scérèn, 2003. Pp. 79–88.

Tolley, A. T. "Defending Ancient Springs." In *Poetry of the Forties.* Manchester, U.K.: Manchester University Press, 1985. Pp. 128–148.

Wardle, Sarah. "Amnesiac Mystique." *Times Literary Supplement,* March 29, 2002, p. 24.

FIONA SAMPSON

(1963—)

Steven Matthews

THE BIOGRAPHY OF the British poet Fiona Sampson initially seems to present divergent interests and commitments. At the outset of her professional career, up until the age of twenty-three, she worked as a classical musician. She was a violinist trained and playing in London, Paris, and such places as the Salzburg Mozarteum, and she was leader of her own string quartet. Her subsequent academic career has taken in philosophy and politics; her artistic management and editorial work has encompassed precise issues of translation alongside promotion of an eclectic range of writing, which absorbs both the mainstream lyric and more experimental poetry that investigates the aftermath of early- to mid-twentieth-century modernism.

On Listening (2007), a collection of prose pieces, includes a section called "Favourite Things," short reviews by Sampson of contemporaries' books. Included in that section are the W. H. Auden–influenced English poets Glyn Maxwell and John Fuller, alongside North Americans Anne Carson and Jorie Graham, the Australian Les Murray, the complexly surreal Irish woman poet Medbh McGuckian, and the Irish-born poet Greg Delanty, who is now based in the United States (where he has taken citizenship). Add these to her inclusion of the Irish Eavan Boland and the English Jo Shapcott and U. A. Fanthorpe, who appear under a separate section called "Reading," and the range of Sampson's attention becomes clear. She is attracted by strong individual voices on the modern poetry scene, whatever their provenance, and she is alert to a range of styles, from the pared-down lyrics of Boland to the unspecified suburbia of Maxwell, the personae of Shapcott, the riddling askance of Murray, and the poetics of process of such as Graham and Carson. The opening essay in *On Listening* finds Sampson declaring her "interest in the way a grammar of thought underpins a poetic" (p. 82). Her rigorous sense of that allegiance between "thought" and poetry frees her interest from all potentially prejudicial response to others' work and opens its possible influence to her.

Sampson's own poetry draws into itself many of these seemingly contending strands in her thought and professional activity. Her early books display a reexploration of the lyric from a sometimes fierce political and gender-focused standpoint. *The Distance Between Us* (2005), which has proved extremely successful in Bulgarian, Hebrew, Albanian, Macedonian and Romanian translation, as well as in its original language, explores a central love relation against the background of European history and landscape. *Common Prayer* (2007) and *Rough Music* (2010) have presented more crucially Sampson's understanding of philosophy and language; but, also, in these latter three poetry collections, which often deploy a more expansive and open formal shape, her interests in the structural musicality of poetry (as evidenced in her 2011 collection of essays *Music Lessons)* are especially to the fore. Each of these books also displays a thematic concurrence with the Eastern European writing with which Sampson has been concerned—home and exile, idiom and locale, brutal history and natural rhythms.

Although her poetry itself bears the imprint, then, of Sampson's plural intellectual foci and commitments, it has also not shied from the more radical consequences of the notion of a life lived in a complex and multifaceted manner. Before launching into close consideration of Sampson's poetry as it has emerged book by book, therefore, it is worth reviewing some of the issues about the modern self and our understanding of identity that she has raised elsewhere. These issues bring pressure to bear upon the many voices, but also the many formal shapes, of her poetry, and they have had a direct consequence for the style and content of much of her poetry across her career.

In the key chapter that she contributed to the coauthored writer's manual *Writing: Self and Reflexivity* (2006), "Memory and History," Sampson considered the role of those two elements in establishing the nature of the self that is translated to the reader through a literary text. In her chapter, Sampson particularly presents an intriguing reflection upon *The Confessions*, the autobiographical text by the eighteenth-century French philosopher Jean-Jacques Rousseau. *The Confessions* is a key text in Western philosophy, for its establishment of the notion that the biographical self is the measure and basis for understanding all experience and for the challenge that it mounts to the notion that there is an external authority which validates or ratifies our conscious understanding of who we are. Sampson's reading of *The Confessions*, however, turns the text back upon its own presumptions, rather in the manner that the French philosopher Jacques Derrida crucially did in the 1970s in his book *Of Grammatology* (1976). Sampson points to the fact that although, in *The Confessions*, Rousseau often somewhat scandalously talked about the most intimate moments or aspects of his life and thought, the book itself presents a strong narrative development based upon standard literary models.

There is a tension, in other words, between the "personal" ad hoc element of *The Confessions* and the book's literary realization. There are also moments in the book where we can see Rousseau, as the man in the present writing down his life, self-consciously looking back at, and judging, the earlier versions of himself that were involved in the experiences of the time that he is writing about. This double consciousness between literary times in his prose forms that "reflexivity" that Sampson is directly involved with in her chapter "Memory and History":

Rousseau's challenge is an interesting one. He makes the paradoxical proposal that a writer can achieve disinterested inquiry—what we think of as something like omniscient narration—by looking at himself. It's a paradox which is at the heart of the book you're reading now [that is, *Writing: Self and Reflexivity*]: and of the writing process itself. For we're suggesting that, through exploring and owning the reflexivity inherent in our writing process—the way it's necessarily engaged with who we are—we can "manage" what's individual in both the process and product and move it outwards to the unknown reader.

(pp. 112–113)

For Sampson, in fact, writing is a "process" because of the way in which it involves a progressive *reading* of the self who creates it. This sense of "process" is something that will be reviewed through the close discussion, particularly of Sampson's more expansive mature collections, that follows below. But Sampson's passionate adherence to the idea of bifurcated (or even trifurcated) modern selfhood, in which identity is rendered a multiple possibility because of such things as memory, which splits us across (or between) personal or historical times, underpins much of her own creative effort.

For Sampson, this "paradoxical" situation of self, which (as it does for Derrida) becomes particularly dramatized within literary texts, unites seemingly divergent moments in the history of poetry, from the "metaphysical" poets of the seventeenth century to the Romantic poets of Rousseau's time, such as William Wordsworth and Samuel Taylor Coleridge. To an extent, therefore, Sampson's sense of "paradoxical" selfhood both resists and queries accepted tropes in feminist readings of women's poetry. Deryn Rees-Jones, for instance, has written in an introduction to the 2005 anthology *Modern Women Poets* that a dramatic poem can provide "a place in which the unstable selfhood of the female poet can comfortably reside, providing a position which problematizes and at the same time explores issues of gender, and identity" (p. 19). Sampson's radical resistance in her own rendering of such selves in her work is one that challenges, or rather subsumes, gendered implications in such common theoretical and literary positions. She often writes consciously as a woman and indicates that the speaker of her poetry is female, yet this is only one facet of the exploration of modern multiplicity on display. Her position is near that of the senior poet Anne Stevenson, who wrote eloquently about "Defending the Freedom of the Poet": "To talk or even to think of women's writing as a category distinct and separated from the rich, multilayered traditions of literature in English is, to my mind, reductionist" (p. 3).

More immediately, the passage cited above from "Memory and History" offers some understanding of the scope of Sampson's own style and literary ambition. The sense of the intimate self becoming the subject of "disinterested inquiry," through the "narration" which that intimate self undergoes in literature, underwrites what could be called the "outside in" manner of much of her poetry. This is a manner in which a piece can move from a seemingly initially gestural, dispersed, or undefined set of descriptive coordinates toward a closer and closer realization of the real nature of the subject of the poem. The poems often progress, in other words, from a rather generalized or abstract perspective and set of terminologies toward a more intimate space in which a crucial aspect of one (and therefore of every) life gets exposed.

The estranging quality of Sampson's own prose as it turns outward to its reader ("It's a paradox which is at the heart of the book you're reading now") is a further aspect of this process. Writing makes the poet reflexively self-aware about her experiences, but it also latterly makes the reader self-aware and self-conscious about theirs. Sampson's writing can sometimes achieve a Brechtian estrangement technique, uncanny in the way it, as it were, turns "outward" toward its reader. An early collection, with a title that would become emblematic for Sampson's oeuvre, *Folding the Real* (2001), presents various occasions in which such eerie reversals within ordinary lives are on display. "Legal and Tender," for instance, begins by contemplating its speaker's outsider status with regard to many of the markers of daily suburban life—the neighbor's dogs, footballs being kicked in a local park, planes flying safely overhead. But, in the poem's final lines, that distanced perspective gathers a more general oddness, as the everyday world is described in the phrase "and everything / is natural without end right to the end" (p. 54) And so the poem ends. We are made dramatically aware through Sampson's arrangement and shaping of her narrative voice in this brief lyric that the end of the poem is covalent with the end of the lives narrated within it, with their death. But we are also made uneasily aware that the "natural" and eternal ongoings of the "everything" that is "life" are themselves, looked at from the poem's perspective, very strange and in fact unnatural. This quality of social and political—as well as literary—estrangement includes the fabled comfort of national life ("we're British").

"Legal and Tender" makes a good example, then, of that further facet of Sampson's reflections on Rousseau in the passage cited above from *Writing: Self and Reflexivity*. The claim that reflexivity enables a writer to "manage" what is "individual in both process and product" suggests that the shape and form of a poem is determined by the encounter that it makes with alternative possibilities of selfhood. It is the staging of that encounter around some defined facet of selfhood that gives a form to the writerly identity, one that is always both performed and performative. The more open and lengthy forms of Sampson's later work reveal her in a more relaxed mode of embodying such paradox or complexity, of allowing the more opaque and hidden aspects of selfhood to emerge through the reflective and gradual course of the writing. The chapter on Rousseau, "Memory and History," takes cognizance of the historically religious aspects of such possibility, the sense of "the holy or mysterious" buried within reality, which the process of the poem might reveal (p. 114). This potential is most consistently presented in Sampson's collection *Common Prayer*. But, pressingly, for Sampson, it is vital that her notion of self as a form of complex possibility, as a dialogue rather than as a mono-vocal entity, is empowering. It represents a political impetus granted not only to writer but also, through the writing, to the reader: "The status of the Romantic self as a *metaphysical* foundation," she says, "is important when ideas about the self are taken as the basis for action, as they are in political philosophy" (p. 116).

Rousseau's dramatization of himself in *The Confessions*, in other words, is coterminous with the direct political involvements he undertook in the fields of human rights and of education. The "disinterested inquiry" he is able to undertake with regard to his own circumstances enables him to respond powerfully to situations in which others' selves are being constricted or unjustly constrained. Sampson's is, therefore, self-consciously a liberal poetics, but one that is considered in its inclusion of multiple viewpoints and voicings that range across key historical brutalities and brutalizations of the twentieth century.

LIFE

Fiona Sampson was born in London on October 7, 1963. She left school at the age of sixteen to become a musician and later studied at the Royal Academy of Music in London (1982–1985). She achieved the Academy's Professional Performance Certificate in 1985. Subsequently, in a shift of focus, she took a degree in philosophy, politics, and economics from Oxford University (1989–1992). She also earned a doctorate in the philosophy of language from the Radboud University of Nijmegen in the Netherlands (2001). While at Oxford, in 1992 Sampson won the university's prestigious Newdigate Prize for poetry, an award made on an annual basis for the best poem presented anonymously to the panel of judges (previous winners include Matthew Arnold, Oscar Wilde, and the recent British poet laureate Andrew Motion). During the time that Sampson was working on her university degrees, she held a series of long-term residencies that established her as a leading pioneer in the use of creative writing in healthcare contexts in the United Kingdom. This interest led to her publication of two major monographs on the subject, *The Healing Word* (1999) and *Creative Writing in Health and Social Care* (2004).

As a postgraduate student, Sampson founded the International Poetryfest in Aberystwyth, Wales (1995–2000). During this phase of her life, she became familiar with trends in modern and contemporary poetry from Eastern Europe, an encounter that has had significant impact upon her more recent life and work. Sampson became editor of the journal *Orient Express*, which she founded and which was concentrated upon making more widely available postcommunist writing in the newly expanding Europe, through the best English translations. Sampson involved herself actively in the processes of translation and publication of the Estonian poet Jaan Kaplinski's *Evening Brings Everything Back* (2004). Sampson was also coeditor—along with Jean Boase-Beier and Alexandra Buchler—of *A Fine Line*, an anthology of contemporary poetry by a range of younger Eastern European writers (2004).

In 2005 Sampson became editor of *Poetry Review,* the only female editor in the near-century of the *Review*'s history with the exception of Muriel Spark (1947–1949). *Poetry Review* is the journal of the Poetry Society, the national body responsible for sponsorship of the medium in the U.K. Sampson's editorship has proved to an extent contentious, in that several women poets initially presumed that the advent of a woman as editor would lead to a policy of positive discrimination toward female writers. Sampson's scrupulous adherence to the notion of aesthetic worth as prerequisite for publication in the *Review* has, however, seen a remaking of it as a top-class forum, in which leading writers from across the globe present new work. Especially influential has been Sampson's commissioning for the *Review* of situational essays from a range of leading writers, including Marjorie Perloff, John Ashbery, Hélène Cixous, the Australian poet John Kinsella, and the Scots writers Don Paterson and John Burnside. These "Centrefolds" have succeeded in acting as foci for vivid discussion about key issues in contemporary writing in English.

PICASSO'S MEN

Sampson's first collection of poetry, *Picasso's Men* (1993), shows some of these themes in potential. The spiky juxtapositions of the phrases in its mainly brief lyrics work to disturb the settled perspective we might expect the poems to take upon the everyday life. Predictably, in a first book, the achievement of some of these poems is not consistently assured, but nonetheless they collectively present an attitude toward their subjects that will broaden and gain in authority rapidly with Sampson's subsequent books.

"The Multiple" is one instance of this. Its five short stanzas present a view of a girl ill in bed in a mocking tone from the poem's speaker. Although the girl seems to be still immature— her childhood dolls watch her as she lies there— what the poem points toward is a much more mature and transgressive sense of her own sexuality that resides within the seemingly normal, if saccharine, and innocent picture the poem starts with. For this young girl sees herself, despite her situation, as a worldly achiever—she has won prizes for her pony-riding—and also as a "Juliet," who, although ill, fantasizes that she's actually waiting for her lover-husband to return to her. The poem is typical from Sampson, in that it reveals that its central character has a different perception of herself to the perception complacently imposed upon her by others. If the charge of this is somewhat undermined by the lapse at the poem's end into a surreal image, it also displays Sampson's early and urgent concern to tackle in her work what she calls here "multiples."

These are "multiples" in the sense of unrealized versions of dream and self-projection that lie within and beneath the everyday and that enable the poems' speakers to engage imaginatively with what seems a uniform and blandly comfortable suburban world all around. It is noteworthy, of course, that Sampson's title here, "The Multiple," together with the term "multiples" applied to such complex personalities, are themselves somewhat askew and odd with regard to current English idiom (the term in fact derives from medical diction for a pregnancy which leads to more than one child being born). Such language adopts the feel of a labeling, almost a prescribed medical or psychological diagnosis— but such uneasiness is a deliberate objective of Sampson's linguistic effects, one that mirrors the mixture of myth and fairy tale with the "normal" and "natural" that such poems present.

There is a strong vein of the grotesque, and even of spite, running through such voiced impatience in *Picasso's Men*. "The Babygod" offers an image of a male child screaming, furious, vomiting, and destructive of the lives of the adults around him. And yet he draws their admiration, as when women dandle him. Characteristically, however, the baby treats his love as a commodity for sale and readily betrays those who fall too easily for his duplicities. His fickleness, and lack of respect for those he is dependent upon for his well-being, are clearly taken to prefigure later behaviors of disrespect toward these, and later, women who dare to love him.

The book title, *Picasso's Men* (Sampson's titles are always key), is a similarly neat inversion of expectation, to that in "The Babygod"; one that, again, works to expose the potentially brutal consequences of the license allowed men. The Spanish painter Pablo Picasso is more renowned for his bullish and libidinous attitude to a series of women than for his attention to other males in his life. So the men in this book conform largely to the type prefigured by this baby; they are brutal pursuers of sex with women who largely wish to retain, or to return to, their previously innocent state. Two poems on consecutive pages, "Flying Nude" and "How Would It Be," reveal the extremes toward which the book pushes these themes. The former poem, a reworking in miniature of typical narratives from Ovid's *Metamorphoses*, sees a terrified and stifled naked woman pursued through a forest by a repulsive male. While the poem mimics the glamour of Ovidian originals, describing its woman in fantastically attractive terms, it ends with her longing for evening time, when she can curl up like a child. The ultimate dream for woman here is disturbingly one of return to a prepubescent state, in which such pursuit by brute males would not happen. The once-classical casting of such yearnings through poetry has become (such is the history of male-female relations), for the speaker of this poem, a harsh caricature.

In a literally repellent move, however, "How Would It Be," on the opposite page to "Flying Nude" (which ended with a rather comforting image of the fantasized escape and quietitude of its young girl), imagines in horrific detail the stripping and pedophilic rape of another girl, so young that she has a pacifier "she plays with still." This poem's title lacks a normal and expected question mark ("How Would It Be"?), because it tells us in dreadful detail how such an attack would be and is—and how it is indicative of other attitudes in society. Such views of disturbing and appalling sexual brutality mark the most memorable tone of *Picasso's Men*, despite their being juxtaposed with other poems that present other views. The poem "Picasso," for example, surprisingly and naughtily (in all senses) relishes a male lover's torso and is a delicious paean of admiration for a form "I often stroke," and one that the speaker imagines, Picasso-like, rendering as a work of art. "Peony" offers a version of pastoral in which a large garden flower offers potential salving consolation through its purple beauty but also through its size. Once again there is a threat beneath the fullness of potential proffered through the poem, one here of verbal violence. But the flower (and poem) "Peony" seems to offer at least a possibility of hope, even as it is strangely and perhaps alarmingly anthropomorphized in the process.

At the center of *Picasso's Men* is the minisequence with which Sampson won the Oxford Newdigate Prize, "Green Thought." Taking its instigation from the Renaissance poet Andrew Marvell's "The Prize" ("like a green thought in a green shade"), this sequence offers a further version of pastoral. The induction poem to "Green Thought" presents a disturbance again on several levels. A male figure (muse?) is figured as erupting into a female child's bedroom as she sleeps, and sowing dreams which are also associated with an "unreason" that threatens to sweep all away before it (p. 14). This unreason is, in its turn, associated with "Poetry," which breaks free from its contained moorings within books on the shelves in the room; and, once again, this presumably young girl displays in this event a disturbingly mature sexuality, dreaming as she does of a mythic lover.

The poems in the main sections of "Green Thought" are dominated, subsequently, by repeated images of this unleashing of potential. They display a series of female protagonists themselves experiencing, or witnessing, eruptions that carry them beyond the known into unknown, and pastoral, worlds. What is shared by the protagonists from each poem, though, is a wish "to step out" into the countryside, to experience immediately its flora and fauna, as the child longs to do in the fourth poem, which also figures her desired version of England as one resplendent with ancient trackways. Although there remains threat, the poems are more celebratory than some others in *Picasso's Men*, although at the same time they are framed by a sense of the unreality and danger of all of this possibility. The concluding framing poem, a reprise of some of the ideas in the induction, sees the speaker once again as a creature of misrule, scattering hope into what seem to be dull lives—but doing so in a way redolent of falsity and destruction. This is a pastoral dreaming that operates in the glamour of beguilement but also in the shadow of the nuclear age. It is, again, askew from contemporary expectation—literally so, in its use of the German adjective *verklarte* ("blissful," "transfigured") to describe potential in the English countryside. There is also something potentially brutal in the (presumably male) voice of this final speaker, offering on the one hand a nature that is full of intrigue, but also, and as a consequence, demanding a dictated response from his audience.

"Green Thought" offers in more complex form a reworking of the themes elsewhere in *Picasso's Men*. Its exploration of thought, or reason, and their dark twins, predicts also Sampson's preoccupation with the "grammar" of thought that poetry particularly enacts. The brutality and threat of male sexuality to women is often not so overtly present in Sampson's subsequent poetry as it is in this first book. But the complications of female innocence and sexuality, and their relation to the imagination, to dreaming, and to artifice and artificiality in a seemingly intransigent and dour contemporary world, all recur in the more mature and achieved books that followed.

FOLDING THE REAL

Sampson's next collection, *Folding the Real* (2001), was her first from an established poetry publisher. It signaled its continuities with the rarer *Picasso's Men* through its republication of the mini-sequence "Green Thought," as well as through its return to some of the themes and issues of the first book. But *Folding the Real* considerably sophisticates those themes, which had sometimes in the first collection taken on a rather essentialized, if vehement, politics in their view of gender violence. This second book, in other terms, views love relations or gender encounters through a more complex lens of difficult and contradictory emotion that is commonly shared but that also bears resonances for the whole possibility of writing poetry, and for creativity per se. As the collection's title indicates, these are poems about making "the real" into something other than itself, origami-like, making of it another form, and kind, of reality.

"Dear Emma," for instance, is a variously perspectived love poem. It has a memory at its center, a memory of an "I" as part of a couple who talked in bed about the child they might have—the Emma of the title. "Emma" is a troublesome notion, however. She seems to be more like a doll than a human child, a "mysterious" presence who emerges from the "half-real," who is contained in herself beyond the imaginings of her putative parents, and who, in her inchoate being, offers to overburden them:

who
can bear the strange
script drifting
by [...]?

(pp. 40–41)

"Emma," as a dreamed-of possibility, is also an alien mode of writing, one that is taken, in the mysterious set of connections and relationships "Dear Emma" presents, as perhaps a signal for the unease existing between the purported lovers themselves. Their joint imaginative product, the little girl who might or not be "real" one day, in her "strange" potential disturbs the love at the heart of their "talk" realizing her. The poem's final two lines, with their awkward line break,

present a surprising separation, within their round of seemingly binding pronouns: "she and / you. You and I." "She," "Emma," is somehow pushed away by this from the speaker; "she" is not something the joint creators "You and I" can actually hold between them. Particular weight is put by this hesitation upon the retrospectively sentimental resonances of that title for the poem, "Dear Emma." By the poem's end, "dear" is a word also applied by the speaker to the lover. It is as though the poem's actual memory is about a rather wistful, clichéd sentimentality that the speaker has outgrown, rather than a purposeful and imaginative engagement of another through love.

Several poems in *Folding the Real*, then, open with an easily achieved potential through relationship before coming to their real center in loss, or what the title of one calls "The Separation." In "How It Was," this takes on a sad actuality in the recounting of an "easy" conception of a child, a conception that leads to a realization of another possible world ("the image of you / I imagined," a nice doubling). But a miscarriage seems both to confirm the separateness of the speaker ("then there was only I") and to provide a stoic (if rather melodramatic) relief that the child has been spared the traumas of attachment in the human world, "love / and all its injuries" (p. 12). The sadness at the child's loss before birth, however, the fact that it remains "unabridged" through memory (and through the poem about it), feeds into the sense of doubleness and doubling that operates more broadly within this second full collection by Sampson.

The curiously titled "The Honeymooneers" enacts this literally. Its opening reminiscence of a scene from a book, which is also a snapshot of "*abandon*" experienced between lovers, is simply juxtaposed in the poem with "*here*," another time in which the two things (the reading of the book and the lovers' experience) are being recalled. What the writing enacts, then, as it declares (in terms predicting those in the essay "Memory and History"), is "*Two presents*. Neither giving / anything to the other" (p. 8). Through writing, it is possible to be in several seemingly congruent present tenses, both "real." But the poem's speaker is able to move deftly between them, allowing the one "present" (the now in which there seems a comfortable reflection "in this winter kitchen" upon the couple[s] who acted wildly in their love before) to nestle neatly alongside the other, in which the lovers' *"abandon"* seems also to be ongoing.

Such themes in the book, notions that poetry is able fully to realize experience, to make it present again both to writer and to audience—but also to form a double-take upon that experience, to place it within a life narrative—come most tellingly together in the book in the title poem, "Folding the Real." An explicatory note to the poem puts us in the realm of Sampson's musical career, informing us that violinists believe that an old instrument retains sounds within itself, sounds created by earlier performers upon it. The interaction any new player has with that past is, then, emblematically realized as a harmonizing with the past:

> uniting
> the sound you will make and the one already made,
> the sound
> waiting in the one actualising—being— [...]
>
> (p. 39)

Partly, this is a remarkable rendition, on different terms, of T. S. Eliot's classic understanding of the relation between "Tradition and the Individual Talent" (1919; collected in *Selected Essays*, 1974). The poem is telling us that any new performance of a work of art is made complex by the way it makes resonate again earlier works and performances, multiple "voices," from the past. "Self," the individual new writer, is only realized from such complexity, both for Eliot and for Sampson.

But "Folding the Real" is also sustained across a single sentence, within a sonnet structure where each poetic line also contains fourteen syllables (there is a sequence of such squared-off, single-sentence sonnets interspersed across this book). What Eliot calls "the historical sense" necessary to any true understanding of the relation of present to past, or self to other, in art, runs oddly, therefore, in this book, through a poetic structure that is determined by arbitrary

mathematical constraints. These are constraints that are advertised in some of the awkward line endings dictated by the syllabics of this sonnet "Folding the Real": "while / the," "a / repetition," for example (p. 39). Sampson, as a result, creates a further level of doubleness, or "folding." The sense in this sonnet, as in other such poems in this periodic sequence, that poetry discovers and presents presence, and that it flows and moves between and across times, memories, and history, is dramatized as being rendered possible only through the artifice and constraints of art. The poem remains a comment upon "the real," a way of "folding" it, but retains a limited presence in itself. As in modern classical music, such as serialism or the atonalism of Arnold Schoenberg, imposed pattern or number serves both to limit the range of possibility within the score or poem and, paradoxically, to intensify and release the "self" within it.

Sampson's attentiveness to such processes in poetry, and her building of reflection and self-consciousness about process into the poetry itself, aligns her work more positively toward a modern American poetics rather than toward a British (or Irish) one. Such British writing remains resolutely dependent still upon a stable, empiricist, understanding, in which memory or visionary reminiscence is readily accessed by the poetry's speaker. Sampson, instead, sometimes creates eerie possibilities out of such (mis-)identification. The poem "The Separation," for instance, seems to be voiced across its length by a male whose female lover has left him, but who seems determined to put a brave face toward the future. "I waved, / jaunty, though I felt myself drowning" is a nice refolding of Stevie Smith's sense of "not waving but drowning," one that captures the boldness of the speaker in this situation (p. 17). Yet, by the poem's final stanza, it appears that the "separation" that might be being talked about in this poem is not a "separation" between lovers but rather between an emotionally undeveloped son and his mother—the poem's references to toys and growing up take on an uncanny, and queasy, edge, the poem now seemingly in an Oedipal voice rather than a mature speaker's.

Other poems in the book use their sense of slippage between possibilities in other ways, to question the specialness of some of the commonly reverenced poetic emotions. "Hotel Boulevard" is a joyful poem that seems to begin in established mode, with delight between lovers at their awakening to a day of new realities and potential ("glad that your body is brown and dry"). But this contentedness rapidly shifts into a demonstration that the possibilities of relationship in themselves exhibit their lack of definiteness:

Now there are two
completenesses. And if two, why not
two million and two? The city suddenly filling up
around you [...]

(pp. 25–26)

Wittily inverting the *aubade* tradition in Western writing, Sampson rejects the normal testy rejection of the business of the new day that threatens to break in upon the exclusive delights of the couple in bed. Instead, she translates the fulfillment and sense of self that can paradoxically be imbued by intimate encounter with another person into delight at the myriad selfhood of the modern city. "Hotel Boulevard" is typical of Sampson's mature poetry, in that it is unafraid to talk rather abstractly as part of its course about the thought and understanding that have been realized within and through the poem, here an "alterity you respect." Unlike much modernist writing, but like the English tradition from Auden onward, this is a poetry that does not go in fear of abstraction but, rather, integrates abstraction into the process and grammar of the poem itself. "Hotel Boulevard" does not reject personal intimacy—at the end, the speaker, who is now revealed as (presumably) female, turns to the "stranger," him.

But in using such moments as models for a mature understanding of modern selfhood, and as a philosophy and politics for modern society, *Folding the Real* shows Sampson presenting a unique voice within contemporary British poetry. What "Drawing the Line" calls "nowness and thisness" (p. 32), or "The Bargain" "a curve into presence" (p. 36), is always placed within a paradigm that alerts the reader to other possibilities, other vocal potential, within and through the time that the poem takes to unfurl itself down the page.

THE DISTANCE BETWEEN US

The Distance Between Us (2005) is a much more *designed* book than Sampson's work had been hitherto. Its physical entity reflects the nature of the issues addressed within it. The book is made up of seven sections; each section is made up nearly always of one brief lyric, and one expansive poem, which deploys the full possibility of modernist typography. The sections are separated by a full blank page, each with the new section number upon it; the fact that the new section's brief poem always appears on the recto sheet means that there are sometimes virtually two empty pages between each (briefish) section. As a result, the book presents a series of defined and crafted moments that are literally "distant" from each other; the reader needs to cross a blank and emptiness in order to "take up" the narrative at each new stage.

The blurb to the book describes this as a verse-novel, which opens with a "love affair in crisis," then moves through various existential questionings raised by these difficulties, to emerge at the end with a joyous reconciliation and lovemaking. While it is possible to see such a pattern subliminally present in the novel, however, it is also the case that the individual sections do not significantly advance the story: it is left to the reader to envisage how they "fit." Certain of the sections ("The Velvet Shutter," "Path") contain moments that provide biographical background to the main female character. Other sections ("Turkish Rondo") seem to provide cultural settings within which the central "romance" takes place. Still others ("Cante Jondo," "Hotel Casino") offer rather abstract meditations on the relationship, intercut with broader reflections upon its relation to other major issues within life. Even the final section, the advertised reconciliatory lovemaking ("The Secret Flowers"), is framed in such a way that the final climax (of lovers and book) is alienated within its context. As the lovers move "beyond our bodies" the scene is envisaged as collapsing around them, and they fly

> through walls beds windows open or shut
> through days opening closing like desert dunes
> like doors
>
> like water
>
> through the long indifferent corridor.

(p. 67)

The poem's bold enactment of climax is brutally placed by this (the book's) final line. It reestablishes that "distance," which has been broadcast so frequently through the book, and its presentation as being paradoxically essential to relationship and proximity, in the poems' view of it. "The Velvet Shutter" has a declarative statement of an understanding that seems to underwrite the philosophical and stylistic choices of much else in the work. In a reminiscence notably about performance, about a violinist on a podium above and before and audience, we are told that

> It's distance that brings you close,
> lets us see my self
> in you
> your self in me.
> Light,
> shadow.

(p. 25)

The typography and vocabulary here is very careful. "My self" is not "myself"; "your self" not "yourself." Traditionally, poetry has largely viewed (love) relations in a Platonic sense, whereby two individuals are part of a lacked whole, which comes together in completion if the relationship is confirmed by experience. Sampson's poetry contradicts the tradition, being founded upon what the earlier poem "Hotel Boulevard" calls "alterity," the proper recognition of the otherness of the lover or other person through the relation with them. "My self" is both a more essential and a newly minted thing, compared with "myself," an established sense of continuous narrative told by the self as to who she/he is. "My self," of course, also enters the notion of distance between the possessive pronoun and the "self"; that self is, therefore, inherently flexible, variable, performative (as it is staged, in other words, at this moment in "The Velvet Shutter"). The typography, which ensures a line break but also a run-on between "in you / your self," is also properly respectful of this otherness; "you," as understood by the "I," is different from the you of "your self," which remains largely unknown to the other person/speaker. The final translation of this, *not* into a binary opposition (light/dark) but rather into a partial relation ("Light / shadow"), further acknowledges a relation through difference, the retention on both sides of something in the respective selves that is not engaged with, or by, or through, the "connection."

The relevance of scrutinizing this seemingly minute detail within such an expansive collection of poems lies in the fact that *The Distance Between Us* is Sampson's most extended and considered meditation upon these issues, which have surfaced in the lyrics of the earlier work. The sense of the flexibility and the performativity of selfhood, of its momentariness, is now reflected in the open-form shifts and movements of the longer poems here. "The Secret Flowers" describes the "sometimes rueful" "impulse to love" shared by and between humans, as "This movement through form" (p. 63). We reach through ourselves and across ourselves in love, and in the process are remade by it. But this is also a poetry that deliberately moves "through form," that breaks down the lyric shapes which had previously characterized Sampson's writing and that now reaches out beyond them to a freer musical possibility.

As a result, the issue of *presence*, the notion that what poetry does is to realize, or re-present, experience tellingly—a notion that had haunted the earlier poems—is here treated much more skeptically and doubtfully. In the early phase of the book (at a time of difficulty, if we go along with the advertised "plotting" of this verse-novel), presence—the possibility of coming near to another—is particularly a painful contention.

The desert-like setting of "Cante Jondo" writes large the barrenness of these debates:

> Can I touch you?
> Putting my hand into the wound of presence
>
> because I don't doubt this truth
> that is a lie,
> that is an ulcer in clear sky?

(p. 16)

In times of difficulty, the establishing confirmations between selves become themselves diseased, something that remains true but that is also false, since the person reaching out to touch the other is no longer necessarily respected or recognized by the other. If the trajectory of the narrative in *The Distance Between Us* is toward resolving such hurtful perplexities, troubling issues remain. The lovemaking in "The Secret Flowers" is, again, specifically geared toward restoration of such confirmation around presence:

> Your bones and inner organs turn
> Towards themselves towards embrace:
>
> *here.*

(p. 63)

This neatly sustains the paradox; through embracing the lover, the self's body is also confirmed in its identity ("themselves"). But as such confirmation is always tentative, the urge remains for the self to become subsumed within the act, or by the lover:

> your mouth squeezing my lip
> till it loses itself
> till my mouth blurs.
> *Overcome me.*
>
> Body begins to clarify itself.
> Touched, its form becomes
> sense.

(p. 65)

The notion that the self must be changed or lost before it can "reform" physically, emotionally, and as a way of comprehending, renders it vulnerable. "*Overcome me*" rests awkwardly as a mode of yearning but also of female compliance.

The Distance Between Us is, like Sampson's previous work, bold in addressing these issues directly. Section 3, which contains "Leda at the Lake" and (the ironically titled) "Brief Encounter," presents disturbing versions of such "overcoming." In the former, Leda, victim of rape by the god Zeus in the form of the swan (and subject of many major previous poems, such as the sonnet by W. B. Yeats), displays a vulnerability: "*Not now* she prays. *Don't let it be now*" (p. 29). But the whole event seems distanced from its mythic associations. It seems part of a film, or to be taking place in a summer suburban garden ("You put the coffee on the terrace"; p. 30). The poem's blaring ending ("Now // Now Now") ambiguously and vindictively seems to celebrate the possibility of such a destructive event within this contained setting.

"Brief Encounter" moves the scene without mediation to the contemporary urban world and, in a prolonged snapshot, gives the story of a rape (or is it a seduction?) at knifepoint:

> The blade on my throat
> is a wound
> in the present,
> it's the precision
> with which the distance between us
> the distance between living and dying
> is measured.

(p. 34)

It is the coolness underpinning such writing, the involvement of the book's title in this abusive scene, which is particularly disturbing. The displaced language of "precision" and of measurement unsettles even the calculated deployment of a by-now-familiar trope for the collection ("wound / in the present"), a trope containing philosophical recognition of personal and physical vulnerability.

Section 3 of *The Distance Between Us*, then, is bold and questionable in its deliberate unbalancing of the ideas that elsewhere govern the book's contextualizing mini-narratives. But disturbance of perspective, challenge to the reader, is also a keynote throughout. "Turkish Rondo" seems initially a straightforward and compelling rendition of the multiethnic society

303

that Britain has become. But it also, as the opening lines make clear, shows how the sense of origins, and of self-definition, continue to be troubling, as does the prospect of assimilation: *"Where'm I from? / Depends who's asking"* (p. 46). This nonwhite Londoner recalls busy family life in the suburbs, including the ethnically governed tensions and name-shifts between the siblings who are attempting to settle there. But Sampson throws the reader out of a complacent acceptance of a situation that has become commonplace in twenty-first-century Britain. At one point, the poem's speaker reflects upon the nature of the poem he is a part of:

What
gives us form? The stories we tell,
the voice we tell them in
I reassure students ...

(p. 47)

The speaker is revealed to have emerged from out of the seemingly disadvantaged ethnic and impoverished past that was described at the poem's beginning to become a college lecturer, rehearsing the weary academic "truisms" about the nature of self and how it is "refracted" by the accent and dialect in which self is narrated. This sudden mechanism of framing the story from within the flow of the poem itself once again alienates a compliant reader into challenging a sense of the nature of what she or he is reading and of how it can be rendered against other experiences of reading similar poems here, containing personae. At one level, it is "reassuring" for the critic of Sampson's poetry to have moments when the mechanisms of her technique are so immediately exposed to and for us. On another level, the poems continue to ask questions of, and about, our own stance toward their distancing and complexly confirmatory strategies.

COMMON PRAYER

Common Prayer (2007) continues something of this challenge about identity, and about the processes of understanding and of reading, from intriguingly different perspectives. Translating these ideas now into a vocabulary derived from contemporary and speculative physics and biology, the book pursues a version of the physical and the metaphysical that seeks a religious radiance through perception. Here, a simple domestic action, like washing dishes, can become access to a ceaseless, bountiful overflowing of wonder:

between house and kitchen
sunlight flocks in a kind of Mobius wave
and return,
a continual pulse-less flow and exchange–
look—

(p. 39)

At such moments, the punning title of the book (itself a variant on the Anglican *Book of Common Prayer*) comes into play. These moments of connection with further possibility, moments underscored by the sophisticated understanding of scientific process that plays through the poems, are, indeed, "common." But they are also moments that poetry, Sampson seems to claim, is uniquely able to show us, to hold up before us, as the difficult abstraction of contemporary scientific "knowledge" is translated into familiar and immediate contexts.

It is key, therefore, that the understanding of "prayer" in the book is a capacious one: "common," here, in the sense of removed from the particular space of the established church and from its established ceremonies or rituals. Like Jorie Graham's *Overlord* (2005), a collection for which *On Listening* reveals Sampson to have a particular liking (pp. 138–140), "prayer" is something that is readily applicable to a range of situations but also something that is staged, a mode of confronting the exterior world, history, and experience. "Attitudes of Prayer" is a minisequence that embraces a scene in which the composer Beethoven works at a late piece of music; a childhood reminiscence and an encounter with the elusive natural world; *and* a meal in the Christian holy site of Nazareth. The sequence does not seek to make a common theme out of these moments, to create a narrative through them, however. Each is an "attitude" in the strict sense, a disposition or positioning (including one of the body) toward communication with a sense of the numinous.

To this extent, *Common Prayer* presents a series of similar "attitudes." Turning to a favorite (post–T. S. Eliot) scene of poetic encounter and revelation, the London Underground railway system, the speaker of one poem, "The Looking Glass," exclaims

> And here it is again:
> a mute, spatial awareness
>
> of how things are,
> unlearnt, unearned;
> its grammar
>
> something understood
> before you stepped into the lights
>
> (p. 14)

The poem echoes the famously celebratory (and grammatically complex!) "Prayer (I)," by the sixteenth-century Anglican cleric and poet George Herbert. Herbert's poem forms a "Prayer" that is essentially a set of descriptive variations about what prayer itself is:

> … Exalted Manna, gladness of the best,
> Heaven in ordinary, man well dressed,
> The milky way, the bird of Paradise,
> Church-bells beyond the stars heard, the soul's blood,
> The land of spices; something understood.
>
> (p. 46)

Herbert captures both the exoticism and unlikeliness of prayer within life, its strange allure and exorbitance, alongside its ordinariness and, yes, commonness. Sampson's "spatial awareness," which is also (handily within a poem, a piece of language) a "grammar," enables a similar range of potentiality. For her, in the early twenty-first century, however, the exotic language within the poetry, what opens it up beyond the quotidian, is not the same as Herbert's, in his poems written at an early phase of geographical exploration and imperial conquest. For Sampson, here, instead, the extraordinary in her poetry's vocabulary is provided by the learned allusions to scientific terms. The "unlearnt, unearned" experience of "how things are" is a very real one, one we can all share. But, in order more fully to understand what is "understood" in such instances, it is necessary to call upon extrapoetic analogies:

> waves of colour-particles
> are washing your hair, they're thrown streaming
> down your back—
> soundlessly
> the whole scarf
> of light, the pulsing crown.
>
> (p. 39)

What this authorization from newly understood natural processes brings to *Common Prayer* is a relaxation in the movement of the poetry itself in the longer poems. "No need to pull these things together, / to lift them out of difference," as "The Earth-Wire" reminds us, since "difference" is the natural condition played upon by these natural forces (p. 32). Such acceptance allows for a considerable unpredictability in the "progression" of the longer poems, which shift deftly between various different moments of recollection, or demonstration, of these larger forces.

This is not to say that the pain of some of these translations of one experience into a wider, other understanding is eradicated. "Night Fugue" opens by marveling at a barn owl as he prepares to hunt, but it is clear about its lack of full ability to articulate what the scene amounts to and in its sense that nature is red in tooth and claw:

> as if feathers are a print
> of something hidden—
>
> the body like music;
> form opening through time
> in a breathing line
>
> a cry.
>
> (p. 60)

Poetic enactment, as a form "opening through time" within the breath of the speaker, also, for all of its articulacy, is a "cry" for a better form of existence. It is also (and this is where Sampson's writing perhaps comes closest to Jorie Graham's) a medium that registers the "cry" of the victims across history: "The Archive" maps the experience of a group of Polish medical doctors, Jews fleeing to havens elsewhere in Europe from the invasion of Nazi and of Russian forces.

The long poems in the book are interspersed with rhymed sonnets, sonnets that play a traditional and historical role, as they had typically in

305

Renaissance verse by such as Edmund Spenser and John Donne, as well as Herbert, in venturing the connection between the human experience of love and connection with the divine. These sonnets offer compelling, but also wry, commentary upon gender relations. "Body Mass" imagines a male's thoughts during copulation, but it also punctures the pretension behind his self-image, as, despite the fantasy he imagines himself enacting:

… it's a local godhead he meets:

how, chasing flights of angels, he
tumbles to earth himself—in *we*.

(p. 28)

These tighter poems, with their wit but also their direct statement of (religious) aspiration, bring out more strongly than the longer works Sampson's alertness to the artifice involved in drawing together such a range of religious and scientific understanding within the defined space of the poem. This is an artifice that is perhaps now more considered in and for itself than in her previous collections.

In a scene on "Trumpledor Beach," the speaker looks back toward the shoreline and the city that overlooks the strand, recognizing the "myth" that the city's lights in the seawater are creating:

These are the fictional angels,
These bursts of supra-natural radiance
You could put your hand through […]

(p. 23)

At such moments in this collection, Sampson acknowledges that poetry must work hard to achieve its moments of true revelation. Too often, it is tempting for the poet simply to point to some visionary instant and proclaim its significance— what, a few lines later, is described as a "brilliant baptism." Such descriptions and religious claims are dangerous, since they skew the quality of perception that the poetry has meticulously (and scientifically) sought to convey. "Trumpledor Beach" attempts another analogy, comparing the shifting sea to the flow of blood around the hu-man body, before seeming to retreat from such potential over a "notional horizon."

Common Prayer, indeed, opens with a signal poem in this regard. "Messiaen's Piano" celebrates the modern French composer's achievement (*On Listening* also contains a meditation involving his work). Olivier Messiaen marvelously included echoes of bird song within his pieces, seemingly making his music a mirror for the natural potential in the world. "Messiaen's Piano" claims an endurance for such writing (it goes on). But, at the same time, the poem acknowledges its lack of meaning for the world that it reflects and creates: "The beautiful world hardly responds / yet these go on" (p. 11). The poem then moves off in its own direction; the absence of impact of the music in the world is read into a situation between a seemingly loving couple, and it ends with premonition of a "perfect fall" for them (into sex? death?) that the music suggests. Yet the poem has given a useful reminder, as others in *Common Prayer* do, of the limits of artistic potential, and therefore of the limits that poetry comes up against *as* prayer. This collection contains many marvelous and obviously "religious" moments—moments ratified by the scientific perception involved. But it also carefully delineates a sense of the boundaries of that perception and of what can be claimed for and about it, a sense that "common" human yearning and "aspiration" does not necessarily achieve the revelation it desires.

ROUGH MUSIC

Rough Music proclaims itself, from its title onward, a very differently ambitious work to the preceding collection. As the first epigraph to the book points out, "rough music," as a phrase, historically relates to street theater, miming, a folk religious "burning of effigies" with some element, also, of scapegoating a local "victim." The high art aspiration of *Common Prayer* is thoroughly grounded, in a work that seems in some senses to be deliberately in dialogue with Samspon's previous collection. A second epigraph to the book, from Emily Dickinson, is more subversive: "I cannot dance upon my toes— / No

Man instructed me—" This lends a gendered edge to the riotous and homely pastoralism of the notion of "rough music": Sampson, as female poet, is wryly proclaiming her rights upon a nimble-wittedness and deft writing within and against what is traditionally male poetic territory, celebration of the local, of the soil, of the radical energies of dialect.

"At Kasmu," a long and philosophical reflection upon the act of writing in and from a specific place, even draws the German thinker about the nature of time, place, and habitation, Martin Heidegger, into its ambit. Reflecting upon a piece of earth in Central Europe that has been successively overrun by forces of occupation (German, Russian), and upon the Heideggerian tradition that casts oblique light upon something of that history, the speaker muses that

I see we still don't know
how to express the *I*, solus, the *eye*
into which all experience flows.

(p. 19)

The familiar pun "I/eye" restores us to the former ground of Sampson's writing, the relation between identity and perception, but now by realizing the limited usefulness of such linguistic consonance. The poem rehearses a series of potential assertions of the "I" against circumstance: the "lying" that the populace had to engage in to counter the Communist regime; a childhood memory of an act of disobedience; a claim by the French theorist Hélène Cixous that "the body writes white." Yet all of these are variously unsatisfactory to the expression of a self-hood at this moment in this location:

I'm a visitor here.
So are these eight—nine—wild swans
gliding out of the shining water
towards the jetty.

(p. 21)

This is a clever inversion. "The Wild Swans at Coole," in which the Irish poet W. B. Yeats counts the annual visitors to the parkland's lake, is a classic proclamation of male at-homeness and dominance within a specific landscape, wearily making the annual migration of the swans

a marker of his own life history. Although "The Wild Swans at Coole" is freighted by fear at its end, uncertainty as to where the swans will be "when I awake some day / To find they have flown away," the spotlight remains firmly upon the sense of the poet within a fixed location (p. 181).

Yeats is, hilariously, sure of the accuracy of his count of the number of swans on the lake ("nine and fifty"). Mockingly, Sampson slips up over hers. Where Yeats registers anxiety in the freedom of the swans to disappear from his view (and his poem) when they fly away, Sampson, in contrast, as a "visitor" to this place, relishes the metaphorical potential of such transience and finds in it a statement of her own situation in the world and in her writing: "I dwell on water / [...] whose instinct is motion" (pp. 21–22). Although her paradoxical at-homeness in such unreliability is seemingly ratified by a male (the final lines point us to a father who aphoristically favors "change"), "At Kasmu" establishes a female poetic out of the fluency that is able to move in a philosophically and literarily informed way between various models and possibilities. This is the "rough" and contingent resolution the complex music of the poem leads us toward.

Other poems in the book draw analogies for this poetic in ways that are by now familiar to the concerted reader of Sampson's poetry. "First Theory of Movement," for instance, links movement to "light. / Flex a bare leg—like this" (p. 14). Poetry as a form of presence; poetry as process. "Light" is "a mineral strain / flowing through [...] eyes" (p. 14). "Amal and the Night Visitors" amusingly, but also movingly, reprises the cultural implications of the fact that "we have no settled home" (p. 47). "We" are gathered up into any space or analogy, but this has harsh and resonant human implications, since "we"

are singing pilgrims
under Lebanon cedars and under the bare standing
  elms of
Somerset, he breaks your heart

(p. 47)

A remembered childhood emotional encounter cuts across and through the rather complacent, if politically correct, adult delight at the liberation and democratic equivalences of the modern world.

Although *Rough Music* delights in movement, in and for its own sake, it also counts something of the cost of unsettledness, the sense that it is possible to become lost through it. The book as a whole, in fact, is haunted by what several poems call "lost girls," girls who, in mythology or the imagination, have been abused and abandoned by men (such poems recall the Ovidian references in Sampson's first work). This interlinking thread across the collection begins in the sequence "Zeus to Juno," where the master god relates (in rather Lawrencian fashion) some of his sexual achievements to his deploring wife. At one point, however, the seemingly neatly contained mythical sequence breaks into shocking contemporary reference:

On a summer day
the lost girl hums—
Kelly, Sarah, Jo, changed
into parable [...]

(p. 13)

The sequence and subsequent poems are a confrontation of the "lost boys" myth that underwrites such literary fantasies as J. M. Barrie's *Peter Pan*, with its charming escapes into worlds of magic and adventure. Sampson's "lost girls" are the battered victims of rape ("body agape"), discarded in the countryside by their male assailants. "Rough" music takes on a harsher common suffering here.

The book's title sequence, "Rough Music or Songs Without Tunes," recasts the myth of Orpheus and Eurydice in the Underworld, ruled by Hades, as a miniature drama. Orpheus emerges as a wan lover, ineffectually lamenting the loss of his wife to the Underworld, and Hades as a tough who equates to the rapists in others of these poems, in a chilling commentary upon what "home" amounts to:

I brought her home—
I bring them all home—

the bruised, the crushed

(p. 26)

While Eurydice shares something of Orpheus's soft-centered view of love, there is also a steeliness to her view that love itself is an "eclipse," is insufficient for fulfilling female potential ("Every girl wants to be free"; p. 27). The sequence ends in unexpected and operatic fashion, however, with Eurydice conforming to a typical Romantic conceit, and going to meet her Death like a lover.

Other poems in the book, and perhaps most notably "The Door," are more adept at handling the complexity of culture clashes and their gender implications. Seemingly adopting a folk-music soul, during a visit through the countryside ("familiar songs / about lost girls, babies who disappear"; p. 38), this sporadically rhyming or half-rhyming tour-de-force rapidly and comically finds itself running out of energy and resource. A visit to a service station seems to reduce everything to the banal, or to a hodgepodge of clichés, and the speaker is forced to confront the fact that this kind of pastoralism has limited running time for the modern poet ("At this rate // you'll have no story left, / just a paraphrase"; p. 40). It is the city that "compels," and that dissipates the "memory" of such Romantic lurches into "nature" as the poem had originally seemingly sought to perform. Rather falsely, we are left to feel, the last stanza seeks to assert that "buried tunes / like grief" (rough music, in other words), do continue even within the city streets (p. 40). This ending manifests recourse to notions of the primitive correlative to moments in modernist writing. Virginia Woolf's Mrs. Dalloway, for instance, hears an "ancient song" sung by a "battered old woman" next to Regent's Park Tube Station (p. 106). In the briefer space of a lyric, Sampson finds it difficult convincingly to posit such breadth of historical and anthropological potential, and this makes for deliberate but questioning awkwardness here, and in other of these poems.

Rough Music as a whole, therefore, might come with time to seem a rewind and review of her career by a poet firmly established and assured in her authority "Nel Mezzo," as the title of one poem has it—in the middle of her life and with an established sense of the complexities and fluency of her potential. This now comes with typical caveats and costs, and with amusing self-denigration, but is a joyous moment for the poetry to expand out from, since, as "Deep Water" puts it, "It seems to me / you're on the high tide of life" (p. 49).

Selected Bibliography

WORKS OF FIONA SAMPSON

POETRY AND ESSAYS

Picasso's Men. Newbury, U.K.: Phoenix Press, 1993.

Folding the Real. Bridgend, U.K.: Seren, 2001.

Hotel Casino. London: Aark Arts, 2004.

The Distance Between Us. Bridgend, U.K.: Seren, 2005.

Common Prayer. Manchester, U.K.: Carcanet, 2007.

On Listening. Cambridge, U.K.: Salt, 2007.

Rough Music. Manchester, U.K.: Carcanet, 2010.

Music Lessons. Newcastle-upon-Tyne: Bloodaxe, 2011.

NONFICTION

Writing: Self and Reflexivity. With Celia Hunt. Basingstoke, U.K.: Palgrave Macmillan, 1986; 3rd ed., 2006.

The Healing Word: A Practical Guide to Poetry and Personal Development Activities. London: Poetry Society, 1999.

Poetry Writing: The Expert Guide. London: Robert Hale, 2009.

VOLUMES EDITED OR TRANSLATED

Creative Writing in Health and Social Care. Editor. With a foreword by Christina Patterson. London and Philadelphia: Jessica Kingsley, 2004.

Evening Brings Everything Back. By Jaan Kaplinski. Translator and editor. Tarset, U.K.: Bloodaxe Books, 2004.

A Fine Line: New Poetry from Eastern and Central Europe. Edited with Jean Boase-Beier and Alexandra Büchler. Todmorden, U.K.: Arc, 2004.

OTHER SOURCES

Herbert, George. *The Complete English Poems*. Edited by John Tobin. Harmondsworth, U.K.: Penguin, 1991.

Rees-Jones, Deryn, ed. *Modern Women Poets*. Newcastle, U.K.: Bloodaxe, 2005.

Stevenson, Anne. "Defending the Freedom of the Poet." *Contemporary Women's Poetry: Reading/Writing/Practice*. Edited by Alison Mark and Deryn Rees-Jones. Houndmills, U.K.: Macmillan, 2000.

Woolf, Virginia. *Mrs Dalloway*. Edited by Claire Tomalin. Oxford: Oxford University Press, 1992.

Yeats, W. B. *The Poems*. Edited by Daniel Albright. London: Dent, 1992.

COLIN THUBRON

(1939—)

Abby Mims

COLIN THUBRON IS most well-known as a travel writer who breaks barriers between the traveler and native cultures, melding with the places he visits through intimate conversation, exhaustive cultural research, and far-flung local adventures. In a time when most writers are drawn to the specific or unique in an attempt to find a niche that has not been filled, Thubron instead has widened his stance in an attempt to understand the largest of both China and the Soviet Union. In doing so, he has gone so far as to learn both Mandarin and Russian, and as a result, observed the interviewer Jeremy Atiyah, "Russian drunks, Siberian fishermen, Uzbeki poets, Mongolian nomads, Shanghai Buddhists and Cantonese restaurateurs (to name but a few) have all enjoyed shooting the breeze over the years with this remarkable Englishman" (p. 2). He broke out critically and popularly with *Among the Russians* (1983), a recounting of a ten-thousand-mile trek through a country that had both terrified and fascinated him as a young boy. His admitted obsession with Russia, Asia, the Middle East, and China propelled his work for the next twenty years and produced five additional volumes of travel narrative. While the names of his English peers such as Jonathan Raban, Paul Theroux, and Bill Bryson are easily recognized outside of Britain, Thubron is not a household name to wider audiences—this seems purely a function of publicity, not talent. Thubron has produced thirteen books of travel writing over the span of his career, gaining him a fellowship to the Royal Society of Literature in 1969 and the Hawthornden Prize and the Thomas Cook Travel Book Award for *Behind the Wall: A Journey Through China* in 1987.

Thubron never carries a camera with him on his journeys, relying only on the power of his words to give us a glimpse into foreign and distant worlds. He takes copious notes in the roughly four months he spends traveling in a given region, yet it usually takes him three or four years to complete a book on the subject. He is considered a master of the genre, in terms of expansive and poetic prose, which provides a sense of history and place, as he infuses the narratives with intimate tales of the people he meets along the way. Despite the fact that he has been criticized at times for maintaining something of a reporter's distance from his subject matter, most readers feel that there is not a complete barrier of objectivity in his writing; sharing as he does his own moments of outrage, sorrow, and shame. Thubron himself seems determined to break through any perceived omniscient objectivity by occasionally breaking up his narratives into different perspectives, shifting from first person to third and so forth, in an attempt to show that the writer is never an all-knowing entity. He is, however, careful not to let much of his own life bleed onto the page, even as those around him are sharing intimate details of their lives.

When Thubron is not traveling or writing about his travels, he is composing fiction, often alternating between the two genres. He has been quoted as saying that the art of travel writing is far easier than that of fiction, simply given that nonfiction is based on outside observations, whereas fiction is a catalog of one's inner world. His fiction is less well known than his travel writing but has been reviewed favorably for many years, beginning with his searing exploration of mental illness, *A Cruel Madness* (1984), which won him the Pen/Macmillan Silver Pen Award. His fiction is intense and psychologically demanding, and it is never without an exploration of the deep themes of life: love, loss, death, and morality. It has been labeled decidedly "British" in its precise and restrained manner, even when Thubron is writing about explosive emotional issues. Often, his protagonists struggle with romantic love that appears hopelessly tied to obsession and tragedy. Reviewers have commented that not only is he unafraid to go to physically dangerous places to write his travel books, he is equally undaunted about going to strange and risky emotional places in his novels.

Thubron was born in London, on June 14, 1939, to an army officer, Brigadier Gerald Ernest Thubron, and Evelyn Dryden Thubron, a homemaker. He grew up wanting to write, and he often recalls his relation on his mother's side to the seventeenth-century poet John Dryden, the first poet laureate of England. Until he was seven, the family lived in a rural area of southeast England; Thubron was sent to boarding school at age eight. The same year the family was relocated to Ottawa, Canada, given that Gerald Thubron was a military attaché to the country. Thubron spent only summers there, but this geographical change had a deep impact on his life. Crossing the Atlantic at least once a year seemed to have stirred an early fascination for travel, and exposure to the North American landscape and culture was a decided contrast to the somber post–World War II English society he had become accustomed to.

In 1953 he enrolled in Eton college, where he excelled in history and English but failed mathematics. He left Eton at age eighteen, knowing only that he wanted to write. His first job in publishing was at Hutchinson in London, where he stayed for four years, eventually becoming an assistant editor. After leaving Hutchinson he began to travel, producing documentaries for BBC television in Turkey, Morocco, and Japan. He returned to publishing for a year in 1964, working in New York for Macmillan, leaving to write full-time in 1965.

He traveled to Damascus soon after, using his life savings to live there for a year and delve into the culture of one of the oldest known cities in the world. He achieved success with his resulting book, *Mirror to Damascus* (1967), and he went on to explore Lebanon and Jerusalem dur-

ing the next few years. Two successive books were published about his travels, *The Hills of Adonis* (1968) and *Jerusalem* (1969), respectively. *Journey into Cyprus* followed in 1975, and then Thubron tried his hand at fiction, producing *The God in the Mountain* (1977) and *Emperor* (1978).

Things shifted some for Thubron in 1978, when a serious car accident left him with a fractured spine and many months of imposed leisure. He decided during that time that his next trips would be to places that he had been taught to fear, primarily Russia and China. A few years later, he embarked on a ten-thousand-mile journey through Russia during Leonid Brezhnev's rule, which resulted in *Among the Russians,* which was soon followed by *Behind the Wall: A Journey Through China* and *The Lost Heart of Asia* (1994). Several years passed before he returned to Russia, this time venturing into the mysterious and barren land of Siberia. *In Siberia* (1999) is a groundbreaking volume of work, demystifying a region that had been little explored by writers from the West. He returned to China nearly fifteen years after *Behind the Wall* to complete *Shadow of the Silk Road* (2006), wherein he traced an ancient two-thousand-mile-long trading route from Xian, China, to the Mediterranean In between these various treks and explorations, Thubron also produced five well-reviewed novels: *A Cruel Madness, Falling* (1989), *Turning Back the Sun* (1991), *Distance* (1996), and *To the Last City* (2002).

EARLY TRAVEL NARRATIVES

Critics often comment that Thubron's first travel narrative, *Mirror to Damascus* in 1967, is perhaps his most personal, as his affection for the city and its people are evident in nearly every line. Thubron himself called the manuscript a labor of love, and it is expressed via his relationships with the Lebanese people he meets throughout the book, from depressed Frenchman to local goatherders. His now-famous gift for striking up intimate conversations was stilted only slightly in this region when tensions mounted between the Arabs and Israelis, and as an Englishman, he was assumed to have Israeli sympathies. Although the people of this ancient place draw him in, its history also fuels his fascination, especially Damascus's status as the world's oldest continuously inhabited city. Syria and Damascus both have a rich and sordid past, given how many conquerers have ruled over this land: Egyptians, Assyrians, Babylonians, Persians, Arabs, Mongols, Turks, and, most recently, the French, from whom Syria gained independence in 1946. Thubron capitalizes on these colorful progressions, managing to weave a varied and complicated history throughout his personal vignettes, which serve as the core of the book.

During his research in 1965, Thubron lived for several months with a Christian-Arab family, yet in order to get a sense of the country's various cultures and religions, he also visits its Jewish and Muslim settlements. Instead of using a car or a bus, Thubron travels by bike to gain a tactile sense of the chaos of the landscape; roads twist, overlap, and often appear to have no traffic rules whatsoever. By traversing these sections of the city in such an intimate manner, Thubron records the changes from one section to the next by recording the alterations that have taken place from culture to culture and age to age. In doing so, he details how the people of Damascus have taken pieces from the cultures of all their conquerers and made them into their own tools and commerce, including the ivory and fabric trades and the legendary Damascus sword blades, polished to a such perfection that it is said one can use them as both a weapon and a mirror.

Critics also note that although Thubron was traveling before the Arab-Israeli War of June 5–10, 1967, the subsequent conflict changed the tone of his book considerably. In 1965, given mounting tensions, the British government implored him to leave the country, but he refused. Although Thubron left the country before violence ensued, this historical event made the present situation in Syria more important than his own desire to linger romantically on its past. He manages these issues successfully, ending the book with themes of resurrection and rebirth, perhaps as much a reflection of his desire for the country as for himself.

Journey into Cyprus (1975), Thubron's foray into Grecian culture, earned his membership into the Royal Society of Literature. This book details his six-hundred-mile trek in 1972 across the island and back, crossing multiple borders where Greece and Turkey were battling. Turkey would invade the country and divide its ethnicities a scant two years later. Thubron ambitiously chooses to walk this route both to be close to the people of Greece as well as to honor the land's history and travel it as previous generations would have. Much of his journey is solitary, as he negotiates his way on little-known paths through farms and pastures used only by farmers and sheepherders. Notwithstanding the fact that the British colonized Cyprus until 1960, most natives greet him as nothing more than a harmless oddity and welcome him into their homes.

In true Thubron style, he manages to find the most colorful people along the way. During his stays in monasteries, flophouses, and a pigsty he meets lute players, fortune tellers, lapsed priests, and a handful of Syrian prostitutes. He skillfully weaves in their stories with descriptions of the beauty of the ancient monument he encounters, describing Roman sewers and a castle once inhabited by Crusaders with an awe that permeates the page.

AMONG THE RUSSIANS

Thubron is most well-known for his influential and highly popular travel book *Among the Russians*, which appeared in 1983 and was republished in 1984 as *Where Nights Are Longest: Travels by Car Through Western Russia*. He embarked on this ten-thousand-mile journey in Moscow, traveling through Leningrad, the Baltic states, and the Caucasus, to regions on the Turkish border and the Ukraine. The spark of his curiosity with Russia began in childhood, as he recalls being afraid of the staggering landmass for as long as he can remember, noting that its topography took up a large portion of a wall in his elementary school classroom. It seems to be the country's massiveness that disturbs him the most, as even when he is traveling deep within

COLIN THUBRON

its center he remarks on an overwhelming feeling of having barely left its edges.

As in most of his travelogues, Thubron balances his own narrative with historical context, and *Among the Russians* focuses on the failure of Communism and the aftereffects of the Second World War. He visited Russia near the end of the Brezhnev era, close the peak of Communism's power, a time when the Russian people had been left with little choice aside from adhering to a blind, steadfast patriotism and a belief system that sought to eradicate any trace of opposition. He captures much of the emptiness of modern Russian life, the endless food lines, unspoken tension, and a pervasive lack of spirituality. There is little hope, and in such bleak circumstances, Thubron observes that what the people are left to do without freedom is simply to drink.

Outrageous stories of drinking and drunkenness are peppered throughout the book, and although Thubron observes that the amount of alcohol consumed here has done nothing but increase the level of domestic abuse, car accidents, infant mortality, and murder, he feels if he is to understand the Russians at all, he must participate. (He does, however, refuse to get drunk, pouring liquor into plants and on the floor so as to keep his wits about himself.) In the case of *Among the Russians,* this often leaves him in the company of dubious travel guides, many of whom he guesses are spies or con-men. Those around him seem to have no sense of restraint, causing Thubron to label vodka as Russia's largest blessing and its largest curse, as it provides its people with oblivion for short periods of time but renders its imbibers relatively senseless.

Some critics labeled Thubron as somewhat naive in this course of his travels, noting the trust he provides his various guides and drivers. After all, he was a high-profile Westerner traveling in a Communist state, and, to this end, Thubron's sense of unease does build some as his narrative develops. His paranoia is confirmed when the KGB arrests him after searching his room, and he near loses a portion of his manuscript notes to officials at the border. In the end, for all his preparation and perceived understanding of the country, Thubron finds himself nearly over-

whelmed by its complications and largess. Overall, *Among the Russians* was well-received by critics, who made note of Thubron's deeply observed insights of the country and its people.

BEHIND THE WALL: A JOURNEY THROUGH CHINA

In the fall of 1985, Thubron embarked on his next ambitious expedition, traversing China by bus, train, and plane with nothing but a backpack to his name. He explored areas from the coastal cities to the edge of the Gobi Desert, and those experiences, combined with an earlier stay on the continent, form *Behind the Wall: A Journey Through China.* The book, popular among readers and critics alike, earned him a Hawthornden Prize and the Thomas Cook Travel Book Award in 1987. Many critics later compared Thubron's account of China to Paul Theroux's *Riding the Iron Rooster* (1988), as both men traveled to China during the same time frame. They often note that while Theroux is sometimes cold and restricted, Thubron writes a nuanced account of a complicated culture and continent.

Shedding the guides and translators of his Victorian predecessors and most travel writers, Thubron goes it alone, using his rudimentary knowledge of Mandarin. He stays in rat-infested hotels, sleeps outside, and eats meagerly. Although he attempts to blend in to Chinese society, he is constantly scrutinized and badgered with questions from Chinese natives. His blond hair and tall stature and the fact that he is traveling solo (and without a camera) make him a prime target for scrutiny, and all the more an outsider. Thubron finds himself thoroughly exhausted from all the attention, and the attention highlights both the regimented togetherness that the Chinese take for granted and provides a case study in aspects of this particular culture's impermeability. At one point, he grows so tired of answering questions about the myths of the West and his own life that he begins to lie to those he encounters, making up a wife and children back in England. This does not mean there is not a sense of joy or adventure in the narrative, as Thubron manages to sleep in Mao's bed in Shaoshan, reach the peak of Mount Emei, celebrate a new monument to Confucius in Qufu, and (after an extensive journey) find the grave of one of his favorite poets, Ki Bai. All the while, he gives a history of these places that is informative and precise, yet rich with rumination.

In the face of his extreme outsider status, Thubron resists falling back on any kind of stereotypes based on his own preconceived notions or beliefs. Perhaps in an attempt to counteract his own prejudices, he presents the reader with individuals from all walks of life. He may talk to a Chinese woman who says that most husbands there still beat their wives, but the conversation will be juxtaposed with the image of a man pushing his wife around a park in her wheelchair. He feels for a grieving widower and comforts a younger man with a broken heart. Still, there is a pervasive shadow of great sameness and repression in what he records: endless crowds of men dressed in black and white, the collective blankness in the looks he receives, the complete lack of political commentary from those he encounters. While this may be just the discomfort of the foreign traveler, the critic John Gittings writes that Thubron's observations may have foreshadowed the uprising that occurred a few years later, writing that he "tapped a deeper truth. One of the most liberating features of the democracy movement in 1989 was that it redeemed so many older Chinese from the shame and self-disgust that they felt ... The cynical, shoving self-interest of the ordinary Beijinger was discarded" (p. 175).

As a result, much like *Among the Russians*, Communism becomes one of the main focuses of *Behind the Wall*. Thubron vigorously disapproves of this form of ideology, and notes its various limits on freedom, from set ages of marriage and the limit of one child per couple to the way the government decides where citizens live and work. The disintegration of any artistic culture in particular via the Cultural Revolution of 1966–1976 seems to be Thubron's understandable Achilles' heel, noting that no "elites" were safe, whether they were doctors, teachers, or scientists. He does not understate the terror of the Maoist regime, which not only tortured and exiled the nation's elites but attempted to kill any form of culture or beauty, including pets and personal gardens. He records the destruction of numerous historical monuments and artifacts, commenting ironically that those left standing are overrun by Chinese tourists taking photos of one another, without bothering to record the magnificence of their surroundings.

Despite the trials and difficulties the Chinese people have endured, Thubron does not leave the reader without hope for China. He recounts the slow resurgence of religious monuments, including Muslim mosques and Buddhist monasteries. There are no easy answers, however, and the book ends with Thubron standing at the edge of classical China, staring out into Gobi Desert and its endless, barren horizon.

THE LOST HEART OF ASIA

Thubron embarked to central Asia during the first six months the USSR was dissolved, the perfect time for a travel writer as the local population was suddenly open to talking about their hopes and expectations after such a radical shift in government and basic ways of life. By pulling out of central Asia for good, the Soviet Union left the world asking questions about what would evolve in terms of the region's cultural, religious, and personal identity. *The Lost Heart of Asia* (1994) attempts to provide some of those answers, for both the region's inhabitants and for Thubron personally, as this trek represented for him the "missing piece" of his decades-long obsession with the European Soviet Union, China, and the Muslim world. Many critics consider *The Lost Heart of Asia* a worthy sequel to Thubron's former efforts, praising him for his grasp of the history of the region as well as for the way he embraces the mysteries within it by drawing out personal stories and opinions from the locals he encounters. As Dervla Murphy writes, "It would have been easy for him [Thubron] to write an excellent book based entirely on a journey through Central Asia's past. He has, however, set himself a far harder task: to present Central Asia now as well as then" (p. 44).

The region has always been a complex combination of culture and identity, placed at the crossroads of Soviet Marxism and the mysticism of Islam. It was originally divided by Stalin into five countries: Kazakhstan, Turkmenistan, Tajikistan, Kirghistan, and Uzbekistan. Its borders were drawn arbitrarily, much the same way Africa was by its colonizers, with no regard to tribal regions or ethnicity. In terms of presenting this kind of complex history, Thubron manages to undo the myth that this region of Asia is entirely wild and remote, and instead he links its past not only to modern China but to India, Europe, and the Near East. Its history is also quite bloody and dramatic, filled with the legends of Genghis Khan and Alexander the Great. Yet once the Mongolian Empire was broken apart in the fifteenth century, and the Silk Road trade routes destroyed, this region no longer threatened the Western world and it was easily conquered by Russia in the nineteenth century.

Thubron travels through these countries by bus, train, and communal taxi and in such a carefully plotted and detailed manner that these states become real places to the reader, both their beauty and ugliness revealed. Most locals had never seen a Westerner before Thubron, but given his adaptable ease and ability to speak Russian, he is accepted everywhere and in many cases taken in as a kind of intimate compatriot. On his part, he accepts any and all invitations, from weddings to an ill-fated dinner involving a course of sheep's head. Thubron takes all of it in stride, and for the middle portion of his journey he travels with Oman, a guide who brings him even deeper into the fragmented cultures he is trying to understand. The people he meets are as varied as any he has encountered on his travels; they range from stranded Russian professionals and Bukhara Jews to underground Sufi sects who are just beginning to enter mainstream society. His chance meetings are vast and provide a depth of understanding to this much misunderstood and, at the time, much forgotten part of the world.

There are some readers, however, who have criticized Thubron's unwillingness to include his own opinions about the plight of those he encounters, as he steadfastly refuses to weigh in on their often dire situations, let alone offer any solutions. Despite this kind of criticism, none of the critics denies the power of Thubron's prose in this volume of travel writing, evident in its opening paragraphs. Thubron records what he sees and feels while flying over Turkmenistan:

> The sea had fallen behind us, and we were flying above a desert of dream-like immensity. Its sands melted into the sky, corroding every horizon in a colourless light. Nothing suggested that were anywhere, or even moving at all. The last solid objects in the universe were the wing-tips of the plane. ... unconsciously I had gone on feeling that somewhere in the core of the greatest land-mass on earth, beyond more familiar nations, there pulsed another country, half forgotten, to which the rest were all peripheral.
>
> (p. 1)

Powerful too, are his own reflections on what it is to be a traveler, and near the end of the book he delves into what transpires as one starts to see a foreign city as less foreign and as partly your own. He experiences his own form of homesickness at times as well, when a memory suddenly strikes and his loneliness is palpable. Thubron seems to be drawing a small parallel between himself an the people of central Asia as they collectively struggle to find religion, meaning, and a way of remaking their lives, searching for comfort in the familiar that is nowhere in sight.

IN SIBERIA

It seems fitting that Thubron's final foray into Russia, the land that intrigued him for more than two decades, would take place entirely in Siberia. Given what the name alone of such a frozen and desolate place has come to symbolize, it is no surprise that Thubron opens *In Siberia* (1999) in part by taking stock of his personal life. To wit, he is sixty, unmarried, and without children. It appears that by going into one of the world's most remote and forbidden places, Thubron hopes to not only find answers about life in Russia after Communism but also answers as to why he has spent the bulk of his life in such outwardly hostile and difficult places. Indeed, critics expressed mystification about Thubron's choice of Siberia:

he is no longer young, and what could be more uncomfortable than traveling into literally the coldest place on earth, where millions of people were worked to death in Joseph Stalin's death camps? But as Thubron told Jeremy Atiyah in 1999:

> When I'm researching for a book, I'm not fussed about comfort. When you travel out of fascination, of course you push yourself. Your own comfort drops away. What depresses me on my trips is if I fail to find that old shaman I want to talk to, not being cold or uncomfortable. In Siberia, discomfort is part of the personality of the land.
>
> (p. 2)

Many viewed *In Siberia* as the denouement of a travel writing career that had spanned more than three decades. For Thubron, it appears that Siberia was instead the ultimate challenge of his already daring career, a final foray into a forbidden territory. After all, before the West won the cold war, only Russians could travel to Siberia, and then as now, little is known about the region beyond rumor and innuendo. In undertaking this volume, Thubron traveled nearly fifteen thousand miles across a country larger that Europe and the United States combined, hoping to find some unifying device or common thread. What he experienced instead was cities in shambles, choked by pollution and full of disillusioned inhabitants who want nothing else than to get out of this hell on earth. In place of a new world order, Siberia has only uncontrolled private business, misguided nostalgia for the czars, and pockets of Orthodox fundamentalism.

Critics raved about this volume of Thubron's work for its prose and its observations of Russian culture, in addition to what Thubron finally reveals about his own intimate history. We are privy to personal details about his teenage years and given a window into this seasoned writer's feelings about his own mortality. As usual, he does not research this strange territory the way others might, by simply exploring the region geographically. He instead climbs down the rungs of Siberian society, exploring one of the key points of the narrative, Thubron's attempt to find some form of religious faith in this "new" Siberia. Much of the optimism Thubron might have hoped to find, however, is frozen among natives whose reindeer herding has gone the way of acid rain and whose children start drinking vodka at the age of twelve. (The bleakness does not stop there, as motor oil is the second drink of choice among those who cannot afford alcohol.) Much of the book is in turn dedicated to the disillusionment and lack of hope Thubron witnesses, and within these pages, he points again and again to the failures of Communism.

Yet even among all this suffering and confusion, Thubron finds a few bright spots in the frozen landscape: a former KGB officer turned Baptist minister, a Polish priest finding Catholic converts, shamans and Buddhist lamas peppered throughout remote villages. Thubron scrapes together enough hope that the critic David Pryce-Jones remarks, "He wanted to find some unity or shape to human destiny, and he has done so. Fear of Russia is a thing of the past, and pity for the living and the dead instead fills this book with the purpose and beauty of prayer" (p. 66).

Many critics predictably compared *In Siberia* to *Among the Russians*, usually with a favorable outcome. Thubron is both older and wiser in his expectations of foreign cultures, and many felt he had expanded his writing style beyond the stereotypical label of the repressed Englishman. Perhaps the biggest shift in Thubron's perception seems to be that his long-ago fears have morphed into compassion, and he has a newfound desire to fully understand a people who will forever symbolize the brutal degradation of Communism.

SHADOW OF THE SILK ROAD

Despite critical assumptions that Thubron was in the twilight of his career when *In Siberia* was published, the publication of *Shadow of the Silk Road* (2006) demonstrated that he was not necessarily going to be slowing down any time soon. In 2003, Thubron decided to traverse the roughly seven-thousand-mile length of an ancient, nearly thirty-five-hundred-year-old trade route most commonly known as the Silk Road. The eight-month journey (interrupted for nearly a year because of war in northern Afghanistan between the Taliban and the United States) took him from the road's origins in Xian, China, through to its end on the shores of the Mediterranean Sea. In addition to the hurdles to travel created by the mounting tensions in Afghanistan, 2003 was the height of the SARS, or yellow pneumonia, epidemic, a time when international travel to China had almost completely ceased. None of these factors daunted Thubron, who, true to form, goes on to eschew all forms of luxurious travel once he reaches China; on the Silk Road, he relies on public buses, the rare hired taxi, and, mainly, his own two feet.

The Silk Road is hailed as the greatest trade route ever in the world, and it can be used to trace the paths of civilization's armies and religions, not to mention the expanse of products it provided in all directions. Silk, gunpowder, paper, the stirrup, and the bridle traveled to Western civilization, while to the East it garnered figs, olives, chariots, and the harp. The "road" itself is more like a series of roads and other means of travel that together served as a kind of relay route for trade; goods were handed off from one person to the next, so despite this transfer of products, cultures never came face to face with one another. This is not to say that pieces of each culture's language, philosophies, and ways of life weren't sometimes attached to the goods that were traded. Thubron demonstrates this phenomenon by describing a mosque where Mandarin mingles with Arabic on the walls, Buddhist cave drawings that include Hindu images, and an archaeological site in Afghanistan that yields an array of cultural artifacts ranging from Egyptian glass to a bust of the Greek god Hercules.

Traversing the Silk Road is for Thubron a key element in understanding the development of modern civilization, while learning how such an important piece of history became virtually extinct. The road closed down slowly over time up until the mid-fifteenth century, when central Asia began to split between the Turks and the Mongols and the Ming Dynasty closed its ports and ceased trading with the outside world. Even as recently as the late 1980s, Thubron's journey would have been impossible, given that portions of the routes in China and Russia were entirely closed, with Afghanistan impassible because of

its ongoing war with the Soviets. In this light, Thubron's timing in 2003 was idyllic in certain ways, as despite the aforementioned obstacles, the road was coming back to life in certain areas. This provided Thubron with a unique opportunity to explore the ways these cultures were opening themselves back up to the world.

The people he meets are as varied as the cultures he explores, particularly when traversing through many places he had previously visited in *The Lost Heart of Asia*. Much of what he records as he travels through the vestiges of Stalin's Russia is nostalgia for the past, along with a longing for the type of structure that Soviet rule afforded the people of Kyrgyzstan, Uzbekistan, Tajikistan, Afghanistan, and Iran. Despite the brutality of Stalin's rule, many people Thubron met along his route still long for the older ways of life or at least some kind of discernible governmental order. One of the most incredible people he encounters is a grandmother whose husband and father were killed by Stalin, yet she still idolizes the brutal dictator. Iran seems to be the country left most confused, particularly in the aftermath of the Islamic revolution. Most Iranians Thubron encounters rely on their religions passions as a means of identity, but at the same time they are frustrated by the ideals of their theocratic government. In a addition, they appear to revile the Western world as much as they are fascinated by it. Thubron uses the example of a young man named Hassed to expand on this paradox; Hassed is obsessed with the chastity of women in his own country, but meanwhile he cannot get enough of the music and videos of Britney Spears.

Thubron's travels through China stand in stark contrast to his travels in the Middle East. It has been fourteen years since he has visited the country, and he is overwhelmed by the explosion of commerce, taken aback by the banks of looming skyscrapers and endless construction sites. He notes that all traces of neighborhood gathering places have been eradicated, and the *hutong* courtyards that remain are reserved for paying tourists, not locals. Thubron does not use the term "globalization" once, yet he seems to be recording its imprints at every turn. Thubron recounts a particularly interesting encounter with a Chinese professor of English, whom he'd met nearly twenty years before, that seems to speak directly to his own concerns about the country's exploding growth. The professor states that neither the English language or the American culture has the ability to translate in any real way to China, and the influx of this foreign culture will eventually erase the essence that *is* China; therefore the professor doesn't really believe in what he's teaching. This view is difficult for Thubron to fathom, particularly given the professor's previous resistance to the Cultural Revolution, to that era's violent oppression and devastating censorship, which forbade any foreign influence on China.

Whatever the ultimate result of the globalization Thubron witnessed, for centuries, the Silk Road served as a tether tying cultures and peoples together. In revealing the past and present of the Silk Road to the reader, he teaches us that no culture or country is ever fixed, that evolution is constant until the national or cultural entity is finished, disappeared, or dead. Sometimes this happens in a way that cannot provide us with the answers we so want in order to understand. In exploring the old site of the city of Khotan, China, Thubron has this revelation:

> Suddenly I came on a heap of skeletons. Their skulls gleamed among scattered shin-bones and rib-cages. ... Soon I was labouring up over a blackened litter of legs and arms and pates. ... the entire slope, I realised, was man-made: I was ascending a hill of compacted corpses. ... I saw a man in the fields. ... What was this place? ... He did not know. ... In rustic Mandarin he recounted a garbled myth of Buddhists butchering Muslims at Friday prayer. So the place opened in my journey like a dark space, awaiting explanation, which never came.
>
> (p. 134)

Many critics commented that in *Shadow of Silk Road,* even as Thubron wrestles with his own demons and need for answers, his writing never lapses into the realm of cliché or takes on the tone of the all-knowing Westerner. He is instead a constant, sympathetic listener and, in turn, a consummate recorder of the world around him. Fittingly, this 2006 book ties together Thubron's decades-long journey exploring this part of the world. With *Among the Russians, Behind the Wall,* and *Shadow of Silk Road,* he has linked for us the paths of civilizations and continents, leaving them to function as one long road to the present.

EARLY FICTION

Thubron wrote two novels early in his career, *The God in the Mountain* (1977) and *Emperor* (1978), neither of which were popularly received yet are reflected on as critically successful forays into the genre. *The God in the Mountain* is based on his travels into the eastern Mediterranean, and it sets up a complex dynamic among its characters, including the impact of modernization on an ancient culture and the aspects of violence that permeate cultural imperialism. It follows the story of Julian Alastos, who is half-Greek and half-English, who has returned to his native home of Kalepia after receiving an education as a mining engineer in England. He joins The Company, a copper-mining operation, which is run poorly by Americans. Alastos has lofty ideals and hopes that this booming industry will improve the lives of his Greek compatriots. When The Company wants to build another site that will not only destroy the land around it but also destroy a shrine to an ancient saint, Alastos must choose between tradition and modern advancements.

In this first work of fiction, Thubron wrestles with large themes while putting his protagonist to several moral tests, and as a result, the novel is filled with a sense of foreboding. Alastos is set up as a perfect man with impeccable morals, who must choose between a cultural loyalty to his country or the potential economic advances of industry in his homeland. When Alastos does decide to reject The Company, and quits to become a teacher in order to better effect his fellow Kalepians, he is immediately disillusioned. His pupils are children both of miners and of fisherman, and as a result, they cannot reach an agreement in terms of The Company's presence in their country. In frustration, he briefly joins a radical group that is set on destroying The Company, helping to blow up a bridge that inadvertently kills an engineer. This is the turning point in the narrative for Alastos, as he realizes he cannot meet his goals with violence. In a final act of irony, he is killed in an effort to stop the two sides from their violent confrontation.

The following year, Thubron wrote *Emperor* (1978), a wholly different book. Here, he focuses on a four-month period in 312 C.E., during Constantine's successful invasion of Italy, reconstructing the circumstances by which the emperor converted to Christianity. The story is told through a series of found documents and letters, which contain various perspectives, including those from Constantine's journal; letters from his estranged wife, Fausta; the book of an elder Greek rationalist; and Synesius, the emperor's secretary. From these imagined documents, Thubron creates a vision for Constantine, which compels him to take over Italy under the sign of the cross. When he commits this act, he forsakes his native sun god and eventually conquers the old with the new.

Although Constantine's conversion occurs while going into battle against his rival emperor, Maxentius, Thubron is less concerned with the details of battle than he is with Constantine's spiritual and religious state. As Constantine undergoes his transformation, he is shown conversing with both a Christian and with the rationalist Synesius, with Synesius usually emerging the victor. Synesius is an atheist and believes Christianity to be irrational, so is roundly disappointed when Constantine makes his choice.

In *Emperor,* as in *God in the Mountain,* Thubron does not provide easy choices for his protagonists. While there is no way of proving or legitimizing Constantine's real motives or emotions for converting, Thubron provides readers with an original interpretation of these historical events and perhaps the underpinnings of Constantine's psychology. At the same time, he uses history to examine the differences between emotion and reason, and the opposition that often exists between tradition and innovation.

A CRUEL MADNESS

Thubron's third novel, *A Cruel Madness* (1984), his first to be widely reviewed, is a novel of pas-

sion, insanity, and despair. It is set in Wales at a local insane asylum, narrated by a schoolteacher, Daniel Pashley, who volunteers at the hospital by teaching English classes. His voice is nothing if not calm and rational—that is, until he sees a woman from his past, Sophia, in the hospital garden. Pashley moves to approach her, assuming that she works at the hospital, but he changes his mind once he discovers she is actually a patient there; he reveals to the reader that he is so drawn to her because they had a deep relationship nearly a decade before, albeit unconsummated. From then on, Pashley uses various techniques to access her (unsure that she will know who he is), but for the most part, Sophia ignores him. His attempts at reaching her become more desperate, including asking her to write two accounts of her feelings for him, one loving and one hateful. When it is revealed that Pashley has written both himself, his reliability as a narrator begins to come into question.

Thubron then increases the tension between reality and insanity by weaving together scenes from the past and present, in order to more fully reveal Pashley's passions and obsessions. As the narrative becomes more fragmented, we learn that Pashley himself is a patient at the asylum, not a volunteer. He decides to go off his medication to escape the hospital with Sophia, but when he turns to a psychiatrist for help, he is told she is not a patient there and never has been. His delusions persist, however, as he imagines escaping with Sophia. The novel ends with Pashley waking up in the ward for the acutely disturbed after being found asleep on the fire escape.

Some critics took issue with this particular unreliable narrator, as the book left many wondering what had actually happened—like Daniel's escape attempt and reunion with Sophia—and what remained a figment of his troubled mind. Others found Thubron's willingness to go deeper into an unstable state of being as a bold move to be applauded, comparing his foray into the microworld of a psychiatric hospital comparable to Thomas Mann's *Magic Mountain* (1924) and Ken Kesey's *One Flew over the Cuckoo's Nest* (1962). As the critic Sharon Dirlam writes:

This isn't just another novel about madness and despair. It is a gripping tale of passion. ... not as distant from "normal" as one might think, but simply a look deeper in the mind than most of us dare to probe. Thubron is incurably curious in his investigations of human depths as well as his travels around the world, and the results are spellbinding.

(p. 22)

FALLING

Thubron returned to the theme of obsessive love in his next novel, *Falling* (1989), but in a more classically Romantic sense. The book is the recounting of a year in the life of the journalist Mark Swabey, starting with his imprisonment for manslaughter and ending with his release. Before Swabey went to prison, he was a man in love with two women: Katherine, a stained-glass artist and his longtime, loyal girlfriend, and Clara the Swallow, a high-wire trapeze performer. The two women are meant to stand in contrast to each other, Katherine as the insecure homebody, self-less and devoted to Swabey, while Clara is exotic, exuding a confidence and self-sufficiency that Swabey finds intoxicating.

The novel opens with a description of Swabey's prison life, but his profession, crime, and complicated love life are revealed slowly, in tightly written and fully absorbing prose. Swabey became obsessed with Clara while covering a small circus for the local paper, and although his lust remains somewhat mysterious in origin, Thubron makes clear that much of it has to do with her daring stunts on the trapeze. He becomes obsessed with Clara, and in turn Katherine becomes obsessed with his obsession, and the three dance around one another, falling in and out of their sordid love triangle. Indeed the theme of "falling" recurs throughout the narrative, from Katherine's stained-glass masterpiece based on the fall of Lucifer from heaven to Clara's literal and tragic plunge from the high wire that leaves her a quadriplegic.

Once Swabey's character comes more fully into view, other characters are given perspectives, including Katherine; Swabey's cell mate, Morgan; Clara; and the prison chaplain. We learn much of the suffering and pain of Katherine, Clara, and Swabey through these various voices, eventually learning that Swabey's love led him to help Clara commit suicide after her fall, for which he is in prison. One of the most compelling voices is that of Katherine, as she attempts to understand her lover's complete absorption in Clara; she observes her as no more beautiful than the average woman, labeling her a "glittering absurdity." At the end of the book, Katherine is left unable to understand her beloved, and Swabey is released from prison. We see him looking down a painfully normal street without the object of his obsession or a loving partner, entirely alone.

While some felt that *Falling* was not as strong as *A Cruel Madness*, critics agreed it was a fascinating exploration of painful mental states, obsessive love, and realms of oddity not often found in the postmodern novel.

TURNING BACK THE SUN

With his fourth novel, *Turning Back the Sun* (1991), Thubron was widely reviewed and praised and was short-listed for the prestigious Booker Prize. His writing evoked comparisons to Graham Greene, in terms of the book's meditation on race relations and love. Although the complex drama is set against a natural landscape, and the region's colonial history drew comparisons to Australia or South Africa, Thubron has said that the seeds for this novel were first planted during his travels to northwest China. There, he observed workers who were sent to remote towns by the government to work and left to endure whatever circumstances befell them.

Thubron's protagonist, Rayner, is subject to a similar fate, as a doctor who has been sent outside the capital of the country to work and live on the plains. Away from the city where he was raised and first fell in love, Rayner is isolated and frustrated by the somewhat archaic peoples he must live among, from the bigoted white men (who, like Rayner, have all been relocated) to the somewhat inscrutable, dark-skinned natives, living in poverty at the edges of town. Rayner does his best to foster some kind of understanding between these two populations, especially when a series of suspicious murders among the whites and a strange skin disease force racial tensions to a fever pitch. In treating the whites afflicted with the disease, which seems to be darkening their skin (with rumors of a plague or poisoning running amok), he attempts to calm his patients and encourages them to be reasonable amid the hysteria. He does this in spite of his suspicion that the aboriginals may have committed the murders, but despite his best efforts, violence ensues. His actions are contrasted with that of his childhood friend, Ivan, who lives in the city and helps the military rule with an iron fist, dominating and abusing those who defy them.

Amid this chaos, Rayner lives much of his days waxing poetic about his life in the city, but he makes little effort to return. His life changes when he visits a dilapidated club in town and begins an affair with an exotic dancer, Zoe. She has been thrown out of the capital city for refusing to dance to please those in power, and she has no desire to return. In the end, Rayner must choose between the woman he loves and moving back to the capital. When he does finally revisit the city, it is not the place he remembers, and he finds it lacking in life and substance. Ultimately, Rayner returns to the plains to practice medicine and live out his life.

Critics noted that Thubron uses a sense of place in *Turning Back the Sun*—be it the wild, untamed country or the repressed, efficient city—as more metaphor than physical landscape. It seems he designed the entire narrative in this way, using it to serve as an allegory on race relations as well as a testimony to the power of memory and nostalgia. As Thubron writes of Rayner's return to the capital, for instance:

> After four days, the city no longer appeared to Rayner in the double focus of memory. It had become real, and so was subtly deconsecrated. Once or twice he found himself looking back on the town with wonder. It was the town that had become memory now, and from this safe vantage point a thousand kilometers to the north, it

seemed to burn in the wilderness with an unholy vigor.

(p. 169)

Much comparison could be made between Thubron's *Falling* to *Turning Back the Sun*, as both protagonists are forced to make difficult, life-changing decisions at the novels' climaxes, having to do with their morals and the women they love. Further parallels are evident between the circus performer Clara of *Falling* and Zoe, both beautiful women who are presented more as objects for men to behold than as fully developed characters. To this end, Thubron is sometimes criticized for writing thin and unflattering portraits of women. Regardless of these criticisms, *Turning Back the Sun* is considered one of Thubron's strongest works of fiction.

DISTANCE

In Thubron's next novel, *Distance* (1996), he delves into the fascinating topic of amnesia, set against the science of astronomy. Edward Sanders, a researcher of black holes, discovers that he is slowly recovering from a serious loss of memory. He does not recall anything from the past two years, including his family and the woman he lives with, Naomi, who is a portrait artist. As the novel unfolds, he recalls pieces of his life, including his mother's death and a love affair with a research colleague, Jacqueline. As he attempts to reconstruct his past, he is pulled between the reality of Naomi, who is nursing him back to health, and his haunting memories of Jacqueline. Sanders does not remember if their affair ended before the accident or if she still loves him, so he remains unable to get her out of his mind. In turn, the narrative structure winds around itself as Thubron weaves pieces of the past into Sanders' present. With this novel, Thubron seems to be saying that without memory and past experience, there is little or no sense of one's self, although critics noted a certain lapse at times in the prose's ability to persuade a reader's suspension of disbelief. It seems obvious that Naomi and Sander's father would have much information to provide Sanders about his past, but they never do. They have decided that it would be more natural and comfortable for him to rediscover his life on his own, no matter how difficult the struggle.

Similar to the protagonists of *Falling* and *Turning Back the Sun*, Sanders is a man obsessed with an ultimately unknowable and unattainable woman, Jacqueline. He remains distanced from Naomi as well, given his inability to remember her, although emotionally powerfully moments occur between them as he rediscovers their love. As Oliver Reynolds commented in the *Times Literary Supplement* regarding Thubron's narrators and their plight, "Disabled by love, the male gazes upward where the female, spotlit by desire remains impossibly aloof" (p. 23).

Despite some strong emotional threads, critics noted that science and intellect overpower the narrative at times, especially during the many ruminations the characters have regarding infinity and the universe. Jacqueline's soliloquies in particular ring more of intellectual exercise than of a true character's voice, and the parallels of Sanders' research of black holes and his amnesiac condition are a bit overdetermined. Essentially, while some critics found the novel entertaining, it is not viewed as Thubron's strongest work.

TO THE LAST CITY

To the Last City, which appeared in 2002, is set deep in the Peruvian Andes, where five ill-prepared travelers find themselves on a journey that will either temper their character or destroy them. The "last city" of their destination is Vilcabamba, the last refuge of the Inca against the Spaniards, subsumed by jungle for four hundred years. Critics view the novel as a brilliant exploration of the psychological challenges of traveling, using five very different characters and points of view to exploit various weaknesses and strengths of mind, body, and spirit. The five characters we learn these life lessons through are Francisco, a Spanish priest; Robert, an English writer; his tough but quiet wife, Camilla; Louis, an overweight Belgian architect; his vain and much younger wife, Josiane; and the group's half-Indian, half-Spanish jungle guide.

Maintaining a rotating point of view can be difficult, but critics found it fitting in *To the Last City*, given the sense that while this group must rely on one another to some degree, they are set apart by their own desires and motivations. Each of them suffers from physical ailments, whether it be Robert's injured knee or Louis' weak heart, not to mention certain mental shortcomings, such as Josiane's overall narcissism, which seems to coincide with Robert's lust for her. Each character in turn is on a personal journey or quest: Robert longs for the inspiration to write a book that will make his career, while Francisco desires absolution for the historical crimes on the people of South American committed by his ancestors. Although each make judgments about his or her fellow travelers, it is the local guide who views the group most transparently. From the beginning, he notes their willful ignorance of the fact that they are a world away from what is familiar or easily navigated, illustrated by his disdain for their carefully packed chocolates and useless cell phones.

All five characters are innocents in some sense, especially in terms of traversing the South American jungle, a stunning, yet unforgiving place. Thubron uses these surroundings as a character that closes in on the tourists as the narrative unfolds. Mountains become menacing, and the landscape as a whole becomes untenable, as a sense of doom begins to permeate the journey. Thubron takes no mercy on these characters, especially as Josiane falls ill and dies, and those left find themselves carrying their dead into the heart of the Inca city. Once there, they must confront both their relationships with one another and the enigmas of the country's sordid past.

To the Last City draws comparisons to works of Arthur Conan Doyle and Gabriel García Márquez as well as to Joseph Conrad's *Heart of Darkness* (1902). Thubron takes on a great challenge in writing about the clash of civilization and the ancient world in a slim volume of fiction, and he succeeds with flying colors. As Robert McCrum writes, "Colin Thubron seems to be a writer, undaunted by immensity of either place or plot. ... *To the Last City* is haunting, passionate and best of all, magnificently fearless."

CONCLUSION

Colin Thubron's contributions to the world of writing, and the travel narrative in particular, are clear. He has taken the art of the genre to new heights with his willingness to take physical and emotional risks over several decades of traveling, seeking out remote locations where comfort and a warm welcome are never guaranteed. His personal preparation for entering a culture is also perhaps unsurpassed, in the way he learns a variety of languages and deeply studies the history of a region in order to bring him closer to the people he travels among. Thubron also remains in a league of his own given how he recreates his journeys on the page, bringing distant places to life with sentences that are full of pitch-perfect images, lyrical prose, and psychological acuity. "Thubron's unique gift to modern literary travel," however, as noted by Ian Thomson reviewing *In Siberia,* is that "he was among the first to abandon conventional travel narrative and focus instead on chance encounters with people. Thubron still is a magician in this field" (p. 10). This truly appears to be Thubron's specialty, the intimacy he builds with people where ever he goes, so that places become much more than geography; they are instead a collection of living, breathing lives, full of hopes and dreams.

Colin Thubron provides us an invaluable first-person account of the places he travels, in a time where most of us want instant results from a search engine, never coming in contact with the subject we are researching. In reviewing *Shadow of the Silk Road,* Benedict Allen writes that Thubron is "a creature of the long search; before ever taking up his backpack, he prepares the intellectual ground ahead. In his London pad he swots up on his Russian and Mandarin, steeping himself in historical and social know-how. ... his solo wanderings are lengthy. ... and they become a lyrical assemblage of telling local humanity."

It seems his appetite for adventure in the place not often traveled is boundless, as is his desire to translate his experiences into a greater understanding of more-remote cultures to the world. Risk appears to be what compels Thubron the most, and for him, forgoing risk seems to be forgoing the way he has learned to live. For most, travel is a form of escape, yet for Thubron it is the opposite; it is a way of confronting the world head-on. He does the same in his fiction, never shying away from difficult subject matter, unafraid to plumb his own emotional depth, daring the reader to come along with him.

Although it might seem that Thubron would be on the cusp of winding down his wild and varied career, readers should not expect him to disappear from the best-seller lists anytime soon. He seems to have a soul destined for adventure. A 2011 volume titled *To a Mountain in Tibet* chronicles a trip he made after the death of his mother and to mark his seventieth birthday, when he journeyed to spend several months in Tibet and made a pilgrimage to the sacred Buddhist mountain of Kailas.

Selected Bibliography

WORKS OF COLIN THUBRON

Nonfiction

Mirror to Damascus. London: Heinemann, 1967.

The Hills of Adonis: A Quest in Lebanon. London: Heinemann, 1968.

Jerusalem. London: Heinemann, 1969.

Journey into Cyprus. London: Heinemann, 1975.

The Venetians. New York: Time-Life, 1980.

The Ancient Mariners. New York: Time-Life, 1981.

The Royal Opera House, Covent Garden. London: Hamish Hamilton, 1982.

Among the Russians. London: Heinemann, 1983.

Behind the Wall: A Journey Through China. London. Heinemann, 1987.

The Silk Road: Beyond the Celestial Kingdom. New York: Simon & Schuster, 1989.

The Lost Heart of Asia. London: Heinemann, 1994.

In Siberia. London: Chatto & Windus, 1999.

Shadow of the Silk Road. London: Chatto & Windus, 2006.

To a Mountain in Tibet. London: HarperCollins, 2011.

FICTION

The God in the Mountain. London: Heinemann, 1977.

Emperor. London: Heinemann, 1978.

A Cruel Madness. London: Heinemann, 1984.

Falling. London: Heinemann, 1989.

Turning Back the Sun. London: Heinemann, 1991.

Distance. London: Heinemann, 1996.

To the Last City. London: Chatto & Windus, 2002.

CRITICAL AND BIBLIOGRAPHICAL STUDIES

REVIEWS AND ARTICLES

Allen, Benedict. "Swap Your Stirrup for My Harp." *Independent,* November 19, 2006.

Dirlam, Sharon. "A Cruel Madness." *Los Angeles Times Book Review,* October 6, 1985, p. 22.

Gittings, John. "Behind the Wall," *Third World Quarterly* 12, nos. 3–4:173–175 (1990–1991).

McCrum, Robert. "Back to the Heart of Darkness." *Observer,* July 28, 2002.

Murphy, Dervla. "Not Only the Past, Brittle with Relics." *Spectator,* September 24, 1994, p. 44.

Pool, Gail. "Where the Nights Are Longest." *Christian Science Monitor,* September 8, 1987, pp. 21–22.

Pryce-Jones, David. "From Fear to Pity." *National Review,* December 20, 1999, pp. 64–66.

Reynolds, Oliver. "Speaking Subjectively." *Times Literary Supplement,* September 20, 1996, p. 23.

Thompson, Ian. "A Thaw in the Gulag: Where Has the KGB Gone?" *Guardian,* October 9, 1999, p. 10.

INTERVIEWS

Atiyah, Jeremy. "Interview with Colin Thubron." *Independent Sunday,* October, 10, 1999, p. 2.

Feldman, Gayle. "The Art of Traveling Well." *Publishers Weekly,* February 28, 2000, pp. 54–55.

Wroe, Nicholas. "Don't Forget Your Toothbrush: A Life in Writing." *Guardian,* September 23, 2000, p. 11.

CUMULATIVE INDEX

All references include volume numbers in boldface roman numerals followed by page numbers within that volume. Subjects of articles are indicated by boldface type.

X

"Y